MICROCOMPUTER USE

Software Applications and Problem Solving with

WordPerfect 4.2 and 5.0

WordStar

Lotus 1-2-3

dBASE III Plus

Teresa Alberte-Hallam
Northern Illinois University

Stephen F. Hallam
Northern Illinois University

HBJ

Harcourt Brace Jovanovich, Publishers
and its subsidiary, Academic Press

San Diego New York Chicago Austin Washington, D.C.
London Sydney Tokyo Toronto

NOTE: This work is derived, in part, from *Microcomputer Use,* Second Edition, by Teresa Alberte-Hallam, Stephen F. Hallam, and James Hallam, copyright © 1988, 1985 by Harcourt Brace Jovanovich, Inc.

PHOTO CREDITS

Page 5: *top left and middle,* courtesy, IBM Corp.; *bottom right,* Werner Kalber, PPS; *top right and bottom left,* © Susan Holtz; **6:** courtesy, IBM Corp.; **7:** courtesy, IBM Corp.; **8:** courtesy, IBM Corp.; **12:** Farmplan; **19:** courtesy, IBM Corp.; **26:** photo courtesy of Hewlett-Packard Co.; **32:** from *Living with Computers,* Second Edition, by Patrick G. McKeown, Harcourt Brace Jovanovich, Inc., Publishers; **88:** photo courtesy of Hewlett-Packard Co.

ISBN: 0-15-558394-8
Library of Congress Catalog Card Number: 88-81029
Printed in the United States of America

Trademark acknowledgments appear on pages 601–602.

PREFACE

The course that uses *Microcomputer Use: Software Applications and Problem Solving with WordPerfect, WordStar, Lotus 1-2-3, and dBASE III Plus* may well be the most interesting and useful one students take. It would be difficult to think of many academic areas in which the developments in technology continue to be so rapid and astonishing, and virtually no career or profession remains untouched by the everchanging role of the microcomputer. Whether students enter business, teaching, or the professions, they will interact with the computer. Facility in microcomputer use is a highly valued asset in the work place.

It is obvious that this skill is desirable. But which aspects of computer use are best to include in a microcomputer course? What types of applications are most appropriate for students? And how can instructors *educate* rather than simply *train* students in microcomputer use? To address these questions, *Microcomputer Use: Software Applications and Problem Solving* uses the following features.

CONCEPTUAL FOUNDATION

Concepts should be stressed along with techniques, so that education and skill building are combined. Different manufacturers of the same type of software give their packages different procedures and capabilities. New versions of the same software package differ from their predecessors (as can be seen in WordPerfect's versions 4.2 and 5.0, presented simultaneously in Chapters 3–5). If students have been taught only which buttons to push—if they have been trained but not educated—then their knowledge will quickly become obsolete. Much better prepared for change are the students who grasp the technological and business needs that the various software packages attempt to meet. In *Microcomputer Use: Software Applications and Problem Solving,* each lesson first presents the concepts—to help educate the user. The tutorials then train the user in which buttons to push to produce specific results.

TUTORIALS AND EXERCISES WITH REAL-WORLD APPLICATIONS

Once they know the conceptual bases for different techniques and applications, students learn best by *doing*. The tutorials and exercises in each lesson of *Microcomputer Use: Software Applications and Problem Solving* follow this "learn by doing" approach. Whenever possible, they focus on practical applications—such as using word processing to produce business letters, resumés, and term papers; using a spreadsheet to prepare an individual budget, analyze financial data, and create charts and graphs to display and compare data more clearly and imaginatively; and using a database to maintain a list of book or compact disk titles or the list of customers and inventories required in many typical business applications.

COMPREHENSIVE, VERSATILE STRUCTURE

Microcomputer Use: Software Applications and Problem Solving is composed of 13 lessons organized into 5 major parts. Part One, Microcomputer Fundamentals, provides an introduction to microcomputer hardware and software, including a discussion of the essential MS-DOS system commands each student needs to prepare a disk for future exercises; Part Two, Word Processing, includes three lessons on word processing; Part Three, Electronic Spreadsheets, has three lessons about spreadsheets; and Part Four, Database Management, presents three lessons about database management. Part Five, Other Microcomputer Applications, contains lessons on using the microcomputer for data communications, statistics and graphics, and various other management applications.

Students who have little or no experience using a microcomputer should certainly begin with Part One. Parts Two through Four can be studied in any order, but it is usually most useful to study the parts in the order presented, especially if output from the spreadsheet or the database management system is to be integrated into a document produced on a word processor.

Each lesson contains an extensive discussion of key concepts, a summary, and exercises that range from simple to challenging. Lessons 1–11, which deal with the operating system and specific software applications, contain tutorials that help students truly understand and appreciate the concepts and reach a competent, confident skill level.

The tutorials and exercises provide over 100 hours of computer lab time. The tutorials teach the use of a software package in a step-by-step manner, taking the student slowly and thoroughly from booting the microcomputer, to entering specific data, to saving data on a file, to retrieving and editing that file, to printing the final product. The exercises, which let students practice their new knowledge, range from simple reinforcement of skills, through mastery of a wide variety of topics, to more difficult, project-length assignments.

SOFTWARE OPTIONS

Students need access to software that is reasonable in cost yet, to the greatest degree possible, full-featured, up-to-date, and similar to what they are likely to find in the work place. In the areas of databases and spreadsheets, identifying the most popular commercial packages is relatively easy: dBASE III Plus and Lotus 1-2-3, both covered here, are currently the most popular packages. In word processing, however, the choice is not so obvious. WordStar has been the industry leader, but WordPerfect is currently the best seller. Therefore, we have included them both. Also, for those who prefer an inexpensive work-alike of Lotus 1-2-3, a VP-Planner/VP-Planner Plus supplement is available. Some schools prefer, and can afford, to purchase sufficient copies of the latest versions of these commercial software packages. Others will opt to use educational versions, which may not contain all the options of the commercial versions but will be more than sufficient for almost every conceivable student application.

Harcourt Brace Jovanovich, the publisher of this textbook, has contracted with the commercial software producers to make the most recent educational versions of several of the above-mentioned packages available at no cost to schools that adopt this book. Specifications for each of these packages are given on page 82 for WordPerfect, page 340 for dBASE III Plus, and on page 547 for VP-Planner Plus. Whether students use the full commercial version or the educational version of the software, *Microcomputer Use: Software Applications and Problem Solving* will fit their needs. For still other schools or individuals who prefer to use software specifically created for educational purposes but featuring the typical "commercial" options, another version of this book—*Microcomputer Use: Word Processors, Spreadsheets, and Data Bases,* Second Edition, by Teresa Alberte-Hallam, Stephen F. Hallam, and James Hallam—is available with accompanying free MicroUSE software for the IBM PC and compatibles.

TIPS ON SELECTION AND COMPARISON OF SOFTWARE

Although students may learn how to apply the personal computer using the currently most popular commercial software packages, they should be introduced to the main features of some of the competing packages, such as SuperCalc, R:BASE, and Paradox. No one software package can suit every need, but each has advantages. *Microcomputer Use: Software Applications and Problem Solving* examines the concerns involved in selecting the appropriate software for word processing, spreadsheet, database, and other applications and briefly presents the main features of over a dozen packages.

OTHER APPLICATIONS

The major portion of the book is devoted to word processing, spreadsheets, and databases, but several other exciting and useful areas of application are also considered: data communications and public-access databases such as

CompuServe, statistical and graphics software, and a variety of other up-and-coming areas, including artificial intelligence and expert systems. For example, CompuServe currently has approximately 400,000 subscribers and, to users who have a PC and a modem access, offers hundreds of valuable online databases, a source we found invaluable in preparing up-to-date material for this book. In fact, our CompuServe electronic address is 72307,450, and we would appreciate hearing from users of *Microcomputer Use: Software Applications and Problem Solving.*

ANCILLARY MATERIALS

The Instructor's Manual that accompanies *Microcomputer Use: Software Applications and Problem Solving* contains suggested course syllabi, instructor notes and activities, and sample test questions. A data disk for student use contains the data from a select number of exercises.

ACKNOWLEDG-MENTS

We are grateful to the instructors and students who have used the first two editions of *Microcomputer Use* and have graciously shared their suggestions for improvement.

We also want to thank the many students and colleagues at Northern Illinois University who read various drafts of the manuscript and worked the tutorials and exercises.

Special thanks go to the people who prepared formal reviews of *Microcomputer Use: Software Applications and Problem Solving:* James Buxton, Tidewater Community College, Virginia Beach Campus; Paulette Gannett, Broome Community College; Martha Hedley, Jim Im, University of New Orleans; Robert Jenkins, Utah Valley Community College; Karen Watterson, and Sharon West, University of South Alabama. This textbook also benefitted from the suggestions of the reviewers of the Second Edition: Gerald Adkins, University of Georgia; Warren J. Boe, University of Iowa; Qwynne Larsen, Metropolitan State College; Carolyn B. Regner, University of Wisconsin, Oshkosh; Paul W. Ross, Millersville University; Leonard Sweet, University of Akron; and John Zales, Harrisburg Area Community College.

We also thank the staff at Harcourt Brace Jovanovich whose support and effort made this book possible: Cate DaPron, Cheryl Hauser, Merilyn Britt, Kay Faust, Maggie Porter, Suzann Nelson, Sarah Randall, and Bill Teague.

Finally, we want to thank our families, especially our daughters, Patricia and Margaret, for their love and understanding during those times when their parents were bleary-eyed and short-tempered from staying up late to meet the hectic deadlines and make the last-minute changes required to keep up with new software releases.

Teresa Alberte-Hallam

Stephen F. Hallam

SOFTWARE LICENSING INFORMATION

The publisher of this textbook has contracted with commercial software firms to make educational versions of WordPerfect 4.2 and dBASE III PLUS available, through instructors, to the students who use this textbook. Instructors who request this software will receive specific instructions on how to inform students of their rights and responsibilities under those license agreements.

In addition, the publisher is required to print the following notices in the Preface. The first notice duplicates the license agreement under which dBASE III PLUS is made available; the second lists in detail the nature of the limitations to the educational version of WordPerfect 4.2.

dBASE III PLUS

Important: Please read this page before using the dBASE III Plus program, a copy of which is being made available to you for use in conjunction with this Textbook pursuant to the terms of this Agreement for educational, training and/or demonstration purposes. By using the dBASE III Plus program, you show your agreement to the terms of this license.

Exclusions of Warranties and Limitations of Liability

THE COPY OF THE dBASE III PLUS PROGRAM MADE AVAILABLE FOR USE WITH THIS TEXTBOOK IS A LIMITED FUNCTIONALITY VERSION OF dBASE III PLUS, AND IS INTENDED SOLELY FOR EDUCATIONAL, TRAINING AND DEMONSTRATION PURPOSES. ACCORDINGLY, THIS COPY OF dBASE III PLUS IS PROVIDED "AS IS," WITHOUT WARRANTY OF ANY KIND FROM ASHTON-TATE OR HARCOURT BRACE JOVANOVICH, INC. ASHTON-TATE AND HARCOURT BRACE JOVANOVICH, INC. HEREBY DISCLAIM ALL WARRANTIES OF ANY KIND WITH RESPECT TO THIS LIMITED FUNCTIONALITY COPY OF dBASE III PLUS, INCLUDING WITHOUT LIMITATION THE IMPLIED WARRANTIES OF MERCHANTABILITY AND FITNESS FOR A PARTICULAR PURPOSE. NEITHER ASHTON-TATE NOR HARCOURT BRACE JOVANOVICH SHALL BE LIABLE UNDER ANY CIRCUMSTANCES FOR CONSEQUENTIAL, INCIDENTAL, SPECIAL OR EXEMPLARY DAMAGES ARISING OUT OF THE USE OF THIS LIMITED FUNCTIONALITY COPY OF dBASE III PLUS, EVEN IF ASHTON-TATE OR HARCOURT BRACE JOVANOVICH HAS BEEN APPRISED OF THE LIKELIHOOD OF SUCH DAMAGES OCCURRING. IN NO EVENT WILL ASHTON-TATE'S OR HARCOURT BRACE JOVANOVICH'S LIABILITY (WHETHER BASED ON AN ACTION OR CLAIM IN CONTRACT, TORT OR OTHERWISE) ARISING OUT OF THE USE OF THIS LIMITED FUNCTIONALITY COPY OF dBASE III PLUS EXCEED THE AMOUNT PAID FOR THIS TEXTBOOK.

Limited Use Software License Agreement

Definitions

The term "Software" as used in this agreement means the Limited Use version of dBASE III Plus which is made available for use in conjunction with this Textbook solely for educational, training and/or demonstration purposes. The term "Software Copies" means the actual copies of all or any portion of the Software, including back-ups, updates, merged or partial copies permitted hereunder.

Permitted Uses

You may:

- Load into RAM and use the Software on a single terminal or a single workstation of a computer (or its replacement).
- Install the Software onto a permanent storage device (a hard disk drive).
- Make and maintain up to three back-up copies provided they are used only for back-up purposes, and you keep possession of the back-ups. In addition, all the information appearing on the original disk labels (including copyright notice) must be copied onto the back-up labels.

This license gives you certain limited rights to use the Software and Software Copies for educational, training and/or demonstration purposes. You do not become the owner of and Ashton-Tate retains title to, all the Software and Software Copies. In addition, you agree to use reasonable efforts to protect the Software from unauthorized use, reproduction, distribution or publication.

All rights not specifically granted in this license are reserved by Ashton-Tate.

Uses Not Permitted

You may not:

- Make copies of the Software, except as permitted above.
- Rent, lease, sublicense, time-share, lend or transfer the Software, Software Copies or your rights under this license except that transfers may be made with Ashton-Tate's prior written authorization.
- Alter, decompile, disassemble, or reverse-engineer the Software.
- Remove or obscure the Ashton-Tate copyright and trademark notices.

- Use the Software or Software Copies outside the United States or Canada.

Duration

This agreement is effective from the day you first use the Software. Your license continues for fifty years or until you return to Ashton-Tate the original disks and any back-up copies, whichever comes first.

If you breach this agreement, Ashton-Tate can terminate this license upon notifying you in writing. You will be required to return all Software Copies. Ashton-Tate can also enforce our other legal rights.

General

This agreement represents the entire understanding and agreement regarding the Software and Software Copies and supersedes any prior purchase order, communication, advertising or representation.

This license may only be modified in a written amendment signed by an authorized Ashton-Tate officer. If any provision of this agreement shall be unlawful, void, or for any reason unenforceable, it shall be deemed severable from, and shall in no way affect the validity or enforceability of the remaining provisions of this agreement. This agreement will be governed by California law

WORDPERFECT

The Limited-Use introductory version of WordPerfect 4.2 (L-WP) is intended to allow one to *learn* the features of WordPerfect 4.2; however, the L-WP is not intended to allow one to print usable academic or professional documents.[1]

Certain limitations *(which should not deter* learning *WordPerfect through the L-WP)* have been encrypted into the L-WP to guard against productive use, and are as follows:

I. One may work with as large a document on screen as desired, but one may only save to disk a data file no larger than 50,000k (appx. 25–30 regular pages).

1. A data file created with the L-WP cannot be imported into regular WordPerfect, nor can a file created in regular WordPerfect be imported into L-WP.

[1]"*WPC" will be automatically printed after each paragraph of text to discourage academic or professional use of the L-WP. *See* paragraph II on page x.

II. Data files of any size may be printed through parallel printer port "1" without defining a printer, but font changes and extended ASCII characters are not allowed. Also, "***WPC**" will be printed after each paragraph.

III. One will be able to learn all the functions of WordPerfect 4.2's speller and thesaurus by calling up the "readme.wp" file and following the step-by-step directions; however, one cannot use the L-WP speller and thesaurus with any of one's own documents because there are only a limited number of words in the L-WP speller and thesaurus. (The regular speller has 115,000 words, and the regular thesaurus has approximately 150,000 words.)

IV. The help file of L-WP allows the user to retrieve the function-key template, but similar to the speller and the thesaurus described above, space will not allow the full help files on the L-WP disk.

L-WP is designed to be used for introductory, word processing courses, and thus far has been well received in these types of environments. Notwithstanding the broad abilities provided in the L-WP, presumably the L-WP will not satisfactorily substitute for regular WordPerfect 4.2, and therefore the full-feature version may be obtained directly from WordPerfect Corporation at a 75% educational discount.

CONTENTS

ONE
MICROCOMPUTER FUNDAMENTALS

Today everyone is talking about the microcomputer, the personal productivity tool. You are bombarded with advertisements proclaiming the values of the microcomputer in the office, at home, and at school. What do you really need to know to use this tool effectively? Part I gets you started by describing hardware and software. It provides the fundamentals you need to study Part II (Word Processing), Part III (Electronic Spreadsheets), and Part IV (Databases). Lesson 1 introduces the hardware typically associated with a microcomputer system. Lesson 2 explains the software concepts.

If you already feel comfortable using a microcomputer, you may want to skip or skim Part I. However, if you are a beginner, Part I is essential for you.

1
Fundamentals of Microcomputer Hardware

LESSON OUTLINE

THE MICROCOMPUTER SYSTEM

Any computer system (including a microcomputer system) has five equally important and mutually dependent components: hardware, software, people, procedures, and databases (see Figure 1-1). **Hardware** consists of the computer equipment and its parts. **Software** is the set of instructions or programs that the computer uses to accomplish certain tasks. PC-DOS (Personal Computer Disk Operating System) or MS-DOS (Microsoft Disk Operating System), the microcomputer operating system used on your microcomputer, is the software used with this book. Together, hardware and software process data to make them more orderly, timely, or accurate than would be possible if people alone did the work. **Data** are facts or figures that can be processed by computers. *People,* the ones who create and use the output of the computer, provide meaning to the results. By analyzing, designing, and programming, people make the hardware and software truly valuable. **Procedures** are instructions telling people how to use and operate a computer system. Some procedures explain how to operate the computer or what to do if an error occurs. User's manuals are a form of written procedures. A **database** is a collection of data organized and stored so that the data can easily be retrieved and processed by computer programs. Part IV of this book devotes three lessons to the use of database management software. As you begin your study of applications software, it is important to realize that such software is only one component of the microcomputer system. All five components—hardware, software, people, procedures, and databases—are dependent on each other and essential to the success of a complete information system.

Of course one of the most important components in an information system is the people who design, build, and use it. Microcomputers are

FIGURE 1-1 All computer systems have five equally important and mutually dependent components: hardware, software, people, procedures, and databases.

especially suitable for one-to-one interaction between a person and a computer (see Figure 1-2). In fact, microcomputers are often called *personal computers,* or simply **PC**'s. With very large computers called

FIGURE 1-2 The microcomputer can be used in a variety of locations where data collection, processing, and analysis are needed most. Compare the size of these microcomputers with the size of the mainframe computer in Figure 1-3.

mainframes, it takes several people, each working with some part of the system, to run a computerized information system (see Figure 1-3). With microcomputer systems, often one person performs all the tasks: identifying a problem to be solved with the computer, designing the program, implementing it, and using the results. With microcomputers the key is that *you* are in control of the system. The microcomputer can become your personal tool to use whenever you decide to use it. However, along with

ONE
MICROCOMPUTER FUNDAMENTALS

Today everyone is talking about the microcomputer, the personal productivity tool. You are bombarded with advertisements proclaiming the values of the microcomputer in the office, at home, and at school. What do you really need to know to use this tool effectively? Part I gets you started by describing hardware and software. It provides the fundamentals you need to study Part II (Word Processing), Part III (Electronic Spreadsheets), and Part IV (Databases). Lesson 1 introduces the hardware typically associated with a microcomputer system. Lesson 2 explains the software concepts.

If you already feel comfortable using a microcomputer, you may want to skip or skim Part I. However, if you are a beginner, Part I is essential for you.

FIGURE 1-3 Mainframe computers are usually placed in large, isolated equipment rooms. Users access the system through terminals.

this freedom and control comes the responsibility of understanding how to properly use the microcomputer system.

HARDWARE: UNDER-STANDING THE PARTS

When you sit in front of a microcomputer, the first thing you see is the hardware. *Hardware* is the physical equipment in the microcomputer system. There are four basic categories of hardware designated by their functions in the microcomputer system: (1) input, (2) processing, (3) output, and (4) storage. Figure 1-4 shows the basic hardware components of any computer system. The size and complexity of the components help determine the computer classification: mainframes (very large computers), minis (medium-sized computers), and micros (small computers).

Typical microcomputer system hardware includes a keyboard, a central processing unit (CPU) or main system unit (also called the main

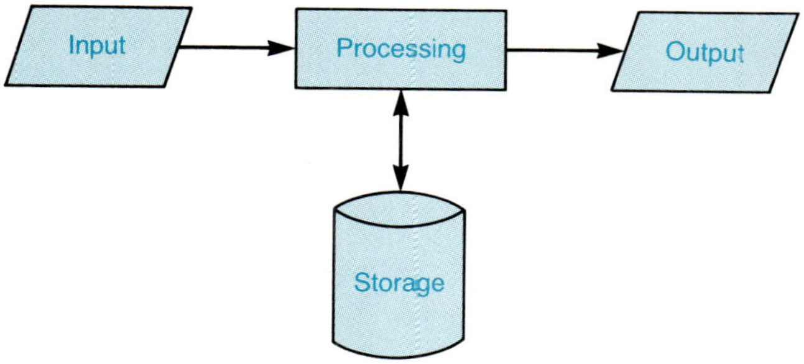

FIGURE 1-4 Computer hardware consists largely of devices to perform the functions of input, processing, output, and storage.

FIGURE 1-5 The general components of microcomputer system hardware: keyboard, CPU, monitor, printer, and disk drive.

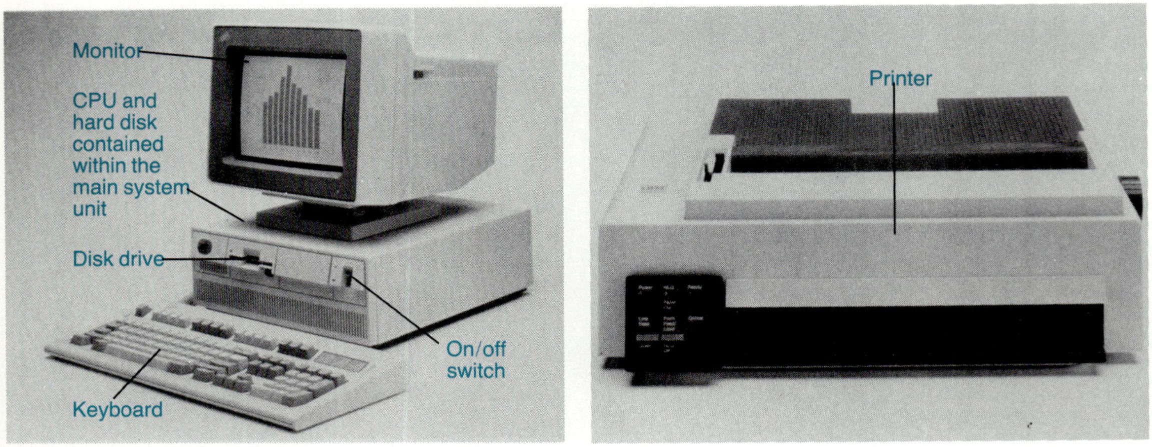

chassis), a monitor, a printer, and disk drives (see Figure 1-5). Often the CPU and disk drives (and sometimes the monitor) are contained within the same unit. Personal computers can range in size from laptop to desktop.

Input Hardware

Keyboards Input hardware provides the computer with data and the instructions for processing. The most common type of input hardware on microcomputers is the *keyboard.* Written text is entered and commands are given by way of the keyboard.

Microcomputer keyboards can generally be described in terms of the style of keys and the special function keys provided. Microcomputer keyboards include keys that are not found on an ordinary typewriter. The Enter key, Control key, Escape key, Caps Lock key, Delete key, cursor or arrow keys, function keys, Print Screen key, and numeric key pad are some of the more common specialized microcomputer keys. As you read the following descriptions of these specialized keys, look at the actual microcomputer keyboard you will be using or refer to Figure 1-6.

The ENTER KEY is used to place data or commands from the keyboard into the computer. The use of the Enter key is commonly indicated by CR (carriage return), Enter, Return, <return>, or the symbol ↵.

The CONTROL KEY is commonly used in combination with regular keys for added commands. The use of the Control key is indicated by the symbol ^, the word *Control,* or Ctrl. Pressing the Control key while pressing another key, such as a letter or number key (like using a shift key on a typewriter), alerts the computer that the letter or number key is to be read as a command and not just a character. The Control key is commonly designated with Ctrl on the key.

FIGURE 1-6 **A variety of keyboards are available for IBM and IBM-compatible microcomputers: *(a)* shows the IBM PC keyboard, and *(b)* displays the IBM enhanced keyboard. All of them share specialized keys, although the placement of the keys may be different. These include the Ctrl key, Shift key, Alt key, Esc key, Del key, Ins key, Caps Lock key, Tab key, the function keys and cursor control keys. More recent model keyboards have 12 function keys across the top.**

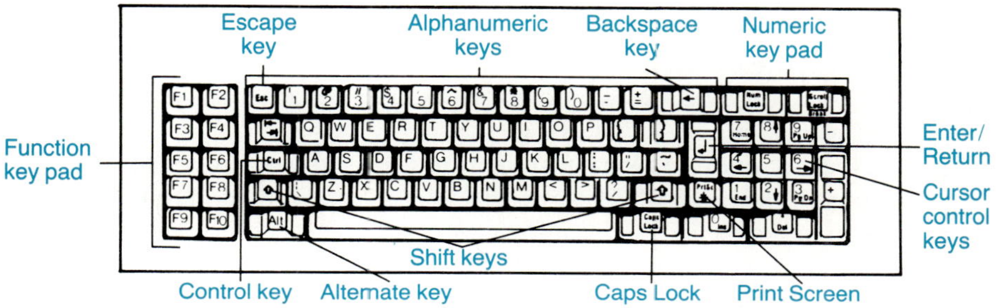

(a)

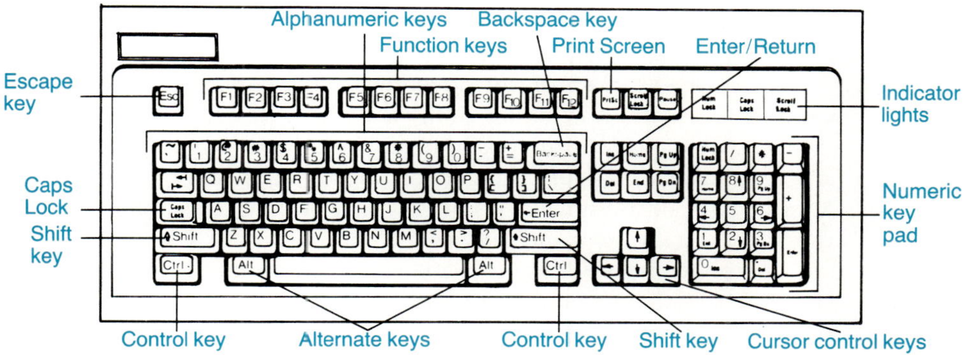

(b)

The ESCAPE KEY (Esc) is commonly used by software packages as a break or cancel key to interrupt or cancel a command. In some cases it may also be used as an alternative to the Control key or to bypass a list, or menu, of commands.

Expert Tip Special lighted indicators on the microcomputer keyboard are a big help—reminding you that you're using the Caps Lock, Num Lock, or Scroll Lock key and thus potentially saving you much editing time. While earlier models of the IBM PC do not have these lights, most IBM compatibles do. And some software, including WordPerfect and Lotus, offer on-screen indicators for these keys. Watch for them.

The CAPS LOCK KEY (Caps Lock) is convenient for entering upper-case letters without continually pressing the Shift key. Note that the Caps Lock key works for alphabetic characters only. Number and special character keys are usually not affected by the Caps Lock key. To get special symbols, such as ! @ # $ % ^ & * ( ) − +, use the Shift key. Also, while the Caps Lock key is in effect, the Shift key will change upper-case to lower-case characters.

The DELETE KEY (Del) is used to delete characters to the left of or directly on the cursor on the entry line, depending on the software used.

The BACKSPACE KEY is commonly used to delete characters to the left of the cursor.

Another common keyboard feature is the NUMERIC KEY PAD. This pad is arranged like a calculator keyboard and is usually placed to the right of the regular keyboard. This allows you to use just one hand to enter numeric data rather than having to reach both hands up to the top row of number keys. Some numeric key pads, such as that on the older models of the IBM PC, can be changed to cursor keys by using the NUMBER LOCK KEY (Num Lock). Newer models, including the IBM PS/2 series, include cursor control keys separate from the numeric key pad. Either set of number keys can be used, but the numeric key pad is a convenient feature for entering a long list of numbers.

CURSOR KEYS control the movement of the cursor on the screen. The **cursor** is usually a blinking line, small box, triangle, or other special character that marks your position on the screen. It shows the location where a character is to be corrected or where data are to be inserted. Cursor keys are typically designated on the keyboard with arrows pointing up (↑), down (↓), right (→), and left (←).

Some keyboards have a HOME KEY that moves the cursor from any position back to the home position at the far upper left corner of the screen or, in some cases, to the top of the document. Other keys include an END KEY that moves the cursor to the bottom of the screen or to the very end of the document and PAGE UP (PgUp) and PAGE DOWN (PgDn) keys to move the screen contents up or down approximately 20 lines, or one screen. The exact operation of these keys is determined by the particular software used.

FUNCTION KEYS are special keys on the keyboard that are defined by the software or programmed instructions stored in the microcomputer. Function keys are sometimes referred to as "soft keys" since they are software controlled. Most applications software, including WordPerfect and Lotus 1-2-3, use function keys to reduce the number of commands you must memorize to use a program. When using a microcomputer with programmed function keys, you can type one key every time a particular set of instructions is needed. In Lotus 1-2-3, by simply pressing [F10], you can print a previously stored graph on the screen. The number and location of function keys depend on the model of the microcomputer. Models of the IBM PC and compatible microcomputers built before 1986 generally have

10 function keys, labeled [F1] through [F10], while newer models, including the Personal System/2, have 12 function keys across the top of the keyboard (see Figure 1-6). Several additional function key commands combine the function keys with the Alt, Ctrl, or Shift keys. For example, WordPerfect offers over forty different function key commands by combining the Control, Shift, and Alt keys with the function keys.

The PRINT SCREEN KEY (PrtSc) is a handy feature commonly found on the IBM PC and compatible microcomputers. By holding down the Shift key and pressing the Print Screen key, you can print the current contents of the screen on paper.

Other Input Devices Although the keyboard remains the most commonly used input device, a number of alternative input devices have been developed, such as the mouse, voice input, and scanners. The purpose of input hardware is to provide the computer with data and the instructions for processing them, regardless of how the device communicates with the microcomputer system.

A **mouse** is a small hand-held pointing device used to move images on the screen, edit or format text, draw or change graphics, and choose commands in certain mouse-supported applications. The mouse comes in a variety of shapes, but the original models were shaped like a small rodent, with buttons for ears and a cord, resembling a tail, connecting the mouse to the microcomputer. None has been known to bite or eat cheese, however. Using the mouse simplifies and adds versatility to most tasks performed with a microcomputer. Instead of pressing direction keys and typing in commands, the user slides the mouse across a small area of the desk top, clicks a mouse button, and thus selects a command from a list of choices shown on the screen. A mouse generally requires a small area of a desk top (about 5 inches wide). The underside of a mouse is generally made of Teflon runners and a rubber ball, but some mouse devices combine a tracking ball and electronic components or optical devices to detect speed and direction of movement.

The microcomputer responds instantly to movements made with the mouse. Slide the mouse, click a button, and the PC immediately reacts with corresponding action on the screen. Figure 1-7 shows how a mouse is used. Applications software used on the IBM PC or compatibles must be configured or specially altered to use the mouse. A mouse is usually purchased separately as an "add-on." Some microcomputers, such as the Macintosh and certain models of the IBM Personal System/2, include the mouse as an integral part of the microcomputer system. Software written for use on these systems usually have a mouse interface built in.

Voice input provides an interesting and perhaps revolutionary dimension to microcomputer use. Instead of entering data at the keyboard, the user provides the input by speaking to an especially equipped microcomputer (see Figure 1-8). Although further development is needed to realize

FIGURE 1-7 A mouse and how it is used. Notice the position of the mouse in the hand and the ease with which the fingers can reach the buttons to give commands. The cursor on the screen mirrors the movement of the mouse.

FIGURE 1-8 Voice input provides an alternative means of entering data and instructions into microcomputers.

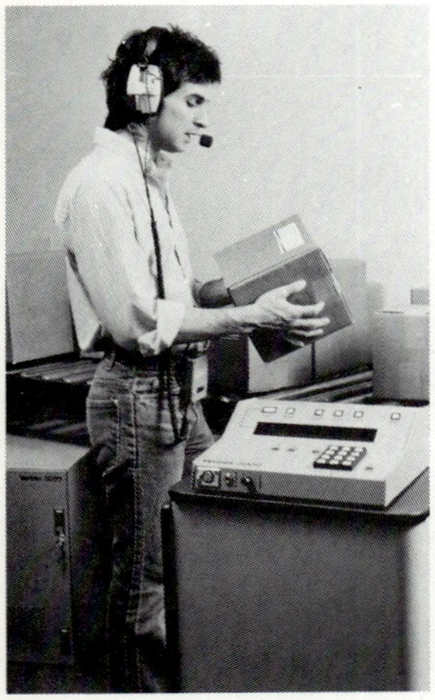

the potential of voice input, even current technology offers the advantages of "hands-off" computing. For example, in some industrial applications, such as at foundries or auto assembly plants, where electronic components could easily become contaminated, the microcomputer is placed in a protective box, and users supply commands by voice through a microphone. Voice input also aids disabled people who cannot use the keyboard or mouse for data entry. The disabled may also give commands through a variety of input devices that detect the slight movements of eyelids, fingers, or even puffs of breath.

Scanners are specialized input devices that let users electronically store graphic images. A page with text or graphics is scanned and translated into binary data and stored (see Figure 1-9). These stored images can then be recalled and inserted into screen presentations or printed documents, such as newsletters and reports. Scanners can also be used to translate printed text into braille for the visually handicapped to read. Scanners may resemble photocopiers, although some handheld models are available.

Scanners have become a popular tool for desktop publishing. **Desktop publishing** permits individuals or small organizations to produce high-quality newsletters, advertising copy, brochures, and other documents that would normally require professional typesetting. With a small amount of training, users can produce professional-looking documents by applying the basic principles of typography, graphics, and aesthetic page layout. Desktop publishing will be described more fully in Lesson 3.

As the types and varieties of input devices continue to grow, microcomputers will become commonplace in a variety of locations and applications.

FIGURE 1-9 **Scanners permit users to translate images into stored data. These can be inserted into documents as illustrations.**

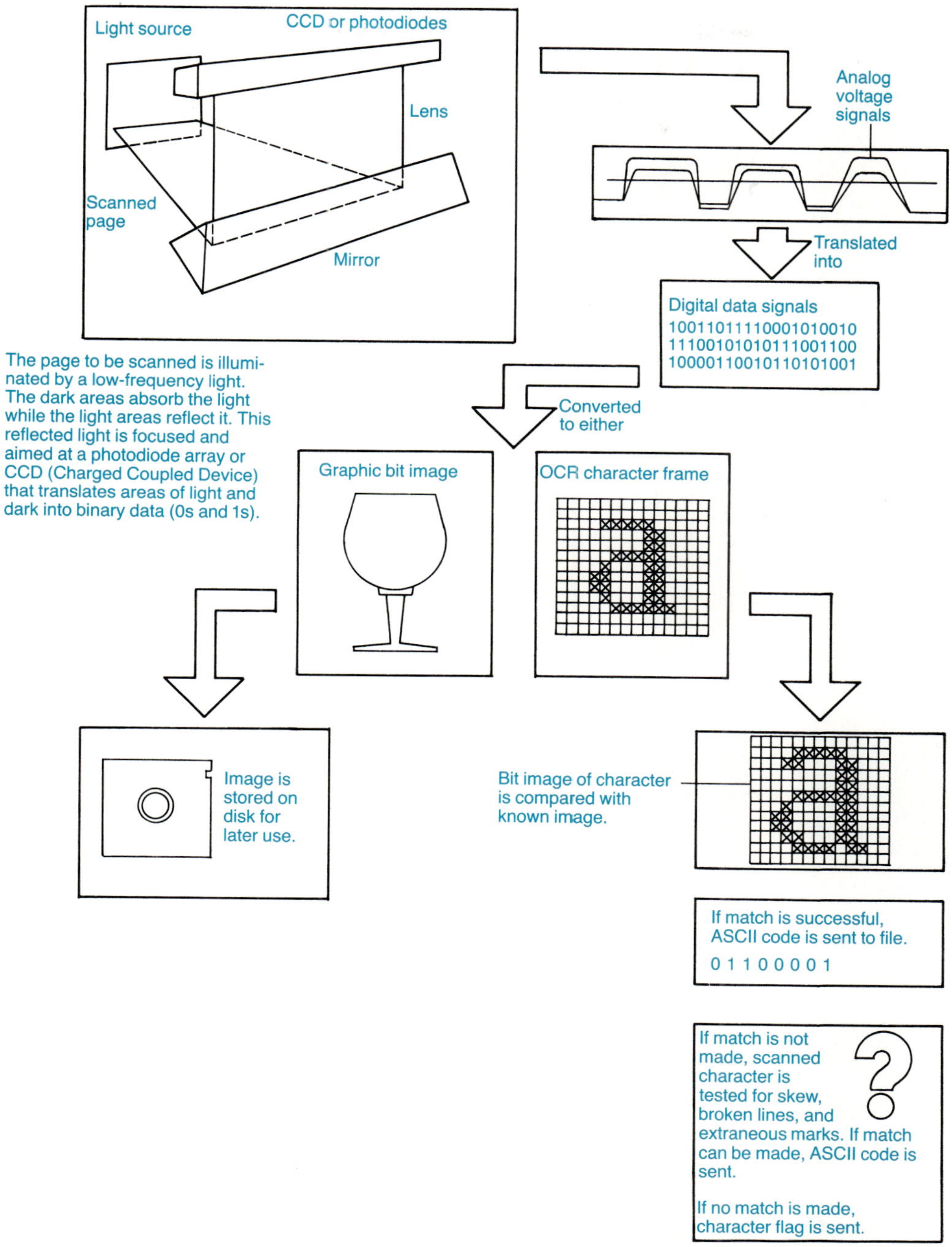

Processing Hardware

Central Processing Unit (CPU) Unfortunately, the main hardware component used in processing, the microprocessor, is hidden from view. We say unfortunately because it is the most spectacular performer in the whole microcomputer system. What it does and how it does it is unique, fascinating, and sophisticated. Yet to most people it is the most abstract part of the microcomputer system. A general idea of how the microprocessor functions helps you understand *how* and *why* the software works.

All computers (mainframes, minicomputers, and microcomputers) have some type of **central processing unit,** or **CPU.** The CPU takes information from primary storage, changes it (for example, by adding another number to it), and then puts it back into primary storage. These three fundamental steps of the computer—(1) fetch, (2) alter, and (3) store—go on at very high speeds (see Figure 1-10). In a microcomputer, the CPU is essentially contained within a single silicon chip called a **microprocessor.** The microprocessor is contained inside the system unit of the microcomputer. The microprocessor typically contains four parts: the arithmetic and logic unit, the registers, an internal control unit, and a bus controller. Primary storage is located separately from the microprocessor (see Figure 1-11).

The **arithmetic and logic unit** carries out the arithmetic operations of adding, subtracting, multiplying, and dividing. It can also logically compare two values to see if one is equal to, greater than, or less than the other. Most other computer functions, regardless of how complicated they may seem, are combinations of these operations.

Registers are small storage areas used to temporarily hold the data

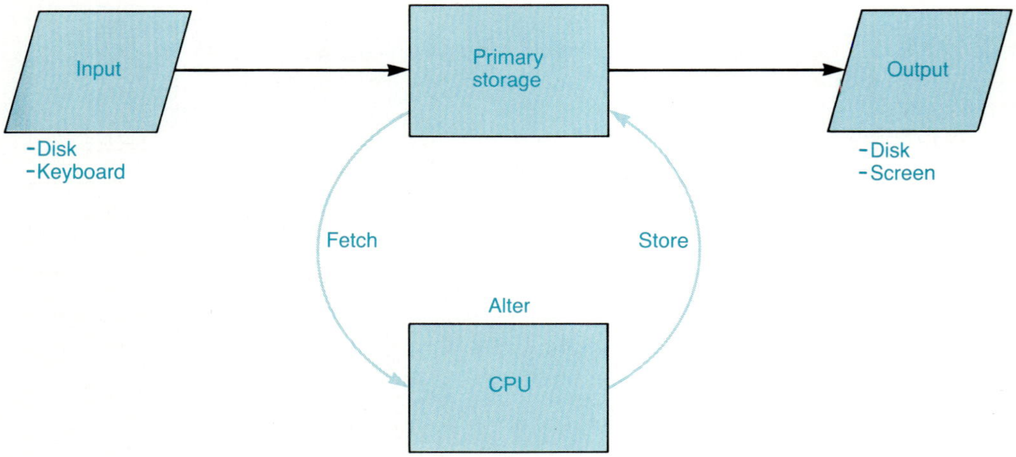

FIGURE 1-10 The CPU takes information from primary storage, changes it, and then puts it back in primary storage. Although the process may seem rather tedious, the computer can do it very quickly.

FIGURE 1-11 The components of a microprocessor: the arithmetic and logic unit, the registers, an internal control unit, and a bus controller. Notice the bus (a data path) and primary storage. Although these are not part of the microprocessor, they are essential to its operation.

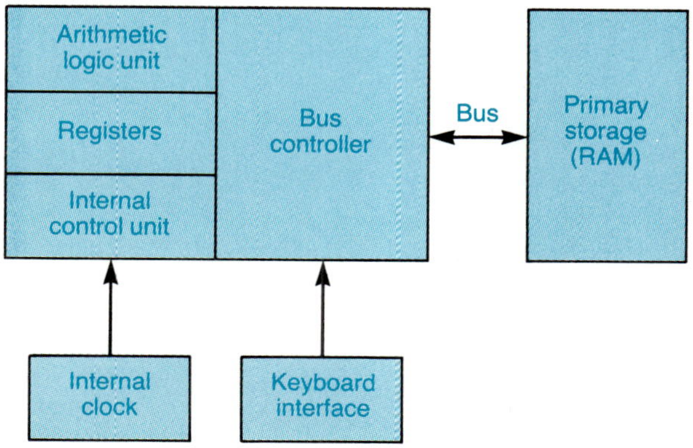

being processed within the microprocessor. All data to be processed must pass through one or more registers to be operated upon.

The **internal control unit** receives timed impulses from the *internal clock* of the microcomputer and regulates the speed and timing of the execution of instructions within the CPU. The faster the internal clock, the faster the CPU can execute instructions. The microprocessor speed is measured in megahertz (MHz).

The **bus controller** regulates the transfer of data to and from primary storage. A **bus** is a group of parallel wire conductors used as a path over which data can be transferred to and from the microprocessor, primary storage, disks, printers, modems, and any other device used as part of the microcomputer system.

Inside the microprocessor all data and instructions are expressed through the **binary numbering system** using on/off switches. "On" is represented by 1 and "off" is represented by 0. Computers use combinations of these codes of 0's and 1's to represent letters, numbers, and other characters and symbols in groups of 8 bits. The binary code is the most fundamental code because it can be related directly to the on or off states of electrical current. The smallest unit of computer storage is the **bit** (*bi*nary digi*t*). Each bit represents one unit of binary code—a 0 or a 1.

This form of storing binary numbers on a computer is referred to as *pure binary.* Actually, pure binary is not used as frequently as a code called ASCII (pronounced *ass-key*) devised by the American National Standards Institute. **ASCII** (an acronym for **American Standard Code for Information Interchange**) assigns a number between 0 and 127 to upper- and

Table 1-1 AMERICAN STANDARD CODE FOR INFORMATION INTERCHANGE (ASCII) DECIMAL VALUES

Decimal	*Symbol/ Function*	*Decimal*	*Symbol/ Function*	*Decimal*	*Symbol/ Function*	*Decimal*	*Symbol/ Function*	*Decimal*	*Symbol/ Function*
32	space	52	4	71	G	90	Z	109	m
33	!	53	5	72	H	91	[	110	n
34	”	54	6	73	I	92	\	111	o
35	#	55	7	74	J	93	]	112	p
36	$	56	8	75	K	94	^	113	q
37	%	57	9	76	L	95	—	114	r
38	&	58	:	77	M	96	`	115	s
39	’	59	;	78	N	97	a	116	t
40	(	60	<	79	O	98	b	117	u
41	)	61	=	80	P	99	c	118	v
42	*	62	>	81	Q	100	d	119	w
43	+	63	?	82	R	101	e	120	x
44	,	64	@	83	S	102	f	121	y
45	–	65	A	84	T	103	g	122	z
46	.	66	B	85	U	104	h	123	{
47	/	67	C	86	V	105	i	124	|
48	0	68	D	87	W	106	j	125	}
49	1	69	E	88	X	107	k	126	~
50	2	70	F	89	Y	108	l	127	Del
51	3								

lower-case letters of the Roman alphabet, to the digits 0 through 9, and to a set of special symbols. Table 1-1 lists the ASCII codes in decimal values and the symbols or functions they represent.

The ASCII code is used for communication between equipment, such as printers, made by different manufacturers; for the interchange of stored text between software; and as a standard code for digital communications over telephone lines.

The next larger unit of computer storage, the **byte,** is the fundamental storage grouping in a computer. One byte in an IBM PC or compatible equals 8 bits. A byte can store an individual character (a letter of the alphabet, a digit, or a punctuation symbol). A byte, therefore, is sometimes referred to as a *character of data.* For example, the letters *RAM* would require three bytes of storage, one for each character. The computer can locate each byte through an individual numeric "address" like the unique numbers for each box in a post office.

The next larger grouping of storage is a **K,** or **kilobyte.** A kilobyte is equal to 2^{10}, or 1,024, bytes. However, 1K is commonly rounded to 1,000 bytes. One page of a single-spaced, 65-character-line, 55-line-per-page document requires approximately 3,575 characters, or bytes, of memory —or approximately 3K. Storage capacity is usually expressed in "K" units. Computer storage is usually available in multiples of 32K bytes. Each 32K-byte unit is capable of storing approximately nine to ten pages of text, depending on the margins and spacing of the pages. A larger measure of storage is a **megabyte** (**M** or **MB**), which is 1,048,576 bytes, or approximately 1 million bytes, of memory.

There are two basic types of storage in a microcomputer: primary storage and secondary storage. Secondary storage holds data and instructions before and after, but not during, processing. Secondary storage is discussed in more detail later in this lesson.

Primary storage is where data and instructions are internally stored during processing. All data and instructions must be placed in primary storage before the microprocessor can process them. Data and instructions that are stored on a disk must be loaded into primary storage before any processing can take place. This loading process actually involves placing a copy of the data or instructions into primary storage while maintaining the original copy on the disk. Primary storage is often referred to as *primary memory* or *main memory* because it is the main or primary place for computer storage. Another common term for primary storage is *RAM.* Primary storage is contained within chips.

A **chip** is a collection of integrated semiconductor circuits contained within a wafer-thin slice of silicon. The microprocessor is commonly referred to as "the chip." However, inside a microcomputer you will find a collection of 20 or more chips with a variety of functions. Some provide storage for the data and instructions during processing; others control the operations of the screen, keyboard, and other components. The development of these tiny chips *(microchips)* has made it possible to manufacture microprocessors of great capacity at a low cost for use in such small items as watches, cameras, and toys. In addition, chips make possible ever smaller but more powerful computers.

To gain a general understanding of a semiconductor and how an integrated chip works, consider the meaning of the word **semiconductor.** A *conductor* is a substance capable of carrying electricity: for example, a copper wire within an electrical cord. A *nonconductor* prevents electricity from flowing: for example, the rubber or plastic insulation on an electrical cord. A semiconductor is between a conductor and nonconductor. A substance is said to be a *semiconductor* if it can carry electricity at a very low energy level.

Silicon is a common element (sand) with an uncommon ability. By adding very tiny amounts of impurities to pure silicon, it can be made to function as a semiconductor. The process of adding impurities is called **doping.** When a positively doped region comes in contact with a negatively doped region, a junction is formed. A **junction** acts like an on/off switch that permits electricity to flow across the junction if it is on and stops the flow when it is off. The flowing state is considered a 1 and the nonflowing state a 0. Semiconductors are therefore capable of storing and processing data and instructions coded as 1s and 0s.

An **integrated circuit** is a collection of thousands of miniature junctions that act as switches to perform the digital logic of the computer. This process requires no moving parts, and the speed is limited only by the size of the circuits and the speed of electricity. This is why electronic computers (including microcomputers) are capable of executing millions of instructions per second.

Although it is fast and relatively inexpensive, semiconductor storage has one major disadvantage: it is volatile. **Volatile storage** requires a constant flow of electricity. If the flow is interrupted, even for a split second, the stored data and instructions are gone forever. Therefore, you should frequently (every 10 minutes or so) store your work on a nonvolatile storage medium, such as a magnetic disk. Some applications software, such as WordPerfect, can automatically back up text at preset intervals. The programs and files stored on your floppy disk will last as long as the files are not erased and the disk is not damaged.

There are two general varieties of semiconductor storage: random access memory (RAM) and read-only memory (ROM). **Random access memory (RAM)** stores data and instructions while they are actively being processed in the microcomputer. RAM, also called *primary storage,* is an electronic scratch pad or *working storage.* When you load the software you are actually moving a copy of a file on the magnetic disk into RAM.

Read-only memory (ROM) stores instructions that cannot be altered or erased. Although programs stored in ROM can be used or read, they cannot be changed by the user and are not affected by changes in electrical current. Therefore, this form of nonvolatile memory is commonly used to store frequently used instructions that can be changed only by the computer manufacturer. Figure 1-12 illustrates the ROM and RAM circuitry and other selected integrated chips commonly found in the IBM Personal System/2.

RAM chips are located either on the main system board, called the **motherboard,** the main computer board containing slots into which other boards may fit, or on **expansion boards,** circuit boards that can be plugged into the main system unit of the microcomputer and used to provide additional features, such as extended color graphics or more RAM storage. These will be discussed in more detail later in the lesson.

Microcomputers are often classified by the type of microprocessor used for processing and the operating system used to run the hardware. Operating systems are discussed in Lesson 2. Microprocessor chips are designed to process data in groups or units. As a general rule, a microprocessor's power is determined by the design of its chip, the number of bits it can process at one time, and its clock speed (the rate at which it works). The higher the number of bits addressed in a register, the faster the

FIGURE 1-12 The ROM and RAM circuitry and other selected integrated chips commonly found in the IBM Personal System/2. These chips help control the operation of the microcomputer hardware.

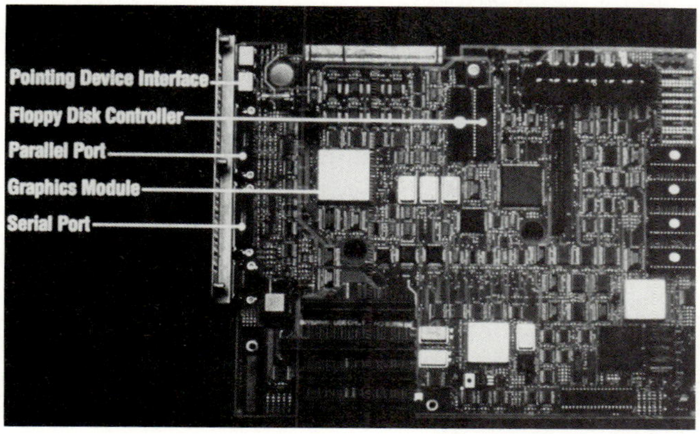

data is processed. The faster the clock speed, the faster the data is processed.

The size of the internal registers determines the word size that can be addressed or processed at one time. A **word** is composed of one or more bytes (8-bit units). If the register size is 8 bits, then the word size is 1 byte; if 16 bits, then a word is 2 bytes; and if 32 bits, then 4 bytes. Machines with larger word sizes are capable of performing more instructions on more data at one time. Some chips, such as the Motorola 68020 and the Intel 80386, have a 32-bit bus and 32-bit internal registers. Such a chip can both transmit (let data or instruction travel on the bus) and process four bytes (one 32-bit word) at a time. Most mainframe computers are 64- or 32-bit machines.

Although some microprocessors, such as the Motorola 68000, can process 32 bits at one time, they require two processing cycles to retrieve 32 bits from storage since they can get only 16 bits at one time. Thus, overall speed of processing depends not only on the word (register) size, but also on bus size.

The most popular microprocessor chip sizes are 8-bit, 16-bit, and 32-bit. Early microcomputers were 8-bit machines; now 16-bit and 32-bit microcomputers are popular. Chips are designed, manufactured, and distributed by particular companies. Some of the most well known are compared in Table 1-2. Notice in Table 1-2 how each chip has particular characteristics and capabilities. Usually, the most recently developed microprocessors can process larger groups of data at once and have more advanced processing capabilities, so the overall processing speed is faster. Currently, 16- and 32-bit microcomputers, such as the IBM PC and Personal System/2 (PS/2) series and the IBM compatibles, are the most widely used,

Table 1-2 A COMPARISON OF SOME POPULAR MICROPROCESSORS

Microprocessor	*Bus Size*	*Register Size*	*Clock Speed*	*Operating System*
Intel 8080	8-bit	8-bit	2 MHz	CP/M*
Zilog Z80A	8-bit	8-bit	4 MHz	CP/M*
Intel 8086	16-bit	16-bit	4.7–12 MHz	MS-DOS**
Intel 8088	16-bit	8-bit	4.7–12 MHz	MS-DOS** PC-DOS*** CP/M 86*
Intel 80286	16-bit	16-bit	10–12 MHz	MS-DOS**
Motorola 68000	16-bit	32-bit	8 MHz	Mac DOS Unix
Intel 80386	32-bit	32-bit	16–25 MHz	MS-DOS** OS/2**** Unix
Motorola 68020	32-bit	32-bit	20 MHz	Mac DOS

*Control Program for Microcomputers
**Microsoft Disk Operating System
***Personal Computer Disk Operating System
****Operating System/2

but 8-bit machines are still used productively. Microcomputers using 32-bit microprocessors, such as the IBM PS/2 Model 80, are becoming popular due to their faster processing speeds, increased memory capacities, and multiple-user capabilities. Such machines can run larger, more complex programs.

Clock speed also influences processing speed. The clock speed of the Intel 8088-based IBM PC is about 4.7 MHz (4.7 million cycles per second), while the clock speed of the IBM PS/2 Model 50, which uses the Intel 80286 chip, is 10 MHz. Several models have been introduced that use the 80386 chip running at 20 and 25 MHz. Some microcomputers have microprocessor chips that can switch to higher clock speeds as needed. Most microcomputer systems have a variety of co-processor chips. A **co-processor** is designed to work with the microprocessor for particular functions. Two of the most popular are the math co-processors 8087 and 80287. By taking over the math processing normally done in the microprocessor, a math co-processor speeds up the system during arithmetic functions, such as calculations with electronic spreadsheets.

It is important to remember that the actual processing speed is dependent not just on the microprocessor but on the entire microcomputer system, including the input (disk access speed), data channels (ports, bus capacity), registers, clock speed, and output channels. Even a slow system can be made faster by adding a hard disk drive or a co-processor. However, all other things being equal, the faster the microprocessor chip, the faster the system (see Figure 1-13).

A **port** is a connection point or interface used to connect various peripheral devices such as printers and modems to the microcomputer. Ports are the channels through which data flow in and out of the computer. Most microcomputers come with two ports: parallel and serial. *Parallel ports* usually connect microcomputers to printers. *Serial ports* usually connect computers to communication devices, including modems. Parallel interfaces transfer data by sending all the bits contained in a byte of storage at one time, like an eight-lane highway, while serial interfaces transfer data one bit at a time, one after another—the microcomputer equivalent of a single-lane road. Thus parallel interfaces transfer data at considerably faster rates than do serial interfaces and are often used in places not visible to the user of a computer, as in a hard disk controller. Sending data over a telephone line requires the use of serial transmission.

However, the true test of a microcomputer is not how fast it processes data, but whether it will economically satisfy *your* processing requirements. The variety of microcomputers available today makes it more important than ever to understand your processing needs before investing in hardware.

Expansion Boards As discussed previously, an *expansion board* or *card* is a printed circuit board designed to add new devices or features to a microcomputer. For example, when you purchase a new device, such as a mouse, to add to your microcomputer, you will receive an expansion board

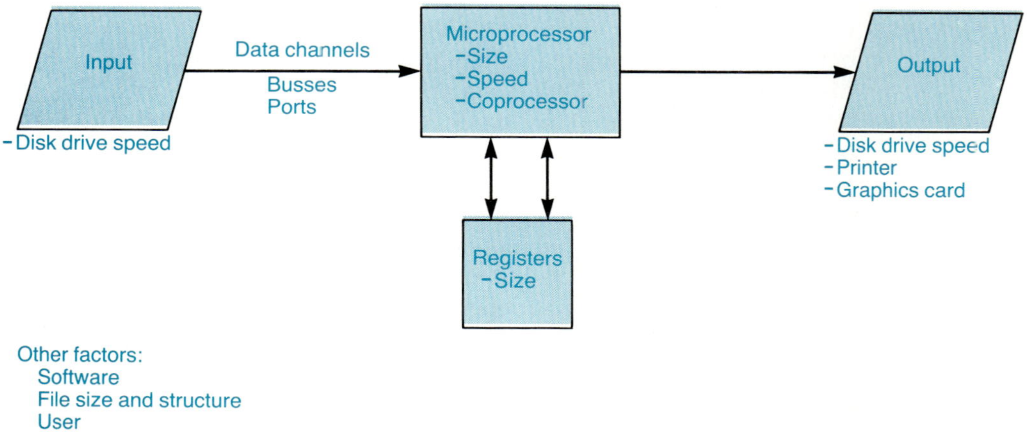

FIGURE 1-13 The speed of the microcomputer system depends on many components in the system.

Table 1-3 COMMON EXPANSION BOARD FUNCTIONS

Disk drive controllers	Control the operation of the disk drives on the microcomputer system.
Video cards	Control the type and quality of the image on the monitor screen.
Modems	Permit communication between computers over phone lines.
Expanded memory cards	Permit RAM to be expanded over ordinary limits.
Accelerator cards	Switch processing to a faster microprocessor, speeding up processing.
Hard disk cards	Contain hard disks for data storage.
Multifunction cards	May contain various features such as additional RAM, a clock/calendar, a parallel port, and a joystick/game port.

that must be plugged into one of the expansion slots of the microcomputer. The device is then plugged into this expansion board through an opening on the back of the microcomputer. The board or a cable connected to the card plugs directly into *expansion slots* contained on the *main system board,* or *motherboard,* of the microcomputer. Expansion boards can be installed to do a wide variety of functions. Expansion board functions are listed in Table 1-3. In fact, some users find these expansion boards so handy and the devices that can be added so numerous that they run out of slots.

Output Hardware

Monitors or Screens The **monitor** is a TV-like screen that is sometimes referred to as a video display terminal (VDT) or cathode ray tube (CRT). Monitors that use only one color (white, green, or red) are called **monochrome** monitors. Monochrome monitors that use green or amber are the most popular for text because they generally have better text resolution, making characters easier to read. However, high-resolution, black-on-white monitors are becoming popular in desktop publishing. *Color* monitors display color images on the screen and are especially useful for displaying graphics. The display on either type of monitor is defined in rows and columns. Alphabetic and numeric characters are formed by dots of light called **pixels.** Each pixel is a tiny dot capable of being turned on or off. In color monitors, pixels can also display colors (see Figure 1-14).

The sharpness or resolution of the image on the monitor is determined by the number of pixels available on the monitor, the video board or chips installed in the microcomputer, and the software used to form characters. As a rule, the more pixels per character, the sharper the image. For example, the standard IBM Color/Graphics Adapter (CGA) display has a resolution of 640 by 200 pixels when used in the high-resolution graphics mode. That is, 200 rows of 640 pixels in each row across the screen. The Enhanced Graphics Adapter (EGA) display has a resolution of 640 by 350 pixels when used in the enhanced resolution graphics mode, provided the

FIGURE 1-14 Characters on the screen are formed by a series of pixels being turned on and off.

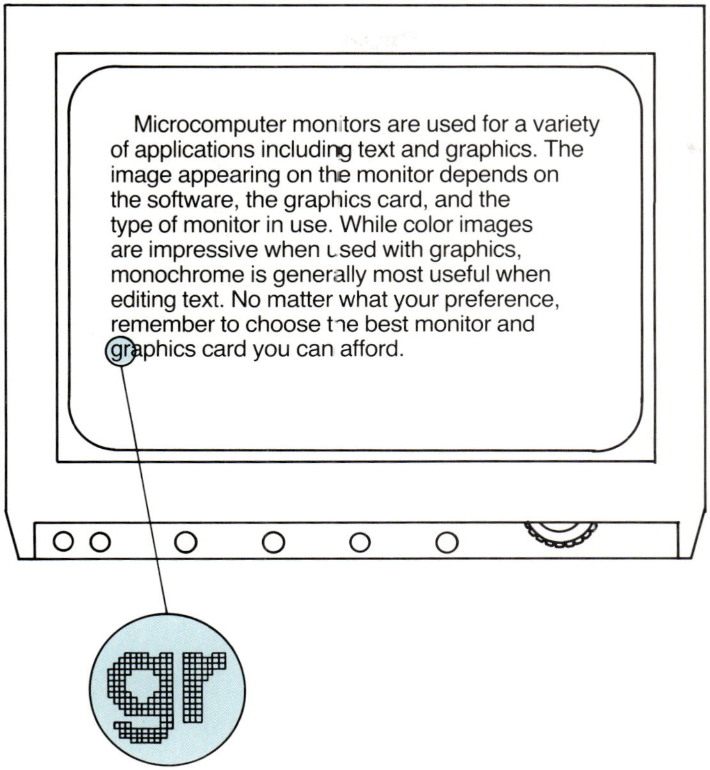

monitor and applications software are capable of EGA display. The Video Graphics Array (VGA) graphics adapter used in several IBM PS/2 models has a resolution of up to 640 by 480 pixels. Images used in computer-aided design (CAD) and computer-aided manufacturing (CAM) may use even higher numbers of pixels for extra sharp, detailed displays.

Printers and Plotters *Printers* provide the paper, or "hard," output from computers. There are two general classifications of printers, depending on how the characters are made on the page. **Impact printers** form the image by using a typing mechanism that directly strikes the paper. With **nonimpact printers** the mechanism produces text without touching the paper. Some nonimpact printers require special paper.

The most popular types of printers used today are dot matrix, daisy wheel, ink-jet, and laser printers. As the name implies, a **dot matrix printer** forms characters with dots. Generally, a dot matrix printer is less expensive (from $150 to $700), more versatile, and faster (from 100 to 400 characters per second) than a daisy wheel printer; however, the print image is usually not as clear because the characters are formed by tiny dots. The dots are formed by pins in the printing mechanism, or *head.* Most dot matrix printers are impact printers, with from 7 to 24 pins in the print head. The more pins in the head and dots used in the character, the better the quality of the print image. Dot matrix printers can print a variety of type styles (such as elite, pica, or italics, compressed or enlarged) as well as graphics. Some even print in color. Compressed print, in which up to 132 characters can be printed on one $8\frac{1}{2}$-inch line, is particularly useful when printing large spreadsheets. (See Figure 1-15.)

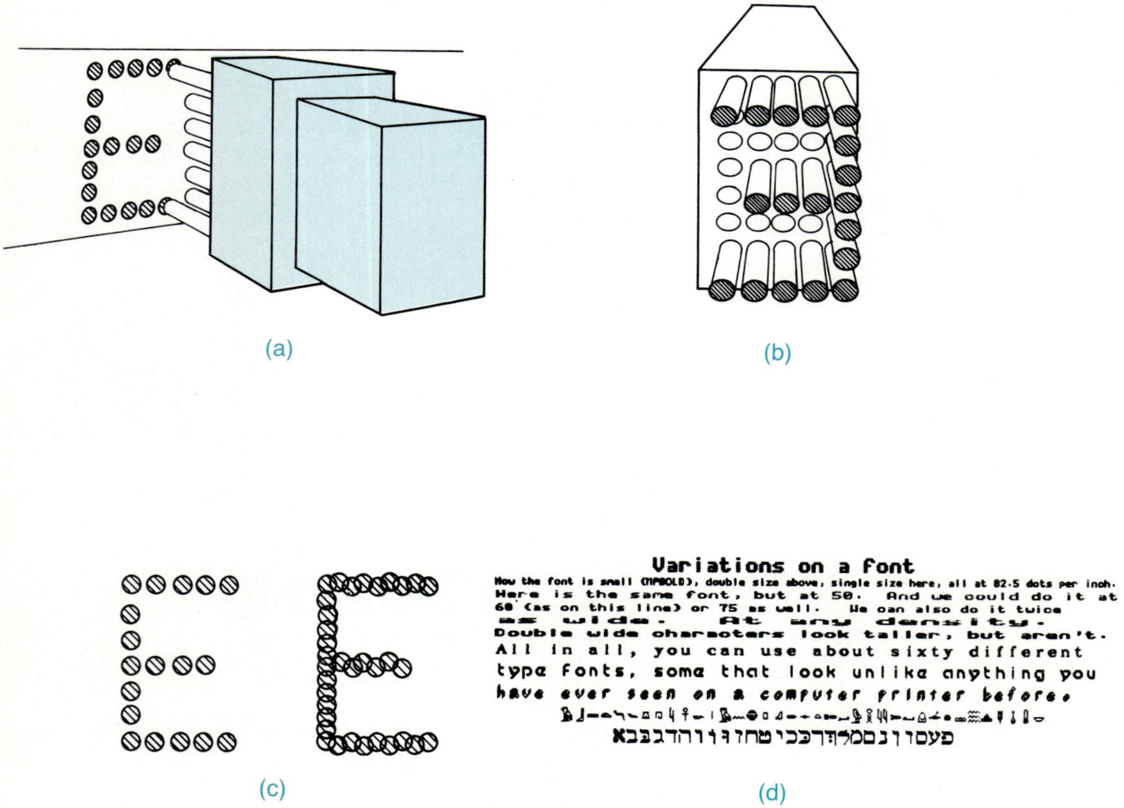

FIGURE 1-15 ***(a)*** **A seven-pin dot matrix print mechanism. In this example, the vertical line of pins strikes the ribbon five times per symbol, forming a five-by-seven matrix.** ***(b)*** **A dot matrix print head printing an** ***E.*** ***(c)*** **Overlapping dots, formed by two or more passes of the print head, improve print quality.** ***(d)*** **Sample output from a dot matrix printer. Notice the variety of styles and sizes available.**

FIGURE 1-16 Daisy wheel printers use a printing wheel shaped like a daisy to produce well-formed, high-quality text. Although users can adjust the pitch (the number of characters per inch), font (character type), and darkness of the typed characters, daisy wheel printers are not as versatile as dot matrix, ink-jet, or laser printers.

A **daisy wheel printer** is an impact printer that uses a print wheel shaped like a daisy flower to produce well-formed characters, called *letter quality,* that resemble typewritten text suitable for printing formal business letters and reports (see Figure 1-16). Daisy wheel printers are slower (12 to 55 characters per second) and generally cannot produce graphics.

Laser and ink-jet printers are nonimpact printers also used to produce letter-quality print. **Laser printers** resemble desktop photocopiers and are fast replacing daisy wheel printers for many office and professional applications. Laser printers use a computer-controlled laser beam to trace an image onto a photosensitive drum (see Figure 1-17). The image is then transferred to paper. The image produced is near typeset quality. Some laser printers can even double as photocopiers. Laser printers can produce a wide variety of print types (called *fonts*) and graphics, from very simple text to very complex combinations of text and graphics. Laser printers are also very fast, printing from 4 to 25 pages per minute. One popular application of laser printers is *desktop publishing.* Using a microcomputer, laser printer, and specialized software, a user can produce professional-quality newsletters, bulletins, and reports. Laser printers are generally quiet and fast but are usually more costly and difficult to maintain than impact printers.

FIGURE 1-17 Laser printers use a process similar to that used in photocopiers. The characters are formed on the paper through electrophotography.

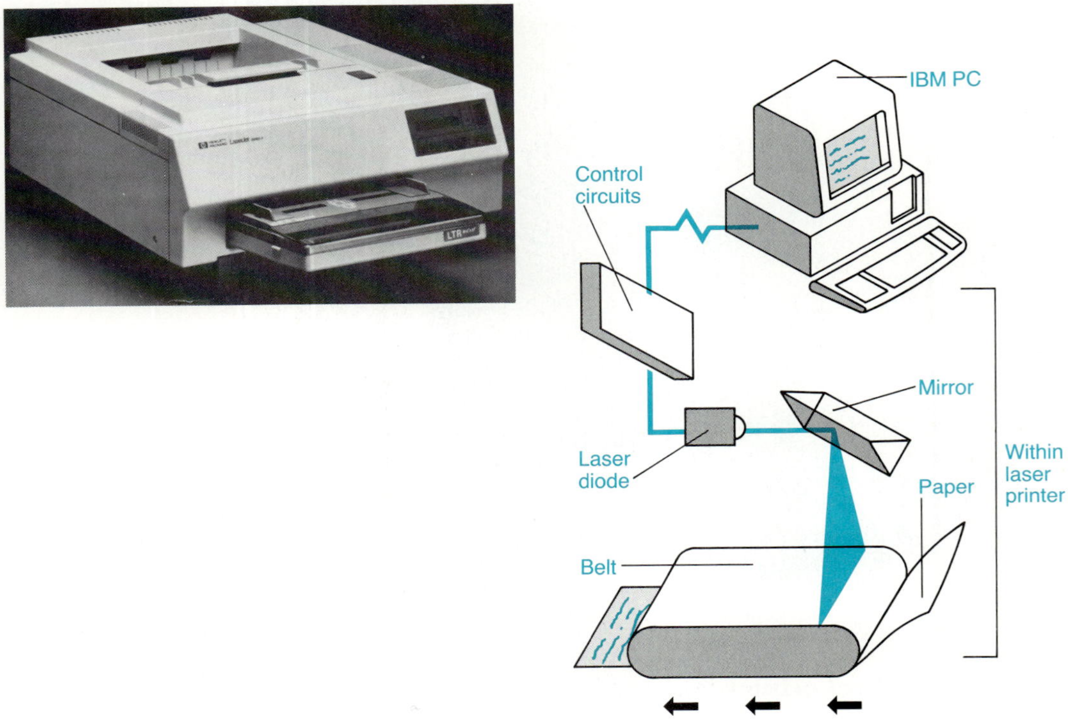

Another type of nonimpact printer known for quiet operation is the **ink-jet printer.** The printer forms the image by spraying ink onto the paper either in a continuous stream or in droplets. Some models of ink-jet printer can produce high-quality color images. Color printers are especially useful for producing color graphics. Multicolored pie charts, bar charts, and line graphs can be used to vividly illustrate data from spreadsheets and other graphics software. Although ink-jet printers are quiet, the printing mechanism can clog and smear characters. (See Figure 1-18.)

Although some printers can produce good quality graphics, the device of choice for producing graphics hard copy is the plotter. **Plotters** work by moving pens, in electronically driven holders, across the paper to produce an image. The advantages of plotters include better resolution (the degree of fineness of the image), speed, variable output size, multiple-color output, stable and long-lived images, easy operation, and compatibility with many computer systems at a relatively low cost. There are two general types of plotters based on their paper and pen movement techniques—*flatbed* and *drum* plotters.

FIGURE 1-18 Ink-jet printers form characters by spraying ink onto the paper.

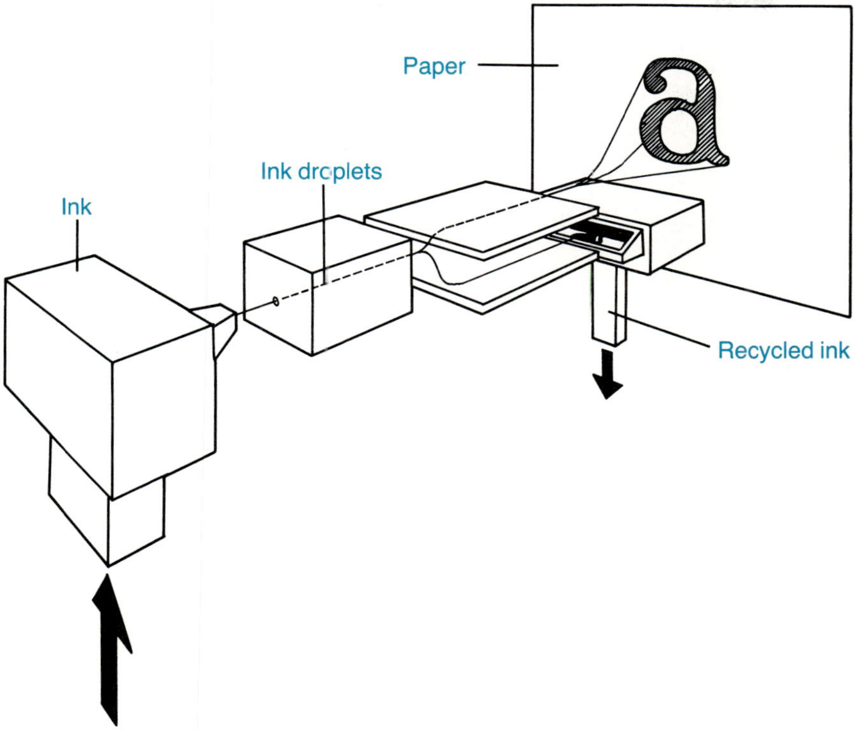

Secondary Storage Hardware

As discussed previously, **secondary storage** is where data and instructions are stored when they are not being processed within the microcomputer. The most common forms of secondary storage in microcomputer systems are disk and tape storage.

Disks A **disk** is a nonvolatile medium used to store programs and data for later use. Recall that programs and data stored in a volatile medium, such as primary storage (RAM), are lost when the power is interrupted or the computer is turned off. A **magnetic disk** is a device used in computers to magnetically store data that can be retrieved directly; the computer can go directly to the location on the disk where the data are stored and retrieve them. Data and instructions are stored as a pattern of magnetic spots that are recorded on and read from tracks on the disks. Once recorded on the surface of the disk, the magnetic spots will remain there even though the electrical flow is turned off.

Disk storage is often referred to as *secondary* or *auxiliary storage,* whereas RAM storage is *primary storage* or *working storage.* Copies of programs and data stored on disks must first be copied or loaded from the disks into primary storage before being processed by the microprocessor. Changes made to the data or instructions must again be saved on a magnetic disk if they are to be stored permanently.

Magnetic disks for microcomputers are either floppy or hard. A **floppy disk** is made of flexible Mylar plastic and comes in a variety of sizes. The most popular floppy disk size is the $5\frac{1}{4}$-inch **minifloppy disk.** The typical $5\frac{1}{4}$-inch, double-density, double-sided floppy disk holds approximately 360K bytes of storage. A **double-sided disk** means data can be written and read from both the top and bottom sides. **Double-density disks** have more storage capacity (40 tracks per inch) per side than single-density disks. **High-density disk drives,** like those found on the IBM AT, typically use $5\frac{1}{4}$-inch disks that can store up to 1.2M bytes on one high-density floppy disk by having 96 tracks of storage per inch.

The $3\frac{1}{2}$-inch **microfloppy** is becoming increasingly popular. Microfloppy disks come in a hard plastic case that fits easily in a pocket. The plastic shell has a shutter to protect the recording surface when the disk is outside the drive, allowing the case to be handled roughly without damage to the enclosed disk. Standard $3\frac{1}{2}$-inch disks, such as those used in laptop microcomputers and the IBM PS/2 Model 30, hold 720K. Microcomputers equipped with high-density disk drives, such as those found on the IBM PS/2 Models 50, 60, 70, and 80, use $3\frac{1}{2}$-inch disks that can hold up to 1.44 megabytes on each disk.

Floppy disks are further classified as hard or soft sectored. These designations do not refer to the hardness of the plastic disk, but rather to whether the sectors are determined by the holes *(hard sectored)* or by the software *(soft sectored).* Most microcomputer disk drives use **soft-sectored disks.**

Figure 1-19 illustrates a $5\frac{1}{4}$-inch floppy disk. In part *(a)* of the figure, notice the common reference points on a $5\frac{1}{4}$-inch floppy disk: the protective plastic sleeve, the labels, the index hole, the write-protect notch, and the read-write head access hole. In part *(b),* notice the *protective plastic sleeve* components, the jacket and liner. They protect the magnetic disk from environmental hazards, including fingerprints. *Labels* are used to describe the contents of the disk. Always label your disk contents with the filename and date.

The **write-protect notch** prevents the drive from writing on protected disks. When the notch on a $5\frac{1}{4}$-inch disk is covered with a tab or tape, the computer can copy or read data from the disk, but the disk is protected so no new data can be written or recorded on the disk. When the notch is uncovered, data can be either copied from or written onto the disk. The smaller microfloppy disks, however, use a sliding write-protect tab built into the rigid case. Both the $5\frac{1}{4}$- and the $3\frac{1}{2}$-inch disks use a *read-write head access hole,* which allows the read-write head to reach the magnetic media. The $3\frac{1}{2}$-inch disk provides a sliding metal covering called a *shutter,* which protects the magnetic media when the disk is removed from the disk drive mechanism of the PC.

FIGURE 1-19 A commonly used $5\frac{1}{4}$-inch floppy disk. Part *(a)* illustrates the common reference points; *(b)* illustrates how the plastic jacket and liner protect the magnetic disk.

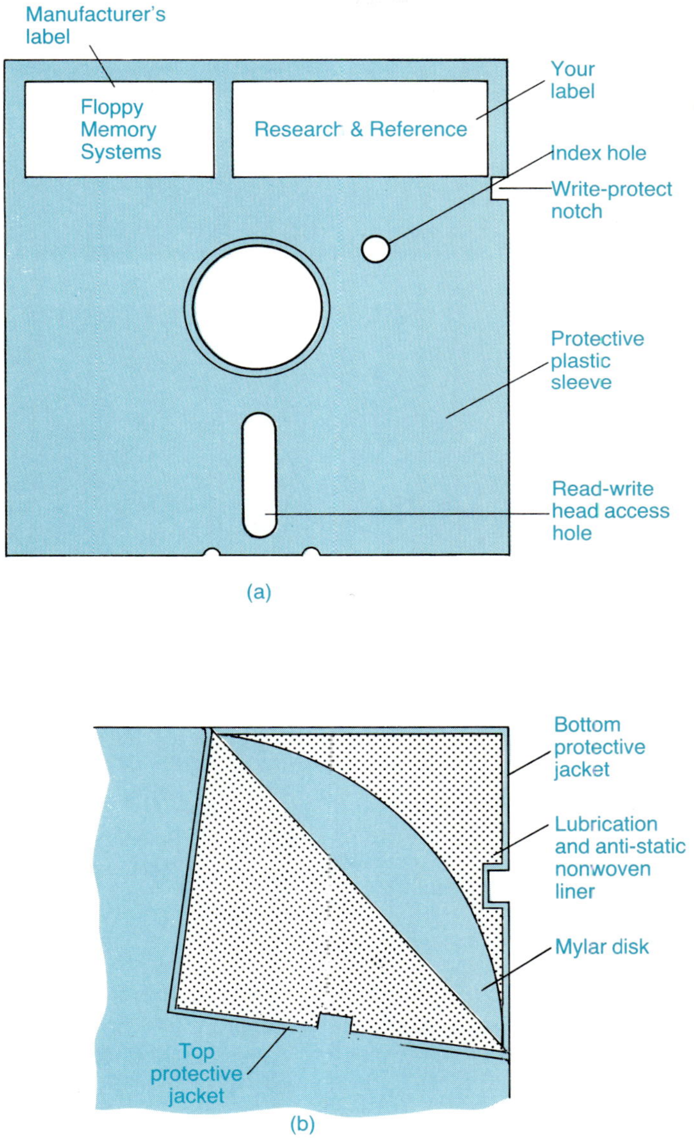

Computers use a **disk map** to relate the items stored on the disk to particular disk sides, tracks, and sectors. Figure 1-20 graphically represents this map. Microcomputers use a variety of disk-mapping schemes to store and find data; therefore, new blank disks must be formatted to correspond

FIGURE 1-20 A representation of a typical formatted floppy disk. The tracks are actually invisible to the eye since they are simply magnetic patterns.

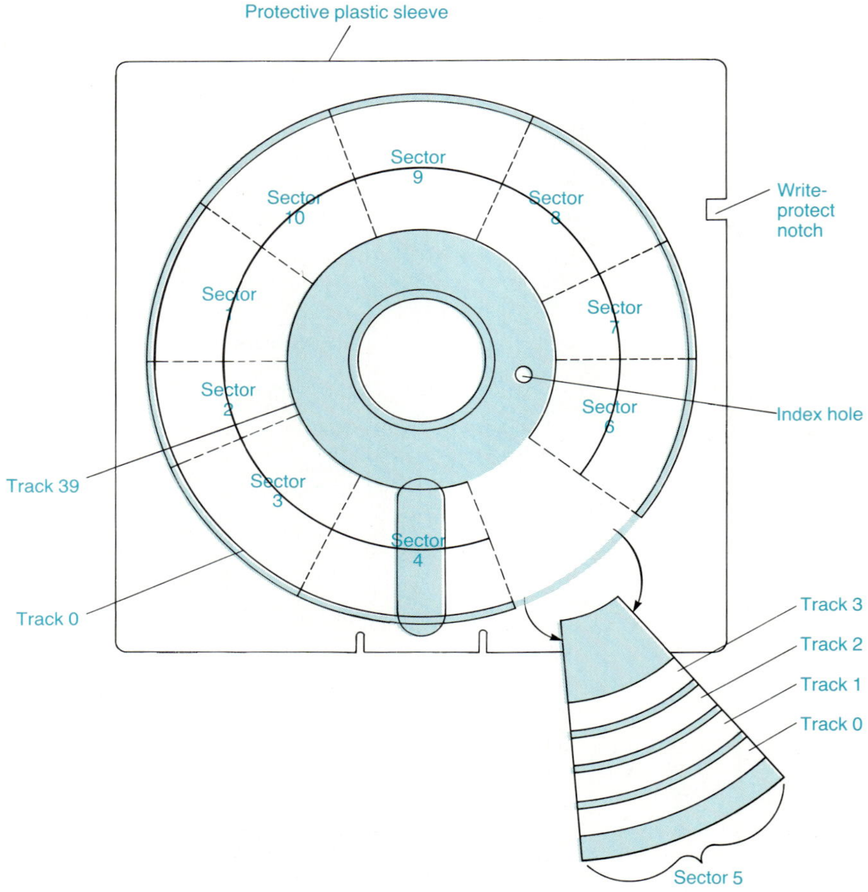

with the particular hardware. **Formatting** is the process of relating the particular microcomputer's disk-mapping scheme to the particular floppy disk. Formatting a disk containing data erases the data stored on that disk. When you buy a new blank disk, it does not contain tracks or sectors. It provides only a blank recording surface. Therefore, you must format it before you can use it. Most microcomputer systems use an operating system utility such as Format to prepare a blank disk for use with a particular microcomputer.

Hard disks have become increasingly common on microcomputers. Hard disks are contained in a unit or installed as an expansion card (see

FIGURE 1-21 Hard disks can be installed as *(a)* an expansion card or as *(b)* a disk unit (with the outer covering cut away). Hard disks greatly increase the storage capacity and access speed of a microcomputer.

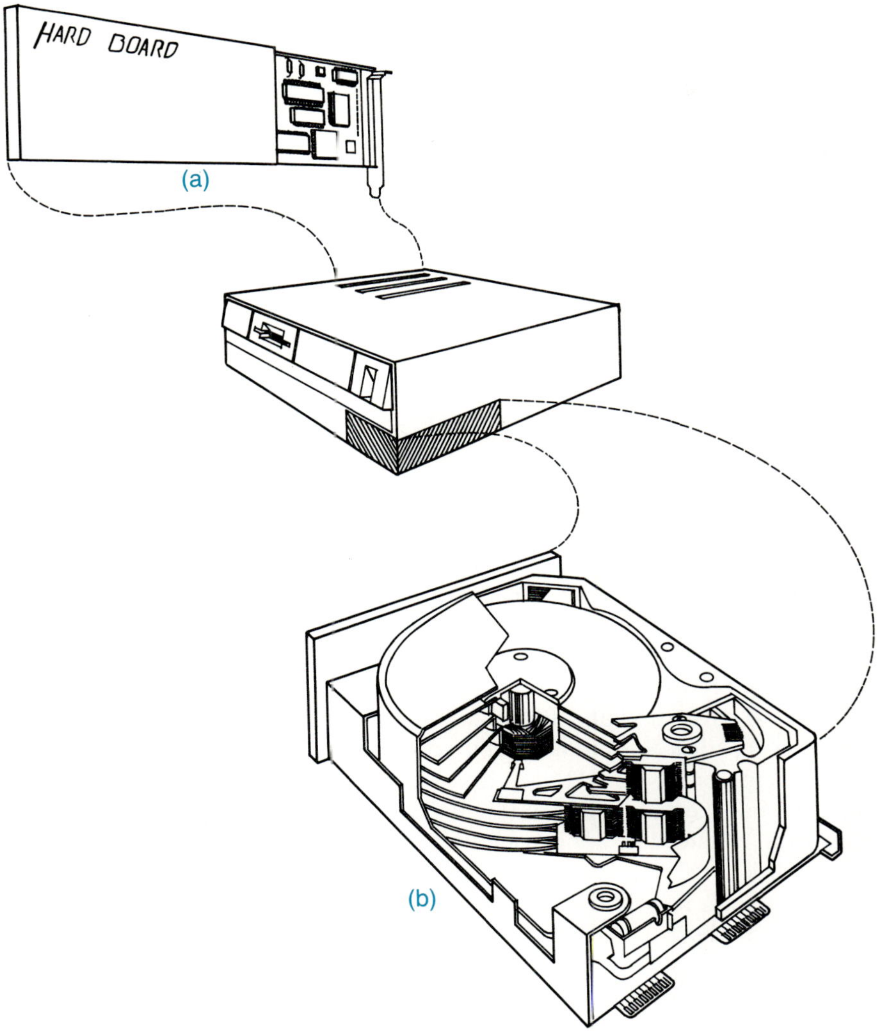

Figure 1-21). A **hard disk,** sometimes called a *Winchester* or *fixed disk,* is an aluminum-alloy disk, coated with continuous magnetic film and covered by an overcoat. The disk and read-write head are sealed within an air-tight container, protecting the disk from environmental pollution. The disk

FIGURE 1-22 Distance between the disk and the read-write head.

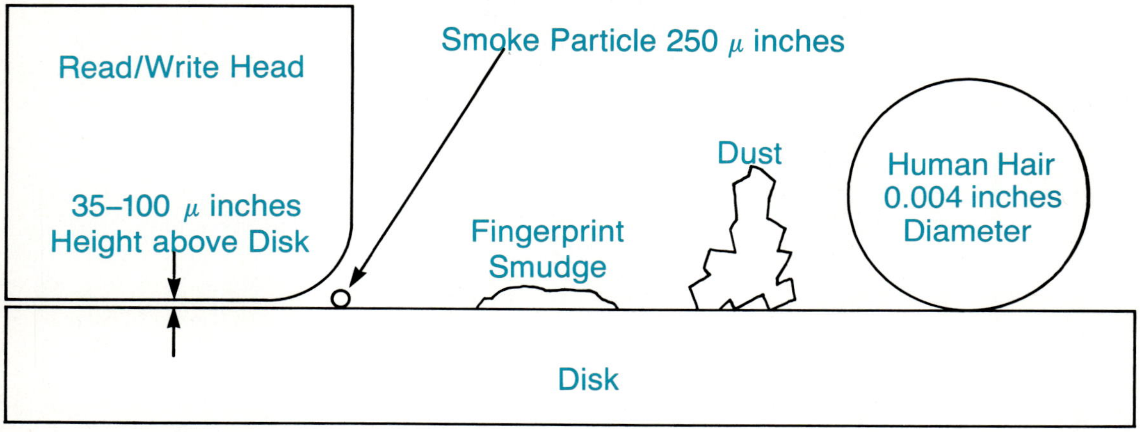

spins at a very high rate, and the read-write head floats just barely above the surface. Figure 1-22 illustrates the distance between the disk and the head compared to some objects we usually think of as being quite small.

Hard disks can hold much more information and work much faster than floppy disks. The typical capacity of a hard disk used in a microcomputer system is 20 to 40 megabytes. However, units are becoming available that can hold 120 or more megabytes. Remember that a $5\frac{1}{4}$-inch floppy disk can hold approximately 360K, or 360,000, bytes. Winchester disks make it possible to have all your software and files on one disk for easy access and use. A hard disk supplements but does not replace floppy disks on a microcomputer system. Floppy disk drives are needed to load programs onto the hard disk, to archive little-used files, or to back up the files on the hard disk. A hard disk microcomputer system usually contains at least one floppy disk drive that is used to load software.

Although it is advantageous to store all your software and data on a single hard disk, a hard disk cannot be removed from the disk drive. Therefore it is essential that important files be copied onto some removable medium, such as a floppy disk or magnetic tape. The disk or tape should then be removed and stored in a safe place.

Tape **Magnetic tape** is often used as backup for a hard disk and is much like the tape used to store music or video. It is coated with magnetic material and uses magnetic codes to store data and instructions. Its big advantages as a backup medium are its low cost and the ease of removing a tape cassette cartridge for storage in a safe location.

TUTORIAL: A TOUR OF YOUR MICROCOMPUTER

To complete this tutorial you need the following:

- Access to the microcomputer system you will use to do the tutorials and exercises in this book

Hardware is just one component of the microcomputer system; however, it is important that you become familiar with the hardware in order to utilize the system. Although each microcomputer system is different, they all share some common elements. This tutorial will help you locate and use these basic hardware components.

Start and Reset the System

Step 1: Locate the on/off switches for the main system unit and the monitor.

The on/off button for the main system unit is usually located on the right side, rear, or front. If you cannot locate the switch easily, check the back of the machine. As you reach around to the back, be careful not to accidentally move the machine off the stand or table.

The on/off switch for the monitor is usually located in the front or rear. Occasionally the switch for the main system unit will also control the monitor.

As fundamental as this may sound, proper use of the on/off switch is important. Improper use can destroy files or even damage your equipment. **Avoid using the on/off switch to reset your microcomputer when you get stuck.** When possible, use the Reset command or button (see below). Follow the software manufacturer's directions when using the on/off switch with floppy disks in the disk drive.

Step 2: Locate the reset button and/or Reset command.

The *Reset command* on most IBM compatibles is a combination of three keys: while holding down both the **Ctrl** and **Alt** keys, press the **Del** key (see Figure 1-23). If the microcomputer has a *reset button,* it is usually located at the rear of the main system unit and is generally small and inconspicuous. If the Reset command fails to work, use the reset button. The reset button or command is to be used when you are stuck, when you cannot get out of a program through normal commands, or when nothing else seems to work. It is important to note that by resetting the machine you lose all contents of primary storage.

Step 3: Turn on the power to the main system unit and the monitor.

Using the on/off switches, turn on the main system unit and the monitor. They may take a few minutes to warm up. Since we have not

FIGURE 1-23 The Reset command is a combination of three keys: Ctrl + Alt + Del.

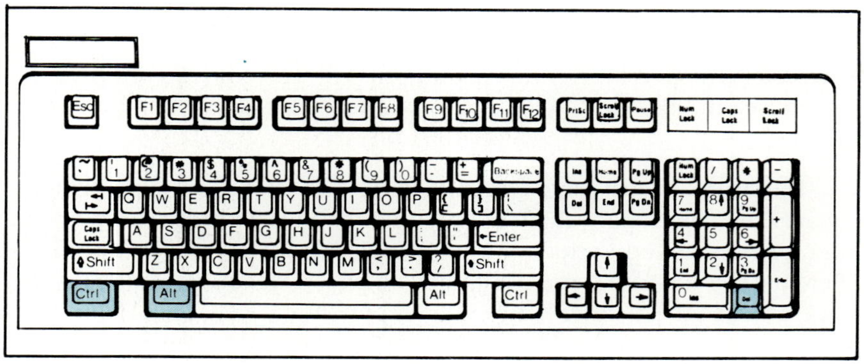

placed a disk in the disk drive, the system will load a small program module stored in the system ROM. This program checks the status of the hardware and loads the operating system when the disk is inserted. It also provides messages on the screen to the user so that the user knows what is going on. It then checks the primary disk drive for a disk containing the operating system. The disk drive indicator usually lights up. Since no disk has been inserted and no operating system loaded, the screen will show a message or prompt explaining that there is a problem—no system has been loaded. The message may even ask for a system disk. (Microcomputer manufacturers differ on the type and scope of these messages.)

Step 4: Reset the system using the Reset command and button.

a. Place a MS-DOS system disk in drive A. Press and hold **Ctrl+Alt** and, while continuing to hold these keys, press **Del.** The system will reset, the screen will go blank, and the system will attempt to restart. This is sometimes called a *warm boot.*

b. After the system requests appear on the screen, if you have a reset button, press it. A reset using the reset button is sometimes called a *cold boot.*

Remember, avoid using the reset button or command unless you have no other way out of a program. You will lose the contents of primary storage and perhaps damage the contents of files. This is particularly true when you are using databases. Databases require a sequence of actions to properly close and save files. A system reset interrupts these actions and may cause unpredictable results.

Locate the Primary Disk Drive

The **primary disk drive** is where the operating system and applications software disk are normally inserted and located. In a dual floppy disk drive system, the primary disk drive is usually drive A. Most microcomputer systems with a hard disk will designate the hard disk as the primary disk drive and name it drive C.

Check to see which disk drive is the primary disk drive. Without inserting a disk, latch and unlatch the drive.

Locate the Brightness and Contrast Controls for the Monitor

Most monitors can be adjusted for brightness and contrast. Brightness and contrast are individual preferences, so find the levels that are comfortable for you. Brightness and contrast controls may be located anywhere on the monitor, although most are located on the front where they are easy to reach.

Locate the Printer and the Printer Controls

Most of the tutorials in this book require you to use a printer. Check with your instructor, lab assistant, or information resource person for details on operating the printer. You should find out how to do the following:

1. *Switch on the printer.*
2. *Switch the printer online and offline. Online* means the computer can transmit data to the printer, and the printer is ready to accept and print data. When a printer is *offline,* no data can be transmitted or printed. This is usually controlled by a switch on the printer. Some printers must be offline to advance paper.
3. *Load the tractor feed paper.* All printers have paper jams eventually, and if you know how to load the tractor feed paper you will avoid delays in printing.
4. *Set the top of form.* A *form* is considered the length of one sheet of paper. For example, most tractor feed paper used with microcomputer printers is perforated every 11 inches. It is important to adjust the paper so that the printing will begin at the top of the form and the text will appear at the proper location on the page. Once the paper has been adjusted, the printer will need to be set to recalculate the number of lines until the top of the next page.
5. *Advance paper by the line or form.* Most printers have switches to advance the paper by the line and by the form.

SUMMARY

In a broad sense, any computer system is composed of hardware, software, people, procedures, and databases. Each component is vitally important to a successful information system. A computer system can also be examined from the point of view of input, processing, output, and auxiliary storage components. In this lesson, major hardware components of a microcomputer system were examined; these included input (keyboard and alternative input devices), processing (microprocessor), output (monitor, printer, and plotter), and auxiliary storage (disks).

EXERCISES

1. Complete the tutorial and answer the following questions:
   a. Where is the on/off switch located?
   b. What messages appear on the screen when the microcomputer system is switched on?
   c. What is the effect of the Reset command?
   d. Does the microcomputer have a reset button?
   e. Where are the monitor brightness and contrast controls located?
   f. What buttons must be pressed to advance the paper in the printer to the top of the next form? What is the sequence?

2. Fill out the microcomputer fact sheet below. Your operating manual, instructor, or designated information resource person should have this information about the microcomputer you will use to do the tutorials and lessons in this book.

   Brand name of the microcomputer: ______________________
   Model number of the microcomputer: ______________________
   Operating system and version used: ______________________
   IBM or IBM-compatible? ______________________
   RAM capacity: ______________________
   ROM capacity: ______________________
   Microprocessor (8-, 16-, or 32-bit): ______________________
   Co-processor: ______________________
   Disk storage capacity
     Number of disk drives: ______________________
     Disk drive capacity in K: ______________________
   Monitor type: ______________________
   Graphics adapter: ______________________
   Printer type: ______________________
   Brand name of printer: ______________________

3. Examine the keyboard on the microcomputer you are using. On the keyboard template in Figure 1-24 mark the appropriate key with the letter immediately preceding the key name below. If the key is not available on your keyboard, put "NA" (not applicable) next to the key name. If your keyboard is different from the one pictured, draw the appropriate placement of the keys.

FIGURE 1-24 Keyboard template to use for Exercise 3.

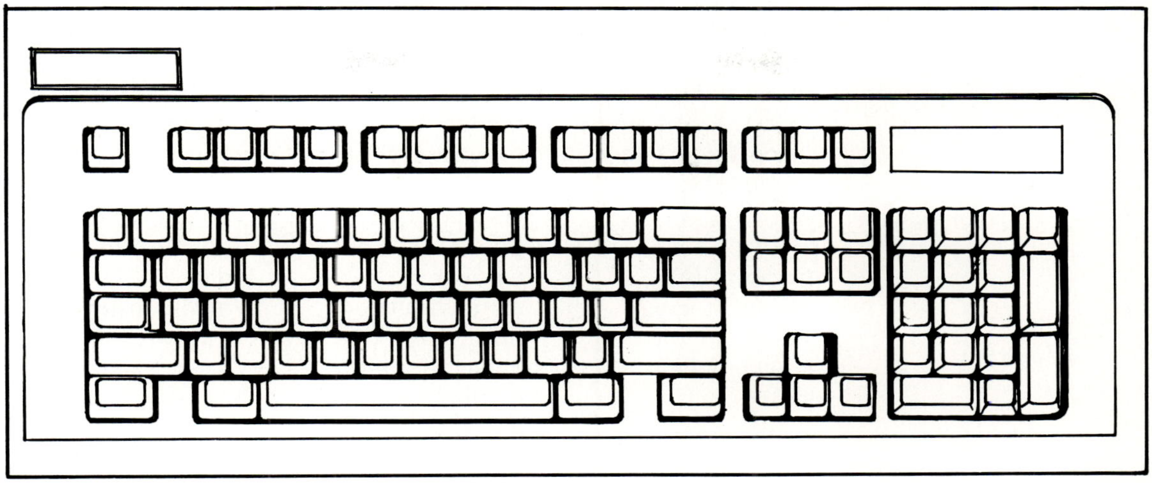

a. Up arrow key
b. [F7] key
c. Esc key
d. PrtSc key
e. Backspace key
f. Enter key
g. Ctrl key
h. Shift key
i. Ins key
j. Home key
k. Num Lock key
l. Down arrow key
m. [F4] key
n. PgUp key
o. Del key
p. Caps Lock key
q. Alt key
r. [F1] key
s. Space Bar
t. Tab key

4. Turn on the microcomputer and the monitor. Most screens will show some image before any instructions have been loaded into the computer. If your microcomputer has automatically loaded a program from ROM, a cursor or a start-up message will appear. Using information from your operating manual, instructor, or information resource person, answer the following questions:
   a. What is the size of the screen (measured diagonally) in inches?
   b. How many columns does the screen show?
   c. Is the monitor monochrome or color?
   d. If the monitor is monochrome, what color is used?
   e. How many pixels does the screen have?

5. Define the following terms:

hardware	cursor	microprocessor
software	mouse	arithmetic and logic unit
data	scanners	registers
procedures	desktop publishing	internal control unit
database	central processing unit(CPU)	bus controller
PC		

bus	volatile storage	laser printer
binary numbering system	random access memory (RAM)	ink-jet printer
bit	read-only memory (ROM)	plotter
American Standard Code for Information Interchange (ASCII)	motherboard	secondary storage disk
byte	expansion board	magnetic disk
kilobyte (K)	word	floppy disk
megabyte (M)	co-processor	minifloppy disk
primary storage	port	double-sided disk
chip	monitor	double-density disk
semiconductor	monochrome	high-density disk drives
doping	pixel	microfloppy
junction	impact printer	soft-sectored disk
integrated circuit	nonimpact printer	write-protect notch
	dot matrix printer	hard disk
	daisy wheel printer	magnetic tape

6. Describe the name, purpose, and action of these specialized keys:
   a. Ctrl
   b. Esc
   c. Caps Lock
   d. Del
   e. Num Lock
   f. Arrow keys
   g. PgDn
   h. End
   i. Home
   j. PgUp
   k. PrtSc
   l. Ins
   m. [F1]
   n. Alt

2
Fundamentals of Microcomputer Software

LESSON OUTLINE

MICROCOMPUTER SOFTWARE

Lesson 1 reviewed the microcomputer system component of hardware, and the exercises helped you become familiar with the hardware used with your microcomputer system. Now we are ready to introduce the next component in the microcomputer system: software. **Software** is generally defined as instructions that direct a computer to process data. These instructions are called *programs.* The term "soft" is used because programs are stored electronically and cannot be physically touched the way you can touch hardware.

There are two general categories of software—systems software and applications software. **Systems software** is a set of programs that coordinates the operations of the various hardware components. Systems software is usually purchased from a software developer and supplied by the computer manufacturer with the hardware. MS-DOS and OS/2, the operating systems supplied with IBM-compatible microcomputers, are examples of a category of systems software. **Applications software** is a set of programs that directs the computer to solve particular problems or to perform certain tasks. Applications software is *user-oriented;* it does what you, the user, want done. Word processing, electronic spreadsheet, and database management software are among the most widely used types of applications software (see Figure 2-1).

Systems Software

Systems software is *computer-oriented;* it takes care of what must be done in order for the computer to operate. The broad category of systems software can be broken down into three divisions: operating systems, utilities, and language processors (see Figure 2-2). As a microcomputer user, you should become familiar with each type of systems software since you will interact closely with them all.

Operating Systems Twenty years ago computer operators were people who worked in computer centers, busily pushing buttons, turning on and off various pieces of equipment and watching over a gigantic mainframe. Such operators were responsible for the smooth operation of the computer system. Today the human operator has been replaced almost entirely by a set of programs called the operating system. An **operating system** supervises the processing of applications programs and all input and output of the microcomputer system. When a microcomputer uses a disk

FIGURE 2-1 The three most widely used types of applications software for microcomputers are word processing, electronic spreadsheets, and data base management.

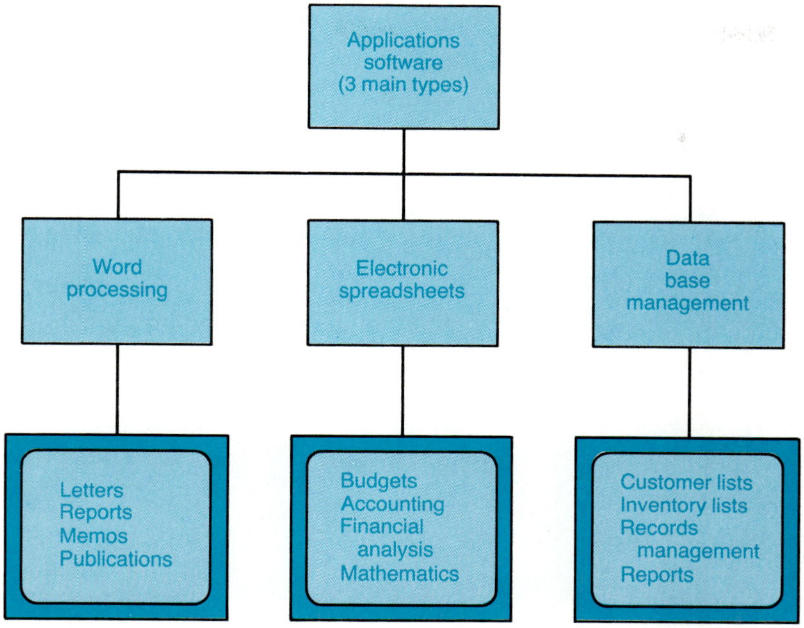

drive, the operating system is often called the **disk operating system** or **DOS.** Operating systems act like air traffic controllers, assuring the orderly, efficient flow of information through the computer. Operating systems translate or interpret human commands into a form the microcomputer hardware can understand (see Figure 2-3). Operating systems also act as intermediaries between applications software and the hardware. All applications software, such as WordPerfect, Lotus, and dBASE III PLUS, interact with the hardware through the operating system. The operating system must be loaded (placed in primary storage) before the applications software can go to work (see Figure 2-4, page 44).

A variety of microcomputer operating systems are available. A particular type and brand is chosen by the hardware manufacturer and then customized for the particular microcomputer. For example, the Apple Macintosh uses Mac DOS, and the Apple II GS uses ProDOS 16.

CP/M-80 (Control Program for Microcomputers) was written by Digital Research and is popular for microcomputer systems based on the 8-bit Z80 chip. CP/M-80 was among the first standard, accessible operating systems for microcomputers. It became one of the dominant operating systems from 1974 until the introduction of the IBM PC and MS-DOS in

FIGURE 2-2 The three main divisions of systems software are operating systems, utilities, and language processors.

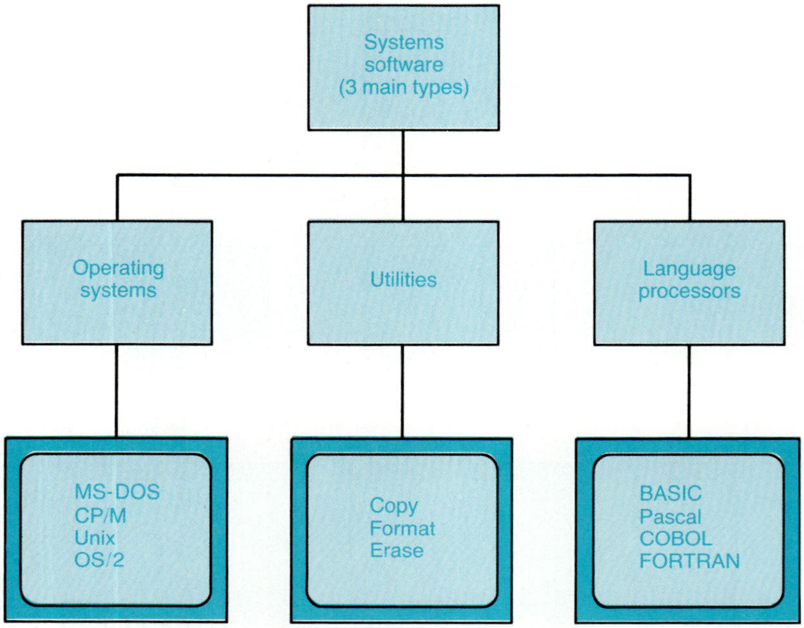

1981. Despite its decline in popularity, CP/M-80 is still widely used on many microcomputer systems. Some microcomputers, such as Apple IIe and Commodore systems, can, with the installation of CP/M-80 expansion boards and additional RAM, access hundreds of business programs written for CP/M-80, such as WordStar (a popular word processing program), SuperCalc (a popular electronic spreadsheet program), and dBase II (a popular database management program).

Unix is a multiuser, multitasking operating system originally developed by Bell Labs (a division of AT&T) in the early 1970s as a program development tool. Since that time, programmers at several universities and at Bell Labs have continued to extend the capabilities of Unix. It was originally used on large multiuser minicomputer systems where several people simultaneously use one computer. However, in recent years Unix has been adapted for use on a wide variety of systems, from microcomputers to mainframes, including more powerful microcomputers based on the Intel 80286, Intel 80386, and Motorola 68000 microprocessors.

Unix is written in a high-level programming language called C. Programs written in C are portable; that is, they can be ported or transmitted from one computer family to another computer family without requiring major rewriting. The portability of Unix from one machine to

FIGURE 2-3 Operating systems translate human commands into commands the microcomputer hardware can understand.

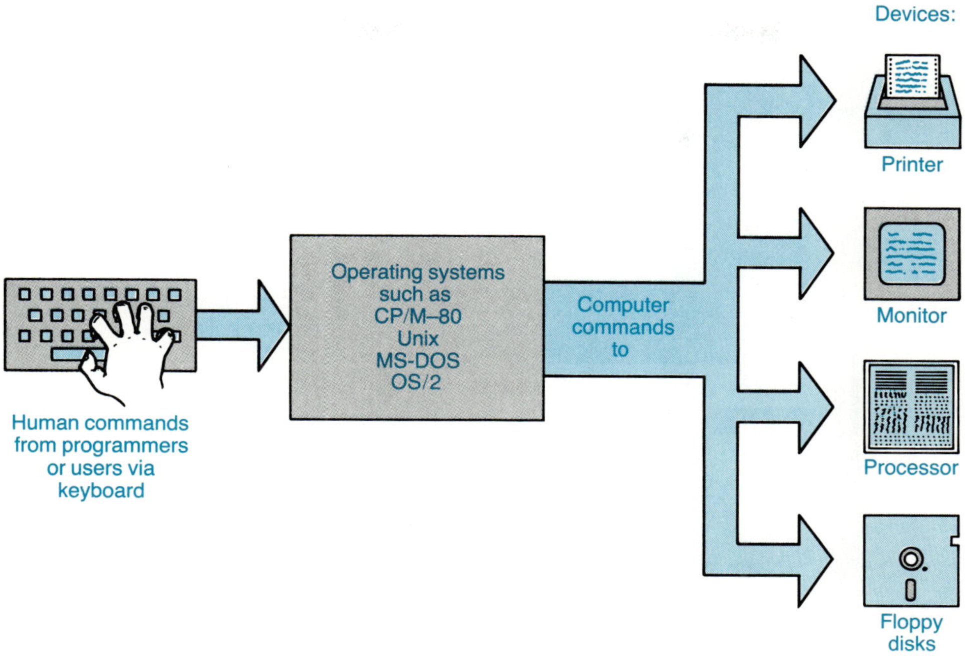

another gives Unix users substantial flexibility in hardware purchase decisions. Applications can be device independent, meaning that the purchase of a particular piece of Unix-compatible applications software does not force the user to install it on a particular type and brand of hardware.

Besides portability and multiuser capability, Unix has many other powerful features not found in most other microcomputer operating systems, including the use of program modules. Software developers can build large applications by connecting small, more manageable modules. A **module** is a program or program segment that is a discrete unit that can be combined with other program units to perform common computer operations such as input, output, and printing. By using modules, programmers can standardize functions, allowing faster, more accurate programming. Unix also allows the easy interconnection of microcomputers using local area networks. A **local area network (LAN)** is a group of personal computers in the same location (such as a building, floor, or room) connected by a common cable and running the same network software.

Despite these advantages, software and hardware developers have been slow to adopt Unix as an operating system. Unix is written primarily

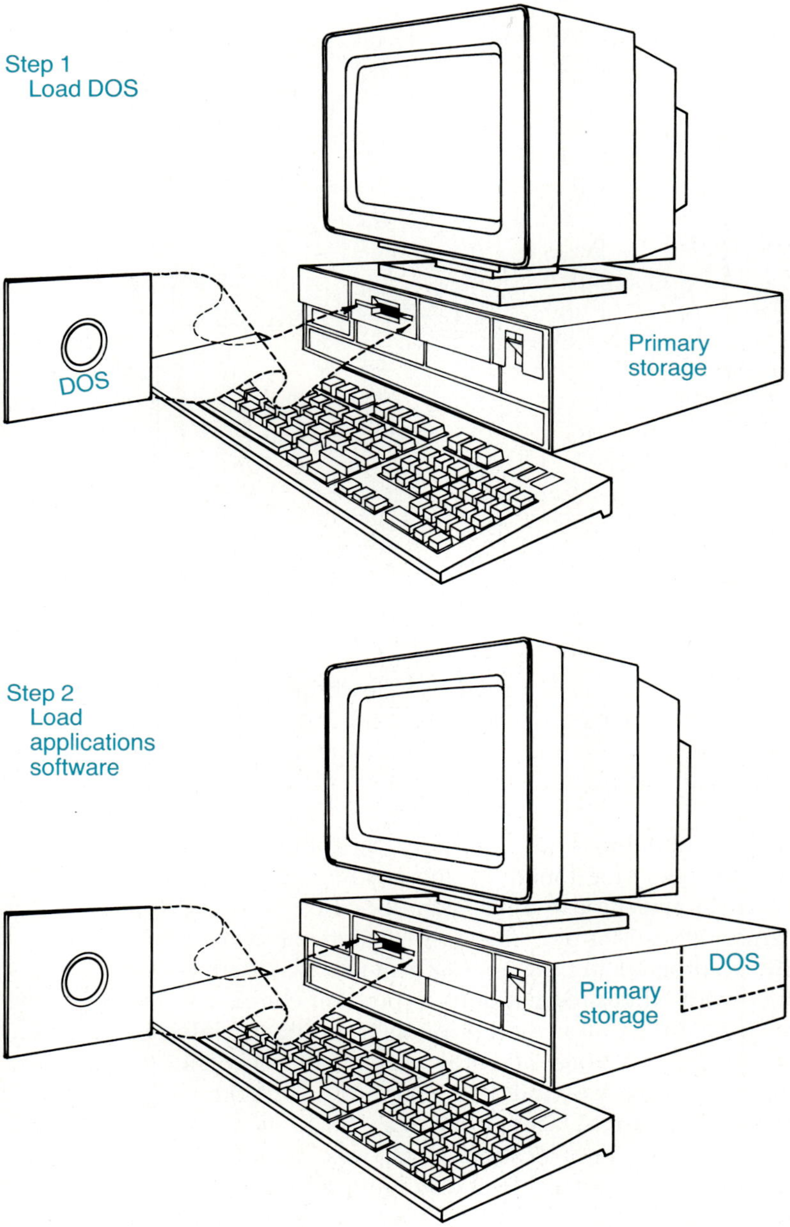

FIGURE 2-4 The operating system (DOS) must be loaded into primary storage before applications software can be loaded. This permits the applications software access to the different components of the microcomputer system.

for programmers and is difficult to learn and use. Fortunately, operating systems developers have begun to modify Unix to make it easier to use. Software packages to merge MS-DOS and Unix permit users to run MS-DOS applications software with the Unix operating system. In addition, more recent versions of popular, more user-oriented software, like MS-DOS, are integrating some of the features of Unix. Some experts predict that the influence of Unix will be greater as microcomputer hardware becomes more powerful and capable of supporting the features of Unix.

MS-DOS (Microsoft Disk Operating System) is the most popular operating system used on 16- and 32-bit microcomputers and is available on a wide variety of microcomputers. The IBM PC operating system is a variation of MS-DOS called **PC-DOS.** Although MS-DOS and PC-DOS are very similar, certain features of PC-DOS make it unique to the IBM PC. Some software that runs on the IBM PC will not necessarily run without modification on a machine using MS-DOS. However, MS-DOS and PC-DOS are so similar that in this book we will use MS-DOS to refer to both PC-DOS and MS-DOS.

Since the introduction of MS-DOS Version 1.0 in 1981, several versions have been developed. *Versions* are like editions of a book. Each is adapted and improved to meet specific needs. A modification of the number following the decimal point, such as 3.0 to 3.1, indicates a minor change from the previous version. A change in the number preceding the decimal point indicates a major change in the operating system. For example, Version 3.0 has several new commands not available in Version 2.0, while Version 3.3 has some minor enhancements on Version 3.0. Each time you start up the microcomputer system, the operating system displays the version number you are using. Table 2-1 lists the different versions of MS-DOS, the changes and improvements in each version, and the reasons for the changes. Several versions of MS-DOS have evolved since its introduction in 1981. Through the development and improvement of the operating system, users can utilize improvements in hardware and software.

It is important to note that different versions of MS-DOS are not always completely compatible. **Compatibility** is the ability of hardware and/or software to interact without special adapters or other devices. It is usually measured on microcomputer systems by the extent to which diskettes and the data and programs contained on the diskettes can be interchanged. There are various levels of compatibility. For example, if two systems are 100 percent compatible, all diskettes designed for one system can be used on the compatible system. When a microcomputer is "100 percent IBM compatible," it should run without modification all software written for the IBM PC. Systems that are partially compatible may require the applications software to be revised in order to work on a particular microcomputer or operating system. For example, not all programs written specifically for the IBM PC using PC-DOS will work on microcomputers using the MS-DOS

Table 2-1 MS-DOS VERSIONS AND FEATURES

Version	*Features*
1.0	CP/M look-alike. Permits users to exchange disks between compatible microcomputers.
1.25	Supports double-sided disks, increasing storage capacity.
2.0	Supports Unix-like hierarchical file structure and hard disks.
3.0, 3.1, 3.2	Offers added support for 1.2 MB floppy disks, higher capacity hard disks, Microsoft networks, and 3½-inch floppy disks.
3.3	Single-tasking operating system for PS/2 systems. Compatible with MS-DOS 3.2 and older models of IBM PC and compatible hardware. Supports 1.4 MB 3½-inch diskettes and hard disks over 32 MB in a partitioned mode as commands to improve system performance.
MS-OS/2	Supports IBM PS/2 microcomputers with basic IBM PC-DOS functions, addresses up to 16 MB of RAM (previous versions of MS-DOS were limited to 640K RAM), virtual memory through segment swapping, multitasking, limited compatibility with older versions of MS-DOS. Contains enhanced windowing, graphics, communications, and networking capabilities as well as built-in extensive help menus and common system interface.

operating system. This is especially true for games and other graphic-intensive applications. If two systems, such as the IBM PC and the Apple Macintosh, are **incompatible,** diskettes cannot be interchanged because they use different operating systems. The software and data files must be extensively modified in order to run on each system.

In addition, files created with one version of MS-DOS may not always be 100 percent compatible with other MS-DOS files. For instance, files collected using Version 2.1 of MS-DOS software are stored on a hard disk differently than files collected using Version 3.1 of MS-DOS. This is an especially critical problem for hard disk users.

While you cannot always be sure that software is 100 percent compatible (using is believing), fortunately, most popular MS-DOS–compatible applications software is designed to work on microcomputers using MS-DOS Version 2.0 or later.

As more powerful microprocessor chips, such as the Intel 80386, become popular, newer versions of MS-DOS are being developed to take advantage of the vast new power of these chips. **OS/2** *(Operating System/2)* is the most recent variation of the MS-DOS operating system for IBM PS/2 Models 50, 60, 70, and 80. OS/2 runs many MS-DOS software applications unchanged. Still, it is not considered 100 percent compatible with all software developed for Versions 2.0–3.3 of MS-DOS. Despite such drawbacks, OS/2 offers significant advantages. Instead of the commands being entered directly at the system prompt (A>), after the operating system is loaded a window appears on the screen, offering several command choices. The user enters a command by highlighting the needed command and clicking a button on a mouse; there are no command names to memorize and no additional typing to do.

Systems can have up to 16 megabytes RAM in primary storage with virtual memory support (previous versions of MS-DOS limited RAM to 640K with no virtual memory support). **Virtual memory** is a technique that transfers data between primary and secondary storage. Software can use secondary storage as if it were primary storage, greatly increasing the amount of primary storage available to the program.

OS/2 also offers users the convenience of **multitasking**—that is, the ability to run two or more software applications at one time. For example, while you are waiting for a complex calculation on an electronic spreadsheet to be completed, you can use word processing to finish a report. In addition, the applications may be shown on the screen simultaneously by way of multiple windows Another feature of OS/2 is its ability to communicate between applications. Results from one program running under OS/2 can be used by another program running under OS/2 at the same time. For example, if you are doing a statistical analysis of data, your graphics software could display the results; no intermediate step of transferring the data is required. OS/2 also offers the advantage of **multiple concurrent communications sessions.** The microcomputer can transmit and receive data from several sources at the same time. If you want to send a file to a friend across the country, while receiving data from another client at the same time, then the OS/2 operating system can support the hardware and software to let you do the job. Another communications feature of OS/2 is *built-in networking* capability. **Networking** is the linking of computers through communications lines. Previous versions of MS-DOS required the user to purchase special enhancements to the operating system to run networking hardware and software. OS/2 also offers sophisticated graphics and enhanced database capabilities. While such features have generally been available on larger computers, OS/2, combined with the 80386 chip, makes such features available to individuals using microcomputers that cost thousands of dollars less than mini and mainframe computers with similar capabilities.

Utilities **Utilities** are programs supplied within the operating system to support the user in the operation of the computer system. Typically, such routine activities as copying disks, copying files, formatting disks, listing file directories, erasing files, and renaming files are included in operating system software. Often these utilities are types of system commands. A **system command** is a communication to the operating system. Such commands request the operating system to carry out a function such as displaying a disk directory, erasing a file, or saving a file. Occasionally such utilities are available within an applications software package. For example, in WordPerfect the user may access a set of file management utilities simply by pressing [F5], Function key 5. Thus the user is saved the time and trouble of memorizing system commands. The applications software acts as an intermediary, telling the operating system what to do.

There are two basic categories of MS-DOS commands—external and internal. **External DOS commands** must have the utility program files present on the disk currently being used. For example, the utility program Format must be present on the disk in drive A (if you have a floppy disk drive system and drive A is usually the default disk drive) when the command Format is invoked. Such program files are usually on the MS-DOS disk and may be copied onto other program disks.

Internal DOS commands are always present whenever MS-DOS has been loaded into primary storage, even after the MS-DOS disk has been removed. Therefore, internal commands can be used even if the MS-DOS disk is not in the disk drive.

If you are using a dual disk drive system, load MS-DOS, or place a copy of the operating system into primary storage, by inserting the floppy disk with the label facing up into disk drive A (generally the left or top drive). The write-protect notch should be on the lefthand side. Latch the disk drive door. Turn on the power switch to the main console unit and, if necessary, turn on the monitor. The microcomputer will take a few minutes to check that the memory and keyboard are working properly. MS-DOS is then copied from the disk into primary storage. The appearance of the **system prompt** (A>) indicates that the operating system has been loaded and is waiting for a command to be typed. The system prompt also indicates the current logged disk drive, usually drive A. All system commands should be entered at the system prompt. To change the current logged disk drive, at the system prompt type

```
A>B:
```

The system prompt will indicate that the logged disk drive has been changed to disk drive B by changing to

```
B>
```

Following the system prompt is a blinking underline symbol called the **cursor.** The cursor indicates where the typed characters will be displayed. The cursor also acts as a prompt, waiting for a command or information to be entered before work can be continued. When entering MS-DOS commands, remember that you can erase any typing errors by pressing the Backspace key. Press the Return key to complete the operation. DOS checks the results; if it detects an error, it will display an error message.

One of the convenient features of MS-DOS system commands is the **wildcard characters.** The wildcard characters of * and ? permit most DOS commands to affect several files with one command. Use the wildcard characters when you want to do the same thing to several files. A ? (question mark) can replace any *single* character, while the * (asterisk) can replace a *group* of characters. For example, the command

```
A>ERASE LETTER?.DOC
```

would erase

```
LETTER.DOC
LETTER1.DOC
LETTER2.DOC
LETTER3.DOC
```

but not

```
LETTER1A.DOC
LETTER1B.DOC
LETTER1C.DOC
```

The command

```
A>ERASE *.BAK
```

would erase all the files on drive A with the .BAK extension, such as

```
LETTER.BAK
REPORT.BAK
TERM.BAK
```

An **extension** is a suffix added to the filename, after the period (.), that helps describe the contents of the file. To find all the files on disk drive B that begin with the letter R, enter the command

```
A>DIR B:R*
```

A list such as

```
REPORT1.DOC
RESUME.DOC
```

will appear.

Despite the obvious advantages of the wildcard commands, they should be used with caution. When combined with the ERASE command, wildcard characters can be very destructive very quickly. For example, suppose you have spent the last three days preparing a report that is due tomorrow. It is 11 P.M. and your only disk is almost filled, so you decide to delete some unneeded backup files. But instead of giving the command **A>**delete b:*.bak, you enter **A>**delete b:report.*. Before you know it, all the files with the filename "report"—with any filename extension—have been erased.

If you give the command

```
A>erase *.*
```

to erase all files on a disk directory, most versions of MS-DOS will display a warning, giving you a chance to change your mind:

```
Are you sure (Y/N)?
```

Any answer except "Y" (yes) will cancel the command. If you type Y, then everything on the disk will be erased in a flash. Use the wildcard characters carefully.

Another convenient feature of DOS is the *Repeat commands.* The [F1] (Function key 1) and [F3] (Function key 3) can save keystrokes by repeating the last command entered. [F1] repeats the last command entered one character at a time, so you can change characters in the command. For example, if you incorrectly entered a command, say,

```
A>DER
```

you could correct it by using the [F1] command to retrieve the **d** and, after you type the **i**, to retrieve the **r**:

```
A>[F1]di[F1]r
```

[F3] repeats the entire command. For example, let's say you are looking at the directory of a series of floppy disks. Instead of typing the Dir command every time you change disks, you can press [F3] and DOS will reenter the Dir command:

```
A>dir
A>[F3]dir
```

Another handy feature of MS-DOS is the *PrtSc key.* You can print the contents of the current screen display simply by pressing the Shift and PrtSc keys simultaneously. To continuously print everything the screen displays, press Ctrl and PrtSc. To turn the printing off, press Ctrl-PrtSc again. For example, press Ctrl-PrtSc and then enter the Directory command

```
A>DIR
```

The disk directory will display on the screen and print at the same time. Note, however, that some applications may not accept the Ctrl-PrtSc command. Also, your printer may not interpret graphic characters correctly, and some strange-looking output may result.

Utility Commands The commands below describe some of the MS-DOS utilities you should be familiar with for day-to-day use. By learning these utilities you will be able to use your microcomputer system more efficiently and effectively. The commands are presented in alphabetical order so they can be located easily. The explanation for each command includes the purpose of the command; whether the command is internal or external; and the format or syntax of the command, including the command options, an example using the command, and additional notes.

Remember the following rules when using these commands:

- MS-DOS does not discriminate between upper- and lowercase letters. All commands, filenames, and parameters may be entered in either upper or lower case.
- The command format or syntax is as follows:
  (1) The commands, listed in upper case in the formats, should be entered without additional spaces. You can, however, enter the command in either upper or lower case.
  (2) Items in square brackets [ ], are optional.
  (3) Items in lower case and angle brackets, < >, are required.
- Remember that the brackets are just a reminder of which parts of the commands are required or optional; you should not type the brackets in the commands. If you get confused about command syntax, look at the examples.

While this is not a comprehensive explanation of all MS-DOS utilities, it gives you the most common uses for these handy "housekeeping" utilities. Check with your instructor or lab personnel for more information on using these and any special DOS utilities for microcomputer networks or hard disk systems.

CLEAR COMMAND (Cls)

Purpose: The Clear command clears the contents of the screen. It does not affect the contents of the file, either in primary memory or on the disk; it simply erases the screen.

Type: Internal

Format:

```
CLS
```

COPY COMMAND

Type: Internal

COPY CON permits you to place directly into a named file characters typed on the keyboard and appearing on the screen.

Format:

```
COPY CON [d:]<filename>
```

Where

[d:] = letter of the drive, followed by a colon, where disk file to be constructed is to be stored. If the disk drive letter is omitted, DOS assumes you want to use the disk in the currently logged drive.

<filename> = the name of the file to be constructed.

Example:

```
A>copy con autoexec.bat
  REM Lotus 1-2-3 is being loaded
  LOTUS
  ^Z
```

would create a file named AUTOEXEC.BAT that would show on the screen the message "Lotus 1-2-3 is being loaded" and then would load Lotus. The ^ Z (Control-Z) is a end-of-file marker. Press and hold the Control key and then press the Z key.

COPY FILE directs DOS to duplicate to another disk one file or a group of files as defined by the command. It also copies one or more files to the same disk, provided the new files have different names than the originals. Wildcard characters can be used to copy a set of files.

Format:

```
COPY [d1:]<filename> [d2:]<filename>[/v]
```

Where [d1:] = letter of the drive, followed by a colon, that contains the source disk of the file(s) to be copied. If the disk drive is omitted, DOS assumes you want to use the disk in the current drive.

[d2:] = letter of the drive, followed by a colon, that contains the target disk of the copied file(s). If the disk drive is omitted, DOS assumes you want to use the disk in the current drive, and the target file must have a new name.

[/v] = verify option to confirm that the copy is exactly the same as the original.

Examples:

```
A>copy letter1.doc b:
```

copies the filename "LETTER1.DOC" to the disk in drive B.

```
A>copy *.doc b:
```

copies all the files on drive A with the suffix "doc" to the disk in drive B.

```
A>copy rpt1.doc b:engrpt.doc
```

copies the file "RPT1.DOC' to the disk in drive B and names the file in drive B "ENGRPT.DOC."

```
A>copy rpt1.doc+rpt2.doc+rpt3.doc bkrpt.doc
```

combines three files to create a new file, "bkrpt.doc".

The /V (verify) option checks that the file contents on the newly copied file exactly match the original file. For example,

```
A>copy letter1.doc b:/v
```

copies "LETTER1.DOC" to the disk in drive B and verifies that the contents match the original file on the disk in drive A.

COPY TO DEVICE can be used to direct a file to a printer.
Format:

```
COPY [d:]<filename> <device>
```

Where

[d1:] = letter of the drive, followed by a colon, that contains the source disk of the file(s) to be copied. If the disk drive is omitted. DOS assumes you want to use the disk in the current drive.
<device> = the name of the output device

Example:

```
A>copy letter1.doc prn
```

sends the contents of the file "LETTER1.DOC" to the printer.

Only files stored in text or in ASCII code should be printed using this method. Other files may contain unprintable codes.

DATE COMMAND

Purpose: The Date command sets the internal calendar of the microcomputer system so that all files are stamped with the date of origin or latest modification.

Type: Internal

Format:

```
DATE [mm-dd-yy]
```

Where

mm = number of month (1–12)
dd = day of the month (1–31)
yy = last two digits of year

Example:

```
A>DATE 12-03-90
```

If the operating system requires the manual insertion of time and date it will, when the system is first turned on, prompt with a message similar to the following:

```
Current date is Tue 1-01-1980
Enter new date (mm-dd-yy):
```

If the date is accepted, the system will prompt for the time. (See TIME for further instructions on setting the time.)

DIRECTORY (Dir) COMMAND

Purpose: The Directory command displays all or specified files in the logged disk directory and indicates the amount of unused disk space remaining on the disk. A **directory** is a list of files and their attributes, including file size and date and time of origin or modification.

Type: Internal

Format:

```
DIR [d:][filename][/w][/p]
```

Where

[d:] = letter of the drive, followed by a colon, that contains the disk whose directory is to be examined. If the disk drive is omitted, DOS assumes you want to use the disk in the current drive.
[filename] = name of the individual file to be located
[/w] = wide option
[/p] = pause option

Examples:

```
A>DIR
```

displays all the files in the logged drive directory:

```
 Volume in drive A has no label
 Directory of A:\

LETTER1   BK!     758   11-20-87    2:12p
LETTER2B  BK!     629    7-15-87    1:00p
LETTER2   BK!     592    4-16-87    9:56a
LETTER3   BK!    5380   12-31-87    1:35p
LETTER1A  BK!    10C7    5-12-87    3:21p
LETTER1B  BK!    2224   12-16-87    1:01p
LETTER    BK!    1169    2-21-87   12:02p
LETTER2A  BK!    2028    1-20-88    7:50p
LETTER    DOC    1168    2-26-88    9:25a
LETTER1   DOC     758    2-26-88    9:25a
LETTER1A  DOC    1007    2-26-88    9:26a
LETTER2   DOC     592    2-26-88    9:26a
LETTER1B  DOC    2224    2-26-88    9:26a
LETTER2A  DOC    2028    2-26-88    9:26a
LETTER2B  DOC     629    2-26-88    9:27a
LETTER3   DOC    5380    2-26-88    9:27a
      16 File(s)   695296 bytes free
```

```
A>DIR *.BK!
```

displays all the files with the .BK! extension:

```
 Volume in drive A has no label
 Directory of A:\

LETTER1   BK!     758   11-20-87    2:12p
LETTER2B  BK!     629    7-15-87    1:00p
LETTER2   BK!     592    4-16-87    9:56a
LETTER3   BK!    5380   12-31-87    1:35p
LETTER1A  BK!    1007    5-12-87    3:21p
LETTER1B  BK!    2224   12-16-87    1:01p
LETTER    BK!    1169    2-21-87   12:02p
LETTER2A  BK!    2028    1-20-88    7:50p
       8 File(s)   695296 bytes free
```

```
A>DIR letter1.doc
```

displays the directory entry for the file named "LETTER1.DOC":

```
  Volume in drive A has no label
  Directory of A:\

LETTER1  DOC    758    2-26-88    9:25a
        1 File(s)    695296 bytes free
```

```
A>DIR/w
```

displays the filenames and extensions in five columns across the screen (this option does not show the file size, date, or time):

```
  Volume in drive A has no label
  Directory of A:\

LETTER1  BK! LETTER2B BK! LETTER2  BK! LETTER3  BK! LETTER1A BK!
LETTER1B BK! LETTER   BK! LETTER2A BK! LETTER   DOC LETTER1  DOC
LETTER1A DOC LETTER2  DOC LETTER1B DOC LETTER2A DOC LETTER2B DOC
LETTER3  DOC
        16 File(s)    695296 bytes free
```

```
A>DIR/p
```

displays one screen at a time (23 lines), pausing at the end of each screen. The listing will continue to the next screen after any key is pressed.

DISKCOPY (DISK COPYING) COMMAND

Purpose: The Diskcopy command makes an exact duplicate of the contents of the source disk onto the target disk.

Type: External

Format:

```
DISKCOPY [d1:] [d2:][/1]
```

Where

[d1:] = letter of the drive, followed by a colon, that contains the source disk to be copied. If the disk drive is omitted, DOS assumes you want to copy the disk in the current drive.

[d2:] = letter of the drive, followed by a colon, of the target disk on which the copy is to be placed. If the disk drive is omitted, DOS assumes you want to copy to the current drive.

[/1] = single-side copy option

Example:

```
A>DISKCOPY A: B:
```

copies the contents of the source disk, the disk in drive A, onto the target disk in drive B.

PC-DOS (the IBM version of MS-DOS) will also format the target disk, if needed. Other versions of MS-DOS may not automatically do so. For more information, see the following discussion on formatting a disk.

Normally, it is not recommended that you use Diskcopy to copy complete disks because it gives an *exact* duplicate of the disk (provided the original disk is not copy protected), including any fragmented sections of files. Instead, use the COPY command,

```
A>copy *.* b:
```

to copy all the complete files from the source disk in drive A to the target disk in drive B. The Copy command organizes files more efficiently on the target disk, leaving more room on the disk.

Another caution about copying: Most microcomputer software is sold with strict limitations on its use. Usually the purchase of the software licenses you to just *use* the software—you do not *own* it. The manufacturers or creators of software are permitting you to use it under certain conditions. Copying of certain software is severely restricted. Illegal copying of a floppy disk that contains programs protected by copyright laws is called **pirating.** At some firms employees caught pirating software are subject to immediate dismissal, and some schools consider pirating software grounds for expulsion.

FORMAT COMMAND

Purpose: The Format command prepares the disk in the default drive so that it can accept data. As discussed in Lesson 1, all disks must be formatted to correspond to the microcomputer's disk-mapping scheme. Formatting prepares a blank disk to accept files by giving addresses for tracks and sectors on the disk. These addresses will be used by the computer to save and later locate files. The formatting process also checks to see that each track of the disk is usable. Therefore, new disks need to be formatted before they can store data. On previously used disks, formatting destroys all data on the disks. Hard disk users should be particularly careful about using the Format command. Accidentally formatting a hard disk containing 20 or more megabytes of data can be disastrous because hundreds of pages of material can be erased in a flash.

Type: External

Format:

```
FORMAT [d:][/S]
```

Where

[d:] = letter of the drive, followed by a colon, that contains the disk to be formatted. If the disk drive is omitted, DOS assumes you want to format the disk in the current drive.
[/S] = system option

Example:

```
A>FORMAT B:/S
```

The /S (System) option places the essential operating system files on the newly formatted disk, creating a formatted system disk. This allows the operating system to load directly from the disk, which is convenient on program disks. A disk that will contain only files—no software—normally will not need the system placed on the disk.

LABEL COMMAND (MS-DOS VERSION 3.xx)

Purpose: The Label command places a volume name of up to 11 characters on a disk. Disk labels help identify the contents of a disk.

Type: External

Format:

```
LABEL [d:][label]
```

Where

[d:] = letter of the drive, followed by a colon, that contains the disk on which the volume label is to be created or altered.
[label] = the volume label to be assigned to the disk in the specified drive.

Example:

```
A>LABEL B:FASSIGNS
```

This label would allow a student to easily identify the disk containing the class assignments for the Fall semester.

To delete a label, do not enter any label name; just press Enter after giving the command.

RENAME COMMAND

Purpose: The Rename or Ren command changes the name of a file to a specified name. It does not copy or alter a file.

Type: Internal

Format:

```
RENAME [d:]<oldname> <newname>
```

Where

[d:] = letter of the drive, followed by a colon, that contains the disk for which the name is to be changed. If the disk drive is omitted, DOS assumes you want to use the disk in the current drive.
<oldname> = the name of an existing file.
<newname> = the new name of file.

Examples:

```
A>RENAME B:LETTER1.DOC LETTER2.TXT
```

changes the name of the file on the disk in drive B from LETTER1.DOC to LETTER2.TXT.

```
A>RENAME B:REPORT1.APR *.004
```

renames REPORT1.APR to REPORT1.004.

```
A>rename b:*.doc *.fal
```

renames the extension of all the files with the suffix .DOC to the suffix .FAL on the disk in drive B.

If the file does not exist or if the new filename already exists, DOS replies, "File not found." If you try to create a new file using an existing filename, DOS replies, "Duplicate filename." Two files on the same disk cannot have identical names.

SYSTEM COMMAND

Purpose: The System command copies the hidden operating files (IBMBIO.COM and IBMDOS.COM) to the newly formatted floppy disk or to a disk that has the first two directory entries empty. Hidden files are not listed when you give the Directory command. With these system files on the disk, the disk becomes self-booting; that is, the essential files of the operating system can be loaded directly from the disk rather than from the MS-DOS operating system disk.

Type: External

Format:

```
SYS [d:]
```

Where

[d:] = the letter of the drive, followed by a colon, that contains the disk that is to hold the system files.

Example:

```
A>SYS B:
```

In order for you to use the Sys command, the disk directory must be empty; or the disk must have been formatted using the /S option; or the disk must have been formatted with the /B option, which formats the disk with eight sectors per track. Some copy-protected disks may require the use of the SYS command to place the operating system on the program disk. Such disks usually leave room for the system files on the first two directory entries.

TYPE COMMAND

Purpose: The Type command causes the contents of a specified file to be displayed on the screen.

Type: Internal

Format:

```
Type [d:]<filename>
```

Where

[d:] = letter of the drive, followed by a colon, that contains the file to be typed. If the disk drive is omitted, DOS assumes you want to use the current drive.

<filename> = name of the file to be displayed.

Example:

```
A>TYPE LETTER1.DOC
```

will display on the screen the contents of the file "LETTER1.DOC."

Only files containing ASCII text will be in an understandable format. If DOS cannot find the named file, it displays "Invalid filename" or "File not found" and returns to the system prompt. Wildcard characters cannot be used with the Type command.

The Type command displays files without stopping, so if the file is longer than the approximately 24 lines on one screen, you can pause the display by pressing the Ctrl-S (any other key will restart the display) or Ctrl-Num Lock keys. Pressing the Control-Scroll Lock keys will restart the scrolling. To print the file as it appears on the screen, type Control-P or Control-PrtSc before entering the Type command.

TIME COMMAND

Purpose: The Time command sets the internal clock of the microcomputer system so that all files are labeled with the time of origin or latest modification.

Type: Internal

Format:

```
TIME [hh:mm:ss.xx]
```

Where

hh = hour of the day, using the 24 hour clock (1–24)
mm = minutes (01–59)
ss = seconds (01–59)
xx = hundredths of a second

Example:

```
A>TIME 13:01
```

If only part of time is entered, the remaining fields will be left as 00, so the time set in the example will be 13:01:00.00. If the operating system requires the manual insertion of time and date, it will, when the system is first turned on, prompt with a message similar to the following:

```
Current time is 0:01:30.00
Enter new date:
```

BATCH FILES

Purpose: Batch files—with the .BAT extension—contain a list of DOS commands (such as DIR, ERASE, or RENAME) or program commands (such as commands to load programs), to be executed when the batch file name is entered. It is not necessary to type the .bat extension when entering the batch filename. For example,

```
A>hkeep
```

is a batch file containing the following commands:

```
dir b:
erase b:*.bak
dir b:
```

First, the Directory command (dir) would show a listing of the files contained in the directory of the disk in drive B. Next, all the files with the .BAK suffix would be erased. The asterisk (*) is a wildcard character, meaning any file with the .BAK would be erased. A new directory listing would appear, indicating that all the .BAK files had been erased.

One of the handiest batch files available in MS-DOS is AUTOEXEC.BAT. When the operating system is loaded, it will automatically execute the AUTOEXEC.BAT file. For example, if you place on your WordPerfect program disk an autoexec.bat file containing the command

```
WP
```

MS-DOS would automatically load WordPerfect after loading the operating system.

To construct a batch file, you can use the COPY CON command explained earlier. Just remember to name the file AUTOEXEC.BAT if you want the file to be executed immediately after MS-DOS has been loaded. You can halt the execution of the batch file at any time by pressing and holding down the Control key and pressing the C key.

Language Processors **Language processors** are programs that read programs written in high-level languages, such as BASIC, COBOL, or FORTRAN, and convert the statements into machine language the computer can execute. A **program** is a set of instructions that causes the computer system to perform specific actions. **Programming** is the act of writing such a set of instructions. The program statements are sometimes referred to as **code,** and writing these statements is called **coding. Machine language** is the actual binary code used by the computer. Ordinarily you would not be using machine language because the language processor automatically converts the instructions into machine language. There are two types of language processors—interpreters and compilers.

An **interpreter** reads a program written in BASIC or another high-level language and converts it, step by step, into machine language. The translation and execution of the program are performed simultaneously, much like a human interpreter translating an on-going conversation between an American speaking only English and a Soviet speaking only Russian (see Figure 2-5).

In contrast, a **compiler** converts an entire high-level program into a machine language program all at once. To again relate this to a conversation between an American and a Soviet, a person acting like a compiler would first read or listen to the entire speech made by the Soviet and then repeat the entire speech in English, getting the meaning correct, if not translating each and every word exactly. In such cases the high-level program is called **source code.** The resulting machine language program is called **object code.** An object code program is more efficient to the computer in terms of

FIGURE 2-5 An interpreter reads a program and converts it line by line into machine language.

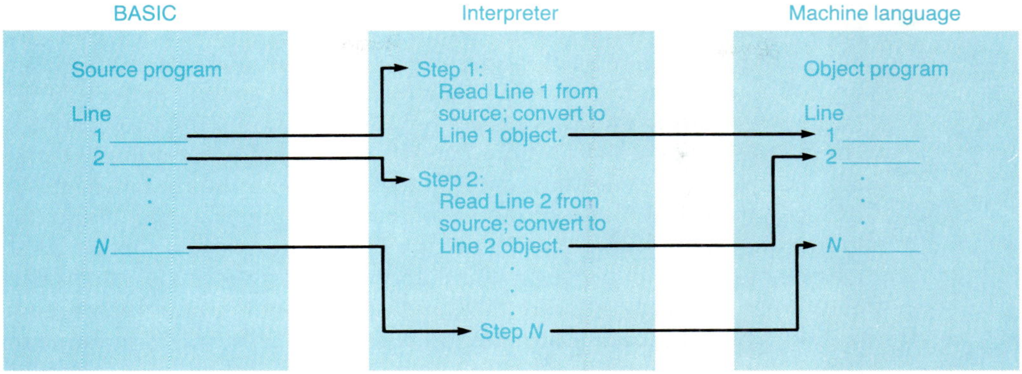

size and speed than the same program would be if processed through an interpreter (see Figure 2-6).

Beginning or occasional programmers usually prefer to use an interpreter because doing so makes it easier to detect and remove errors (**bugs**). Most interpreters have built-in error detection and error messages. Some even have facilities for tracing errors. An interpreted program can be halted and corrected anywhere within the program. More experienced, professional programmers may prefer compilers because of the added speed of execution, efficiency in storage space used, and protection from program pirating. Most commercially available software (called **software packages**) use an object code, so the buyer cannot see exactly how the

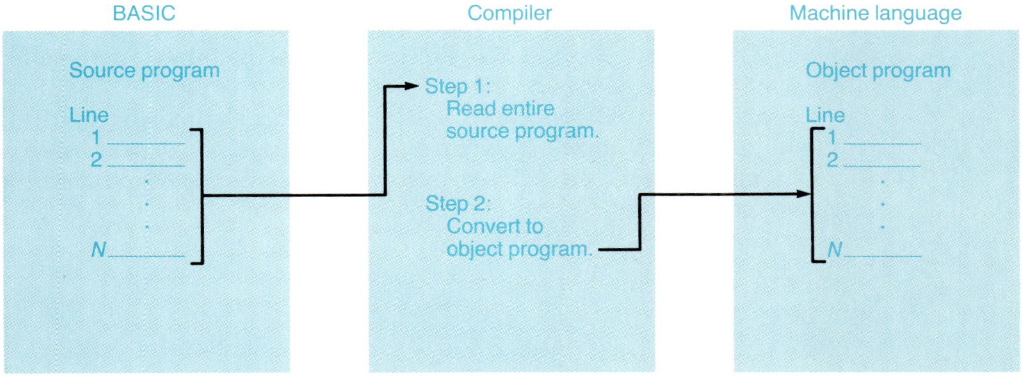

FIGURE 2-6 A compiler translates an entire program at once, converting the source code into machine language object code. Only the object code is used when the program is executed.

program was written. This makes it less likely the buyer will alter the program code and try to resell the program to others. There are several programming languages available for use on microcomputers. Among the most popular are BASIC, Pascal, and C.

BASIC (*B*eginners *A*ll-Purpose *S*ymbolic *I*nstruction *C*ode) is either built in or supplied with almost all microcomputers, including the IBM PC (whose version of BASIC is called BASICA) and most IBM compatibles (usually GW-BASIC). It was introduced in 1965 by Professors John Kemeny and Thomas E. Kurtz at Dartmouth College as an easy-to-use language for college students, available only on mainframe computers. Designers quickly adapted BASIC for the microcomputer because it required so little RAM (remember that the first microcomputers had 4K to 8K RAM, versus the 640K RAM standard on most MS-DOS machines today), was relatively easy to learn and code, and was cheap to license. The most common forms of BASIC are written and licensed by Microsoft, including the most popular forms found on IBM and IBM-compatible microcomputers, BASICA and GW-BASIC. Microcomputer BASIC is hardware and operating system independent, interactive, and easy to learn (some people even think it is fun). **Interactive** means that BASIC can be programmed to prompt the user for data, have the user enter data, and then process the supplied data all while the program is executing.

A simple BASIC program is composed of a set of numbered lines that give commands to the computer. Each statement line gives an order to the computer. The orders are executed in line number order. An example of a simple BASIC statement is

```
10 PRINT "I CAN PROGRAM A COMPUTER"
```

Notice the line number preceding the BASIC command Print.

The statement orders the BASIC *interpreter* to print the phrase contained in the quotes: "I CAN PROGRAM A COMPUTER" (see Figure 2-7).

A **program** is a collection of these orders or commands with a common goal. Running the program is the step-by-step execution of the orders contained in the program. An example of a simple BASIC program to calculate gross pay is

```
10 LET HRWK=40
20 LET RATE=5
30 LET PAY=HRWK*RATE
40 PRINT "PAY FOR THIS WEEK IS ";PAY
```

Notice the line numbers (10, 20, 30, 40) and the arithmetic operator of "*" for multiplication.

FIGURE 2-7 A program statement orders the interpreter to execute the command contained in the statement.

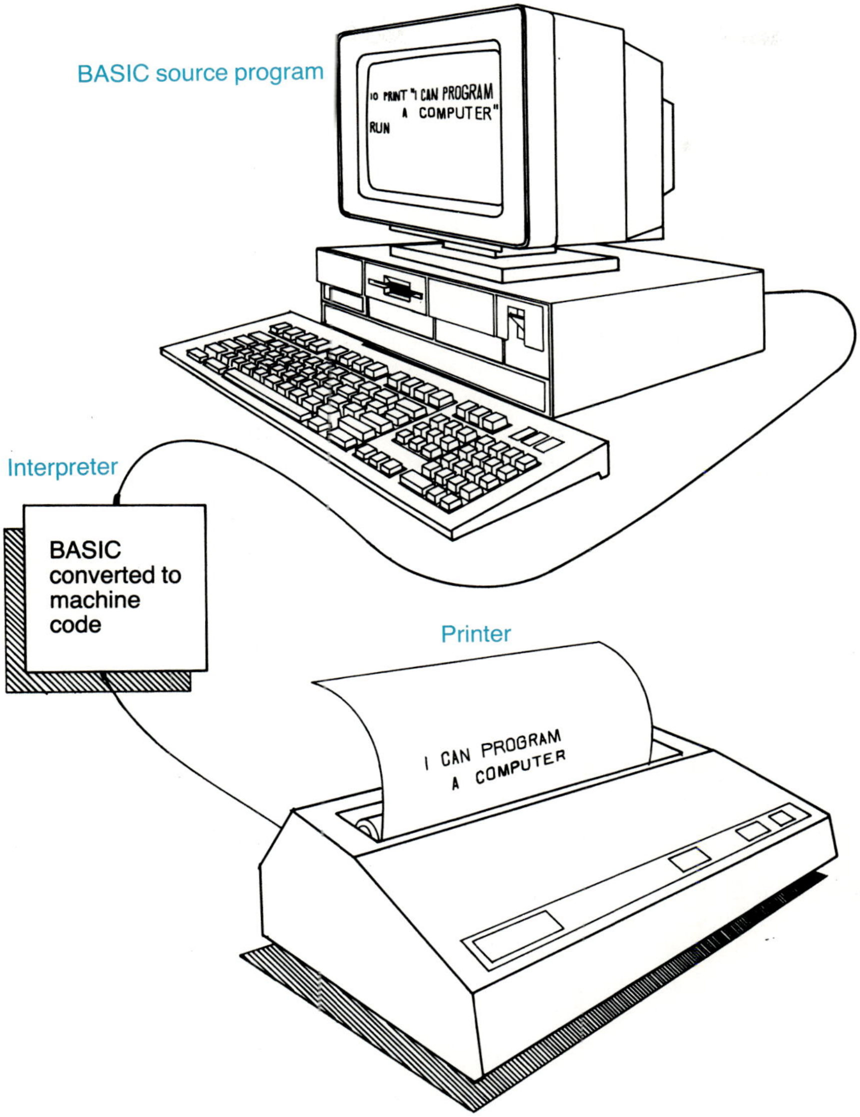

Statement 10 defines HRWK, hours worked per week, as 40; RATE, pay rate per hour, as 5 (dollars); and PAY, gross pay for the week, as equal to hours worked per week multiplied by rate per hour. The values are stored by the interpreter within RAM and used as needed in calculations.

While BASIC is relatively simple to use, most BASIC programs written for microcomputers lack the structure considered proper by professional programming standards. Some programmers refer to common microcomputer BASIC as "street language"—very adaptable but easily abused. One major cause of abused structure is the use of the BASIC command GOTO. This command causes the computer to next execute the statement whose number immediately follows the words GOTO. Frequent use of this GOTO command causes the program to jump around, making it difficult for users (and even the author of the program) to follow the logic. Fortunately, newer versions of BASIC are including more features of structured programming that give BASIC some manners.

Modern programming techniques expect program logic to be structured. **Structured programming** generally uses only simple logic structures, including sequential structures, conditional structures, and looping structures (see Figure 2-8). The program should have only one entrance and one exit from a structure and should minimize the use of branching instructions such as GOTO. The program should use the "top-down" approach; that is, the main function should be defined and then continually refined, or broken down into smaller function components or modules. When sequential structures are used, the instructions or routines are executed in the order written or numbered. Structured programs are generally easier to debug (find and correct errors) and maintain.

The syntax limitations of the most popular forms of microcomputer BASIC make it difficult to follow good structured programming techniques. While some structured techniques can be used, BASIC is not a good language to teach students structured programming. However, newer versions of BASIC, such as True BASIC and Better BASIC, have been designed to encourage good structured programming techniques. Also, BASIC compilers, such as Turbo BASIC and Quick BASIC, are now available to microcomputer users.

Pascal is growing in popularity with microcomputer users because of its more powerful commands and easy-to-follow structure. Like BASIC, Pascal was designed as an instructional language. Unlike BASIC, Pascal is a structured language that encourages good structured programming practices. Programs can easily be broken into modules or procedures. Each set of variables in a module can be defined independently.

C is the favorite language of the software developers of IBM and IBM-compatible microcomputers. It was invented at Bell Laboratories in the early 1970s and was originally designed for and used with the Unix

FIGURE 2-8 The three simple logic structures used in structured programming. *(a)* Sequential structures execute instructions one after another in the same sequence as they are numbered or written. *(b)* Looping structures execute a set of instructions repeatedly. *(c)* Conditional structures test to see if a condition is true or false. If a condition is true, then one set of instructions is executed; if a condition is false, then an alternate set of instructions is executed.

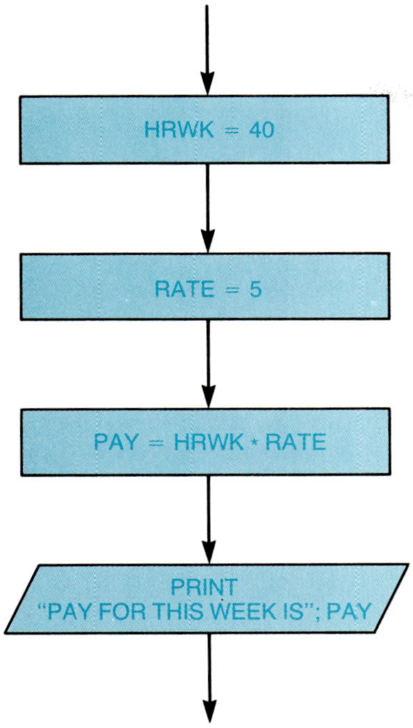
HRWK = 40
RATE = 5
PAY = HRWK * RATE
PRINT
"PAY FOR THIS WEEK IS"; PAY

(a)

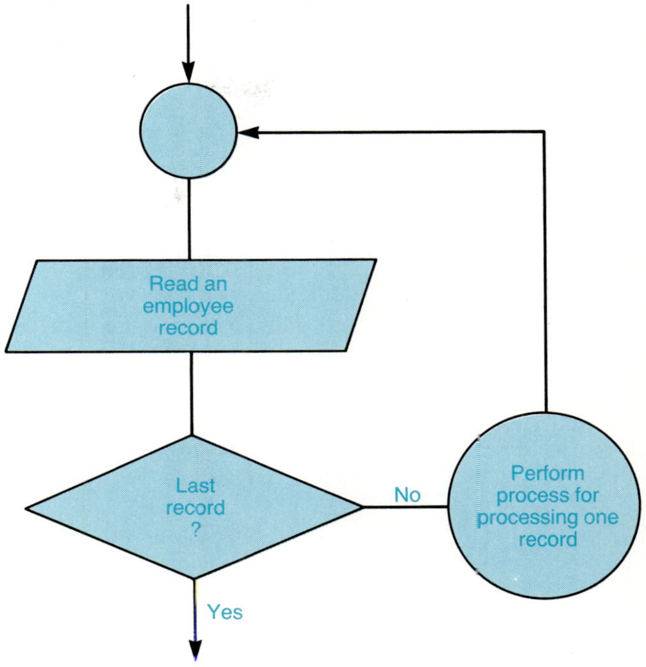
Read an
employee
record
Last
record
?
No
Perform
process for
processing one
record
Yes

(c)

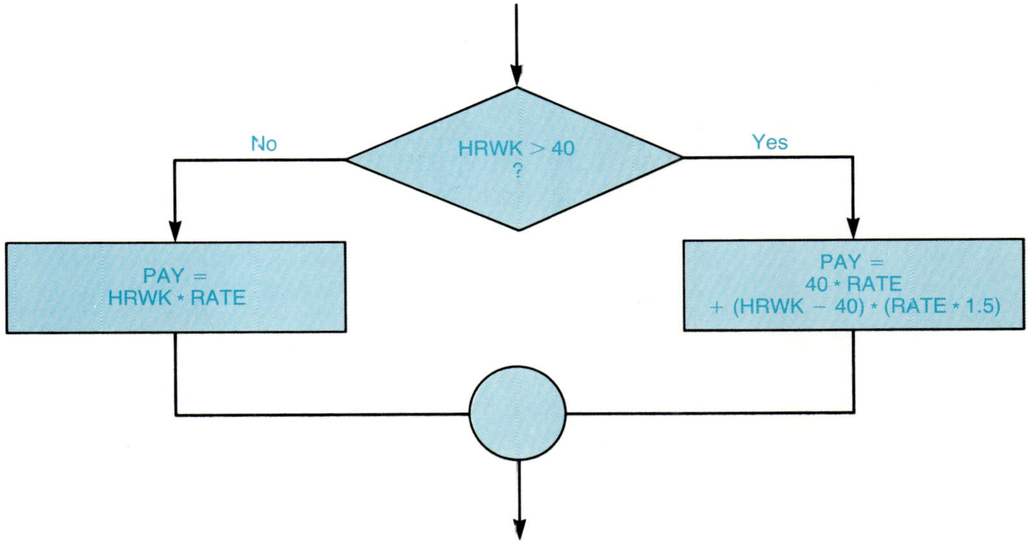
No
HRWK > 40
?
Yes
PAY =
HRWK * RATE
PAY =
40 * RATE
+ (HRWK − 40) * (RATE * 1.5)

(b)

operating system. Programs written in C are *portable;* that is, they can be moved or ported to another computer system quickly and easily. Like Pascal, C is a structured programming language but offers the programmer the additional power of directing special operations of the computer.

Applications Software

Applications software refers to programs designed to solve specific problems. Applications software can be divided into *user-written software* and *purchased software (software packages).* Software that requires no user programming at all is called **turnkey.** The user simply inputs data into the package and receives output. The user is unable to access the actual program code in order to alter it or change the format of the output in any way.

Custom programming may still be necessary in some cases. But if appropriate software is already available at a reasonable cost, many users prefer to buy applications software from professional software companies called **software houses.** Often, purchased software is better written, executes faster, and is easier to implement than custom programs a user may write. However, if the needed software is unavailable, users must write their own, a challenge some people enjoy.

One way to clarify the relative merits of programming in a computer language versus using applications packages is to reexamine the definition of programming. A general definition of a *computer program* is a set of instructions that causes the computer system to perform specific actions. *Programming* is the act of writing such a set of instructions. This definition includes the actions people perform when they use applications software that requires instructions to accomplish specified exercises. Therefore when we talk about computer programming, we are treating applications software as a high-level *problem-solving* language that allows the user to concentrate more on the problem to be solved and less on coding. We use the term *coding* when referring to the writing of a computer program in a specific programming language, such as BASIC or Pascal. Notice in Figure 2-9 that the higher the complexity of the software, the lower the user involvement in coding. The applications software takes care of the details that can make coding a tedious, time-consuming chore.

Some applications software, such as WordPerfect and Lotus 1-2-3, permit users to condense a series of commands into one or two keystrokes. A series of commands is stored to be executed at one time, much like a program written in BASIC. These may be contained within a file, as in *macros,* or stored in a separate file, as in *execute files.* Complex programming logic can be included in such files.

At one extreme is software that is written by the user in machine language or binary code. The writer must be highly skilled at programming. Each action performed by the computer must be programmed as a separate command. At the other extreme are turnkey systems where the user just turns on the machine and does no programming.

FIGURE 2-9 **A graph showing the level of complexity of software versus the user involvement in coding. User involvement is high in machine-level language programming; more complex software such as word processors and spreadsheets require less user involvement in coding.**

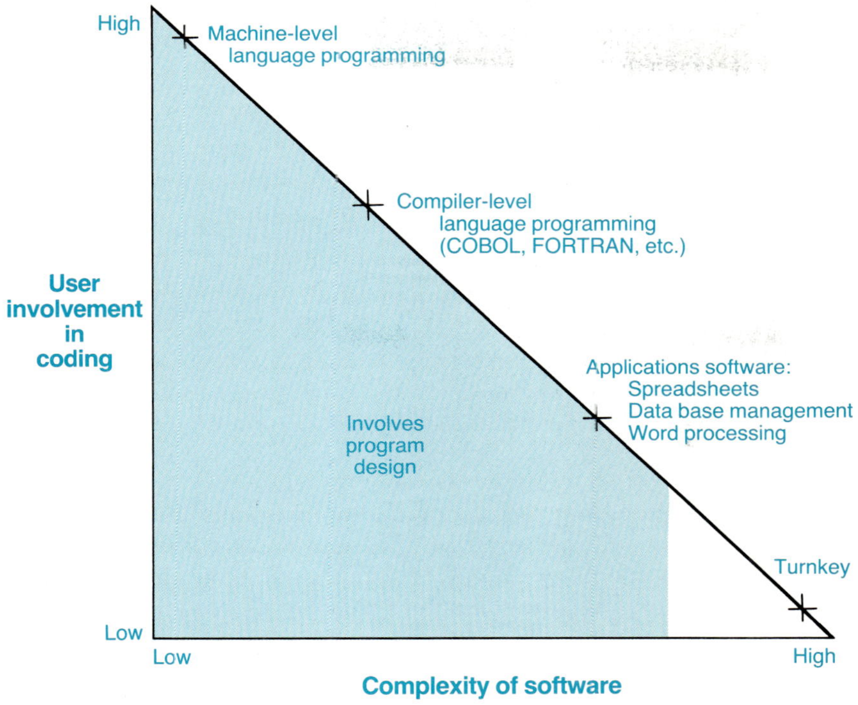

Between these two extremes lie applications software such as WordPerfect, Lotus 1-2-3, and dBASE III, to help users do word processing, electronic spreadsheet, and database management applications.

SYSTEMS ANALYSIS AND DESIGN PRINCIPLES APPLIED TO APPLICATIONS SOFTWARE

Since applications software packages are so flexible and fast, it is often unnecessary to do the elaborate steps of systems development associated with systems design using programming languages. However, even with applications software packages it is possible to use the systems analysis and design approach to consider the problems to be solved by the microcomputer and applications software. **Systems analysis** is the study of an activity or problem to determine the purposes or goals and how they should be achieved. **Systems design** is the definition of the system and the working relationship of the parts of the system. Often included in systems design is the programming of the software needed in the system.

Although the users of applications software do not have to spend as much time defining programming logic and coding language statements as do the users of BASIC or Pascal, they do need to accomplish the essential tasks of systems analysis and design: to define their goals and the steps needed to meet these goals. One approach to take with applications software is the general problem-solving approach:

1. Define the problem to be solved. What is it that you want to accomplish? What is the goal of the application?
2. Gather and analyze relevant data. Get the information you need to make a decision and analyze it.
3. Test possible solutions. Try out different alternatives to figure out which ones work.
4. Implement the best solution available.

By using this method of problem solving we focus not on coding but on the steps needed to *solve the problem.*

Of course, as situations change, the solution you have implemented may need to be changed and some or all of the steps repeated.

This same general problem-solving approach can be applied to computer applications, but with important improvements. The computer's speed, accuracy, and flexibility make it possible to consider the process a cycle. Alternatives can be tested and revisions made quickly and easily.

Some people refer to the computer's ability to allow additional testing and revisions as the "What if?" feature. One application is a preliminary budget for a small business. It could take a bookkeeper hours to complete a budget manually. Even the most efficient bookkeeper would hesitate to make any changes unless they were absolutely necessary. However, if this same budget is placed on an electronic spreadsheet, the manager can consider many alternatives (i.e., "Should we spend more on advertising?" "What if utilities go up 15 percent next year?" "Can we afford to give our workers a raise?") before making decisions. The budget is stored electronically and can be revised over and over without affecting the original copy stored on the disk.

Many types of applications software are available to help users with problem solving, including word processing (all documents become drafts, to be constantly improved and refined without the entire document having to be retyped), database management (making it easy to ask such questions as "How many clients have overdue accounts of more than $500?"), project management (providing answers to "When do we need to start work on this project?" and "How will staffing affect the deadline?"), and accounting (telling us, for example, the dollar value of current accounts receivable).

In Figure 2-10, analysis and design steps are shown as a program flowchart with a loop going from Step 3 (testing) back to Steps 1 through 3.

FIGURE 2-10 The four steps in the analysis and design process using applications software.

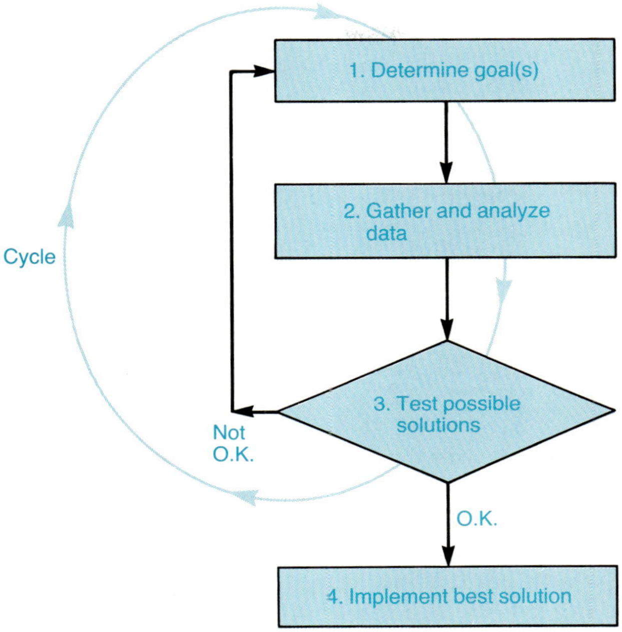

Computers make it easy to repeat these steps until the user is satisfied with the results. However, the microcomputer system is a tool that makes the problem-solving process faster, not necessarily more accurate. So remember to check your results carefully.

The applications software described in this book allows you to solve problems using the three most popular forms of applications software word processing, electronic spreadsheets, and database management systems. After spending a few hours of your time reading this book and using the software, you will be able to solve problems that would have, just a few years ago, required months or years of training in programming. After you have learned about this applications software, you will be able to spend more time creatively solving problems.

TUTORIAL 1: FORMATTING A DISK

To complete this tutorial you need the following:

- MS-DOS system disk
- At least one new blank floppy disk

While completing this tutorial you will learn how to

- Format a disk

Following are the steps necessary to format a floppy disk on the IBM PC (MS-DOS Versions 2.xx–3.xx). The Format Utility prepares a blank disk to accept files by giving addresses to the disk tracks and sectors. Any previous contents of the formatted disk will be destroyed.

Step 1: Load the operating system.

a. If necessary, put the MS-DOS disk in disk drive A.

b. Turn on the microcomputer and monitor.

c. After the system checks the keyboard and memory status, if the system requires manual setting of the time and date, the date prompt appears:

```
Current date is Tue 1-01-1980
Enter new date (mm-dd-yy):
```

Enter the correct date. Remember to insert hyphens between the month (1 through 12), date (01 through 31), and year. For example, February 10, 1989, would be 02-10-89. Typing errors can be erased by pressing the Backspace key. Press the Enter or **Return** key to complete the operation.

d. If the date is accepted, DOS will prompt for the time:

```
Current time is 0:01:30.00
Enter new time:
```

Enter the correct time. Remember to type the numbers for the hour and minutes using the 24-hour clock (i.e., 13:57 should be entered for 1:57 P.M.). The system will automatically take care of seconds and hundredths of a second.

If the time is accepted, the operating system prompt should appear:

```
A>
```

indicating that the operating system is loaded into primary storage, the active disk drive is drive A, and the computer is ready to receive your commands.

Step 2: Format the disk.

a. Place a **new** floppy disk in disk drive B. (Hard disk drive users should use the floppy disk drive [usually A].) Latch the disk drive door. *The*

MS-DOS disk must go in drive A, and the blank disk must go in drive B. **Make sure you are not formatting a software disk or a disk with needed files.**

If you are using a floppy disk drive system, type the command

```
FORMAT B:
```

Hard disk drive users should type

```
FORMAT A:
```

Press **Return.**

A prompt appears directing you to insert a new disk and to strike any key when ready. Since you have already placed a new disk in the drive, press any key, such as the Space Bar, to start the formatting of the disk. This process should take 2 to 5 minutes.

b. After the formatting is completed, a prompt appears asking if you would like to format another disk. If you would like to format another blank disk, press **Y**; if not, press **N**.

c. After you are finished formatting the disk in drive B, remove both disks and replace them in their envelopes. Your disk is now ready to accept the new files you create.

TUTORIAL 2: USING MS-DOS SYSTEM UTILITIES

To complete this tutorial you need the following:

- MS-DOS System disk containing the MS-DOS utilities
- Blank formatted disk created in Tutorial 1

While completing this tutorial you will learn how to

- Use Copy Con to create files
- Use wildcard characters
- Use the MS-DOS utilities to
  - Obtain a listing of files and disk space
  - Change the logged disk drive
  - Rename a file
  - Copy a file
  - Erase a file

Following are the steps necessary to use the MS-DOS utilities. Hard disk drive users should contact their instructor or lab personnel to find out which utilities are available and any possible command changes.

Step 1: Load the operating system (if it is not already loaded).

In Tutorial 1, you loaded MS-DOS by placing the MS-DOS disk in drive A and turning on the machine. Here is an alternative method for loading the operating system.

a. With the microcomputer turned on, insert the MS-DOS disk in disk drive A. Latch the disk drive door.

b. Reset the system by pressing the **Ctrl + Alt** keys; while holding down these keys, pressing the **Del** key. After a few moments, the data prompt should appear.

c. Set the date and time using the instructions in Tutorial 1. The system prompt (A>) appears when the system has been successfully loaded. This whole process is called a **warm boot.**

Step 2: Create files using the Copy Con command.

a. Place the blank, formatted disk in drive B.

b. After reading the discussion below, enter

```
COPY CON:B:filename
```

Notice the use of **B:** to tell DOS to place the newly created file on the disk in drive B. Be sure to put the colon after the disk drive designation.

Create your own filename for *filename,* such as your initials and a number (TAH1). Here are some rules for filenames when you are using MS-DOS.

1. Name files so you and the operating system can tell them apart on the disk. Duplicate names are not permitted on the same disk.
2. Make names as descriptive about the contents as possible. Avoid names that are too short, cute, abstract, or obscene.
3. A filename can be up to eight characters long.
4. Filenames can contain any letter or number. Although DOS allows ! @ # − $ % & ( ) { } ' we strongly suggest you avoid such special characters since not all applications software packages accept these special characters. Stick to letters and numbers.
5. Filenames can be upper or lower case; MS-DOS doesn't distinguish between upper and lower case.
6. Remember, a suffix, called an **extension,** may be added to the filename to help describe the contents. It can be up to three characters long, uses the same valid characters as filenames, and must be separated from the name by a period.

Table 2-2 EXAMPLES OF LEGAL AND ILLEGAL FILENAMES AND EXTENSIONS

Legal Filenames	*Illegal Filenames*	*Reasons*
R	REPORT1987.RPT	Too long
88BUDGET	BUDGET.1988	Extension too long
BTS81388.LET	BTS 91488.LET	Blanks not allowed
TERMPAP.DOC	TERM,445.DOC	Commas not allowed

WordPerfect uses the extension BK! to name back-up files automatically created by the software. Back-up files will be discussed in Lesson 3, Fundamental Concepts of Word Processing. dBASE III Plus uses the extension .DBF to distinguish database files. Avoid these filename extensions and other illegal filenames when naming your files. (See Table 2-2.)

After you name your file, press **Return.**

c. Type

```
This is the first sample file.
```

Press **Return.**

Next, press and hold the **Ctrl** key and, while holding the **Ctrl** key, press **Z**. On the screen

```
^Z
```

appears. Press **Return.**

The file will be written to the disk in drive B.

d. Create three more files (for a total of four new files). Make sure to give each file a different filename and contents and precede the filename with **B:**, to indicate that the file is to be stored on the disk in drive B.

e. After creating the four new files on the disk in drive B, check to make sure that all of the files are properly stored on the disk in drive B.

Type

```
dir b:
```

Press **Return.**

A listing of all four files should appear on the screen. If you are missing files, just repeat the steps needed to create the files. Make sure to check the disk in drive A, using the Dir command. Erase any files *you* erroneously placed on MS-DOS disk using the MS-DOS Del or Erase command.

Step 3: Use the MS-DOS utilities.

a. Enter the Directory command

```
dir
```

(Remember that in MS-DOS you can use either upper- or lower-case letters.)

Press **Return.**

The Directory command gives you a listing of the files contained on the MS-DOS disk.

Notice the number of bytes left or "free" on the disk. Determine how many kilobytes (K) you have remaining on the disk by dividing 1,024 (the number of bytes in a K), or approximately 1,000, into the total number of bytes shown on the screen.

Use the directory command with the pause option and wide option. Long listings, such as those found on the MS-DOS disk, are easier to see when you use these options. Type

```
dir /p
```

Press **Return.**

After looking at the directory page by page, type

```
dir /w
```

Press **Return.**

Notice how the /w option prints only the filenames.

b. Use wildcard characters.

1. Use the wildcard characters to locate all the files on drive A with the .EXE extension. .EXE files are program files that the system will load and execute. Type

   ```
   *.EXE
   ```

   Press **Return.**

2. Try out the wildcard characters to find those files on drive A starting with the letter "F". Type

   ```
   F???????.*
   ```

   Press **Return.**

3. Repeat the directory command to get a listing of disk drive B. Type

```
DIR B:
```

Press **Return.**

c. Rename a file. At the system prompt enter the command to rename a file from disk drive B. Type

```
rename b:oldname newname
```

Substitute for *oldname* the name of one of the files you created with Copy Con. Remember to type the filename **exactly** as it appears on the screen. Substitute for *newname* any new filename. Make sure to avoid any existing filenames or an error message will result.

Press **Return.**

Repeat the directory command to see if your file has been properly renamed.

d. Erase files. Now let's remove any unneeded files and regain some disk space. Type the command to erase all the files on disk drive B. Type

```
erase b:*.*
```

Press **Return.**

If your system asks you if you are sure you really want to do this, double-check that you have entered the correct command (drive B), and press "Y." Within a few seconds the files will have been erased.

e. Change the logged disk drive. At the system prompt, type

```
B:
```

Press **Return.**

Notice how the system prompt changes to B:.

Step 4: Turn off the microcomputer.

After returning to the system prompt, remove the disks from the drives and turn the microcomputer off. **Remember to always return to the system prompt before removing the disk or turning off the machine.** Otherwise, file contents may be lost or damaged.

SUMMARY

Software is the instructions that make the hardware work. Although there is a large variety of software available for the microcomputer, software can be grouped into systems software (coordinates the operations of the hardware components) and applications software (directs the computer to solve particular problems or applications). Systems software includes operating systems, utilities, and language processors. Applications software includes user-written programs and purchased software. The use of applications software, such as word processors, electronic spreadsheets, and database management systems, allows the user to spend less time coding and more time concentrating on the actual solution to the problem.

EXERCISES

1. Supply the MS-DOS utility for the operations listed below. For example,

   Delete a file from disk in drive B: *DELETE B:filename*

   a. Copy all files from the disk in drive A to the disk in drive B
   b. Format the disk in drive B (Make sure there is nothing on the disk you do not want erased)
   c. Rename all the files on drive B with the suffix of DOC to BAK
   d. Make an exact duplicate of the disk in drive A to the disk in drive B
   e. Display all the files on the disk in drive B, pausing at the end of each screen
2. Define the following terms:

software	OS/2	interpreter
systems software	utilities	compiler
applications software	external DOS commands	source code
operating system	internal DOS commands	object code
disk operating system (DOS)	networking	bugs
CP/M-80	system prompt	software packages
Unix	cursor	BASIC
module	wildcard characters	interactive
local area network (LAN)	extension	structured programming
MS-DOS	directory	Pascal
PC-DOS	pirating	C
compatibility	language processors	turnkey
incompatibility	program	software houses
virtual memory	programming	systems analysis
multitasking	code	systems design
multiple concurrent communications sessions	coding	
	machine language	

3. What is the difference between the MS-DOS utilities Copy *.* and Diskcopy?
4. Name the three most popular operating systems.
5. What version of operating system does your microcomputer use?
6. Create an additional formatted disk. Write down the steps and commands you use to create the disk.
7. Create a file from the console using the Copy command. Then clear the screen and list the file contents on the screen. Print the file contents on a printer. Write down the steps and commands you use.
8. Complete Tutorial 1: Formatting a Disk. Use the Ctrl-PrtSc command to print a copy of the entire tutorial while you complete it. Keep a diary of any problems or difficulties you experience while completing the tutorials.
9. Complete Tutorial 2: Use the PrtSc command to record your filenames and disk space.
10. What is the relationship between the level of complexity of software and the user involvement in coding?

TWO
WORD PROCESSING

Word processing software is the most popular applications software used on microcomputers, and for good reason: word processing frees you from tedious and time-consuming retyping and editing chores. Word processing does not necessarily *make* you a better writer, but it does *permit* you to be a better writer. To put it simply, word processing gets rid of all those excuses for not having a perfect term paper, letter, memo, resumé, or report. Remember the headaches of erasing typing errors or typing a page over and over? With word processing those problems are all behind you. Word processing permits you to get everything just right. If you find you have continually misspelled "computers" (for example, "computors"), just give a few commands, and the word processing applications software will change the spelling throughout your term paper. By the time you finish this section, you will know how to make corrections electronically by using word processing software.

SOFTWARE SPECIFICATIONS

Students who will be using the Limited-Use introductory version of WordPerfect 4.2 (L-WP), made available through the publisher of this textbook, are referred to the Preface for a complete list of the limitations of this version of the software. Briefly, the limitations include the following:

1. The maximum size data file that can be saved to disk is 50,000K (approximately 25–30 regular pages).
2. A data file created with L-WP cannot be imported into regular WordPerfect, nor can a file created in regular WordPerfect be imported into L-WP.
3. Data files may be printed through the parallel printer port "1" without a printer being defined, but font changes and extended ASCII characters are not allowed.
4. "*WPC" will be automatically printed after most paragraphs.
5. The speller and thesaurus are limited to only a few words for demonstration purposes only.
6. The help file is restricted to a display of the function key template.

These limitations will be noted as appropriate in Lessons 3–5.

3

Fundamental Concepts of Word Processing

LESSON OUTLINE

WHAT IS WORD PROCESSING?

In formal terms, **word processing** is the electronic, automated processing or manipulation of words using a specialized applications program designed to compose, revise, print, and file written documents. Word processing is a specialized form of data processing in which the data are characters and words. A **character** is any letter, number, or symbol you can type on a keyboard or input through other hardware (for example, a mouse or voice device). These characters can be grouped into words, sentences, paragraphs, and pages. The largest grouping is called a **document.** Typical documents include memorandums, letters, term papers, reports, and manuscripts.

To use word processing effectively, you must understand how and why it works. Computers can process **soft** (electronic) **words.** The words stored within the primary storage of a word processing system (the microcomputer system) are termed "soft" because they are not in a physical form. They are merely *electrical impulses.* As you type, each keystroke is converted by the computer into a series of 0's and 1's. Every letter, number, punctuation mark, or even blank space you type becomes a string of 8 binary digits (bits), or 1 byte. Each byte of primary storage has a unique address. Therefore, the microcomputer, aided by word processing software, can directly access each character you create. Individual characters or groupings of characters in words, sentences, or paragraphs can be moved around and processed with ease. For instance, to erase (delete or overstrike) a typed character, you instruct the word processor to enter another keystroke character into the same byte, replacing the old letter or character with the new. RAM has a feature called **destructive write.** That is, writing a new character to a byte causes what was previously stored in that byte to be destroyed (actually just replaced) by the new entry (see Figure 3-1).

WHAT IS WORD PROCESSING USED FOR?

Word processing can be used for anything that can be put down in writing. You can recognize potential word processing applications by looking for the following characteristics on a project or task:

1. Repetition
2. Editing

FIGURE 3-1 A representation of how a byte is replaced in random access memory (RAM) by using the feature of destructive write.

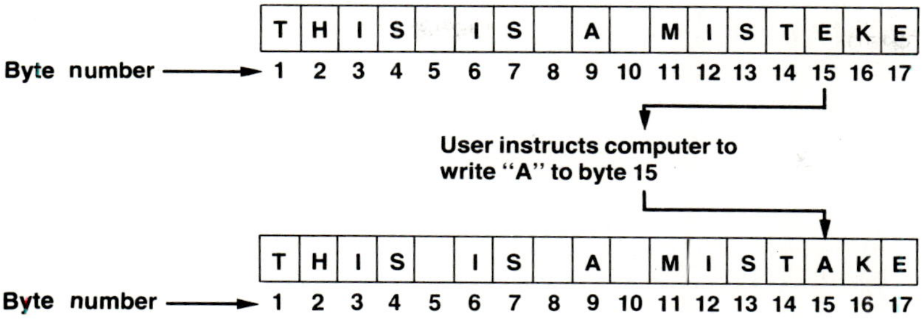

3. Revisions
4. Variable and fixed parts
5. The need for quality appearance

Word processing is especially useful for *repetitive* tasks, such as preparing a large number of similar letters with some individual touches. For example, you plan to send resumés to a series of employers but want each resumé to appear to be individually typed. Instead of duplicating the resumés by expensive typesetting or photocopying, you can print each resumé individually using word processing software.

Another application for word processing is *editing* and rewriting. **Editing** involves correcting spelling, grammar, and sentence structure and, in general, "cleaning up" the writing. For example, when working on an important report or speech, you may want to make frequent changes and corrections. Such editing is fast and easy with word processing because it is done electronically.

Revisions are changes that must be made in a document, such as new dates, procedures, and prices. Such changes can be made on an electronically stored document in a word processing system by simply retrieving the document and entering a few simple commands such as Search and Replace.

Many documents are a mixture of *variable and fixed parts.* For example, you plan to send out letters to 35 clients. Each letter has a different name, address, and salutation, but the body of the letter is essentially the same. Once the basic letter has been typed and saved on the disk, the word processing software allows you to tailor each letter to the person receiving it without retyping the entire letter. You can collect the individual information, such as name, address, and salutation, on a separate file. A series of letters can then be printed by merging the fixed text in the basic letter file with the individual variable information in the other file (see Figure 3-2).

Preprinted forms are another example of documents with variable and fixed parts. The part that is preprinted is fixed, but the part to be filled in is variable. With a word processor, the equivalent of the preprinted material can be stored as a document. To complete the variable part, the user merely retrieves the stored document and inserts the variable items. Today, some firms use a laser printer that can, together with the proper word processing software, create the printed form at the same time it prints in the variable items.

If you need a document that has a *quality appearance,* with no correction-fluid marks, erasures, or penciled-in changes, then a microcomputer with word processing software is the answer.

An increasingly popular use of word processing is **desktop publishing.** Desktop publishing permits individuals or small organizations to produce high-quality, professional-looking text and graphics using the basic principles of typography, graphics, and page layout. Through the use of desktop publishing systems that include sophisticated laser printers, scanners, page composition software, and word processing software, the quality of output can be dramatically increased, so the term "quality appearance" has a whole new meaning (see Figure 3-3).

In addition to benefitting from the typical applications, many people find that they simply enjoy the freedom and convenience of using a word processor. For some individuals, word processing has made the composition of text easier and more creative. Some authors say that word processing permits them to "write now, edit later." Of course, you'll experience a certain period of frustration while learning to use the software, but once you get through that initial stage, word processing can make writing and typing faster and more productive than ever before.

A writer often uses a word processor first to hold the outline of a story, article, report, or book. Then the author inserts material within that outline, thus using the word processor not only to produce a copy with a cleaner appearance, but also to produce a product that sticks to the planned outline.

PLANNING WORD PROCESSING APPLICATIONS

The computer aids the problem-solving process by making it easier to test many possible solutions to problems. The computer can also make it easier to adapt to changing goals. As goals, data, and alternatives (solutions) change over time, electronically stored documents can be easily changed to keep pace. This flexibility is most noticeable in word processing. Words, lines, paragraphs, and even larger segments of text can be altered, deleted, or moved to achieve a better result.

FIGURE 3-2 Variable and fixed parts of letters can be combined to produce a large number of "personalized" letters quickly and efficiently.

FIXED PART
Letter File Named
INTERV.LET

```
..FILE INTERV.LET } Name of Fixed File
.mt10 } Format Commands
.OP
.DF INTERVLI.DAT } Name of Data File with Variable Parts
.RV NAME1,ADDRESS1,ADDRESS2,NAME2,POSITION } Names of the Variables to Read
                                             from the Variable File
September 14, 1985

&NAME1&
&ADDRESS1&
&ADDRESS2&

Dear &NAME2&:

Our office has received your resume and letter applying for the
position of &POSITION&.  Please call my office as soon as
possible to schedule an interview to further discuss your
qualifications for this position.  Interviews can be scheduled on
Mondays, Wednesdays, and Fridays, from  9 a.m. to 3 p.m.  Please
be prepared to supply references at that time.

Thank you for your interest in Applied Technologies and I look
forward to meeting you soon.

Sincerely,


Mary C. Mahoney
Personnel Officer



MM/ss

.pa } Page Break Command
```

VARIABLE PART
Data File Named
INTERVLI.DAT

```
 NAME1      ADDRESS1            ADDRESS2            NAME2     POSITION
Keum Kim, 227 Locust St., "DeKalb, Illinois 60115", Ms. Kim, Accountant
Dick Brown, 498 College Dr., "DeKalb, Illinois 60115", Mr. Brown, Manager
Steve Franey, 87 Fair Rd, "Forrest, Illinois 65578", Mr. Franey, Purchasing Officer
Catherine Albert, 990 Oak Dr, "Houston, Texas 77030", Ms. Albert, Programmer
Donna Kotecki, 689 Glen Cir., "Naperville, Illinois", Ms. Kotecki, Lawyer
Lyle Smith, 290 Elm St., "DeKalb, Illinois 60115", Mr. Smith, Consultant
```

Resulting Merged Letter

```
September 14, 1985

Keum Kim
227 Locust St.
DeKalb, Illinois 60115

Dear Ms. Kim:

Our office has received your resume and letter applying for the
position of Accountant.  Please call my office as soon as
possible to schedule an interview to further discuss your
qualifications for this position.  Interviews can be scheduled on
Mondays, Wednesdays, and Fridays, from  9 a.m. to 3 p.m.  Please
be prepared to supply references at that time.

Thank you for your interest in Applied Technologies and I look
forward to meeting you soon.

Sincerely,


Mary C. Mahoney
Personnel Officer



MM/ss
```

FIGURE 3-3 An example of a desktop publishing system with printed output produced with a laser printer. As the cost of such systems declines and the technology develops, such high-quality output is becoming more common.

Perhaps the most important goal that word processing will help you accomplish is clearer written communication. By learning to master the various software commands, you will find yourself less constrained by the process of typing, correcting errors, and rewriting—and freer to be more creative and effective in your written communications.

You may want to produce an impressive report or a resumé that is totally free of errors and looks well organized. Plan the content by preparing an outline identifying main topics and subtopics. While the specific organization and topics included in an outline are largely a matter of training and personal preference, outline processing software can make this process much easier, especially when you are planning a large document such as a report. Outline processing software can be purchased separately (such as Think Tank and PC Outline) or included in the word processing software (such as WordPerfect and Word). Such software, sometimes called "idea processors," allow users to change sections of outlines quickly and easily (see Figure 3-4).

In WordPerfect 4.2 the outline processor is activated by pressing Alt-[F5] (Shift-[F5] in WordPerfect 5.0). Every time you start a new paragraph by pressing the Return, a new section of the outline is inserted. You go to the lower levels of the outline by pressing the Tab key.

Plan the document appearance by determining the margins, tabs, line length, page length, and other general features of the printed result. All word processing software have specific default format settings that may be changed using format commands. For example, WordPerfect has the default settings of 1-inch margins on sides, top, and bottom; 6 lines per inch; single spacing; tabs every 5 spaces; and 10 pitch, or 10 characters per inch. Some software, such as Word, WordStar 2000, and WordPerfect 5.0 provide a **style sheet**—a group of preset format commands that can be used with any document.

After you have determined the goal of your writing project, gather the notes, articles, books, and other material or data you need to prepare your document. Analyze the data to determine which material will really contribute to the desired result.

As you actually enter the material into the computer using word processing software, you can revise and edit, testing alternative approaches. This is where word processing is so valuable. For example, if you are preparing a resumé, you can consider many different arrangements and select the style that you think will most impress an employer. Or if you need to change the margins on a 20-page report, just enter a few simple commands to justify the paragraphs and the job is done.

Implementation of a word processing project means printing the document and presenting it to the reader. Although every writer hopes that this is the final step, sometimes the reader (instructor, editor, or supervisor) has suggestions for improvement. With the document still stored electronically, such revisions are simple to make.

FIGURE 3-4 An outline for a report done with an outline processor. The numbers on the left are section headings. These can be deleted if necessary. Entire sections of the outline can be moved. Text inserted under the headings (stored separately and not appearing in the figure) will be moved when the headings are moved. Changes in the level and order of the headings in the outline affect the text contained in the document.

```
I.   The Problem
     A.   Expenses exceeding income for third year
     B.   No improvement in foreseeable future
II.  Possible solutions
     A.   Staff
          1.   Across-the-board pay cuts
               a.   Advantages
                    (1)  No one loses job
                    (2)  Share burden
               b.   Disadvantages
                    (1)  Cut productive and non-productive
                         employees pay
                    (2)  May be putting off the inevitable
          2.   Layoffs
               a.   Advantages
                    (1)  Get rid of non-productive, non-essential
                         employees
                    (2)  Good employees retained
               b.   Disadvantages
                    (1)  Making the decision of who goes
                    (2)  Hard on fellow employees
          3.   Early retirement
               a.   Advantages
                    (1)  Keep good young talent
                    (2)  Make room up top for new ideas
               b.   Disadvantages
                    (1)  Lose the most experienced managers
                    (2)  Expensive
                    (3)  Hard on morale of the organization
```

To clearly understand how problem solving using word processing is actually done, let's consider the major categories of commands common to all word processing, regardless of the particular type of hardware and software being used.

THE FIVE CATEGORIES OF COMMANDS OF WORD PROCESSING

There are five major categories of word processing commands:

1. Creating
2. Editing
3. Formatting
4. Printing
5. Document handling

FIGURE 3-5 **A screen from a newly opened document on WordPerfect version 4.2. Like a blank sheet of paper, the screen will accept the new text you create. However, changes are much easier to make on the screen than on a sheet of paper. Version 5.0 will show inches (1″) for the line (Ln) and position (Pos) numbers.**

Creating a document involves the opening, naming, and original typing or keystroking of a document. A newly opened document appears as a blank screen ready to accept lines of text (see Figure 3-5). By giving this empty document a new unique filename, you are creating a new document. As you type, the characters you enter are becoming a part of that new document. The document is being stored keystroke by keystroke in the primary storage area of the computer. To produce a copy of that document on disk storage, you must save the document by using a Save command.

Editing includes the deletion, overwriting, or insertion of text. When you indicate that you want to edit a previously created and stored document, the word processing software will retrieve it and display it on the screen. All word processors have commands that allow the user to delete or replace characters, words, lines, and blocks of text and insert other characters in their place.

Formatting is the alignment or positioning of the text in a document. This function includes setting margins, line spacing, page breaks, and other placement options. All word processors provide com-

FIGURE 3-6 Formatting commands change the appearance of a document onscreen and as it is printed. Although these two resumés contain the same text, they differ in appearance through the use of formatting commands.

RESUME

STEPHEN B. FARMER

HOME ADDRESS	SCHOOL ADDRESS
208 West Elm Street	407 University Avenue
Joliet, Illinois 62345	Dekalb, Illinois 60115
(312) 555-1234	(815) 555-9876

EMPLOYMENT OBJECTIVE:
Seeking full-time marketing position in consumer products with major corporation.

EDUCATION:
B.S. in Business Administration, Northern Illinois University, expected May 10, 1989.
Major in Marketing Management.
GPA: overall 3.5 on 4.0 scale, 3.75 in major courses.

HONORS AND AWARDS:
Dean's List of Students with GPA above 3.25, 1987-1988
President of Student Marketing Management Association, 1987-1988.
Treasurer of Resident Hall Student Association, 1987.

EMPLOYMENT RECORD:
Sales Representative, Joliet Microcomputer Sales Company, Summer 1988. Position involved sales of microcomputers, printers, disks, software, and other computer supplies.

Counter Sales, MacDonalds, Joliet, Summer 1987. Position involving taking and filling orders from customers, and handling money.

REFERENCES FURNISHED UPON REQUEST.

RESUME

STEPHEN B. FARMER

EMPLOYMENT OBJECTIVE:
Seeking full-time marketing position in consumer products with major corporation.

EDUCATION:
B.S. in Business Administration, Northern Illinois University, expected May 10, 1989.
Major in Marketing Management.
GPA: overall 3.5 on 4.0 scale, 3.75 in major courses.

HONORS AND AWARDS:
Dean's List of Students with GPA above 3.25, 1987-1988
President of Student Marketing Management Association, 1987-1988.
Treasurer of Resident Hall Student Association, 1987.

EMPLOYMENT RECORD:
Sales Representative, Joliet Microcomputer Sales Company, Summer 1988. Position involved sales of microcomputers, printers, disks, software, and other computer supplies.

Counter Sales, MacDonalds, Joliet, Summer 1987. Position involving taking and filling orders from customers, and handling money.

REFERENCES FURNISHED UPON REQUEST.

HOME ADDRESS:	SCHOOL ADDRESS
208 West Elm Street	407 University Avenue
Joliet, Illinois 62345	DeKalb, Illinois 60115
(312) 555-1234	(815) 555-9876

mands that allow the user to select a variety of formatting options (see Figure 3-6).

Printing is the production of hard copy from a stored document. The final document is printed on paper according to special format instructions that position the text the way you want it to appear as printed output. Some word processors are designed to print on only the more common models of printers, called "standard" printers, but others allow the user to specify a wide variety of makes and models of printers, including ink-jet and laser printers.

Document handling is the use of special commands to copy, delete, or rename files. Keeping track of your word processing documents is similar to maintaining a filing system. The careful word processing user will find it helpful to systematically organize documents according to topic, date, or another meaningful scheme.

WORD PROCESSING FEATURES

Word processing software offers many features that make the creating, editing, and printing of text faster and easier. These include cursor movement; overwriting, deletion and undoing; replacement and insertion; and word wrap.

Cursor Movement

Cursor movement is one of the fundamental operations in word processing. The **cursor** is the symbol on the screen (a blinking line, square, or rectangle) indicating the position of entry on the screen.

Expert Tip: When you use a typewriter, you use the Space Bar to move to where you want to start typing. If you use the Space Bar when using word processing software, however, it will insert **hard spaces** into the document, placing the ASCII code characters in the file as if text were there (see Figure 3-7). Although such hard blank spaces may look identical to **soft spaces** (inserted by the software for formatting purposes), such unwanted hard spaces have to be deleted if the document is to be properly reformatted. Remember to use the cursor control keys when you move the

```
Soft▲spaces▲are▲spaces▲inserted▲by▲the▲word▲processing▲software▲■■
to▲format▲the▲text▲on▲the▲screen.▲▲Hard▲spaces▲are▲inserted▲by▲■■■
the▲user▲with▲the▲space▲bar,▲or▲tab▲key.▲▲Since▲hard▲and▲soft▲■■■■
spaces▲are▲treated▲differently▲on▲the▲screen▲and▲in▲a▲document,▲■■
it▲is▲important▲for▲you▲to▲know▲the▲difference▲and▲to▲insert▲hard▲
spaces▲only▲when▲necessary.▲


C:\MAIN\WP\FIG3-7.ART                     Doc 1  Pg 1  Ln 15    Pos 10
```

(a)

```
Soft spaces are spaces inserted by the word processing software
to format the text on the screen.  Hard spaces are inserted by
the user with the space bar, or tab key.  Since hard and soft
spaces are treated differently on the screen and in a document,
it is important for you to know the difference and to insert hard
spaces only when necessary.


C:\MAIN\WP\FIG3-7.ART                     Doc 1  Pg 1  Ln 15    Pos 10
```

(b)

FIGURE 3-7 **A graphic representation of the difference between hard spaces (symbolized by △) and soft spaces (symbolized by □) using WordPerfect. Part (*a*) shows the screen as it actually appears; (*b*) shows the codes contained within the document. Hard spaces should be inserted only when necessary. The triangle and square are not ASCII code symbols.**

cursor. Treat the Space Bar as you would a character key; use it only when you really want hard spaces added in the text.

How do you move the cursor? The direction and length of cursor movement are controlled by the cursor control keys. **Cursor control keys** move the cursor in four directions—up, down, left and right. There are two general types of cursor control keys used with microcomputer word processing software: the arrow keys and optional cursor control keys.

The **arrow keys** are marked with arrows indicating up (↑), down (↓), left (←), and right (→) movement. Some microcomputers, such as older models of the IBM PC, may combine the cursor control keys with the numeric keys (see Figure 3-8). To enter numbers using the numeric key pad, depress the Number Lock key. Releasing the Number Lock key returns the numeric keys to cursor control keys. Other models with the enhanced keyboard, such as the IBM AT and IBM Personal System/2 series, have separate cursor control and numeric keys (see Figure 3-9). In most cases the cursor control keys are separate from the regular keys on the keyboard.

Optional cursor control keys are regular keys on the keyboard (such as *E, S, D,* or *X*) that are given command power when they are

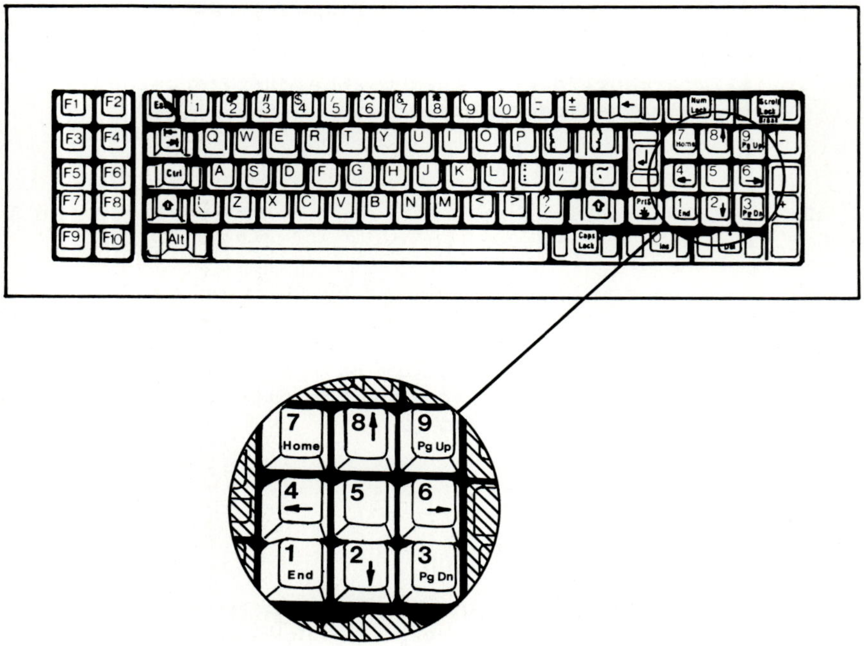

FIGURE 3-8 Arrow cursor control keys as found on the IBM PC. Notice the combination of the numeric key pad and the cursor control keys. The cursor direction is indicated by the arrow on the key.

FIGURE 3-9 Arrow cursor control keys as found on the IBM PS/2 enhanced keyboard. Notice how the numeric key pad and the cursor control keys are separate. The key pad can still be used for cursor control when it is not in the Num Lock mode.

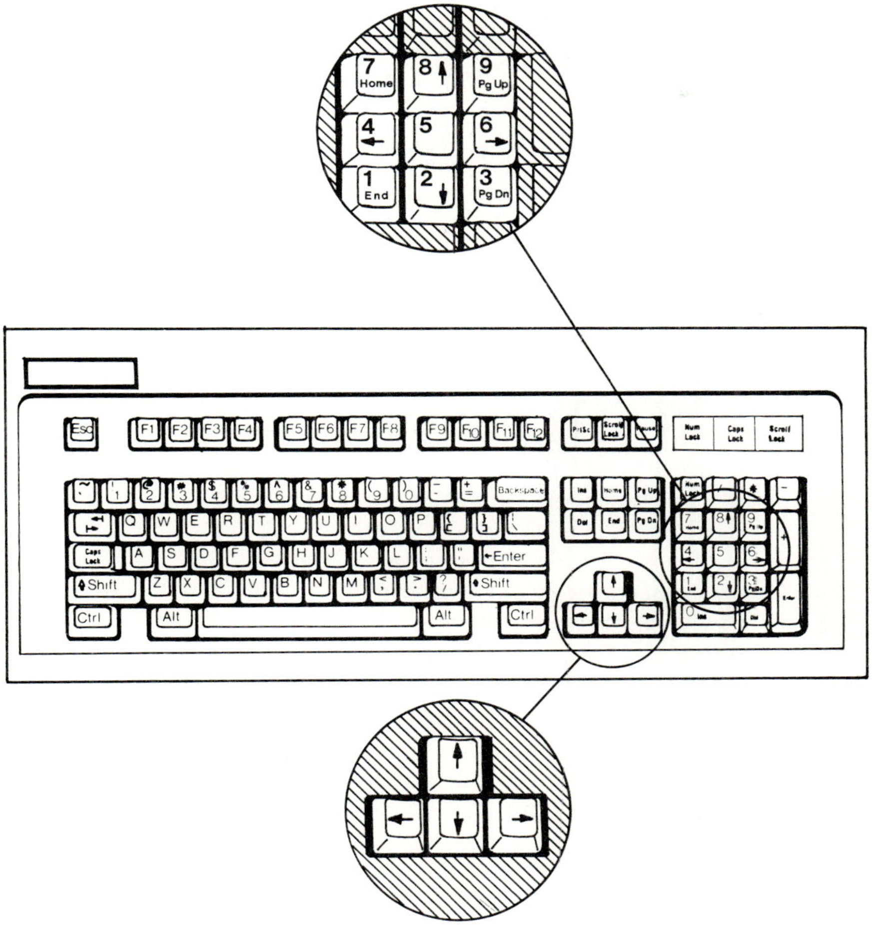

teamed up with the Control and/or Escape key. The Control key is most commonly used. In WordStar and other word processing software systems, the cursor can be controlled by a set of keys arranged in a diamond on the keyboard (see Figure 3-10). By pressing the Control key (indicated with a ^ or Ctrl) and *E* (to move up), *S* (to move left), *D* (to move right), or *X* (to move down), you can move the cursor to any location on the screen. The commands can be in upper or lower case.

Most people find the arrow keys easier to use initially. However, there are some good reasons for knowing how to use the optional cursor control

FIGURE 3-10 The optional cursor control keys as used in WordStar. Notice how the points of the diamond indicate the direction of movement controlled by each key.

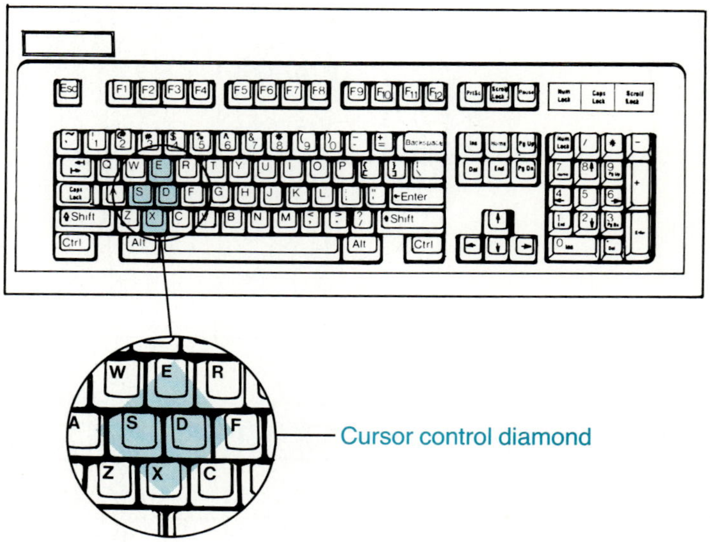

keys. You can do cursor movement without significantly changing the position of your hands on the keyboard. This increases your speed and accuracy, especially if you have some keyboarding or typing skill. Some microcomputers, especially those using CP/M and Apple operating systems, may not have arrow keys that work with certain applications software.

The WordStar cursor control key letters—*E, S, D,* and *X*—have no mnemonic significance; they do not stand for anything. They were chosen solely because of their positions on the keyboard. (Of course, you can make up your own memory jogger, such as SEXD.) The position of each key in the cursor control diamond mimics the direction of the cursor movement.

In addition to the arrow keys, other keys and key combinations can be used to quickly move the cursor through the document—by moving the cursor word by word, or by scrolling the document. **Scrolling** is the movement of a portion of a document up, down, or from side to side so that other parts of the document can be seen on the screen. In WordPerfect the command to move the cursor word by word is a combination of the Control key and the left or right arrow. The scrolling commands use combinations of the Home, End, and arrow keys, as well as the PgUp and PgDn keys, to move the cursor quickly through the document. In addition, WordPerfect offers a command to go to a particular page. Table 3-1 lists the most frequently used cursor movement and scrolling commands in WordPerfect.

Table 3-1 CURSOR MOVEMENT COMMANDS USED IN WORDPERFECT

Action	*Command*
Character right	Right arrow
Character left	Left arrow
Word right	^ Right arrow
Word left	^ Left arrow
Beginning of line	Home Left arrow
End of line	Home Right arrow *or* End
Line up	Up arrow
Line down	Down arrow
Page up	PgUp
Page down	PgDn
Screen up	− (numeric key pad)
Screen down	+ (numeric key pad)
Top of screen	Home Up arrow
Bottom of screen	Home Down arrow
Top of current page	^ Home Up arrow
Bottom of current page	^ Home Down arrow
Top of File	Home Home Up arrow
End of File	Home Home Down arrow
Go to Page	^ Home *page number*
Go to Beginning of Block	^ Home Alt-F4
Go to Original Position	^ Home ^ Home
Repeat command *n* times	Escape, *n*

Overwriting and Deletion and Replacement

There are two general methods of changing characters in a word processing document: (1) overwriting and (2) deletion and replacement.

Overwriting changes a character by *replacing* the incorrect character with a new character. The previous text is removed from primary storage and from the screen. WordPerfect calls this **typeover.**

Overwriting is usually controlled through the use of the *insert function.* When the insert function is *on,* overwriting is impossible because the newly typed characters are inserted between existing characters. Therefore, to overwrite you must turn the insert function *off* (press the Ins key). You can then, for instance, type over an *e* to correct it to read *a* (see Figure 3-11). To return to the insert mode, use the same command (Ins key) again. With WordPerfect the status line at the bottom of the screen indicates whether the insert function is on or off. Most word processing software have some procedure for overwriting and inserting text.

Another valuable editing feature of word processing is **deletion,** which permits fast removal of unwanted text. *Delete* commands can be used to remove a specified group of characters (one character, a word, a

```
                                        123 East Street Apt. 21
                                        Iowa City, Iowa 52204
                                        (402) 555-9876
                                        May 4, 1989


Ms. Shirley Swanson
Vice President for Personnel
NewSoft Corporation
56 High Tech Drive
Naperville, Illinois 60234

Dear Ms. Swanson

Your ad in the Chicago Tribune on April 30 states that you are
looking for a person with experience using word processing,
spreadsheets, and date bases plus a fundamental understanding of
IBM PC-compatible hardware and software.  The ad further states
that position will be available beginning June 1 and will
continue full-time throughout the summer.  I believe your
position describes my qualifications and employment interests.

My resume is enclosed for your consideration.  The resume does
Typeover                                      Doc 1  Pg 1  Ln 18      Pos 31
```

(a)

```
                                        123 East Street Apt. 21
                                        Iowa City, Iowa 52204
                                        (402) 555-9876
                                        May 4, 1989


Ms. Shirley Swanson
Vice President for Personnel
NewSoft Corporation
56 High Tech Drive
Naperville, Illinois 60234

Dear Ms. Swanson

Your ad in the Chicago Tribune on April 30 states that you are
looking for a person with experience using word processing,
spreadsheets, and data bases plus a fundamental understanding of
IBM PC-compatible hardware and software.  The ad further states
that position will be available beginning June 1 and will
continue full-time throughout the summer.  I believe your
position describes my qualifications and employment interests.

My resume is enclosed for your consideration.  The resume does
Typeover                                      Doc 1  Pg 1  Ln 18      Pos 31
```

(b)

FIGURE 3-11 An illustration of overwriting a character using WordPerfect and the typeover function. The "e" in "date" is replaced simply by the typing of an "a."

Table 3-2 DELETE COMMANDS USED IN WORDPERFECT

Action	*Command*
Delete cursor character	Del
Delete character left of cursor	Backspace
Delete word at the cursor	^ Backspace
Delete from cursor to the end of the line	^ End
Delete from cursor to the end of the page	^ PgDn
Delete *n* lines	Esc *n* ^ End
Restore the previous deletion (Cancel or Undo command)	[F1]

line, or a block) from a document, including hard spaces and end-of-paragraph markers.

Delete commands differ in effect and scope. For example, the commands in Table 3-2 permit you to delete characters, words, or lines quickly and easily.

WordPerfect uses the Delete key to delete the character currently marked by the cursor, as well as the space it occupied. The Backspace key removes the character directly to the left of the cursor character.

A deletion can be cancelled and the characters restored at the *current* location of the cursor with the **Restore command** ([F1] in WordPerfect). The latest deletion will be replaced at the current cursor location (see Figure 3-12). While the Restore command is found on many popular word processing software packages, be aware that some word processing software do not have this undo feature, in which case when something is deleted it is gone, unless you can retrieve it from a file stored on disk.

To **insert** (add) characters into existing text, first be sure the insert mode is *on*. In WordPerfect, if the filename appears in the left bottom corner, or if this space is blank, then the insert mode is on. If the word "typeover" appears, then the insert mode is off. Position the cursor over the letter (or space) that will *follow* the character of text you wish to add, and type in the new character. The current cursor character will automatically be moved to the right to make room for the new one. (Contrast this with overwriting, in which the insert mode is off and the existing text is actually replaced by a new character.) Figure 3-13 shows how we correct the word "spreasheets" by inserting a *d*.

Word Wrap

Word wrap automatically moves any text that goes beyond the right margin down to the next line. As you enter characters, use the Return key only at the end of paragraphs. Instead of listening for the typewriter bell at the right margin and hitting the carriage return, you simply keep on typing. As you type past the right margin, the words automatically move down to

FIGURE 3-12 After multiple character deletion using the Delete to End of Line command (^End) in WordPerfect. The deleted line can be retrieved at the current cursor position when the user presses the Undo Command ([F1]).

```
experience with my own microcomputer, I think I can be of service
to NewSoft.  Your consideration of my application is
appreciated.  I will be calling in a few days to answer any
additional questions you may have concerning my qualifications
and supply references.  Please call me if you have any questions.


C:\MAIN\WP\FIG312B.ART                  Doc 1  Pg 1  Ln 18     Pos 10
```

(a)

```
With my previous work experience, courses at Iowa, and personal
experience with my own microcomputer, I think I can be of service
to NewSoft.  Your consideration of my application is
appreciated.  I will be calling in a few days to answer any
additional questions you may have concerning my qualifications
and supply references.  Please call me if you have any questions.


Undelete: 1 Restore; 2 Show Previous Deletion: 0
```

(b)

the next line (see Figure 3-14). Some word processing software combine word wrap with hyphen-help, which suggests how a word should be hyphenated to fit on a line.

It is time to start using WordPerfect. The commands found in WordPerfect are similar to those found in several popular word processing software packages, and the fundamental concepts presented are common to word processing applications software.

FIGURE 3-13 Inserting text with WordPerfect. Notice how the previous text is moved over. The insert mode, indicated by the filename on the status line, must be on if new characters are to be added.

```
          My resume is enclosed for your consideration.  The resume does
          not explain that I have just completed a course where I was
          required to do several projects using word processing,
          spreasheets, and data base management software.  While enrolled
          in that course I decided to use the extra money earned last
C:\MAIN\WP\SS5489.WPC                           Doc 1  Pg 1  Ln 27     Pos 15
```

(a)

```
          My resume is enclosed for your consideration.  The resume does
          not explain that I have just completed a course where I was
          required to do several projects using word processing,
          spreadsheets, and data base management software.  While enrolled
          in that course I decided to use the extra money earned last
C:\MAIN\WP\SS5489.WPC                           Doc 1  Pg 1  Ln 27     Pos 15
```

(b)

Note that, in the word processing tutorials in Lessons 3, 4, and 5, we refer to two versions of WordPerfect: version 4.2 and version 5.0. Version 5.0, released in April 1988, is a significant update from version 4.2 and contains significant refinements. These include the following:

References specific to the Limited-Use version of WordPerfect 4.2 (L-WP) will appear as glosses in the margin.

- Absolute measures of inches replace characters and lines for margins and spacing measurements. For example, in WordPerfect 4.2, having a 1-inch right margin would mean setting the margin at 10 spaces. With version 5.0, the margin is 1″. A $1\frac{1}{2}$-inch margin is 1.5″. This allows users to mix different typeface sizes on the same line.

- "Intelligent printing" capabilities allow much greater flexibility in using fonts with specific printers. WordPerfect 5.0 adjusts the base font and font changes to the selected print driver. Font sizes, appearance, and color codes can all be incorporated in a document quickly and easily. This permits users with sophisticated printers, such as laser printers, to use WordPerfect for desktop publishing.

FIGURE 3-14 A representation of how word wrap works. Notice that the word processing software automatically moves the word down to the next line.

```
Word wrap is a feature that automatically moves any text that goes
goes beyond the right margin to the next line.  As you type past
the right margin, the words simply move down to the next line.

C:\MAIN\WP\WORDWRAP.WPC                        Doc 1  Pg 1  Ln 1      Pos 10
```

- Embedded formatting codes have been expanded and are more descriptive. For example, in version 4.2, boldfacing is indicated by the codes [B][b], while in version 5.0 it is indicated by the codes [BOLD][bold].
- Graphics can be recalled and incorporated into documents.
- A sophisticated screen preview feature allows users to see the page as it will be printed, including incorporated graphics and font changes.

Although WordPerfect Corporated tried to minimize the changes to the function key commands, the increased capabilities required that seven keys be moved or renamed. The commands in the tutorial include both sets of commands. Read the instructions carefully to make sure you are pressing the right commands for the version you are using.

In version 5.0 the following changes have been made to the function key commands.

Command	*Action*
Format (Shift-[F8])	The page, print, and line format keys used in version 4.2 have been combined on a single key. The menu for the format key gives the choices for Line, Page, Document, and Other. Each option will show additional subfunctions.
Font (Control-[F8])	This key replaces and expands the Pitch/Font selection under the Print Format command in version 4.2. This key should be used to choose font size, appearance, base fonts, and color.
Style (Alt-[F8])	This new function key command allows users to store and recall styles. **Styles** are a combination of formatting codes and/or text.
Graphics (Alt-[F9])	This key permits users to add four different types of graphics (figure, table, text, and user-defined), as well as horizontal and vertical lines, to a document.
Date/Outline (Shift-[F5])	The date and outline functions were combined on this key.
Setup (Shift-[F1])	This handy key allows you to "customize" WordPerfect to your individual needs. Selections include backup options, cursor speed, display options, fast save, initial settings, keyboard layout, location of auxiliary files, and units of measure.

Before starting the tutorials, remember the following command conventions:

Command	*Action*
[F1]	Press the function key alone.
Shift-[F1]	The dash (-) means to press and *hold* the first key (in this case the Shift key) and, while still pressing the first key, press the function key ([F1]).
Home Home Down Arrow	The space between the commands means to press each key separately. For example, this command means to press the Home key twice and then press the Down Arrow key.
^Return	The caret (^) is the symbol for the Control key. Press and *hold* the Control key and, while still pressing the Control key, press the second key.

TUTORIAL: CREATING AND PRINTING A LETTER USING WORDPERFECT

To complete this tutorial you need the following:

- A WordPerfect disk
- A formatted disk for files
- An installed printer connected to the microcomputer

While completing this tutorial you will learn how to:

- Load WordPerfect
- Create, edit, and save a letter
- Print a letter

In this tutorial you will create a cover letter written by a student applying for a summer job at the imaginary NewSoft Corporation.

Create the Document

There are four basic steps in creating a new document using word processing software: (1) load the operating system into primary storage, (2) load the word processing software into primary storage, (3) insert new text into the document, and (4) assign the document a unique filename.

Step 1: Load the operating system (MS-DOS) into primary storage.

In order to use any applications software, including WordPerfect, you must first load the operating system into primary storage. Some hardware and/or software permit an abbreviated version of the operating system to be placed on the same disk that contains the applications software, provided there is room on the disk. Others require the operating system to reside on a separate disk that must be inserted into the disk drive every time the microcomputer is started or reset. It is usually more convenient to have the operating system on the applications software disk because it reduces disk handling.

The details of loading the operating system were covered in Lesson 2, but we will briefly review the process here.

a. If the WordPerfect disk contains the operating system, insert the WordPerfect disk in disk drive A and latch the disk drive door. Otherwise, use the MS-DOS disk to load the operating system. Remember that the disk is usually inserted label side up with the write-protect notch on the left.

b. Turn on the microcomputer and monitor. If the computer is already on, give the Reset command (simultaneously press the three keys labeled Ctrl, Alt, and Del).

c. After the system checks the keyboard and memory status, if the system requires manual setting of the time and date, enter the required information. Remember to use the 24-hour clock. For example, April 29, 1989, would be entered as 4-29-89, and 1:15 p.m. would be entered as 13:15. Press the Enter key at the end of each entry. When you see the MS-DOS system prompt of A>, you have completed loading the operating system and are ready to load WordPerfect.

Step 2: Load WordPerfect into primary storage.

If necessary, remove the MS-DOS disk and place the WordPerfect disk in the disk drive.

Enter the command to load WordPerfect. Type

```
WP
```

Press **Return.**

Users of L-WP will see, in addition to the copyright screen, a screen listing the limitations of the software.

After the initial copyright notices appear, a blank screen appears, ready to receive your typed text. Your screen should be similar to Figure 3-5. If you are using WordPerfect 5.0 your screen may be slightly different.

Step 3: Insert new text into the document.

a. Examine the screen features. At this point let's assume that you have properly loaded the operating system and the word processing software. By opening the document, the word processing software has established a blank work area, or storage area, in primary storage and is now ready to accept data into the file.

Think of this screen as a page. Unlike a printed page, however, the screen has features unique to word processing.

1. At the bottom of the screen is the *status line.* **Doc 1** tells you that document 1 is currently on the screen. WordPerfect can handle two documents at once, a very convenient feature. **Pg 1,** the page indicator, matches the page number that will be printed when the document is printed. **Ln 1,** the line indicator, shows the number of the line on which the cursor is located. **Pos 10,** the position indicator, indicates the position of the cursor on the line. (Remember that the first column on the screen is actually column 10 on the printed page). If you are using WordPerfect 5.0, the line indicator (Ln 1") and position indicator (Pos 1") show *inches.*

   Keep your eye on the position indicator as you use the following features.

2. Press the **Caps Lock Key.**

   Notice how the Pos symbol changes to **POS.**

   Type your name and press **Return.**

   Remember, if you press the Shift key when the Caps Lock is on, characters will be entered as lower case.

   Press the **Caps Lock key** again to return to the original **Pos** symbol.

3. Now press the **Number Lock key.**

   The Pos symbol flashes to warn you that you will now enter numbers when pressing the arrow keys. Press the **arrow keys** and notice that numbers are entered. Press **Return** at the end of the line. Press the **Number Lock key** again to cancel the number entry.

4. If the boldface option is on, the position number changes to show boldfacing (the exact appearance depends on the monitor and the WordPerfect installation).

   Press **[F6]** for boldfacing and type your address. Notice how the characters on the screen appear distinctive.

   After you have typed your address, press **[F6]** or press the **Right arrow** and **Return** to end the boldfacing.

5. Underlining is another print enhancement used to improve the appearance of a document. The position indicator also changes when the underline command is entered.

   Press **[F8]** for underlining and type your phone number.

   Notice how the position indicator and characters on the screen are different from those for boldfacing.

   End the underlining by pressing **[F8]** or press the **Right arrow** again and **Return.**

   The position indicator will return to the original appearance.

6. The status line also contains information about the insert mode and filename as well as prompts asking for further information.

   Press the **Insert key.**

   Notice the word "Typeover" on the left side of the status line. This indicates that the insert mode is off and that previous entries will be replaced rather than moved over. Press the **Insert key** once again to return to inserting characters. Once the typeover message has disappeared, the space remains blank. However, once you have saved the file, the filename will appear on the status line. Software prompts and messages will also appear in this space at appropriate times.

7. WordPerfect attempts to show, as closely as possible, how the text will actually look on paper. Thus, control codes and other special symbols are hidden so that they will not clutter the text. However, placement of these commands is crucial. You can make such codes and symbols (including printing enhancements) visible simply by giving the Reveal Codes command.

   Press **Alt-[F3].**

   Notice that the screen becomes divided. The top portion shows the text normally, while the bottom window shows the text with the embeddedcodes. [B][b] or [BOLD][bold] surround characters to be boldfaced while [U][u] or [UND][und] surround the underlined characters. [HRt] indicates a hard return inserted by the user, and [SRt] indicates the soft return placed by the software. Although this system of formatting codes may seem intimidating at first, the codes are quite easy to read and use. They are all English language abbreviations rather than cryptic codes.

   Press **Alt-[F3]** to remove the Reveal Codes window.

8. There are a template and a help menu to remind you of commands. A **template** is a small plastic overlay to fit above or around the function keys as a reminder of the function key commands. Since WordPerfect combines the function keys with the Control, Shift, and Alt keys to carry out various commands, the WordPerfect template is color coded so users can see which key combination to use. WordPerfect also has extensive on-line help, including a help menu and explanations. Press **[F3]** twice to see the on-screen template. The on-line help feature will be discussed further in Lesson 4.

   Press the **Space Bar** or the **Return** to exit the help function.

*Online help in L-WP consists of the onscreen template, which is accessed by pressing **[F3]** only once.*

9. Clear the screen by pressing the **Exit** command **[F7].**

   At the prompt you will see

```
Save Document?(Y/N)Y
```

Type

N

The prompt will change to

```
Exit WP?(Y/N)N
```

Type

N

A new blank screen will appear.

b. Type the letter exactly as shown in Figure 3-15, including the spelling and typing errors (maybe you'll add a few of your own). You will correct them later.

Remember to use your Tab key to move the cursor to the proper columns for the inside address. Use the Return key as a marker for the end of paragraphs. **Do not press the Enter key or the Return key at the right margin! Let the word wrap feature handle this.** The print and formatting commands will not work properly if you insert Returns at the end of every line. If you are accustomed to a regular typewriter, you will be in the habit of listening for the bell indicating the right margin, and you may find it difficult to break the habit of pressing the Return key at the right margin. With a word processor, use the Return key to start a new paragraph, not a new line. This is the most common error made by beginners, so do not feel discouraged if it takes some practice before you are accustomed to letting the word wrap feature do its job.

Edit the Document

One of the handiest features of word processing is the ability to edit documents quickly. To see this firsthand, you are going to edit the letter you just entered.

Step 1: Correct the errors.

Make the corrections either by deleting the errors and typing in the corrections or by typing over the errors. Use the arrow keys to move the cursor to the different errors and correct those errors. Remember to use the keys or commands shown in Tables 3-1 and 3-2.

Step 2: Realign the paragraphs.

As you correct errors and insert new material between existing words, you may notice that the line extends beyond the right margin. Don't panic!

Column 50

Press the TAB key 8 times → 123 East Street Apt. 21 RETURN
Iowa City, Iowa 52204 RETURN
(402) 555-9876 RETURN
May 4, 1989 RETURN RETURN

Column 10 on screen

Ms. Shirley Swanson RETURN
Vace President for Personnel RETURN
NewSoft Corporation RETURN
56 High Tech Drive RETURN
Naperville, Illinois 60234 RETURN RETURN

Dear Ms. Swanson: RETURN RETURN

Yaur ad in the Chicago Tribune on Aprol 30 stated that you are looking for persom with experience using ward processing, spreasheets, and date bases plus a fundamantal understanding of IBM PC-compatible hardwere and software. The ad further states the position will be available begining June 1 and will continue full-time throughout the summer. I believe your position describes my qualifications and employment interests perfectly. RETURN RETURN

My resume is enclosed for your consideration. The resume does not explain that I have just completed a cursr where I was required to do several projects using word processing, spreadshets, and data base management software. While enrolled in that course I decided to use the extra money earned last summer working for TechMARK as a microcomputer salesperson to purchase my own microcomputer systam. I have installed several expansion boards and have become even more acquainted with the hardware and softwore. This semester I am enrolled in two microcomputer related courses: Computer Graphics and Data Communications. I hove also completed the course called Systems Analysis and Design. RETURN RETURN

By June 1 I will have completed my jnior year at the University of Iowa and will be living in Naperville with my parents. I will be returning to Iowa for my senior year starting the last week in August. RETURN RETURN

With my previous work experience, courses at Iowa, and personal experience with my own microcomputer, I think I can be of service to NewSoft. Your consideration of may application is appreciated. I will be calling in a few days to answer any additional questions you may have concerning my qualifications and supply references. Please call me if you have any questions. RETURN RETURN

Press the TAB key 8 times → Sincerely, RETURN
RETURN
RETURN
RETURN
Pat Allen RETURN

WordPerfect will handle it. Whenever you make changes to the text, WordPerfect automatically rewrites the document on the screen so that the changes fit into the format of the margins, tabs, or other formatting options. Although the automatic rewrite may be turned off, most users find this feature very convenient and leave it on. The paragraph will be realigned provided you have avoided using the Return key at the end of every line.

Step 3: Add a print format command.

After entering the letter, you need to turn off the page number. Move the cursor to the left edge of the screen, before all formatting codes.

Press **Home Home Home Up Arrow.**This will move the cursor to the first available position for formatting commands.

Version 4.2 users press the Page Format command, **Alt-[F8],** to see the Page Format menu (see Figure 3-16). This menu gives you several choices for changing the appearance of your document:

1. Page Number Position specifies the location of page numbers and, if desired, suppresses page numbering.
2. New Page Number specifies the number to use when page numbering starts.
3. Center Page Top to Bottom centers text vertically on a page.
4. Page Length changes the length of the page as well as the number of text lines per page.
5. Top Margin specifies a top margin other than the 1-inch default setting.
6. Headers or Footers specify text to be printed at the top (header) or bottom (footer) of each page of your document.
7. Page Number Column Position specifies the column position of the page number.
8. Suppress for Current Page Only allows you to turn off page numbering headers and footers for the current page.
9. Conditional End of Page allows you to specify a condition that must be met to keep lines of text together on one page.
10. Widow/Orphan allows you to specify that a single line of a new paragraph not appear by itself at the bottom of a page (widow) or at the top of a new page (orphan).

FIGURE 3-15 The letter, complete with errors, to be used in the tutorial. Users of WordPerfect 4.2 should follow the instructions for columns. Version 5.0 users will use inches instead of columns. Column 10 will be 1 inch and column 50 will be 5 inches.

```
Page Format

     1 - Page Number Position

     2 - New Page Number

     3 - Center Page Top to Bottom

     4 - Page Length

     5 - Top Margin

     6 - Headers or Footers

     7 - Page Number Column Positions

     8 - Suppress for Current page only

     9 - Conditional End of Page

     A - Widow/Orphan

Selection: 0
```

(a)

```
Format

     1 - Line
              Hyphenation                  Line Spacing
              Justification                Margins Left/Right
              Line Height                  Tab Set
              Line Numbering               Widow/Orphan Protection

     2 - Page
              Center Page (top to bottom)  New Page Number
              Force Odd/Even Page          Page Numbering
              Headers and Footers          Paper Size/Type
              Margins Top/Bottom           Suppress

     3 - Document
              Display Pitch                Redline Method
              Initial Codes/Font           Summary

     4 - Other
              Advance                      Overstrike
              Conditional End of Page      Printer Funtions
              Decimal Characters           Underline Spaces/Tabs
              Language

Selection: 0
```

(b)

FIGURE 3-16 (*a*) Version 4.2 Page Format menu; (*b*) version 5.0 Format menu. Notice that users can select from many options for changing the appearance of a document.

If you are using WordPerfect 5.0, press **Shift-[F8]**. Your Format menu will be different and will include the following:

1. *Line* controls hyphenation, justification, line height, line numbering, line spacing, right and left margins, tabs, and widow/orphan protection.
2. *Page* controls page centering (top to bottom), odd/even page forcing, headers and footers, top and bottom margins, new page number, page numbering, paper size and type, and suppression of page formatting.
3. *Document* controls the commands for displaying pitch, initial codes and fonts, redline method, and inclusion of a document summary.
4. Other options include commands to control the page advance, conditional end of page, decimal characters, foreign language characters, overstrike, printer functions, and underlining of tabs and spaces.

If you are using WordPerfect 4.2, press

1

A second menu appears with nine (0–8) options for placing the page number on the page. Since we want to suppress the page number, press

0

Press **Return.** Users of WordPerfect 5.0 should press **P** for Page. The Format:Page menu appears. Notice the options for changing the format of the page. Press **9 1** to suppress the all page numbering, headings, and footers. Press **[F7]** to return to the document. The page number will not be printed.

Step 4: Proofread the document carefully.

It is more difficult than you may imagine to find all your errors as you proofread. Your mind plays tricks, so that you "see" what you *think* you typed, not necessarily what you really did type. You may want to print the letter before proofreading; some people find it easier to locate errors on a printed document than on the screen. Some expert proofreaders may actually read a manuscript backwards, making it more difficult for their minds to trick them into "seeing" what isn't really there. Others read the material out loud or have someone else read it out loud to them. Still others slide a piece of paper or a ruler down the page as they proofread, concentrating on only one line at a time. Learn to develop good proofreading skills. It doesn't do much good to learn to use a word processor if you fail to find and correct mistakes.

Once you are sure that all errors have been corrected, you are ready to save the document.

Save the Document

One lesson most students learn the hard way is the importance of periodically saving their work on a disk. A document is saved when the text contained in **working storage** (the contents of RAM) is written on **permanent storage** (the disk). Remember, until you save your letter on a disk, it is stored in volatile primary storage only. Your letter can disappear if there is any interruption in the electrical supply or if you shut off the computer. When you save a document or file on a disk, the computer actually makes a copy of what is currently in primary storage and places the copy on the disk. At that moment, two copies of your file exist, one on the disk and one in the primary storage area of the microcomputer.

We recommend that you save your work every 10 minutes. In this way, if something should happen accidentally to erase your working storage, you will have lost only the last 10 minutes worth of effort. In fact, WordPerfect has the option of installing a special automatic timed backup feature that allows the user to set the number of minutes between each automatic save operation. Also, when you save the document as you exit the program normally at the end of a work session, {WP}BACK.1 or WP{WP}.BK1 (depending on the version you are using)—the special file used for automatic backups—is automatically erased. However, if you experience some problem (such as a power interruption or system reset), and WordPerfect was not exited normally, the special file is retained and can then be renamed and edited.

Despite safeguards against accidental loss of a file, WordPerfect still requires you to save your file before exiting the software normally. It is a common, but troublesome, oversight to fail to save the latest working storage version. It is easy to forget that you are working on a primary storage copy of the file and not directly on the file stored on the disk. Remember to save your latest working storage version on a disk before quitting and turning off the computer.

There are two basic ways to save a document using WordPerfect: (1) save and continue and (2) save and exit. See the table on p. 113.

To save the file for the first time, press **[F10].** WordPerfect then prompts for a filename.

Remember, a filename must be unique to that particular disk yet follow a convention or series of rules and guidelines to help you determine the type and content of the document when you look at a directory of filenames on the disk, using either the MS-DOS Directory command (DIR) or the List File command [F5] in WordPerfect. For example, you may decide to start all your correspondence with the initials of the recipient and the

Action	*Commands*
Save and Continue:	
To save a file for the first time	[F10] <filename> Return
To save a previously saved file under the same name	[F10] Return Y
To save a previously saved file under a new name	[F10] <filename> Return
Save and Exit:	
To save a previously saved document and edit another document	[F7] Y Return Y N
To save a file and exit WordPerfect	[F7] Y Return Y Y

date. Thus, a letter sent to John Doe on May 4, 1989, would be named JD5489.LET. Here are some suggested guidelines.

1. Use extensions (suffixes) to describe the nature of the contents, such as .LET for letter, .DOC for document, or .RPT for report.
2. Avoid using restricted extensions such as .BK! (back-up files created by WordPerfect), .DBF (database files created by dBASE III Plus), and .WKS, .WK!, .PIC, .PRN, and .CAL (common extensions used by spreadsheet software such as Lotus 1-2-3 and VP-Planner).
3. The name should begin with a letter and must be no more than eight characters long.
4. Avoid using special symbols and punctuation marks in the name. Although WordPerfect will accept such symbols, not all software is as forgiving and you may have difficulty interchanging files with other software.
5. Also, do not use blank spaces within the name.

Good naming habits are especially important when you are creating and using a large number of files on a hard disk.

Remember to specify a filename prefix for the disk drive—typically A: or B: for a floppy disk drive and C: for a hard disk drive. Word processing software used on MS-DOS systems accepts either upper- or lower-case letters in filenames and extensions and automatically changes lower-case commands or filenames into upper case.

Be aware that back-up files and other files automatically created by the software can use up disk space faster than you might realize. Back-up files,

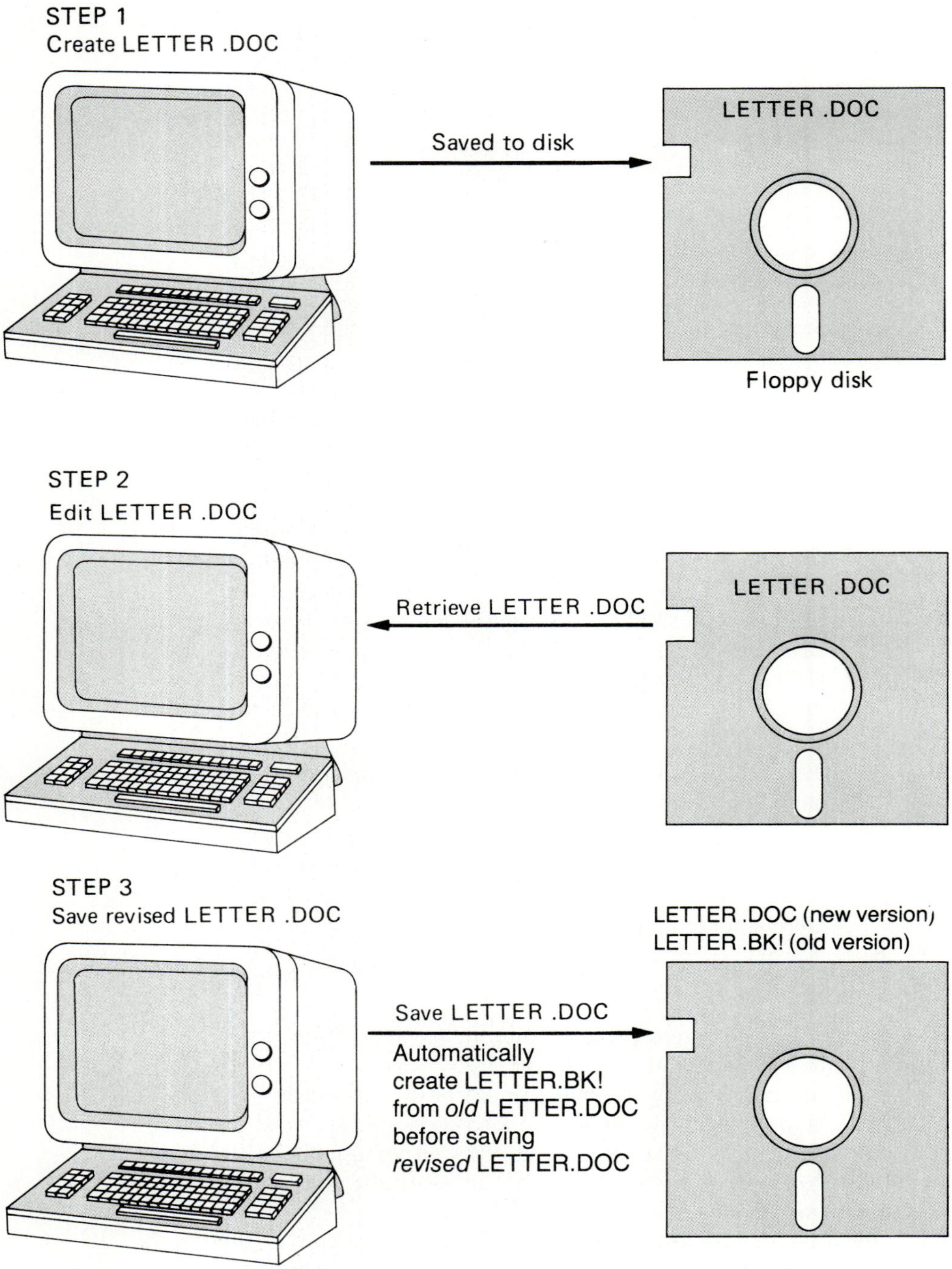

FIGURE 3-17 Back-up files (designated by .BK!) are created from saved copies of previous documents.

for example, automatically double the amount of disk space needed to store a file. Figure 3-17 is an illustration of how back-up files are created. Notice that the action of saving after editing an existing file causes the software to automatically create a copy of your old file, giving you two files where previously there was only one. (Later, when you use dBASE III Plus, you will find the database software automatically creating several files on your data disk).

Also be aware that these back-up files are stored on the same disk and, unlike the automatic back-up files, are not destroyed when the software is exited properly. If that disk is lost, damaged, or destroyed, both the original and back-up files will be gone. To prevent such a disaster, copy all important files on a separate disk.

What happens if you give an improper filename? That depends on the word processing software. Some just refuse to use it and will give you an error message. WordPerfect will truncate names that are too long, and will continue to the next operation when a space is placed in the name.

For your first document, use a complete file specification of B:SS5489.LET. At the prompt

```
Document to be Saved:
```

type

```
B:SS5489.let
```

Press **Return.**

If you have previously saved the file, WordPerfect will prompt with the previously saved filename. If you want to save the file under the same name, press **Return.** At the prompt

```
Replace <filename> (Y/N) N
```

respond

```
Y
```

The revised file will replace the old file.

One way to speed up the process of saving a file and continuing with your editing is to construct a macro. A **macro** is a set of commands, instructions, or text stored as a group and executed when you enter the name of the macro. Let's construct a simple macro named Alt-S as a Save and Continue Macro.

Press ^ **[F10].** The prompt will change to

```
Define Macro:
```

Press **Alt-S.** The prompt will begin to flash, indicating that all your keystrokes are being recorded. Press **[F10] Return Y.**

Now end the macro definition. Press ^ **[F10].**

Now, every time you want to save a document that has been saved previously, just press Alt-S. The sequence of commands will automatically be invoked.

Print the Document

WordPerfect offers a variety of print options that make it quick and easy to print a document. There are two commands available to print a document: the List Files command [F5] and the Print command (Shift-[F7]). Printing from the List Files Screen is generally quicker and easier. However, printing from the Printer Control Screen gives you greater control over the print commands. For now we are going to use the List Files command. The Printer Control Screen will be discussed further in future lessons. Before printing a document, check that your computer is properly connected to a printer that is turned on and ready. There are two basic steps to printing a document: (1) accessing the print options, through either the List Files or the Printer Control Screens, and (2) producing the document on a printer.

Step 1: Access the List Files Screen.

To print a document located on the current disk, press **[F5].** A prompt appears, asking you to specify which directory and files to list. For example,

```
Dir A:\*.* (Type = to change default Dir)
```

To change the default directory to disk drive B, type

```
=B:
```

Press **Return.**

The prompt will change to

```
Dir=B:\*.*
```

WordPerfect is asking if the directory of all the files on disk drive B is what you want. Since it is, press **Return.**

The List Files Screen gives you several command options: (1) Retrieve (recall a file from disk into WordPerfect to the current cursor position; (2) Delete; (3) Rename (Move/Rename in version 5.0); (4) Print; (5) Text In (retrieve a MS-DOS text file); (6) Look (show the contents of a file); (7) Change Directory (Other Directory in version 5.0) (change the default directory or create new directories); (8) Copy; and (9) Word Search (show the files containing specified words). Name Search in version 5.0 locates files by the entered filename.

Move the highlight to the name of the file that you want to print, SS5489.LET.

Step 2: Print the document.
Type

```
4
```

to select the Print option. A prompt may appear:

For users of L-WP, the document will begin to print as soon as "4" is typed.

```
Page(s): (All)
```

Press **Return.** You may return to creating or editing another document by pressing

```
0
```

If you need to stop the printing, enter a command from the Printer Control screen. To access the Printer Control commands, press Shift-[F7] and type **4** for the Printer Control option. Press **C** for Cancel Print Job(s).

Step 3: Proofread the printed document and correct any remaining errors.

Check carefully for errors and correct any remaining ones. After making any changes, save your file with the Save and Return macro (Alt-S).

Print the document, following the previous instructions.

Quit WordPerfect

As fundamental as this may sound, it is very important to quit WordPerfect properly to make sure files are properly saved and closed. Always return to the system prompt (A>) before removing the WordPerfect disk or turning off the microcomputer.

When you are satisfied with your letter, press **[F7].** WordPerfect will prompt

```
Save Document? (Y/N)Y
```

If you have not made any changes since the file was saved, the message

```
(Text was not modified)
```

In L-WP, the software will not display this message. Rather, the software will simply save the file to disk.

will appear on the status line. If changes were made to the file, no prompt will appear.

If you need to save the file, press **Return.** Otherwise, press **N.**

At the prompt

```
Exit WP? (Y/N)N
```

press

```
Y
```

After the system prompt reappears, remove the disks and turn off the microcomputer.

SUMMARY

This lesson has defined word processing: what it is, how it is used, and what its major functions are. Word processing is the automated processing of words using a specialized applications program. Word processing permits people to change, edit, and print written documents easily.

Characteristics of potential word processing applications can be put into five major categories: (1) repetition, (2) editing, (3) revisions, (4) variable and fixed parts, and (5) quality appearance. The major functions of word processing are (1) creating, (2) editing, (3) formatting, (4) printing, and (5) document handling.

The functions of creating, editing, formatting, saving, and printing are used to produce a letter. Editing is the recalling, deletion, overwriting, and inserting of text. Saving copies the document to a disk file. Printing produces hard, or printed, copy from a stored document.

Word processing software offer features that make the creation, editing, and printing of text faster and easier. These include cursor movement; overwriting, deletion, and undoing; replacement and insertion; and word wrap. Cursor movement permits users to move the cursor, or point of entry, on the screen using the cursor control keys. Overwriting changes characters by replacing the incorrect character with a new character. Deletion is the removal of unwanted characters. Undoing returns the deleted characters to the screen. Insertion moves the characters over to make room for newly inserted characters. Word wrap automatically moves down to the next line any text that goes beyond the right margin.

These commands and features are used in the tutorial to create and print a letter using WordPerfect.

EXERCISES

1. List the five characteristics of word processing applications. Then indicate the most appropriate characteristic(s) for each application listed below.

   a. term paper

   b. personal letter

   c. letter to customers

d. report to stockholders

e. resumé

f. columns of numbers

2. Define the following terms:

word processing	document handling	status line
character	cursor movement	scrolling
document	cursor	insert
soft words	hard spaces	deletion
destructive write	soft spaces	Restore command
editing	cursor control keys	word wrap
revisions	arrow keys	template
desktop publishing	optional cursor control keys	working storage
style sheet	overwriting	permanent storage
creating	typeover	macro
formatting		
printing		

3. What is the purpose of planning word processing applications?

4. What is the difference between working storage and permanent storage? Why is it important to understand the difference?

5. Create your own filenames for word processing documents with the following contents:

   a. letter to John Kenney, dated December 12, 1989

   b. book report for American History 202

   c. resume for summer jobs

   d. term paper for Business Law 217

   e. letter to a friend named Pat McDonald sent on February 18, 1989

6. Practice using WordPerfect by completing the tutorial, Creating and Printing a Letter. Then repeat the tutorial, creating your own letter to apply for a summer job; include the following changes:

   a. With the MS-DOS Copy utility, on the disk in drive B, copy the corrected letter SS5489.LET. Assign the new file a name based on a new addressee. For example, if you plan to change the addressee from Ms. Shirley Swanson to Mr. Jim Torma, and you plan to date the letter September 17, 1989, you would name the file JT91789.LET. Please do not use this filename; it is only an example. Give the letter your own unique filename.

   b. Use your own local address and phone number to replace the inside address and phone number. Replace the date with the date you completed the tutorial. The current inside address and date are

123 East Street Apt. 21
Iowa City, Iowa 52204
(402) 555-9876
May 4, 1989

c. In a local newspaper find an ad for a microcomputer-related position.

d. Change the information in the letter to match the position in the ad. Be sure to change the addressee's name and address (Ms. Shirley Swanson, etc.), the newspaper name (*Chicago Tribune*), the date of the ad (April 30), and the name of the company (NewSoft) referred to in the letter.

e. If you have taken or are enrolled in any other computer-related courses, substitute these course titles for those mentioned in the sentence "This semester I am enrolled in two microcomputer-related courses: Computer Graphics and Data Communications. I have also completed the course called Systems Analysis and Design." Otherwise, delete the sentence and substitute any other relevant information.

f. Substitute your own information for other details contained in the letter, such as your current semester (junior year), school (University of Iowa), home town (Naperville), and name (Pat Allen).

g. Save and print the letter.

7. Create your own letter to a friend, relative, or business acquaintance. Write down the steps necessary to create, edit, save, and print the document.

8. Supply the WordPerfect commands necessary to complete the functions below:

a. Change the insert function to Typeover
b. Delete the current cursor character
c. Scroll the page up
d. Go to the bottom of the file
e. Delete character to the left of the cursor
f. Save the document and return to editing
g. Go to page number
h. Change the left margin
i. Reveal the WordPerfect Onscreen Template
j. Delete the current word
k. Save the text and exit to MS-DOS

4
Word Processing Applications

LESSON OUTLINE

Word Processing Functions
- Editing
- Formatting
- Saving
- Printing

Additional Word Processing Features
- Help Menus
- Block Operations
- Search and Replace
- Text Formatting

Tutorial: Creating a Resumé

Summary

Exercises

Lesson 3 introduced several important concepts essential to your general understanding of word processing. In Lesson 4 we will expand on these concepts and produce a resumé to illustrate the commands and techniques needed to create, edit, format, save, and print a finished resumé. The tutorial then uses the example letter from Lesson 3 to illustrate various printing techniques.

WORD PROCESSING FUNCTIONS

In Lesson 4 you will use some of the more sophisticated features of word processing to edit, format, save, and print a document. Let's briefly review the definition of each of these four functions of word processing.

Editing

Editing is the correcting of errors and rewording of existing text. For an existing document to be edited using word processing, it must be retrieved from secondary storage on the data disk and stored as a working copy in primary storage. The computer simply makes a *copy* of the file to be edited and stores this new copy in primary storage. People speak of this retrieval process as if the file were actually moved from one place to another. However, the data disk still contains the original version until the newly edited version with the identical document name is stored on the same disk after the editing process is completed.

To edit a document, you will use the cursor movement commands, the delete commands, and the insert commands you learned in Lesson 3 and apply block commands we will discuss in this lesson. Most word processing software systems allow users to insert and overwrite text as well as mark and move blocks.

Some word processing software, such as WordStar, have a status line at the top of the screen indicating whether the insert mode is on or off. Others, such as WordPerfect, have a status line at the bottom indicating when the typeover mode is active. Thus, if the insert mode is on, you place new keystrokes in the document by pushing the existing material to the right. If the insert mode is off or TYPEOVER is the condition, then you place new keystrokes on top of the existing material, and overwrite the old text with the new.

Formatting

Formatting is the alignment or positioning of the various parts of a document. Formatting includes changing margins, switching from double to single spacing, determining the number of lines on a page, and other placement options. Often word processing software uses format commands embedded directly in the file. Sometimes these commands are visible, as are the dot commands used in WordStar. A **dot command** directs the printer to format the output. Some software, such as WordPerfect, normally hide such commands, showing only the effect on the screen. Formatting commands will be explained more fully later in this lesson.

Saving

Saving a document copies the working copy in primary storage onto a disk. The document is saved in magnetic form, so it can be retrieved later. Since any interruption in the electrical flow to the computer will cause the material being held in primary storage to be lost, it is a good idea to save your document every 10 to 15 minutes. In this way you will never lose more than that amount of work due to a power failure or an accidental erasure.

Printing

Printing produces the document on paper. A printed document, or **hard copy,** is normally a copy of a file stored on a disk or onscreen. Some word processing software, can print only documents that are first stored on a disk file, while others, including WordPerfect, permit you to print a document that is not yet stored on a disk. Note that producing a printed report does not erase or alter the copy stored on the disk.

ADDITIONAL WORD PROCESSING FEATURES

Word processing packages offer many advanced features to increase efficiency and make the software easy to use. Some of these special features, including menus, search and replace, onscreen and print formatting, chain printing, and block commands, are discussed in the following sections.

Help Menus

As explained in Lesson 3, a menu is a list of available functions and the commands necessary to use them. Most word processing software, including WordPerfect, have menus. Some offer menus that are displayed constantly on the screen, while others have **on-demand menus** that display a menu only after you enter the proper command. Some have extensive, multilevel menus, while others offer only single-level menus listing fundamental commands. For example, WordStar has several levels of command menus, as illustrated in Figure 4-1. Figure 4-2 is an example of the WordStar Edit Menu. Notice on the left of the menu the commands to show additional menus. WordPerfect offers extensive online help by way of the Help key, [F3]. If you press the Help key and another function key, a complete explanation of the function key command and the command

FIGURE 4-1 WordStar has several different levels of command menus.

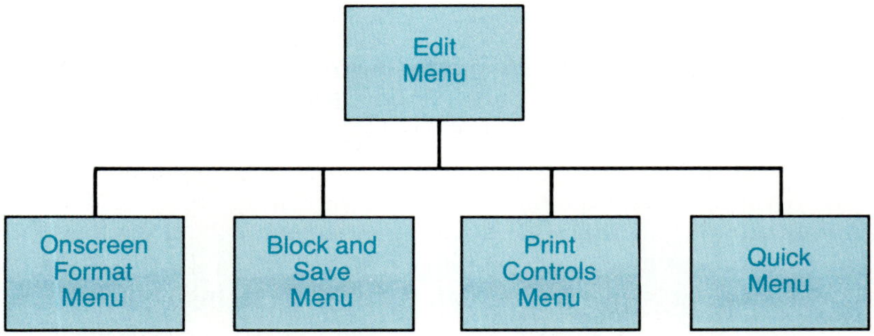

options replaces the text on the screen. For example, if you press the Help key ([F3]) and then press the List Files command ([F5]), an explanation of the List Files command appears on the screen. If you press the Help key twice, the function key template will appear, as in Figure 4-3, helping you locate the needed function key command. The document reappears when the next key is pressed. Remember, the template for version 5.0 will be slightly different.

When you first see all those commands listed they may look rather overwhelming. You may say, "How can I learn all those commands at once?" Fortunately, you do not have to learn them all at once. Although WordPerfect is rich in features, you learn the commands as you need them. Practice is the key to learning how to use any word processing software. Help ([F3][F3]) is always available to remind you of the commands. If you need help using the software, refer to this book, the WordPerfect reference guide, or the onscreen help.

```
 C:FIG42.WPC          P01 L01 C01 Insert Align
                              E D I T   M E N U
   CURSOR       SCROLL        ERASE     OTHER                MENUS
^E up        ^W up         ^G char   ^J help             ^O onscreen format
^X down      ^Z down       ^T word   ^I tab              ^K block & save
^S left      ^R up screen  ^Y line   ^V turn insert      ^P print controls
^D right     ^C down      Del char   ^B align paragraph  ^Q quick functions
^A word left    screen     ^U unerase ^N split the line  Esc shorthand
^F word right                        ^L find/replace again
```

FIGURE 4-2 An example of the WordStar Edit Menu. Notice that commands are grouped according to type and action. The commands to recall additional menus are listed in the right column of the screen so users can easily recall needed menus.

FIGURE 4-3 (*a*) The WordPerfect Help onscreen template for version 4.2. The user can request information about the commands simply by pressing the appropriate function key. WordPerfect combines the functions keys with the Alt, Ctrl, and Shift keys to offer more than 40 function key commands. (*b*) Version 5.0 (page 126) users will find their template slightly different. The Setup command (Shift-[F1]), Date/Outline command (Shift-[F5]), Graphics command (Alt-[F9]), Font (Ctrl-[F8]), Format (Shift-[F8]), and Style (Alt-[F8]) are new key assignments.

WordPerfect 4.2 Template (IBM Layout)

F1	Shell SUPER/SUBSCRIPT Thesaurus Cancel	Spell <-SEARCH Replace Search->	F2
F3	Screen SWITCH Reveal Codes Help	Move ->INDENT<- Block ->Indent	F4
F5	Text In/Out DATE Mark Text List Files	Tab Align CENTER Flush Right Bold	F6
F7	Footnote PRINT Math/Columns Exit	Print LINE FORMAT Page Format Underline	F8
F9	Merge/Sort MERGE E Merge Codes Merge R	Macro Def. RETRIEVE TEXT Macro Save Text	F10

Legend:
Ctrl + Function Key
SHIFT + FUNCTION KEY
Alt + Function Key
Function Key alone

(a)

FIGURE 4.3 (continued) part (b)

WordPerfect 5.0 Template (IBM Layout)

	Shell	Spell	
F1	SETUP	<-SEARCH	F2
	Thesaurus	Replace	
	Cancel	Search->	
	Screen	Move	
F3	SWITCH	->INDENT<-	F4
	Reveal Codes	Block	
	Help	->Indent	
	Text In/Out	Tab Align	
F5	DATE/OUTLINE	CENTER	F6
	Mark Text	Flush Right	
	List Files	Bold	
	Footnote	Font	
F7	PRINT	FORMAT	F8
	Math/Columns	Style	
	Exit	Underline	
	Merge/Sort	Macro Def.	
F9	MERGE CODES	RETRIEVE	F10
	Graphics	Macro	
	Merge R	Save	

Legend:

Ctrl + Function Key
SHIFT + FUNCTION KEY
Alt + Function Key
Function Key alone

Block Operations

Block operations quickly and easily perform the "cutting and pasting" of editing. A **block** is a segment of text. The user defines size of the segment, using **block markers** at the beginning and end of the block or highlighting the text to be included in the block, as in Figure 4-4. Once you define the block, you can move, copy, save, print, and delete it. Block commands permit various editing tasks, such as moving a sentence or deleting or moving a paragraph. You can define only one block at a time but can change the size and content of the block at any time. Although the specific block operation commands may differ, most word processing software have some block operations.

In WordPerfect, you can mark any size block of text, from a single character to the entire document, by pressing Alt-[F4]. After you enter this command, a flashing message—*Block On*—appears on the status line, indicating that as you press any cursor movement key, WordPerfect will mark the block by highlighting the affected text. The cursor movement keys can be used to mark all the text to be included in the block operations. WordPerfect block operations include moving, deleting, underlining, boldfacing, centering, converting to upper or lower case, printing, sorting, searching, marking, saving, appending, and spell checking. To mark only a few characters or words, use the arrow keys or the Control-arrow key combination. To mark a few lines of text, press the down arrow. To block a paragraph, press Return while the blocking is on. WordPerfect

FIGURE 4-4 **A block is a section of text that can be moved, copied, or deleted. Block operations make the revision and editing of text much easier. In WordPerfect a block is highlighted in reverse video.**

```
or faculty electronic mailbox, and send and receive files.  Many
university computer centers, however, are so heavily utilized
with current processing needs that they are unable to
realistically add these features.  Constant busy signals and slow
response time can quickly discourage students and faculty from
using electronic communications, and what could be a valuable
tool becomes an annoying burden.  This is especially true for
-------------------------------------------------------------------------
managers and other adult learners who are often overwhelmed by
other demands and are less tolerant of delays.
     Another approach is to set up a microcomputer or
minicomputer as a dedicated communications hub.  Low cost
bulletin board software enables a personal computer equipped with
a smart modem to automatically answer incoming calls, receive and
transmit messages, and establish an electronic bulletin board and
electronic mail.  If conferencing is desired, then multiple
modems and phone lines and more sophisticated software are
required.  Such a plan also requires someone, perhaps the
professor or a program administrator, to monitor and maintain the
system.  In addition, users may be required to call long-distance
to access the system, because the university may be located in a
different town or calling region.


Block on                                   Doc 2  Pg 2  Ln 14     Pos  43
```

will extend the block to the end of the paragraph. If you want to mark a block to a particular character, type that character after turning the blocking on. If you mark too much text, use the opposite cursor movement key to reduce the block borders.

To cancel the block marking, press the Cancel command [F1], or press Alt-[F4] again. To remark the same block, press Alt-[F4] to turn the blocking on and then press ^Home (the GoTo command) twice.

WordPerfect has a handy feature that allows users to copy, move, or delete sentences, paragraphs, and pages without marking the block. If you know that the text is a discrete unit, such as a complete sentence, paragraph, or page, you can avoid having to mark the block by pressing the Move command ^[F4]. Figure 4-4 is an example of a block using WordPerfect.

Search and Replace

Search and replace is an editing feature that directs an electronic search through a document to locate characters and, if specified, replace the characters. The search option allows the user to locate specific characters in a document. The search and replace option will locate and also replace

```
                         FAIR WARS

     One of the biggest travel bargins of the year is airline
fairs.  In recent weeks airline fairs have decreased from 40 to
50 percent.  AirHwy has been a leader in cutting fairs.  In those
markets where AirHwy flies, fairs have been between 30 to 50
percent lower.  Even competing airlines must admit that low fairs
have really revolutionized the concept of air travel.  No longer
is air travel reserved for the rich.  Fairs are so low that
almost everyone can afford to fly.  Who knows how low these fairs
will go?  Of course, there is always the danger of too much of a
good thing.  Airlines might find the fairs too low to meet
-> Srch: fairs
```

(a)

```
                         FAIR WARS

     One of the biggest travel bargins of the year is airline
fairs.  In recent weeks airline fairs have decreased from 40 to
50 percent.  AirHwy has been a leader in cutting fairs.  In those
markets where AirHwy flies, fairs have been between 30 to 50
percent lower.  Even competing airlines must admit that low fairs
have really revolutionized the concept of air travel.  No longer
is air travel reserved for the rich.  Fairs are so low that
almost everyone can afford to fly.  Who knows how low these fairs
will go?  Of course, there is always the danger of too much of a
good thing.  Airlines might find the fairs too low to meet
expenses.
Replace with: fares
```

(b)

these characters. The software does the tedious work of looking at each word to see if it matches the word or phrase requested in the search. For example, remember the last time you prepared a long report and realized after you were finished that you had spelled a word wrong throughout the entire report? If you had been using word processing software, the search and replace feature could have found every instance of the exact match of the characters and corrected them, such as replacing "fairs" with "fares" in Figure 4-5.

Search and replace generally has two options. You may examine each occurrence of the designated word or phrase and confirm each change, or you may specify **global replacement,** which changes all the occurrences of a particular word or phrase throughout the document without pausing for user confirmation.

Search and replace is one of WordPerfect's most useful features for editing text. You can search for any combination of up to 59 characters and search either backward or forward in the document, specifying upper-case, lower-case, and wildcard characters. Forward search ([F2]) directs the search from the location of the cursor to the end of the document. Backward search (Shift-[F2]) searches from the cursor back to the beginning of the document. To limit WordPerfect's search to a complete word, just enter a space before and after the search characters. Pressing Home-[F2] will extend the search into the special hidden formatting features such as headers, footers, footnotes, and endnotes. Lower-case letters in the search string match both lower-case and upper-case letters, while upper-case letters match only the upper-case letters in the document.

You can use the key combination of ^V ^X as a wildcard character when searching for words or phrases in the document. It can be substituted for any character or group of characters. For example, if you search for *comp ^X,* WordPerfect would locate *computer, compare, company,* and so forth.

The replace option (Alt-[F2]) permits users to search and replace characters from the location of the cursor to the end of the document, with or without confirming each replacement. The Replace function matches the upper and lower case of the original entry. Control characters and hidden function codes can also be replaced. Pressing Home Alt-[F2] will extend the search and replace into headers, footers, footnotes, and endnotes.

Figure 4-5 is an example using WordPerfect to search for the word

FIGURE 4-5 An example of global search and replace in WordPerfect. Notice in (*a*) the prompt in the lower left corner asking for the characters to be located ("fairs"). In (*b*) the user is prompted for the replacement characters ("fares").

"fairs" and replace it with "fares." Notice that the word "Fairs" is replaced but "FAIRS," in upper-case letters, is not.

Text Formatting

The **text formatting** function of word processing lets you alter the appearance of a document by adjusting the page layouts, including margins, spacing, justification, headers, footers, page numbers, pagination, and centering. There are two basic types of text formatting in word processing—onscreen formatting and print formatting.

Onscreen formatting is the change of the appearance of the text on the screen, by specific commands, to match the printed output. For example, if you change the margins from 65 characters per line to 40, onscreen formatting allows you to see on the screen the results of the change. If you give the command to center a line of text, onscreen formatting shows the centering on the screen.

If the text on the screen is shown essentially as it will appear on the printed page, then the word processing software is WYSIWYG, or "What You See Is What You Get." Most popular commercial word processing software have some degree of WYSIWYG. Some, like WordPerfect 4.2, show on the screen almost all formatting changes; however, not all of them display page headers, footers, or page numbers as they will be printed. Print enhancements such as italics or elaborate typefaces will not be shown on the screen, but will be printed. However, due to advances in software and graphics capabilities, some word processing software, including the new WordPerfect version 5.0, can show certain typefaces, as well as graphics, on both the screen and the printed page.

Onscreen formatting features vary from package to package. Several word processing software packages, including WordPerfect, offer onscreen formatting of columns. Two general types of text columns are available. In **newspaper-style columns,** the text is continuously written down the first column to the bottom of the page; then the text continues at the top of the second column. Both columns are left and right justified. **Parallel columns** are used for text that is printed across the columns, such as lists and command descriptions. Figure 4-6 illustrates these two types of columns in WordPerfect. You will have the opportunity to use some of these onscreen formatting capabilities in the tutorial.

Print formatting adjusts the text for the printer, but does not necessarily show the adjustment on the screen. An example of print formatting is right justification. **Justification** is the alignment or realignment of text in a document to specific margins. With left justification (the most common type of justification) the left margin is straight but the right margin is "ragged." Most books, newspapers and magazines, however, are printed in columns with both right and left margins justified. The text of this book is also right and left justified. Figure 4-7 shows the different forms of justification. Right justification is usually not visible on the screen but is printed correctly.

FIGURE 4-6 Example of (*a*) newspaper-style and (*b*) parallel columns. Such sophisticated on-screen formatting makes it easy to arrange the text on the screen as it will appear when printed.

```
Desktop publishing is the              Of course, AppliTechnology
newest concept in word                 Inc. is in the forefront of
processing.  Some even feel            this technology.  We have
that it revolutionized how we          recently purchased rights to
think about words.  Words will         one of the most popular
no longer be isolated from             desktop publishing software
graphics.  The user can freely         packages, Lazerrighter.
manipulate images just as              Lazerrighter permits users to
easily as text.  Of course, as         quickly and easily integrate
the hardware and software              text and graphics without
comes down in price, and               investing a lot of extra money
becomes easier to use, more            in additional hardware or
and more desktop publishing            software.  It accepts text
applications will become               files in the format of several
popular.                               popular word processing
                                       packages.
```

(a)

```
DESKTOP PUBLISHING                 ADVANTAGES
APPLICATIONS

Company newsletters                Can integrate text and
                                   graphics
                                   Professional appearance
                                   No more cutting and pasting

Sales Reports                      Effective use of photographs
                                   in reports
                                   Charts easily integrated
                                   Professional appearance
                                   Save time

Personnel Procedures               Graphics can illustrate
                                   important safety procedures
                                   Easier to read and understand

Forms                              Cheaper
                                   Can keep them up-to-date
```

(b)

Print formatting instructions can be embedded in the text file or in commands given when the document is printed. Figure 4-8 is an example of a print formatting command in WordPerfect to print a heading, including a date, and a page number on each page. The WordPerfect heading will not appear on the screen but will appear when the document is printed. You

FIGURE 4-7 Examples of right and left justification. The first paragraph is right and left justified; the second paragraph is only left justified.

```
Word processing is a very effective tool for people who write.
It frees them from tedious typing chores.  Word processing can be
used for anything you put down on paper, from personal letters to
manuscripts.  The hardest part about getting started in word
processing is learning the commands.  For most of us it takes
practice and patience.  It is obvious that word processing is
here to stay for a long time.

Word processing is a very effective tool for people who write.
It frees them from tedious typing chores.  Word processing can be
used for anything you put down on paper, from personal letters to
manuscripts.  The hardest part about getting started in word
processing is learning the commands.  For most of us it takes
practice and patience.  It is obvious that word processing is
here to stay for a long time.
```

can make the commands visible by using the Reveal Codes command (Alt-[F3]).

Some word processing software combine onscreen and print formatting by using commands within the document file to control special print features that enhance the appearance of the document when it is printed.

```
          REST AND LUNCH PERIODS


A.    Rest Periods:  Electronic Assembly Inc. provides for rest

      periods during the course of the day.
                                                  Doc 2  Pg 1  Ln 1      Pos 10
{ ▲    ▲    ▲    ▲    ▲    ▲    ▲    ▲    ▲    ▲ ]  ▲    ▲    ▲    ▲    ▲
[Hdr/Ftr:1,1;Personnel Procedures Draft February 19, 1989[HRt]
][Pos Pg#:7][Spacing Set:2][C][U]REST AND LUNCH PERIODS[u][c][HRt]
[HRt]
A.[->Indent][U]Rest Periods[u]:  Electronic Assembly Inc. provides for rest[SRt]

periods during the course of the day.[HRt]
```

FIGURE 4-8 An example of print formatting commands in WordPerfect version 4.2. The command codes appear in brackets on the bottom of the screen when the user gives the Reveal Codes command (Alt-[F3]). [Hdr/Ftr:1.1;Personnel Procedures Draft February 19, 1989[HRt]] defines the heading, while [Pos Pg:7] directs the software to print the page number in position 7, the bottom right of every page. [Spacing Set:2] sets the document at double line spacing. Special print features of centering and underlining are noted by the [C], [c], [U], and [u]. [HRt] indicates a hard return, while [SRt] indicates a soft return. Version 5.0 formatting commands are slightly different.

These include such special print effects as **double striking** (typing each character twice to darken the image); **boldfacing** (typing each character twice, with the print head slightly moved); **overstriking** (typing one character, such as a slash, over another); **subscripting** (typing one character below another); **underlining;** and **superscripting** (typing one character above another). See Figure 4-9 for examples of boldfacing, overprinting, subscripting, superscripting, and underlining.

Note: *Subscripting and superscripting are not available in L-WP.*

Some word processing software packages—for example, WordStar—offer specialized effects, such as extended and condensed print, especially for dot matrix printers. And laser printers, increasingly available to individual users, have combined sophisticated hardware and software to offer a wide variety of typefaces.

Some word processing software packages use special characters, placed within the text, to control formatting commands. These special characters include the hidden function codes used with WordPerfect as well as the dot commands used for print formatting with WordStar. *Dot commands* are entered into the text to control the format of the text when it is printed. They begin with a period or a dot in column 1 followed by a two-letter code.

Some of the most useful formatting commands control page headings, page numbering, and page breaks. A **page heading,** or **header,** is the title or other words you want printed at the top of every page. A **page footing,** or **footer,** is whatever you want printed at the bottom. Most word processing software have **page number omission** to shut off the automatic page numbering feature. Use the **page number setting** feature to start numbering pages at some number other than 1. **Page offset** allows the left margin of the document to be shifted on the printer. A **page break** command ends a page of printing and begins a new page. If a page break command is not entered, the word processing software automatically prints whatever number of lines you have specified for the length of a page. This often results in the illogical splitting of paragraphs or in section titles "floating" at the bottom of a page. Some word processing software, including WordPerfect, offer **conditional page breaks** in which a page

Print Enhancement	WordPerfect Command	Embedded Code	Appearance
Boldfacing	[F6]	[B]word[b]	**important**
Underlining	[F8]	[U]word[u]	distinguished
Overstriking	Shift-[F1],3	[Ovrstk]	A/
Superscript	Shift-[F1],1	[SuprScrpt]	10^9
Subscript	Shift-[F1],2	[SubScrpt]	14_2

FIGURE 4-9 WordPerfect offers several print enhancements, including boldfacing, underlining, overstriking, superscript, and subscript. These are examples of the codes as they appear in version 4.2.

```
the page break will be located.  A line will appear and a new
page will be started.
     If a conditional page break is inserted, you decide where
the page break should be inserted.  For example, if you decide
------------------------------------------------------------------------------
that you want a table to be printed on one page, then insert a
conditional page break command and include how many lines are to
remain together.
     If you want to determine where a new page will start, insert
the hard page command.
==============================================================================
A page break will be indicated on the screen by a line and a new
page will appear
                                       Doc 2  Pg 2  Ln 49    Pos 31
```

(a)

```
the page break will be located.  A line will appear and a new
page will be started.
------------------------------------------------------------------------------
     If a conditional page break is inserted, you decide where
the page break should be inserted.  For example, if you decide
that you want a table to be printed on one page, then insert a
conditional page break command and include how many lines are to
remain together.
     If you want to determine where a new page will start, insert
the hard page command.
==============================================================================
A page break will be indicated on the screen by a line and a new
page will appear
                                       Doc 2  Pg 4  Ln 3     Pos 27
```

(b)

break will be inserted if a specified number of lines of text do not fit on a page. For instance, in WordPerfect, if you place the command for Conditional End of Page to keep five lines together (Alt-[F8]) but they do not all fit on the current page, the page break will occur at the command. **Unconditional** or **hard page breaks** cause the printer to start printing on a new page. Figure 4-10 illustrates conditional and unconditional page breaks.

WordPerfect offers a wide variety of formatting options via the Format command (Alt-[F8] or Shift-[F8]). (See Figure 3-16). For formatting long documents, one of the more useful options is the Widow/Orphan Protection feature. Remember, a **widow** is a first line of a paragraph appearing alone at the bottom of a page, with the rest of the paragraph appearing at the top of the following page. An **orphan** is the last line of a paragraph appearing alone on the first line of a page, with all of its preceding text at the bottom of the previous page. When the Widow/Orphan protection is turned on, the software prevents widows and orphans from occurring (see Figure 4-11).

Another useful formatting feature is the ability to change margins, line spacing, and tabs. A **margin** is the amount of space left between the edges of the paper and the text printed on the paper. For example, an instructor may tell you to leave a $1\frac{1}{2}$-inch margin on the left side and a 1-inch margin on the right. You put the margins at the appropriate settings so that the text will be printed at the proper distance from the edges of the paper. Please note that WordPerfect 4.2 starts printing text in column 10 on both the screen and the paper. WordPerfect 5.0 uses inches, so the margin is 1 inch.

A **tab** is a point where the cursor will stop when the Tab key is pressed. Tabs are used for indenting text and lining up columns, and most word processing software permit the user to set or remove tab stops as needed. To use the tab, press the Tab key. For example, to indent 10 spaces or 1 inch, press the Tab key twice. The cursor will automatically indent 10 spaces and start entering text in the next space. Please note that these 10 spaces or 1 inch are interpreted as "hard" spaces, just as if a letter or a number had been entered, and they must be removed through deletion.

FIGURE 4-10 An example of a conditional page break and a hard page break using WordPerfect. The single dashed line is the soft page break inserted by the software at the end of the page, while the double dashed line is the unconditional or hard page break inserted by the user. (*a*) illustrates where the page break would be inserted without the conditional page break command. Notice that the paragraph is broken up by the page break. When a conditional page break command is inserted, as in (*b*), the page break is inserted if a specific number of lines of text, in this case 10 lines, do not fit on a page. The software then inserts the page break on the line directly below the conditional page break command.

FIGURE 4-11 An illustration of a widow and an orphan using WordPerfect.

```
  A widow is the first line of a paragraph that appears alone at
---------------------------------------------------------------
the bottom of a page, with the rest of the paragraph appearing at
the top of the following page.


An orphan is the last line of a paragraph that appears alone on
the first line of a page, with all of its preceding text at the
bottom of the previous page.  When the Widow/Orphan protection is
turned on, the software prevents either widow or orphans from
---------------------------------------------------------------
occurring.
```

"Soft" spaces are spaces inserted by the word processing software for page appearance. Since they are soft, they do not need to be removed through deletion.

Line spacing is the distance between lines of text. For example, if the line spacing is set for double spacing there is one extra line of space between each line of text. Single spacing has no extra space between lines of text. Most term papers are double spaced; letters and memos are usually single spaced.

In WordPerfect you use the Format key (Shift-[F8]) to change tabs, margins, and spacing.

Each type of formatting has advantages and disadvantages. Onscreen formatting is especially useful for situations in which you must see the finished product before it is printed, for example, to satisfy yourself that items are properly placed on the cover sheet of a report that must have a specific appearance. Print formatting is convenient when one document may have to be printed in several different formats. For example, if you are going to submit drafts of a report to several agencies and each requires a different print format, the print format feature allows the document to be stored in one manner but easily reformatted and printed in several different formats. Microsoft Word, WordStar 2000, and WordPerfect 5.0 offer **style sheets** in which the set of formatting commands for each style is stored separately and can be called up and applied to specific documents. In general, new versions of word processing software offer increasingly more onscreen formatting features, so the user can get a better idea how the text is going to look—before it is printed.

TUTORIAL: CREATING A RESUMÉ

To complete this tutorial you need the following:

- A WordPerfect disk
- A disk containing the files from Lesson 3
- A standard printer connected to the microcomputer

While completing this tutorial you will learn how to use

- boldfacing
- block movement
- format commands of margins, page breaks, tabs, indent, and centering
- print options
- file retrieval

In this tutorial you will create a resumé for a fictitious person called Pat Allen, the same fictitious person who wrote the cover letter in Lesson 3. Remember to follow instructions for the version of WordPerfect you are using.

Create the Document

As explained in Lesson 3, there are three basic steps for creating a new document: (1) load the operating system into primary storage, (2) load the word processing software into primary storage, and (3) insert the new text into the document. Below we will briefly review the steps. If necessary, refer to Lesson 3 for more detailed information.

Step 1: Load the operating system into primary storage.
Load the operating system and, if necessary, set the time and date. When you have the system prompt (A>) on the screen, load WordPerfect.

Step 2: Load WordPerfect into primary storage.
If necessary remove the system disk. Then insert the WordPerfect disk in drive A and the files disk (the disk on which you stored your files from Lesson 3) in drive B. Latch the disk drive doors. Type

```
WP
```

Step 3: Insert the new text into the document.

a. Enter the heading. The heading is centered and boldfaced to improve its appearance and to get the reader's attention.

1. Enter the command to center the text. Press **Shift-[F6].** Notice that the cursor moves to the center of the line.
2. Enter the command to boldface the heading. Press **[F6].** Notice that the position indicator on the status line changes appearance. The code will not appear on the screen, but you can make it visible by pressing the Reveal Codes command, Alt-[F3].
3. Enter the document title. Press **Caps Lock** and type

   ```
   RESUME
   ```

   Notice that the text is centered as it is entered. Remember that, if you use the Shift key while the Caps Lock key is on, characters will be printed as lower case.
4. End the boldfacing by repeating the boldface code **([F6])** or press the **right arrow key.** It is very important to remember to end the boldfacing.

   Press **Return** *twice.*

   Repeat the same steps to center and boldface the name.
5. Center the name. Press **Shift-[F6].**
6. Boldface the name. Press **[F6].**
7. Type

   ```
   PAT ALLEN
   ```

8. Turn off the boldfacing. Press **[F6]** or press the **right arrow key.**
9. Press **Return.**

If the centered line does not turn out the way you want, and you would like to delete the entire line and start over, move the cursor to the beginning of the line (Home Left Arrow) and use the Delete to End of Line command (^ End). Be careful to position the cursor on the exact line you want to delete. WordPerfect has a nice feature you can use in case you delete the wrong line. Press the Cancel command ([F1]) and the deleted line will reappear at the current cursor position. WordPerfect temporarily saves the previous three deletions and lets you retrieve either of them.

The boldfaced title and name should appear on the screen in a different shading or color. This is an example of onscreen formatting. Notice that you can see instantly whether the text has been properly boldfaced.

b. Enter the address headings. The headings HOME ADDRESS and SCHOOL ADDRESS are created by using the boldface command, the Caps Lock key, and the Tab key.

1. First, insert two blank lines so the section headings begin two lines below the main headings. Press **Return** *twice.*
2. With the **Caps Lock** *on,* type

   ```
   [F6]HOME ADDRESS[F6]
   ```

3. Press **Tab** *five times.* Your cursor should be in column 45 or 4.5 inches. Type

   ```
   [F6]SCHOOL ADDRESS[F6]
   ```

   Press **Return.**
   Press the **Caps Lock key.**

   In WordPerfect the tab stops are automatically fixed at 5-space or $\frac{1}{2}$ inch intervals. However, you can change the tab settings using the Line Format or Format command. In version 4.2 the Line Format command modifies the format that determines line length and spacing, including tabs, margins, hyphenation, and alignment character. In version 5.0, the Format command controls all of the formatting commands. An alignment character is used for aligning text and/or numbers when the Tab Align is used with WordPerfect. For example, if you have a column of numbers to enter and you want them aligned on the decimal point, the alignment character would be a period (.). Let's set the tabs to make entry of the addresses quicker and easier.

4. Press the Line Format or Format command, **Shift-[F8].** To choose the Tabs option, press

   ```
   1
   ```

   Version 5.0 users only should also press **8.**

5. The ruler line appears. The "L" indicates where the tab stops have been set (see Figure 4-12). Delete all of the preset tabs by pressing the Delete to End of Line command, ^ **End.**
6. Set the new tab stops. Version 4.2 users type

   ```
   15
   ```

   Version 5.0 users type **1.5.**
   Press **Return.**
   Version 4.2 users type

   ```
   50
   ```

   Version 5.0 users type **5.**
   Press **Return.**

FIGURE 4-12 A ruler line with WordPerfect. A "L" appears where the tab stops have been set.

```
                    RESUME

                   PAT ALLEN















L....L....L....L....L....L....L....L....L....L....L....L....L....L....L....L...
567890123456789012345678901234567890123456789012345678901234567890123456789012 3
    10        20        30        40        50        60        70        80
Delete EOL (clear tabs); Enter number (set tab); Del (clear tab);
Left; Center; Right; Decimal; .= Dot leader; Press EXIT when done.
```

Exit from the tab ruler line by pressing the Exit command, **[F7]** until the editing screen appears.

You can set the tabs at as many points as you want in a document. Remember, however, that only the text after the tab setting is changed.

7. In typing home and school addresses, move to the tab stops you have just set. Press **Tab** before entering each line of the addresses.

   Press **Tab** and type

```
880 West Elm Street
```

   Press **Tab** and type

```
123 East St. Apt. 31
```

   Press **Return.**
   Press **Tab** and type

```
Naperville, Illinois 60234
```

   Press **Tab** and type

```
Iowa City, Iowa 55204
```

Press **Return.**
Press **Tab** and type

```
(312) 555-1234
```

Press **Tab** and type

```
(402) 987-9876
```

Press **Return** *twice.*

8. Reset the tab stops to the default setting. Press **Shift-[F8] 1.** Version 5.0 users press **8.** When the tab ruler line appears, version 4.2 users type

```
0,5
```

Version 5.0 users type **1, .5**

To delete a tab, move the cursor to the tab stop you wish to delete, and press the Backspace. Or enter the column number or inch and press the Del key.

Press **[F7]** until you return to the resumé.

c. Enter the sections. On a resumé, section headings are used to highlight the areas of interest. Each heading will be typed in upper case and boldfaced.

1. Press the **Caps Lock key.** Type

```
[F6]EMPLOYMENT OBJECTIVE:[F6]
```

Press **Return.**

2. Press the **Caps Lock** key. Press the →Indent key, **[F4].** When you give the Left Indent command at the beginning of a paragraph, the text in the paragraph will be indented as it is typed until you press Return to signal the start of a new paragraph. **Do not use the Return key to move to the next line. Let word wrap do the work.** Type

```
Seeking full-time summer position working
with microcomputer hardware and software.
```

Press **Return** *twice.*

3. Press the **Caps Lock key.** Type

   `[F6]EDUCATION:[F6]`

   Press **Return.**

4. Another formatting feature of WordPerfect is the Hanging Indent command. The first line in a paragraph begins at the left margin, while the remaining lines are indented to the first tab stop. Let's use this feature on the resumé to help distinguish the different educational accomplishments.

   Press the **Caps Lock key.**

   Press **[F4] Shift-Tab** (the Hanging Indent command) to move the first line of the paragraph one tab stop to the left. Type

   ```
   Currently pursuing B.S. in Business
   Administration, University of Iowa.
   Expected graduation date, May 20, 1989.
   Majoring in Management Information
   Systems. Overall GPA 3.4 on 4.0 scale and
   3.5 in major.
   ```

   Press **Return** *twice.*

5. Repeat the **Hanging Indent command** and type

   ```
   High school diploma from Naperville High
   School, 1985, with 3.88 GPA (top 10
   percent of class). Member National Honor
   Society, and Computer Club. Participated
   in band and yearbook.
   ```

   Press **Return** *twice.*

6. Press the **Caps Lock key.** Type

   `[F6]HONORS AND AWARDS:[F6]`

7. Press the **Caps Lock key.** Press **Return.** Press the **Hanging Indent command** and type

   `The University of Iowa Dean's List, 1988.`

   Press **Return** *twice.*

   Press the **Hanging Indent command** and type

   ```
   Elected president of Lincoln South
   Residence Hall Association, 1987 and 1988.
   ```

   Press **Return** *twice.*

8. Press the **Caps Lock key.** Type

```
[FG]EMPLOYMENT RECORD:[FG]
```

9. Press the **Caps Lock key.** Press **Return.** Press the **Hanging Indent command** and type

```
Current: Computer Lab Assistant, Business
Microcomputer Laboratory, University of
Iowa. Assist students in lab in using
IBM-compatible microcomputers and software
including Lotus 1-2-3, dBase III Plus, and
WordPerfect.
```

Press **Return** *twice.*

10. Repeat the **Hanging Indent command** and type

```
Summer 1988: Sales Representative,
TechMARK Incorporated. Sold various models
of microcomputers and helped customers set
up hardware and software for home and
small business use. Gained experience
dealing with people in addition to
handling a variety of technical problems.
```

Press **Return** *twice.*

11. Repeat the **Hanging Indent command** and type

```
Summer 1987: Sales Clerk, Kay's Department
Store. Sold electronics including
televisions, VCRs and stereos. Gained
experience meeting people and handling
money.
```

Press **Return** *twice.*

12. Press the **Caps Lock key.** Type

```
[FG]REFERENCES FURNISHED UPON REQUEST[FG]
```

Press **Return.**

Compare the document on the screen with Pat Allen's resumé in Figure 4-13 to make sure you have entered the text correctly.

FIGURE 4-13 Pat Allen's resumé after it has been entered.

```
                              RESUME

                            PAT ALLEN

HOME ADDRESS                          SCHOOL ADDRESS
     880 West Elm Street                   123 East St. Apt. 31
     Naperville, Illinois 60234            Iowa City, Iowa 55204
     (312) 555-1234                        (402) 987-9876

EMPLOYMENT OBJECTIVE:
     Seeking full-time summer position working with microcomputer
     hardware and software.

EDUCATION:
Currently pursuing B.S. in Business Administration, University of
     Iowa.  Expected graduation date, May 20, 1989.  Majoring in
     Management Information Systems.  Overall GPA 3.4 on 4.0
     scale and 3.5 in major.

High school diploma from Naperville High School, 1985, with 3.88
     GPA (top 10 percent of class).  Member National Honor
     Society, and Computer Club.  Participated in band and
     yearbook.

HONORS AND AWARDS:
The University of Iowa Dean's List, 1988.

Elected president of Lincoln South Residence Hall Association,
     1987 and 1988.

EMPLOYMENT RECORD:
Current:  Computer Lab Assistant, Business Micropcomputer
     Laboratory, University of Iowa.  Assist students in lab in
     using IBM-compatible microcomputers and software including
     Lotus 1-2-3, dBase III Plus, and WordPerfect.

Summer 1988:  Sales Representative, TechMARK Incorporated.  Sold
     various models of microcomputers and helped customers set up
     hardware and software for home and small business use.
     Gained experience dealing with people in addition to
     handling a variety of technical problems.

Summer 1987:  Sales Clerk, Kay's Department Store.  Sold
     electronics including televisions, VCRs and stereos.  Gained
     experience meeting people and handling money.

REFERENCES FURNISHED UPON REQUEST
```

Step 4: Save the document and return to editing.

Before you start to change the document, save the document and return to editing. Since the document needs to be named, use the Save command instead of the Save macro.

Press **[F10].** At the prompt, enter the name of the file. Type

B:RESUME.DOC↵

The file is to be stored on disk drive B. "RESUME" is a name that starts with a letter, contains no blanks or punctuation, has eight or fewer characters, and reminds you of the contents of the file. ".DOC" is an extension added to remind you that this is a document file rather than a worksheet or database file.

Press **Return.**

Now, when you need to save the file while editing, you can press the Save macro you constructed in the tutorial in Lesson 3. When necessary, press Alt-S to save the file.

Step 5: Print the document.

In the tutorial in Lesson 3 you used the List Files command to print a document; this time you are going to use a new command to print. Be certain, before entering the Print command, that the microcomputer is properly connected to a printer and the printer is turned on and ready.

The Print command (Shift-[F7]) offers several options for printing documents.

> *Full Text* (or *Document* in version 5.0) *and Page* lets you print the entire document or a page that is currently in RAM, even if you have not saved it. This is a quick and easy way to check your work.
>
> *Print Control* (*Control Printer* in version 5.0) gives you complete control over the printing, including choice of printer, number of copies, selective page printing, pausing print jobs, canceling print jobs, and stacking several print jobs.
>
> *Type-thru* (*Type Through* in version 5.0) lets you use WordPerfect like a typewriter, a handy feature when you want to type an envelope or a form.

Version 5.0 offers additional options including *View,* which lets you see the formatted document before it is printed.

After the printer is connected, turned on, and online, press **Shift-[F7]** and type

1

to select the quick draft printing option. After a few seconds, a draft of the resumé will be printed. Use this printed copy to check your work. Notice the placement of the text on the page, including margins and centering. In Step 6 we will adjust the format of the document to change the appearance of the text on the page.

Step 6: Format the document.

a. Change the margins. As explained previously, the *margins* are the amount of blank space left on the sides of the document. The default margin is column 10 or 1 inch on the left and column 74 or 1 inch on the right. Since 10 spaces equal 1 inch, the current margin setting would provide a 1-inch margin on the left and right sides.

The Line Format or Format key, Shift-[F8], lets you set new left and right margins. Let's experiment with the appearance of the resumé by adjusting the margins.

1. Move the cursor to the top of the document. Remember to always move the cursor to the first position of the document before entering formatting codes that affect the entire document. You cannot see these formatting codes, but where you place them can have a big effect on the document. Use the Reveal Codes command if necessary to find any hidden codes.

   Press **Home Home Home Up Arrow.**

   Use the **Reveal codes command (Alt-[F3])** to check cursor placement. Press **Alt-[F3]** again.

2. Select the Margins command. If you are using version 4.2 press **Shift-[F8] 3.** The current margins are displayed and you are prompted for a new left margin. Since we are going to change the margin to $\frac{1}{2}$ inch, type

   5

   Version 5.0 users press **Shift-[F8] 1 7 .5.**

   Press **Return.**

   Press **Return** again to leave the right margin unchanged. *If necessary,* press **[F7]** to return to the editing.

   The text is adjusted to the new left margin. When you want to check the current settings of margins in the document, use the Tab Ruler command of ^[F3] 1 Up Arrow Return. To remove the Tab Ruler, press ^[F3] 1 Down Arrow Return.

3. Print the resumé by pressing **Shift-[F7] 1.** Notice that the text is now shifted over five spaces.

b. Add a print format command. Since your resumé is a single page, you will not want a page number printed on the bottom of the page. Although your copy of WordPerfect may be installed to suppress the page number, let's be absolutely sure no page number will be printed. A print format command is added to the document to turn off the automatic page numbering, as follows.

If necessary, move the cursor to the start of the document. Press **Home Home Home Up Arrow.**

Insert the command for turning the page numbering off. If you are using version 4.2 press **Alt-[F8] 1 0 0.** Version 5.0 users press **Shift-[F8] 2 9 1.** Press **[F7].**

If, in the future, you want to turn the page numbering back on, use the Page Format or Format command to select the new page number by pressing Alt-[F8] 2 (Shift-[F8] 2 7 for version 5.0 users) and the page number desired. Before finishing the formatting of the document center the text on the document.

If you are using version 4.2 press **Alt-[F8] 3.** Version 5.0 users press **Shift-[F8] 2 1.** The text will be centered from the top to bottom of the document.

If necessary, press **Return** until the document reappears.

c. Use the Reveal Codes command to return the margins to their original settings.

With the Reveal Codes command you can edit the hidden format commands.

Press **Alt-[F3]**. The format codes appear at the bottom of the screen below the ruler line and the text appears above the ruler line (see Figure 4-14).

With the arrow keys, move the cursor to the space directly after the margin set code ([Margin Set:5,74] or [L/R:0.5″, 1″]).

Press the **Backspace key.** The margin set command will be deleted and the margin will revert to its original, default settings.

Press **Alt-[F3]** to return to the letter.

d. Save the document. Using the Save macro, press **Alt-S.**

Edit the Document

Now that you've created and saved the document, you can use some of the sophisticated editing commands available with WordPerfect.

Step 1: Proofread the document.

a. Print the document. Press **Shift-[F7] 1.**

```
                         RESUME

                        PAT ALLEN

   HOME ADDRESS                      SCHOOL ADDRESS
             880 West Elm Street               123 East St. Apt. 31

C:\MAIN\WP\FIG4-14.ART                 Doc 2  Pg 1  Ln 1      Pos 5
{                                                         ]
[Margin Set:5,74] [Pos Pg#:0][Center Pg] [HRt]
[C][B]RESUME[b][c][HRt]
[HRt]
[C][B]PAT ALLEN[b][c][HRt]
```

FIGURE 4-14 An illustration of the screen after the Reveal Codes command (Alt-[F3]). Notice the formatting codes at the bottom of the screen. Version 5.0 formatting codes will be slightly different.

b. Check the document. Now is the time to *carefully* proofread the document. Do not be concerned if it takes a few tries to get the resumé perfect. A resumé is not something you do every day, and accuracy is more important than speed. Careful proofreading is so important that you may want to use some of the professional proofreading techniques, such as reading backwards, holding a piece of paper under the line you are reading, or having someone else read the text to you aloud.

Step 2: Correct all errors.

Use the cursor movement and delete keys to correct any errors.

Step 3: Mark and move a block of text.

Move the "EMPLOYMENT RECORD" section to before the "EDUCATION" section to give emphasis to the employment history. To rearrange the document, you will need to define the section called "EMPLOYMENT RECORD" as a block and then move the block to where you want it.

Mark the block. In order for the word processing software to know which text is to be included in the block, you must show it where the block begins and ends. This is called **marking a block.** For a block command to be carried out, the block must be highlighted (see Figure 4-15).

```
Elected president of Lincoln South Residence Hall Association,
     1987 and 1988.

EMPLOYMENT RECORD:
Current:  Computer Lab Assistant, Business Microcomputer
     Laboratory, University of Iowa.  Assist students in lab in
     using IBM-compatible microcomputers and software including
     Lotus 1-2-3, dBase III Plus, and WordPerfect.

Summer 1988:  Sales Representative, TechMARK Incorporated.  Sold
     various models of microcomputers and helped customers set up
     hardware and software for home and small business use.
     Gained experience dealing with people in addition to
     handling a variety of technical problems.

Summer 1987:  Sales Clerk, Kay's Department Store.  Sold
     electronics including televisions, VCRs and stereos.  Gained
     experience meeting people and handling money.

REFERENCES FURNISHED UPON REQUESTED

Block on                                   Doc 2  Pg 1  Ln 29    Pos 10
```

FIGURE 4-15 The highlighted block that indicates which segment of the text is to be affected by the block operation. The illustration shows the section of the resumé titled "EMPLOYMENT RECORD" marked using WordPerfect.

To mark a block, move the cursor to where you want the block to begin. Place the cursor on the first character in the line containing the title "EMPLOYMENT RECORD."

Use the Reveals Code command, **Alt-[F3],** to make sure the cursor is positioned before the boldface code ([B]or [BOLD]) that comes before the title 'EMPLOYMENT RECORD."

Press **Alt-[F4]** to turn the block on. Press **Alt-[F3]** to return to the letter.

Mark the end of the block by using the arrow keys to move the cursor to the last character of the block, one space beyond the period at the end of the word "money" (see Figure 4-15).

WordPerfect versions differ on the steps necessary to move a marked block. Version 4.2 requires users to *cut* the block so the block no longer appears on the screen. The user then moves the cursor to the desired location and retrieves the block. Version 5.0 users have a simplified procedure in which the user gives the move block command, the text is automatically removed from the screen, the cursor is moved to the desired location, and the user presses Return to retrieve the block.

For version 4.2, move the block by following these instructions:

Press the Move command to cut a block, **^[F4].** Notice the options at the bottom of the screen. We are going to use the Cut Block option to remove the marked block and place it in temporary storage. Press **1**. The most currently cut block will then be retrieved using the Move Retrieve Text command.

Move the block. Using the **arrow keys,** move the cursor to the blank line directly above the title "EDUCATION" in column 1. Press **Return** to insert a blank line. With the **arrow key,** move the cursor back up one line. Press the command **^[F4] 5** to retrieve the block. Press **Return** to move the paragraph down one line.

If you are using version 5.0, use the following instructions to move the block.

Press the Move command, **^[F4] 1,** to move a block. Options appear across the bottom of the screen. Press **1** to choose Move. The block immediately disappears from the screen and is placed in a temporary buffer.

With the **arrow keys,** move the cursor to the blank line directly above the title "EDUCATION" in the first column. Retrieve the block by pressing **Return.**

Check the document to make sure all the spacing is correct. Add lines where necessary. Use the arrow keys to move the cursor to the line directly above the line "REFERENCES FURNISHED UPON REQUEST." Check carefully the number of blank lines between the title and the section above. There should be one blank line. If there are too many lines, delete the blank lines by placing the cursor on the blank line directly above the title in column 1 and pressing the Delete key, marked **Del.**

The extra line will disappear, and the title will move up one line. Delete as many lines as necessary to leave only one blank line between the title and the preceding sections.

Step 4: Save the document.

Now that you have completed moving the block, enter the macro to save the file, **Alt-S.**

Step 5: Merge two documents.

Merge the resumé with the cover letter you completed in the tutorial for Lesson 3 so they can be printed together. To do this, you will move the cursor to the end of the document, retrieve the letter file, and then store the revised resumé, using a new filename to preserve the original resumé.

a. Move the cursor to the bottom of the document. Press **Home Home Down Arrow.**

Press **Return** to insert a blank line. Your cursor should be in the first column of a blank line at the bottom of the document.

Insert a hard page break. Press **^Return.** A double dashed line will appear on the page, indicating the beginning of a new page.

b. Retrieve the letter onto the new page. Use the Retrieve command, **Shift-[F10],** and insert the needed filename, SS5489.LET. Or use the List Files command Retrieve option: Press **[F5] Return,** place the cursor on the needed file, and press **1.** If you are using version 5.0, press **Y** at the prompt.

c. Using the WordPerfect date function, change the date in the letter to today's date.

Delete the old date in the letter.

Move the cursor to the column at which you want the first character of the date inserted.

Press **Shift-[F5].**

Several options appear on the status line. Choose the option to insert the date code. In version 4.2, press **3.** In version 5.0, press **2.** This inserts the date with the WordPerfect function code. When you first insert the code, the current date and/or time is displayed. Then, whenever you retrieve or print the document, the current date appears.

d. Save the file using a new name. Press **[F10].** At the prompt

```
Document to be saved:B:\RESUME.DOC
```

type

```
B:RESLET.DOC
```

to indicate that you have combined the resumé and the letter. Notice that WordPerfect automatically clears the old name from the prompt and inserts your new name. You can also revise filenames by moving the cursor and inserting or deleting characters.

Print the Document

As discussed earlier, versions 4.2 and 5.0 have some different print functions and commands. However, they share many of the same functions.

a. If you are using version 4.2, use the following steps to print a document. To print a document using the Print Control screen, press **Shift-[F7]** and type

4

The Printer Control screen will appear (see Figure 4-16).

The Printer Control screen gives you greater control than any other method of printing a document. By using this screen you can print a portion of a document; stop (S) and resume (G) printing; stack several print jobs in a queue; cancel specific or all print jobs in the queue (C); rush a print job to the top of the queue (R); display all files placed in the print queue; change the printer to be used, the number of copies, or the binding width for all jobs in the queue by using the Select Print Options menu (1); display the installed printers and the eight fonts supported by WordPerfect; and install new printers.

Not all of these features are available in L-WP. Specifically, L-WP will not allow the user to change either the printer to be used or the binding width, display the printers and fonts supported, or install new printers.

Print RESLET.DOC by pressing the Print a Document option. Type

P

b. Version 5.0 users have several options for controlling the printer. Press **Shift-[F7].** The Print menu appears. As explained earlier, the *Full Document* option will print the document currently in RAM, while the *Page* option will print the current page. *Document on Disk* lets you print a file or selected pages of a file on disk. After entering the name of the file, you can indicate which pages are to be printed and then press Return to print the entire document. *Control Printer* provides several options for managing printing jobs, including cancelling the printing of one or more document (Cancel Job), changing the priority of printing jobs so one job can be moved to the front of the queue (Rush Job), showing a list of the documents to be be printed (Display Jobs), restarting the printer after a printing job has been interrupted (Go), and interrupting the printing of a document (Stop). *Type Through* allows the computer to be used like a typewriter. Each character typed is immediately sent to the printer (Character Type Through) or is

FIGURE 4-16 (*a*) The Printer Control screen for version 4.2 of WordPerfect. (*b*) The Print screen for WordPerfect version 5.0. Notice the Control Printer option (4), which permits users to cancel, rush, and display print jobs as well as start and interrupt printing.

```
Printer Control
                                          C - Cancel Print Job(s)
1 - Select Print Options                  D - Display All Print Jobs
2 - Display Printers and Fonts            G - "Go" (Resume Printing)
3 - Select Printers                       P - Print a Document
                                          R - Rush Print Job
Selection: 0                              S - Stop Printing


Current Job

Job Number: n/a                           Page number:  n/a
Job Status: n/a                           Current Copy: n/a
Message:    The print queue is empty

Job List

Job  Document          Destination          Forms and Print Options
```

(a)

```
Additional jobs not shown: 0

      Print

          1 - Full Document
          2 - Page
          3 - Document on Disk
          4 - Control Printer
          5 - Type Through
          6 - View Document
          7 - Initialize Printer

      Options

          S - Select Printer          HP LaserJet Series II
          B - Binding                 0"
          N - Number of Copies        1
          G - Graphics Quality        Medium
          T - Text Quality            High



      Selection: 0
```

edited and sent a line at a time (Line Type Through). *View Document* lets users view the format of a document before it is printed. When diplayed all format settings and text will be made to look as much like the printed page as possible, including, when possible, boldfacing, italics, and other chosen fonts and enhancements. *Initialize Printer* loads the marked soft fonts (programmed instructions for the creation of characters on a laser printer) into the chosen printer. *Select Printer* allows the user to define the printer and select a printer for document. *Binding* permits users to shift the text to the right for odd-numbered pages and to the left on even-numbered pages, for binding on two-sided copies. *Number of Copies* permits the user to enter the number of copies to be printed. *Graphics/Text Quality* determines the resolution of print for graphics and text in a document. Type **3**

A prompt appears:

```
Document name:
```

Type the name of the document you are going to print:

```
B:RESLET.DOC
```

Press **Return.**

Notice that we enter the complete filename, including the disk drive. Make sure to spell the filename exactly as it is stored or you will receive an error message.

After the name has been entered, the prompt changes to

```
Page(s): All
```

If you want to print an entire document, press Return. If you want to print specific pages, you can enter a page range by typing the numbers of the first and last pages to be printed separated by a hyphen. For example, if you want to print pages 67 through 85 of a document, type 67-85. If you want to print from page 67 to the end of a document, type 67-. If you want to print from the beginning of a document to page 67, type -67. To print individual pages—such as 12, 19, 33, and 56 through 58—type 12,19,33,56-58.

Since in this case you want to print the entire document, press **Return.**

Quit WordPerfect

Like most software, WordPerfect expects users to properly exit the software.

Press the Exit command **[F7].** A prompt appears on the screen:

```
Save Document? (Y/N)Y
```

If you need to save the document, answer

```
Y
```

and press Return at the filename prompt. Also press

```
Y
```

at the prompt to replace the file. If you press N, any changes made to the document since the previous save will be lost. The original document will remain on the disk.

At the prompt to exit WordPerfect, type

```
Y
```

After the system prompt reappears, remove the disks and turn off the microcomputer.

In addition to using word processing software to type your resumé, you can customize parts of your resumé to fit the type of job you are applying for. You may want to slightly change the section on employment objectives to more nearly meet the type of job, or you may want to emphasize or de-emphasize particular courses or experiences, depending on the position you are considering. In this way you can send out many resumés, each one custom-made. Also, each can be an original rather than a photocopy.

An interesting method for customizing documents is to use **boiler-plate** paragraphs. For example, a section of your resumé may be particularly appropriate if you are applying for a sales position. Rather than retyping it every time you prepare a custom-made resumé, save the section in a file. You can then recall or read the file into a new file whenever you need it.

SUMMARY

This lesson described the fundamental word processing steps necessary to edit, format, save, and print documents. Editing involves correcting errors, inserting new material, and rearranging blocks of text. Formatting is the alignment or positioning of the text. There are two types of formatting: onscreen formatting (changing the appearance of the document on the screen) and print formatting (using commands that are embedded in the text to control printer operations). Saving a document copies the document and stores it on a secondary storage device, such as a floppy disk. After an edited document has been saved, it can be printed.

EXERCISES

1. Define the following terms:

editing	parallel columns	page offset
formatting	print formatting	page break
dot command	justification	conditional page breaks
saving	double striking	unconditional (hard) page breaks
printing	boldfacing	widow
hard copy	overstriking	orphan
menu	subscripting	margin
on-demand menu	superscripting	tab
block	underlining	line spacing
block markers	page heading (header)	style sheets
cursor movement	page footing (footer)	marking a block
search and replace	page number omission	boiler-plate
global replacement	page number setting	
onscreen formatting		
newspaper-style columns		

2. Specify the WordPerfect command needed for each option listed below.
   Center text on a line
   Boldface text
   Change the left margin
   Reset tabs to the default option
   Underline text
   Hanging Indent
   Print a document that is currently in RAM
   Reveal codes
   Mark a block

3. Match the term on the left with the description on right.

_____	justification	a.	locates specific characters in a document
_____	conditional page break	b.	the amount of space left between the edges of the paper and the text printed on the paper.
_____	block	c.	A type of column in which text is continuously written down the first column to the bottom of the page and continues at the top of the second column
_____	widow	d.	the alignment or realignment of text in a document to specific margins

____	menu	e.	a first line of a paragraph appearing alone at the bottom of a page, with the rest of the paragraph appearing at the top of the following page
____	newspaper	f.	a type of command in which text is moved to the next page if a specific number of lines of text do not fit on a page
____	global replacement	g.	a segment of text defined by defined markers
____	search option	h.	a list of available functions and the commands necessary to use them
____	margin	i.	the changing of all the occurrences of a particular word or phrase throughout the document without user confirmation

4. Match the item on the left with the action on the right.

____	[F7]	a.	moves to the beginning of a document
____	Shift-[F8]	b.	boldfaces characters
____	[F10]	c.	changes the format of a document
____	Shift-[F7]	d.	inserts a hanging indent
____	Home Home Down Arrow	e.	saves a document
____	[F6]	f.	prints a document using the Printer Control or Print menu
____	[F4] Shift-Tab	g.	permits users to do a variety of file operations from one screen
____	Shift-[F10]	h.	moves to the bottom of a document
____	[F5]	i.	helps
____	[F3]	j.	turns the block marker on
____	Home Home Up Arrow	k.	retrieves a file
____	Alt-[F4]	l.	quits a document

5. Fill in the blanks.
   a. A type of help that offers onscreen information after the proper command has been given is called ____________.
   b. A type of command that allow you to move, copy, save, and print a segment of text is called ____________.

c. If you want to locate a group of characters in a document without having to read the text you can use the ____________ command.

d. A type of format in which text is continuously written down the first column until it reaches the bottom of the page and then continues at the top of the second column is called ____________

e. The alignment or realignment of text to specific margins is called ____________.

f. The command that permits the retrieval of deleted text is called the ____________.

6. A resumé should be neatly organized and totally free of errors. A word processing software package can be of great help in meeting those objectives. In this exercise, use the tutorial as a model to prepare your own resumé.

   a. Using the guidelines below, revise the resumé in the tutorial to be your own resumé. Replace the name, addresses, job objectives, educational history, and employment history with information about yourself.

   b. After you have completed the resumé, retrieve the cover letter you prepared in Lesson 3 and the resumé.

Make sure the cover letter and the resumé each start on a new printed page.

The steps in the preparation of a resumé are as follows:

Step 1: *Determine goals.* Resumés are usually prepared with the goal of obtaining a particular job. Sometimes, however, they are used to accompany articles for publication or for background information to introduce a speaker or consultant. The resumé should present the most important information relevant to the purpose you intend for it.

Step 2: *Gather data.* Collect the data you will need to answer the following questions:

- Where can someone contact you? List home and work or school addresses and phone numbers.
- What is your objective? List employment objective or other goals.
- Where have you worked, spoken, or written before? List these items in chronological order, most recent first.
- What is your educational level? List degrees, dates, majors, universities, and grade point averages.
- What honors or awards have you earned that are especially relevant to the objective of this resumé?

- Are you willing to have the reader contact references? If yes, then describe how.

Step 3: *Test alternative solutions.* This involves setting up the resumé according to some style. For example, some people like to see their names and addresses centered at the top of the page, but others prefer everything starting at the left margin. Some prefer one-page resumés while others like to elaborate on certain experiences or qualifications using more than one page.

Step 4: *Implement the best solution.* After testing various formats, select the one that most clearly meets your goals. Then save and print your document. If possible, use a letter-quality printer.

7. Create three files with three different employment objectives to be included in a resumé. Label the files GOAL1.DOC, GOAL2.DOC, and GOAL3.DOC. Then create three different versions of the resumé created in Exercise 4 by following these steps.
   a. Open a new file with a new filename to create a new resumé. With the Retrieve command, read the file you created for your resumé in Exercise 4 into the newly opened file.
   c. Mark the contents of the Employment Objectives section (not the heading) as a block and delete it using the Delete Block command.
   d. Save this file. For example, name it NEWRES.DOC.
   e. Open a new file to create another new resumé.
   f. With the Retrieve command, read the file you saved in step d into the newly created file. This is the file from which the employment objectives are missing.
   g. Place the cursor under the Employment Objectives heading and, with the Retrieve command, read the contents of GOAL1.DOC into the file.
   h. Save this file. For example, name it NEWRES1.DOC.
   i. Repeat steps e through h, giving new names to the newly created files—for example, NEWRES2.DOC and NEWRES3.DOC. Read GOAL2.DOC into NEWRES2.DOC and GOAL3.DOC into NEWRES3.DOC. When you are finished you should have three new resumés with three different job objectives.
   j. Print a copy of each resumé. Use Shift-PrtSc to print a copy of the disk directory listing the files created during this exercise.
8. Assume you have used the search and replace feature to find "January 3, 1989," and replace it with "January 9, 1990." The following dates

appear in the document. Indicate whether or not the computer will find each item and replace it; if not, explain why not.

a. January 3, 1889,
b. January 3, 1989,
c. January 3, l989,
d. January 3, L989,
e. January 3 1989,

5

Advanced Word Processing Applications

LESSON OUTLINE

In the past few years the power and flexibility of word processing software packages have increased dramatically. Features that were once found only in software costing thousands of dollars are now commonly found in software costing less than $500. As you completed the tutorials and exercises in Lessons 3 and 4, you became familiar with the commands and features used to create, edit, print, and save a document. This lesson emphasizes the advanced features that make word processing an even more powerful tool—including mail merge, spell checking, electronic thesaurus, windows, multiple document editing, outlining, text marking for table of contents, indexing, lists, and macros. While you may not use these advanced features as readily as you use the commands to move the cursor or delete characters, they can change and improve the quality of your writing as well as its appearance.

ADVANCED WORD PROCESSING FEATURES

Mail merge operations insert fields, files, and keyboard input into specific places in a form to automate the production of letters, mailing labels, personalized mass mailings, order forms, contracts, and other documents. A simple merge combines a list of names and addresses with a form letter to produce a personalized letter for each person named on the list.

Mail Merge

Merge operations essentially involve using two files: (1) a **secondary merge file** that holds a list of variable data items arranged in a specific order and named or assigned a code and (2) a **primary merge** or **master file** that contains the fixed text and the data names or codes that will be replaced with the specific data items from the secondary merge file when the merge operation is performed.

Outline Processors

We all know that outlines are helpful tools in organizing any report, paper, or speech; however, most writers find updating an outline a tedious task. Fortunately, computerized outline processors have come to the rescue. An **outline processor** automatically constructs and maintains an outline as it is created and edited. The processor inserts the proper indentation levels and numbering as the items are entered. If a level is deleted, the outline is revised and renumbered. Most outline processors, such as Think Tank, can maintain several levels. Some people consider outline processors as "idea processors" since they help encourage organized thought. Most allow users to define outlining styles and the numbering conventions to be used.

WordPerfect provides a comprehensive outline processor. To activate it, version 4.2 users enter the Mark Text command (Alt-[F5]) and choose the Outline option (1). Version 5.0 users should press Shift-[F5]4. Once the Outline mode is turned on (indicated by the change in the status line), the Tab and Return keys work differently. The Return key adds an outline number that is of the same level, such as from I. to II., while the Tab key steps the outline up or down to the next level—say, from I. to A. or from B. to (1). WordPerfect keeps track of the outlining levels as you do your work.

The Define option lets you change the numbering style. There are three predefined styles: paragraph—1. a. i. (1) (a) (i) 1); outline—I. A. 1. a. (1) (a) i); and legal—1. 1.1. 2. 2.1., etc. Users can also create their own styles using the options listed on the Options menu. End the outlining by repeating the outline command.

Word Processing Enhancements

"To err is human . . . ," the old saying goes. Fortunately there is microcomputer software to correct human errors in word usage and spelling. Of course, even the best software cannot totally eliminate such problems, but the three features described below can help a great deal.

Spell Checker After a document has been created, you may want to check it for proper spelling by using a software package called a spelling checker. A **spelling checker** is a program that compares each word in a document to a stored list of properly spelled words called a **dictionary.** If a word cannot be found in the dictionary, the spelling checker records it as a mismatch, meaning that the word is either misspelled or is not listed in the software's dictionary. The spelling checker marks or writes a list of mismatched words for the user to review. Each listed word can be corrected, ignored, or added to the dictionary.

Some spelling checkers assist in the decision by showing the context of the word in the text or by suggesting alternative spellings for the word. The dictionaries used by spelling checkers generally contain 20,000 or more frequently used words, plus the capacity to add more. In addition to the main dictionary, some spelling checkers permit you to set up specialized dictionaries for technical terms that will be used only in particular documents. WordStar offers specialized medical and legal dictionaries as add-ons, a feature that keeps the main dictionary at a reasonable size to save time when the computer searches through it. You can specify which dictionary you want to use to check a particular file.

Some spelling checkers are integrated with word processing software, such as WordPerfect; others can be purchased separately and used with most word processing software. Popular brands include Lightning, Random House, Webster's New Word, and Super SpellGuard.

WordPerfect contains a full-feature spelling checker called the Speller. This fully integrated package includes features such as a 115,000-word dictionary (290K); on-screen spellchecking; page, document, and block checking; automatic correction of words; pattern and phonetic lookup, flagging of double occurrence of a word; easy addition or deletion of words from the dictionary; and word count. To use the Speller, just press ^[F2]. Notice in Figure 5-1 that the screen is divided in half. The upper half contains the document, with the unmatched word highlighted. The lower half contains a list of suggested alternative spellings for the word. You can choose one of the alternative spellings by pressing the letter, or you can select a numbered option from across the bottom. The Speller has completed the operation when the word count appears on the status line.

The Limited Use version of WordPerfect 4.2 (L-WP) does not include the full Speller. Students using L-WP can learn more about how this feature operates by calling up the file README.WP and following the step-by-step directions. The same holds for the electronic thesaurus (see below).

Electronic Thesaurus The purpose of a thesaurus is to help you find the right word and use it at the right time. An **electronic thesaurus** is a convenient and fast way of looking up alternative terms, including synonyms, antonyms, and related terms. In WordPerfect, the user places the cursor on a word, presses the Thesaurus command (Alt-[F1]), and within a

```
primary merge or master file that contains the fixed text and the

data names or codes that will be replaced with the specific data

items from the secondary mege file when the merge operation is

performed.  Figure 5-1 is an illustration of merge operations

using WordPerfect.



=====================================================================

  A. mere                     B. merge                    C. mete
  D. mag                      E. maggie                   F. magi
  G. midge                    H. mig                      I. mug
  J. muggy



Not Found!  Select Word or Menu Option (0=Continue): 0
1 Skip Once; 2 Skip; 3 Add Word; 4 Edit; 5 Look Up; 6 Phonetic
```

FIGURE 5-1 Correct spelling can be done more quickly and easily using a spell checker. This figure illustrates WordPerfect's Speller. Notice how the unmatched word is highlighted and a list of alternative spellings is given below. The user can select an alternative word by pressing a letter or can choose one of the options listed at the bottom of the screen.

FIGURE 5-2 An illustration of WordPerfect's electronic thesaurus. A list of synonyms and antonyms appears on the bottom half of the screen.

```
checker marks or writes a list of mismatched words to be reviewed

by the user for further action.  Each listed work can be

 action (n)
  1 A  motion                   action (ant)
    B  movement                  6    inactivity
                                      settlement
  2 C  act
    D  deed
    E  endeavor

  3 F  gesticulation
    G  gesture
    H  motion

  4 I  effect
    J  operation
    K  performance

  5 L  case
    M  lawsuit
    N  proceeding
1 Replace Word; 2 View Doc; 3 Look Up Word; 4 Clear Column: 0
```

few seconds several synonyms and antonyms for the word appear on the screen (see Figure 5-2). By choosing an option, the user can replace the word, view more of the document, look up a specific word, look up other levels of meaning, or clear the cursor column to make room for other words.

In WordPerfect both the spell checker and the electronic thesaurus are totally integrated; that is, they work entirely within the word processing program. There is no need to leave the word processor and load another software package.

Grammar Checker One of the most popular add-on software packages for word processing software is the **grammar checker.** Grammar-checking software scans the document and flags suspected errors in punctuation and grammar, such as placement of periods, verb agreement, and double negatives. It also rates the text for reading level. While grammar checkers are not a substitute for a good editor, they can improve writing and catch some mistakes.

Multiple Document Editing Some word processing software permits users to work with two documents at one time. Each document is kept in a separate document window. A **window** is the portion of the document currently visible on the screen. The user edits the document by switching from one window to the next.

FIGURE 5-3 Multiple windows let users see two documents at once on the screen. Notice that the documents are identified by name and number on the status line.

```
There are three predefined styles:  paragraph, 1. a. i. (1) (a)

(i) 1); outline - I. A. 1. a. (1) (a) i); and legal, 1. 1.1. 2.

2.1., etc.  Users can also create their own style using the

available options listed on the Options menu.  To begin and end

outlining, type Alt-[F5] 1.  Figure 5-2 is an example of an
C:\MAIN\WP\MUC6P167.WPC                    Doc 1  Pg 3  Ln 21     Pos 10
{  ▲   ▲   ▲   ▲   ▲   ▲   ▲   ▲   ▲   ▲   ▲   ▲  ]▲   ▲
          1.   Systems Software
               a.   Operating Systems (MS-DOS)
               b.   Utilities - Hand-outs
               c.   Language Processors
          2.   Applications Software
               a.   Word Processing - Text
               b.   Spreadsheets - Numbers and Formulas
               c.   Database Management Systems - Files
     D.   Hands-On:
          1.   Finding Features on the Microcomputer
               a.   On/Off Switch
               b.   Keyboards
C:\MAIN\WP\EMBAAGD.DOC                     Doc 2  Pg 1  Ln 31     Pos 39
```

Some word processing software, including WordPerfect, permit multiple windows on the screen simultaneously. The user can view and edit two or more documents at one time. The windows are identified by the document number (Doc 1 and Doc 2) on the status line. Figure 5-3 is an example of multiple document editing using two windows on the screen.

With WordPerfect, press the Switch key, Shift-[F3], to move to the second document window. The document indicator will switch from Doc 1 to Doc 2. To show two or more documents on the screen at the same time, press the Screen command, ^[F3], and choose the Window option, 1. WordPerfect will then ask for the number of lines in the window. Change the number of lines displayed on the screen to a number between 1 and 22 or press the Up arrow key until the screen is the desired number of lines. Press Return when you are finished. Normally there are 24 lines on the screen.

Manuscript Preparation Features

Word processing software that assist in the preparation of long manuscripts include features that create and organize footnotes and endnotes, table of contents, lists, outlines, indexes, number lines, citations, and table of authorities. These specialized word processing features are becoming more and more commonly available.

A **footnote** is an explanatory comment or reference note at the bottom of a page, keyed to a specific part of the text on the page. Footnotes are usually numbered with superscript numerals. **Endnotes** are similar to footnotes, but appear at the end of a chapter, section, or document. Their reference numbers are usually printed on the same line as the note, rather than superscripted. The WordPerfect command for footnotes in version 4.2 is ^[F7] 1 <note> [F7] and the command for endnotes is ^[F7] 5 <note> [F7]. The version 5.0 command for footnotes is ^[F7] 1 1 <note> [F7] and for endnotes is ^[F7] 2 1 <note> [F7]. The footnote or endnote command is placed within the body of the text, at the point the note number would be placed. WordPerfect will then print the footnote or endnote in the proper location, automatically subtracting the number of lines the footnote requires from the number of text lines available (including any footers or headers on the page).

A **table of contents** is an outline, including page numbers, of the contents of a long document. An **index** is an alphabetical listing of names, places, and topics, along with the numbers of the pages on which they are mentioned or discussed. A **concordance file** is a file containing all the words and phrases to be searched for and marked as index entries. A **table of authorities** lists all the citations referred to in a legal document. A **citation** is a reference to a particular legal statute, case, or article. WordPerfect uses the Mark Text key (Alt-[F5]) to create a table of contents, lists, outlines, indexes, concordances, and number lines and to record all citations, from which it generates a table of authorities. To use these features, the user must first define the option and then mark the text to be included under each category using block commands and the Mark Text command, a task made much easier by macros.

Macros

A **macro** is commands, instructions, or text stored as a group and executed by pressing a few keys or evoking the macro name. A macro turns a long complicated series of commands into a simple keystroke. Macros can be as elaborate or as simple as needed. The macro feature in WordPerfect allows you to record any keystrokes, both text and WordPerfect commands, under one name and then play them back exactly as they were recorded. You can define a macro to perform any job you would do with WordPerfect. You've already created a macro in Lesson 3 to save a document. Now you can apply the same steps to any WordPerfect task. There are four basic steps to defining a macro:

1. Begin defining the macro. Press ^[F10].
2. Enter the name of the macro. The name can be two to eight characters or a combination of the Alt key plus any letter from A to Z. Temporary macros that are erased after WordPerfect is exited can be named with a Return key or one character.

3. Type the keystrokes to be included in the macro.
4. End defining the macro. Press ^[F10].

Once a macro has been defined, you can execute it by pressing Alt-[F10] and entering the name of the macro or, if you named the macro with the Alt key, by holding down the Alt key and then typing the letter used to name the macro.

Data Interchange with Other Software Packages

Word processing software is an even more effective tool when it can use data and information from other programs, including other word processing, spreadsheet, and database software packages. Numeric data can be collected and manipulated using the spreadsheet, and the results can be printed in a report. A database can be used to collect and select variable data, such as names and addresses to be mail merged with a form letter. You may want to interchange documents with another department that uses a different word processor. Data interchange greatly expands the usefulness of your computer system.

The data interchange capability of word processing software differs from software to software. Some software have limited conversion capabilities. For example, WordStar 4.0 will generally accept a document in the DOS text file format (also called ASCII format). However, in the process specialized formatting codes are lost, requiring the user to strip the returns from each line, using special utility programs, before the document can be edited.

Fortunately, most spreadsheet and database management software can generate files that can be inserted into word processing documents. For example, if you use Lotus 1-2-3 to output a spreadsheet to a disk file, this file can then be retrieved or read into a word processing document. dBASE III Plus can copy or report to a disk file that is readable by the word processing software.

In L-WP, the user cannot save a document on the screen to a DOS text file format, a locked document format, or other word processor formats. Files saved under L-WP are usable only under L-WP.

WordPerfect includes a built-in Text In/Out feature to save a document as an ASCII DOS text file or import a DOS text file into WordPerfect (see Figure 5-4). With this feature you can import or export files to and from other programs or use WordPerfect as a program text editor for programming languages such as BASIC. No special formatting codes are added to the document.

To save the document on the screen as a DOS text file for use in another program or to prepare the document to send to an output device, press the Text In/Out command, ^[F5]1, and enter the filename for the document. All WordPerfect formatting codes are deleted. The soft returns ([SRt]) and soft page breaks are converted to hard returns ([HRt]), and hard returns become carriage return-line feeds. To read a DOS text file into WordPerfect, press ^[F5]2 and enter the filename of the document to be retrieved. The "Text In" option on the List Files menu can also be used to read in files. When you retrieve a DOS text file, the end of each line normally contains a hard return ([HRt]). Although this is desirable if you are

FIGURE 5-4 The WordPerfect Text In/Out screen. With WordPerfect's flexible importing and exporting options, files can be easily interchanged among users with different software packages.

```
Document Conversion, Summary and Comments

     DOS Text File Format
          1 - Save
          2 - Retrieve  (CR/LF becomes [HRt])
          3 - Retrieve  (CR/LF in H-Zone becomes [SRt])

     Locked Document Format
          4 - Save
          5 - Retrieve

     Other Word Processor Formats
          6 - Save in a generic word processor format
          7 - Save in WordPerfect 4.1 format

     Document Summary and Comments
          A - Create/Edit Summary
          B - Create Comment
          C - Edit Comment
          D - Display Summary and Comments

Selection: 0
```

using a program, these hard returns will make it difficult to reformat text in a word processing document. WordPerfect has two import options: one that places hard returns at the ends of lines and one that places soft returns at the ends of lines.

The Convert utility is not available in L-WP.

WordPerfect also has a special utility, loaded separately, called Convert, for converting documents directly from one of the several popular formats to WordPerfect format and vice versa, including WordStar, Multi-Mate, seven-bit transfer format, and spreadsheet DIF format (see Figure 5-5). The convert utility is not available in L-WP. This powerful and handy program lets you convert a WordPerfect document into any of these five formats: Revisable-Form-Text (a format used by IBM mainframes), Navy DIF (Navy document interchange format, not a spreadsheet format), WordStar (a popular word processing format that can sometimes be used as an intermediate format), MultiMate (a popular word processing format), and seven-bit transfer format (a format used for transferring over communications lines via modems).

COMPARING AND SELECTING SOFTWARE

Selecting the right word processing software package is an important part of using word processing. If the word processing software does not fit your needs, then time, money, and effort will be wasted. This discussion provides a general approach to, plus some specifics about, the process of selecting word processing software. While you may not be in a position to buy software in the immediate future, these guidelines can help you appreciate the importance of understanding the software specifications.

FIGURE 5-5 An illustration of the WordPerfect Convert utility options. Notice the wide variety of data formats available.

```
Name of Input File? jb2389.let
Name of Output File? jb2389.ws


1 WordPerfect to another format
2 Revisable-Form-Text (IBM DCA Format) to WordPerfect
3 Navy DIF Standard to WordPerfect
4 WordStar 3.3 to WordPerfect
5 MultiMate 3.22 to WordPerfect
6 Seven-bit transfer format to WordPerfect
7 Mail Merge to WordPerfect Secondary Merge
8 WordPerfect Secondary Merge to Spreadsheet DIF
9 Spreadsheet DIF to WordPerfect Secondary Merge

Enter number of Conversion desired 1

1 Revisable-Form-Text (IBM DCA Format)
2 Final-Form-Text (IBM DCA Format)
3 Navy DIF  Standard
4 WordStar 3.3
5 MultiMate 3.22
6 Seven-bit transfer format

Enter number of output file format desired
```

The first question you might ask when considering different word processing software packages is "Where do I begin?" If you are a novice in the field of word processing, the task can be confusing. If you ask experienced users what they think, you will find almost all of them have strong feelings, positive or negative, about the word processing software they use. If you talk to a salesperson, your choices may be limited to the particular software the store sells, rather than the one that best suits your needs. Instead of one clear-cut answer to your needs, you may get contradictory advice.

How do you sort it all out and make a sensible decision? It is important to remember that no single word processing software package does it all. Every software package has strengths and weaknesses, and the final selection depends on your personal preferences and applications. You must weigh the advantages and disadvantages of the numerous software alternatives. To make the process less confusing and more organized, use the general four-step problem-solving approach:

1. Define your goals
2. Gather data
3. Test alternatives
4. Implement the best solution

Step 1: Define Your Goals

What do you really want the word processor to do? The first step in deciding which software is best for you is to determine your word processing goals and constraints. Goals should specify how you plan to use the word processing software. Constraints include how much money you have to spend and the hardware you are planning to use. For example, the goal of a student may be to have word processing software that helps produce term papers and reports that have a neat, organized appearance. In addition, the software should work on the particular microcomputer available in the dormitory or lab and cost less than $100.

As situations change, so do the goals for the word processing software. For example, a manager of a small office may have a larger budget than the student but may be more concerned about the speed of the commands or the compatibility of the word processing software with other computers within the firm. If long reports are frequently used, then software programmed to handle lengthy documents should be considered. Some software, such as PC-Type and Nota Bene, limit the size of the document to the primary storage capacity of the computer. This type of software provides faster editing, because the document is processed entirely within primary storage rather than using the slower disk memory. However, the advantage of speed may be offset by the disadvantage of the limited size of each document. Other word processing software, such as WordPerfect, Microsoft Word, and WordStar, limit file size by the room on the disk. Everyone wants word processing software that is easy to learn and to use. The issue is to balance the ease of use with the features needed to achieve the main goal.

In general, if your goal is to use word processing to do simple, occasional letters and small reports, look for software that is simple to use, is inexpensive, and enables you to edit quickly. If you need to prepare lengthier, more complex documents, then look for more sophisticated features, such as the ability to move text around easily; search operations; on-screen formatting display; block operations, including copy, move, and delete; screen display of 80 columns per line; and large file size. Another consideration might be vendor assistance, such as a toll-free phone number to call for help, newsletters to keep you informed of new developments, and free or inexpensive updates of software. Other special features allow for ease of footnoting, indexing, outlining, spell checking, thesaurus checking, and mail merging. Flexibility of printer choice and the use of special characters, such as boldface, underlining, superscripts, subscripts, graphics, and mathematical symbols, are still other considerations.

Step 2: Gather Data

Where can you collect data regarding the numerous microcomputer software packages available for word processing? There are a variety of sources. Magazines such as *Byte, PC World, PC, Personal Computing,* and *Infoworld* are readily available at most newsstands. Several offer regular features reviewing software; many offer special "buyer's guides" editions.

Look for recent articles. Microcomputer software prices and specifications are updated frequently. Read several of these articles to get a variety of opinions before making up your mind. Remember, however, that the author of each article has his or her bias too.

Another valuable source of information is other people currently using word processing. Seek out users with applications similar to yours. Perhaps a friend will let you try out his or her word processing software. Often local **users groups,** clubs of people who share an interest in a particular computer or software, can supply valuable information. Some groups even operate local electronic bulletin boards that can be accessed by people with a microcomputer, a modem, and communications software. **Electronic bulletin boards** provide the electronic version of a community bulletin board where people can leave messages, ask others for assistance with a particular problem, or even advertise software or hardware for sale. Seek out others who have similar word processing applications and hardware. They can give you clues on the advantages and disadvantages of particular software.

A third source of information is your local computer store. Most sell a variety of word processing software packages and can provide a reasonable amount of information about the products they sell. Of course, the same cautions about personal bias apply. It is a good idea to first examine the other sources of information so you will not be overwhelmed by a salesperson's use of such jargon as "proportional print," "virtual storage," and "on-screen justification." You need to determine whether a salesperson is factually describing a product or merely trying to make a sale. Studying this book will help you cut through some of the jargon.

Step 3: Test Alternatives

You can test alternative word processing software packages through friends, at work or school, in information centers, and at your local computer store. **Information centers** set up by organizations, such as corporations, schools, or colleges, may provide users with information about and hands-on experience with hardware and software. When you have the opportunity, ask to try out the word processing software packages that meet your needs. If you happen to have exactly the same computer and printer available, you can achieve the equivalent of a "test drive." Sit down at the computer, insert the word processing disk, and actually create a letter or short report to test the editing and formatting features you need. Try to work alone with the software before you decide to buy. If the "test drive" is impractical, you may have to be satisfied with a demonstration before purchasing the product. If software have **"shrink-wrap" licenses,** you automatically agree to the license requirements by breaking the plastic shrink wrap enclosing the software. Such software generally cannot be returned since the dealer cannot sell the software after the wrapping is opened. However, there may be a demonstration disk you can try. A demonstration disk often contains most, but not all, of the features and functions of the regular software disk. For example, the functions of saving a file and printing a file may be omitted, thus allowing a potential customer to test the software but not use it for any actual jobs.

Step 4: Implement the Best Solution

After testing various software packages, decide which package would best suit your needs *and* your budget. Prices range from around $50 to over $500. The more advanced the features, the more expensive the software tends to be. For instance, Bank Street Writer is designed for beginning microcomputer users and is priced accordingly. It is written primarily for home use. However, low price does not always mean few features. Some sophisticated packages are available at reasonable cost.

Some word processing software, such as WordStar, are "bundled" with several microcomputers. **Bundled software** is software that is sold as a package with the microcomputer hardware. When you buy the hardware, you get the software free or at a very reduced price. WordStar offers features that would be used in most offices and for professional applications. Remember that price is not necessarily a good indicator of value, since whatever the price, you are wasting your money unless you use the software.

It takes practice to *really* learn how to use word processing software. Unfortunately, many people buy a software package and never seem to find the time to *really* use it enough to break through the initial barrier caused by their lack of practice. Most software is easiest to learn when you have a practical reason for learning it. However, do not attempt a last-minute project or one that is too complex so you get discouraged by trying to learn too much too soon. Start with some simple but practical applications, such as the tutorials and exercises in this text. Work on these projects and practice regularly. Your skills will grow each time you use the word processor. Word processing is, of course, easier when you have typing skills and really becomes a powerful tool in the hands of a touch typist. However, "hunt and peck" typists can also benefit from it.

Once you have made your decision and bought, used, and learned the word processing software, be ready for the new and improved versions to tempt you. The four steps in software selection really form a cycle. As new software becomes available or as your needs change, it pays to stay flexible and consider going back to Step 1 to reassess your goals and needs. Perhaps you have bought a hard disk and can use a more complex word processor because more storage space is available. Maybe you now want to merge files and produce mass mailings that your current word processing software cannot handle. The area of computers, especially microcomputers, is constantly evolving. Expect new developments in word processing to occur on a regular and frequent basis. Keeping up to date in this dynamic area is an exciting challenge.

One consequence of the ever-changing field of computers in general and word processing specifically is the need for a spirit of curiosity and adventure. If you simply give up when you meet a problem, you will find word processing very frustrating. However, if you have the spirit of adventure and are willing to experiment and be persistent, you can use such experiences as an opportunity for growth. If you are having difficulties using the software, call the store where you bought the software, call the vendor by using the toll-free number, seek help from others who use the software, or in some way meet the challenge. Then you can soon become an expert and have a right to feel proud of what you have accomplished. You will have succeeded where others have given up.

A CHECKLIST OF WORD PROCESSING FEATURES

The following checklist can be used to systematically evaluate the various word processing software packages. The checklist is organized around major and miscellaneous factors you should consider when purchasing word processing software. If the software you are considering has a particular feature, put a check mark beside it on the list. Some features may be more important than others to you, depending upon your goals.

Hardware Requirements

_____ Is the software compatible with your existing microcomputer and its operating system?

_____ Does the microcomputer have sufficient RAM?

_____ Do you have sufficient disk storage?

_____ Is the software better suited for a hard disk?

_____ Is the software compatible with your printer?

_____ What is the limit on document size?

Documentation

_____ Are onscreen as well as manual tutorials available?

_____ Are the tutorials and manuals easy to understand and use?

_____ Are help menus available and easy to use and understand?

_____ Is phone support available?

_____ Is the phone support toll-free?

_____ Does the manufacturer offer phone support at reasonable hours?

_____ Is the dealer familiar with the software?

Cursor Movement

_____ Does the software offer full function cursor control? (The cursor can be moved by character, word, sentence, paragraph, and page.)

_____ Does the cursor control use the arrow keys?

_____ Is the cursor control diamond available?

_____ Can a mouse be used with the software?

Editing Features

- ____ Does the software offer full feature deleting? (Deletions can be by character, word, line, paragraph, block, and file.)
- ____ Can a block be easily marked, copied, moved, or deleted?
- ____ Can text that is accidentally deleted be retrieved?
- ____ Is it easy to insert additional material within existing text?
- ____ Can a character or string of characters be found and replaced?

Onscreen Display

- ____ Does the screen display what you get on the printer?
- ____ Are boldfacing and underlining displayed clearly on the screen?
- ____ Can the text be left and right justified?
- ____ Is right justification shown on the screen?
- ____ Can the software generate and display graphics on the screen, including headers and footnotes?
- ____ Are multiple windows available?

Formatting

- ____ Is word wrap available?
- ____ Is text justification automatic?
- ____ Is paragraph reform easy after inserting text?
- ____ Are embedded format commands available?
- ____ Can margins and tabs be changed easily?
- ____ Is page format flexible, or does it require a predefined format?
- ____ Are page numbers easy to add?
- ____ Does the text require separate formatting before printing?
- ____ Are conditional page breaks available?

Special Print Attributes

- ____ Are the special print attributes that you need available? (i.e., underlining, boldfacing, double striking, proportional printing, superscripts and subscripts, compressed printing, overstriking)
- ____ Are these special attributes visible on the screen?

Printing

- ____ Can you edit a file while another file is being printed?
- ____ Can multiple copies of one document be printed at one time?
- ____ Can single sheets and continuous forms be used conveniently?

_____ Can several documents be linked together, or chained, for printing?

_____ Can you select just one particular page in a document to be printed?

_____ Can printing be interrupted and restarted?

_____ What kind of printers are supported?

Miscellaneous Features

_____ Can the word processing software be integrated with spreadsheet and database software?

_____ Does it offer a built-in or an add-on mail merge feature?

_____ Does it offer a built-in or an add-on spell checker?

_____ Is a back-up copy automatically generated?

_____ Does it automatically create an index of key words?

_____ Can you define your own command macros?

_____ Are there others you know who are satisfied users?

_____ Is the vendor willing and able to offer help?

_____ Is the accompanying manual easy to understand and use?

_____ Is the cost reasonable for the features provided?

Cost of the software: $_____ versus Your budget: $_____

COMPARING WORD PROCESSING SOFTWARE PACKAGES

Table 5-1 provides a comparison of eight widely used word processing software packages—WordStar 4.0, PFS Professional Write, MultiMate, Samna Word IV, Word, WordPerfect 5.0, WordStar 2000, and Manuscript 1.0. Of course, as improvements are made and newer versions become available, the information on this chart may change. Use Table 5-1 to compare the features of the sophisticated word processing software available today. Think about how these software tools can be useful to you and to organizations today.

The characteristics used for comparison are organized into the categories of hardware requirements, documentation, cursor movement, editing features, onscreen display, formatting, special print attributes, printing, document handling, special features, cost, and additional notes. Most of these characteristics have already been described in this book; however, the following brief descriptions of some new terms will be helpful in fully understanding Table 5-1.

Software that is **copy protected** comes on a disk that cannot be easily copied. This is particularly inconvenient for people who own microcomputers with hard disks. They typically copy the software onto a hard disk.

Table 5-1 A COMPARISON OF WORD PROCESSING SOFTWARE PACKAGES

SOFTWARE NAME	*WordStar (4.0)*	*PFS Professional Write (1.0)*	*MultiMate (3.31)*
HARDWARE REQUIREMENTS			
Microcomputer/Operating system	MS-DOS	MS-DOS	MS-DOS
Minimum RAM	256K, 320K to use thesaurus	320K	256K
Number of disk drives	1, 2 recommended	2	2
DOCUMENTATION			
Help menus	yes	yes	yes
On-line help	yes	yes	yes
On-screen tutorial	yes	no	yes
CURSOR MOVEMENT			
Arrow keys	yes	yes	yes
Cursor control diamond	yes	no	no
Full feature cursor movement	yes	yes	yes
Supports mouse	no	no	no
GoTo function	yes	no	yes
EDITING FEATURES			
Mnemonic commands	no	no	yes
Full feature deleting	yes	yes	yes
Search and replace	yes	yes	yes
Block delete, move, and copy	yes	yes	yes
Undo function	yes	yes, for block deletions only	no
ON-SCREEN DISPLAY			
Displays as printed (WYSIWYG)	yes	yes	yes
Boldface and underlining displayed	yes	essentially	no/highlighted
On-screen justification	yes	yes	no
Line and box drawing capability	yes	yes	no
Windows per screen	1	1	1
FORMATTING			
Header/Footer function	yes	yes	yes
Lines per header/footer	multiple	2	5
Embedded print format commands	dot commands	yes	yes
Conditional page breaks	yes	no	yes
Column function	yes	no	yes
SPECIAL PRINT ATTRIBUTES			
Underline	yes	yes	yes
Boldface	yes	yes	yes
Proportional spacing	yes	no	yes
Super/Subscript	yes	yes	yes
Overstrike	yes	yes	yes
PRINTING			
Edit during printing	yes	no	yes
Single sheet printing	yes	yes	yes
Number of printers supported	100+	80+	400+
DOCUMENT HANDLING			
Automatic backup	yes	no	no
Automatic file save	no	no	yes
SPECIAL FEATURES			
Mail-merge printing	yes	yes	yes
Spelling checker	yes	yes	yes
Glossary	no	no	yes
Thesaurus	yes	yes	no
Table of contents function	no	no	no
Outline function	no	no	no
Automatic indexing	yes	no	no
Style sheet	no	no	no
Macros	yes	yes	no
Math capability	yes	no	no
LIST PRICE	$395	$199	$495
ADDITIONAL NOTES		maximum file size 64K	

Samna Word IV (4.0)	*Word, PC (3.11)*	*WordPerfect (5.0)*	*WordStar 2000 Plus*	*Manuscript (1.0)*
MS-DOS	MS-DOS	MS-DOS	MS-DOS	MS-DOS
360K	256K	384K	256K	512K
2	2	2	hard disk recommended	requires hard disk
yes	yes	yes	yes	yes
yes	yes	yes	yes	yes
yes	yes	yes	yes	no
yes	yes	yes	yes	yes
no	no	no	no	no
yes	yes	yes	yes	yes
no	yes (Microsoft)	no	no	no
yes	yes	yes	yes	yes
yes	no	no	yes	no
yes	yes	yes	yes	yes
yes	yes	yes	yes	yes
yes	yes	yes	yes	yes
yes	yes	yes	yes	no
yes	yes	yes	partial	no
as inverse video	exactly	yes (view)	yes	no
yes	yes	yes	yes	yes
yes	no	yes	no	no
2	8	2	3	2
yes	yes	yes	yes	yes
limited by page	unlimited	unlimited	limited by page	1
yes	no	yes	yes	no
yes	yes	yes	yes	yes
yes	yes	yes	yes	yes
yes	yes	yes	yes	yes
yes	yes	yes	yes	yes
yes	yes	yes	yes	yes
yes	yes	yes	yes	yes
yes	yes	yes	yes	yes
yes	yes	yes	yes	no
yes	yes	yes	yes	yes
100+	100+	200+	220+	25
yes	yes	yes	yes	no
no	no	yes	no	no
yes	yes	yes	yes	yes
yes	yes	yes	yes	yes
yes	yes	yes	yes	no
no	yes	yes	no	no
yes	yes	yes	yes	yes
yes	yes	yes	no	yes
yes	yes	yes	no	yes
no	yes	no	no	yes
yes	no	yes	no	no
yes	yes	yes	no	no
$595	$450	$495	$595	$495
	multiple fonts preformatted options			

However, copy-protected software normally must remain on the floppy disk, forcing the use of the slower, more awkward floppy disk. Backup or replacement copies must usually be purchased from the manufacturer.

Word processing software with **fully formed graphics** have sophisticated graphics software built into the programs, so the user can make charts and graphs within the word processing document.

Multiple windows enable the screen to be split into two or more parts. Various parts of the document can be viewed at one time. For example, the upper half of the screen could contain the outline and the lower half could contain text.

Word processing software with a **separate formatting program** requires the user to run the program formatting the document file before printing. Such formatting programs can be memory- and time-consuming. However, if a document must be formatted several different ways, the formatting program would make this job easier and faster than reformatting manually within the document.

Proportional printing relates the amount of space allocated to a printed character to the size of that character. For example, an *i* is smaller than an *m*. However, most printers allocate exactly the same space to both letters, squeezing the *m* so it fits. Proportional printing gives space to a character in proportion to the amount of space it needs.

Compressed print is an option usually available only for dot matrix, ink-jet, and laser printers. The characters are printed smaller, usually 14 to 17 characters per inch. The smaller the character, the more characters can be fit on one line.

One of the most frustrating parts of word processing is the amount of time it takes to print a document while you are waiting to work at the microcomputer. With **print spooling,** the word processing software permits a document to be printed while the user continues to edit documents with the word processing software.

The **mail merge** feature permits variable parts to be merged with a document. The most common use for this feature is the merging of names and addresses with form letters.

As word processing software has become more sophisticated, **keyboard macros** have become available. Several individual commands can be grouped and later entered more simply by pressing a single key or a few keystrokes.

TUTORIAL: PLANNING AND WRITING A TERM PAPER USING WORDPERFECT

To complete this tutorial you need the following:

- WordPerfect disk
- WordPerfect Spell disk (except for users of L-WP)

- Files disk used in Lessons 3 and 4
- An installed printer connected to the microcomputer

While completing this tutorial you will learn how to

- Use outlining
- Use formatting commands, including margins, headings, page numbers, centering, and double spacing
- Use search and replace
- Use spell checking and thesaurus
- Create footnotes
- Use two-document editing and windows
- Insert the date of printing using the Date Function

So far you have learned how to use word processing to edit, format, save, and print short documents. This tutorial uses a report as an example of a longer and more complicated document. As we have seen, editing and revising, especially on longer documents, are easier when you use word processing.

Suppose you have been asked to investigate and discuss the topic of the history of word processing software. The report you produce should meet the following standards of style:

- The report must be double spaced and have a 1-inch top margin and a 1-inch right margin. The first page of text should have a top margin of $1\frac{1}{2}$ inches.
- A title page is required, containing the title of the paper centered both vertically and horizontally in the middle of the page, followed by your name, the course name and number, and the instructor's name, each centered.
- Each page of the report should have a page heading that includes the title of the report, the date, and the page number.
- The report is to be footnoted, and at least five references should be consulted and cited.

You already know how to load the operating system and the word processing software into your computer. If you need a reminder, see Lesson 3 or Lesson 4. Remember to watch out for the correct version when entering commands.

Create an Outline

Use the outline capacity of WordPerfect to plan the document.

Step 1: Define the outline.

Version 4.2 users press **Alt-[F5].** The options for marking text appear. Press

```
1
```

to turn the outlining function on. Version 5.0 users press **Shift-[F5] 4.**

Step 2: Enter the outline.

Press **Return** to insert the first level number. Press **Indent ([F4])** to indent the text.

If you press Tab by mistake (the level number is reduced to the next lower level and moved to the next tab stop), press Shift-Tab (the Margin Release command) to return to the next higher level.

Type

```
Introduction
```

Press **Return**.

Notice that the next level number (II.) appears. Press **Indent [F4].** Type

```
The History of Word Processing
```

Press **Return.**

Press **Tab.** Notice that the level number is reduced to the next lower level (A.)

Continue entering the outline, using Figure 5-6 as your guide.

Turn the outlining off. Version 4.2 users press **Alt-[F5] 1** and version 5.0 users press **Shift-[F5] 4.**

Step 3: Save and exit the outline.

Press **[F7].**

At the prompt for the filename, type

```
B:TERMOUT.DOC
```

At the prompt for exiting WordPerfect, type

```
N
```

The empty screen will reappear.

Create and Format the Report

If you have properly opened an empty file, the next step is to format, or set up, the document according to the required standards of style. As we discussed earlier, some word processing software permit very flexible

FIGURE 5-6 An outline for the term paper to be entered in the tutorial.

```
I.   Introduction
II.  History of Word Processiing
     A.   Data Processing
     B.   Electric Typewriters
     C.   Word Processing Systems
     D.   Word Processing Software for Microcomputers
III. Who Uses Word Processing?
     A.   Executives
     B.   Professionals
IV.  The Industry Standard?
     A.   WordStar
     B.   WordPerfect
V.   Summary and Conclusions
```

formatting. All margins (top, bottom, right, and left) are adjustable through formatting commands. Most word processing software packages have **default** settings for formatting requirements. The default format settings are usually the common settings for a standard business letter. Therefore, if you add no formatting commands on your own, the document you create will be formatted according to the default settings.

Step 1: Insert the format codes.

Document-inclusive format codes—including headings, page numbers, and Mark Text definitions—should have the format codes placed, whenever possible, at the beginning of a document. This makes them easier to use and revise.

Move to the beginning of the page.

Press **Home Home Home Up Arrow.**

a. Insert the formatting code to place headings, including page number, at the top of each page.

1. Version 4.2 users press **Alt-[F8] 6.** Version 5.0 users press **Shift-[F8] 2.**
2. In version 4.2 a Header/Foot Specification Menu will appear (see Figure 5-7). Select Type **1** (Header A) and Occurrence **1** (Every Page). In version 5.0 the Format: Page menu appears. Press **3 1 2.**
3. The Heading editing screen appears. Type

   `A Short History of Word Processing`

   Space over *3 spaces.* Do NOT press Return.
4. Enter the date function into the heading so the date of the paper will reflect the day the report was printed.

FIGURE 5-7 The Header/Footer Specification screen.

```
Header/Footer Specification

     Type                                Occurrence
     1 - Header A                        0 - Discontinue
     2 - Header B                        1 - Every Page
     3 - Footer A                        2 - Odd Pages
     4 - Footer B                        3 - Even Pages
                                         4 - Edit

     Selection: 0                        Selection: 0
```

Version 4.2 users press **Shift-[F5] 3.** Version 5.0 users press **Shift-[F5] 2.** Today's date will appear on the heading line. Remember that this date will change. **Space** over *3 spaces.* Do NOT press Return.

5. Insert a page number for each page by inserting the ^B code. Type

   Page

   Press the **Space** bar. Press and hold the **Control key,** and, while holding the Control key, press

   B

   Press **Return.**
   Exit the heading page by pressing **[F7].**

b. Suppress the heading for the title page.

1. When the Page Format or Format: Page screen reappears, if you are using version 4.2, type

   8

   Version 5.0 users press **9.**
   A new screen appears with several options for suppressing the page format for the current page.

2. Since we want no headings or page numbers printed on the title page, version 4.2 and 5.0 users type

   1

   Version 5.0 users should press **0** (zero) to return to the Format: Page screen.

c. Turn on the Widow/Orphan protection.

1. If you are using version 4.2, when the Page Format screen reappears, press

   `A`

2. At the prompt, press

   `Y`

3. Version 5.0 users press **0** (zero) *again* to return to the Format menu. Press **1 9 Y 0** (zero).

d. Enter the Center Page Top to Bottom command. This command will affect this page only. Version 4.2 users, when the Page Format screen reappears, press

`3`

Version 5.0 users should be at the Format menu. Press **2 1 0** (zero). WordPerfect accepts the code very quickly and it may seem as if nothing has happened, but if you look at the hidden codes, the Center Page code ([Center Pg]) will have appeared.

e. Exit the Page Format or Format screen. Press **0** or **Return.**

Step 2: Insert the title page contents.

a. Enter the text.

1. Type

   `A SHORT HISTORY OF WORD PROCESSING`

   Press **Return** *twice.*

2. Type

   `by`

   Press **Return** *twice.*

3. Type your name.
   Press **Return** *four times.*

4. Type

```
Prepared for
```

Press **Return** *twice.*

5. Type the lines below and press **Return** after each line.

```
Introduction to Information Systems
Information Systems 110
Dr. Joseph Baumgart
Spring 1990
```

Version 4.2 users press **Shift-[F5] 1** to insert today's date. Version 5.0 users press **Shift-[F5] 2.**
Press **Return.**

b. Center the text by marking and centering the block.

1. Move the cursor to the first letter of the title. Press **Alt-[F4].**
2. Move the cursor to the first column of the line directly beneath the date.
3. Press the Center command, **Shift-[F6].** At the prompt, type

```
Y
```

The text will automatically be centered on the line and on the page. Remember all those times you had to count the number of characters in a title or the number lines on a page, and then backspace or use the carriage return to get the same result?

c. Start a new page. Press the Hard Page command, ^ **Return.**

Step 3: Format the report.

Although the formatting for most of the document has already been defined on the title page, there are some commands that affect only the paper.

a. Turn on the page numbering and set the page number to 2.

1. Version 4.2 users press the Page Format command, **Alt-[F8].** Version 5.0 users press the Format command, **Shift-[F8].**

2. Version 4.2 users when the Page Format screen appears, press option

   `2`

   for new page number. Version 5.0 users, at the Format menu, press **2 6.**
3. At the prompt or line asking for the new page number, press

   `1`

   Press **Return.**
4. Version 4.2 users will be prompted asking for numbering style. Choose Arabic. Press

   `1`

5. Press **Return** until you return to the document.

b. Set the line spacing to double spacing.

1. Version 4.2 users press the Line Format command, **Shift-[F8].** Version 5.0 users press the Format command, **Shift-[F8].**
2. Version 4.2 users have the line format options appear on the status line. To choose the spacing option, press

   `4`

   Version 5.0 users, at the Format menu press **1 6.**
3. At the prompt or line for spacing, type

   `2`

   Press **Return** until the document screen returns.

c. Adjust the top margin to 1 $\frac{1}{2}$ inches.

1. Version 4.2 users press the Page Format command, **Alt-[F8].** Version 5.0 users press the Format command, **Shift-[F8].**

2. With version 4.2, when the Page Format screen appears, choose option

   ```
   5
   ```

   to change the Top Margin.

3. With version 4.2, the prompt asks for the number of half lines for the top margin. Since there are 12 lines per inch, add 6 lines to add $\frac{1}{2}$ inch to the top margin. Type

   ```
   18
   ```

   Press **Return** *twice.*

4. Version 5.0 users, at the Format menu, type **2 5 1.5** and press **Return** until the document reappears.

Step 4: Enter the text.

As you enter text, you will have footnotes to enter as well. When the report is printed, they will appear at the bottom of the page on which they are cited.

a. Type the text as it is written below. Remember to use the Tab when necessary and to let word wrap do its work. *Use the Return key only at the end of a paragraph.* Press Tab, when necessary, to indent paragraphs.

```
     At what point in history did word
processing begin? It depends on how word
processing is defined. To quote the authors
of THE NAKED COMPUTER, a humorous almanac of
computer lore, "One of the most common and
useful applications for a personal computer
is writing, called word processing."
```

Do not press Return.

1. Insert a footnote. Press the Footnote command, ^ **[F7].** Footnote and endnote options appear on the status line. Since a footnote is to be created, press

   ```
   1
   ```

   Version 5.0 users *only,* press **1** again to create the footnote.

The footnote screen appears, with a "1" to indicate that this is footnote number 1. Type

```
Rochester, Jack B., and John Gantz, The
Naked Computer (New York: William Morrow
1983), p. 29.
```

Press **[F7].**

2. Continue with the paper. Do not press Return before entering the following text. It should be in the same paragraph as the text preceding the footnote.

```
They say the term grew out of data
processing, which is a computer working
with numerical information as opposed to
the written language. "Next to liquor,
word processing is a writer's best
friend," says one writer we know.
```

3. Insert a footnote. Press the Footnote command, ^ **[F7] 1** (version 5.0 users press **1** again), and type

```
Ibid.
```

Press **[F7].**

4. Continue with the paper. Press **Return** and insert the command to change the top margin back to 1 inch. Version 4.2 users press **Alt-[F8] 5.**

At the prompt, type

```
12
```

Press **Return.** Version 5.0 users press **Shift-[F8] 2 5 1** and **Return** until the document reappears on the screen.
Continue typing the text.

```
    One way to mark the beginning is to
consider some developments in typewriting
technology in the 1960's. In July 1961,
IBM first presented its Selectric
typewriter, a speedy electric model with
changeable print balls that gave users
more control over the type-face and type
size in their documents.
```

5. Insert a footnote. Press ^ **[F7] 1** (version 5.0 users press **1** again) and type

   Ellison, Carol, "The Trek from Typewriters," PC Magazine (Feb. 29, 1988), p. 96.

   Press **[F7].**

6. Continue with the paper. Do not press Return; continue with the same paragraph.

   In 1971, a full ten years later, Wang Labs introduced Wang 1200, a typing workstation with a small screen and the ability to store up to 133,000 characters on cassette tape.

7. Insert a footnote. Press ^ **[F7] 1** (version 5.0 users press **1** again) and type

   Ibid.

   Press **[F7].**

8. Continue with the paper. Do not press Return; continue with the same paragraph.

   Five years later Wang introduced a system it called the WPS, which stood for Word Processing System and the term was born.

9. Insert a footnote. Press ^ **[F7] 1** (version 5.0 users press **1** again) and type

   Ibid.

   Press **[F7].**

10. Continue with the paper. Do not press Return; continue with the same paragraph.

    Also in 1976, Michael Shrayer produced Electric Pencil, the first popular word processing program for microcomputers.

11. Insert a footnote. Press ^ **[F7] 1** (version 5.0 users press **1** again) and type

```
Williams, Gregg, and Mark Welch, "A
Microcomputing Timeline," Byte (Sept.
1985), p. 200.
```

Press **[F7]**.

12. Continue with the paper. Press **Return** and type

```
    Following those initial steps in the
1960's and '70's, a flood of developments
hit. WordStar was born in 1979, IBM
Displaywriter in 1980, Volkswriter,
EasyWriter, and WangWriter in 1981,
MultiMate with WordMate and Wordperfect in
1982, Microsoft Word, PFS:Write, and
Version 3.3 of WordStar were all
introduced in 1983, and since then
practically every product mentioned has
introduced one or more major new versions.
```

13. Insert a footnote. Press ^ **[F7] 1** (version 5.0 users press **1** again) and type

```
Ibid.
```

Press **[F7]**.

14. Continue with the paper. Press **Return** and type

```
    Today many journals--PERSONAL
COMPUTING, BYTE, PC MAGAZINE, FAMILY &
HOME-OFFICE COMPUTING, and many
more--feature new word processing software
reviews practically every month. Some,
such as INFOWORLD and COMPUTERWORLD, are
produced in newspaper-style format every
week and manage to fill approximately 100
pages per week with articles and ads
concerning new developments.
```

Press **Return** *twice.* Continue the paper.

```
WHO USES WORD PROCESSING?
    Some folks may still view personal
computers and word processing as only the
tools of secretaries and technical nerds,
and not of executives and other
```

```
high-ranking professionals. However, even
arch conservative William F. Buckley, Jr.,
is a regular user. Buckley says those who
say you cannot love the written word
unless you set it down by pencil on a
legal pad are just foolish.
```

15. Insert a Left/Right indent to set off the quote below. The Left/Right indent command indents the text in the paragraph to the left tab and the right margin an equal amount. Press **Return**.
    Press **Shift-[F4]** and type

```
Writing is menial work. It is not
artistic, unless one is a calligrapher.
So, then, why not attempt to abbreviate
that work? . . . Progressive conservatives
should pass a law making it unlawful not
to use a computer.
```

16. Insert a footnote. Press ^ **[F7] 1** (version 5.0 users press **1** again) and type

```
Buckley, William F., Jr., "The
Conservative Computer," in Digital Deli,
Steve Ditlea, ed. (New York: Workman
Publishing, 1984), pp. 362-363.
```

    Press **[F7]**.

17. Continue with the paper. Press **Return** and type

```
Numerous other surveys and reports
indicate that top executives are using
word processing to help them prepare
speeches, draft reports and memorandums,
and, with the aid of spelling checkers and
grammar checkers and outline processors,
improve the quality of their writing.
Former President Jimmy Carter tells of the
sheer fun he had learning to use his new
word processor after he left the White
House and began to write a series of
```

18. Insert a footnote. Press ^ **[F7] 1** (version 5.0 users press **1** again) and type

```
Carter, Jimmy, and Rosalynn Carter,
Everything to Gain (New York: Random
House, 1987), p. 18.
```

Press **[F7].**

19. Continue with the paper. Do not press Return; continue with the same paragraph.

```
Professionals in practically all walks of
life have found that a PC and a word
processing package do more than merely
speed up the typing process. They actually
aid their ability to communicate.
     Word processing traces its roots back
into data processing and typewriting, but
it was the invention of the transistor in
1948 by John Bardeen, Walter Brattain, and
William Shockley of Bell Laboratories and
its use in the microcomputer in the early
1970's that really propelled word
processing into its current state of
popularity. That current state includes
numerous vendors retailing word processing
software; in fact the February 29, 1988,
issue of PC Magazine reviews 55 packages.
With so many products to choose from, how
does the potential buyer know which to
select? One approach is to go with the
industry standard; the so-called IBM of
word processing software.
```

Press **Return** *twice.* Continue the paper.

```
THE INDUSTRY STANDARD?
     A few years ago WordStar was the
standard in American offices. Its
mail-merge and spelling checker came at an
additional cost, but today its vendor,
MicroPro, offers those features and many
others as part of the standard package
called WordStar Professional, Release 4.0,
retailing at $395.00. Currently the
```

```
industry leader in sales is WordPerfect,
by Wordperfect Corp., selling for $495.00.
```

20. Insert a footnote. Press ^ **[F7] 1** (version 5.0 users press **1** again) and type

```
Seymour, Jim, "Word Processing: Fast,
Flexible, and Forward Looking," PC
Magazine, Feb. 29, 1988, pp. 92-104.
```

Press **[F7].**

21. Continue with the paper. Do not press Return; continue with the same paragraph.

```
Wordperfect is described as featuring easy
import of files created in other leading
programs, mail-merge, outlining,
redlining, table of authorities, unlimited
toll-free telephone support, plus an
energetic Wordperfect forum on CompuServe,
offering on-line advice, utilities, and
free updates of program add-ons.
```

22. Insert a footnote. Press ^ **[F7] 1** (version 5.0 users press **1** again) and type

```
Ibid., p. 324.
```

Press **[F7].**

23. Continue with the paper. Do not press Return; continue with the same paragraph.

```
To quote Dr. Edward Mendelson, a
contributing editor of PC Magazine and a
professor of English at Columbia
University, "If you use Wordperfect,
you're using the industry standard. It has
supplanted the once-standard WordStar, and
with good reason."
```

24. Insert a footnote. Press ^ **[F7] 1** (version 5.0 users press **1** again) and type

```
Mendelson, Edward, "Wordperfect," PC
Magazine Feb. 29, 1988, p. 326.
```

Press **[F7].**

25. Continue with the paper. Press **Return** *twice* and type

```
SUMMARY AND CONCLUSION
    Word processing can trace its recent
history from the early 1970's and has been
greatly affected by the boom in personal
computer sales, especially since the
introduction of the IBM PC in August of
1981. The IBM PC legitimized the
microcomputer industry to the rest of the
world and established the preeminence of
the Intel 8086 family of processors and
the Microsoft MS-DOS operating system.
```

26. Insert a footnote. Press ^ **[F7] 1** (version 5.0 users press **1** again) and type

```
Williams and Welch, p. 205.
```

Press **[F7].**

27. Continue typing the paper. Do not press Return; continue with the same paragraph.

```
Since then, dozens of word processing
packages have been marketed and word
processing has spread from the secretary's
desk to the desks of the executive and the
home office worker. WordPerfect is now the
industry standard, but WordStar and many
others are also popular. The laser printer
and desktop publishing software now make
it possible for individuals to produce
high-quality documents with just a few
hundred dollars worth of hardware and
software.
```

Step 5: Save the document.

Press **[F10]** and name the document

```
B:TERMtah.DOC
```

substituting your initials for tah.

Edit the Document

Step 1: Spell check the document to find spelling errors.*

Press ^ **[F2] 3** to check the entire document. If necessary, insert the disk containing Spell and spell check the document.

*Users of L-WP should check for spelling errors manually.

Step 2: Do a global Search and replace the word "Wordperfect" with "WordPerfect" without confirmation of each word replacement.

a. Move to the beginning of the document. Press **Home Home Up Arrow.**

b. Press **Alt-[F2].** At the prompt

```
w/Confirm? (Y/N) N
```

type

```
N
```

c. At the prompt

```
→Srch:
```

type

```
Wordperfect
```

Press **[F2].**

d. At the prompt

```
Replace with:
```

type

```
WordPerfect
```

Press **[F2].** Within a few seconds, the word is replaced and you can continue editing.

Step 3: Print the document.
Press **Shift-[F7] 1** to print a copy of the document stored in RAM.

Step 4: Proofread the document.
Check the document carefully and mark any errors and awkward page breaks.

Step 5: Correct any errors.

a. Correct any errors, using the Insert and Delete commands.

b. You can edit footnotes by giving the Footnote command, selecting the edit option, and pressing the number of the footnote to be corrected.

c. If necessary, insert a conditional page break. For example, if the page break came directly under the subsection title "SUMMARY AND CONCLUSION," as in Figure 5-7, place the cursor on the line directly above the title, in the first column. Version 4.2 users, press the Page Format command, **Alt-[F8],** and select the Conditional End of Page,

9

Type

10

for the total number of lines to keep together. Press **Return.** The page break will be placed directly above the title.

Version 5.0 users should press **Shift-[F8] 4 2 10** and press **Return** until the document reappears.

Save the Document

Use the Save Macro (Alt-S) or the Save command ([F10]) to save the document.

Print the Document

Before printing the term paper, check the paper alignment in the printer for proper spacing. Make sure you use a printer ribbon that has enough ink to print a clear image. Use paper that is as close to standard typing paper as possible. Wide "green bar" paper (computer paper with green bars) should be avoided. If you need to use bond paper and your printer will not accept single sheets of paper, some stores carry continuous feed computer bond paper with connected sheets of paper for printers. If you use continuous feed paper, you will need to "burst" or separate the perforated pages for your printed report. Be sure to make a copy of your report before submitting it.

Step 1: Select the Print options.

a. Use the Print command to print the document using the Printer Control options. Press **Shift-[F7] 4.**

b. Print two copies of the document. Version 4.2 users:

1. At the Print Control screen, choose Select Print Options by pressing

   1

2. At the Select Print Options screen, choose Number of Copies by pressing

`2`

3. Press

   `2`

   and press **Return** *twice.*

4. At the Print Control screen, choose the Print option by pressing

   `P`

   and then enter the name of the document to be printed. Type

   `B:TERMtah.DOC`

   substituting your initials for tah. Press **Return.**

   Version 5.0 users: at the Print menu, press **N 2 Return 3** and enter the document name, B: TERM tah. DOC, substituting your initials for tah. Press **Return** until you return to the document.

Exit WordPerfect After you have printed the document successfully, exit WordPerfect using the Exit command. Press **[F7].**

After the system prompt has reappeared, remove your disks from the disk drive.

SUMMARY

Lesson 5 discussed some of the advanced word processing applications available with today's software packages, including mail merge, spell checking, electronic thesaurus, windows, multiple document editing, outlining, text marking for table of contents, indexing, lists, and macros. The lesson also addressed the difficult problem of selecting the word processing software package best for you. The four-step, general problem-solving approach can help you decide. First, determine what your goals and word processing needs are. Second, gather data about features and costs. Third, actually test the software before you buy. Fourth, purchase the software that best fits your goals and then practice using it. Use the checklist of word processing features for help regarding creating, editing, formatting, printing, and other concerns.

EXERCISES

1. Define the following terms:

mail merge operations	master file	dictionary
secondary merge	outline processors	electronic thesaurus
primary merge file	spelling checker	grammar checker

window	users groups	multiple windows
footnote	electronic bulletin boards	separate formatting program
endnotes	information centers	proportional printing
table of contents	"shrink-wrap" licenses	compressed print
index	bundled software	print spooling
concordance file	copy-protected software	keyboard macros
table of authorities	fully formed graphics	
citation		
macro		

2. Matching

a. mail merge	An explanatory comment or reference note at the bottom of a page, keyed to a specific part of the text on the page.
b. multiple document editing	A program that compares each word in a document to a stored list of properly spelled words.
c. grammar checker	The ability to work on two documents at one time.
d. electronic thesaurus	A set of commands, instructions, or text stored as a group and executed by pressing a few keys or evoking the name.
e. spell checker	Scans the document and flags suspected errors such as placement of periods, verb agreement, and double negatives.
f. footnote	An outline, including page numbers, of the contents of a long document.
g. table of contents	A tool for looking up alternative terms, including synonyms, antonyms, and related terms.
h. macros	Inserts fields, files, and keyboard input into specific places in a form to automate the production of documents.

3. Prepare a short paper using some of the manuscript preparation techniques described in Lesson 5. Include in the paper the advantages of using these computerized techniques. How much time do you think you saved?

4. Review several issues of such popular microcomputer magazines as *Byte, PC, PC World,* and *Personal Computing* and report on the articles that review word processing software. Find information about three word processing software packages. Note the name, cost, operating system needed, and other hardware and storage requirements for each.

   NAME: ______________________________

   COST: __________ OPERATING SYSTEM NEEDED: __________

   PRIMARY STORAGE REQUIREMENT: __________________

   OTHER HARDWARE REQUIREMENTS: __________________

   ____

   NAME: ______________________________

   COST: __________ OPERATING SYSTEM NEEDED: __________

   PRIMARY STORAGE REQUIREMENT: __________________

   OTHER HARDWARE REQUIREMENTS: __________________

   ____

   NAME: ______________________________

   COST: __________ OPERATING SYSTEM NEEDED: __________

   PRIMARY STORAGE REQUIREMENT: __________________

   OTHER HARDWARE REQUIREMENTS: __________________

   ____

5. Interview three frequent users of word processing software. Ask them how they selected the particular package they are now using. (A user may be an individual or an organization.) Ask what features are most important to them and why. Make special note of the particular goals each person or organization wants to accomplish with the word processing system.
6. Visit several microcomputer stores in your area to see which word processing packages are available and which ones are the most popular with the store's customers and why. Take along the checklist provided earlier in this lesson and use it to compare at least three different word processing software systems.
7. Find out if there are any microcomputer users groups in your area. How were the groups formed, and what activities do they sponsor?
8. Determine if one or more electronic bulletin boards are available in your area. Find out what types of services are available on the bulletin

boards. Do users advertise hardware and software for sale? Can users ask for help from other bulletin board users regarding problems they are having with their word processing system?

9. Prepare your own term paper or report by completing the tutorial, including the following changes:
   a. Instead of a page heading, insert a page footing. Make sure the page numbering is in the right-hand corner of the page.
   b. Have the page heading printed with boldface print enhancement.
   c. Underline all section headings.
   d. After you have completed the term paper or report, open a new file and write a one-to-two page report on the differences between preparing a paper using a typewriter and using a word processor. If the report fills only one page, make sure to turn the page numbering off.
   e. Print both reports.

THREE
ELECTRONIC SPREADSHEETS

The three chapters in Part III focus on the concepts and techniques employed in the effective use of electronic spreadsheets. You will discover what electronic spreadsheets are, what their basic components are, how they originated, and how to recognize potential spreadsheet applications. You will learn how to properly design spreadsheets so they can be efficiently used for "What if?" analysis. Electronic spreadsheet software packages contain commands to create, revise, format, print, and store spreadsheet files.

Along the way you will learn by using Lotus 1-2-3, currently the most popular spreadsheet software package. The tutorials explain the specific Lotus 1-2-3 commands and describe step by step how to load, revise, print, and save the revised spreadsheets on your own file disk. By the time you complete the tutorials and exercises you will be prepared to recognize potential uses of electronic spreadsheets and design and create your own spreadsheets using Lotus 1-2-3. Because you will learn concepts, not just memorize specific commands, you will also be ready to consider other commercial spreadsheet software packages, such as SuperCalc, VP-Planner, Symphony, Quattro, and Excel, plus spreadsheet software that will be created in the future.

SOFTWARE SPECIFICATIONS

Harcourt Brace Jovanovich has made available to adopters of the VP-Planner Supplement that is available with this textbook the educational version of a Lotus 1-2-3 work-alike, VP-Planner Plus. Please see page 547 of Appendix B and page 5 of the VP-Planner Supplement for information about the capabilities of this software package.

6
Fundamental Concepts of Electronic Spreadsheets

LESSON OUTLINE

WHAT IS AN ELECTRONIC SPREADSHEET?

The electronic spreadsheet is to numbers and formulas what word processing is to words. An **electronic spreadsheet** is an all-purpose tool that can be used to help solve almost any problem involving numbers and formulas. The most common business application is budgeting, but the potential applications are limited only by your imagination. In physical terms, an electronic spreadsheet is an electronic version of a paper spreadsheet (Figure 6-1).

A paper spreadsheet is simply a large sheet of paper on which rows and columns are laid out in a grid on standard forms. The paper spreadsheet has been used for years to prepare tables, budgets, and other forms of analysis. Information is handwritten and corrected by hand.

The unique characteristics of the electronic spreadsheet, however, make it much more powerful and versatile than its paper counterpart. For one thing, electronic spreadsheets are generally much larger. Spreadsheet size ranges from 64 to 9,999 or more rows and from 32 to 256 or more columns. One of the most popular electronic spreadsheets, Lotus 1-2-3 (Figure 6-2), can provide over 2 million cells, depending on the primary storage capacity of the microcomputer.

A **cell** is formed by the intersection of a row and a column. Each cell can be visualized as a storage location where you can store text, values, or formulas. The large number of cells allows space for a vast amount of information on one spreadsheet. For example, monthly budget projections for the next five years can be produced on one electronic spreadsheet instead of on a 5-foot-wide sheet of paper.

Along with the advantage of size, electronic spreadsheet software has dozens of built-in formulas or functions. Electronic spreadsheets include mathematical, statistical, and financial formulas that permit you to analyze the data contained on the spreadsheet quickly, easily, and accurately. These formulas can be used simply by entering the formula name. All formulas, no matter how complex, will be calculated accurately and within a short time.

FIGURE 6-1 An example of a paper spreadsheet. Notice the number of rows (the numbered horizontal lines) and columns (the numbered vertical lines) available on a standard spreadsheet. Electronic spreadsheets offer many more rows and columns.

Income Statement for
Associated Technologies Incorporated
For the Year Ended December 31, 1990

	1	2	3	4
Revenue from Sales				
Gross sales		500000		
Less returns & allowances		7000		
Less discounts		3000		
Net sales			490000	
Cost of Goods Sold				
Inventory, January 1, 1990		55000		
Purchases	252000			
Less returns & allowances	5000			
Less discounts	3000			
Net purchases		244000		
Total merchandise for Sale		299000		
Less merchandise inventory,		35000		
December 31, 1990				
Cost of goods sold			264000	
Gross Profit on Sales			226000	
Operating Expenses				
Selling Expenses				
Salaries - sales	60000			
Advertising	10000			
Depreciation - Fixtures	1000			
Packaging	4000			
Total selling expenses		75000		
Administrative Expenses				
Salaries - administrative	55000			
Salaries - office	12000			
Rent expense	4000			
Depreciation - office equip.	1000			
Total administrative expenses		72000		
Total operating expenses			147000	
Net income before taxes			79000	
Federal income taxes			14950	
Net Income after Taxes			64050	

FIGURE 6-2 The paper spreadsheet from Figure 6-1 converted to its electronic equivalent.

```
b   ----------------A---------------:B:-----C-----:---D----:----E---:
 1 INCOME STATEMENT FOR
 2 ASSOCIATED TECHNOLOGIES INCORPORATED
 3 FOR THE YEAR ENDED DECEMBER 31, 1990
 4
 5 Revenue from Sales
 6   Gross Sales                                     $500,000
 7     Less Returns and Allowances                     $7,000
 8     Less Discounts                                  $3,000
 9   Net Sales                                                 $490,000
10
11 Cost of Goods Sold
12   Inventory, Jan. 1, 1990                          $55,000
13   Purchases                              $252,000
14     Less Returns @ Allowances              $5,000
15     Less Discounts                         $3,000
16      Net Purchases                                $244,000
17
18   Total Merchandise for Sale                      $299,000
19     Less Merchandise Inventory                     $35,000
20       December 31, 1990
21       Cost of Goods Sold                                    $264,000
22
23 Gross Profit on Sales                                       $226,000
24
25 Operating Expenses
26   Selling Expenses
27     Salaries-Sales                        $60,000
28     Advertising                           $10,000
29     Depreciation-Fixtures                  $1,000
30     Packaging                              $4,000
31       Total Selling Expenses                       $75,000
32
33   Administration Expenses
34     Salaries-Administrative               $55,000
35     Salaries-Office                       $12,000
36     Rent Expense                           $4,000
37     Depreciation-Office Equip              $1,000
38       Total Adm. Expenses                          $72,000
39
40 Total Operating Expenses                                    $147,000
41
42 Net Income Before Taxes                                       79,000
43 Federal Income Taxes                                          14,950
44
45 Net Income After Taxes                                        64,050
```

Another advantage of electronic spreadsheets is flexibility. Changes can be made quickly and easily on a spreadsheet because all the information, including the values and formulas, once inserted, is stored electronically in primary storage. In fact, changes are so easy to make that electronic spreadsheets are widely used to test the effect of changes. This is called **"What if?" analysis.** For example, you may construct a spreadsheet to project your room and board costs for the next school year. Then you can test how the changes in expenses (rent, utilities, deposits, food) and incomes (jobs, grants, loans, parental support) affect your plans. You are essentially asking "What if I get a more expensive apartment?" "What if I get a part-time job?" and "What if I spend less on my car?"

A specialized type of "What if?" analysis is called **sensitivity analysis.** A result, such as net profit, is calculated at various levels of some other variable or set of variables, such as selling price or advertising expense, to see how much net profit changes with a small change in the selling price or advertising expense. If a small change in selling price results in a large change in net profit, then net profit is said to be highly sensitive to the selling price. Alternatively, if net profit changes very little or not at all when advertising expenses change, then net profit is insensitive to advertising expenses.

In summary, electronic spreadsheets are much more versatile than their paper counterparts. Errors can be easily corrected; data can be changed simply by a new value being typed in a cell; the contents in some cells can be determined by formulas, and the formulas can be recalculated easily. The work space provided by an electronic spreadsheet is large. The biggest advantage offered, however, is the ability to help decision makers try out alternatives. Once an electronic spreadsheet is properly built, it is so easy to ask numerous "What if?" questions that decision makers can try out more possibilities and, it is hoped, make more informed decisions.

BASIC COMPONENTS OF AN ELECTRONIC SPREADSHEET

The basic components of an electronic spreadsheet are rows, columns, cells, labels, values, variables, and formulas.

A **row** is a horizontal area across a spreadsheet; a **column** is a vertical area from the top of a spreadsheet to the bottom. Most electronic spreadsheet software packages state their capacity in terms of the maximum number of rows and columns allowed (see Figure 6-3).

The space formed by the intersection of a column and row is called a **cell.** Each cell can hold a value (number), formula (expression), or label (text). Most spreadsheet packages use letters to name the columns and numbers to identify the rows. Cell location is indicated by the column letter and row number—sometimes referred to as the cell **address.** For example, in Figure 6-3, the cell B8 would be located in column B (the second column from the left side of the spreadsheet) and in row 8 (the eighth row from the top of the spreadsheet). A group of adjoining cells that form a square or rectangular pattern is called a **range.** A range is similar to a block in word processing. Ranges are usually referred to by the cells marking the top left and bottom right of the range. Figure 6-4 shows a range in Lotus 1-2-3. In *(a),* cell B7 is the top left of the range and cell E19 is the bottom right. Therefore the range coordinates are B7 to E19, or B7.E19.

Some software, including Lotus 1-2-3, Excel and VP-Planner permit ranges to be named so they can be referred to by name rather than by cell coordinates. In a similar fashion, a series of keystrokes can be placed in a

FIGURE 6-3 A column and a row on the screen of an electronic spreadsheet. The column is vertical while the row is horizontal. A cell is the intersection of a column and a row. The cell pointer is located in the active cell where entries will be placed.

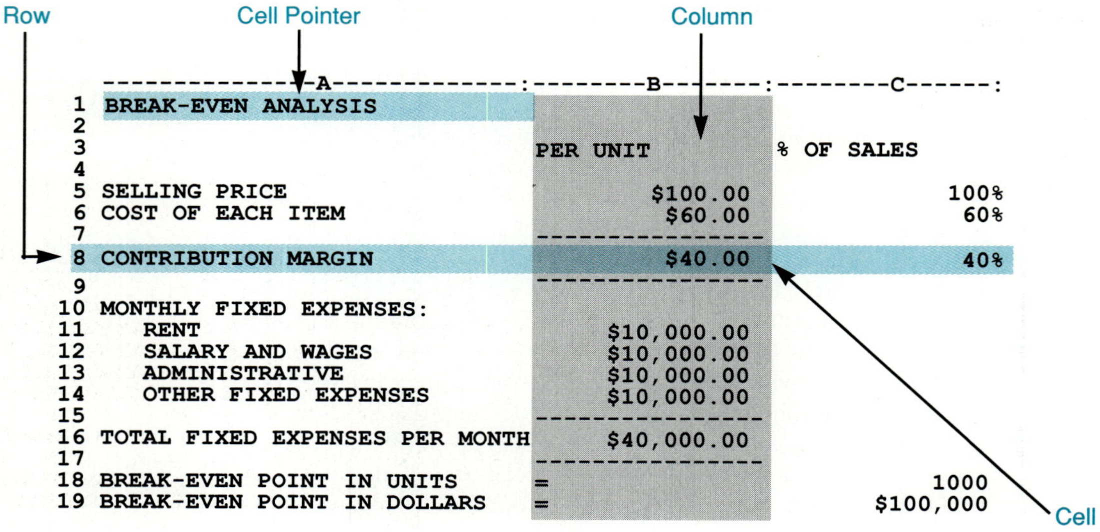

spreadsheet, grouped together, and labeled. Such a grouping of spreadsheet commands is called a **macro.** The user can execute the commands by invoking the macro name.

The far upper left-most cell on a spreadsheet, cell A1, is referred to as the **Home position.** The cell where the cell pointer is currently located is called the *current* or *active* cell. For example, in Figure 6-3, cell A1 is the current cell.

A **label** is any descriptive text used primarily to provide headings for the rows and columns. For example, in Figure 6-5, A1, A8 through A20, and A6 through F6 are labels. They are all text (alphabetic characters), and they describe the contents of the rows and columns. Numbers such as dates and years can also be labels. The numbers are forced to be text by the insertion of a label-prefix character before the number is typed. Since labels, values, and numbers are justified differently in the cell, sometimes it is advantageous to have numbers treated as text. The label-prefix character differs from software package to software package. Lotus 1-2-3 and VP-Planner use a single quote mark (').

A **constant value** is a number that is entered in the spreadsheet as data. Values that do not change when the formulas are recalculated are called **constants.** Values that decision makers can alter are called **decision variables;** they do not vary as the model is run, but the decision maker may change them before running the model again. In Figure 6-5, for

FIGURE 6-4 **A range is a rectangular or square block of cells. Part *(a)* shows a range; *(b)* is not a range since the cells do not form a continuous square or rectangle.**

```
E19: 625                                                        POINT
Enter range to format: B7..E19

                A                   B         C         D        E
1    INCOME AND EXPENSE STATEMENT FOR MARCH 1990
2    ==================================================================
3    OPERATING ACCOUNT EXPENSES  CURRENT   EXPENSES BUDGETED CUM.
4                                MONTH     TO       EXPENSES ACTUAL
5                                EXPENSES  DATE     TO DATE    1989
6    ------------------------------------------------------------------
7    Salaries & Wages               43223    361043    37850   337845
8    Health Insurance                1470     11409    12040    12553
9    Retirement                       778     13398    16400    14243
10   Social Security                 3176     26248    22720    25846
11   Unemployment Insurance             0       972     2160      594
12   Workers' Comp. Insurance         409      3272     2280     1799
13   Other Employ. Benefits            88      1888      880     5715
14
15   SUBTOTAL SALARIES & WAGES      49144    418230    94330   398595
16
17   Office Supplies                  409      5080     4800     3900
18   Food & Beverages                 410      5197     3960     4304
19   Other Supplies                    80       742      840      625
20
                                                    CALC
```

(a)

```
B7: 43223                                                       READY

                A                   B         C         D        E
1    INCOME AND EXPENSE STATEMENT FOR MARCH 1990
2    ==================================================================
3    OPERATING ACCOUNT EXPENSES  CURRENT   EXPENSES BUDGETED CUM.
4                                MONTH     TO       EXPENSES ACTUAL
5                                EXPENSES  DATE     TO DATE    1989
6    ------------------------------------------------------------------
7    Salaries & Wages               43223    361043    37850   337845
8    Health Insurance                1470     11409    12040    12553
9    Retirement                       778     13398    16400    14243
10   Social Security                 3176     26248    22720    25846
11   Unemployment Insurance             0       972     2160      594
12   Workers' Comp. Insurance         409      3272     2280     1799
13   Other Employ. Benefits            88      1888      880     5715
14
15   SUBTOTAL SALARIES & WAGES      49144    418230    94330   398595
16
17   Office Supplies                  409      5080     4800     3900
18   Food & Beverages                 410      5197     3960     4304
19   Other Supplies                    80       742      840      625
20
                                                    CALC
```

(b)

FIGURE 6-5 An example electronic spreadsheet showing labels, values, and variables. Formulas that produced the variables are not visible in this screen display but are shown in Figure 6-6.

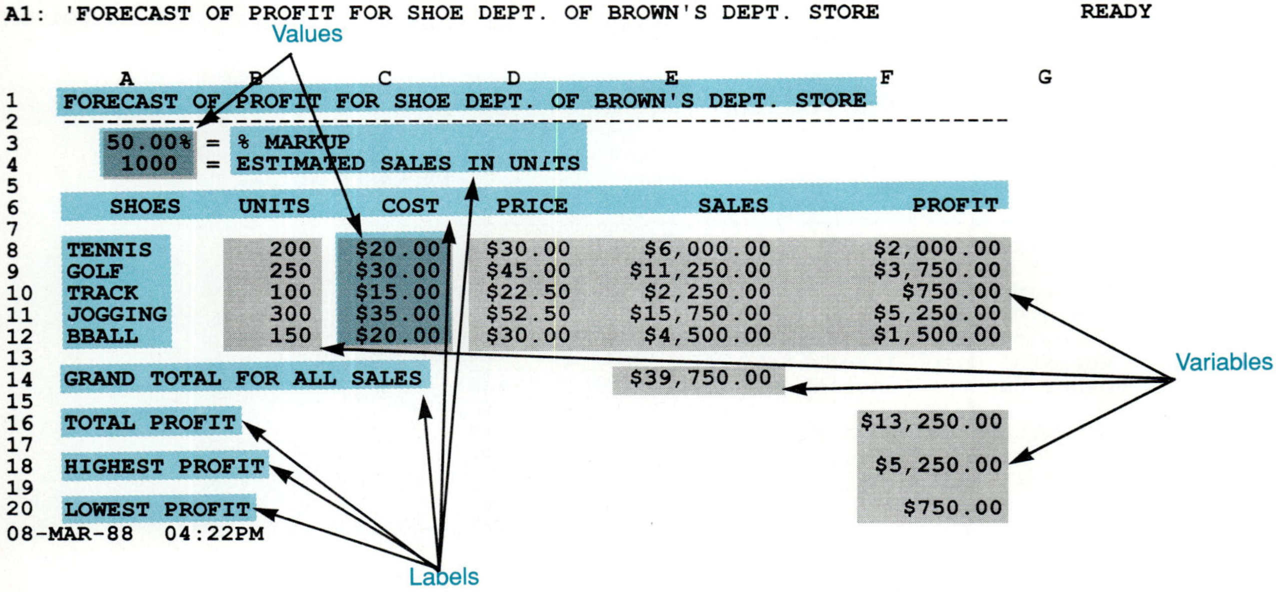

example, the amounts entered for cells A3, A4, and C8 through C12 are constant values. They are entered directly into the worksheet and are not the result of a formula. A3 and A4 are also called decision variables, because the decision maker will likely want to change them to test the effect of various levels of markup and estimated sales on profit.

Variables are quantities that are the result of a calculation by a formula. Every time the values that make up the formula are changed and the formula is recalculated, the resulting variable is subject to change. For example, if you multiply price by number of units, the result is a variable. It varies according to the price and also the number of units. In Figure 6-5, for example, the contents of cells B8 through B12, D8 through F12, E14, and F16 through F20 are variables.

A **formula** is the symbolic expression of a rule or principle or calculation, such as +B5*D5. This formula would be interpreted by the computer as "Take the value stored at cell B5, multiply it by the value stored at cell D5, and store the results in the current cell (that is, the cell where the pointer is now located)." Figure 6-6 is a view of the spreadsheet in Figure 6-5 with the formulas visible. Notice that the variables shown in Figure 6-5 are the result of the formulas stored in the spreadsheet. Also notice that most of the formulas contain cell addresses rather than values.

FIGURE 6-6 The same electronic spreadsheet as in Figure 6-5 with the formulas visible. Notice that the formulas refer to the cell addresses as well as the values. The Lotus command to produce this output from a prepared spreadsheet is /Worksheet Global Format Text. Also, the columns might need to be widened using /Worksheet Global Column-Width followed by the necessary column width.

```
A1: 'FORECAST OF PROFIT FOR SHOE DEPT. OF BROWN'S DEPT. STORE              READY


        A        B        C        D           E               F          G
1   FORECAST OF PROFIT FOR SHOE DEPT. OF BROWN'S DEPT. STORE
2   ----------------------------------------------------------------
3      50.00% = % MARKUP
4        1000  = ESTIMATED SALES IN UNITS
5
6      SHOES    UNITS      COST     PRICE          SALES            PROFIT
7
8   TENNIS        200        20 +$A$3*C8 +B8*D8        +E8-(B8*C8)
9   GOLF          250        30 +$A$3*C9 +B9*D9        +E9-(B9*C9)
10  TRACK         100        15 +$A$3*C1 +B10*D10      +E10-(B10*C10)
11  JOGGING       300        35 +$A$3*C1 +B11*D11      +E11-(B11*C11)
12  BBALL         150        20 +$A$3*C1 +B12*D12      +E12-(B12*C12)
13
14  GRAND TOTAL FOR ALL SALES        @SUM(E8..E12)
15
16  TOTAL PROFIT                                       @SUM(F8..F12)
17
18  HIGHEST PROFIT                                     @MAX(F8..F12)
19
20  LOWEST PROFIT                                      @MIN(F8..F12)
08-MAR-88   04:35PM
```

Electronic spreadsheets also have several built-in formulas or **functions** to calculate averages, standard deviations, net present values, numerous trigonometric functions, and many other frequently used calculations. Labels, values, and variables are visible in the cells on the spreadsheet. While formulas are usually not visible on the screen in the cells, they are visible on the first line in the control panel when the cursor is placed in the cell. Notice in Figure 6-5 that the formula is visible in the control panel.

HOW DID ELECTRONIC SPREADSHEETS GET STARTED?

The first popular electronic spreadsheet, VisiCalc, was invented by Dan Bricklin while he was a student at Harvard Business School. He had spent many hours with a paper spreadsheet and a calculator totaling columns of numbers for course homework in accounting and finance. Convinced there had to be a better way, he and Bob Frankston developed a computer program to do the calculations. The program provided the equivalent of a paper spreadsheet with 63 columns and 254 rows. Their invention, VisiCalc, revolutionized spreadsheet work and, some computer experts claim, was the single biggest reason for the boom in sales of microcomputers during the late 1970's and early 1980's.

In the years since VisiCalc's introduction, spreadsheets have become more flexible, powerful, and versatile. Spreadsheets such as Lotus, Quattro, and Excel have taken advantage of the increased processing capabilities of newer, more powerful 32-bit computers. These software programs contain options such as larger electronic spreadsheets, computer graphics (pictures or charts drawn by the computer program), and data management (the ability to select certain files and extract and output information according to a particular format) within the same package. Add-on software (enhancements to the original software, sold separately by either the original software manufacturer or other software houses), such as HAL, an English language interface for Lotus, and Freelance, a sophisticated graphics package, greatly enhance the capabilities of electronic spreadsheets.

CHARACTERISTICS OF POTENTIAL ELECTRONIC SPREADSHEET APPLICATIONS

Spreadsheets are valuable to mathematicians, statisticians, and chemists, and in a variety of scientific and engineering areas. Currently, the most widespread business use of electronic spreadsheets is in the area of budgets and planning. Business plans often involve calculating anticipated budgets, looking at sales figures or other income items, recalculating budgets, and then repeating the process over and over. In fact, it is the use of electronic spreadsheets in business decision making that has helped create the massive demand for microcomputers in business, even in organizations that have used large computer systems for many years.

Some personal uses of electronic spreadsheets include personal financial management (household budgeting, checkbook balancing, computation of financial net worth, income tax preparation, investment analysis, insurance analysis, and record keeping), small business accounting, property management, scheduling, check lists, mailing labels, inventory, payroll. Teachers use electronic spreadsheets in place of grade books to record and calculate students' total points and percentages. Church treasurers find them handy to keep track of budgets and donations. Wine connoisseurs can even keep track of their wine cellars. What is the common thread among all these diverse uses of electronic spreadsheets? When should you use an electronic spreadsheet?

A potential spreadsheet application must first be a problem that can be expressed in mathematical terms and laid out in rows and columns. There are five other characteristics to look for as well: repetition, editing, revisions, variable and fixed parts, and need for quality appearance. If the problem is mathematical, can be expressed in columns and rows, and involves one of these five characteristics, it is probably worth your time and effort to use an electronic spreadsheet.

Planning, designing, and entering an electronic spreadsheet requires an investment of time. This investment starts paying off when you use the spreadsheet several times. Therefore, one of the characteristics for a potential electronic spreadsheet application is **repetition.** You may be able to finish a one-time-only project using your calculator, pencil, and paper spreadsheet faster than you could design an electronic spreadsheet. However, if you need to do the same spreadsheet task over and over or even every day, week, or month, you should consider using an electronic spreadsheet. You may find it easier than using paper and pencil, even in single-use applications.

Editing involves correcting typing errors; moving labels, formulas, and figures; and, in general, refining the electronic spreadsheet. Before electronic spreadsheets, it was not unusual for someone to erase and re-erase items on a paper spreadsheet until the paper had holes in it. Often the entire spreadsheet would have to be thrown away and redone completely. In contrast, on an electronic spreadsheet, columns and rows can be moved, inserted, deleted, and changed with ease. Users correct errors by simply reentering the right data. Some electronic spreadsheets permit you to edit an individual entry by commands similar to a text editor in a word processor. Once changed, row and column totals and other formulas are recalculated either automatically or on request.

Revisions are purposeful changes made in the spreadsheet. Frequently they are caused by organizational changes in assumptions about plans, updated information, and the desire to examine "What if?" situations. As a decision maker looks at the results of a budget or other planning document, questions often arise about the consequences of changes. What if sales were to drop by 10 percent? What if production had to be increased by 25 percent? These and many other revisions can be handled easily by electronic spreadsheet software. You can adjust the appropriate figure or formula and have the electronic spreadsheet recalculate the answers quickly. This ability to adjust the spreadsheet quickly to answer current or future questions is one of the strongest reasons why electronic spreadsheets are so popular.

Many potential spreadsheet applications are composed of *fixed and variable parts.* A **fixed part** does not change as other parts change. For example, most budget reports consist of income and expense account titles and various formulas that do not vary from month to month. A **variable part** is subject to frequent change as the result of some other change. For example, the cost of goods sold may change each month in direct proportion to increases or decreases in sales. Electronic spreadsheets allow for some of the data to be fixed or constant, while other data are variable and based on some formula. Some electronic spreadsheet software permits you to protect row and column labels and formulas to prevent accidental changes. These frequently used labels and formulas can be arranged to create a master electronic spreadsheet. The master electronic spreadsheet is copied each time a new spreadsheet is started. The format is then standardized. These standardized formats for electronic spreadsheets are called **templates.**

The need for a **quality appearance** is also a strong reason for using electronic spreadsheet software. If you are presenting a budget to the company president, you are concerned about the appearance of the work, as well as the accuracy of the data and computations. Some word processing software will permit the spreadsheet to be printed within a word processing report, provided the results of the spreadsheet have been output to a disk file.

In addition to these characteristics, some people simply enjoy working with electronic spreadsheets. They find that they try out more options and discover relationships among various technical or managerial issues they might not have discovered unaided by electronic spreadsheet software. You might find you enjoy doing work that is neat and accurate and you may discover many applications not considered here.

THE MAJOR FUNCTIONS OF ELECTRONIC SPREADSHEETS

There are five major functions common to electronic spreadsheet software:

1. Creating
2. Revising
3. Formatting
4. Printing
5. File handling

Each electronic spreadsheet software package has its own set of commands to carry out these functions. However, all share these common groups of commands.

Creating an electronic spreadsheet involves the opening of a file and the original entry of labels, formulas, and values in the spreadsheet. Once a file has been opened, a blank spreadsheet appears, ready for data entry. The user creates the spreadsheet by moving the cursor to the desired cells; typing in the needed labels, formulas, and values; and saving the spreadsheet on disk.

Revising is the deletion, replacing, and/or insertion of entries in an electronic spreadsheet. Entries can be changed by cell, column, or row, including the changing of formulas, values, or variables. Most spreadsheet software provide an editing command that allows the user to make minor changes to the cell entries. Additional rows and columns can be inserted easily.

Formatting is the adjustment of the display formats. Format options available in many electronic spreadsheet software include numeric display (integer, general, or exponent numbers), precision (number of decimal places shown in a number), column width, and display of label borders and formulas.

Printing is producing a copy of a spreadsheet as output. The output can be sent to a disk file where it is stored or to a printer where a paper copy (hard copy) is printed.

File handling includes the consolidation and loading of files into other spreadsheets. Files can be copied, deleted, or moved.

ESSENTIAL FEATURES OF ELECTRONIC SPREADSHEETS

The four essential features you need to know about before creating your own spreadsheet are the screen, cursor movement, scrolling, and data entry.

The Screen

When most electronic spreadsheets appear on the screen, there are a row of letters across the top of the screen and a column of consecutive numbers down the left side of the screen.

The screen can be divided into two parts: the control panel and the window worksheet. The **control panel** consists of lines displaying information about where you are, what you are doing, and what you can do next (see Figure 6-7). It is located at the top of the screen in Lotus 1-2-3 and at the bottom in VP-Planner.

The first line of the control panel indicates the current cell's address and contents, telling you where you are on the worksheet. The second line is sometimes referred to as the **prompt line.** When the slash key is pressed, the prompt line shows menu items and prompts. When entries are typed, it shows the newly entered cell contents. The third line shows the submenus and descriptions of the menu items highlighted in the second line. Prompts are also displayed on this line.

As you enter new labels, formulas, or values, they appear on the second line. When you press the Return key, the contents of the line disappear and then reappear within the cell.

The **worksheet** is the large area on the screen where the actual work of the spreadsheet is done. There are two parts of the worksheet: the border and the cell.

The **border** is the edge of the worksheet that defines the rows and columns. It is located along the top and left sides of the screen. In standard practice spreadsheet software names the columns A, B, C, and so forth. Rows are usually named 1, 2, 3 and so on. Lotus 1-2-3 names the 256 columns A, B through Z, AA, AB through AZ, BA, BB through IV. Rows are numbered 1 through 8,192. As discussed earlier, using the combination of the column and row names, you can locate each cell individually using the cell address. For example, the cell in the upper left-hand corner of the worksheet is column A, row 1. Thus, the cell is referred to by an address called A1. The "A" and "1" are called the **coordinates.** The cell to the

FIGURE 6-7 The Lotus 1-2-3 screen or worksheet window. Notice the control panel with the current cursor position, the mode indicator displaying the current mode of operation, the date and time indicator, and the status indicator displaying the recalculation mode.

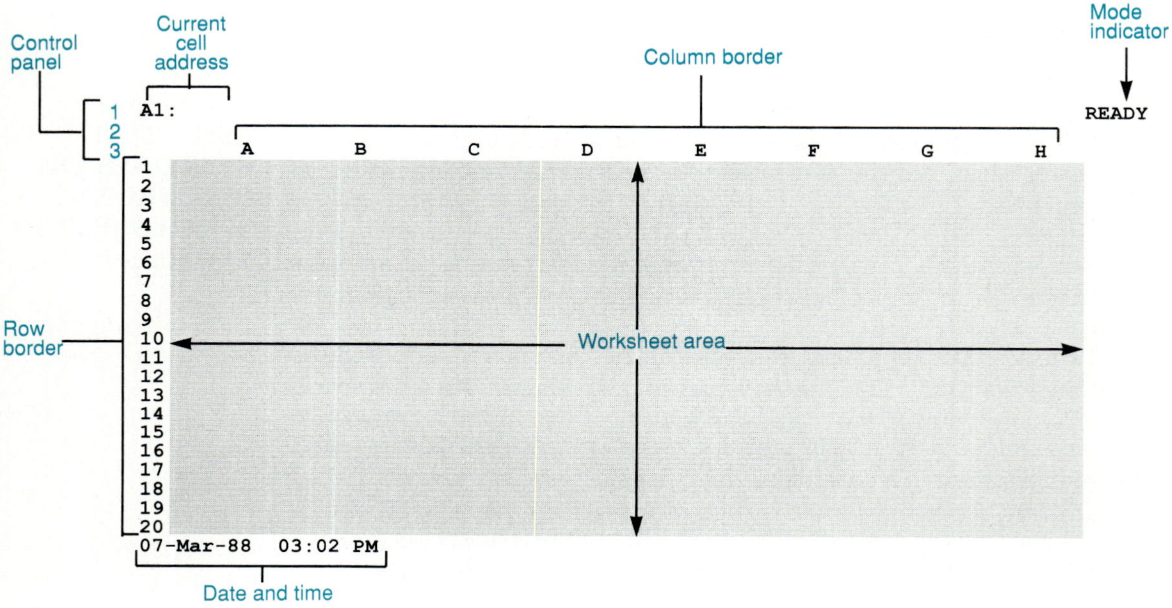

immediate right of A1 is labeled B1. The cell immediately below cell A1 is labeled A2, and so on.

The **cell pointer** is the highlighted bar on the worksheet. It marks the active cell location where data can be entered. VP-Planner calls it a **cell cursor.** Its width depends on the width of the column it is currently occupying. The short blinking line within the cell pointer is the **cursor.** When data is entered into a cell, the cursor in the cell pointer moves to the second line of the control panel, the entry line.

Some electronic spreadsheet software have editing features that permit you to change the contents of a cell by using a built-in text editor. After you give the appropriate editing command ([F2] in Lotus), the current cell's contents will appear on the entry line for editing. When you have made the necessary changes, press the Return key; the edited cell's contents disappear from the entry line and appear in the cell (see Figure 6-8).

After you press the slash (/) key, the second line shows a list of ten available commands. Figure 6-9 is an illustration of the prompts available to

FIGURE 6-8 The built-in text editing feature of Lotus 1-2-3. Notice how the lengthy formula can be edited without the user having to reenter the entire formula.

```
A16: (C2) [W12] @IF(A10=0,A9*(1+A7)^A8,@NA)                           EDIT
@IF(A10=0,A9*(1+A7)^A8,@NA)

        A          B        C        D        E        F        G
1   COMPOUND INTERST ANALYZER
2   ==============================================================
3   To use this analyzer you need to know three of the following:
4   Simple interest rate, term in months, present value, or future value
5   ==============================================================
6             8  <--Simple annual interest rate, 0 if unknown
7         0.67%  <--Yield this monthly interest rate
8            88  <--Term in months, enter 0 if unknown
9          5000  <--Present value, enter 0 if unknown
10            0  <--Future value, enter 0 if unknown
11  ==============================================================
12  Solution:
13           NA  <--Mo. int. rate or yr. rate of--->      NA
14           NA  <--Term in months
15           NA  <--Present value
16    $8,972.44  <--Future value
17
18
19
20
07-Mar-88  09:06 PM
```

you on the Lotus and VP-Planner main menu of commands when you press the slash key. Table 6-1 lists the commands and gives a short explanation of each. Advanced spreadsheet software have a rich and highly developed set of commands, all with full English-language prompts. Remember, you can get even more information about either VP-Planner or Lotus command options by pressing the Help key, [F1].

Before you start using the worksheet on your screen, you need to understand the fundamentals of moving the cursor around the spreadsheet, entering data into the cells, and changing the contents of the cells.

Cell Pointer Movement

Cell pointer movement is the changing of the position of the cell pointer to permit the entry or editing of labels, formulas, or values in cells. In electronic spreadsheets, the cell pointer can be moved one cell at a time, up, down, right, or left. Some electronic spreadsheets let you tell the cell pointer to go to a specific cell through the GOTO command ([F4] in Lotus). Most spreadsheet software have some provision for moving the cell pointer directly to the edges of the worksheet. Some keyboards, such as the one on the IBM PC, use the Home key to return the cell pointer to cell A1.

Table 6-2 (p. 220) lists the cell pointer movement commands in Lotus on MS-DOS microcomputers. The ^ sign indicates that you should press

Command option

Description of highlighted command

```
D26: +$D$8                                                                  MENU
Worksheet  Range  Copy  Move  File  Print  Graph  Data  System  Quit
Global, Insert, Delete, Column, Erase, Titles, Window, Status, Page
        A        B        C        D        E        F        G        H
21
22                               Through  Through  Through  Through  Through
23                               Year--   Year--   Year--   Year--   Year--
24                                     1        2        3        4        5
25                              ---------------------------------------------
26  Cumulative Investment        $11,000  $11,000  $11,000  $11,000  $11,000
27  Cumulative Savings            $5,000  $10,000  $15,000  $20,000  $25,000
28                              ---------------------------------------------
29  Net Position                ($6,000) ($1,000)   $4,000   $9,000  $14,000
30                              =============================================
31
32
33
34
35
36
37
38
39
40
```

(a)

As the main menu command option changes, the second level of options changes.

```
D26: +$D$8                                                                  MENU
Worksheet  Range  Copy  Move  File  Print  Graph  Data  System  Quit
Format, Label, Erase, Name, Justify, Protect, Unprotect, Input, Value, Transpose
        A        B        C        D        E        F        G        H
21
22                               Through  Through  Through  Through  Through
23                               Year--   Year--   Year--   Year--   Year--
24                                     1        2        3        4        5
25                              ---------------------------------------------
26  Cumulative Investment        $11,000  $11,000  $11,000  $11,000  $11,000
27  Cumulative Savings            $5,000  $10,000  $15,000  $20,000  $25,000
28                              ---------------------------------------------
29  Net Position                ($6,000) ($1,000)   $4,000   $9,000  $14,000
30                              =============================================
31
32
33
34
35
36
37
38
39
40
```

(b)

Table 6-1 LOTUS COMMAND GROUPS

Command		*Action*
/W	Worksheet	Allows user to insert or delete columns and rows, change standard column width, control order of calculation, divide screen into windows, and define other worksheet characteristics.
/R	Range	Affects groupings of cells to change display format, make cells blank, name cells, or protect cells in a range.
/C	Copy	Duplicates the contents of one or more cells into another cell or group of cells. Original cells remain unchanged.
/M	Move	Places a cell or group of cells into a new location. Contents of original cells are removed.
/F	File	Allows the saving and retrieval of spreadsheet files to and from disks. Also used to combine worksheet files, exchange data with other software systems, and maintain file directories.
/P	Print	Prepares the spreadsheet for printing by setting up the page size and margins and defining page headers and footers. Prints the worksheet.
/G	Graph	Used to define the type of graph (pie, bar, or line), define titles and legends, view the graph on the screen, and save graphs for later printing using the PrintGraph feature.
/D	Data	Allows the use of the worksheet as a database. Includes the commands for defining and using data management functions. If certain structured questions (queries) are asked, records can be sorted and selected for processing. Also, command lets user obtain certain statistical calculations, such as regression analysis.
/S	System	Temporarily suspends operations of the spreadsheet and accepts DOS commands (Release 2 only). User can then reenter 1-2-3 by typing EXIT at the system prompt.
/Q	Quit	Ends the 1-2-3 session and returns to the Lotus Access Menu.

and hold the Control (Ctrl) key and, while pressing the Control key, press the next character key.

Scrolling

Scrolling is the movement of not just the cursor but a portion of the spreadsheet on the screen. If you move the cell pointer beyond the right edge of the screen, the spreadsheet scrolls left so that another portion of it becomes visible to the right. In the same fashion, if you move the cell pointer to the bottom row on the screen and then try to move it one or

FIGURE 6-9 The Lotus main menu of commands. As the pointer highlights a command option, such as "Worksheet" in *(a)*, the third line displays a second level of options for the highlighted command. *(b)* As the pointer is moved along the line containing the main menu command options, the second level of command options changes to show the description of the highlighted command.

Table 6-2 CELL POINTER MOVEMENT COMMANDS IN LOTUS

Command	*Resulting Cursor Movement*
←	Cell left
→	Cell right
↑	Row up
↓	Row down
PgUp	Scroll window up 20 rows
PgDn	Scroll window down 20 rows
Home	Cell pointer moved to cell Al
End + arrow	Cell pointer moved to highest number cell that is not empty
[F5] + cell address	GOTO specific cell

more rows further down the screen, the spreadsheet scrolls or moves up on the screen.

The entire spreadsheet may be much larger than the part you see on the screen at any one time, thus scrolling is an essential feature for electronic spreadsheets. You can scroll up, down, left, and right. The cell pointer remains on the screen. The visible work space is called the

```
D9: (C0) +C5-(C6+C7)                                                 READY

               A                          B             C           D
5      Gross sales                                  $500,000
6        Less returns & allowances                    $7,000
7        Less discounts                               $3,000
8                                                 ------------
9      Net sales                                                $490,000
10
11   Cost of Goods Sold
12     Inventory, January 1, 1990                    $55,000
13     Purchases                          $252,000
14       Less returns & allowances          $5,000
15       Less discounts                     $3,000
16     Net purchases                                $244,000
17                                                -----------
               A                          B             C           D
45   Federal income taxes                                        $14,950
46                                                           ------------
47   Net Income after Taxes                                      $64,050
48
49
50
```

FIGURE 6-10 **A worksheet that is longer than one screen size (approximately 20 lines) displayed using multiple windows. The second window is marked by the horizontal column designation. Although the worksheet is larger than one screen, notice how different segments of the worksheet are visible in each window. The bottom line is visible in the lower window.**

window. This window is normally about 8 columns wide and about 20 rows deep, depending on the software, the size of the monitor screen, and the width of the columns. Some electronic spreadsheets permit multiple windows. The monitor screen is split into two or more sections, either vertically or horizontally. A portion of the spreadsheet can be displayed in each section. Cells that are not normally seen on the same screen can be viewed at the same time. The windows can be synchronized (meaning both windows scroll in unison) or unsynchronized. Figure 6-10 is an example of a Lotus 1-2-3 worksheet with multiple windows.

Data Entry

Data entry is the process of putting text (labels), formulas, and numbers (values) into cells in a spreadsheet. The type of data in a cell determines what can be done with the cell. For example, cells with text cannot be used to calculate values. Attempting to use labels in a formula can result in an error message. With some spreadsheet software, before you type the first character to be entered in the cell, you must press a key that will tell the software what is being entered. However, most versions of spreadsheet software, including Lotus 1-2-3, SuperCalc4, and VP-Planner, automatically convert label and number cell entries into the proper data type.

A cell can contain text (a label), expressions (formulas), or numbers (values). Table 6-3 contains examples of the different types of cell contents.

You place *alphabetic text* in a cell by simply typing the entry. Lotus automatically classifies the entry as a text or label entry. If you want to have a number, such as a year (1989), treated as a label, enter a single quotation mark (') before typing the number. This signals to Lotus that it should consider the number as text. Most electronic spreadsheets have ways to "fool" the software into considering numbers as text.

You enter a *value* by simply typing the number. A positive number is placed in a cell by starting the entry with a number. Negative numbers are preceded by a minus sign (−). If the first character you type is a digit, a plus (+), a minus (−), a decimal point (.), or a left parenthesis, Lotus assumes you are entering a value or a formula.

You enter a *formula* in Lotus by first entering a plus sign (+) and then simply typing it as is. After you have entered the number or formula and have pressed Return, the software looks at the entry. If the entry is

Table 6-3 EXAMPLES OF DIFFERENT KINDS OF CELL CONTENTS

Text	*Values*	*Formulas*
Income	45,000	@SUM(B5.B8)
'1990	90	@IF(B5>B6),0,1
Expenses	43	+57+45+2
Name	.006	+B5*(C5−C4)

acceptable, the software will perform the computation and the result will appear in the current cell. If the number or formula is not acceptable, a beep will sound, an error message will be displayed, and the erroneous formula will be displayed as text. The entry must be changed by replacing, editing, or deleting.

After you have keyed the label, formula, or value, you need to direct the software to place the entry into the cell and store it in working storage. You do this by pressing the Return key or an arrow key that places the entry into the cell and moves the cell pointer simultaneously.

Remember, **built-in functions** are formulas already stored in the spreadsheet program that save you the trouble of writing your own formulas to perform commonly used formulas or functions, such as calculating the sum of the values in several cells, finding the maximum value in a row or column or area, calculating the average value in some area of the spreadsheet, and calculating the net present value (one that is especially popular in business classes). Built-in functions greatly enhance the usefulness of electronic spreadsheets by making complex analysis available quickly and easily.

Most electronic spreadsheets require a special key to distinguish built-in functions from other formulas and text. Lotus 1-2-3 requires the "at" sign (@). For example, in @SUM(C1.C7), C1 is the beginning of the range of cells to be summed, and the cell following the period, C7, is the end of the range. Some spreadsheets use a colon (:), while Lotus 1-2-3 uses a period (.) or double period (..) to separate the beginning cell and the ending cell in a range.

Most spreadsheet software packages, such as SuperCalc4, Excel, and Quattro, contain a hundred or more built-in functions. Lotus 1-2-3 has an extensive repertoire of them.

A function has two parts: the name of the function and its arguments. The name describes what the function does. Arguments are values used in the calculations. For example,

```
@AVG(B4:D6)
```

function name   function arguments

AVG is an abbreviation for Average. In the argument above, the range is separated by a colon. Other arguments may require commas. Arguments can be any of the following:

- Numeric Value, such as 123.89
- Cell Range Name, such as SALES
- String Value, such as "Total Sales"

- Formula, such as (D3*37)/12
- Cell Address, such as B27
- @Function, such as @SUM(C1..C10)
- Cell Range, such as C1..C10

The eight categories of built-in functions in Lotus 1-2-3 are

1. Mathematical functions
2. Statistical functions
3. Logical functions
4. Financial functions
5. Date and Time functions
6. Special functions
7. String functions
8. Database Statistical functions

Many of the functions will be described later. For now, review some of the most commonly used Lotus built-in functions in Table 6-4.

Correcting errors involves correcting typographical errors and other mistakes on the spreadsheet. Errors can be corrected three ways depending on the timing and scope of the error. If you make an error while typing something in the prompt area and you detect the error before entering it in a cell, backspace over the error and type in the correct copy. Press the Return key or arrow key to enter the data into the cell indicated by the cursor position.

If you have already entered data into a cell and then discover an error, replace the cell contents simply by moving the cell pointer to the cell with the error and entering the correct data. Your newly typed data will replace the entry that was previously stored in the cell.

You can avoid retyping complex cell contents, such as a long formula, by using available editing features. For example, Lotus 1-2-3 uses the Edit key [F2]. The cell contents will appear on the entry line. Simple editing features, such as inserting (adding new characters within the line by pushing over existing text), deleting (removing the characters and the space occupied by the characters), and overwriting (replacing characters with new characters), permit you to change the cell contents without retyping the entire entry.

If you start typing a command for a cell and decide not to complete it, you can change your mind by pressing the Escape key (Esc) once or twice. The contents of the entry line will be gone, and you can start fresh.

Table 6-4 COMMONLY USED LOTUS BUILT-IN FUNCTIONS

Function	*Brief Description*
@IF(cond,x,y)	Puts *x* in cell if *cond* is true and *y* in cell if *cond* is false.
@NOW	Puts serial number for current date and time in the cell. If cell is formatted as a date field, then serial number is converted to standard date format.
@CTERM(int,fv,pv)	Number of compounding periods for an investment of present value *pv*, to grow to future value *fv*, earning a fixed periodic interest rate *int*.
@FV(pmt,int,term)	Future value of series of equal payments, each of amount *pmt*, earning periodic interest rate *int*, over the number of payment periods in *term*.
@IRR(guess,range)	Internal rate of return for the series of cash flows in *range*, based on the approximate percentage *guess*.
@NPV(int,range)	Present value of a series of future cash flows in *range*, discounted at periodic interest rate *int*.
@PMT(pmt,prin,int,term)	Amount of the periodic payment *pmt* needed to pay off principal *prin* at periodic interest rate *int* over the number of payment periods in *term*.
@PV(pmt,int,term)	Present value of a series of equal payments, each of amount *pmt*, discounted at a periodic interest rate *int* over the number of payment periods in *term*.
@RATE(fv,pv,term)	Periodic interest rate necessary for present value *pv* to grow to a future value *fv* over the number of compounding periods in *term*.
@TERM(pmt,int,fv)	Number of payment periods of an investment, given the amount of each payment *pmt*, the periodic interest rate *int*, and the future value of the investment *fv*.
@AVG(list)	Average of the values in *list*.
@COUNT(list)	Number of non-blanks entered in *list*.
@MAX(list)	Maximum value in *list*.
@MIN(list)	Minimum value in *list*.
@STD(list)	Standard deviation of the values in *list*.
@SUM(list)	Sum of values in *list*.
@VAR(list)	Population variance of the values in *list*.
@NA	No value available for this cell.
@ROUND(x,n)	*x* rounded to *n* places.

If you have accidentally entered data in a cell that was to be left blank, put your cell pointer on the affected cell and enter /Range Erase. The cell will be left blank.

Of course, if you decide to start over again, you can always remove the entire worksheet from primary storage with the /Worksheet Erase command in Lotus 1-2-3. The worksheet is erased from the screen and from RAM. Removing the contents of a spreadsheet is a drastic step. It deletes from RAM everything you have put on that spreadsheet. If you plan to reuse the spreadsheet, it is important to save it on a disk (/File Save in Lotus) before clearing it from the screen. Most software verifies the /Worksheet Erase command to prevent you from erasing a worksheet by mistake. Lotus will prompt you:

```
No Yes
Do not erase the worksheet; return to READY mode.
```

Only if you answer "yes," the current worksheet is cleared and you get to start fresh.

Relative Addressing in Lotus 1-2-3

As previously described, cells are addressed by the column letter followed by a row number, such as C2 for the third column, second row. When cells are included in formulas, the user needs to know the differences among a relative address, an absolute address, and a mixed address. A **relative address** can be adjusted or changed as the formula or cell is moved or copied. Such movement may also be caused by a row or column being inserted or deleted. Relative addressing also makes it possible to copy formulas so that they are adjusted to their relative placement in the worksheet. Relative addresses would commonly be used in summing the columns in a particular row. By your copying that formula into several other cells down a column, the formula will automatically adjust so that it sums the columns in successive rows down the spreadsheet. For example, if cell D1 contains the formula A1+B1+C1 and is copied down column D from D1 to D2 through D4, the formulas will be these:

Cell	Formula
D2	A2+B2+C2
D3	A3+B3+C3
D4	A4+B4+C4

An **absolute address** stays fixed regardless of any copying or moving of cells. In Lotus 1-2-3 and VP-Planner, you denote absolute addressing by typing a dollar sign ($) before both the column and the row components of the cell address (e.g., $B$4, +$H$21+$J$10). The cell addresses that have a dollar sign before them will not change, even if columns or rows are inserted or deleted. In formula-driven spreadsheets, the decision variables are often conveniently located at the upper left-hand corner of the worksheet and, when included in a formula, are often designated as absolute addresses. The examples in the tutorial and exercises that follow will illustrate this further.

A **mixed address** allows the user to fix either the column portion or the row portion of the cell reference, leaving the other component relative.

In Lotus 1-2-3, the part that is absolute or fixed must be preceded by a dollar sign ($). For example, $A4 has column A fixed but the row component can be adjusted; A$4 has row 4 fixed but the column component can be adjusted.

Copying

The Lotus 1-2-3 Copy command is one of the most important commands in the building of models. Often, models used in business contain a set of formulas that can be repeated for each month, product, employee, or customer. For example, if sales for a particular firm are expected to grow at the rate of 2% per month, then the sales formula would be 1.02 multiplied by sales from the previous month. The user would define the formula for January of a particular year and then copy that formula for February through December, allowing the cell reference to adjust so that for February it computes January sales times 1.02, for March it computes February sales times 1.02, and so forth. The user would want to refer to the growth rate in absolute terms and the month in relative terms.

To understand the power of the /Copy command, consider a firm's Profit and Loss Statement that may contain 40 to 50 rows of accounting items, many of which are determined by formula. Once the user defines the formulas needed for one month, say, January, then the Copy command can be used to copy the pattern of formulas for the next eleven months, thus saving hours of typing and reducing possible typing errors.

The 1-2-3 Function Keys

As explained in Lesson 2, IBM and IBM-compatible personal computers have on the keyboard ten or twelve keys called function keys. A **function key** is a specialized key whose function is controlled by the software. Rather than being labeled Del or Shift or Ctrl, function keys are labeled F1, F2, F3, . . . F10. Such keys will have a different function depending on the software you are using. Table 6-5 lists the functions assigned to each of the function keys by Lotus 1-2-3 and VP-Planner.

Many of these functions will be described more fully in the tutorials. However, for now you may find the [F1] Help key especially useful. If you want to learn more about the 1-2-3 system at any time, simply press [F1]. When you are using any command and need a hint or further explanation regarding that command, simply press [F1] and a Help message that relates to that specific command will appear. To end a Help session, press Escape.

The second function key that beginners often find helpful is the [F2] Edit key. If you find, after entering a formula, that you have made an error, press the [F2] key to edit the formula in the current cell instead of retyping the entire formula. When you are editing an entry, the Home key takes you to the beginning of the line, End takes you to the end of the line, and Return completes the entry.

Table 6-5 THE LOTUS 1-2-3 FUNCTION KEYS

Function Key		*Lotus 1-2-3 Function*
[F1]	Help	Get Help information regarding the current operation.
[F2]	Edit	Edit the contents of the current cell.
[F3]	Name	Name a range.
[F4]	Abs	Insert Absolute Address code ($) into formula.
[F5]	GoTo	Go To a particular cell address.
[F6]	Window	Switch Windows.
[F7]	Query	Repeat /Data Query command.
[F8]	Table	Repeat /Data Table command.
[F9]	Calc	Recalculate the spreadsheet.
[F10]	Graph	Display a graph.
[F11] or Alt+[F1]	Compose*	Compose accented and other special characters in Lotus International Character Set.
[F12] or Alt+[F2]	Step*	Turn on single step mode for macro execution for macro debugging.

***In Release 1 of Lotus 1-2-3, [F11] or Alt+[F1] enables the Step mode. See the Release 1 Lotus manual for more details.**

DESIGNING A SPREADSHEET

Design is an important part of learning how to use electronic spreadsheets. Spreadsheet design is a process where selected needs and goals of an organization or individual are defined and subsequently expressed in a spreadsheet. A spreadsheet is a type of model. A **model** is a symbolic representation or example used to help visualize or test something that cannot be easily or directly observed. A spreadsheet can be considered a model in that it allows us to utilize the "What if?" approach to problem solving. It enables us to see what would happen if a particular value in the spreadsheet were changed. The following principles are involved in the development of any good model and apply to designing a good spreadsheet as well:

1. Define goals.
2. Keep it simple.
3. Keep it flexible.
4. Be complete.

The first step in designing a spreadsheet is to *define your goals.* What is the spreadsheet supposed to tell you? You have to know what you want. This starts with a careful definition of the problem to be solved.

Most people find it difficult to define a problem. Usually they get trapped into describing, and trying to fix, only the symptoms. The key is to formulate a good problem statement. A good problem statement should be accurate, precise, and complete. It should include all the relevant information needed for the solution. The problem should be stated in a simple declarative sentence. All facts relevant to the problem should be included, along with all assumptions. Figure 6-11 is an example of how a spreadsheet model may be requested.

Simplicity is the second principle of a good model. Some people try to include all the variables found in the real-life situation; however, the purpose of using a model is to make a complex problem simpler and easier to understand. For instance, if your task is to model the budget for a firm, including all the factors that influence national inflation will force you to spend a great deal of time creating the model and will probably raise more questions about the validity of the model than it will answer. Instead, you

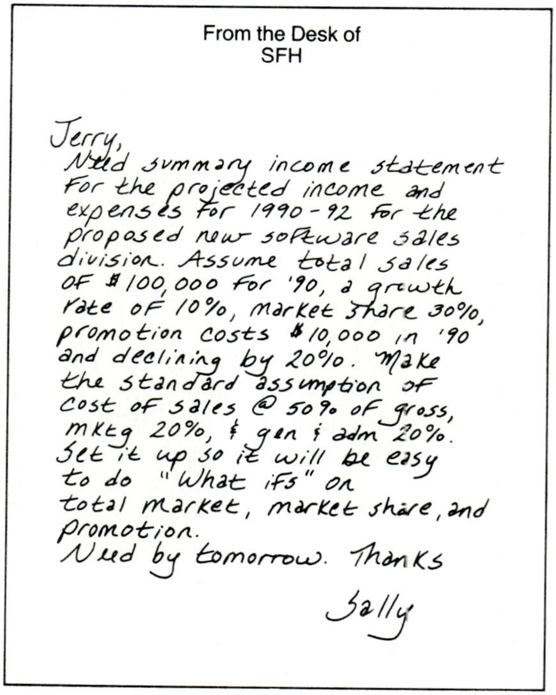
From the Desk of
SFH

Jerry,
Need summary income statement for the projected income and expenses for 1990-92 for the proposed new software sales division. Assume total sales of $100,000 for '90, a growth rate of 10%, market share 30%, promotion costs $10,000 in '90 and declining by 20%. Make the standard assumption of cost of sales @ 50% of gross, mktg 20%, & gen & adm 20%. Set it up so it will be easy to do "What ifs" on total market, market share, and promotion.
Need by tomorrow. Thanks

Sally

FIGURE 6-11 A boss may request an assistant to prepare a summary income statement, so she and other managers can make some decisions about a new proposed department, in this case a software sales department.

should simply state your assumptions about inflation and focus on the firm's likely sales and expenses. The general rule is *Keep it simple.* Figure 6-11 could include many other variables, such as income taxes, depreciation, and how software sales may affect other sales. However, Sally Hanson doesn't seem to think such things are really that important to the critical decision, that is, whether or not to go into the retail software business. Therefore, the spreadsheet should not include these other variables, but instead should be kept simple.

Keeping a model *flexible* means considering other uses of the model whenever possible. Could your spreadsheet be designed to be useful in other departments as well as your own? Can your spreadsheet be easily changed to accommodate "What if?" questions or changes that are likely to occur over time? Will you be able to use the spreadsheet next month or next quarter? To design the model with flexibility in mind, you must consider more than your immediate needs.

A *complete* model includes all the truly important formulas and relationships needed to describe the situation being modeled. Leaving out a potentially large expenditure, for example, could make your budget very unrealistic. Sometimes the rule of being complete seems to run counter to the rule of keeping it simple. The trick is to do a complete job in the simplest form possible. If a model has been designed with clear goals and is simple, flexible, and complete, it should gradually gain acceptance by demonstrating usefulness over time. In the spreadsheet requested by Sally Hanson, the model would not be complete without consideration of such major factors as cost of sales ($150,000), promotion ($10,000), marketing ($60,000), and general and administrative expenses ($60,000) in 1990. It is also important, in this example, to consider more than one year and the various growth rates or, in the case of the special software promotion expenses, rate of decrease.

Now that we have considered the four principles of good model building, let's consider the steps used to design effective spreadsheets. These steps are really variations of the process of systems analysis and design used with information systems.

1. Determine the desired result or goal of the spreadsheet.
2. Define the formulas, values, and variables needed to produce the desired result.
3. Design the desired output to be produced as a result of the model.
4. Hand-check the calculations.
5. Enter data into the electronic spreadsheet.
6. Check the spreadsheet calculations.

Step 1: Determine the desired result or goal of the spreadsheet.

Goals should be put down in writing and should be as specific and quantifiable as possible. Can the goal be expressed in a number? If the goal of the spreadsheet is to aid in making a decision (such as "At what price should we market our product?") then determine what variables will be involved. For example, if the goal of the spreadsheet is to determine which bank to use for a loan, variables such as amount of the principal, interest rate charged, and payback period might be the decision variables, and monthly payments and total cost of the loan might be the appropriate resulting variables.

The goal in our example is to be able to test the consequence of various levels of estimated total market, market share, and promotion on net income before taxes.

Step 2: Define the formulas, values, and variables needed to produce the desired result.

Think about how the problem might be expressed in formulas. Before inserting a number as raw data, ask if this value depends on, or can be determined by, some relationship to another variable. Such a process results in a spreadsheet that is formula driven. Ideally, the user should be able to just change a decision variable, such as interest rate in the loan example mentioned in Step 1, and the rest of the spreadsheet should be so formula driven that the new result is produced automatically.

The formulas needed in our example include

ESTIMATED TOTAL MARKET FOR 1991 = ESTIMATED TOTAL MARKET FOR 1990 * 1.15

ESTIMATED TOTAL MARKET FOR 1992 = ESTIMATED TOTAL MARKET FOR 1991 * 1.15

MARKET SHARE FOR 1991 AND 1992 = MARKET SHARE FOR PREVIOUS YEAR * 1.10

ESTIMATED $ SALES = (ESTIMATED TOTAL MARKET) * MARKET PORTION

COST OF SALES = (ESTIMATED $ SALES) * 50 PERCENT

GROSS MARGIN = (ESTIMATED $ SALES) − (COST OF SALES)

PROMOTION FOR 1991 AND 1992 = PROMOTION FOR PREVIOUS YEAR − (PROMOTION FOR PREVIOUS YEAR * 0.2)

MARKETING = (ESTIMATED $ SALES) * 20 PERCENT

GENERAL AND ADMINISTRATIVE = (ESTIMATED $ SALES) * 20 PERCENT

TOTAL EXPENSES = PROMOTION + MARKETING + (GENERAL AND ADMINISTRATIVE)

NET INCOME BEFORE TAXES = (GROSS MARGIN) − (TOTAL EXPENSES)

Step 3: Design the desired output to be produced as a result of the model.

Spreadsheet design is greatly influenced by the end user (the person using the result) and the content of the spreadsheet. Will that person want all of the details or just the decision variables and the result? The spreadsheet **planning guide** shown in Figure 6-12 can help in designing a layout of the spreadsheet.

	A	B	C	D	E	F	G	H	I	J
1										
2										
3										
4										
5										
6										
7										
8										
9										
10										
11										
12										
13										
14										
15										
16										
17										
18										
19										
20										
21										
22										
23										
24										
25										
26										
27										
28										
29										
30										

FIGURE 6-12 A blank planning guide for a spreadsheet. Notice how the columns and rows are similar to those on an electronic spreadsheet. However, columns cannot be widened, so sometimes it is necessary to squeeze in formulas.

FIGURE 6-13 A suggested model for designing formula-driven spreadsheets. As a rule, titles are placed on the top so the contents of the spreadsheet are easily seen; row labels are placed in the left column; the decision variables that are likely to be changed in the "What if?" analysis are in the upper left corner; and the results are in the lower right corner. Very large spreadsheets should begin with a directory showing the user the cell addresses for each major portion of the spreadsheet.

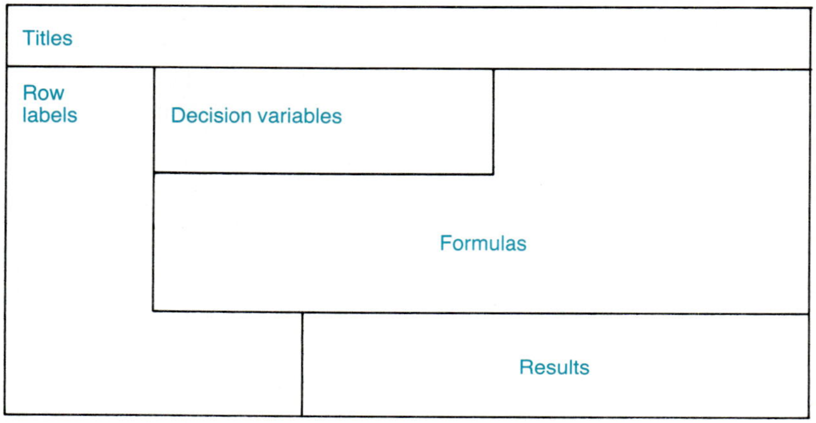

As a rule of thumb, decision variables are usually put in the upper left-hand corner of the spreadsheet, and resulting variables are usually placed at the lower right, the so-called "bottom line" (see Figure 6-13). This general design lets users easily see the decision variables affecting the process and the resulting variables. Such designs are also easy to change and recalculate if the spreadsheet you use has been designed to be formula driven. **Formula-driven** spreadsheets get results from formulas rather than from directly entered data. For example, in Figure 6-14, a simple spreadsheet for calculating gross pay, the basic formula for gross pay is HOURS * PAY PER HOUR. There are two ways of getting the results (GROSS PAY): We could just multiply the actual amounts, 40 * 8.00, or we could define two variables and then use the variables in the formula, HOURS = 40, PAY PER HOUR = 8.00, HOURS * PAY PER HOUR = 320.00. In a spreadsheet, instead of variable names, we generally use the cell addresses. Therefore, if the value for HOURS is in cell C10 and the value for PAY PER HOUR is stored in cell B10, the formula is written and the results are shown in cell D10, which has become +B10*C10. Note that the asterisk denotes multiplication. While this may seem like a long way to go for a simple answer, the advantage of this approach becomes obvious when you are designing large spreadsheets or spreadsheets with many potential changes, such as templates. By putting the decision variables in the upper

FIGURE 6-14 ***(a)*** **An example of an electronic spreadsheet to calculate a simplified payroll.** ***(b)*** **The formulas rather than the results are shown, so you can see how the spreadsheet has been designed to be formula driven.**

```
      |      A      ||    B   ||      C      ||       D      ||    E   ||    F   ||    G   ||
1     PAYROLL SUMMARY FOR JUNE, 1990
2     Today's Date      7/ 1/90              FICA                    .8%
3     Beginning Date    6/24/90              State Tax              1.0%
4     Ending Date       6/30/90
5     Days in Report          7
6     ==================================================================
7     NAME            PAY PER   HOURS        GROSS PAY     NET PAY
8                     HOUR
9     ------------------------------------------------------------------
10    Albert, J.          8.00           40        320.00    314.24
11    Bell, J.            7.55           37        279.35    274.32
12    Bonnaci, R.         9.00           40        360.00    353.52
13    Davidson, K.        8.90           39        347.10    340.85
14    Jensen, J.         10.00           40        400.00    392.80
15    Kiederlein, E.      9.50           40        380.00    373.16
16    Mahoney, M.         7.50           40        300.00    294.60
17    Nenonen, J.         8.50           38        323.00    317.19
18    Zimmerman, C.       9.00           40        360.00    353.52
19
20    TOTALS                            354       3069.45   3014.20
```

(a)

```
      |      A      ||    B   ||      C      ||       D      ||    E   ||    F   ||    G   ||
1     PAYROLL SUMMARY FOR JUNE, 1990
2     Today's Date    DATE(7,1,1990)         FICA         .008
3     Beginning Date  DATE(6,24,90)          State Tax    .010
4     Ending Date     DATE(6,30,90)
5     Days in Report  B4-B3+1
6     ==================================================================
7     NAME            PAY PER   HOURS        GROSS PAY     NET PAY
8                     HOUR
9     ------------------------------------------------------------------
10    Albert, J.      8         40           B10*C10       D10-((D10*E2)+(D10*E3))
11    Bell, J.        7.55      37           B11*C11       D11-((D11*E2)+(D11*E3))
12    Bonnaci, R.     9         40           B12*C12       D12-((D12*E2)+(D12*E3))
13    Davidson, K.    8.90      39           B13*C13       D13-((D13*E2)+(D13*E3))
14    Jensen, J.      10        40           B14*C14       D14-((D14*E2)+(D14*E3))
15    Kiederlein, E.  9.50      40           B15*C15       D15-((D15*E2)+(D15*E3))
16    Mahoney, M.     7.50      40           B16*C16       D16-((D16*E2)+(D16*E3))
17    Nenonen, J.     8.50      38           B17*C17       D17-((D17*E2)+(D17*E3))
18    Zimmerman, C.   9         40           B18*C18       D18-((D18*E2)+(D18*E3))
19
20    TOTALS                    SUM(C10:C18) SUM(D10:D18) SUM(E10:E18)
```

(b)

left and referring to the cell addresses in formulas within the spreadsheet, you can quickly change the spreadsheet by entering just a few numbers. Incorrect placement can cause erroneous results.

That is why, whenever possible or practical, spreadsheets should be designed to be formula driven. However, if a variable is used only once in a spreadsheet, it is unnecessary, and even unwise, to use that value as a variable.

Step 4: Hand-check the calculations.

Too often people assume that because something came out of a computer it is correct. The computer, if improperly programmed, can make bigger errors much faster than a human. Computers are not capable of having "hunches" or spotting results that just don't look right. Although some error flags can be built in, most errors must be discovered by the user. One helpful suggestion is to first enter numbers in the spreadsheet that are easy to calculate by hand. For example, in the loan example already mentioned in Step 1, use a loan amount of $1000, a time period of 10 years, and an interest rate of 10 percent for an easy-to-calculate result of $1000 for the total cost of the loan.

Step 5: Enter data into the electronic spreadsheet.

Some people like to start with this step. Perhaps if you are a very experienced spreadsheet builder, this approach will work. For most of us, however, the careful planning outlined in Steps 1 through 4 will pay dividends. Good spreadsheet design dictates that data be entered only after the planning and design are complete. Labels should be entered first, then formulas, and finally values.

As you enter the values, turn off the recalculation mode so the worksheet does not recalculate the entire spreadsheet every time you enter new data. This recalculation is very time consuming, especially with large worksheets. Double check to make sure you are putting the right formula in the right cell address. Carefully check formulas for proper syntax and labels for proper spelling. Although changes are relatively easy to make with an electronic spreadsheet, some errors are difficult to catch once your spreadsheet has been constructed. In the software sales example, we can see that ESTIMATED $ SALES should be $300,000 since it is 30 percent of the ESTIMATED TOTAL MARKET of $1,000,000. COST OF SALES should be checked in each year to assure it is 50 percent of ESTIMATED $ SALES, such as $150,000 in 1990. TOTAL EXPENSES can easily be added up to check the total of $130,000. NET BEFORE TAXES is GROSS MARGIN minus TOTAL EXPENSES, or $150,000 − $130,000 = $20,000 in 1990.

Step 6: Check the spreadsheet calculations.

Once the electronic spreadsheet has been constructed, turn on the recalculate mode, put in the same data as you entered in Step 4, and check the computer's results against the hand-calculated results. Be prepared to edit and correct entries. When people construct spreadsheets, experience teaches them when an answer is too far off to be reasonable. Unfortunately, computers have no such sense. **Spreadsheet auditing** is the careful checking of an electronic spreadsheet for errors, incompleteness, and inaccuracy. Even the most experienced model builder should be on the lookout for errors.

Once the spreadsheet is completed you can print it on paper or create an output file, a text file that is the equivalent of the printed

```
TO:         Sally Hanson
FROM:       Jerry Worker
DATE:       February 28, 1989
SUBJECT:    Projected Income for New Software Department

The Summary Income Statement you requested is shown below.  I
assumed the total market for software in our market area is
$1,000,000 per year and will grow at the rate of 15% per year.  I
also assumed our share of that market will be 30% in 1990 and
will grow at the rate of 10% per year in 1991 and 1992.  We will
expect to incur  extra promotion expenses for this product line
of $100,000 per year with a planned decrease of 20% in 1991 and
1992.  Marketing and general and administrative expenses are
estimated at 20% of gross sales.
    As you can see, the market, market share, and promotion costs
are all clearly identified at the top left of the spreadsheet and
the spreadsheet will automatically recalculate net income before
taxes for any value you decide to test in those variables.
Please let me know whether or not this spreadsheet meets your
approval.


 PROJECTED INCOME STATEMENT FOR NEW SOFTWARE DIVISION
 * DECISION VARIABLES       1000000.00    = EST. TOTAL MARKET IN $
 *                                  30    = % MARKET SHARE
 *                            10000.00    = PROMOTION COSTS
 ***************************************************************
                                  1990          1991          1992
  EST. TOTAL MARKET         1000000.00    1150000.00    1322500.00
  MARKET PORTION                   0.3          0.33         0.363
  EST. $ SALES               300000.00     379500.00     480067.50
  COST OF SALES              150000.00     189750.00     240033.75
                          ----------------------------------------
  GROSS MARGIN               150000.00     189750.00     240033.75

  OTHER EXPENSES:
    PROMOTION                 10000.00       8000.00       6400.00
    MARKETING                 60000.00      75900.00      96013.50
    GEN AND ADMIN             60000.00      75900.00      96013.50
                          ----------------------------------------
   TOTAL EXPENSES            130000.00     159800.00     198427.00

   NET BEFORE TAXES         $20,000.00    $29,950.00    $41,606.75
                          ========================================

To me the new venture looks profitable.  What do you think?
```

FIGURE 6-15 The output file from the Projected Income Statement worksheet incorporated within a memo.

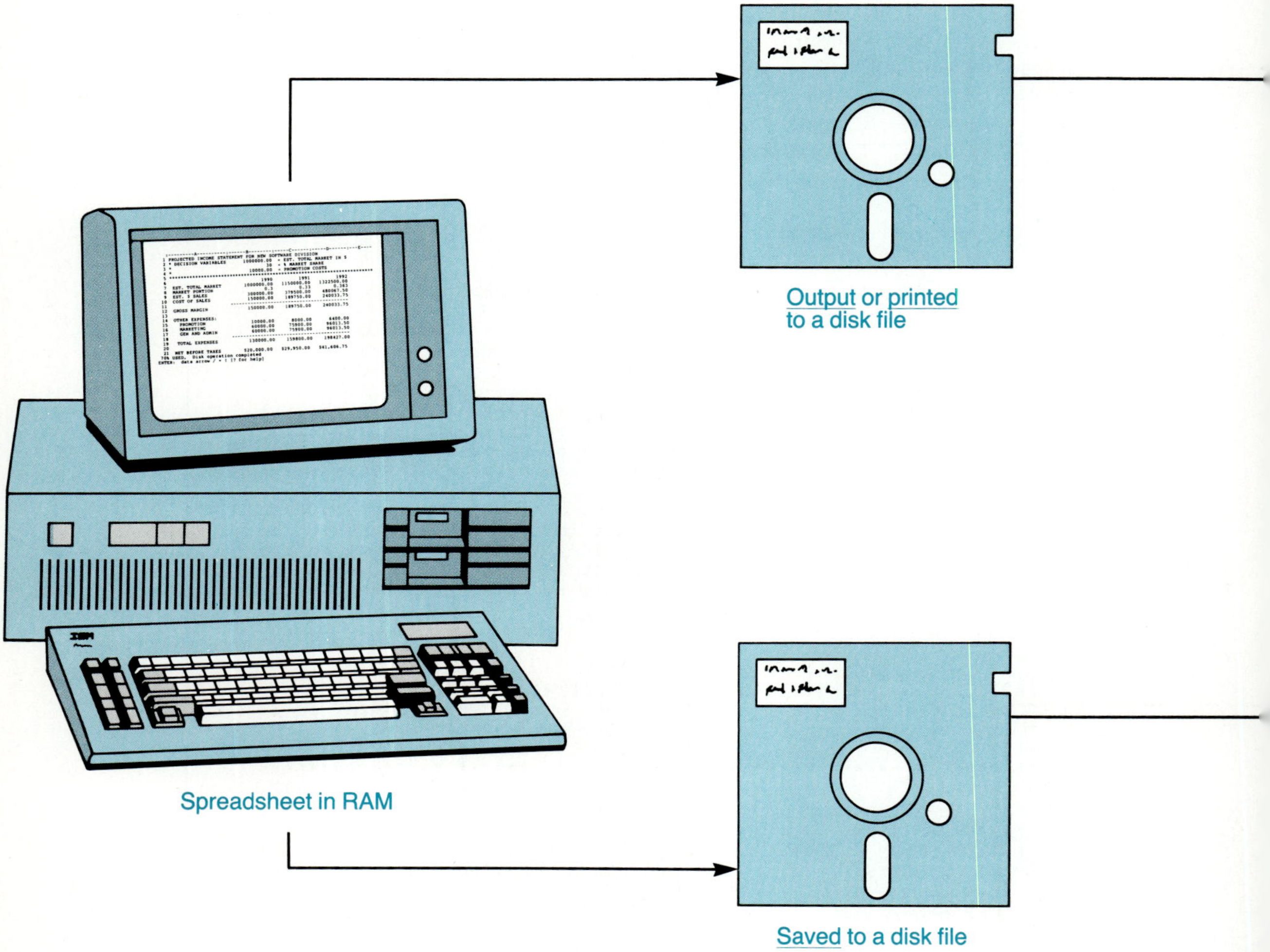

FIGURE 6-16 ***(a)*** **The user creates output files by printing the results of an electronic spreadsheet to a disk file, creating a text file. These files can then be printed within word processing documents.** ***(b)*** **When a worksheet file is saved, a copy of the spreadsheet, including the formulas, is saved on the disk and can be retrieved only by use of the spreadsheet software. Such a saved copy cannot be effectively processed by a word processor.**

TO: Sally Hanson
FROM: Jerry Worker
DATE: February 28, 1989
SUBJECT: Projected Income for New Software Department

The Summary Income Statement you requested is shown below. I assumed the total market for software in our market area is $1,000,000 per year and will grow at the rate of 15% per year. I also assumed our share of that market will be 30% in 1990 and will grow at the rate of 10% per year in 1991 and 1992. We will expect to incur extra promotion expenses for this product line of $100,000 per year with a planned decrease of 20% in 1991 and 1992. Marketing and general and administrative expenses are estimated at 20% of gross sales.

As you can see, the market, market share, and promotion costs are all clearly identified at the top left of the spreadsheet and the spreadsheet will automatically recalculate net income before taxes for any value you decide to test in those variables. Please let me know whether or not this spreadsheet meets your approval.

PROJECTED INCOME STATEMENT FOR NEW SOFTWARE DIVISION

* DECISION VARIABLES	1000000.00	= EST. TOTAL MARKET IN $
*	30	= % MARKET SHARE
*	10000.00	= PROMOTION COSTS

	1990	1991	1992
EST. TOTAL MARKET	1000000.00	1150000.00	1322500.00
MARKET PORTION	0.3	0.33	0.363
EST. $ SALES	300000.00	379500.00	480067.50
COST OF SALES	150000.00	189750.00	240033.75
GROSS MARGIN	150000.00	189750.00	240033.75
OTHER EXPENSES:			
PROMOTION	10000.00	8000.00	6400.00
MARKETING	60000.00	75900.00	96013.50
GEN AND ADMIN	60000.00	75900.00	96013.50
TOTAL EXPENSES	130000.00	159800.00	196427.00
NET BEFORE TAXES	$20,000.00	$29,950.00	$41,606.75

To me the new venture looks profitable. What do you think?

(a)

Spreadsheet can be seen by loading into RAM

(b)

spreadsheet on an electronic file, that can later be incorporated within a word processing document. In this way a spreadsheet can be a part of a memo or report. In Lotus use /Print File and provide a print filename different from the name used to save the actual spreadsheet file (see Figure 6-15, page 235). Remember that output files must be "printed" to disk files before they can be printed using word processing software. Figures 6-16*(a)* and *(b)*, pages 236–37, illustrate how output files are created.

Now let's apply these electronic spreadsheet concepts by creating a spreadsheet using Lotus.

TUTORIAL: CREATING AND PRINTING A NEW SPREADSHEET USING LOTUS 1-2-3

To complete this tutorial you need the following:

- MS-DOS system disk
- Lotus 1-2-3 system disk
- A previously formatted data disk
- A printer connected to the microcomputer

While completing this tutorial you will learn how to

- Load Lotus 1-2-3
- Create, edit, and save a spreadsheet
- Print a spreadsheet

The specific Lotus 1-2-3 commands used within this tutorial are

- 123—To load the Lotus 1-2-3 spreadsheet system into RAM.
- /C (Copy)—To copy the contents of a cell or a range of cells to another cell or range. When a formula is copied, the cell references will change relative to the appropriate row or column unless the user surrounds the constant parts of the formula with dollar signs, as in +$A$4*B10 where A4 will stay constant and B10 will be adjusted relative to the row and column.
- @SUM(range)—To use the Lotus 1-2-3 built-in function to sum or total a designated part of a row or column.
- @NOW—To use the Lotus 1-2-3 built-in function to print the current system date.
- /F S (File Save)—To store a copy of the spreadsheet on the floppy disk. You will be prompted to supply a name for the file. Like all MS-DOS

filenames, it must be eight characters or fewer, contain no embedded blanks, and have no punctuation characters.

- /P P R A1..G16 G (Print to the Printer the Range A1 through G16 Go)—Prints to the printer.
- /P F filename R A1.G16 G (Print to a disk File with filename the Range A1 through G16 Go)—Allows user to direct a copy of the output to a disk file, to be retrieved later by a word processor and edited or included in a larger report.
- /Range Format Currency 2—To change the display format so the values have dollar signs, commas, decimal points, and rounding as is customary for currency values.
- /Range Label Prefix Center—To center the text in a range of cells.
- /Range Label Prefix Right—To right justify the text in a range of cells.
- /Worksheet Column Set-width 10—To change the column width to 10. This command changes only the column where the pointer is; therefore it must be repeated for each column in which the width must be changed.
- /Q Y (Quit Yes)—To command the computer to conclude the session. It is vitally important to save your work **before** quitting, because the action of quitting causes all work in RAM to be erased immediately.

As part of this tutorial, you will also enter numeric data, alphabetic data, and labels. Simply type in numeric and alphabetic data while the pointer is at the appropriate cell and enter them into that cell by pressing Return or any of the arrow keys.

In this tutorial you are going to create a spreadsheet to analyze the cost of the payroll for the imaginary Fast Data Services, Inc. Refer to Figure 6-17 to see the planning guide for the spreadsheet to be completed in this tutorial. Notice the placement of the labels and formulas. The objective of the spreadsheet is to make it easy for a decision maker to analyze the effect of proposed new pay rates for the five hourly workers—Steve, Ken, Jim, Joe, and Cecilia—who currently earn $6.00 per hour and are asking for a raise to $7.00. The design makes it easy for the decision maker to test various "What if?" situations with different current pay rates and proposed pay rates.

Create the Spreadsheet

There are three basic steps to creating an electronic spreadsheet: (1) load the operating system into primary storage, (2) load the electronic spreadsheet software into primary storage, and (3) enter the spreadsheet contents (labels, formulas, and values) into the spreadsheet.

FIGURE 6-17 The planning guide for the first spreadsheet. Notice the placement of the labels, values, variables, and formulas.

	A	B	C	D	E	F	G	H	I	J
1	FAST DATA SERVICES, INC.									
2	EMPLOYEE PAY RATE ANALYZER									
3	----	----	----	----	----	----				
4	6	← CURRENT HOURLY PAY RATE								
5	7	← PROPOSED NEW HOURLY RATE								
6	----	----	----	----	----	----				
7			CURRENT	NEW	DOLLAR					
8	WORKER:	HOURS:	PAY:	PAY:	CHANGE					
9										
10	STEVE	10	A4 * B10	B10 * A5	D10 - C10					
11	KEN	20	A4 * B11	B11 * A5	D11 - C11					
12	JIM	15	A4 * B12	B12 * A5	D12 - C12					
13	JOE	30	A4 * B13	B13 * A5	D13 - C13					
14	CECILIA	40	A4 * B14	B14 * A5	D14 - C14					
15	----	----	----	----	----					
16	TOTALS:	@SUM (B10..B15)	@SUM (C10..C15)	@SUM (D10..D15)	@SUM (E10-E15)	← COST OF CHANGE				
17										
18										
19										
20										
21										
22										
23										
24										
25										
26										
27										
28										
29										
30										

Step 1: Load the operating system.

To load the operating system, follow the procedures described on page 72 until you see the operating system prompt (A>) on the screen. Make sure the system date and time are correctly set. As explained in earlier lessons, it may be necessary to use a separate operating system disk. If you are using a hard disk system or networked system, your loading instructions may differ. Contact your instructor or lab supervisor for more information.

Step 2: Load the electronic spreadsheet software into primary storage.

a. If necessary, remove the MS-DOS disk from drive A and insert the Lotus 1-2-3 disk into drive A and the previously formatted data disk into drive B. Latch the disk drive doors.

b. Enter the command to load Lotus 1-2-3. Type

`123`

Press **Return.** Figure 6-18 is an example of how the screen should appear.

Step 3: Enter the contents of the worksheet.

a. Take a few seconds to explore the screen and the spreadsheet. Notice the features on the screen. The letters across the top designate the columns, and the numbers down the side designate the rows.

The control panel is at the top of the screen. Remember, the first line tells you the location of the cell pointer, the second line is blank but will display either menu prompts or entries, and the third line will show additional menus and prompts.

In the upper right corner is an area called the **mode indicator.** It indicates the current status of the spreadsheet. When the word READY appears in the area, the spreadsheet is ready to accept data or commands.

In the top left corner is the pointer address, "A1." This indicates that the active cell, or the cell in which the spreadsheet cursor is currently located, is column A, row 1. To see the mode indicator change, press the **slash key (/).** The second line changes to show the

```
A1:                                                                    READY


        A         B         C         D         E         F         G         H
1
2
3
4
5
6
7
8
9
10
11
12
13
14
15
16
17
18
19
20
31-Mar-88  10:37 AM
```

FIGURE 6-18 **The Lotus 1-2-3 screen before data is entered.**

next level of menu options, and the mode indicator changes to MENU. To return to the READY mode, press **Esc** to back out of the menu.

To scroll down the worksheet to see how the borders change, press the **PgDn key.** The row numbers will change but the columns will remain the same. To scroll across the worksheet, press the **right arrow key** several times.

Move to the corners of the worksheet. Press the **End key** and then the **right arrow key.** This command will move the pointer to the last column on the far right side of the spreadsheet.

Press the **End key** and then the **down arrow key** to move the pointer to the last row.

Press the **Home key** to return the pointer to position A1.

Note that no matter where you are on the spreadsheet the display area, called the **window,** displays only 20 lines and approximately 8 columns. Since the user can change the width of the columns, the number of columns displayed in a window can vary.

Now examine the bottom center of the screen. Notice the date and time. Lotus 1-2-3 has functions that allow you to reference the time and date within the spreadsheet to provide a date for your output. As you use Lotus 1-2-3, also watch for error messages that may result from your mistakes. The computer will sound a brief beep tone and an error message will appear, providing a very brief explanation of the error. When you make an error, press the Escape key or Return to erase the error message and continue.

b. Plan the layout of the spreadsheet. The goal of this initial spreadsheet is to examine the effect of pay rate change on the total payroll of a small firm employing five workers: Steve, Ken, Jim, Joe, and Cecilia. We will assume that all five workers will be paid the same hourly rate, but each worker has been assigned to work different hours during the week: 10, 20, 15, 30, and 40, respectively.

Remember, the spreadsheet has been designed to allow the decision maker to quickly see how much it would cost to raise the workers' pay from $6 per hour, the current rate, to $7 per hour, the proposed new rate. Of course, we have made it easy to test various other "What if?" alternatives, such as $6.50 and $6.75. The hourly rate is the decision variable and should therefore be clearly labeled and placed in the upper left-hand corner where it can be easily seen and changed. The formulas for determining each employee's total wages and the total wages for all the employees should depend on the value of the decision variable.

Now that you have considered the design for the spreadsheet, you are ready to enter the contents. Remember, if you make a typing error before you press the Return key, use the Backspace key to delete the error and then type the correction. Cancel any command by pressing the Esc key before pressing the Return key. If you have already entered the error, simply type the entry over again until it is correct.

c. Format the spreadsheet. Change the width of column A to 20 spaces to accommodate the length of the employee names. If necessary, use the arrow keys to move the cursor to column A. Type

```
/W
```

This is the slash command to use the worksheet menu options. As was discussed earlier, *slash commands* use a "/" (slash) to tell the computer that you are going to enter a command. The letter indicates which command. Remember, the slash commands are listed in Table 6-1.

The prompt line will show a choice of worksheet menu options, including Column. Since column A is going to be widened, choose the column width option by moving the pointer to the listed option, or by pressing the first letter of the option. In this case, press

```
C
```

The prompt line immediately changes to a new set of options:

```
Set-Width Reset-Width Hide Display
```

To change the width of column A from 9 spaces to 15 spaces, press

```
S
```

and type

```
15
```

Press **Return.** Notice how the border containing the column letter A widens.

d. Enter the worksheet contents. Worksheet contents should generally be entered in the following order:

1. Column and row headings and labels
2. Formulas needed for variables, including built-in formulas
3. Values

Although maintaining this order may seem rather unnecessary when you are using a small spreadsheet such as in our example, you will find that, as your spreadsheet applications grow in size and complexity, this order will prevent time-consuming mistakes.

Set the keyboard to produce all capital letters by pressing the **Caps Lock key.** The message CAPS will appear at the bottom right of the screen. If you make a typing error, backspace using the Backspace key and type the correction. Back out of or cancel any command by pressing the Escape key before pressing the Return key. If you have already pressed the Enter or Return key, then simply type the entry over again or use the Edit command, [F2].

Below is a list of cell contents to enter. Notice the repeat entry command (\) used in cell A3. The dash will be repeated across the column. The cell contents are then copied across the spreadsheet with the /Copy command. Press the Return key or an arrow key after typing each entry to place it into the current cursor cell. (Hint: Use the arrow key to simultaneously place the entry in the cell and move the cursor. It saves a lot of keystrokes.)

In Cell	Enter
A1	FAST DATA SERVICES, INC.
A2	EMPLOYEE PAY RATE ANALYZER
A3	\-

(That last item is the backslash key followed by a hyphen. It fills the cell with hyphens to make a dashed line.)

Copy the dashes from A3 to B3 through F3. With the pointer at cell A3, press

```
/C
```

The prompt line in the control area changes to

```
Enter range to copy FROM: A3..A3:
```

Press **Return.** This will define the range where the dashed line will be copied from.

The prompt line changes to

```
Enter range to copy TO: A3
```

With the **arrow key,** move the cell pointer to cell B3.
Press **.** (period) to anchor the beginning of the range.

With the **arrow key,** move to cell F3. Notice how the newly defined range is highlighted as you move the cell pointer.

Press **Return** to complete the Copy command. Notice how the dashed line now extends along row 3 from column A through F.

Continue entering the cell contents:

In Cell	Enter
B4	'<--CURRENT HOURLY PAY RATE
B5	'<--PROPOSED NEW HOURLY RATE
A6	\-

Press

/C

At the "From" cell range prompt (A6..A6), press **Return.** At the "To" cell range prompt, move the pointer to B6 and press **.** (period) to anchor the beginning of the range.

Move the pointer across row 6 to column F and press **Return,** thus copying the dashed line across row 6.

Continue entering the cell contents.

In Cell	Enter
A8	WORKER:
B8	HOURS:
C7	CURRENT
C8	PAY:
D7	NEW
D8	PAY:
E7	DOLLAR
E8	CHANGE:
A10	STEVE
A11	KEN
A12	JIM
A13	JOE
A14	CECILIA
A15	\-

Copy the dashed line in A15 to B15 through F15, following the instructions listed above and substituting the correct cell addresses.

In Cell	Enter
A16	TOTALS:
F16	'<--COST OF CHANGE
C10	+$A$4*B10

Copy C10 to C11 through C14.

Type

/C

Press **Return.**

To define the destination, move the pointer down to C11 and type **.** (period). Move the pointer down the column to C14 and press **Return.** The formula will be copied and adjusted. The cells will show 0 (zero) since no values have been inserted in the worksheet.

Continue entering the cell contents.

In Cell	Enter
D10	+$A$5*B10

Copy D10 to D11 through D14, following the instructions listed above and substituting the correct cell addresses.

In Cell	Enter
E10	+D10-C10

Copy E10 to E11 through E14, following the instructions listed above and substituting the correct cell addresses.

In Cell	Enter
B16	@SUM(B10.B15)

Notice that you can enter the ranges by typing them in as shown or by using the pointer method used earlier. To use the pointer method, first enter @SUM(and then move the pointer to B10 and enter **.** (period). Move the pointer down the column to B15 and press Return. Then enter the ending parentheses. The advantage of the pointer method is that you can see the range highlighted on the screen. Note also that cell B15 contains a dashed line rather than a value to be added to the total. This cell is included in the range so that another row could be added (if a new employee were hired, for example), and the range in the @SUM function would automatically be adjusted to include the new row.

Provide totals for the rest of the columns by copying the contents of B16 to C16 through E16.

In Cell	Enter
A4	6
A5	7
B10	10
B11	20
B12	15
B13	30
B14	40

Your totals should be 115, 690, 805, and 115.

e. Save the worksheet contents. Although the worksheet is not yet completed, it is always a good idea—just as it is in word processing—to save partially completed works and thus avoid any disasters. The /File Save command places a copy of the worksheet contained in RAM onto a disk file.

To save the work you have completed, type

```
/F S
```

Where

/F = File
S = Save

Lotus 1-2-3 then prompts you for a filename.

```
Enter save file name: A:\
```

Backspace to delete A:\ and type

```
B:TUTOR1
```

Press **Return.** Lotus 1-2-3 will automatically assign a filename extension of .WK1 to the stored worksheet. Within a second or two, the worksheet in primary storage will be copied onto the disk in drive B. Note that it will also remain in RAM and on the screen until you remove it by using the /Worksheet Erase command, so you can continue refining the spreadsheet without fear of accidentally erasing it. Once it is stored on disk, you can retrieve it at any time by using the /File Retrieve command.

Format the Spreadsheet

Formatting is the adjustment of display formats, such as numeric display, precision, and column width. Such commands can improve the appearance and readability of a worksheet. These commands are discussed in more detail in Lesson 7. Please note that formatting commands change the *appearance* of a worksheet. They do not change the actual contents of the file.

a. Change the format of cells C10 through E16 to currency format. The currency format adds the value 0.005, rounding the number to the nearest penny, displays it with two decimal places, and aligns the decimal places. Formatting of a group of cells is done through the /Range Format command.

Move the pointer to column C. Type

```
/R F C 2 Return C10.E16
```

Where

/R = Range
F = Format
C = Currency
2 = decimal places
C10.E16 = the range to be formatted

Press **Return.**

Notice how the appearance of the cell entries changes. The entries are rounded to the nearest penny with two decimal places.

b. Change the format of rows 7 and 8. To center the text using the /Range Label-prefix command, type

```
/R L C
```

Where

/R = Range
L = Label
C = Center

Lotus 1-2-3 will prompt for the range of cells to be altered. Use the pointer to specify which cells are to be centered.

Press **Esc** to "de-anchor" the pointer. Now you can move the pointer to the first cell to be included in the range.

With the arrow keys, move the pointer to cell B7. Notice how the cell reference in the prompt changes as you move the pointer to the desired cell. When the pointer is in cell B7, press **.** (period) to anchor the new beginning cell.

Move the pointer to cell E8. Press **Return.** The text entries in cells B7 through E8 will be centered.

c. Change the format of cell A16 to right justify the text. Individual cells, also called *fields,* can be formatted.

Move the pointer to cell A16. Type

```
/R L R
```

Where

/R = Range
L = Label
R = Right

Press **Return.** This formats a single cell or field so that the text is aligned against the right margin (right justified).

d. Insert today's date with the @NOW function. Users often want the spreadsheet to contain the current date. MS-DOS provides the date (although many users skip over it when they sign on, so the system date may not be correct), which can be inserted into a spreadsheet by use of the built-in function @NOW. To display the current date as it is normally shown, move the pointer to the bottom of the spreadsheet, to cell A18. Type

```
Today's Date:
```

Move the pointer to cell A19 and enter

```
/R F D 1
```

Where

/R = Range
F = Format
D = Date
1 = the date format

Press **Return.**

This will cause the date to be displayed in the (DD-MMM-YY) format. For example, if the date is March 3, 1990, then the @NOW function will display 03-Mar-90. The column width must be at least 10 spaces.

Type the function that will cause the date to be placed in the cell. Press **Esc** until you return to the READY mode. Enter

```
@NOW
```

Remember that the date will be changed to the current system date each time the file is retrieved and printed.

Save the spreadsheet on the disk. Press

```
/F S
```

for File Save. At the prompt

```
Enter save file name: b:tutor1
```

press **Return.** The prompt changes to

```
Cancel Replace
```

Choosing Cancel will rescind the command. Selecting Replace will cause Lotus 1-2-3 to replace the previously stored file with the newly revised file of the same name. Select

```
R
```

Within a second or two, the worksheet in primary storage will be copied onto the disk in drive B. Recall that it will also remain in RAM and on the screen until you remove it by using the /Worksheet Erase command. Once it is stored on disk, you can retrieve it at any time by using the /File Retrieve command.

Print the Spreadsheet

There are two ways to print a spreadsheet: on paper and on a disk file. A spreadsheet printed on a disk file can then be included in word processing documents.

To print a spreadsheet on paper, make sure your computer is connected to a printer and the printer is ready to receive data. Type

```
/P
```

A new prompt appears:

```
Printer File
```

If you select "Printer," a copy of the worksheet file, specially coded to be printed, is sent to the printer. If you select "File," the specially coded copy is sent to a disk file. Such output files are stored differently than files that are saved. Output files can be used in word processing or other text documents or printed using the Copy Prn system command in MS-DOS.

Type

```
P
```

to select the option of printing the worksheet on the printer. Lotus 1-2-3 offers a wide variety of print options. *Range* lets the user specify the cells to be printed; *Line* will advance the printer one line; *Page* will advance the printer to the top of the next page one page; *Options* lets the user specify headers, footers, margins, borders, setup codes, and page length; *Other* lets the user print the worksheet as is (As-Displayed) or with formulas visible (Cell-formulas) and formatted or unformatted; and *Align* resets the top of the page.

Specify the range to be printed. Type

```
R A1.G19
```

Press **Return.**

Check again to make sure your printer is connected, turned on, and loaded with paper. Type

```
G
```

for Go, to print the worksheet contents that are currently in the specified range.

Print a worksheet using the output option. This is also a good time to learn how to create a spreadsheet file that can later be accessed by the word processing software and included as part of a memo or report.

Press **Esc.** The printer prompt will reappear:

```
Printer File
```

Type

```
F
```

for file. Then, at the prompt, give the file a name. Backspace to delete A:\ and type

```
B:TUTOUT
```

Since this is an output file and *not* a spreadsheet file, Lotus 1-2-3 will assign a different file extension of .PRN.

Lotus 1-2-3 will then prompt for the print range. Since we have already specified a range, press

```
G
```

for Go. Within a few short moments the spreadsheet will be printed to a disk file.

Press **Esc** until the READY mode reappears.

Examine the printed spreadsheet. If there are errors, repeat any of the above steps until you are satisfied with the printed result.

Save the worksheet again to save the printing settings. Press

```
/F S Return R
```

Quit Try as many "What if?" analyses as you want. For instance, change the proposed new hourly rate or the hours for each worker. The original worksheet is saved on the disk, so these changes will not affect it. Notice that each time a new value is entered in this decision variable location, the entire spreadsheet automatically recalculates and cell G16 provides the user with the cost of the proposed new pay rate.

If you have made any changes to the spreadsheet, remember to save the spreadsheet using the /F S command. To quit this tutorial session, type

```
/Q
```

If you are ready to quit, without needing to save any additional changes, enter **Y** for **Yes** and the worksheet disappears. If your disk contains the 1-2-3 Access System, you may need to enter E for Exit to return to the system prompt (A-).

Remove the disks from both drives, turn off the computer, remove your printed spreadsheet from the printer, turn off the printer, and take a moment to review what you have learned.

You have created a spreadsheet using Lotus 1-2-3, printed out the results, and saved the spreadsheet on a floppy disk. Now you are ready to tackle even more interesting assignments.

SUMMARY

An electronic spreadsheet is an all-purpose tool that can be especially helpful solving problems involving numbers and formulas. Paper spreadsheets with preprinted rows and columns and spaces for column headings and row labels have been used by accountants and others for many years. Electronic spreadsheets offer greater size, flexibility, and speed of calculation than paper spreadsheets, as well as built-in mathematical functions, making them a natural for "What if?" analysis.

A potential spreadsheet application must be a problem capable of being expressed in mathematical terms and laid out in rows and columns. Other characteristics include repetition (a task that must be frequently repeated), editing (the need to correct errors and rearrange layouts), revisions (frequent small changes that require recalculation of the entire spreadsheet), variable and fixed parts (using standardized formats or templates for the fixed parts and blanks to fill in for the variables), and, finally, the need for quality appearance (for formal reporting and presentations to groups).

The five major functions common to electronic spreadsheet software are creating (opening a blank worksheet area and entering labels, formulas, and values, and saving the worksheet on a disk file), revising (deleting, replacing, and inserting changes), formatting (adjusting the display formats), printing (producing paper or disk output), and file handling (copying, deleting, and consolidating spreadsheets).

EXERCISES

1. List the six characteristics of an electronic spreadsheet application. Name the most appropriate characteristic(s) for each of the applications listed below.
   a. monthly budget report
   b. projected income report
   c. departmental quarterly reports
   d. stockholder's report
2. What are the advantages of an electronic spreadsheet over a paper spreadsheet?
3. List five personal uses of electronic spreadsheets applicable to the "typical" student.
4. What are the six steps of designing an effective spreadsheet? Why are these steps important?
5. Define the following terms:

electronic spreadsheet	quality appearance	active cell
cell	model	control panel
range	planning guide	status area
macro	formula driven	status line
Home position	spreadsheet auditing	cursor
label	creating a spreadsheet	entry line
sensitivity analysis	revising a spreadsheet	prompt line
value	formatting a spreadsheet	slash commands
constant	printing a spreadsheet	worksheet
variables	file handling for spreadsheets	border
functions	prompt area	address
formula	worksheet window	coordinates
editing		cursor movement
revisions		scrolling
fixed part		titling
variable part		data entry
template		built-in functions

6. Match the following Lotus 1-2-3 slash commands on the left with the proper actions on the right.

/W	____	Commands that affect only a designated area of the spreadsheet
/R	____	Commands that affect the entire spreadsheet
/C	____	Leaves Lotus and erases the spreadsheet in RAM
/M	____	Prints spreadsheet
/F	____	Enters graphing command set
/P	____	Data commands
/G	____	Goes to MS-DOS system
/D	____	For saving or retrieving files
/S	____	Rows or columns relocated
/Q	____	Duplicates cell or range

7. Enter the Lotus 1-2-3 built-in arithmetic functions appropriate for the following results.
   a. Returns the percent of a loan payment
   b. Returns the average
   c. Returns the sum of the values in the range
   d. Maximum value in a list
   e. If *a* is true, *b* is entered into the cell; if *a* is false, *c* is entered into the cell
   f. Returns the number of numeric items in the list
8. Match the Lotus 1-2-3 commands with the function keys.

[F1]	____	Step
[F2]	____	Compose
[F3]	____	Help
[F4]	____	Edit
[F5]	____	Name
[F6]	____	Abs
[F7]	____	GOTO
[F8]	____	Window
[F9]	____	Graph
[F10]	____	Calc
[F11]	____	Table
[F12]	____	Query

9. On a copy of the blank planning guide in Figure 6-12, indicate the placement of the decision variables, formulas, and bottom line for the design of a formula-driven spreadsheet for projecting a budget.
10. Practice using Lotus 1-2-3 by completing the tutorial, Creating and Printing a Spreadsheet Using Lotus 1-2-3. Then revise the spreadsheet to include the following changes.

a. With the MS-DOS Copy utility make, on the disk in drive B, a copy of the spreadsheet you created in the tutorial. Assign a new filename based on your name and date of completion of the exercise. For example, if your name is Joan Williams and you completed the exercise on June 11, 1990, you would name the file JW61190. Lotus 1-2-3 will assign the filename extension. *Please do not use this filename; it is only an example.* Give the spreadsheet its own unique filename.

b. Load Lotus 1-2-3 and the newly copied spreadsheet. Use the /File Retrieve command to load the spreadsheet. Press **/F R** and enter the name of the newly copied spreadsheet. Press **Return.**

c. Replace the current company name of "FAST DATA SERVICES" with a new name. For example, Joan Williams could name the company "JOAN WILLIAMS CONSULTING, INC."

d. Starting in A10, insert 5 new rows, using the following instructions:

(1) With the arrow keys, move the cursor to cell A15. Enter

```
/WIR  A15.A19
```

(2) Insert five new employees, including employee name (WORKER) and hours worked (HOURS). *Do not insert the current pay (CURRENT PAY), new pay (NEW PAY), or dollar change (DOLLAR CHANGE), since these are calculated variables.*

(3) Copy the formula in C14 to cells C15 through C19.

(4) Copy the formula in D14 to cells D15 through D19.

(5) Copy the formula in E14 to cells E15 through E19.

(6) The totals across the bottom are automatically adjusted to include the new inserted rows.

e. At the bottom of the spreadsheet, insert your name and, if you have not already done so, today's date using the @NOW function.

f. Save the spreadsheet using the new filename.

g. Print the worksheet using the Print option.

11. Create your own Lotus 1-2-3 spreadsheet to calculate your current college expenses and income. Use a planning guide to design the spreadsheet. For expenses include room and board (or rent, food, and utilities), tuition, books, and entertainment. For income, include all sources of income, including scholarships, loans, summer jobs, part-time jobs, and parents. Enter, save, and print the worksheet. Write down the steps necessary to create, edit, save, and print the spreadsheet.

12. A study of the daily high temperatures in four cities has yielded the data listed below. Create a spreadsheet that will calculate the high, low, and average temperatures for each of the four cities over the ten-day period. Use the following data, substituting your name:

TEMPERATURE STUDY Prepared by: *your name*

DATE:	Chicago	New York	Tampa	Houston
01-Jan	10	25	75	65
02-Jan	15	22	70	58
03-Jan	12	34	67	48
04-Jan	−4	32	70	50
05-Jan	−3	30	73	65
06-Jan	0	39	68	56
07-Jan	2	10	69	57
08-Jan	5	12	71	58
09-Jan	7	10	70	59
10-Jan	15	11	71	56
High:				
Low:				
Average:				

13. High Tech Sales Co. sent five of its sales representatives on a 16-day sales trip. At the end of the trip each sales representative was required to submit a daily expense record. The sales manager would like a spreadsheet showing the daily expenses for each person, the total per day, the total per person, the grand total, and the daily average for each person. Use the following data, substituting your name and today's date:

HIGH TECH SALES CO.
Sales Rep. Expenses
As of: *today's date* Prepared by: *your name*

Date:	Mary	Jack	Cecilia	Joe	Jim	Totals
	2/1	20.50	45.30	32.40	45.10	34.30
	2/2	45.30	32.00	45.00	45.00	56.00
	2/3	32.10	32.00	56.00	50.00	67.00
	2/4	12.20	34.00	43.00	50.00	76.00
	2/5	34.50	43.00	43.00	65.00	76.00
	2/6	65.80	45.00	34.00	76.00	87.00
	2/7	45.00	45.00	23.00	87.00	98.00
	2/8	56.00	45.00	32.00	54.00	76.00
	2/9	34.00	43.00	32.00	45.00	78.00
	2/10	34.00	56.00	34.00	65.00	65.00
	2/11	56.00	54.00	45.00	65.00	75.00
	2/12	78.00	55.00	56.00	52.00	75.00
	2/13	32.00	45.00	43.00	34.00	85.00
	2/14	56.00	43.00	54.00	43.00	82.00

HIGH TECH SALES CO. (*Continued*)
Sales Rep. Expenses
As of: *today's date*   Prepared by: *your name*

Date:	Mary	Jack	Cecilia	Joe	Jim	Totals
	2/15	67.00	33.00	56.00	65.00	75.00
	2/16	71.00	23.00	34.00	54.00	96.00
Totals:						
Average:						

14. The Heavy Duty Trucking Co. is involved in negotiations with its truck drivers regarding hourly wages. The truck drivers want a 10% increase and management says it can afford only a 5% increase. As the negotiations proceed, there will be a need to rapidly calculate any proposed percentage increase. Design a spreadsheet to quickly calculate the current pay, the proposed pay, the dollar increase per truck driver, and the total dollar increase depending on the percentage increase being negotiated. To display a value as a percentage, enter /Range Format Percent 2 and specify the range. For example, if the user enters a value such as 1.23 into the cell, the display will be 123.00%; 0.01 would be 1.00%; 1 would be 100.00%, and so forth. Use the following data, substituting today's date (using the @NOW function) and your name:

Heavy Duty Trucking Co.   Today's date:
Truck Driver Wage Study   Prepared by: *your name*
5.00 <-- Proposed Percentage Wage Increase

Driver:	Current Hours:	Proposed Rate:	Current Rate:	Proposed Pay:	Dollar Pay:	Increase:
Mary	30	12.50				
Katie	35	12.50				
Terri	38	10.00				
Jeanne	38	10.00				
John	37	10.00				
Cecilia	35	15.00				
Joe	40	18.00				
Jim	35	12.00				
Ken	34	13.00				
Steve	35	19.00				
Totals:						

For the proposed rate in cell D8, use the formula +C8+(C8*$A$3) and copy it down the range of column C. In this way any percent entered in A3 will cause the spreadsheet to automatically recalculate using the newly proposed percentage wage increase. For the Current pay in cell E8, use the formula +B8*C8 and copy it down the range of the column. For the proposed pay in cell F8, use the formula +B8*D8 and copy it down the column. For the dollar increase in cell G8, use +F8−E8 and copy it down column G. Use the @SUM(range) to total columns B, E, F, and G.

15. The Heavy Duty Trucking Co. has to consider various prices of diesel fuel for its fleet of nine trucks. The transportation manager says she has to consider not only the price but the mileage the trucks obtain from the various brands of fuel. Create a spreadsheet that will allow the transportation manager to consider various proposed prices per gallon and various estimates of percent increases or decreases in miles per gallon to be obtained with proposed brands of fuel. Use the following data, substituting your name and today's date:

Heavy Duty Trucking Co.
Fuel Price/Mileage Study

1.00 <--Current Price/Gal. Prepared by: *your name*
1.10 <--Proposed Price/Gal. Prepared on: *today's date*
10.00 <--Est. Percent Increase or Decrease in Miles/Gal. Rating

Tractor Number:	Current Miles/ Month:	Current Miles/ Gal :	Current Cost:	Proposed Miles/ Gal :	Proposed Cost:	Dollar Increase (Savings):
	205	700	6.70			
	304	2000	7.70			
	333	300	7.80			
	345	1000	7.90			
	360	1200	10.00			
	456	1200	11.00			
	457	1800	12.00			
	458	1900	11.00			
	501	3000	14.30			
Totals:						

16. Create a spreadsheet that will compare the sales for last year to the sales for this year for Synozyn, Inc. Column A should contain the names of the five departments, column B last year's sales figures, column C the dollar change, and column D the percent change. To display a value enter /Range Format Percent 2 and specify the range. Use the following data:

SYNOZYN INC.
Sales Comparison

Dept.	Last Yr.	This Yr.	Change	% Change
Hardware	50000	60000		
Software	40000	45000		
Books	10000	20000		
Consulting	20000	30000		
Instruction	10000	15000		
Totals				

17. Prepare a payroll register for Blackburn Consultants. In cell D1 put today's date by entering @NOW and using /Range Format Date. Select option 1, which is (DD-MMM-YY). Set the column width to 10 spaces using /Worksheet Column Set-Width 10. Use column A for the employee names, column B for total hours, column C for rate, and column D to multiply total hours for each employee by rate to determine gross pay. In column E, calculate each employee's percent of the total payroll. Use the following data, substituting your name for the author's and inserting today's date:

BLACKBURN CONSULTANTS
Payroll Register
For the week ending 27-Feb-90 Prepared by: Steve Hallam

Employee:	Total Hours:	Rate:	Gross Pay:	Percent of Total:
Alberte, John	40.0	7.50		
Alberte, Jeannette	35.5	6.50		
Brown, Richard	40.0	10.00		
Crowley, Robert	25.0	6.00		
Dunlop, Kelly	27.0	6.00		
Franey, Rita	40.0	8.50		
Hallam, Jerome	40.0	9.50		
Totals:	=========		=============	

Total the columns where the double lines are shown.

18. Prepare an instructor's grade book for a course called MATH 101, Section 2. Use column A for the students' names, column B for exam 1, column C for exam 2, column D for each student's total on the two exams, and column E for each student's percent of the total possible.

For cell D1, use the @NOW and the Date format. Calculate the average for columns B and C and D using @AVG(range). For those columns, calculate the standard deviation, using @STD(range); the highest score, using @MAX (range); and the lowest score, using @MIN(range). Use the following data, substituting your name and today's date:

MATH 101, SECTION 2
FALL 1990
AS OF THE DATE OF *today's date* Prepared by: *your name*

Names:	Exam 1	Exam 2	Total	Percent
Anderson, Ellen	97	97		
Bach, Jan	78	96		
Beard, Dorothea	78	95		
Behrens, Curt	98	92		
Bickle, Barbara	78	99		
Bishop, Helen	69	94		
Brieant, Marcia	95	87		
Brown, Patricia	87	86		
Cleland, Clifford	67	91		
Total Possible:				
Average:				
Standard Deviation:				
Highest Score:				
Lowest Score:				

19. Prepare an Income Statement for Hallam's Hardware Company using the data provided below. Column A contains the labels for the areas of revenue and expense, column B contains the values and formulas, and column C contains a calculation of each item as a percent of gross sales. In cell C6 use the formula +B6/$B$6 (Gross Sales/Gross Sales) and then use the /Copy command to replicate that formula down column C. Use formulas to fill in all the blank areas in column B; for example, the formula for B8 is +B6−B7 (Gross Sales−Sales Returns+Allowances), the formula for B14 is +B12−B13 (Purchases−Purchases Returns+Allowances), and so forth. As a final check on your work, Net income before taxes should be $12,282.00, which is 14.69% of Gross Sales. Substitute your name and today's date.

HALLAM'S HARDWARE COMPANY
Income Statement for the Year Ended December 31, 19xx
Prepared by: *your name* On: *today's date*

Revenue:		% Gross Sales
Gross Sales	$83,597.00	100.00%
Less: Sales returns and allowances	$790.00	
Net Sales		
Cost of goods sold:		
Merchandise inv, Jan 1, 19xx	$8,750.00	
Purchases	$49,400.00	
Less Purchases returns & allowances	$275.00	
Net purchases		
Add Freight-in	$1,100.00	
Net cost of purchases		
Goods available for sale		
Merchandise inv, Dec 31, 19xx	$8,950.00	
Cost of Goods Sold		
Gross Profit from Sales		
Operating Expenses:		
Selling Expenses:		
Sales Salaries	$8,200.00	
Rent expense, selling space	$4,800.00	
Advertising expense	$900.00	
Freight-out & delivery expense	$1,350.00	
Store supplies used	$425.00	
Depreciation exp, store equipment	$775.00	
Total selling expenses		
General & Adm expenses:		
Office salaries	$3,100.00	
Rent expense, office space	$600.00	
Expired insurance	$65.00	
Office supplies used	$125.00	
Depreciation exp, office equipment	$160.00	
Total gen. & adm. expenses		
Total operating expenses		
Net income before taxes		
	= = = = =	

20. Suppose you have won $5,000 in a lottery. You want to put your winnings in a money market fund and let the sum accumulate interest until the total reaches $9,000. If the money market fund earns 8 percent compounded monthly, how long will you have to wait before you have $9,000? Set up the spreadsheet as follows:

```
COMPOUND INTEREST ANALYZER
= = = = = = = = = = = = = = = = = = = = = = = = = = = = = = = = = = = = = = = = = =
To use this analyzer you need to know three of the following: Simple interest rate, term in months,
persent value, or future value

= = = = = = = = = = = = = = = = = = = = = = = = = = = = = = = = = = = = = = = = = =
        8  <--Simple annual interest rate, 0 if unknown
    0.67%<--Yields this monthly interest rate
        0  <--Term in months, enter 0 if unknown
     5000  <--Present value, enter 0 if unknown
     9000  <--Future value, enter 0 if unknown
= = = = = = = = = = = = = = = = = = = = = = = = = = = = = = = = = = = = = = = = = =
Solution:

       NA  <--Mo. int. rate or yr. rate of --->      NA

    88.46  <--Term in months

       NA  <--Present value

       NA  <--Future value
```

The formulas to produce the solutions in cells A13 through A16 are shown below:

```
Solution:

    @IF(A7 =0,@RATE(A10,A9,A8),@NA)          ← Mo. int. rate
    @IF(A8 =0,@CTERM(A7,A10,A9),@NA)         ← Term in months
    @IF(A9 =0,A10*(1+A7) ^ -A8,@NA)          ← Present value
   @IF(A10 =0,A9*(1+A7) ^ A8,@NA)            ← Future value
```

7
Electronic Spreadsheet Applications

LESSON OUTLINE

Lesson 6 introduced several important concepts essential to your general understanding of electronic spreadsheets. In Lesson 7 we will expand on these concepts and use several additional electronic spreadsheet features.

ADDITIONAL ELECTRONIC SPREADSHEET FEATURES

Electronic spreadsheet software, particularly recent versions, have additional features that change the screen operation and appearance, adjust cell content display on the screen and in output, adjust spreadsheet operation, create graphs, and offer data management. These features advance the electronic spreadsheet far beyond the capabilities of the paper spreadsheet. Let's discuss these features and how they work.

Titles

Title lock and *windowing* permit the user to see more than one section of the worksheet on the monitor at one time. The **Title Lock** command (sometimes called *Titles command)* locks or freezes designated rows and/or columns in place on the screen. Once a row and/or a column has been defined as a title, you can scroll the worksheet past the fixed set of titles and they will remain on the screen, regardless of their relative position on the worksheet. For example, the titles option (/Worksheet Titles Vertical) was used in the Lotus 1-2-3 worksheet in Figure 7-1 to fix the students' names in the left-most column on the screen regardless of which other columns are on the screen. This enables the user to move columns on the far right side of the worksheet next to the title column. The instructor can easily refer to the students' names when looking at columns normally scrolled off the screen, such as the students' final percentages.

Windows

Most electronic spreadsheet software packages permit you to split the worksheet on the screen into multiple parts or **windows.** The window command (/Worksheet Windows) permits you to see different sections of the spreadsheet that may not normally be visible on one screen, such as the top and bottom of a large spreadsheet. Each section may contain several columns or rows and may be split either horizontally or vertically. The split may be placed in any row or column, except those at the edge of the screen. Most spreadsheet software will allow the screen to be split into two windows, but some, such as Multiplan, allow the user to split the screen

FIGURE 7-1 A Lotus 1-2-3 worksheet used as an instructor's grade book. Column A (highlighted) has been defined as a title. The pointer has been moved to column W. The students' names remain in the left-most column on the screen, but columns B through R have scrolled off the screen.

W17: (F0) U [W8] @SUM(B17..U17) READY

	A	S	T	U	V	W	X	Y	Z	AA
1	SPRING 1990 GRADEBOO									
2	10-May-90					TOTAL				
3		BASIC 2	BASIC QZ	FINAL		POINTS	PRCT	GRD		
4	Date Due	4/22/90	4/29/90	5/5/90						
5	Pts per assignment	30	30	250		1000				
6	Points awarded	30	30	250		1000	100			A
14	CARLSON, MARY	30	27	184		810	81	B	3	0
15	CLARKE, MELISSA	0	18	184		738	74	C	2	0
16	DAVIDSON, KAREN	0	16	172		688	69	C	2	0
17	GOLICK, RICHARD	29	21	208		865	87	A	4	1
18	GRANSEE, MARIE	30	27	158		737	74	C	2	0
19	HANNUS, SUSAN	29	16	156		729	73	C	2	0
20	HANS, RACHEL	30	28	148		719	72	C	2	0
21	JENSEN, JIM	30	23	182		824	82	B	3	0
22	JOHNSON, SUSAN	25	18	156		724	72	C	2	0
23	KRAKAWAK, ABBY	28	23	136		674	67	D	1	0
24	KRUGER, JOHN	30	16	170		762	76	C	2	0
25	LEGRANDIE, MARIE	27	20	178		771	77	C	2	0
26	MCCLORY, RICHARD	25	22	182		767	77	C	2	0
27	MICHAELS, KEITH	30	30	188		774	77	C	2	0

CALC

into as many as eight windows. Of course, the screen may become cluttered if too many windows are used. Figure 7-2 is an illustration of a screen split into two windows using Lotus 1-2-3. Notice that rows 1 through 13 are in the top window and rows 23 through 28 are in the bottom window. The column designators of A through E just below row 13 mark the dividing line between the top and bottom windows.

In some cases, software may permit each window to act like an autonomous copy of the same worksheet. Different format specifications, such as column width, can be set for each window. Windows can be **synchronized,** so that cell pointer movement in one window causes a similar movement in the other window, or **unsynchronized,** meaning that movement of the pointer in one window does not affect the other window. The flexibility of window options depends on the software package.

Since the cell pointer can be in only one window, a command must be used to switch the cell pointer and the entry cell from one window to another. For example, in Lotus 1-2-3, if you have defined two horizontal windows, the pointer is placed initially in the upper window. To switch it

FIGURE 7-2 A screen split horizontally into two windows using Lotus 1-2-3. Notice how the pointer can be placed in only one window at a time. Multiple windows allow users to see two divergent areas of a large worksheet at one time.

```
A3: [W31] 'OPERATING ACCOUNT EXPENSES                                    READY

                 A                        B         C        D        E
1   INCOME AND EXPENSE STATEMENT FOR MARCH 1990
2   =================================================================
3   OPERATING ACCOUNT EXPENSES     CURRENT  EXPENSES BUDGETED CUM.
4                                  MONTH    TO       EXPENSES ACTUAL
5                                  EXPENSES DATE     TO DATE    1989
6   -----------------------------------------------------------------
7   Salaries & Wages                  43223   361043    37850   337845
8   Health Insurance                   1470    11409    12040    12553
9   Retirement                          778    13398    16400    14243
10  Social Security                    3176    26248    22720    25846
11  Unemployment Insurance                0      972     2160      594
12  Workers' Comp. Insurance            409     3272     2280     1799
13  Other Employ. Benefits               88     1888      880     5715
                 A                        B         C        D        E
23  Property Insurance                  468     3746     4040     3960
24  Utilities                          2735    21021    22000    20638
25  Bldg/Grounds Maint. Service        1620    13582    10840    11071
26  Bldg/Grounds Maint. Supplies        277     1422     1800     2319
27  Maint.-Prod. Equip.                 146     4056      760      771
28  Maint.-Other Equip.                 135     3916     3640     3759
                                                  CALC
```

to the lower window, press [F6] if you are using Lotus 1-2-3 or VP-Planner. If you have defined two vertical windows, the pointer is placed initially in the left window and can be switched to the right window with the same pointer switch command.

Formatting

The display of the cells contents is changed with **format commands.** Such commands are similar to word processing formatting commands; they determine how the worksheet is displayed on the screen or in output (printed or disk file). As explained in Lesson 6, formatting is the adjustment of the display formats. Formatting commands change only the *appearance* of the cell contents, not how the entry is actually stored in the computer's memory. Format commands permit you to tailor your output to make a professional-looking and easy-to-understand worksheet.

Typical format options include choice of numeric display (integer, general, or exponent numbers), specification of precision (decimal places shown in a number), setting of column width, and several choices concerning the display of label borders and formulas. The original setting for each of these options is referred to as the **default setting.**

Formatting commands usually include commands for right and left *justification* of cell contents, where the cell contents are aligned with the right or left cell boundary; dollar and cents or *currency* format, where numbers are displayed with two places to the right of the decimal point and rounded to the nearest penny; and *integer* or *fixed format,* where numbers are displayed rounded to the nearest integer. Other commonly found format commands display numbers in exponential or scientific form or percent. Some spreadsheets have formats that show the formula rather than the resulting variable in the cell. The Lotus 1-2-3 command is /Worksheet Global Format Text.

Most electronic spreadsheets have the option of changing an individual cell, a block, or a segment of cells (usually a column or row) or of making changes affecting the entire spreadsheet, called **global format commands.** In Lotus 1-2-3 you use the /Worksheet Global Format command for global changes and the /Range Format command to change a single cell or block of cells.

The format options for a single cell, column, row, or range of cells override the global options. For example, in Figure 7-3, if you use the global option to display the worksheet in currency format (/Worksheet Global Format Currency 0), but you want the numbers in row 9 to appear as

```
A1: [W20] 'MARKET ANALYSIS FOR NEW PRODUCT                            READY

            A                  B        C        D        E        F
1    MARKET ANALYSIS FOR NEW PRODUCT
2                        1000000 <--EST. OF TOTAL MARKET IN UNITS
3                            15%<--EST. OF RATE OF MARKET GROWTH PER YEAR
4                            10%<--EST. OF OUR MARKET PORTION
5                         $3.50 <--PLANNED SELLING PRICE PER UNIT
6                            60%<--EST. OF COST OF SALES AS % OF $ SALES
7
8                           1990     1991     1992
9    EST. TOTAL MARKET   1000000  1150000  1322500
10   EST. $ SALES       $350,000 $402,500 $462,875
11   COST OF SALES      $210,000 $241,500 $277,725
12                      ---------------------------
13   GROSS MARGIN       $140,000 $161,000 $185,150
14
15   OTHER EXPENSES:
16     PROMOTION         $10,000  $10,000  $10,000
17     MARKETING         $20,000  $20,000  $20,000
18     GEN. AND ADMIN.   $15,000  $15,000  $15,000
19                      ---------------------------
20   TOTAL EXPENSES      $45,000  $45,000  $45,000
08-Mar-88  09:42 AM
```

Cells are formatted as fixed, percent, or currency

Rows are formatted as fixed with no decimal places

The Worksheet Global Format is currency with no decimal places

FIGURE 7-3 An example of how the format options for a single cell or block of cells override the global format commands.

integers, the command to change row 9 (/Range Format Fixed 0 B9.D9)· would override the global format commands.

In Lotus 1-2-3 the options available after you enter /Worksheet Global are Format, Label-Prefix, Column-Width, Recalculation, Protection, Default, and Zero. The Format option allows you to set the format for the entire spreadsheet. The choices are Fixed, Scientific, Currency, General, +/−, Percent, Date, Text, or Hidden. If a few parts of the spreadsheet have to be set in a different format, remember that a range format will override a global format.

The Label-Prefix option sets the label alignment for the entire spreadsheet so that labels are aligned to the left side or right side of the cells or are centered. Column-Width sets the column width for the entire spreadsheet. Recalculation allows a choice of automatic, manual, natural order, column order (Columnwise), row order (Rowwise), or a setting of the iteration count (Iteration). **Iteration** is the number of times Lotus recalculates all formulas during recalculation of the worksheet. **Recalculation** is calculation of formulas on the worksheet after the values in the cells have been entered or changed. The most common use of the recalculation option is for a user to set the recalculation to manual while entering a large amount of new data into an existing spreadsheet. *Manual recalculation* is the recalculation of the worksheet only when a command is given. This allows data to be accepted without the entire spreadsheet being recalculated after each data entry. Of course, it is then vital that the user recalculate the spreadsheet after all the data are entered by pressing the recalculation command. In Lotus 1-2-3 and VP-Planner, the command is [F9]. *Automatic recalculation* updates the results of the worksheet formulas each time a value is entered or changed. It is more convenient after the data is already entered and one or two values are changed, such as when you are doing "What if?" analysis.

The *protection* option keeps a user from accidentally changing vital formulas or other important parts of a spreadsheet. If a user is supposed to enter data in only a specific area of the spreadsheet, then those specific cells are unprotected. The *Default* option defines the default disk and printer settings. The *Zero* option turns zero suppression on or off; if it is on, then cells evaluating to zero will be blank instead of displaying 0.

Order of recalculation refers to the sequence or order the electronic spreadsheet uses when it recalculates the formulas and functions. Recalculation may be done in several ways, including natural, column, or row order. In **natural order** (Natural), before recalculating a particular formula, the software recalculates any other values on which the formula depends. With **column order** (Columnwise) the recalculation starts at the top of column A and continues to the bottom of the column. It continues to recalculate columns B, C, and so on until the entire worksheet is recalculated. **Row order** (Rowwise) recalculates the worksheet starting at the beginning of row 1 and continuing to the end of row 1. It continues to recalculate rows 2, 3, and so on until the entire worksheet is recalculated.

To see the importance of proper recalculation order, consider Figure 7-4 *(a), (b),* and *(c).* Figure 7-4*(a)* is a simple spreadsheet used to total expenses for two salespeople, John and Mary. All the data is entered as 100, so you can see that the column totals should be 400 and the total for both salespeople should be 800. Notice we have put the total in two places, cell E4 and cell B11.

Now consider Figure 7-4*(b).* The global option for recalculation order has been set to column-by-column, and Mary's "Other Expenses" in cell C7 have been changed to 200. Now Mary's total should be 500, and the total for both John and Mary should, of course, be 900. However, examine cell B11; the total is 800, not 900. Why did this error occur? Cell B11 is the result of B9 + C9. Because the recalculation was done columnwise, column B is recalculated before column C, so C9 is still 400 when B11 is calculated.

Now consider Figure 7-4*(c).* We have changed the global recalculation option to rowwise and changed Mary's "Other Expenses" in cell C7 back to 100. Of course, the totals for John and Mary should be 400, and the combined total for both should be 800. However, examine cell E4. It is 900. Why did this error occur? Cell E4 is B9 + C9. Because the recalculation was done on a row-by-row basis, E4 was recalculated before C9 changed from 500 to 400. E4 is in row 4 and C9 is in row 9, so row 4 is recalculated before row 9.

Do you see now why the order of recalculation can be so important? Such errors are easy to see when the spreadsheet is small and the calculations are simple. However, in a spreadsheet containing thousands of cells and thousands of calculations, the designer must be careful to lay out the spreadsheet so that formulas have the proper values available when formulas are calculated.

In both the cases in Figures 7-4*(b)* and 7-4*(c),* the user can obtain the correct answer with Lotus by pressing the recalculation key, [F9], again. On the second recalculation, cell C9 would have contained the proper sum and the B9 + C9 formula in cells B11 and E4 would have provided the proper answer. However, an inexperienced spreadsheet user may not know this trick and may produce erroneous results. Even with spreadsheet packages using forward referencing (the software goes forward in the worksheet, calculates the other formulas, and returns to complete the current formula), it is important to carefully check results using sample data.

Most spreadsheets will let you select the order of recalculation through commands. Since the order of recalculation can change results, you should always consider the recalculation order when designing and constructing a worksheet. Most spreadsheet software use the natural or dependency order of recalculation.

FIGURE 7-4 ***(a)*** **The worksheet properly recalculated using the default recalculation mode for Lotus. Note the totals in cells E4 and B11. If the worksheet is properly recalculating, these two results should match.** ***(b)*** **With the Global option set to column-by-column recalculation, cell B11 will be in error if you change cell C7 to 200 and recalculate once. Cell E4 will be correctly updated as 900, but B11 will remain 800.** ***(c)*** **With the Global option set to row-by-row, cell E4 will be in error. If you change cell C7 back to 100, cell E4 will remain 900, but cell B11 will be correct at 800.**

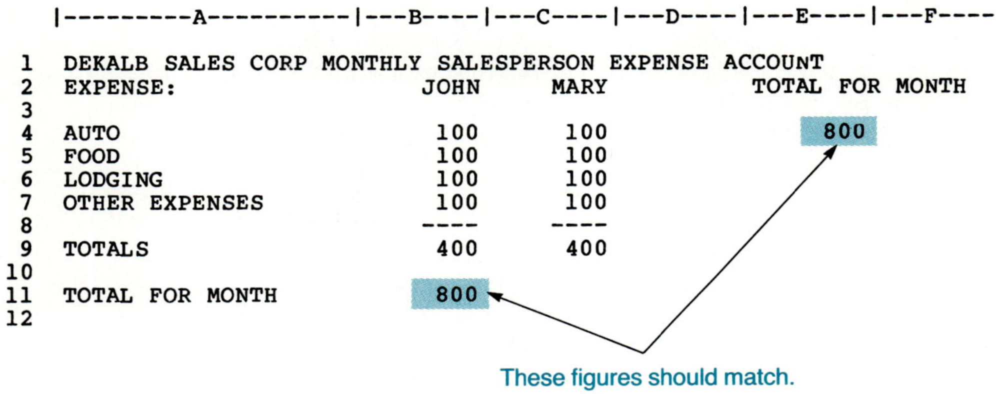

(a)

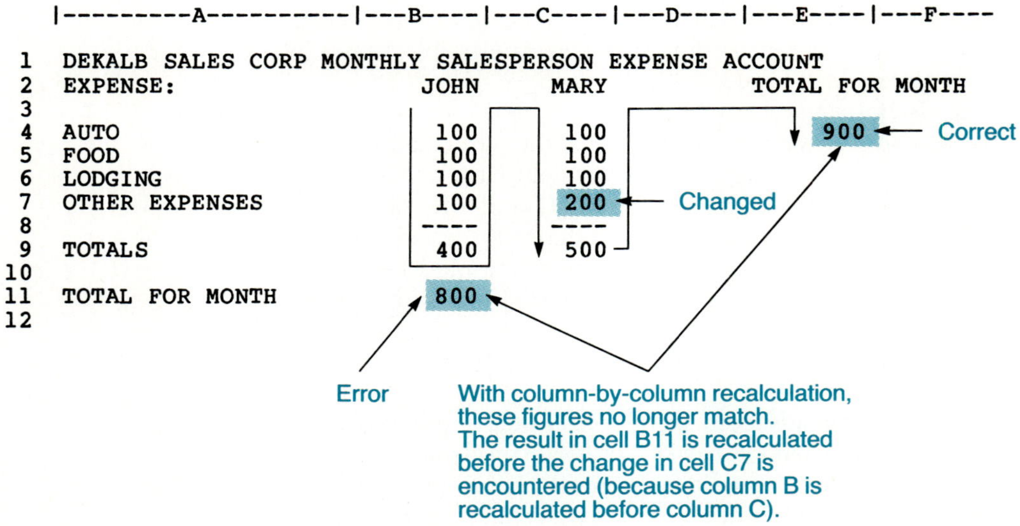

(b)

FIGURE 7-4 (continued)

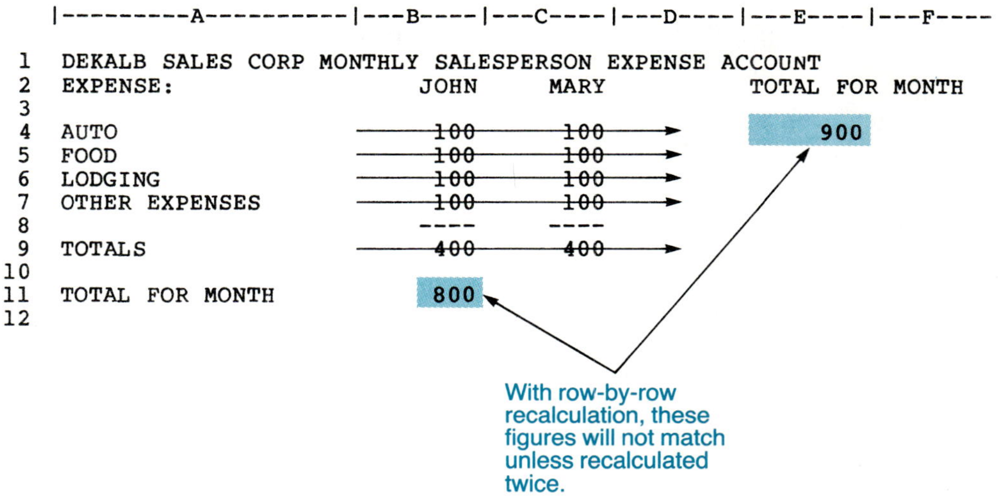

(c)

In some situations, however, it is necessary to enter the recalculation command two or more times to obtain the correct results from a spreadsheet. If some cells depend on values from other cells that have not been recalculated yet due to the rowwise recalculation order, it may be necessary to repeat the Recalculate command until all the cells are properly recalculated. Often such recalculations can be avoided by proper layout of the spreadsheet, but sometimes multiple recalculation is unavoidable. Some software, including Lotus 1-2-3, have an **iteration control option** that specifies the number of times (usually 1 through 50) a worksheet is to be recalculated when the recalculation is set to natural and the worksheet includes a circular reference. You can minimize these recalculations by keeping referenced cells above and/or to the left of the formulas that reference them.

Replication is the copying of cell contents from one cell or range of cells to another cell or range of cells. Replication is called **copying** in Lotus 1-2-3. The importance of the Copy command was discussed in Lesson 6. Spreadsheet software have a variety of commands and options to let users copy cells. The most common use for such commands is to duplicate formulas, automatically placing the same formula into a specified range of cells while letting the computer automatically adjust cell references. Remember, a *range* is a group of adjacent cells specified by the addresses of the first and last cells in the group. If the range is more than a single column or row, then it is called a **block range** and is specified by

FIGURE 7-5 ***(a)*** **An illustration of a block replication. The replication is from the block B5 through B10 to the blocks starting in cells C5 and D5. Only the first row or cell in the receiving block need be named in the /Copy command.** ***(b)*** **The same spreadsheet after the block is replicated. Notice the entire block is replicated.**

```
B10: @SUM(B5..B8)
Enter range to copy FROM: B5..B10                                  POINT

            A             B        C        D        E        F
1   PROJECTED EXPENSES FIRST QUARTER 1990
2
3                       JAN      FEB      MARCH
4
5   SALARIES                5000
6   UTILITIES               1000
7   INSURANCE                200
8   MAINTENANCE              200
9
10  TOTAL EXPENSES          6400
11
12
13
14
15
16
17
18
19
20
08-Mar-88   09:46 AM
```

(a)

```
B5: 5000                                                           READY

            A             B        C        D        E        F
1   PROJECTED EXPENSES FIRST QUARTER 1990
2
3                       JAN      FEB      MARCH
4
5   SALARIES                5000     5000     5000
6   UTILITIES               1000     1000     1000
7   INSURANCE                200      200      200
8   MAINTENANCE              200      200      200
9
10  TOTAL EXPENSES          6400     6400     6400
11
12
13
14
15
16
17
18
19
20
08-Mar-88   09:47 AM
```

(b)

reference to the addresses of the upper left-most and lower right-most cells. When copying, you need to specify a *source* range (signified by the "From" prompt in Lotus) and a *target* range (signified by the "To" prompt in Lotus). The **source range** is the cell or group of cells you want to copy. The **target range** is where you want the copied cells to be placed. (See Figure 7-5). Replication is the most practical method of copying similar formulas or data into spreadsheet cells.

Copying is useful for duplicating any type of cell entry. However, its real strength is in duplicating formulas while adjusting the formula for the cell location. You might want to think of this feature as being similar to describing to someone how to do one column or row of calculation and then telling that person to do the rest of the worksheet in a similar fashion. Copying formulas from the source range and duplicating them exactly in the target range is called **absolute replication** (see Figure 7-6). Replicating the formulas so that the references to other cells are adjusted to the target range is called **relative replication** (see Figure 7-7). The formulas are adjusted to their relative location on the spreadsheet.

Spreadsheet software differ on the commands and procedures for replication. As discussed in Lesson 6, with Lotus 1-2-3, cell addresses that

```
A1: (T) +$A$1                                                         READY

          A        B        C        D        E        F        G        H
1    +$A$1    +$A$1    +$A$1    +$A$1    +$A$1    +$A$1    +$A$1    +$A$1
2    +$A$1    +$A$1    +$A$1    +$A$1    +$A$1    +$A$1    +$A$1    +$A$1
3    +$A$1    +$A$1    +$A$1    +$A$1    +$A$1    +$A$1    +$A$1    +$A$1
4    +$A$1    +$A$1    +$A$1    +$A$1    +$A$1    +$A$1    +$A$1    +$A$1
5    +$A$1    +$A$1    +$A$1    +$A$1    +$A$1    +$A$1    +$A$1    +$A$1
6    +$A$1    +$A$1    +$A$1    +$A$1    +$A$1    +$A$1    +$A$1    +$A$1
7    +$A$1    +$A$1    +$A$1    +$A$1    +$A$1    +$A$1    +$A$1    +$A$1
8    +$A$1    +$A$1    +$A$1    +$A$1    +$A$1    +$A$1    +$A$1    +$A$1
9    +$A$1    +$A$1    +$A$1    +$A$1    +$A$1    +$A$1    +$A$1    +$A$1
10   +$A$1    +$A$1    +$A$1    +$A$1    +$A$1    +$A$1    +$A$1    +$A$1
11   +$A$1    +$A$1    +$A$1    +$A$1    +$A$1    +$A$1    +$A$1    +$A$1
12   +$A$1    +$A$1    +$A$1    +$A$1    +$A$1    +$A$1    +$A$1    +$A$1
13   +$A$1    +$A$1    +$A$1    +$A$1    +$A$1    +$A$1    +$A$1    +$A$1
14
15
16
17
18
19
20
                                                 CIRC
```

FIGURE 7-6 An example of absolute replication. Notice that the cell reference is duplicated exactly when copied from the source cells into the target cells. In Lotus 1-2-3, the dollar sign ($) before each part of the cell address signals to the software an absolute cell reference. Compare this with Figure 7-7.

FIGURE 7-7 **An example of relative replication. Notice how the cell references in the formulas are adjusted as the formulas are copied from the source cells to target cells.**

A1: (T) +A1 READY

	A	B	C	D	E	F	G	H
1	+A1	+B1	+C1	+D1	+E1	+F1	+G1	+H1
2	+A2	+B2	+C2	+D2	+E2	+F2	+G2	+H2
3	+A3	+B3	+C3	+D3	+E3	+F3	+G3	+H3
4	+A4	+B4	+C4	+D4	+E4	+F4	+G4	+H4
5	+A5	+B5	+C5	+D5	+E5	+F5	+G5	+H5
6	+A6	+B6	+C6	+D6	+E6	+F6	+G6	+H6
7	+A7	+B7	+C7	+D7	+E7	+F7	+G7	+H7
8	+A8	+B8	+C8	+D8	+E8	+F8	+G8	+H8
9	+A9	+B9	+C9	+D9	+E9	+F9	+G9	+H9
10	+A10	+B10	+C10	+D10	+E10	+F10	+G10	+H10
11	+A11	+B11	+C11	+D11	+E11	+F11	+G11	+H11
12	+A12	+B12	+C12	+D12	+E12	+F12	+G12	+H12
13	+A13	+B13	+C13	+D13	+E13	+F13	+G13	+H13
14								
15								
16								
17								
18								
19								
20								

CIRC

require absolute replication are preceded with a dollar sign ($) (see Figure 7-6). SuperCalc4 can, upon request, prompt the user after the Replicate command, asking if cell references are to be absolute or relative [see Figure 7-8*(a)*]. If the relative option is chosen, the software prompts the user at each cell reference in the formula to see which are to be adjusted [see Figure 7-8*(b)*].

Spreadsheet Graphics

Spreadsheet graphics use charts and graphs to present complex numeric information contained within an electronic spreadsheet in a more comprehensible format. The graphics software contained within spreadsheets such

FIGURE 7-8 **Spreadsheet software takes a variety of approaches to specify which cell references are to be copied exactly (absolute replication) and which are to be adjusted when copied (relative replication). SuperCalc4 asks the user which cell references are to be adjusted (relative) and which are to remain the same (absolute). *(a)* If the user specifies relative replication, then the software prompts at each cell reference in the formula to see if the user wants it relative or absolute. *(b)* If the user replies no ("N"), then the cell reference remains the same, as in the cell references to cells G4, G5, and B6. However, if the user replies yes ("Y"), then the cell reference is adjusted to the relative position in the worksheet, as with the cell references to D10 through D16.**

```
CALC   A        B       C       D                E              F            G
1    MONTHLY PAYROLL:                  LOOKUP(MONTH(D4),A25:A36)
2   ============================================================================
3   Today's Date          DATE(2,17,90)                 Deduction Percentages
4   Payroll Start Date    DATE(2,1,90)                  Fica         0.071
5   Days this period      D3-D4+1                       State        .01
6   Recalculate YTD? Y                                  Insurance    25
7                              Gross              Total         Net          YTD
8         Employee    St       Salary            Deduct         Pay        Gross
9   ============================================================================
10                                     -((G4+G5)*D10+B6) D10+E10     IF(C6="Y",G10
11                                                                   IF(C6="Y",G11
12                                                                   IF(C6="Y",G12
13                                                                   IF(C6="Y",G13
14                                                                   IF(C6="Y",G14
15                                                                   IF(C6="Y",G15
16                                                                   IF(C6="Y",G16
17  ============================================================================
18  TOTALS                SUM(D10.D1 SUM(E10.E16)      SUM(F10.F1 SUM(G10.G16)
19
20
Source cell E10. Adjust G4 (Y or N)?
Copying to... 11
 25>-((G4+G5)*D10+B6)
MENU  Confirm adjustment for each cell reference                    CAPS
```

The adjustment inquiry

(a)

```
CALC   A        B       C       D                E              F            G
1    MONTHLY PAYROLL:                  LOOKUP(MONTH(D4),A25:A36)
2   ============================================================================
3   Today's Date          DATE(2,17,90)                 Deduction Percentages
4   Payroll Start Date    DATE(2,1,90)                  Fica         0.071
5   Days this period      D3-D4+1                       State        .01
6   Recalculate YTD? Y                                  Insurance    25
7                              Gross              Total         Net          YTD
8         Employee    St       Salary            Deduct         Pay        Gross
9   ============================================================================
10                                     -((G4+G5)*D10+B6) D10+E10     IF(C6="Y",G10
11                                     -((G4+G5)*D11+B6)             IF(C6="Y",G11
12                                     -((G4+G5)*D12+B6)             IF(C6="Y",G12
13                                     -((G4+G5)*D13+B6)             IF(C6="Y",G13
14                                     -((G4+G5)*D14+B6)             IF(C6="Y",G14
15                                     -((G4+G5)*D15+B6)             IF(C6="Y",G15
16                                     -((G4+G5)*D16+B6)             IF(C6="Y",G16
17  ============================================================================
18  TOTALS                SUM(D10.D1 SUM(E10.E16)      SUM(F10.F1 SUM(G10.G16)
19
20
  E10          Form=-((G4+G5)*D10+B6)
Width: 18  Memory: 273  Last Col/Row:H36
  1>
READY F1:Help F3:Names  Ctrl-Break:Cancel                           CAPS
```

The adjusted cell reference. The other cell references are replicated absolutely.

(b)

as Lotus 1-2-3, SuperCalc4, Excel, and Quattro, is a set of programs that interprets graphically on a screen, printer, or plotter the data contained in the spreadsheet file. The software permits the user to easily enter labels, legends, and other descriptive headings on the graphics produced. Some of the more common graphics available with electronic spreadsheets are **bar charts** and **elaborated bar charts** (a series of horizontal or vertical bars representing data); **pie charts** (divisions of a quantity shown proportionately as pieces of a pie); **line graphs** (data represented by lines connecting plotted points); and shading and color to enhance the presentation of data.

In addition to spreadsheet software, several add-on software packages are available to expand and enhance the graphing of worksheet data. These packages, such as Freelance and Harvard Graphics, can directly use the data contained within the worksheet without transferring or translating the data into a different format. In a later tutorial you will create several graphs using Lotus.

Print Options

As discussed previously, **printing** is the reproduction of a copy of the entire electronic spreadsheet or a portion of it as output. The output can be sent to a disk file where it is stored or to a printer where a paper (hard copy) is printed. Most electronic spreadsheets permit files to be printed directly from working storage without first being stored on disk.

Printing from a spreadsheet can be done in two ways: range or block printing and spreadsheet printing. **Range** or **block printing** is the printing of a group of adjacent cells that make up partial rows and/or partial columns of a spreadsheet. **Spreadsheet** or **worksheet printing** is the printing of an entire worksheet. In addition, most spreadsheet packages offer a wide range of print options to allow users to customize reports. Headings, footings, margins, borders, and page length are among the adjustable print options. Figure 7-9 shows the screen display for choosing print options for Lotus.

Because spreadsheets are often wider than the width of a standard page, most spreadsheet software have techniques for printing large worksheets. These include using compressed print (print that is smaller, compressing more characters per inch than standard type), automatically dividing the worksheet into several pages, and printing the worksheet on its side. The option chosen depends on the size of the worksheet, the capabilities and limitations of the printer, and the type of paper (single sheet versus continuous feed). Most electronic spreadsheet software have print format commands available to change the way the output is printed. If the spreadsheet is printed as output to a disk file, then it can be edited and printed using word processing software such as WordPerfect or WordStar.

Now that you have read about these additional electronic spreadsheet features, let's use Lotus to specifically illustrate some of them.

FIGURE 7-9 **The Lotus options using the command /Print printer options.**

```
B5: 5000                                                                MENU
Header  Footer  Margins  Borders  Setup  Pg-Length  Other  Quit
Specify header line
             A              B        C         D         E         F
1   PROJECTED EXPENSES FIRST QUARTER 1990
2
3                        JAN      FEB      MARCH
4
5   SALARIES                 5000     5000      5000
6   UTILITIES                1000     1000      1000
7   INSURANCE                 200      200       200
8   MAINTENANCE               200      200       200
9
10  TOTAL EXPENSES           6400     6400      6400
11
12
13
14
15
16
17
18
19
20
08-Mar-88  09:51 AM
```

TUTORIAL: RETRIEVING AND EDITING AN EXISTING SPREADSHEET USING LOTUS 1-2-3

To complete this tutorial you need the following:

- MS-DOS system disk
- Lotus 1-2-3 system disk
- The data disk containing the Lotus 1-2-3 spreadsheet you created and saved in the previous tutorial
- A printer connected to the microcomputer

While completing this tutorial you will learn how to

- Copy and rename a Lotus 1-2-3 spreadsheet file
- Use various formatting commands to improve the appearance of the resulting spreadsheet

- Create and view onscreen several Lotus 1-2-3 graphs that illustrate parts of the spreadsheet
- Create and print graphs

The specific Lotus 1-2-3 commands used within this tutorial are

- /File Directory—To change the directory disk drive to B:.
- /File Retrieve TUTOR1.WK1—To retrieve a previously stored worksheet.
- /File Save TUTOR2.WK1—To make a copy of TUTOR1.WK1.
- /Worksheet Column Set-width—To use the pointer to change the column width to 10 spaces.
- Edit key [F2]—To change the contents of cells.
- /Worksheet Titles Vertical—To lock a column as titles.
- /Worksheet Window Horizontal and Vertical—To split the worksheet into horizontal and vertical windows.
- /Worksheet Window Synchronized—So both windows will scroll simultaneously.
- /Worksheet Global Recalculation Manual—So the worksheet will recalculate only upon command.
- /Graph Type Pie X—To create a pie chart and designate the X range, which is the range used to label the slices of the pie.
- /Graph View—To see the graph displayed on the screen.
- /Graph Save—To save the graph so it can be recalled using PrintGraph and printed.
- /Graph Name—To name the graph so it can be recalled to view on the screen.
- PrintGraph—To print the saved graph.
- /Graph Quit—To leave the graphing mode.
- /Graph A—To set the first data range, which in this case defines the data to be used to determine the size of each pie slice.
- /Graph B—To set the second data range, which in this case defines different patterns to be used in the slices of the pie chart.
- /Graph Type Stacked Bar—To create a stacked bar chart.
- /Graph Type Line—To create a line chart.

- /File Save—To save the spreadsheet.
- /Quit Yes—To leave Lotus 1-2-3.

This tutorial builds on the one you previously completed by illustrating how to copy an existing spreadsheet into another file with a new filename, edit the spreadsheet for proper appearance, and use several of the graphics capabilities of Lotus 1-2-3. Figure 7-10 shows how the spreadsheet should appear as we begin this tutorial. The steps we shall carry out include the following: (1) load Lotus 1-2-3 and load the copy of the original spreadsheet, (2) edit the spreadsheet, and (3) create several graphs.

Revise the Spreadsheet

Revising a spreadsheet is much like creating a spreadsheet. The three basic steps are similar: (1) load the operating system, (2) load the electronic spreadsheet software and spreadsheet into primary storage, and (3) change the spreadsheet.

Step 1: Load the operating system.

To load the operating system, do the procedures described earlier until you see the operating system prompt (A>) on the screen. As

```
A19: (D1) [W15] @NOW                                                    READY

          A          B        C        D        E        F        G
1   FAST DATA SERVICES, INC
2   EMPLOYEE PAY RATE ANALYZER
3   ------------------------------------------------------------
4                  6 <--CURRENT HOURLY PAY RATE
5                  7 <--PROPOSED NEW HOURLY RATE
6   ------------------------------------------------------------
7                           CURRENT     NEW    DOLLAR
8   WORKER:         HOURS:    PAY:      PAY:    CHANGE:
9
10  STEVE               10   $60.00   $70.00    $10.00
11  KEN                 20  $120.00  $140.00    $20.00
12  JIM                 15   $90.00  $105.00    $15.00
13  JOE                 30  $180.00  $210.00    $30.00
14  CECILIA             40  $240.00  $280.00    $40.00
15  ------------------------------------------------------------
16         TOTALS:     115  $690.00  $805.00   $115.00 <--COST OF CHANGE
17
18  Today's Date:
19       19-Sep-88
20
19-Sep-88  02:54 PM
```

FIGURE 7-10 TUTOR1.WK1 at the start of the tutorial.

explained in earlier lessons, it may be necessary to use a separate operating system disk. Users of hard disk systems or networks should contact the instructor or lab personnel for specific loading procedures.

Step 2: Load Lotus 1-2-3 and the spreadsheet.

a. Load the spreadsheet software. When the screen shows the A> prompt, remove the MS-DOS system disk from drive A, insert the Lotus 1-2-3 system disk in drive A, and enter

```
Lotus
```

Press **Return.**

The 1-2-3 Access System menu will appear. Notice the options across the top of the screen:

Option	*Action*
1-2-3	Loads the 1-2-3 worksheet.
PrintGraph	Accesses the Lotus Graphics Printing program so graphs that have been saved using Lotus 1-2-3 can be printed.
Translate	Permits files to be interchanged between Lotus and other programs, including 1-2-3 Release 1A; dBase II; dBase III; files stored in the .DIF format; Jazz; Symphony Versions 1.0, 1.1, and 1.2; and VisiCalc.
Install	Accesses the utility programs to install Lotus 1-2-3 for different types of microcomputer hardware, including different graphics cards, monitors, and printers.
View	Loads an introduction to Lotus 1-2-3.
Exit	Leaves the menu and returns to the operating system.

With the highlight on the 1-2-3 option, press **Return.**

b. Change the logged disk drive with the /File Directory command. When the blank worksheet appears on the screen, first change the logged disk drive. Type

```
/F D
```

A prompt appears asking for a path or a directory. Type

```
B:
```

Press **Return.** Now all worksheet files will be retrieved from and stored to the disk in drive B.

c. Retrieve the previously stored file, TUTOR1.WK1, with the /File Retrieve command. Type

```
/F R
```

Lotus 1-2-3 will supply a list of the files with the .WK1 extension currently stored on the logged disk drive, B. Remember, if you are using Lotus 1-2-3 Version 1a, the filename extension will be .WKS. If necessary, use the arrow keys to move the highlight to **TUTOR1.WK1.** Press **Return.**

The previously stored worksheet appears on the screen. The screen should now look similar to Figure 7-10.

d. Make a copy of TUTOR1.WK1 with the /File Save command. You now have a copy of TUTOR1.WK1 in RAM and the original on a disk file. If you save the copy in RAM with a new filename, TUTOR2.WK1, then TUTOR1.WK1 remains on the disk as it was originally stored. Type

```
/F S
```

At the prompt

```
Enter save file name:
```

type

```
TUTOR2
```

Press **Return.** The copy currently in primary storage will be renamed TUTOR2. When you save the file on the disk, the new TUTOR2.WK1 and the original TUTOR1.WK1 will both be on the disk.

Step 3: Edit the spreadsheet.

a. Widen columns B, C, D, and E. Since we changed the format to currency in the preceding tutorial, some spaces are used for the dollar sign, the decimal point, possible left and right parentheses for negative values, and commas every three spaces to the left of the decimal point. Therefore, the largest value that could be displayed in a nine-space cell is $999.99. The value 1000 would be formatted as $1,000.00 and would require ten spaces, counting the space for the $ sign, the comma, and the decimal point. In fact, if the resulting variable were a negative number, requiring left and right parentheses, eleven spaces would be required. However, it is unlikely that a payroll would ever show a negative number. Therefore, ten spaces will be sufficient. The default of nine spaces is adequate for the values used to this point. However, suppose the decision maker wants to see the cost of the proposed pay rate after one *month* rather than one *week*. Assume that the hours worked after four weeks are now four times the current hours. In cell B14 enter

```
160
```

to see the effect of column width on cell contents. Notice that cells C16, C17, and D14, change to asterisks when the new value is entered. The asterisk display is an indication that the value is too large to fit into the nine-space cell. The new pay changes to all asterisks when Cecilia's hours are changed from 40 to 160 because 160 times 6.5 is $1,040.00, which exceeds the nine spaces.

To handle all these formatting problems, move the pointer to column C and type

```
/W C S
```

Where

/W = Worksheet
C = Column
S = Set-Width

The prompt appears:

```
Enter column width (1..240): 9
```

Press the **right arrow key** *once*. Notice that both the column width number and the actual width of the column on the screen increase as you press the right arrow key. When necessary, you can reduce the column size by pressing the left arrow key.

Press **Return** to accept the column width of 10. Increase the width of columns D and E using the same commands. Change cell B14 back to a reasonable number by typing

```
25
```

b. Add last names to the worker names using the Edit command, [F2]. Move the pointer to cell A10. Press the Edit key, **[F2].** Change the worker names as follows:

In Cell	Enter
A10	Abbott, Steve
A11	Boulder, Ken
A12	Hall, Jim
A13	Johnson, Joe
A14	Wax, Cecilia

Make sure to use upper- and lower-case letters. Use the arrow keys to move the edit line cursor. Delete characters using the Delete or Backspace key. Insert or overwrite characters using the Ins key. Complete the editing and place the edited line in the cell by pressing Return or pressing the up or down arrow keys.

c. Use Title Lock to see how Lotus 1-2-3 freezes designated rows and/or columns on the screen. Move the pointer to column B. Type

```
/W T V
```

Where

/W = Worksheet
T = Titles
V = Vertical

Scroll the pointer to column J. Notice that column A remains locked on the screen.

Titling can be done horizontally for specific rows, vertically for specific columns, or both. To clear a title, move the pointer back to column B and type

```
/W T C
```

d. Use windows to view sections of the spreadsheet that you may not normally see on one screen at one time. Lotus 1-2-3 lets you split the screen into two windows. Move the pointer to the row that will be the top of the lower window: row 9. Type

```
/W W H
```

Where

/W = Worksheet
W = Window
H = Horizontal

Notice that Lotus 1-2-3 has drawn a new column border. Notice also that the pointer is in the top window. With the **arrow keys,** move the pointer to column H. The top, active window scrolls while the bottom window remains the same. These windows are *unsynchronized. Synchronized* windows scroll simultaneously.

Synchronize the windows by moving the pointer to cell A1. Type

```
/W W S
```

Where

/W = Worksheet
W = Window
S = Synchronize

Move the pointer to column H. Notice that both the upper and lower screens scroll simultaneously.

Move the pointer to cell A1. Clear the windows by typing

```
/W W C
```

Where

/W = Worksheet
W = Window
C = Clear

Try the vertical windows. Move the pointer to column B. Type

```
/W W V
```

Notice that the border appears at column B. Also notice that the *active* window is the left window. Move the pointer to the right window with the window command **[F6].** Clear the window using the command

```
/W W C
```

e. Change the Recalculation mode. As explained within the lesson, when you are entering data for a large worksheet, it is usually faster to turn off the automatic recalculation and manually recalculate the worksheet after all the values have been entered. Lotus 1-2-3 uses the /Worksheet Global command to change recalculation mode. Type

```
/W G R M
```

Where

/W = Worksheet
G = Global
R = Recalculation
M = Manual

Now when you want to recalculate the worksheet, press the recalculation command, [F9].

To see how manual recalculation works, move the cursor to cell A5 and type a new number, such as 11. The calculated entries on the spreadsheet remain the same. Press **[F9].** Almost instantly the worksheet is updated. To return to the original PROPOSED NEW HOURLY RATE, type

```
7
```

Press **[F9]** again to recalculate the worksheet.

Step 4: Create graphs.
Creating a graph for viewing on the screen is easy in Lotus 1-2-3.

a. Produce a pie chart of the current pay of the five employees. Move the pointer to A10 and enter

```
/G T P X
```

Where

/G = Graph
T = Type
P = Pie
X = Range for labels

The X range will contain labels. Define the X range to be A10 through A14. At the prompt, press **.** (period). With the **arrow keys,** move the pointer from A10 to A14. Press **Return.**

Define the A range to be C10 through D14. Type

```
A
```

Move the pointer to C10 and press **.** (period). With the **arrow keys,** move the pointer from C10 down to C14. Press **Return.**

Type

```
V
```

to view the graph. The screen should now display a pie chart with the workers' names used as labels. Note also the percentages within parentheses. These represent the proportion of the total payroll for each employee.

Press **Return** to return to the Graph menu. Type

```
Q
```

to quit the graph mode and return the display to the spreadsheet.

b. To provide different patterns for each of the pie slices, move the cell pointer to cell F10.

In Cell	Enter
F10	1
F11	2
F12	3
F13	4
F14	5

Each number represents a different pattern for each section of the pie.

Now move the cursor to F10 and enter

```
/G B
```

At the prompt

```
Enter second data range: F10
```

press **.** (period).

Move the pointer from F10 down to F14 and press **Return.** Type

```
V
```

Your screen will show a pie chart with each slice containing a different pattern. Up to six patterns are allowed.

Press **Return** to return to the graph menu.

Type

```
Q
```

to quit the graph mode.

c. Construct an "exploding" pie chart by first adding 100 to any one of the values in cells F10 through F14.

Move the pointer to F14 and type

`105`

Press **Return.** Type

`/G V`

The display should show Cecilia's slice of the pie as separated or exploded from the rest of the pie.

Press **Return.**

d. Name the graph. When a graph is *named,* you can recall it quickly without having to redefine the graph. To name the graph, at the Graph submenu, type

`N C`

Where

N = Name
C = Create

You are then prompted for a graph name. The name, which can be up to 14 characters long, should be as descriptive as possible so a graph can be recalled quickly and easily. Since this is an exploding pie chart, type

`EXPLODINGPIE`

Press **Return.**

In addition to naming the graph, you must use the /File Save command to attach the named graph to the current worksheet. If the contents of the graph have been changed, due to changes in the worksheet, use the /Graph Name Create command and the /File Save command again. You can then recall the graph using the /Graph Name Use command.

e. Save the graph. In order to print a graph later, you must save it with the /Graph Save command. A graph cannot be revised after it is saved. Remember, if you want to use a graph again, or modify it later, you must create a name for it using the /Graph Name Create command. To print the graph using the PrintGraph utility, use the /Graph Save command. At the Graph submenu, press

`S`

At the prompt for the graph name, type

`Graph1`

Press **Return.**

f. Experiment with several other types of graphs.

1. To display a stacked bar chart, change the second data range. Press

   `B`

   Type

   `D10.D14`

   Press **Return.**
   Define the graph type. Press

   `T`

   for Type. Press

   `S`

   for Stacked Bar chart.
   To view the chart, press

   `V`

   Your display will show a stacked bar chart with each vertical bar representing the current pay and the projected pay for each of the five employees. Press **Return** to return to the Graph submenu.
   Name and save the graph following the instructions listed above. Give it the graph name **STACKEDBAR** and save it with the name **GRAPH2.**

2. To display a line graph, define the graph type. Press

   `T`

   for Type. Press

   `L`

   for Line chart.

To view the chart, press

```
V
```

Your display will show a line chart with the lower line representing current pay and the upper line representing projected pay. Each employee is marked with a small rectangular symbol. Press **Return** to return to the Graph submenu.

Name and save the graph following the instructions listed above. Give it the graph name **LINE** and save it with the name **GRAPH3.**

Printing the Graphs

In order to print a graph, Lotus 1-2-3 requires the use of the PrintGraph utility on the Lotus 1-2-3 Access System menu. You must first exit the 1-2-3 worksheet and return to the Lotus 1-2-3 Access System menu. Once the PrintGraph option has been chosen from the option line, you may need to replace the Lotus 1-2-3 System disk with a PrintGraph Utility disk. Remember, it takes *much* longer to print graphs than text, and not all printers are capable of printing graphs. Lotus must be using a printer that is capable of producing graphics and that has been properly installed for Lotus 1-2-3. However, once you overcome these obstacles, the sight of a graph you produced from your worksheet is very satisfying.

Step 1: Quit and save.

a. Press

```
Q
```

to Quit the graph mode.

b. Save the file. Press

```
/F S
```

to save the current version of this spreadsheet. Remember, you have named and saved the graphs, but you have not saved the worksheet. At the prompt for the filename, press **Return.** Press

```
R
```

to replace the file.

The latest version of the spreadsheet will be copied to the disk.

c. Print the worksheet. While in the READY mode, type

```
/P P R Return Go
```

d. Now enter

```
/Q
```

to Quit Lotus 1-2-3. At the prompt, press

```
Y
```

for Yes.

Step 2: Load PrintGraph.

After you quit Lotus 1-2-3, the Lotus 1-2-3 System Access menu will appear, with options listed across the top of the screen. Move the cursor to PrintGraph and press **Return** or type **P.**

If you are using a floppy disk system, you will be prompted to insert the PrintGraph Disk into your disk drive. Remove the Lotus System disk and insert the PrintGraph disk. Press **Return.**

After the PrintGraph copyright notice appears for a moment, the PrintGraph Main Menu will appear. The options are *Image-select* to find and mark graphs to be printed; *Settings* to specify the graphics printer and the appearance of the printed graph; *Go* to print the document; *Align* to tell PrintGraph where the top of the page is; *Page* to advance the page in the printer; and *Exit* to end the PrintGraph session.

Step 3: Print the graph.

a. Press

```
I
```

to select Image-Setting. A listing of your saved graphs should appear. Once you have inserted the proper disk, or have the disk or directory listed, you should see a listing of the graph files you have saved. If necessary, change the logged disk drive using the Settings Hardware Graphs-Directory options.

b. Select the graph to be printed. To select a graph file, move the highlight with the up or down arrow keys. Highlight **GRAPH1.** To view the highlighted graph, press the GRAPH key, **[F10].** Press **Esc** to return to the file menu. Press the **spacebar** to mark or unmark a choice. A marked file is indicated by the symbol "#" next to the graph file. Although we can select several graphs to be printed at one time, let's try just one first, so we can be sure that the settings are working properly. Mark **GRAPH1** and press **Return.**

c. Check that microcomputer and printer are properly connected and that the printer is on and ready to go.

d. Press

`Go`

Within a few minutes your printer should begin printing. Remember that printing a graph takes much more time than printing a spreadsheet or a word processing document.

e. Print the remaining graphs, GRAPH2 and GRAPH3.

Quit

After you have printed the graphs, return to the Lotus 1-2-3 Access System menu. Type

`E Y`

to Exit. After the Lotus 1-2-3 Access System menu reappears, press

`E`

for Exit and return to the system prompt. Turn off the microcomputer. Congratulations! You have learned how to use the effective tool of graphics.

SUMMARY

Modern electronic spreadsheet software packages provide several features that enhance the appearance of the spreadsheet on the screen and on the printed page. Title lock commands allow the user to define particular rows or columns as titles that will remain on the screen as the rest of the spreadsheet is moved around. Windows provide for splitting the screen into two or more segments, allowing the user to see two or more distant parts of the spreadsheet at once. Various formatting options can be used to give the spreadsheet a more professional appearance. Such options usually include various forms of numeric display, such as integer or exponential form, various settings of the decimal point precision, rounding of numbers, and the use of asterisks to form a bar chart. Global options allow the user to change the order the spreadsheet follows in recalculation and to choose whether or not the recalculation is automatic and whether or not replication of formulas is absolute or relative.

Spreadsheet graphics provide the user with still another presentation form. Most allow the user to present values in pie charts, bar graphs, and line graphs. The software may be a separate graphics package or be a part of the spreadsheet software package. Packages such as Lotus 1-2-3, Excel, SuperCalc4, and others provide rather extensive graphics as an integral part of the spreadsheet commands.

Printer options provide choices regarding the type of print used, the size of page, the portion of the spreadsheet printed per page, and the creation of titles. Some software packages come with special printing enhancements that rotate a wide worksheet so it can be printed down the printed page rather than across.

EXERCISES

1. Describe each of the following spreadsheet features and comment on the usefulness of each:
   a. title lock
   b. windows
   c. formatting
   d. global options
   e. graphics
   f. print options
   g. data management

2. Define the following terms.

title lock	natural order	bar chart
windowing	dependency order	elaborated bar chart
synchronized window	column order	line graph
unsynchronized window	row order	pie chart
default settings	iteration control option	exploded segment
global format command	replication	printing
iteration recalculation	range	worksheet printing
order of recalculation	block range	block printing
	source range	data management
	target range	formula-driven spreadsheets
	absolute replication	user-defined formats
	relative replication	configuration
	spreadsheet graphics	

3. Supply the Lotus 1-2-3 command(s) to complete the following operations:
   a. Change the recalculation mode from automatic to manual.
   b. Erase the entire worksheet from primary storage.
   c. Change the appearance of the entire worksheet to scientific notation.
   d. Save the output file so it can be printed in a word processing file.
   e. Copy the range of B2 to B3.B8.
   f. Lock the titles horizontally.
   g. Change the format of a column worksheet to currency.
   h. Save a file.
   i. Globally format the worksheet using the currency format.
   j. Change the column width to 23 spaces.

4. Match the Lotus 1-2-3 commands on the left with the proper actions on the right.

a.	+C8*E8	____	Replicates from C8 to C9 through C12.
b.	/C C8 C9.C12	____	Formats the current column to 20 spaces.
c.	/W T H	____	Multiplies the contents of C8 times E8.
d.	/W C S 20	____	Locks a horizontal title.
e.	/W G F	____	Displays the global format options.
f.	/R L R	____	F8+F9+F10+F11+F12+F13.
g.	/W G F C	____	Formats the entire spreadsheet in currency format.
h.	/W G F S	____	Text in ranges right justified.
i.	@sum(F8.F13)	____	Puts entire spreadsheet in scientific notation.

5. Describe the steps necessary to use the /File Save command to save the spreadsheet created in the tutorial.
6. Describe the steps necessary to produce printed output from the tutorial spreadsheet.
7. Describe the steps necessary to print a bar graph from the tutorial spreadsheet.
8. Describe what happens if you try to read into a word processing document the spreadsheet saved with the /File Save command instead of the results saved with the /Print File command.
9. Using Figure 7-4 (a), (b), and (c), explain how the recalculation order and the placement of formulas within the spreadsheet can produce erroneous results. How could the spreadsheet in Figure 7-4 be redesigned so this would not be a problem?
10. Retrieve the worksheet completed in the tutorial in Lesson 7 and produce a bar graph with the names of the workers as the X axis range, the current pay for the five workers as the A data range, and the new pay as the B data range. Use the Options Titles command to enter "Fast Data Services, Inc." as the first graph title line, "Prepared by: *Your Name*" as the second graph title line, "Workers" as the X axis title, and "Pay" as the Y axis title. Use the Options Legend command to enter "Current Pay" as the legend for the A range and "New Pay" as

the legend for the B range. View the bar graph on the screen and save the graph as B:EXER710 to be printed out later.

11. Practice using Lotus 1-2-3 by completing the tutorial, Retrieving and Editing an Existing Spreadsheet Using Lotus 1-2-3. Then revise the spreadsheet to include the following changes.

    a. Following the steps described in the tutorial, make a copy of TUTOR2.WK1 and assign a new filename based on your name and the date of completion of the exercise. For example, if your name is John Smith and you completed the exercise on May 21, 1990, you would name the file JS52190. Lotus 1-2-3 will assign the filename extension. *Please do not use this filename, it is only an example.* Give the spreadsheet its own unique filename.

    b. In cell C1, use the @NOW function to insert the date you completed the exercise.

    c. Replace the current company name of "FAST DATA SERVICES" with a new name—for example, "MY-T-FAST HAMBURGER PALACE."

    d. Edit the worksheet, revising CURRENT HOURLY PAY RATE to 7 and PROPOSED NEW HOURLY RATE to 10. Recalculate the spreadsheet using the Recalculate command. Widen any columns if necessary.

    e. Save and print the worksheet.

    f. Produce, save, and print an exploding pie chart with labels and different patterns for each section of the pie.

    g. Remove the second data range and produce, save, and print a bar chart.

12. Using the spreadsheet you created in Lesson 6 for Synozyn, Inc., create a pie chart with an X range listing the five departments and an A range showing the percent change. Move to cell F6 and use the command /Data Fill F6.F10 Start: 1 Step: 1 Stop: 5 to create a column to be used as the B range to produce different cross-hatch patterns in each slice of the pie. Define the B range as F6 . . F10 and view the graph. Use Options Titles to enter a first title of "Synozyn Inc. Sales Comparison" and a second title of "Prepared By: *Your Name.*" Save and print both the graph and the worksheet.

13. Using the gradebook you created in Lesson 6, add the scores for four more exams to the worksheet using the /Worksheet Insert Column D1 . . G1 to insert four columns. The TOTAL column will be moved to column H. With the pointer in cell B7, use /Worksheet Titles Vertical to lock Column A as a title. Move to cell H7 and notice that Column D is now next to Column A. Move back to cell D7 and enter the new scores listed at the top of page 295:

Anderson, Ellen	90	89	98	90
Bach, Jan	78	89	78	89
Beard, Dorothea	91	89	78	87
Behrens, Curt	67	78	67	69
Bickle, Barbara	90	78	87	67
Bishop, Helen	67	50	98	99
Brieant, Marcia	78	89	84	79
Brown, Patricia	70	89	98	99
Cleland, Clifford	89	69	76	87

Move to cell B16 and use /Copy FROM: B16..B22 TO: C16..G16 to replicate the dashes and formulas over the new columns. Move to H7 and enter @SUM(B7..G7) to compute the proper total for Anderson, Ellen. Then use /Copy FROM: H7 TO: H8..H15 to compute the proper total points for the other students. In cell H17 enter @SUM(B17..G17) to compute the new total possible. Also use the /Copy command to copy dashed lines across the newly added columns. Move to cell L7 and notice that the TOTAL and PERCENT columns (H and I) have moved beside column A. Save and print the spreadsheet.

14. Retrieve the TEMPERATURE STUDY worksheet you prepared for Exercise 6-12, insert ten new rows beginning at row 13, and add the following data:

DATE:	**Chicago**	**New York**	**Tampa**	**Houston**
11-Jan	20	12	80	66
12-Jan	10	10	81	61
13-Jan	0	12	76	50
14-Jan	−4	5	78	60
15-Jan	−1	8	79	67
16-Jan	−9	9	65	56
17-Jan	−1	10	59	49
18-Jan	2	9	60	50
19-Jan	10	12	69	56
20-Jan	11	15	78	65

Edit cells B24, B25, and B26 (High:, Low:, Average:) so their ranges will be (B3 . . B22) and copy these formulas from B24 . . B26 to C24 . . E24. Move to A3 and create a window by entering /Worksheet Window Horizontal. Use [F6] to toggle from the upper window to the lower window. With the upper window displaying rows 1 and 2, toggle to the lower window and scroll down until line 24 is at the top of the lower window, thereby making it possible for you to see the top and the bottom of the spreadsheet on the same screen. Beginning in D1, enter "Prepared by: *Your Name*" and, in G1 (or the first available blank cell in row 1), use @NOW to date your worksheet. Save and print the spreadsheet.

15. Retrieve the High Tech Sales Co. Sales Rep. Expenses worksheet created in the Lesson 6 exercises. In cell A7 use /Worksheet Titles Horizontal to define rows 1–6 as titles and move the cursor to A37 to position row 24 below row 6 so the totals and averages can be seen directly below the column labels. Save and print the spreadsheet.

16. Retrieve the Heavy Duty Trucking Co. Truck Driver Wage Study spreadsheet created in the Lesson 6 exercises. Assume we now have new hours for each of the truck drivers. Before entering the new data, use /Worksheet Global Recalculation Manual to halt the automatic recalculation with each new data entry. Enter the following new data:

Driver	Hours
Mary	40
Katie	50
Terri	45
Jeannette	45
John	40
Cecilia	40
Joe	35
Jim	40
Ken	35
Steve	37

Press [F9] to recalculate the spreadsheet. Restore the automatic recalculation, save the spreadsheet with a *new name,* and print out a series of spreadsheets for proposed percentage wage increases of 5%, 6%, 7%, 8%, and 9%.

17. Retrieve the Heavy Duty Trucking Co. Fuel Price/Mileage Study spreadsheet created in the Lesson 6 exercises. For the estimated percent increase in miles/gallon rating, enter 0.20 in cell A5. Then create a line graph with the tractor numbers as the X axis range, the current costs as the A data range, and the proposed costs as the B data range. For the first title enter "Heavy Duty Trucking Co. Fuel Study." For the second title enter "Prepared by: *Your Name.*" For the X axis title enter "Tractor Number" and for the Y axis title enter "Cost." Set the A legend to "Current Cost" and the B legend to "Proposed Cost." View the graph and, if it's satisfactory, save it.

8

Advanced Spreadsheet Applications

LESSON OUTLINE

This lesson addresses several additional spreadsheet features. Included first is the use of a spreadsheet to create a simple database and perform statistical analysis of the data. Also addressed is the issue of comparing and selecting electronic spreadsheet software packages using the general analysis and design process described in Lesson 2 (see Figure 2-10). A checklist is provided as a general guide to the selection process, and features of some of the most popular spreadsheets are summarized. The tutorials guide you through the steps needed to use a Lotus database and Lotus macros.

Like word processing software, electronic spreadsheet software should be selected to fit your particular needs. Once you obtain a basic understanding of how useful such software can be, you may want to purchase one of the popular commercial packages for your personal or professional use. The guidelines discussed in this lesson will help you understand the main features of and differences among commercial software packages. Electronic spreadsheet software is evolving rapidly, and as your understanding of the software grows, you will be better equipped to take advantage of these expanding capabilities.

DATA MANAGEMENT

Starting in Lesson 9, we discuss data management software, such as dBASE III Plus. However, several spreadsheet packages also offer some data management functions. Especially useful with spreadsheet software is the capability to analyze the data using certain statistical procedures, such as regression analysis. In this section we will examine the basic concepts of data management and demonstrate selected data management functions, using the Data Management feature of Lotus 1-2-3 as an example.

Data management is the use of electronic spreadsheet commands to sort, search, and extract selected data contained within a spreadsheet. This extracted data can then be printed to an output block, written to a disk file, or saved as a separate spreadsheet. Data contained within the spreadsheet in column and row form can be sorted, selected, and reported much like a series of index cards. This permits the data contained on the spreadsheet to be used in a variety of ways, such as to produce mailing lists, personnel lists, work schedules, training schedules, customer/client lists, rate tables, and daily/weekly logs. Figure 8-1 is an example of a worksheet using the database capabilities of Lotus 1-2-3 to keep track of an inventory of compact disk recordings.

A Lotus 1-2-3 database can contain both numeric values and labels. The database occupies a grouping or range of rows and columns on the

FIGURE 8-1 **With a database in Lotus 1-2-3, a user keeps track of her compact disk recordings. She can enter, search, and select recordings according to specified criteria. (*a*) The entries appear in random order. (*b*) The entries are sorted in ascending order first by artist name (Primary Sort Key) and second by the name of the recording (Secondary Sort Key). (*c*) The Primary Sort Key is the music classification, and the Secondary Sort Key is the name of the recording** ***[continued on pp. 300–301].***

COMPACT DISK COLLECTION

NAME	ARTIST	MUSIC	TYPE
In Search of the Turtle's Navel	Ackerman, William	New Age Jazz	CD
Haydn Cello Concerti	Ma, Yo-Yo	Classical	CD
Invisible Touch	Genesis	Rock	CD
Winter into Spring	Winston, George	New Age Jazz	CD
Emotion	Striesand, Barbra	Vocal	CD
Please Please Me	Beatles	Rock	CD
A Hard Day's Night	Beatles	Rock	CD
Sampler #2	Narada Artists	New Age Jazz	CD
Handel Music for the Royal Fireworks	English Concert	Classical	CD
Beethoven Symphonie No. 9	Karajan Berlin Philhamoiker	Classical	CD
The Bridge	Joel, Billy	Rock	CD
They Don't Make Them Like They Used To	Rogers, Kenny	Country	CD
Riptide	Palmer, Robert	Rock	CD
Hot Together	Pointer Sisters	Rock	CD
Beethoven Sonatas Volume 2	Ma, Yo-Yo and Emanuelax	Classical	CD
Gustav Holst The Planets	Karajan Berlin Philhamoiker	Classical	CD
With the Beatles	Beatles	Rock	CD
The Beatles for Sale	Beatles	Rock	CD
Perhaps Love	Domingo, Placido	Vocal	CD
Third Stage	Boston	Rock	CD

(a)

standard worksheet area. In database management, a collection of data about one item or entity is called a **record** and on a spreadsheet is held in one row or portion of a row. The top row of a spreadsheet database holds the labels that describe the type of data stored in each column (such as NAME, STREET ADDRESS, CITY, STATE, ZIP, and AMOUNT ORDERED). The labels used to describe and name the columns in a database are called **field names** and the columns themselves are called **fields.** Lotus 1-2-3 Release 2 has a limit of 256 fields per database. The number of rows (records) can be as many as the 1-2-3 spreadsheet allows (over 8,000 in Release 2), but the practical limitations of RAM in your computer may determine the maximum size of the database.

Lotus 1-2-3 allows you to enter data into a simple database structure in which each record is a row and each column is a field. Database commands then allow you to sort your data using label or numeric fields as sort keys and to locate and list data records that match the criteria you specify. Other database commands allow you to average, sum, and count selected records.

COMPACT DISK COLLECTION

NAME	ARTIST	MUSIC	TYPE
In Search of the Turtle's Navel	Ackerman, William	New Age Jazz	CD
A Hard Day's Night	Beatles	Rock	CD
Please Please Me	Beatles	Rock	CD
The Beatles for Sale	Beatles	Rock	CD
With the Beatles	Beatles	Rock	CD
Third Stage	Boston	Rock	CD
Perhaps Love	Domingo, Placido	Vocal	CD
Handel Music for the Royal Fireworks	English Concert	Classical	CD
Invisible Touch	Genesis	Rock	CD
The Bridge	Joel, Billy	Rock	CD
Beethoven Symphonie No. 9	Karajan Berlin Philhamoiker	Classical	CD
Gustav Holst The Planets	Karajan Berlin Philhamoiker	Classical	CD
Haydn Cello Concerti	Ma, Yo-Yo	Classical	CD
Beethoven Sonatas Volume 2	Ma, Yo-Yo and Emanuelax	Classical	CD
Sampler #2	Narada Artists	New Age Jazz	CD
Riptide	Palmer, Robert	Rock	CD
Hot Together	Pointer Sisters	Rock	CD
They Don't Make Them Like They Used To	Rogers, Kenny	Country	CD
Emotion	Striesand, Barbra	Vocal	CD
Winter into Spring	Winston, George	New Age Jazz	CD

Secondary Sort Key   Primary Sort Key

(b)

Although the database commands within most spreadsheet packages are somewhat limited, they can be useful when relatively small and simple databases are being maintained and analyzed, when other database software is not available, and when the needed data analysis is easily accomplished using spreadsheet functions. For example, many people find the regression analysis function available within the Data feature of Lotus 1-2-3 sufficient for many of their forecasting needs.

Data Query

Among the most useful features of Lotus 1-2-3 is the data query feature. Use **data query** commands to search a database for a particular record, copy records from a database to a separate part of the worksheet, extract records with no duplication, and remove selected records. Lotus offers four different query options:

Find locates and highlights selected records in a database.

Extract locates selected records and places them in a designated area of the worksheet.

COMPACT DISK COLLECTION

NAME	ARTIST	MUSIC	TYPE
Beethoven Sonatas Volume 2	Ma, Yo-Yo and Emanuelax	Classical	CD
Beethoven Symphonie No. 9	Karajan Berlin Philhamoiker	Classical	CD
Gustav Holst The Planets	Karajan Berlin Philhamoiker	Classical	CD
Handel Music for the Royal Fireworks	English Concert	Classical	CD
Haydn Cello Concerti	Ma, Yo-Yo	Classical	CD
They Don't Make Them Like They Used To	Rogers, Kenny	Country	CD
In Search of the Turtle's Navel	Ackerman, William	New Age Jazz	CD
Sampler #2	Narada Artists	New Age Jazz	CD
Winter into Spring	Winston, George	New Age Jazz	CD
A Hard Day's Night	Beatles	Rock	CD
Hot Together	Pointer Sisters	Rock	CD
Invisible Touch	Genesis	Rock	CD
Please Please Me	Beatles	Rock	CD
Riptide	Palmer, Robert	Rock	CD
The Beatles for Sale	Beatles	Rock	CD
The Bridge	Joel, Billy	Rock	CD
Third Stage	Boston	Rock	CD
With the Beatles	Beatles	Rock	CD
Emotion	Striesand, Barbra	Vocal	CD
Perhaps Love	Domingo, Placido	Vocal	CD

Secondary Sort Key (NAME) — Primary Sort Key (MUSIC)

(c)

Unique locates selected records and places them in a designated area of the worksheet, but includes no duplicate records. Only unique records are listed.

Delete finds and deletes selected records. The other records are adjusted to fill in blank rows.

Before these query commands can be used, an input range and a criterion range must be defined. An **input range** is the area of the worksheet to be searched. The input range must include the row of field names since this row acts as a reference when Lotus tries to match the criterion. The first step in using any query command is to set up the input range so Lotus knows what area of the database to search. The /Data Query Input command lets the user specify the input range.

The **criterion range** establishes the criterion to be used to search for matching records. For example, "all students with grade point average of more than 3.00" could be a criterion for searching the database. The criterion range is made up of two or more rows. The first row contains the field names from the input range. These field names must match exactly, since both are used as cross-references when the database is being searched. One way to make sure of the name match is to copy the names from the input range to the criterion range. The second row and any additional rows contain the actual criterion.

After the input and criterion ranges are set up, the database can be searched with the Find command. After the search criterion is specified in the criterion range, the Find command places the pointer on the matching record in the database range, thus highlighting the record so it is easy to "Find."

To use the Extract command, it is necessary to define an output range. An **output range** is a designated place on the worksheet where selected records are copied and placed if they meet the stated criterion in the criterion range. Like the criterion range, the output range must contain the field names from the database. Even though the user needs only to define the output range as only a single row (the one containing the field names), Lotus uses the area below these field names to copy the selected records.

Now that we've discussed the general rules for setting up the database for querying, let's see how they work using the following example.

Consider the following small set of data regarding the name, age, and sex of the members of a family:

NAME:	AGE:	SEX:
Steve	24	M
Cecilia	28	F
Ken	25	M
Jim	26	M
Joe	27	M

One advantage of using a spreadsheet to do database operations is that entering such data into a spreadsheet is easy. We just load the spreadsheet software, enter the labels (NAME:, AGE:, and SEX:) in row 1, and enter the data (columns A, B, and C) in rows 2 through 6. Then, for example, we could sort the data in ascending order according to the age of each individual, using the Lotus Data Sort command. To illustrate, if the command

```
/Data Sort Data-Range A2..C6 Primary-Key B2 A Go
```

were inserted, within a few moments the sorted data would appear on the screen:

```
NAME:     AGE:      SEX:
Steve     24        M
Ken       25        M
Jim       26        M
Joe       27        M
Cecilia   28        F
```

Notice that we specified both the range to be sorted (A2..C6) and the starting cell of the primary key (B2), we selected ascending order (A), and we directed the computer to start (Go).

Another convenient data management function is Data Fill. The user fills a range of cells with values by specifying the starting value, defining the amount the value increases in each successive cell, and giving the ending value. For example, suppose we want to add and fill a column in our tiny database, such as

ORDER:	NAME:	AGE:	SEX:
1	Steve	24	M
2	Ken	25	M
3	Jim	26	M
4	Joe	27	M
5	Cecilia	28	F

First, we use the /Worksheet Insert Column A1 command to add the column. After entering the column label ("ORDER:"), we use the Data Fill command to fill the column. For example, let's move the cursor to cell A2 and enter the command

```
/Data Fill A2..A6 Start: 1 Step: 1 Stop: 5
```

Notice we specify the range (A2 through A6), the starting value (1), the increment or step value (1), and the ending or stopping value (5).

Remember, in order to have Lotus query the database to find certain records and place them in a separate area of the worksheet, you need to define three areas of the spreadsheet: one to contain the database (Query Input), one to define the criterion (Query Criterion), and, finally, one to contain the extracted data (Query Output). Lotus uses the command

```
/Data Query Input A1..D6
```

to define the area containing the database.

Define the criterion area by first copying the column headings used in the database. It is important that the headings be exactly the same, so use the Copy command to make a duplicate:

```
/Copy from A1..D1 to A10..D10
```

Second, use the Lotus command

```
/Data Query Criterion A10..D11
```

to define the two rows that will hold the criterion or basis of the data query.

Third, define the output area by first copying the column headings used in the database, using the command

```
/Copy from A1..D1 to A13..D13
```

Then label the output area with a heading, for example,

```
ITEMS EXTRACTED FROM DATABASE ABOVE USING CRITERION LISTED BELOW
```

Last, define the output area by using

```
/Data Query Output A13..D13
```

to define the top row containing the column labels. The records we extract will be listed directly below these labels.

To see how the Find command works, we must first define a criterion for a data query by entering a specific criterion in row 11 of the query area. For example, if you were looking for someone who is 26 years old, you would move to cell C11 and enter 26. Then you would enter the Data Query command

```
/Data Query Find
```

and the row containing

```
3 Jim     26 M
```

should be highlighted in reverse video. The highlighting indicates that the data manager has found the record that met the criterion of AGE=26. You would then press Return and enter

```
Extract
```

The screen would contain

```
ORDER:          NAME:             AGE:          SEX:
    1           Steve              24             M
    2           Ken                25             M
    3           Jim                26             M
    4           Joe                27             M
    5           Cecilia            28             F

ORDER:          NAME:             AGE:          SEX:
                                   26
ITEMS EXTRACTED FROM DATA BASE ABOVE USING CRITERION LISTED ABOVE
ORDER:          NAME:             AGE:          SEX:
    3           Jim                26             M
```

To extract all the males in the database, you would need to quit the query, enter

```
/Range Erase C11
```

to erase the 26 from cell C11, move to D11, enter an M for Male, and then enter

```
/Data Query Extract
```

The output range A14..D17 should immediately be filled with

```
ORDER:      NAME:       AGE:    SEX:
1           Steve       24      M
2           Ken         25      M
3           Jim         26      M
4           Joe         27      M
```

To see how the [F7] Query function key can be used to quickly toggle in and out of the Data function, press [F7] and enter F in cell D11. Press [F7] again and the output range should immediately change to

```
ORDER:      NAME:       AGE:    SEX:
5           Cecilia     28      F
```

Now let's examine a criterion that will extract all males over 24 years old. You would press [F7] and, in cell C11, enter

```
+C2>24
```

In cell D11, you enter the criterion

```
M
```

and press [F7] again. The output area would contain

ORDER:	NAME:	AGE:	SEX:
2	Ken	25	M
3	Jim	26	M
4	Joe	27	M

Notice that Steve is excluded because he is not over 24 years old (he is exactly 24) and that Cecilia is excluded because she is female. Note that the formula in C11 must begin with a plus sign "+" and that the cell C11 contains "0." As a data criterion +C2>24 makes sense, but as a formula in the spreadsheet at cell C11 it produces an answer of zero.

Regression

Another data management feature in Lotus is regression. **Regression** is a statistical method used to predict the value of one variable given the value of another (simple regression) or several other (multiple regression) associated variables. For example, in a simple regression, someone might attempt to predict a grade point average given the number of study hours or attempt to predict the number of traffic accidents given the speed limit. An example of multiple regression would be predicting a firm's sales for next year given last year's sales, the amount spent on advertising, the amount spent on new product development, and the amount spent on commissions for sales representatives. For both types of regression, the primary objective is to predict the value of one variable (the **dependent variable)** given that the value of an associated variable or the values of a set of associated variables (the **independent variable** or variables) are known. For linear regression (whether simple or multiple), it is assumed that the independent and dependent variables are linearly associated; that is, when graphed the relation will be a straight line.

In Lotus the /Data Regression command permits users to apply simple or multiple linear regression analysis. After selecting the /Data Regression command, the user defines the independent variables by selecting the X-Range option and entering the range—by address or by name—or the columns containing the data representing the independent variables. Up to 16 variables can be included, each with up to 8,192 values. Then the user defines the dependent variable by selecting the Y-Range option and entering the range that contains the column of data representing the dependent variable. This column must contain the same number of rows specified for the X range. Next, the Output-Range is defined. Like the Output range in Data Query, this area on the spreadsheet will receive the output. The range should be at least nine rows deep and two columns wider than the number of independent variables. The user can specify the output range by name or address or by entering the address of the cell that will become the top left corner of the output range. Next, the user selects the Intercept option Compute to allow Lotus to calculate the Y intercept. Then the user selects Go to execute the analysis and place the result in the output range.

In order to understand how the regression command works, let's consider the following example. Assume you have the data for the last ten years regarding the amount a firm has spent on Research and Development (R&D) and Advertising (ADV). Also, you have the Sales Income (SALES) for each year. Assume you have entered the following data with all the dollar amounts expressed in thousands:

	A	B	C	D
1	YEAR	R&D	ADV	SALES
2	1	19	10	100
3	2	20	11	101
4	3	22	11	102
5	4	23	14	103
6	5	23	12	103
7	6	24	14	104
8	7	26	15	107
9	8	25	16	108
10	9	27	16	110
11	10	28	17	111

It is reasonable to assume that SALES are related in some way to the year, the amount spent on Research and Development, and the amount spent on Advertising. If we tried to forecast sales for the eleventh year, we could reasonably assume that sales would be some function of YEAR + R&D + ADV. What we need to know is how much weight to assign to each factor. Although a detailed discussion of the statistical topic of multiple regression analysis is beyond the scope of this book, the technique for using Lotus to compute a multiple regression is simple. Assuming you have entered the above data, the next step is to enter

```
/Data Regression X-Range A2..C11
```

to designate the independent variables as the area of the spreadsheet containing the values for YEAR, R&D, and ADV. Then enter

```
Y-Range D2..D11
```

to designate SALES as the dependent variable. Then enter

```
Output-Range A12
```

to specify where Lotus should begin to place the output it will produce as a result of the regression analysis. Next enter

```
Intercept Compute
```

so that Lotus will calculate where the regression equation will intercept the Y axis. Then enter

```
Go
```

and within a second the following output will be displayed:

```
                 Regression Output:
Constant Regression Output: 94.55357
Std Err of Y Est               0.938364
R Squared                      0.960247
No. of Observations                  10
Degrees of Freedom                    6
```

The general mathematical form for a model with more than one independent variable is

$$Y = A + B1*X1 + B2*X2 + B3*X3 + \ldots + Bn*Xn$$

where, in this case,

Y = forecasted Sales
A = constant (94.55357)
B1 = coefficient of the first independent variable YEAR (0.998724)
B2 = coefficient of the second independent variable R&D (0.080357)
B3 = coefficient of the third independent variable ADV (0.216836)

For example, if

YEAR = 11
R&D = 30
ADV = 20

then the forecast would be

SALES = 94.55357 + 0.998724*11 + (0.080357*30) + (0.216836*20)

SALES = 112.2869

To facilitate "What if?" analysis, put the decision variables on the screen in a place that is easy to see and change. For example,

```
X Coefficient(s)    0.998724   0.080357 0.216836
Std Err of Coef.    0.557767   0.524561 0.436956
```

The formula to calculate the forecast at G6 is

+D13+C19*G2+D19*G3+E19*G4

This formula makes it easy to change the amount we plan to spend on R&D or ADV and to see what the resulting SALES forecast will be. Just change the values in G3 or G4 and watch Lotus calculate a new forecast.

More Graphing Techniques

The graphing techniques in Lotus provide a handy way to compare the actual sales to the predicted sales. Let's use column E to contain the results of the regression model for each of the ten historical periods. First we must set up the equation formula so it can be copied easily. Move the pointer to G6 and press [F2] to edit the formula. Insert dollar signs around each of the parts of the formula that will not change as a result of going from year to year. Move to cell E2 and enter

```
+$D$13+$C$19*A2+$D$19*B2+$E$19*C2
```

Copy this by entering

```
/Copy from E2..E2 to E3..E11
```

Adjust the format for column E by entering

```
/Range Format Currency 1 Return E2.,E11
```

Increase the column width by entering

```
/Worksheet Column Set-Width 12
```

Label the column by moving to E1 and entering

```
PREDICTION
```

Now the spreadsheet shows in column D the actual historical sales figures and in column E the sales figures that would be predicted by the regression formula. To see how close the predicted values are to the actual ones, let's graph both sets of values using line graphs. Begin the graphing by entering

```
/Graph Type Line X A2..A11 Return
```

to define the type of graph we want (a line graph) and the area of the spreadsheet to plot along the horizontal (X) axis (A2..A11). Then enter

```
A D2..D11
```

to define the data to be plotted on the vertical (Y) axis. Then enter

```
B E2..E11
```

to define the second set of data to be plotted on the vertical (Y) axis. Now press Q to Quit the description of the graph and press V to View what we have created so far. You should have two lines on the graph: one with the data points marked with small boxes (the actual sales) and the other with the data points marked with small crosses (the predicted sales). To make the graph more readable, press Return and enter

```
Options Legend A ACTUAL Return
```

to make the word "ACTUAL" a label on the legend for the small boxes. Then enter

```
Legend B PREDICTED Return
```

to make the word "PREDICTED" the label on the legend for the small crosses. Add a title line to the graph by entering

```
Titles First FAST DATA INC. Return
```

and

```
Titles Second Last 10 Year's Sales Return
```

and

```
Titles X-Axis YEARS Return
```

and

```
Titles Y-Axis SALES (000's) Return Quit
```

Then enter

```
View
```

to see what the graph now looks like. Repeat any of the above steps if you need to correct any typing errors. When you are satisfied that the graph is correct, save it as a separate file by entering

```
Save GRRESS.PIC Return
```

to save the graph as GRRESS.PIC on the currently logged disk. Note that Lotus 1-2-3 Release 2 will automatically add the .PIC suffix if you do not. Now the graph is saved so it can be printed later using the PrintGraph feature of Lotus 1-2-3.

If you have recently had to compute a multiple regression problem by hand, you will appreciate how easy Lotus makes this tedious task. If you have recently used a statistical software package such as MicroStat, then you may be disappointed at how tedious Lotus is at solving a multiple regression problem. However, not everyone has access to a statistical software package. And Lotus provides the user with the flexibility of using the results of the regression computations in other parts of the spreadsheet, a feature that makes the results more meaningful to some users.

MACROS IN LOTUS

On a spreadsheet, a **macro** is a range that contains a set of keystrokes used as a series of spreadsheet commands. A **macro name** is the range name given to a macro. A macro name is created by using the /Range Name Create command followed by a range of cell coordinates. The keyboard macro commands names have a special format: \ A . . \ Z (the backslash followed by one of the 26 letters of the alphabet). Therefore, only 26 keyboard macros can be named within one spreadsheet. To cause Lotus 1-2-3 to execute the macro, you hold the [Alt] key down while pressing the letter that names the macro.

The list of commands within the macro is sometimes called the **macro body.** The macro body is stored in spreadsheet cells, just as numbers, labels, and formulas are. A macro cell entry usually begins with an apostrophe (') so that Lotus 1-2-3 will not interpret the slash as a signal to start executing a command right away. The apostrophe causes Lotus 1-2-3 to temporarily think of the macro as a label. The macro is entered as a series of vertical cell entries. Lotus 1-2-3 will execute the macro instructions from left to right and from top to bottom. When it reaches a blank cell, it will stop. Therefore, it is very important not to put any blank cells within the body of a macro.

Some software packages, such as Excel and SuperCalc4, have an automatic macro-building feature that allows the software to "learn" the keystrokes as the user enters them. Additional software packages, such as HAL and LEARN, can be added to give Lotus 1-2-3 this ability, but the standard Lotus 1-2-3 Release 2 does not provide automatic macro-building. It does, however, provide an extensive set of **macro commands** that are enclosed in braces, { }, and are used only within macros to simplify various cursor movements (such as {GOTO} to go to a cell); to simulate the pressing of a function key (such as {CALC} for [F9]); or to perform other functions, such as simulating the pressing of the Return key (the tilde, ~) or waiting for a user to input a value into a cell {?}.

Most people create macros by putting in the commands as you normally would but writing down on paper the keystrokes as they are entered. Each time you press Return or a function key or use the arrow keys to move about, write down the corresponding macro command as in Table 8-1.

After you write the macros on paper, it is common practice to enter them in an area of the spreadsheet away from the regular formulas and data entry area, such as row 1 of column AA (assuming, of course, that this area is not already used). Column AA could contain the macro names, column AB the macro commands, and column AC a description of what each macro does. If column AB contains several macros, then there should be at least one blank row between each macro. You must give each macro a range name, using the /Range Name Create command, and start each macro name with a backslash so that you can invoke it by holding down the Alt key and the single letter naming the macro.

After testing the macros to be sure they perform as needed, save the worksheet. If you need to interrupt a macro while it is executing, press Ctrl and Break simultaneously. The spreadsheet will return to the READY mode. If there is an error in the spreadsheet, Lotus will display ERROR in the mode indicator. To clear the error message and return to READY mode, press the Esc key.

Use macros whenever you need to automate spreadsheet operations or repeat a spreadsheet routine. A macro will save keystrokes or reduce the chances of your making a typing error. The {?}~ macro is especially useful in making your spreadsheets **interactive,** that is, in displaying a prompt to the user and then waiting for the user to enter a reply at the keyboard.

The most common error made in writing macros is to forget to include the ~ signal where needed to simulate the pressing of Return. Perhaps the next most frequent error is to forget to name the macro using the /Range Name Create command. The second tutorial in this lesson provides practice in creating and using a Lotus 1-2-3 macro.

Table 8-1 COMMONLY USED LOTUS 1-2-3 MACRO COMMANDS

	Macro	*Description*
POINTER MOVEMENT		
	{up}	pointer up one row
	{down}	pointer down one row
	{left}	pointer left one column
	{right}	pointer right one column
	{home}	jump to cell A1
	{end}	jump to first blank cell
	{pgup}	jump up 20 rows
	{pgdn}	jump down 20 rows
	{bigleft}	jump left one screen
	{bigright}	jump right one screen
FUNCTION KEYS		
	{edit}	[F2] edits current cell contents
	{name}	[F3] menu of the current range names in point mode
	{abs}	[F4] relative, absolute, or mixed addressing in POINT/EDIT
	{goto}	[F5] moves pointer to cell address that you enter
	{window}	[F6] switches between windows
	{query}	[F7] repeats the last /DataQuery command
	{table}	[F8] repeats the last /DataTable command
	{calc}	[F9] recalculates the spreadsheet
	{graph}	[F10] displays the last graph specified
SPECIAL KEYS		
		press the [Enter] or [Return] key
	{esc}	press the [Esc] key
	{bs}	press the [Backspace] key
	{del}	press the [Del] key as in Edit mode
	{~}	the tilde character itself (not interpreted as [Enter] or [Return])
	{{} or {}}	the left or right brace
	{?}	pause and wait for keyboard input, completed by pressing the [Enter] or [Return] key

COMPARING AND SELECTING SOFTWARE

The quest for *the* best spreadsheet software package may seem awesome, given the multitude of spreadsheets available and the length of the list of options. However, it is possible to apply common problem-solving techniques and select the spreadsheet software package that best meets your individual needs. Remember, as with any major software purchase, you need to *define your goals* and constraints. You should have a clear idea of how you will use the electronic spreadsheet you plan to purchase. Make out a list of possible applications. Include information such as how large the spreadsheets must be, how often they will be used, what reporting capabilities are needed, what kinds of calculations will be performed on the spreadsheet, and what formatting options you will require. Once you have your written list of basic goals, the next step is to ask just how the various features of different spreadsheets can contribute to or detract from those goals. For example, if your basic goal is simply to learn about spreadsheets and solve simple problems, a large complex package may be more of a hindrance than a help. On the other hand, if you know that the types of problems you will be facing require the use of particular trigonometric functions, statistical routines, or multi-dimensional worksheets, then your goal should be to find a package that combines the right functions and routines.

To keep your goals realistic, it is necessary to recognize any constraints or limitations on your selection of software. Possible constraints include your budget, the microcomputer hardware you plan to use, and compatibility with other software you use. Everyone operates within some monetary constraints; the challenge is to reach your goal or come as close to it as possible within those constraints. Fortunately, there are numerous spreadsheet packages available for just a few hundred dollars or less. At the other extreme are very powerful software packages, priced at several thousand dollars, that can operate on several mainframes and minis. Systems such as the Interactive Financial Planning System (**IFPS**) can link up to a firm's accounting information system to obtain data and can employ very sophisticated simulation techniques.

Other constraints relate to hardware and operating systems. Some spreadsheets, such as **Jazz,** can be run on the Macintosh. A large number of electronic spreadsheet software packages have been written to run on the IBM PC and compatible microcomputers with 256K or more. The most popular is Lotus 1-2-3, which requires PC-DOS or MS-DOS with a minimum of 256K. If you have already chosen or purchased the hardware and the operating system, then you must purchase spreadsheet software that is compatible.

Next, *gather data* about what spreadsheet packages are compatible with your hardware and operating system. How much do they cost? What features do they have? Good information is as close as your nearest magazine counter. There are dozens of magazines for the computer user, with articles about a wide variety of computer interests. Articles about spreadsheets tend to be in the more business-oriented publications, since spreadsheet software is very popular in business.

Such data quickly become outdated, so look for the most recent articles you can find. Magazines and periodicals such as *Infoworld, PC,* and *Computerworld* are good sources of information. Since electronic spreadsheet software is rapidly changing and is popular, you should have no trouble finding several current articles that are aimed directly at the question of selecting the most appropriate spreadsheet.

Other sources of data include your local computer store and people you know who are regular users of spreadsheets. Local **user's groups** (clubs of people who own similar equipment or software) and computer salespeople may be able to give you more information and assistance. Before soliciting their help, however, read some articles on packages you are interested in to help you better understand what these experts tell you.

In addition to gathering information about the features of spreadsheets on the market, you should gather information about the types of problems you expect to encounter while using the spreadsheet. Will you need certain built-in functions? Will you need an extremely large worksheet? Will you need to share data and output from the spreadsheet with other software, such as word processing and database management? Do you need graphics? If so, is it important for the graphics to be in color? What formatting and printing features are especially important for the types of problems you will be addressing?

If onscreen menus are important to you, examine the menus available on several packages. For example, some spreadsheets, such as Lotus 1-2-3 and Excel, offer extensive full-word prompts and step-by-step menus. Examine the user's manual and other training material. Is the manual clear and easy to understand? Is it easy to find information in the manual? Talk to other users and examine the documentation yourself for clarity and completeness. Some of the more popular spreadsheets have a wide range of supplementary "how-to" books available in bookstores. Some spreadsheets have onscreen interactive tutorials that teach you at the computer how to use the spreadsheet.

A CHECKLIST OF ELECTRONIC SPREADSHEET FEATURES

Another tool in the quest for an objective analysis is the following checklist. The checklist provides a reasonably comprehensive list of important considerations. It is organized around the categories of creating, revising, saving, printing, and miscellaneous features.

Creating a Spreadsheet

_____ Can the package be loaded on your existing hardware and operating system?

_____ Does the spreadsheet offer sufficient rows and columns?

_____ Does it have all the built-in formulas and all the commands that will be needed?

_____ Can several spreadsheets be linked?

_____ Is the user's guide easy to understand and use?

_____ Are the menus helpful in creating a spreadsheet?

_____ Can column widths be changed individually?

_____ Can you select automatic or manual recalculation?

Revising a Spreadsheet

____ Are formulas displayed in the prompt area?

____ Is it easy to change a cell entry?

____ Is it easy to insert a new column or row?

____ Is it easy to delete a column or row?

____ Are cell references automatically adjusted after inserting a new column or new row?

____ Does it have built-in editing features?

____ Can reports be edited using integrated word processing software?

Saving a Spreadsheet

____ Can the spreadsheet and associated graphics be saved so that they can be retrieved by other software such as word processors and/or a database manager?

____ Does the system automatically create a back-up copy of the spreadsheet to guard against accidental erasure?

____ Will the spreadsheet work with floppy disk drives or is a hard disk needed?

____ Is it easy to save a spreadsheet and reload a saved spreadsheet?

Printing a Spreadsheet

____ Can the program be configured to work on your current printer?

____ Will the program automatically configure your printer to print compressed print?

____ Is it easy to print either the entire spreadsheet or any desired block?

____ Can you select the number of copies to be printed?

____ Can printing be interrupted and then resumed easily?

____ Will it rotate the spreadsheet 90 degrees so wide spreadsheets can be printed lengthwise down continuous paper?

Miscellaneous Features

____ Is it highly rated in the computer magazine reviews?

____ Do you know of any satisfied users of this software who are using it for applications similar to yours?

____ Does the vendor offer telephone support? If so, is it toll-free? How many hours per day and days per week?

_____ Will updates be offered to current users at reduced prices?

_____ Is there a window function allowing you to split the screen into two or more parts so you can see different parts of the spreadsheet at once?

_____ Will the spreadsheet sort data into numeric and alphabetic sequence?

_____ Does it provide the arithmetic, trigonometric, or financial functions you will need?

_____ Does it provide graphics? How extensive (bar, pie, line, and other types of charts) are they?

_____ Is color an option?

_____ Does it work with a mouse?

_____ Does it include a database to aid in the collection, editing, and organization of the data, or integrate with an existing database management system?

_____ Does it allow you to link worksheets?

Cost of the software: $_____ versus Your budget: $_____

Once you have gathered information about the problems you expect to solve and the prices and features of spreadsheets on the market, the next step is to *test possible solutions.* How can you obtain an objective analysis of the alternative solutions? The suggestions presented so far should help, but nothing is as good as a "test drive." Try out the spreadsheet software using a sample spreadsheet problem. If this is not possible, you may want to purchase the software and test it on your own microcomputer or on the one you will be using. Check with the salesperson first to see if a free demonstration version is available or if you may return the package if it does not meet your needs. Several software companies offer demonstration disks free or at minimum price. Such versions usually contain all the features but do not allow files to be saved or printed.

After defining your goals, gathering your data, and testing the possible solutions, it is time to *implement the best possible solution* by deciding which spreadsheet package to purchase. If you have done your job thoroughly, the actual purchase of the right package should be an easy task.

Once you make the purchase, work with the package. Try the various commands that you have not used before. Much of learning how to use the software comes from experimenting on your own.

The microcomputer software world is dynamic. New and improved products are coming on the market almost daily. Thus, even though you

Table 8-2 A COMPARISON OF SPREADSHEET SOFTWARE PACKAGES

SOFTWARE NAME	*Lotus 1-2-3*	*SuperCalc4*
HARDWARE REQUIREMENTS		
Operating system	PC/MS-DOS	PC/MS-DOS
Minimum RAM	256K	256K
Requires hard disk	no	no
Color/graphics board required	for onscreen graphics display	for onscreen graphics display
Color display	graphics only	worksheet and graphics
Copy protected	yes	no
CHARACTERISTICS		
Spreadsheet size (rows by columns)	8,192 × 256	9,999 × 255
Number of windows	2	2
On-screen graphics	yes	yes
Number of graphic types	6	7
Internal macros	yes	yes
External macros	no	yes
Uses math co-processor	yes	yes
FEATURES		
On-screen tutorial	yes	no
Online help	yes	yes
Supports mouse	no	no
Supports EMS	yes	yes
Sorts data	yes	yes
Data query	yes	yes
Multiple regression	yes	no
Worksheet linkage	no	no
ADDITIONAL NOTES	Extensive prompts Complex command structure Powerful built-in functions Widely used in business Advanced features require extensive study and practice	Simple command structure Date and calendar functions Extensive data import and export utilities Can read and write to Lotus files Graphics directly accessible from spreadsheet Sophisticated graphics options Includes sideways print utility

have purchased your new spreadsheet software package, you will want to continue to watch for even better versions in the future.

FEATURES OF POPULAR SPREADSHEET SOFTWARE PACKAGES

As discussed in Lessons 6 and 7, electronic spreadsheets have evolved into sophisticated tools used in the analysis of financial and other numeric problems. A number of new software packages have become available in the last few years. Some of the most popular are Lotus 1-2-3, SuperCalc4, Multiplan, Quattro, and Microsoft Excel. These all have the basic components, functions, and features common to all spreadsheets. However, there

Multiplan	*Excel*	*Quattro*
PC/MS-DOS	PC/MS-DOS 3.0	PC/MS-DOS
256K	640K	384K
no	yes	no
no	yes	recommended
no	yes	yes
no	no	no
4,095 × 255	16,384 × 256	8,192 × 256
8	limited by available RAM	2
no	yes	yes
not applicable	44	10
yes	yes	yes
yes	yes	yes
yes	yes	yes
no	yes	no
yes	yes	yes
yes	required	no
no	yes	yes
yes	yes	yes
yes	yes	yes
yes	yes	no
yes	no	no
Automatic linking of spreadsheets	Requires 80286 or 80386 processor Can view spreadsheet and graph simultaneously Complete laser printer support including fonts Database forms for data entry Microsoft Windows permit integration with other software Supports dynamically linked worksheets	Can load and use files created by Lotus 1-2-3, dBASE, and Paradox Understands 1-2-3 macros 100 built-in financial and statistical functions Pop-up menus Custom menus available Transcript feature records all keystrokes

are differences in the size, complexity, and scope of the software. Table 8-2 compares the features of these popular spreadsheet packages in detail to help you choose the correct software.

Lotus 1-2-3

Lotus 1-2-3 is to the IBM PC what VisiCalc was to the Apple computer. Lotus was introduced in 1983 by Lotus Development Corporation for use on the IBM PC and quickly became so popular that some say it established the IBM PC standard for business software. Lotus 1-2-3 was the brainchild of Mitch Kapor, a programmer who had written VisiTrend/Plot, a graphics package designed to chart VisiCalc data. With the proceeds from the sale of

VisiTrend/Plot, he formed the Lotus Development Corporation and set out to improve the electronic spreadsheet and simplify the steps needed to produce spreadsheet graphics. These improved features, combined with astute marketing by Lotus, made Lotus 1-2-3 an immediate success. It continues to be one of the top-selling software packages of all time.

Lotus 1-2-3 hardware requirements include a minimum of 256K RAM, two disk drives, and a color/graphics board. Lotus is normally run on the IBM PC and compatible microcomputers, although it has been specially adapted to run on certain non–IBM-compatible machines.

Lotus 1-2-3 characteristics include a large spreadsheet offering 8,192 rows and 256 columns for a total of 2,097,152 cells, depending on the amount of available RAM. Also included in the spreadsheet are powerful financial and statistical functions, including multiple regression, and extensive prompts and menus. Lotus solves the problem of forward references in calculations. A **forward reference** occurs when a formula being calculated depends upon the result of another formula that has not yet been calculated. If Lotus 1-2-3 finds such a reference, it goes forward to calculate the other formulas and returns to complete the current formula.

Among the additional features are internal and external macros, graphics, data management, and keyboard programming. Remember, a *macro* is a set of commands, instructions, or text stored as a group so the user can execute it simply by pressing a few keys or by calling the name of the set. **Internal macros** are stored within an individual worksheet and apply only to that worksheet. **External macros** are stored in separate files and can be recalled from any worksheet. Lotus 1-2-3 was one of the first software packages to integrate graphics and data management software with the spreadsheet. Users exit the spreadsheet, load the graphics software, and print bar, line, and pie charts without extensive data conversion.

Although Lotus is a very popular package, some say it is one of the most underutilized because the elaborate command structure and powerful features require skill and practice. Some people use Lotus as an expensive calculator, not using the extensive capabilities of the software. Others use it to do everything from database management to word processing, which is, perhaps, an error of equal proportion in the opposite direction. See Table 8-2 for additional information about Lotus 1-2-3. Figure 8-1 is an example of a Lotus 1-2-3 worksheet.

SuperCalc4

Since the introduction of Lotus 1-2-3 in 1983, other software producers have been working to "catch up." **SuperCalc4** is one of the foremost competitors, offering an integrated package of spreadsheet, graphics, and data management software. SuperCalc4 is the most powerful package in the SuperCalc family. Computer Associates, the software producers, have developed SuperCalc (for CP/M and Apple II), SuperCalc2 (a more powerful CP/M version), and SuperCalc3 and SuperCalc4 (for the IBM and compatibles). A special version of SuperCalc3 (SuperCalc3a) is available for Apple II machines.

Hardware requirements for SuperCalc4 include a minimum of 256K RAM, MS-DOS Version 2.0 or higher, a minimum of two disk drives, and a graphics card. As in Lotus 1-2-3, the number of rows and columns depends on the amount of RAM; the maximum available is 9,999 rows by 255 columns for a total of 2,549,745 cells. With color monitors, color is used not only for color graphic display but also for highlighting within the spreadsheet. For example, cells with negative balances are shown in red. SuperCalc4 automatically senses and uses the 8087 mathematics coprocessor when it is installed in the microcomputer. Recall from Lesson 1 that a co-processor is designed to work with a microprocessor (in this case the Intel 8088) for particular functions. By taking over the math processing normally done in the microprocessor, the entire system is speeded up when math functions, such as those in electronic spreadsheets, are being done. This permits very fast recalculations, especially for scientific applications.

As in Lotus, a menu of available commands is displayed after the slash key (/) is pressed. As in Lotus, these are full-word commands. The user chooses a command by pressing the first letter of the command. For example, to format a cell, column, row, or an entire spreadsheet, the user gives the command/F. Further format options are then displayed on the prompt line. This prompting approach makes SuperCalc4 one of the easiest spreadsheet packages to learn. In addition to the straightforward command structure, SuperCalc4 manuals and tutorials are considered some of the best in the industry. Another convenient yet idiosyncratic feature is **cursor direction after data entry.** The user enters data by pressing the Return Key. The pointer or cell cursor is automatically moved to the "next" cell. The direction of the pointer or cell cursor movement is determined by the direction of the latest cell movement. If the pointer or cell cursor was moving down, pressing Return would cause the pointer or cell cursor to enter the entry line and continue the downward movement.

Files from other versions of SuperCalc, including SuperCalc and SuperCalc2, are compatible with SuperCalc4. SuperCalc4 can easily read or write spreadsheets saved in the Lotus format. Unlike Lotus 1-2-3 graphics, the graphics function of SuperCalc4 permits the user to construct, display, and print pie, bar, and line charts (including stacked bar in which each bar is subdivided into two or more variables) without exiting the spreadsheet. In contrast, users of Lotus 1-2-3 must exit and load software from a different floppy disk to print graphs. Therefore, technically, SuperCalc4 can be considered more integrated than Lotus. In addition, the graphics capabilities are considered some of the best in the software industry. In addition to these features, SuperCalc4 offers both *internal macros* (recall that these are groups of commands stored within a particular worksheet and applicable only to that worksheet) and *external macros* (remember that these are

FIGURE 8-2 A SuperCalc4 worksheet. Notice the position of the prompt area at the bottom of the screen. Like Lotus 1-2-3, SuperCalc4 also offers full-word prompts.

```
CALC              A                     B         C         D         E         F
1    INCOME AND EXPENSE STATEMENT FOR MARCH 1990
2    ===========================================================================
3    OPERATING ACCOUNT EXPENSES  CURRENT   EXPENSES BUDGETED CUM.      PRIOR
4                                MONTH     TO       EXPENSES ACTUAL    MONTH
5                                EXPENSES  DATE     TO DATE      1989  CUM.
6    ---------------------------------------------------------------------------
7    Salaries & Wages                43223    361043     37850    337845    317820
8    Health Insurance                 1470     11409     12040     12553      9939
9    Retirement                        778     13398     16400     14243     12620
10   Social Security                  3176     26248     22720     25846     23072
11   Unemployment Insurance              0       972      2160       594       972
12   Workers' Comp. Insurance          409      3272      2280      1799      2863
13   Other Employ. Benefits             88      1888       880      5715      1800
14
15   SUBTOTAL SALARIES & WAGES       49144    418230     94330    398595    369086
16
17   Office Supplies                   409      5080      4800      3900      4671
18   Food & Bevrages                   410      5197      3960      4304      4787
19   Other Supplies                     80       742       840       625       662
20
Arrange  Blank  Copy  Delete  Edit  Format  Global  Insert  Load  Move  Name
Output  Protect  Quit  Save  Title  Unprotect  View  Window  Zap  /more
  2>/
MENU  Sort spreadsheet (entire or partial) by a column or row
```

Slash commands

groups of commands stored in a separate file). See Table 8-2 for more information concerning SuperCalc4. Figure 8-2 is an example of a SuperCalc4 worksheet. Notice the position of the prompt area and the full-word prompts similar to Lotus.

Multiplan

Multiplan, produced by Microsoft, is a spreadsheet program available for use on a variety of microcomputers, including PC/MS-DOS, Apple, Apple CP/M, and Apple Macintosh. Hardware requirements depend on the operating system used, but for MS-DOS systems, Multiplan requires a minimum of 256K RAM and two disk drives. A color board is not required, but color spreadsheet display is available with color monitors. Graphics and data management are not available with Multiplan. Multiplan provides 4,095 rows and 255 columns for 1,044,225 cells. Although the spreadsheet size is considerably smaller than Lotus 1-2-3 (2,097,152 cells) or SuperCalc4 (2,549,745 cells), Multiplan can construct huge worksheets of almost unlimited size by linking a series of smaller spreadsheets. As changes are made to one of the smaller linked spreadsheets, the results are automatically updated to the others. While other spreadsheets may offer this feature, Multiplan makes it particularly easy to do.

Another distinctive feature of Multiplan is the number of windows. While Lotus 1-2-3 and SuperCalc4 have a two-window maximum, Multiplan can display up to eight windows simultaneously.

Like Lotus 1-2-3 and SuperCalc4, Multiplan also allows you to refer to a cell or group of cells by *range name* rather than by cell coordinates. Thus one area of the spreadsheet might be called "REVENUE," another "EXPENSES," and another "NET INCOME." Formulas can then be developed using the names rather than giving cell coordinates. Instead of "A3−C3=E3," a formula would read "GROSS INCOME − EXPENSES = NET INCOME." Like SuperCalc4, Multiplan can also solve formulas involving circular references. A **circular reference** occurs when the formula to calculate one cell depends on the results of a formula in a second cell and the formula of the second cell also depends on the results in the first cell. For more information concerning Multiplan, see Table 8-2. Figure 8-3 is an example of a Multiplan worksheet. Like Lotus 1-2-3 and SuperCalc4, Multiplan offers extensive prompts and information on the screen. However, notice the window numbers, reminding the user that Multiplan is a multiwindow spreadsheet.

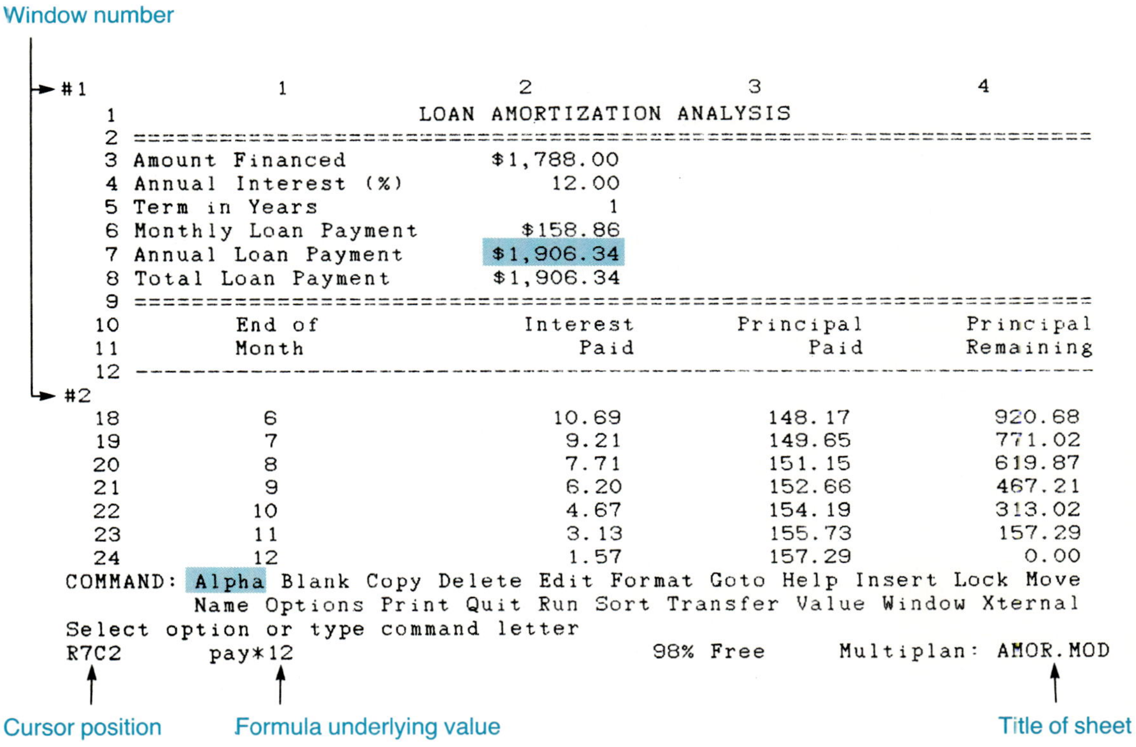

FIGURE 8-3 An example of a Multiplan worksheet. Notice the window numbers and the extensive full-word prompts.

Excel

Microsoft Excel is a powerful spreadsheet designed especially to take advantage of the capabilities of new, more powerful microcomputers, laser printers, and high-resolution monitors. Hardware requirements include the 80286 or 80386 microprocessor, VGA or EGA graphics card, 640K memory, hard disk, MS-DOS version 3.0 or higher, and a 1.2-megabyte high-density disk drive. A mouse is highly recommended. Excel combines the capabilities of a very powerful spreadsheet, the flexibility of a fast database, and the brilliance of stunning graphics. Spreadsheets can be as large as 256 columns by 16,384 rows. Display and linking of multiple spreadsheets and charts is limited only by memory. Such charts and worksheets may be viewed on the screen simultaneously. It recalculates only those cells where the data have been changed. It has 131 built-in worksheet functions and 224 macro functions. A macro recorder stores a sequence of commands as they are entered as a macro. Menus, dialogue boxes, and on-line help may be customized by the user. Files are compatible with those created by Lotus 1-2-3, Symphony (.WKS and .WK1), dBASE II, dBASE III, and Microsoft Multiplan (SYLK). Lotus 1-2-3 macros can be translated using a feature called a Macro Translation Assistant. Built-in auditing features allow users to name and attach notes to individual cells. For example, a user can add an explanation about where a particular value was derived. Microsoft Excel offers complete laser printer support, including multiple fonts, borders, shading, custom number format, and color. User assistance includes an interactive online tutorial, Help, Undo, and familiar standard function and cursor movement keys. An additional bonus is the use of database forms for simplified data entry.

Quattro

In the last few years, several spreadsheet packages have been developed as Lotus 1-2-3 clones. **Clones** use commands and menu structures similar to the original software package, but are offered at reduced prices, usually with other enhanced features. **Quattro** by Borland International is designed as a clone of Lotus 1-2-3. Like 1-2-3, the worksheet is a 256 by 8192 cell matrix, and it offers better graphics, simple database functions, and macros. It even uses slash key command menus similar to those of Lotus 1-2-3. However, Quattro has several enhanced features to win over potential Lotus users. First, Quattro offers quick and easy installation. Once installed, Quattro loads quickly from a hard disk. The file conversion feature allows users to load worksheets stored in a variety of popular formats, including Paradox, dBASE II or III, Symphony, and Lotus 1-2-3 Release 1A or 2.0 or Educational. Users can save files in their original format just by entering the proper extension. Menu structure can be customized to be identical to Lotus 1-2-3, or Quattro's own pull-down menu system can be used. Menus are "pulled down" when the user moves the cursor to the desired command on a menu line located at the top of the screen. A window then appears on the top of the screen containing further command options. The cursor is placed on one of the options and the Return key is pressed to implement the command.

Quattro also offers Menu Builder, which permits users to customize the menus any way they like. Additional features also include search and replace, where users can locate cell contents or format codes and revise them automatically, as well as color display. An especially interesting feature is Transcript, which saves all keystrokes to a separate disk file. If a file is deleted or lost, the last version of the worksheet can be loaded and played back. Macro construction is quick and easy, with a Learn mode to automatically record keystrokes and a split screen debugger that lets users see the macros on the top screen as they are executing in the screen below.

Recently, new software packages that enhance Lotus or other spreadsheets or extend the spreadsheet features described so far have entered the market. **HAL,** for example, is a Lotus 1-2-3 **add-on** (software developed to work with another software package and purchased separately) that allows spreadsheet users to give English-like commands. For example, instead of referring to cells by coordinates, HAL allows you to refer to cell locations by row and column labels. Also, commands look like English verbs rather than cryptic abbreviations. If you need a particular sequence of commands executed repeatedly, then HAL has a **learn feature** that stores the sequence of commands as a macro. HAL even has an undo command to bring back deleted worksheets.

Other, less commonly used software packages, such as **Javelin,** feature several aids to modeling and incorporate several statistical routines commonly used in model testing and validation. Among the features included are regression, analysis of variance, and chi-square.

The Lotus add-on package **1-2-3 Forecast** provides the user with a menu of common forecasting techniques. Data from a Lotus worksheet can be transferred to 1-2-3 Forecast for further analysis using various forecasting techniques. Yet another product, **VP-Planner,** has gained popularity as a less expensive clone of Lotus 1-2-3. Remember, a **clone** imitates well-known hardware or software by appearing or operating nearly identically to the original hardware or software. VP-Planner contains many of the Lotus 1-2-3 features plus some features found in these add-on packages.

Now let's try out more features of Lotus.

TUTORIAL 1: CREATING AND USING A LOTUS DATABASE

To complete this tutorial you need the following:

- Lotus 1-2-3 system disk
- A data disk

While completing this tutorial you will learn how to

- Use Lotus 1-2-3 as a database manager
- Create an input area for the data
- Create a criterion area
- Create an output area
- Sort the database
- Find selected records in the database
- Extract selected records from the database

The purpose of this tutorial is to gain experience creating and using a database as part of a Lotus 1-2-3 spreadsheet. You are to set up a database for a portion of the personnel records of FAST DATA INC. For each employee, set up a record containing the employee's NAME, DEPT, STATUS, OFFICE, and SALARY as listed below:

NAME	DEPT	STATUS	OFFICE	SALARY
JENSEN, BONNIE	ADM	PARTTIME	208	30000
MONSELL, GLORIA	ADM	FULLTIME	306	40000
KIEDERLEN, ED	SALES	FULLTIME	201	50000
BROWN, PAT	R&D	PARTTIME	205	35000
MARIS, TINA	SALES	PARTTIME	206	20000
JENSEN, JAMES	SALES	FULLTIME	207	60000
ANDERSEN, ELLEN	R&D	FULLTIME	301	40000
KIEDERLEN, ANN	ADM	FULLTIME	303	50000
MONSELL, RANDY	R&D	FULLTIME	305	45000

Use this database to practice using the data management functions of sorting, finding, and extracting.

Step 1: Create the database.

a. Load MS-DOS and Lotus 1-2-3 as described in previous lessons.

b. Enter the data.

1. When Lotus 1-2-3 is in READY mode, enter the data as listed above, putting the column labels (NAME; DEPT; STATUS; OFFICE:, SALARY) in row 3 and columns A, B, C, D, and E, respectively.
2. Increase the width of Column A to 16 spaces. Type

```
/W C S 16
```

Where

/ W = Worksheet
C = Column
S = Set-Width
16 = Width

Press **Return.**

3. Starting in row 4, enter the records, starting with JENSEN, BONNIE and continuing down through MONSELL, RANDY in row 12.
4. In cell A13, type

```
\-
```

Press **Return.**

5. Copy the dashed line from A13 across the row to B13 through E13. Enter

```
/C from A13..A13 to B13..E13
```

6. In cell B14 enter

```
CRITERION AREA
```

Copy the labels from row 3 to row 15 by entering

```
/Copy from A3..E3 to A15
```

7. Put a dashed line in row 17 by entering

```
/Copy from A13..E13 to A17
```

8. In cell B18 enter

```
OUTPUT AREA
```

Copy the labels from row 3 to row 19 by entering

```
/Copy from A3..E3 to A19
```

c. Check your entries carefully. Correct any typing errors by moving to the needed cell, pressing [F2], and editing the cell contents.

d. Save the spreadsheet by typing

```
/File Save PERSONEL
```

(Remember a file name can be only eight characters long, so the word PERSONNEL will not qualify.)

Step 2: Use the data commands.

a. Sort the names into alphabetical order. Press

```
/D S D A4.E12
```

Where

/D = Data
S = Sort
D = Data Range (range of records to be sorted)

Press **Return.**
Press

```
P A4 Return A Return G
```

Where

P = Primary Key
A4 = Key field
A = Ascending Order
G = Go

Almost instantly the records will be reordered. ANDERSEN, ELLEN should be at the top and MONSELL, RANDY at the bottom.

b. Find who is in office 207. Move the cell pointer to cell D16. Enter

```
207
```

Press

```
/D Q I A3.E12 Return C A15.E16 Return F
```

Where

/D = Data
Q = Query
I = Input
A3.E12 = the range to be searched
C = Criterion (set the range containing the criterion)
A15.E16 = range containing the criterion
F = Find

The row meeting the criterion—row 7, JENSEN, JAMES—should be highlighted. Press **Return.** Enter

```
Q
```

for Quit.

c. Extract the records of the R&D department. Erase the contents of cell D16. Move the pointer to the cell and type

```
/Range Erase Return
```

Enter a new criterion. Move to cell B16 and type

```
R&D
```

Press **Return.**
Press

```
/Data Query Output A19..E19 Return Extract Quit
```

Examine rows 20 through 22 to see if they contain the records of the three employees in R&D.

d. Extract the records of the SALES department. Move to B16 and enter

```
SALES
```

Press **[F7].** The [F7] function key executes the last Query command using the new criterion. The rows 20 through 22 should contain the records of the three employees in the SALES department.

e. Experiment with other extract criteria. When you finish, save the worksheet and quit.

TUTORIAL 2: MACROS IN LOTUS

To complete this tutorial you need the following:

- DOS and Lotus 1-2-3 disks
- Data disk
- A printer properly installed for Lotus

While completing this tutorial you will learn how to

- Use the @PMT built-in formula to calculate a loan payment amount.
- Use a macro to accept user input and calculate a loan payment amount.

The specific commands introduced in this tutorial include

- /Range Erase range, to erase previous data from an area.
- /Worksheet Global Recalculate Manual, to set the worksheet so that it does not recalculate every time a value is entered into a cell. Instead, the spreadsheet should recalculate only when the Recalculate command is entered.
- {GOTO}, used within a macro to cause the pointer to go to a specific cell.
- {CALC}, used within a macro to cause the spreadsheet to be recalculated.
- /Range Name Create, to define a name and a range for a macro.
- @PMT(prin,int,term), to calculate the periodic payment necessary to pay off the principal (prin) at the periodic interest rate (int) over the term of the loan.

The goal of this spreadsheet is to allow a user to enter the principal, term, and interest rate for a loan and have a macro do the rest of the work. Usually macros are placed out of the sight of the user; however, so that you may see exactly what the macro looks like as it is working, we will place the macro and the rest of the spreadsheet where everything can be clearly seen on one screen.

Step 1: Load DOS and Lotus 1-2-3.
Follow the procedures described previously.

Step 2: Set up the display part of the spreadsheet.
The part of the spreadsheet that the user will see is included within columns A and B and within rows 1 through 9.

a. Set the width of the columns of the worksheet. If necessary, move the cell pointer to column A. Set the width of column A to 25. Press

```
/W C S 25
```

Where

/W = Worksheet
C = Column
S = Set-Width
25 = width of the column

Press **Return.**

Change the width of column B to 15, column C to 1, and column D to 25 by repeating the steps listed above, substituting the appropriate number for the width of the column. Remember to place the cell pointer in the appropriate column before entering the commands to change the width.

b. Change the format of the columns. Move the cursor to cell B1 and change the format to currency. Type

```
/R F C 2
```

Where

/R = Range
F = Format
C = Currency
2 = number of decimal places

Repeat the steps for cells B5 and D9.

At the prompt for the range, press **Return.** Move the cursor to cell B3 and change the format to percent. Type

```
/R F P 2
```

Where

/R = Range
F = Format
P = Percent
2 = number of decimal places

At the prompt for the range, press **Return.**

In Cell	Enter
A1	PRINCIPAL--------------------->
A2	TERM IN MONTHS---------------->
A3	INTEREST AS DECIMAL ------>
A5	MONTHLY PAYMENT------------->
A9	PRESS [Alt] +A to enter another loan

Remember, if you need to correct any entered cell, use the Edit function [F2].

Step 3: Set up the Macro in column D.

In Cell	Enter
D1	'/REB1..B3~/REB5~/WGRM

This ' must precede any macro that begins with a slash, so that 1-2-3 does not think it is a slash command to be executed now.
REB1..B3~ tells 1-2-3 to Range Erase the cells B1 through B3; the ~ causes a Return.
/REB5~ causes cell B5 to be erased.
/WGRM causes a Worksheet Global Recalculate Manual command to turn off the automatic recalculation mode.

D2 {GOTO}A1~{GOTO}B1~{?}~

{GOTO} is a macro command causing the cursor to go to in this case, cell A1. The is the macro symbol for pressing Return. The {?} is a macro command causing the spreadsheet to wait for the user to input data.

D3 {GOTO}B2~{?}~

Causes the spreadsheet to go to cell B2 and wait for the user to input data.

D4 {GOTO}B3~{?}~

Causes the spreadsheet to go to cell B3 and wait for the user to input data.

D5 {CALC}~

Causes the spreadsheet to recalculate.

D6 '/CD9~B5~

Causes the contents of cell D9 to be copied to cell B5.

D7 `{GOTO}A9~`

Causes a move to cell A9, where the user is asked to press Alt+A to enter another loan.

D9 `@PMT($B$1,$B$3/12,$B$2)`

Uses the built-in Payment function to calculate the monthly payment on a loan for which the principal is found in B1, the interest rate in B3, and the term in B2. Note that all three cell references are absolute references. The user will always put the input data in those three cells, and as we copy the formula to cell B5 we do not want it to change relatively by the action of cell D6 in the macro.

Move the cursor to D1 and type

`/R N C`

Where

/R = Range
N = Name
C = Create

When prompted for the name of the range, enter

`\A Return D1.D9`

To invoke the macro, press and hold the **[Alt]** key. While pressing the Alt key, press **A.**

Step 4: Input values.

Remember that in most cases the spreadsheet designer would put the macro out of sight. We are putting it in column D so you can see how it works. After pressing [Alt]+A, input

In Cell	Enter
B1	1000
B2	24
B3	.1

The spreadsheet should look like the following:

```
PRINCIPAL--------------->  $1,000.00  /REB1..B3~/REB5~/WGRM
TERM IN MONTHS---------->         24  {GOTO}A1~{GOTO}B1~{?}~
INTEREST AS DECIMAL----->     10.00%  {GOTO}B2~{?}~
                                      {GOTO}B3~{?}~
MONTHLY PAYMENT--------->     $46.14  {CALC}~
                                      /CD9~B5~
                                      {GOTO}A9~
PRESS [Alt] + A to enter another loan                $46.14
```

Try other values to see just how easily the user could make use of such a spreadsheet, even if he or she knows very little about Lotus 1-2-3.

Step 5: Save the spreadsheet and quit.

When you have finished trying several possible principals, terms, and interest rates, save this spreadsheet by typing

```
/F S MACRO1
```

Where

/F = File
S = Save
MACRO1 = filename

Check to make sure your filename includes the proper disk drive.
Press **Return.**
Quit Lotus 1-2-3 by entering

```
/Quit Yes
```

At the system prompt, turn off the computer to end this session.

SUMMARY

This lesson discussed several advanced electronic spreadsheet features, including data management, statistical analysis, graphic techniques, and macros. Data management is the use of electronic spreadsheet commands to sort, search, and extract selected data contained within a spreadsheet. In Lotus 1-2-3 the database is a grouping or range of rows and columns on the worksheet. Each row is one record within the database. Data is located and extracted using data query commands. Among the most useful statistical analysis techniques available with Lotus is regression. Regression is a statistical method used to predict the value of one variable given the value of another or several associated variables. In Lotus, the /Data Regression command permits users to apply simple or multiple linear regression analysis. A macro is a range on a spreadsheet that contains a set of keystrokes used as a series of spreadsheet commands. Macros permit Lotus users to customize and simplify using electronic spreadsheets.

In comparing spreadsheet software, apply the four-step problem-solving approach. Define your goals for using a spreadsheet package and determine your budget and hardware constraints. Gather data about the available software by reading magazine articles, talking to users, and visiting several retail computer stores. Test the alternatives by trying them out and by using the checklist provided within this lesson. Select the spreadsheet software that best meets your objectives and plan to spend time learning to use it effectively. Expect new and better products to become available in the future.

EXERCISES

1. Define the following terms:

data management	macro body	Multiplan
record	macro commands	circular reference
field names	interactive	Microsoft Excel
fields	IFPS	clones
data query	Jazz	Quattro
input range	user's groups	HAL
criterion range	Lotus 1-2-3	add-on
output range	forward reference	learn feature
regression	internal macro	Javelin
dependent variable	external macro	1-2-3 Forecast
independent variables	SuperCalc4	VP-Planner
macro	cursor direction after data entry	

2. Prepare a list of the limitations for the microcomputer that you are using. This should include RAM size and number and types of disk drives. List three electronic spreadsheet software packages that would work on the microcomputer you are using.
3. Interview two businesspeople who use electronic spreadsheets. Ask each person to describe how he or she decided on the software package currently used. What would these users do differently if they were once again going to purchase a spreadsheet package?
4. Match the following features with the appropriate spreadsheet software package:
   a. Lotus 1-2-3
   b. VP-Planner

c. Multiplan
d. Quattro
e. Excel

_____ Allows several small worksheets to be easily linked together and updated in an integrated fashion

_____ One of the foremost competitors of Lotus 1-2-3, offering an integrated package of spreadsheet, graphics, and data management software

_____ Considered the standard because of its widespread popularity among business users

_____ A powerful software package designed to work with 80286 or 80386 microprocessors, laser printers, and high resolution monitors

_____ Has menu feature which permits users to customize menus

_____ Command structure mimics Lotus 1-2-3, yet offers several unique features, including printing graphs from within worksheets

5. Retrieve the spreadsheet created in the first tutorial in this lesson and saved as PERSONEL. Starting in A1, enter "NEWSYS EMPLOYEE DATABASE Prepared by: *Your Name.*" In F1 enter today's date using the @NOW function, the date format, and a column width of 10. At A2 enter \– and copy it across row 2. With the cursor at A3 insert a new row and enter "INPUT AREA." With the cursor at A14 insert 10 new rows and enter the following new data:

NAME	DEPT	STATUS	OFFICE	SALARY
CUMMINGS, BOB	ACCY	FULLTIME	210	50000
ENGSTROM, JOHN	ACCY	PARTTIME	211	20000
FITZGERALD, NORMA	ACCY	PARTTIME	212	25000
FLEMAL, MARY LOU	ACCY	PARTTIME	213	20000
HARREL, LISA	SALES	PARTTIME	310	23000
KING, TED	MIS	FULLTIME	401	50000
LEONARD, HENRY	MIS	FULLTIME	402	55000
MASON, NAN	MIS	PARTTIME	403	39000
MULLIKIN, BRIAN	SALES	FULLTIME	404	40000
NENONEN, JANE	SALES	PARTTIME	405	30000

Sort the database into alphabetic ascending order and print it.

6. From the database that resulted from your completing Exercise 8-5 above, extract the records of all employees in the ACCY department and print the output range.

7. From the database that resulted from your completing Exercise 8-5 above, extract the records of all employees earning over $40,000. You will need to enlarge the Input range to include the newly added records. The criterion under the SALARY heading would be +E5>40-000. The cell will display 0, but after the Extract command is executed the output area will list the seven employees with salaries over $40,000. Print the output range.

8. Given the following set of data, use the/Data Regression command to find R squared and the regression equation.

y	x1	x2	x3
100	10	20	78
101	10	21	79
103	11	22	80
104	12	23	80
108	13	25	81
110	14	26	82
113	15	27	82
118	16	28	84
120	17	32	85
125	18	35	87

9. Write down the exact keystrokes needed to compute the regression in Exercise 8 above. Create a macro in cell F4 to cause the regression to be computed using just the range name Alt+R.

FOUR
DATABASE MANAGEMENT SYSTEMS

Although word processors and spreadsheets are very useful applications for microcomputers, database management systems can be even more useful. Information is power, so knowing how to use a database management system to store, process, and retrieve information quickly and accurately can be a powerful asset.

Some people believe that a database is a vast storehouse of information magically compacted within a computer and that by using some complex computer logic the computer programmer can retrieve answers to all sorts of questions. Lessons 9 through 11 strip away some of the magic and complexity. Lesson 9 explains the fundamental concepts, while Lessons 10 and 11 present more advanced features of the commonly used commercial database systems, such as dBASE III Plus, Paradox, and R:base System V. As you learn the concepts of database design and the particular techniques of dBASE III Plus, currently the best-selling database software package on the market, the mystery of database management will be revealed to you, and this powerful tool will be added to your arsenal.

SOFTWARE SPECIFICATIONS

Harcourt Brace Jovanovich has made available to users of this textbook the educational version of dBASE III Plus. This software has all the features of the commercial version of dBASE III Plus with the following restrictions:

- Each file is limited to 31 records. dBASE does not warn the user when more than 31 records have been created on a given file. If the 31-record limit is exceeded the user will be denied access to that file. A commercial version of dBASE III Plus can be used to access the file and delete the excess records.
- Each record can contain up to 256 fields.
- There is no restriction on the number of files that can be created.
- The word "demo" appears at the dot prompt.
- A special routine is required for installing, loading, and using this version of dBASE on your microcomputer. See Appendix A, pages xxx–xx, for instructions on how to use the routine.

9
Fundamental Concepts of Databases

LESSON OUTLINE

WHAT IS A DATABASE?

A **database** is an orderly collection of one or more related files containing data related to a specific type of application. Everyone uses databases. You've used a database if you have looked up a book in a card catalog in a library, searched for an item in a department store catalog, checked a stock quotation in a stock market report, or looked for a term in the glossary of a textbook. All of these examples contain data that are organized and presented in a way that makes it easy to find specific items. A card catalog is organized in alphabetical order by author, by title, or by subject. A department store catalog might be organized into categories of children's clothes, women's clothes, men's clothes, hardware, and so on. A stock market report is organized alphabetically by the name of the corporations, such as International Business Machines (IBM) and General Motors (GM). The glossary for this book lists in alphabetical order the defined terms.

Despite these common, everyday examples, not all collections of data are databases. For example, a textbook is not a database; a newspaper is not a database. How is a glossary different from a textbook? How is a stock market report different from a newspaper containing the report? The answer is in organization around one or more keys. A **key** is a field that uniquely identifies a record. In some files the key is simply the number of the record, determined by the sequential order in which the record was added to the file. That is, the first record placed in the file is number one, the second record is number two, and so forth. Other nonsequential examples include a social security number for an employee, an account number for a customer, and a part number for an inventory item. A glossary or a stock market report is organized around one or more keys, so users can quickly find exactly the data needed. If you own IBM stock, you want to be able to quickly find the current selling price by looking for the unique key or identifier—in this case the letters IBM. If you are looking for a definition of a specific word, you can look in a glossary organized alphabetically around the key words to be defined and find it without reading the entire book.

Today, a **computerized database** usually means a collection of one or more related files stored compactly and electronically on a disk and accessed through a computer. When the database is computerized, large quantities of data can be added, edited, accessed, and manipulated quickly.

A **database management system (DBMS)** is a software tool that aids in the design, creation, updating, searching, and rearranging of a database and reporting from a database. Examples of popular DBMS's for mainframe and minicomputers include DB2, IMS, and SQL/DS from IBM; IDMS/R from Cullinet; ADABAS from Software AG of North America; and TOTAL from CINCOM Corp. Examples for microcomputers include dBASE (II, III, III Plus, and IV) from Ashton-Tate; R:base 5000 and R:base System V from Microrim Inc.; Paradox from Borland Software; Oracle from Oracle Corp.; and many others (see Figure 9-1).

The purpose of a database is to make it possible for users to easily select data needed to answer important questions. The key to building a successful database is to correctly anticipate what questions users are likely to ask regarding the data. Then the designer, with the help of the database software, needs to provide the links or connections within the collection of one or more related files. The person creating the design must use human understanding to achieve the orderliness. The computer merely provides the speed, flexibility, and efficiency plus some tools to help the database designer and the user. This lesson examines those tools and the basic concepts needed to use them.

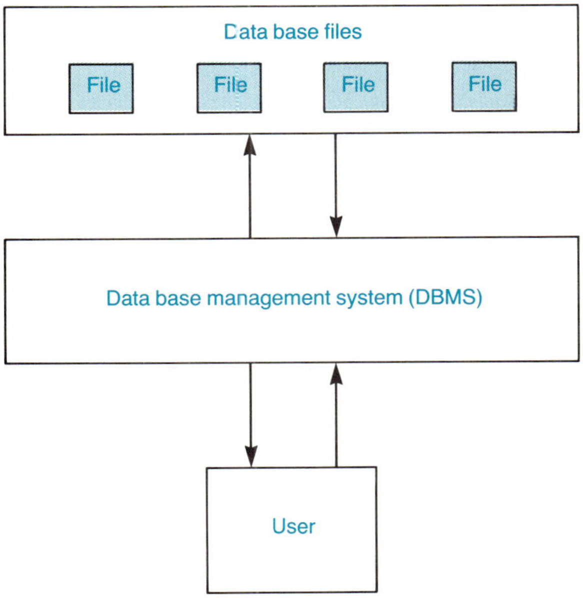

FIGURE 9-1 A database management system (DBMS) aids in the design, creation, updating, searching, and rearranging of a database and reporting from a database.

BASIC COMPONENTS OF A DATABASE

The first step in using a database is to understand its basic components: file, record, and field.

A **file** is an orderly collection of records, such as a file of customers, a file of all clients, a file of all students, or a file of all sales. A **record** is an orderly collection of data fields about one subject or entity, such as one customer, one client, one student, or one sales transaction. A **field** is a set of spaces containing data describing or identifying one entity, such as the customer's name, the client's account number, the student's grade, or the amount of a sales transaction. Several related fields make up one record; several related records make up one file; and several related files make up one database.

One way to picture the concept is to think of a filing cabinet as a database. A particular drawer might contain the name and address file for all the company's employees: the employee file. Within that drawer are folders, one for each employee constituting a record for a single employee and arranged in alphabetical order by employee last names. Each individual folder is similar to a record in a database file. If the filing cabinet is a four-drawer cabinet, the other drawers might contain files for customers in

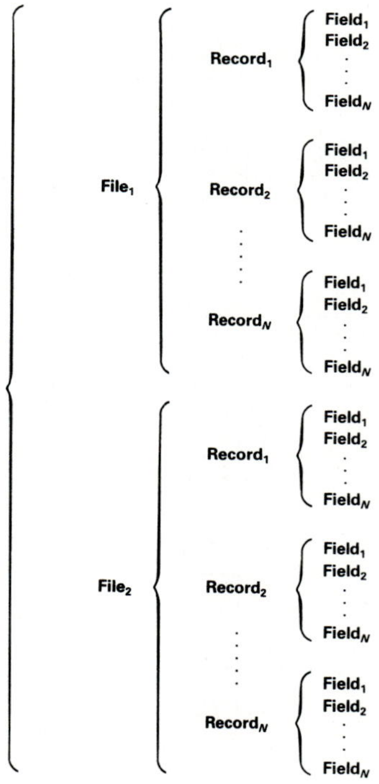

FIGURE 9-2 A database is made up of an orderly collection of fields, records, and files.

one drawer, suppliers in another, and products in the fourth. Figure 9-2 illustrates and compares the different components of a database.

PLANNING DATABASE APPLICATIONS

Perhaps the most difficult decision for a database designer to make is the identification of the entity from which the definition of a record flows. An **entity** is a person, place, or thing that is identified and described by the fields or attributes in a record. In some cases, it is easy; a single customer is an entity and each record in a customer file is about one customer, or a student is an entity in a student file and each record contains data about one student. However, what is an entity in a church membership file? If each person who attends is defined as an entity, then we would have to keep redundant data, such as address and phone number, for each individual in a family living at the same address. If we define the family as an entity, then some members of one family may attend the church, but others may not attend or may attend a different church. Is a person an entity for the database if he or she attends only at Christmas and Easter? Does a person have to be baptized or make a financial pledge of support to the church in order to be considered an entity in such a database?

A sales transaction file may present similar confusion. Consider a customer who calls in an order for ten different products, ordering various amounts of each product. Is this one entity or ten? Suppose the customer calls back in a few minutes to say he forgot to order an eleventh item. Is this a new entity or a change to a previous one? Suppose 60 days later the customer pays half of his bill. Which products are now paid for?

How can such questions be answered? There is no one answer; it depends on the type of questions that will need to be answered. For example, if the primary purpose of the church database is to answer financial questions regarding pledges made, then it may make sense to define an entity as an individual pledge, whether the pledge was made by one individual or by a family. If the purpose is to answer questions about which members have been baptized, confirmed, married, and so forth, then it is necessary to maintain information about each individual member. For the business, it may make sense to count all the sales made during one business day to one customer as an entity if the purpose is mainly to bill the customer on a periodic basis. However, if a manager needs to frequently answer a customer's questions about particular products being manufactured to the customer's specifications, then the sale might be separated into separate entities for each product the customer orders. The database management software can help create a database after one or more knowledgeable human beings have thought about these issues and have made decisions based upon the future questions to be answered by the database.

The next issue requiring human decision making is the grouping of records into files. Should we have a separate name and address file plus a separate customer account balance file for our customers, or should we include both in one larger file? How many different files does a university need in order to hold the necessary student information? Should information about a student's grades be on the same file as information needed at the health center regarding insurance coverage?

One principle to follow is to *minimize redundant data;* that is, do not try to record and maintain the same data on multiple files. However, this may create a file that is larger than the capacity of your computer system or one that takes too long to process efficiently.

Another principle to follow is to *maintain the integrity of the data;* that is, the data should be accurate and up-to-date and consistent if it appears in more than one file. When a customer moves, for example, we need to establish a database system that will accurately update the customer's address in all the files where that information is kept.

So, although it seems simple to create a database by simply answering the software's prompt for a database name, we really have to think about the problem to be solved by the database. We need to clearly define the problem and anticipate the questions that are likely to be asked of the system. Also, we must consider the constraints imposed by the physical and practical limitations of disk storage space and the speed of processing one large file versus a series of related smaller files. As with word processing and spreadsheet software, one capability provided by a good database management system is the ability to modify the structure of a database after the initial design. There are times when it is simply impossible to anticipate all the future needs of the decision makers who will be using the database.

Before a person can effectively use a database management system to create a new database, considerable thought should be given to the questions users may want answered from the data, the type of data available to put into the database, and the capabilities of the particular database software. In other words, what kind of information or output does the user need from the database? Despite what you might see in movies about the intelligence of computers, they cannot provide answers to questions not previously anticipated or retrieve data not previously stored and labeled for future retrieval. If the database is not properly designed and constructed, it can be of only limited usefulness. A database management system can, if properly designed and constructed, search a huge database and retrieve a specific data item with blinding speed. Let's consider the characteristics of potential data base applications, so that we can recognize where a database can be used effectively.

CHARACTERISTICS OF POTENTIAL DATABASE APPLICATIONS

A potential application for a database can be found wherever there is a need to organize and store a large amount of data for quick retrieval of specific items. A business manager may need to quickly determine whether or not a specific product is in inventory, whether or not a potential customer has a good credit record, how many times a particular product has been returned defective, and so on. Databases are often used to produce customized mailings in which, for example, the target customer lives in a particular zip code area, has an income above a particular level, and drives a particular model car. A student may create her own database to systematically collect bibliographic references for a research paper. All these applications have common characteristics: large quantities of data, repetition, frequent retrieval and revision of data, need for specialized or ad hoc reporting, shared data, and data that can be structured and organized using common fields.

Computerized databases are particularly valuable when you need easy access to *large quantities of data.* What constitutes a "large" quantity of data depends upon your point of view. Insurance companies need to store hundreds of data items for each of their thousands, or perhaps millions, of customers. Because the processing of data is such a major part of what insurance companies do, they are known to have some of the largest database applications and use some of the largest computers made. Government agencies such as the Social Security Administration and the Department of Defense maintain huge databases. On the other hand, an individual with a home computer may decide to use a database to store addresses of 20 to 30 friends and relatives.

For example, if you are researching a term paper and need to collect and organize a bibliography of 20 sources, then it is probably not in your best interest to computerize your bibliographic database. You can do it manually by placing the needed information on index cards. However, if you are researching a dissertation with over 2,000 sources, then you must be able to select the information you need and report on it easily. Of course, databases are used for much larger and more complex files. Banks with hundreds of customers and thousands of transactions were among the first businesses to computerize their databases. Lawyers use databases to keep track of legal documents used in large, complex cases, while schools use databases to keep student files. If you must collect and access a large quantity of data, then a computerized database may be the tool you need.

Repetition refers to the need to repeatedly search for particular data items within a large database. Going through a pile of index cards, looking up account numbers, or tracking down inventory may not be a problem when done occasionally, but multiply the time and energy required to do this by hundreds of times, and the need for a computerized database becomes critical. Large businesses and governmental agencies as well as individuals need to consider which files are best left in paper form in a file cabinet. If the data processing activity is seldom repeated, then a database may be more troublesome than convenient.

Frequent revision results when the data changes often and the decision makers need the most up-to-date information. For example, the number of seats left on a particular airline flight must be revised frequently as ticket agents and travel agents from all over sell tickets for that flight. Yet when you call a travel agent you want to know right away whether or not a seat is available for you. One of the first large-scale uses of computerized databases was for airline reservations, which require thousands of retrievals and revisions.

If you need to produce *specialized* or *ad hoc reports* from files, then a computerized database may suit your needs. Users can request information from specified records and fields, using custom-designed reports. The software then does the picking and choosing, instead of the user. For example, if you call a travel agency to arrange plane tickets for a trip, the travel agent will access the airline reservation system via a terminal, and the agent's terminal screen will display information about open flights to your destination, prices, and accommodations available. This information on the agent's screen is an example of an ad hoc report. The report answers such specific questions as "What flights are available on TWA from Chicago to New York next Saturday morning?" The travel agent did not have to write a new program to get the needed report or even tell the computer where to position the information on the screen. Instead the agent simply asked the question in a manner understandable to the database management software, and the software did the rest. Most database management systems, even simple ones for a personal computer, provide a way for the user to generate such ad hoc reports by simply asking questions in a prescribed manner.

Shared data refers to data that more than one user might need, possibly at the same time. For example, the database that describes the products currently available in a firm's inventory may be needed by several clerks simultaneously. Most sophisticated database management software provide support for **networking,** in which more than one user can access one file simultaneously while coordinating concurrent processing. Each user may have a terminal or even a computer, but the database physically resides at only one location. A DBMS with networking capabilities allows each of several users to have access to a single database. While more than one user can access a file, only one user can use a particular record at a time. Some database management software offer security protections, such as passwords and locked records, that prevent unauthorized users from accessing or revising sensitive records.

Structured data is data that can be organized into files, records, and fields. There must be some standardization to the way the data is expressed. For example, the employee database may contain such structured data about each employee as identification number, name, department, initial date of employment, home address, and home phone number. However, it may not be possible to really describe a human being in a database structure if what we mean to describe is that person's inner feelings, personal code of ethics, fears and aspirations, and the like. These things do not fit into neat categories such as a numeric field nine digits wide with two positions to the right of the decimal place or an alphabetic field ten characters wide. A person's inner feelings may be too complex to truly capture in a database, and it may be foolish to even try.

In summary, when you encounter a situation in which a large quantity of data needs to be organized and stored for frequent retrieval, the data need to be frequently updated or revised, people ask questions requiring ad hoc reports, more than one user needs to share the same data (perhaps in a network of personal computers or terminals connected to a common data source), and the data themselves can be structured and organized into fields, records, and files, you have found a good application for a database and database management software.

TYPES OF DATABASE MANAGEMENT SOFTWARE

Database management software for microcomputers can be categorized into several broad groups: single-file databases, multiple-file databases, and relational databases.

A **single-file database** provides the customary functions of creating, updating, searching, and reporting, but the database consists of just one file. For many applications such a limitation is not serious; the needed data can easily be placed into a single file, and the questions users are likely to ask require only data within that file.

Most single-file database software and all relational systems require each file to be a flat file. A **flat file** is organized in rows and columns, and each row contains the same number of columns. A flat file is called "flat" because it has just two dimensions, like a flat surface. But instead of thinking of the dimensions as length and width, think of them as rows and columns, similar to a spreadsheet. In fact, some spreadsheets, including Lotus 1-2-3 and VP-Planner, can operate as flat-file databases when using the data management commands supplied with the software. If you have completed the tutorial in Lesson 8, you have created and used a flat file.

Some single-file databases include more advanced features, like automatic date fields (the date is placed into the record automatically), complex report options, and multilevel indexing and sorting (features that permit reorganization of records within the databases). Many single-file databases are menu-driven and have sophisticated user interfaces that make manuals and detailed instructions almost unnecessary. **Menu driven** means users are prompted with choices and do not have to directly enter commands. In contrast, a **command driven** software system requires the user to enter coded commands rather than simply selecting from a menu. While the single-file database is not as advanced as other types of databases, its strength is its ability to collect, reorganize, and report information quickly and easily. Single-file databases are also easy to learn and typically less expensive. Figure 9-3 illustrates a single-file database.

Examples of single-file database software for MS-DOS systems include Alpha/three, by Alpha Software Corp.; Reflex: The Database Manager, by Borland; PC-File/R and PC-File III, from Buttonware Inc.; and PFS:Professional File, from Software Publishing Corp.

A **multiple-file database** can perform all the functions of a single-file database, but can contain more than one file. An essential requirement

FIGURE 9-3 Single-file databases hold records sequentially within one file. While more limited than relational and programmable databases, single-file databases are a very useful tool.

NAME	SSN	MAJOR	YEAR	GPA
ABRAHMS, PETER	904546576	MATH	4	3.50
BROWN, PATRICIA	234345443	MIS	2	4.00
CRANDALL, GERALD	454566765	MIS	3	2.00
DONNELLY, JAMES	555654665	LA&S	3	2.50
EISNER, WILMA	676767876	LA&S	3	2.90
FRANEY, RITA	223454323	ACCY	4	3.90
GRADEY, PATRICK	343245443	ACCY	3	3.00
HOLKOLM, JENNIE	454576677	MIS	4	3.00
HOLLAND, MARGARET	768897768	MATH	1	4.00
IMBODEN, THOMAS	678654765	MIS	3	2.90
JACKSON, LARRY	765575650	LA&S	1	3.90
KELLERMAN, NANCY	999787666	MATH	2	3.00
LAPINSKI, NICHOLAS	675890954	MATH	4	3.00
MAHONEY, MARY	767567556	MIS	3	4.00
NEWMAN, RALPH	777997779	MATH	3	3.50
ORTMAN, HAROLD	689090098	MATH	2	2.00
PORTERFIELD, HARRY	889723312	LA&S	1	3.00
RICHMAN, DALE	867999999	LA&S	3	4.00

END OF REPORT - HIT <CR>

of a multiple-file database is the ability to link two or more files together, although there is much variety in how various software systems accomplish this.

A **relational database** can contain multiple flat files and is capable of searching and retrieving data from more than one of the flat files within the database; however, there must be a defined relationship between the files. Figure 9-4 represents how a relational database works. For example, suppose data about a firm's customers, such as name, address, and phone number, are contained on one file and data about customers' credit accounts are on another. Perhaps only a small portion of the customers are authorized to purchase on credit, so the customer file contains 10,000 records whereas the credit customer file contains only 1,000 records. Therefore, it would not be reasonable to put all the data on one file because the fields for credit information would be blank for 9,000 of the 10,000 records.

However, a credit manager might want a list of the phone numbers of all credit customers who have overdue bills in excess of $500, so she can call to ask for payment. A relational database system could provide this information as long as there is a relationship between the customer file

FIGURE 9-4 An example of a relational database.

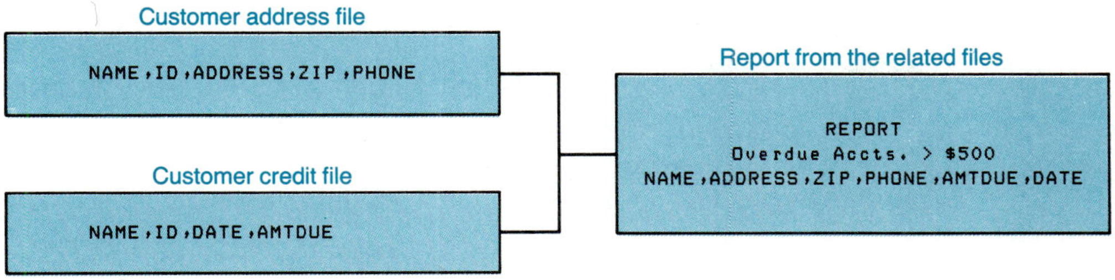

containing the phone numbers and the credit file containing the data about overdue bills. A likely relationship would be a customer identification number that would be the same for one customer on both files. If, for example, the database software found that customer number 10010 has an overdue account owing more than $500, the software can search the other file to find customer number 10010 and print out that customer's phone number and other important information, such as name, amount due, and date of last payment.

All relational databases today are based upon concepts first publicly proposed by Dr. E. F. Codd in a paper titled "A Relational Model of Data for Large Shared Data Banks" in *Communications of the ACM,* June 1970. Codd suggested a theoretical method for representing databases on concepts developed in the field of relational algebra. Until the early 1980s, the idea was of only theoretical interest. At that time, mainframe-oriented relational database management software systems such as Oracle were introduced. Now there are several such systems for microcomputers, including dBASE III Plus from Ashton-Tate, R:base 5000 and R:base System V (R:base stands for Relational Database) from Microrim Inc., Knowledgeman from Micro Database Systems Inc., Personal Pearl from Pearlsoft, Inc., Ingres from Relational Technology Inc., and Paradox from Borland. There are versions of Oracle for both mainframes and personal computers.

A **programmable database system** combines the functions of the other database systems mentioned so far, plus the user can write programs to further process the data and create custom-designed reports. Some database management systems, such as dBASE, provide a built-in set of commands for programming, while others allow the user to incorporate programs written in such standard languages as Turbo Pascal, C, BASIC, and COBOL. The user has the option of using the simpler functions to simply search and retrieve specific data items or of writing programs to apply formulas, repetitive processes, and logical processes and actually process or transform the data to create new data files and reports. Microcomputer programmable databases include Condor 3, dBASE II and III Plus, R:base Series 5000 and System V, Oracle, and Revelation.

Regardless of the level of complexity or the cost of the database management system, the software must be able to perform certain functions. The following section examines the most basic of those functions.

FUNCTIONS OF DATABASE MANAGEMENT SOFTWARE

There are eight major command functions common to database management software. These are creating, data entry, editing, retrieving and reporting, organizing, modifying, pointing, and file handling.

Creating

Database **creation** is the describing of the database contents to the database management software. Before data can be collected, manipulated, and stored, the database file must be named, and the structure of the database must be defined. The definition must include the name, type, and size of the fields contained within the database file. When a new database file is named, the database management system establishes a storage area on the disk to hold the data and the database file that is to be recalled in the future. Like the filenames assigned to word processing documents and electronic spreadsheets, database filenames follow certain rules or conventions, depending on the particular database software. For example, in dBASE III, a database filename can include up to eight characters, the first of which must be an alphabetic character. The filename cannot contain spaces or symbols other than an underscore. Filenames should be significant and meaningful.

In addition to establishing a name for the database file, the creator must define the database structure, including the description of each data field within each record contained in the file. Each field has at least four characteristics to be defined: the field name, the type of information the field will contain, the width of the field in characters, and the number of spaces after the decimal point (for numeric fields).

Field names also have naming conventions determined by the database software. In dBASE III, each field name may be up to ten characters long and may include letters, digits, and embedded underscore characters, such as FIRST_NAME, but it must begin with a letter. Certain reserve words, including commands, must be avoided. Duplicate field names in a single file are not permitted.

Although database software may differ on the particular procedures followed to define fields, there are, in general, five field types. **Alphanumeric** or **character fields** generally include alphabetic or alphanumeric data such as names, addresses, or descriptive information. A common example of a character field containing numbers is a social security number containing hyphens, such as 123-45-6789. Fields that are to be alphabetically sorted must be defined as character fields. However, such fields cannot be included in mathematical operations.

Numeric fields contain numeric data to be used in mathematical operations such as adding and subtracting. Once the user has defined a numeric field, it is usually necessary to define the number of decimal places to the right of the decimal point. Dollar signs and commas are not entered as part of the value. You will also need to consider the size of the largest possible value that might be stored in the field.

Some database software offer **date fields** to help you enter calendar dates. The format of the field is strictly defined by the software rather than by the user. For example, with dBASE, calendar dates are typically arranged in mm/dd/yy fashion. December 25, 1991, would be 12/25/91.

Logical fields generally accept only one character indicating a true or false value. Logical fields are sometimes called **Boolean fields,** after George Boole, an English mathematician and logician (1815–64). Boolean variables consist of two possible values, typically 1 (to represent true) or 0 (to represent a false logical condition). Some systems provide for T or F (true or false) or Y or N (yes or no) to be used in logical fields. A logical field consumes only one space, but it can be a handy identifier of active or inactive customers, people who have or have not paid their dues, or admitted or nonadmitted students.

Some database software offer **memo fields** to hold large amounts of text, such as additional miscellaneous information, that cannot be manipulated (sorted, indexed, searched, used in functions, or connected to other fields or files) later. Table 9-1 lists examples of the different types of data fields.

Data field width is the maximum number of characters allowed in the field. This depends on the type of field being used. With character or memo fields, the width determines the length of the text that can be entered in the field. The user defines the width of the field, considering such constraints as reporting needs and maximums allowed by the

Table 9-1 EXAMPLES OF DATA FIELDS

Nature of Data Field	*Type of Data Field Description Needed*
Social security numbers	Numeric if in the form 123456789 but character if 123-45-6789
Dollar amounts	Numeric if in the form 123.56 but character if $1,123.99
Phone numbers	Numeric if in the form 1231234 but character if 123-1234
Dates	Some database systems allow various forms for dates; if the software does not provide for specific date fields, then usually character if in mm/dd/yy form
People's names	Character or alphabetic
Addresses	Character or alphanumeric

software. The size of the field should be determined by the size of the largest data item. In other words, how many characters do you need to make the data contained in the field meaningful? Frequently, alphabetic data is abbreviated to fit into a field; you especially may have noticed this characteristic of data extracted from a database if your last name is longer than 15 characters, the number of spaces normally allocated to people's last names. A date field is usually eight characters wide and stores the numeric codes for the month, day, and year and the symbols (usually slashes or hyphens) that separate the codes. Logical fields are usually one character wide. Numeric field width needs to be defined by the maximum number of digits allowed in the value, including, if used, the sign (positive or negative) and the decimal point. Then the number of digits to appear to the right of the decimal point should be specified.

After a database structure has been defined, the structure is saved to a disk file, and the database file is ready for data entry. Figure 9-5 is an example of a dBASE III Plus screen after the structure of a file named EMPLOYEE has been defined.

Data Entry

Data entry is the placing of data into defined fields on the record in the database file. Before data can be entered into the file, the user must tell the database management software which file to use. For example, in dBASE III, if no database file is currently in use, the software prompts the user for the name of the file using the Set Up command (see Figure 9-6).

```
                                                   Bytes remaining:   3940
 CURSOR  <-- -->  |   INSERT     |   DELETE      | Up a field:     ↑
  Char:    ←  →   | Char:   Ins  | Char:    Del  | Down a field:   ↓
  Word:  Home End | Field:  ^N   | Word:    ^Y   | Exit/Save:     ^End
  Pan:    ^←  ^→  | Help:   F1   | Field:   ^U   | Abort:          Esc

     Field Name  Type       Width  Dec          Field Name  Type      Width  Dec

  1  IDNO        Numeric        5    0
  2  LNAME       Character     20
  3  FNAME       Character     20
  4  MINITIAL    Character      1
  5  DEPT        Character      5
  6  STARTDATE   Date           8
  7  BENEFITS    Logical        1

MODIFY STRUCTURE |<C:>|EMPLOYEE          |Field: 1/7      |  |       Caps
                          Enter the field name.
Field names begin with a letter and may contain letters, digits, and underscores
```

FIGURE 9-5 An example of a structure of a database file named EMPLOYEE using dBASE III Plus. Notice the field names, types, and widths of the fields.

FIGURE 9-6 **Examples of the on-screen prompts used with dBASE III Plus.**

```
Set Up  Create  Update  Position  Retrieve  Organize  Modify  Tools  03:15:33 pm

 Database file              MUCFIG.DBF
 Format for Screen          TRADEMK.DBF
 Query                      FIGURES.DBF
 Catalog                    NEIGHBOR.DBF
 View                       EMPLOYEE.DBF
 Quit dBase III PLUS

Command: USE C:
ASSIST          <C:> MUCFIG              Rec: 123/123

           Position selection bar - ↑↓.  Select - ↵.
                    Select a database file.
```

Once the correct file has been defined, an entry screen may appear. For example, with dBASE III Plus, a full-screen entry form is available when you use the Append command (see Figure 9-7).

You place data into a field by typing in the data and pressing the Return key. The entered data must meet the defined characteristics of the field, including width and type (character, numeric, logical, date, or memo). Invalid data, such as character data in a numeric field, may get the response of a beep or no response at all; the typed characters will not appear on the screen.

Most database management software offer a wide selection of editing commands to be used with data entry—such as cursor control commands, including the arrow, Backspace, and Delete keys. In Figure 9-8, notice the menu of commands at the top of a dBASE III Plus screen. These will be detailed in the tutorial later in this lesson.

In dBASE III Plus, you end data entry by pressing the Return key at the first field of the first blank record. Unlike word processing and electronic spreadsheet software, database management software typically does not have a Save function. Saving of files is completely controlled by the database management software. For databases containing thousands, or even millions, of records, it simply would not be practical to have to re-save the entire database each time a change was made to an individual field in a record.

FIGURE 9-7 Adding new records to a database file using the Append command in dBASE III Plus.

```
CURSOR    <-- -->  |          UP    DOWN  |  DELETE      | Insert Mode:  Ins
  Char:    ←  →    | Field:   ↑     ↓     | Char:   Del  | Exit/Save:   ^End
  Word: Home End   | Page:   PgUp  PgDn   | Field:  ^Y   | Abort:        Esc
                   | Help:    F1          | Record:^U    | Memo:       ^Home

IDNO         40002
LNAME        ULEMEN
FNAME        JERALD
MINITIAL
DEPT
STARTDATE
BENEFITS

APPEND      |<C:>|EMPLOYEE          |Rec: 7/7         |     |    Caps
```

Editing

Editing is the changing, replacement, or deletion of the contents of a data record. This typically involves searching the database to find the record or set of records desired, displaying the records one at a time on the screen in some predetermined order, and then allowing the user to make changes using commands similar to the editing features in a word processing software system. The user can move the cursor to any character in the record using the arrow keys, delete errors with the Backspace and Delete keys, insert correct data, insert additional data on the record, and move on to subsequent records in the file. This provides the user with a convenient method for changing data items such as the address of a client, for recording the payment toward a customer's account, for adding sales transactions at the end of a business day, for closing accounts of customers who have moved far away or died, and for correcting all types of data errors. Once these changes have been completed, the database software must reorganize the database into proper sequence and update the disk to properly reflect the current condition of the database. Figure 9-8 shows the full-screen editing features available on dBASE III Plus. Notice the menu of cursor control and editing commands available.

Record deletion is usually a two-step process. For example, in dBASE III Plus, the records to be deleted are first described using a conditional statement or, when the dBASE III Plus Append command is used, are marked. A delete message appears on the status bar or an asterisk appears next to the record when the file is listed. Figure 9-9 shows examples of dBASE III Plus commands for deleting records. Since deleting a record is a drastic step, most database management software, including dBASE III Plus, verify the operation. dBASE III Plus marks the file that is to be deleted

FIGURE 9-8 Editing a current data record using dBASE III Plus. Notice the menu of editing commands at the top of the screen.

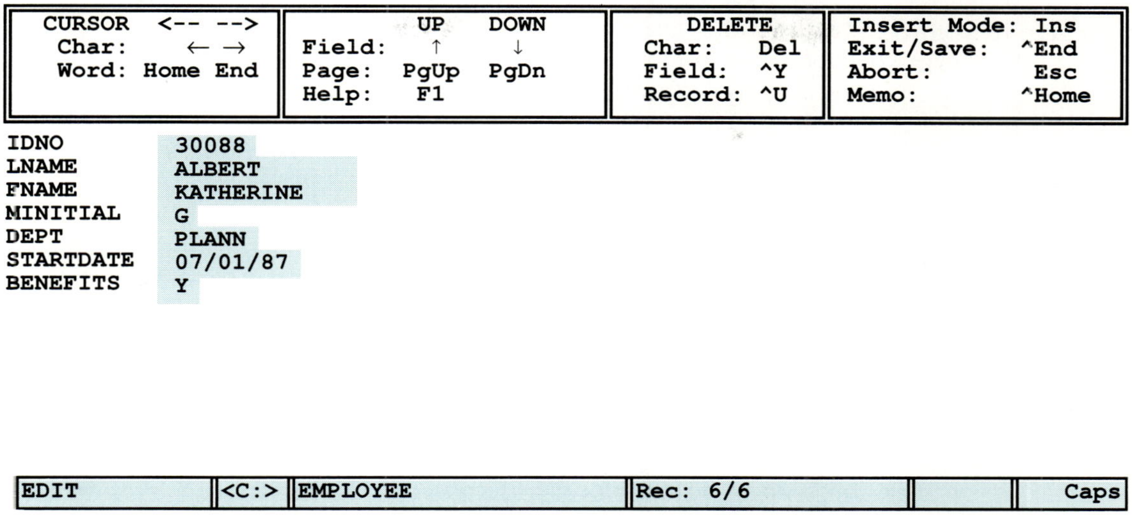

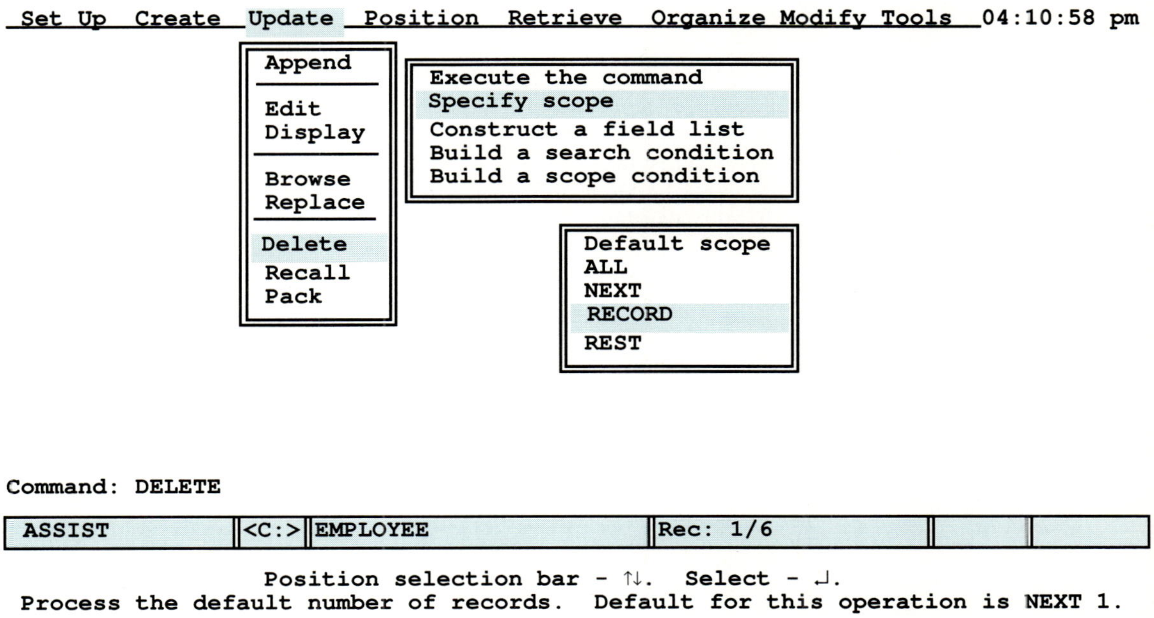

FIGURE 9-9 An example of record deletion using dBASE III Plus.

and then requires an additional command (Pack) before finally removing the record from the file (see Figure 9-10).

Retrieving and Reporting

Any user of a database is primarily interested in retrieving and reporting information from the database. The **retrieve and report function** causes the database software to search the records in one or more files within the database, retrieving particular records requested by the user and reporting those records to the user either by displaying them on the screen or by printing them. Some software systems provide a standardized report format, so the user does not need to describe just how each data item will be positioned on the screen or page. Others require the user to first build a report file describing in detail the desired position of all fields and the headings, labels, and other details of the report. Still others allow a standardized report to be used as a default, but leave the user free to customize the report format if desired. Some database software permit reports to take the form of mailing labels, which is very convenient when a database is used for mass mailings.

An essential concept to understand about the retrieve and report function is the need for the user to properly describe to the software the logical conditions that specify the data needed for the report. Such logical conditions are in the form of a statement composed of database names, record names, field names, and relational operators and logical operators. Logical conditions are also used to describe records for editing and deletion as well as reporting. **Relational operators** include the following:

Operator	*Description*
<	Less than
>	Greater than
=	Equal to
<=	Less than or equal to
>=	Greater than or equal to
<> or #	Not equal to
$	Substring comparison

Logical operators include the following:

Operator	*Description*
NOT	Logical *not*
AND	Logical *and*
OR	Logical *or*
( )	Parentheses for grouping

FIGURE 9-10 **dBASE III Plus marks the record to be deleted and then requires an additional command (Pack) before removing the record from the database.**

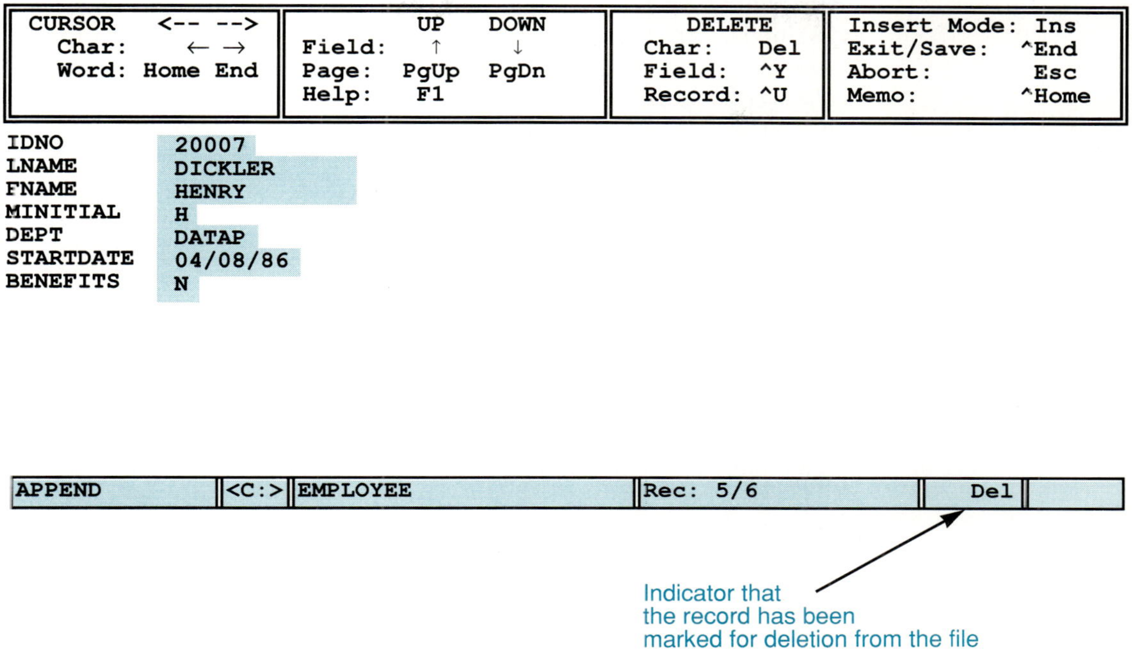

Some software, such as dBASE, require the use of single periods before and after the logical operators. For example, with dBASE the statement

```
DISPLAY FOR AGE>=20 .AND. (MAJOR='HISTORY' .OR. MAJOR='MATH')
```

would retrieve from a file containing the field names AGE and MAJOR those records in which the AGE is a value greater than or equal to 20 and the MAJOR is HISTORY or MATH. The on-screen display so created would not include anyone younger than 20 and would also exclude anyone whose major was anything but history or math. More examples will be illustrated in the tutorial found later in this chapter. **Mathematical operators** include the following:

Operator	*Description*
+	Addition
-	Subtraction
*	Multiplication
/	Division
** or ^	Exponentiation

Organizing

Organizing is the physical or logical rearrangement or duplication of a database file. The major types of commands to help organize a database include index, sort, and copy. **Indexing** a file causes the software to create another file holding the key field and the prescribed order. The records contained in the file are not physically rearranged, but the file can be printed or otherwise processed in the indexing order. **Sorting** causes the records contained in the file to be physically rearranged. The typical sorting function actually creates a copy of the original file, but the new file contains the records in the desired sorting order. Often a user may desire that the file be sorted once into alphabetical order by customers' last names or numerical order by account numbers, for example. If the user then wants to see a listing of customers arranged in ascending order by the amount of customers' purchases, indexing would be used for this report. Indexing by amount of purchase would allow the printing of a report in the desired order, but there would be no need to physically sort the file and waste the file space needed to hold the new file a sort would create.

The **copy** function simply causes the computer to copy the file and store it on the disk. This function can be used to create a backup of the original file or to selectively copy certain fields or certain records, thereby making a file that is a subset of the original file. Some database management systems make use of the Copy command to allow the user to move the data from one file structure into a modified structure. The user creates the new structure by defining the records in terms of the field names, sizes, and characteristics and then copies the data from the old file structure into the new structure, avoiding the need to rekey the data (see Figure 9-11).

Modifying

Modifying is the revision of the database already in use. The user modifies the various names and characteristics in the database files, records, and fields. If the user has created files containing descriptions of report formats or has described relationships between files, these too may need to be modified as needs change. The Modify function provides the flexibility users want, so they can adapt the database to better serve needs that change over time.

Pointing

Pointing, or **positioning,** is the movement of the pointer anywhere in the database. A **pointer** is the address or location of the next record in the file. Commands that cause the pointer to find a particular record include Seek, GOTO, and Locate. These cause the computer to position the pointer at a particular record so that record can, for example, be displayed. To cause the computer to advance the pointer one record in the file, dBASE uses the Skip command. To skip forward, a positive number is used; to move backwards, a negative number is used.

There are also commands to position the pointer at the top or bottom of the file and to continue moving in the direction already begun. These commands allow the user to search around in the file much as he or she might search around in a drawer of a filing cabinet.

FIGURE 9-11 The copy function permits the contents of a database file to be copied to a new database file, provided the fields have identical names.

File of Students Enrolled in CIS 101
File structure

Field definitions:

NAME	TYPE	LENGTH	PRECISION
NAME	CHARACTER	25	
SSN	NUMERIC	9	0
MAJOR	CHARACTER	4	
YEAR	NUMERIC	1	0
GPA	NUMERIC	4	2

Data contained in fields with *identical names* are copied to the file.

File of Students Enrolled in CIS 101A
File structure

Field definitions:

NAME	TYPE	LENGTH	PRECISION
NAME	CHARACTER	25	
SSN	NUMERIC	9	0
MAJOR	CHARACTER	4	
YEAR	NUMERIC	1	0
GPA	NUMERIC	4	2
SEX	CHARACTER	1	

File Handling

File handling functions take care of various housekeeping tasks, such as telling the computer which disk drive will hold the database, erasing files or databases, creating backup files, listing the structure of files, and perhaps connecting your database to other software, such as a word processor or spreadsheet.

In the previous paragraphs we provided a general introduction to database software functions from a conceptual point of view. In the tutorial that follows we will provide specific commands in dBASE III Plus that will enable you to create a database, insert data, and produce a printed report.

INTRODUCTION TO dBASE III PLUS

Up to this point we have discussed databases and database management software in general terms, only occasionally referring to a specific dBASE III Plus command. Now, however, you are about to start your first dBASE III Plus tutorial, and you will need to become familiar with specific dBASE III Plus features and commands.

dBASE III Plus is the name of a software package (a collection of computer programs) marketed by Ashton-Tate, Inc., of Culver City, California. Currently, dBASE III Plus is the most popular database management system for personal computers. It is considered a relational database manager; that is, the software helps you create and maintain relational databases.

Ashton-Tate, Inc., defines a relational database as one in which the data are arranged in the form of a matrix, with the rows of the matrix forming the individual records in the database and the columns of the matrix forming the individual fields of information, across all records. With this database, users can establish a relationship between two or more databases by using a common key field of information. For example, the user can access an inventory file, and using the PART_NUMBER as the key for each inventory record, list all the transactions for this PART_NUMBER from a transaction file. Or, for example, a program to produce paychecks may access both a personnel master file and a payroll master file, using the employee social security number on each record in each file as the common link between the two files.

There are several versions of dBASE from Ashton-Tate. This book describes dBASE III Plus Version 1.1 with The Assistant. Although command structures of the different versions of dBASE look similar, The Assistant looks quite different from the dBASE prompt. Without The Assistant (sometimes called Assist) the user sees only a single dot as the prompt to show that dBASE is loaded and ready to receive the first command. The Assistant provides a set of commands across the top of the screen in a fashion similar to Lotus. When the cursor is moved to a command, additional menus appear on the screen to show the user the various choices that accompany the command. The Assistant displays several levels of menus, called **submenus,** that continue to prompt the user through routines of many steps. Figure 9-12 shows the various command options available through The Assistant.

Some users think The Assistant is a wonderful tool; others (usually more experienced computer users) think it is tedious. We recommend that beginners start with The Assistant; when they are more experienced, they can leave The Assistant by pressing Escape one or more times until the dot prompt appears on the screen. They can then type the commands instead of selecting from the menus. Even in the native dBASE mode, if users forgot what choices are available, they can get assistance simply by typing HELP followed by the command in question. Further, as a short-cut, all dBASE commands can be abbreviated to their first four letters. To recall The Assistant, just type Assist at the dot prompt.

The features of dBASE can be grouped into four basic processes: creation, editing, sequencing, and reporting. The dBASE **creation** process involves naming the database and describing each field in terms of the field name, field type, field size, and number of positions to the right of the decimal point. This process is similar to the one you used in Lotus when you gave the spreadsheet a filename, put labels at the top of columns, set

FIGURE 9-12 **A representation of the levels of Assistant menus. As the highlight is moved across the menu line, the submenus will appear.**

```
Set Up                    Create                Update
Database file             Database file         Append
                          Format
Format for Screen         View                  Edit
Query                     Query                 Display
                          Report
Catalog                   Label                 Browse
View                                            Replace

Quit dBASE III PLUS                             Delete
                                                Recall
                                                Pack

Position          Retrieve      Organize
Seek              List          Index
                  Display       Sort
Locate            Report
Continue          Label         Copy

Skip              Sum
Goto Record       Average
                  Count

Modify            Tools
Database file     Set Drive
Format            Copy file
View              Directory
Query             Rename
Report            Erase
Label             List structure

                  Import
                  Export
```

the columns to the needed width, and specified the necessary format. In fact, Lotus 1-2-3 can be used to create and process a simple database, as illustrated in Lesson 8.

The **editing** process allows you to browse through the records to locate typing errors and correct them in a fashion similar to the way you have corrected errors in word processing and spreadsheets: deleting records, adding or appending records to the file, and employing several other editing techniques. Although editing in database management is similar to editing in word processing or spreadsheets, a major difference involves the way your work is saved to the disk file. With word processing and spreadsheets you were warned repeatedly that the changes you were making were being made only to the working copy temporarily stored in

RAM and that it was essential, upon completion of any editing, to re-save the entire word processing document or spreadsheet file on the data disk. dBASE III Plus periodically writes to disk the records you have edited *while* the editing process is taking place. You must, however, be very careful to *always properly exit* dBASE III Plus so that any records being temporarily held in RAM during editing will be replaced on the data disk and files will be closed and saved before you turn off the computer.

dBASE provides two basic forms of **sequencing:** physical sorting and logical indexing. **Physical sorting** involves the copying of the file arranged in some specifically requested numeric or alphabetical order. **Logical indexing** involves the creation of an index file but not another database file. The index file provides the various sequencing orders using only the record numbers and does not actually re-arrange the records in the file. You will learn more about dBASE III Plus indexing and sorting in Lesson 10.

Finally, the **reporting** process involves the creation of a **report format file,** which describes each report in terms of report headings, column headings, fields to be included, groupings of records within the report, and fields to be totaled. The report format file and the database file are combined later, when you execute the command to actually display a report on the screen or print it on a printer. Thus the formats for displaying or printing a report are not kept as part of the data file. In this manner, one database file can be used for numerous different reports. Reporting is discussed and used in Lesson 10.

dBASE III Plus assigns extensions to filenames. Table 9-2 lists these extensions and their meanings.

Table 9-2 dBASE III PLUS FILE EXTENSIONS

Extension	*Description*
.DBF	Database file.
.DBT	Memo file.
.NDX	Index file.
.PRG	Program file.
.FMT	Format file
.LBL	Label file
.MEM	Memory file
.FRM	Report form file
.TXT	Text output file
.CAT	Catalog file
.QRY	Query file
.SCR	Screen file
.VUE	View file

Since this book deals with many microcomputer applications besides those of dBASE III Plus, it should not be considered a complete reference to all the dBASE III Plus commands and features. However, anyone who purchases dBASE III Plus receives various reference guides or manuals along with the software. Further, dBASE III Plus provides a comprehensive HELP function within the software. Lessons 9–11 will, however, present a foundation in the general concepts of database systems and enough specifics about dBASE III Plus to enable you to use it for most of the typical database applications.

TUTORIAL: CREATING A DATABASE USING dBASE III PLUS

To complete this tutorial you need the following:

- MS-DOS system disk or MS-DOS installed on the dBASE III Plus disk
- dBASE III Plus disk
- A data disk to hold your first database

While completing this tutorial you will learn how to

- Load dBASE III Plus
- Create a single-file database by describing the fields in the records and entering some sample data
- Create and produce a query to display answers to specific questions concerning the data in the database

For this tutorial, assume that you have been asked to create a database single flat file called CLIENTS to hold data about the clients of the law office of Hallam, Hallam, and Hallam, better known as Hallam3. We will record each client's account number (ACCTNO), first name (FNAME), middle initial (INITIAL), last name (LNAME), street address (ADDRESS1), city (CITY), state (STATE), Zip code (ZIP), amount owed (AMT), and payment date (PAYDATE).

The firm is new and the number of clients is rather small (fewer than 100). The firm hopes to grow, but for now we will input only a sample of five. Cash flow is a major problem for this fledging law firm, and it needs to keep its billing current or it may not be able to pay the rent for its plush office suite. The first goal of the database, therefore, is to produce a list of the clients whose bills are overdue, so Hallam3 can send Bruno, its newly hired bill collector, to personally collect all overdue bills.

This tutorial is divided into three major parts: (1) create the database by naming it, and name and describe each of the fields within the file; (2)

input data to the CLIENTS database; (3) produce a query that will cause certain records to be selected and displayed on the screen.

Step 1: Load the operating system and dBASE III Plus.

a. Load MS-DOS following the procedures described in earlier lessons.

b. At the A> prompt, if necessary, remove the MS-DOS system disk from drive A. Insert the dBase III Plus system disk and type

```
DBASE
```

Press **Return.**

A copyright notice is displayed on the screen. This screen disappears after a few seconds or when you press the Return or the Enter key.

c. The dBASE Assistant menu screen is displayed (See Figure 9-13). If the dot prompt (.) appears on the screen, type

```
ASSIST
```

and press **Return.** The Assistant menu will appear.

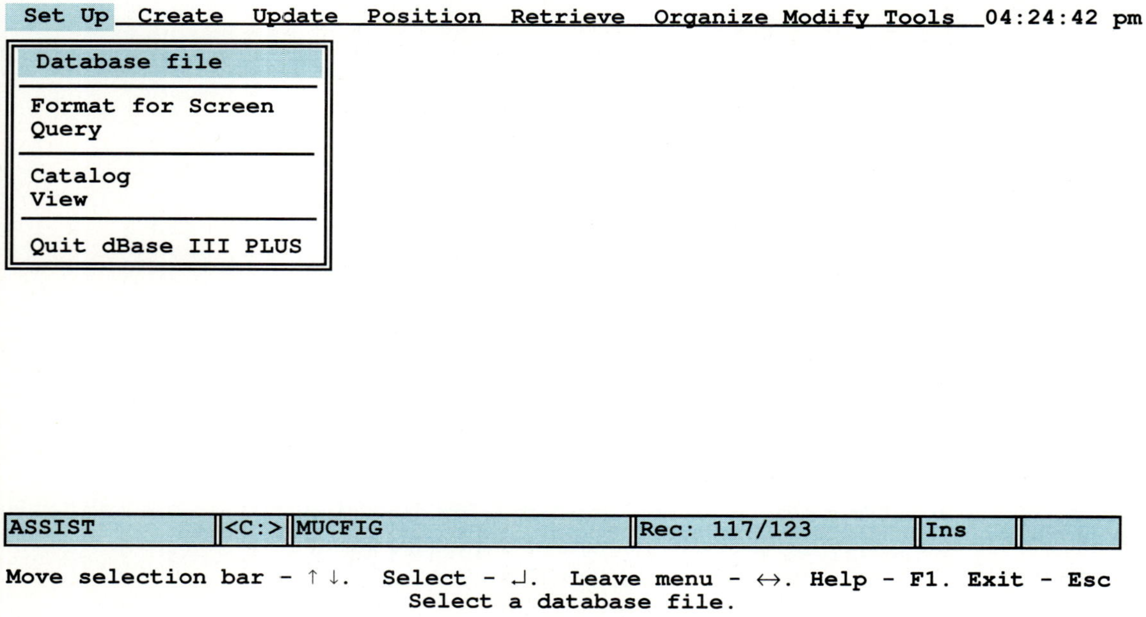

FIGURE 9-13 **After dBASE III Plus is loaded, the dBASE Assistant menu screen is displayed. Notice the menu line across the top of the screen.**

Move the cursor across the line of commands by pressing the right arrow key.

Notice the **pull-down menus,** sometimes called **submenus,** that drop down from the top of the screen under each command as you move the cursor across the line of commands. You can use the up and down arrows to highlight choices within each pull-down menu. You can get helpful information about each choice by pressing the [F1] Help key. Let's try out one of these Helps.

Move the cursor to **Create.** The first choice in the pull-down menu, **Database file,** will be highlighted. Press **[F1]**.

A message defining Create appears, followed by the command format. The words in all capital letters are dBASE III Plus commands; the angle brackets, < >, indicate a *required* entry; and the square brackets, [ ], indicate an *optional* extension.

Other parts of the Assistant screen include the action line, the status bar, the navigation line, and the message line (see Figure 9-14). The **action line,** the line above the bar near the bottom of the screen, displays the command being generated by your menu or submenu selection. The **status bar,** which can be found near the bottom of the screen, displays information about the current status, such as the current disk drive, the file in use, whether various options are in use, whether a record has been marked for deletion, and whether the Caps Lock or Num Lock key is on. The **navigation line,** just beneath the status bar, provides instruction for moving from one menu option to another or from one submenu to another. Finally, the **message line,** just below the navigation line, provides an explanation of the current

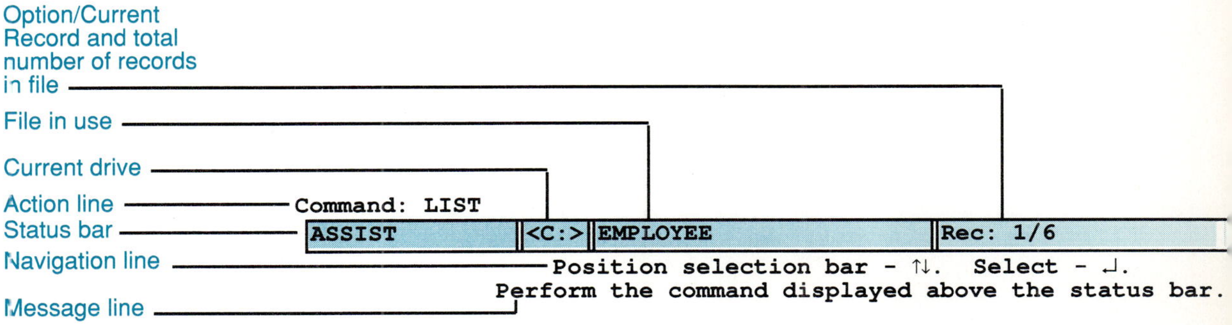

FIGURE 9-14 **The Action line describes the current commands. The Status bar describes the mode (ASSIST), the current logged disk drive (<C:>), the data file currently in use (EMPLOYEE), the number of the record currently in use, the total number of records in the file (Rec: 1/6), and other messages, including records that have been deleted, insert mode, and numeric lock status. The Navigation line offers cursor movement options. The Message line gives further information about actions.**

menu option along with any action you are to take if you choose that option.

As discussed before in the lesson, earlier versions of dBASE did not have the extensive menus of The Assistant. The only feature on the screen was the single dot prompt, indicating that dBASE was ready to receive a command from the user. For example, rather than selecting Create from a menu, the user would type Create. To experience this low level of assistance, press the **Escape** key twice.

A dot appears in the lower left corner of the screen, while the status bar and message line remain on the screen. This dot command is the dBASE command prompt. Whenever this dot is on the screen, dBASE is ready to accept a command.

You may not want to venture away from the Assistant screen for a while (you'll have an opportunity in Lessons 10 and 11). But even at the dot command prompt, help is always available. Type

```
HELP
```

Press **Return.** The Help Main Menu appears (see Figure 9-15). Spend some time exploring the Help feature.

Move the highlight by pressing the up or down arrow keys. Press **Return** to select any Help explanation.

```
                                                MAIN MENU

          Help Main Menu
          ==============

          1 - Getting Started
          2 - What Is a ...
          3 - How Do I ...
          4 - Creating a Database File
          5 - Using an Existing Database File
          6 - Commands and Functions


HELP        |<C:>|           |          |     |     |
 Position selection bar - ↑↓.  Select - ↵.  Exit with Esc or enter a command.
                 ENTER >
```

FIGURE 9-15 The Help Main Menu is available whenever the user types "HELP" at the dot prompt. Notice the different categories of help available, just by moving the highlight to the appropriate category and pressing Return.

To leave Help, press **Esc.**

Return to the Assistant. At the dot prompt, type

```
ASSIST
```

Press **Return.**

It is very important to properly exit any database management system, because open files are not yet properly closed. If a file has had records added to it and is not closed properly, the end-of-file marker will be misplaced and records may be lost. There are two ways to quit dBASE: first, you can press Esc until the dot prompt appears and then type QUIT; or, while in Assist, you can position the cursor on the Set Up command, move the highlight with the down arrow to the Quit dBASE III Plus choice on the pull-down submenu, and press Return.

Quit using either method. If you have properly quit dBASE, the message

```
*** END RUN   dBASE III PLUS
```

appears on the screen and the system prompt reappears.

At the system prompt, type

```
DBASE
```

and press **Return** to reload dBASE III.

Step 2: Create a database.

a. Open and name the database. At the Assistant Main Menu, move the highlight to **Tools** and select **Set drive.** Press **Return.** A submenu appears listing the potential disk drives.

If you are using a typical dual floppy disk system, select **B:** and press **Return.**

Now your database will be stored on the floppy disk in drive B. Of course, if you are using a hard disk system, select the appropriate drive.

Using the left arrow key, move to **Create** on the Assistant Main Menu.

Press **Return** to select the **Database file** option. The submenu to the right should highlight **B:.**

Press **Return** and a prompt appears:

```
Enter the name of the file:
```

Type

`CLIENTS`

for the name of the file and press **Return.**

b. Define the database fields. After you press Return, the screen changes to help you describe the first field in the file. See Figure 9-16.

Enter

`ACCTNO`

Press **Return.**

Notice the navigation line (the next to bottom line), which now contains the message

`Press SPACE to change the field type.`

Press **Space** to see how the field types change. Each time you press the Space Bar, the field Type changes—from Character to Numeric to Date to Logical to Memo and back to Character. As the field type changes, the Message Line at the bottom of the screen changes to briefly describe each data type. You can also enter the field type directly by typing the first letter of the field type.

```
                                                     Bytes remaining:   4000

 CURSOR   <--  -->  |    INSERT     |    DELETE     | Up a field:      ↑
   Char:    ←  →    | Char:   Ins   | Char:    Del  | Down a field:    ↓
   Word:  Home End  | Field:  ^N    | Word:    ^Y   | Exit/Save:     ^End
   Pan:    ^←  ^→   | Help:   F1    | Field:   ^U   | Abort:          Esc

    Field Name  Type       Width   Dec          Field Name  Type       Width   Dec
    ==============================              ==============================
  1             Character

 CREATE        |<B:>|CLIENTS            |Field: 1/1        |    |  Caps
                            Enter the field name.
 Field names begin with a letter and may contain letters, digits, and underscores
```

FIGURE 9-16 After you press Return, the screen changes to help you describe the first field in the file.

The ACCTNO field is numeric, so press the **Space Bar** until **Numeric** appears under Type in the highlight. Press **Return.**

The cursor automatically moves to the Width area. Notice the message line informs you that numeric fields are 1 to 19 digits wide, including the decimal point and sign.

Type

```
3
```

Press **Return.**

The cursor moves to the Dec area so that you can enter the number of positions to the right of the decimal.

Enter

```
0
```

Make sure you press the numeral zero and not the letter O. If you try to enter a character in a numeric field, dBASE will beep a polite reminder.

Press **Return.**

This completes the definition of your first data field. Continue defining the data fields for the CLIENTS file. For the rest of the fields, enter the following data:

FIELD NAME	TYPE	WIDTH	DEC
FNAME	Character	10	
INITIAL	Character	1	
LNAME	Character	15	
ADDRESS1	Character	25	
CITY	Character	15	
STATE	Character	2	
ZIP	Character	5	
AMT	Numeric	8	2
PAYDATE	Date	Press Return.	

The field width for Date is automatically set at 8 characters.

After entering all the data fields, press **Return.**

The navigation line below the status bar provides the prompt

```
Press ENTER to confirm. Any other key to resume.
```

If the field names, types, widths, and decimal positions all appear correct to you, press **Return.** The navigation line says to please wait and then it prompts:

```
Input data records now? (Y/N) _
```

Press

Y

and the screen changes, providing a form to be filled in for the first record in the file. See Figure 9-17.

Step 3: Input the data.

Although dBASE files can hold thousands of records, dBASE is fully operational even with a few records. To get started using dBASE, enter the following five records at the appropriate fields. Here are some tips for entering data:

- When you are entering data in fields, if the data extends into the last place in the field, the cursor will automatically move to the next field. You should not need to press Return to move to the next field.
- When you are entering numbers with a decimal point, if there are only zeros after the decimal point (for example, 100.00), you do not need to press the decimal point or enter the zeros. Just type the entries that come before the decimal point and press Return.
- When you are entering dates, *do not* type the slashes (/). Just enter the numbers for the month, day, and year. The cursor will automatically move to the proper place in the date and insert the slashes.

```
CURSOR   <-- -->  |            UP    DOWN  |     DELETE     | Insert Mode:    Ins
 Char:     ← →    | Field:     ↑      ↓    | Char:     Del  | Exit/Save:     ^End
 Word:  Home End  | Page:    PgUp   PgDn   | Field      ^Y  | Abort:          Esc
                  | Help:     F1           | Record:   ^U   | Memo:         ^Home

ACCTNO
FNAME
INITIAL
LNAME
ADDRESS1
CITY
STATE
ZIP
AMT                     .
PAYDATE              /  /

CREATE       |<B:>|CLIENTS              |Rec: None        |      |      Caps
```

FIGURE 9-17 After defining the record fields, press Y and the screen will change, providing a form to be filled in for the first record in the file.

- Remember to always type two numbers each for the day and the month. For example, January 1, 1989, should be typed as 010189.
- Beeps that sound while you are entering data indicate that you have reached the end of a field and the cursor has moved to the next field, or that you have made an error. In general, do not ignore the beeps.

ACCTNO	FNAME	INITIAL	LNAME	ADDRESS1	CITY	STATE	ZIP	AMT	PAYDATE
101	Craig	A	Abbott	1512 Margaret Lane	DeKalb	IL	60115	500.00	01/15/88
102	Ellen	P	Anderson	213 River Drive	DeKalb	IL	60115	200.00	02/15/88
103	Barbara	K	Bickle	1732 Raintree Court	Sycamore	IL	60178	250.00	02/15/88
104	Robert	M	Harkness	350 South Malta Road	Malta	IL	60150	975.00	12/15/87
105	Elizabeth	M	George	315 North Maple	Waterman	IL	60556	450.00	12/15/87

Step 4: Extract data from the database.

Now that you have a small database, you can recall data in a variety of ways. For instance, a listing of all the entered data can be placed on the screen or printed. First create a list on the printer. Press **Return.**

a. When you have typed in all the above records, a quick way to examine what you have entered is to use the Retrieve/List command.

Move the highlight to **Retrieve** and select **List** from the submenu.

From the submenu which then appears to the right, select **Execute the command.** At the prompt

```
Direct the output to the printer? [Y/N]
```

reply

N

for No. The listing will be displayed on the screen. Press **Return** to clear the screen.

If your computer is properly connected to a printer, repeat the above sequence of commands but answer

Y

to the prompt

```
Direct the output to the printer? [Y/N]
```

Since the records are too long to fit across one line of either the screen or the printer, dBASE III Plus automatically wraps each record to the second line as needed. Later when you use the Report option, you will format the fields so they can be read more easily.

b. The data **query** function allows the user to locate a specific record using a specific set of defined conditions. dBASE III Plus offers easy-to-use data query. Let's examine the Query option under the Create command. Suppose we need to find all the clients on our database who owe more than $350.00.

Highlight **Create** and **Query** and press **Return.** A side menu appears, listing the disk drive options. Highlight **B:** and press **Return.** A prompt asks for the name of the query file, where the search specifications will be stored for later use.

```
Enter the name of the file:
```

To avoid confusion about which query file belongs to which database, give them the same name. A filename extension of .QRY will distinguish the query file from the database file, which has the extension .DBF.

Type

```
clients
```

Press **Return.**

dBASE will accept upper- or lower-case names as equivalent.

The screen changes to show **Set Filter** highlighted at the very top of the screen. The Query menu bar, which contains the options for building a search condition, appears. Below the menu bar is a table, the **query form,** which will display the conditions as you enter them. Each line in the query form represents a search condition. A box appears, containing a highlighted bar and an arrow (▶) that prompts for the field name to be used for the search.

Press **Return.**

A side menu lists the fields in the CLIENTS file. Figure 9-18 is an example of how your screen may look. Notice the listing on the upper right of the screen.

Select the field named AMT. Move the cursor down to highlight **AMT.** Press **Return.** Notice that, in the query form, the field name is placed on line 1. The prompt changes to Operator.

Press **Return.** The submenu presents the choices of logical operators to be used in the search.

FIGURE 9-18 **A side menu lists the fields in the CLIENTS file. This is an example of how your screen may look. Notice the listing of the fields on the record on the right side of the screen.**

```
Set Filter          Nest              Display              Exit  02:25:36 pm
 Field Name                 ▶           ACCTNO
 Operator                               FNAME
 Constant/Expression                    INITIAL
 Connect                                LNAME
                                        ADDRESS1
 Line Number          1                 CITY
                                        STATE
                                        ZIP
                                        AMT
 Field Name         Type    Width  Decimal  PAYDATE         Connect

 CLIENTS->ACCTNO    Numeric   3       0

 3
 4
 5
 6
 7

CREATE QUERY  <B:> B:CLIENTS.QRY          Opt: 1/10
  Position selection bar - ↑↓.  Select - ↵.  Leave menu - ↔.
           Select a field name for the filter condition.
```

```
=   Equals
>   More than
>=  More than or equal
<   Less than
<=  Less than or equal
<>  Not equal to
```

Move the cursor to highlight > **More than.** Press **Return.** In the query form, notice that **More than** is placed in the Operator Column on line 1. dBASE prompts for the next part of the query definition, Constant/Expression.

Press **Return.** The value 350 should be displayed. If not, type

```
350.00
```

Press **Return.**

Connect is highlighted. Since we are not going to connect logical expressions in this example, press **Return.** A new list of submenu options appears:

```
No combination
Combine with .AND.
Combine with .OR.
Combine with .AND..NOT
Combine with .OR..NOT.
```

Press **Return** to select No combination. Line Number is highlighted.

Type

```
1
```

to select the Query in Line 1. Press **Return.**

Move the top highlight to **Display** and press **Return.** The screen should now show the first eight fields of the first record in the file to meet the Query condition of having an AMT > $350.00. Figure 9-19 is an example of how your screen may look.

To see the other two fields on this record, press **PgDn.**

Continue pressing **PgDn** to see all the records that meet the Query condition.

```
Set Filter              Nest              Display              Exit 03:13:07 pm

ACCTNO        101
FNAME         Craig
INITIAL       A
LNAME         Abbott
ADDRESS1      1512 Margaret Lane
CITY          DeKalb
STATE         IL
ZIP           60115
```

Line	Field	Operator	Constant/Expression	Connect
1	AMT	More than	350	
2				
3				
4				
5				
6				
7				

```
CREATE QUERY  ||<B:>||B:CLIENTS.QRY  ||Rec: 1/5  ||  ||
Next/Previous record - PgDn/PgUp.  Toggle query form - F1.  Leave option - ↔.
        Display records in the database that meet the query condition.
```

FIGURE 9-19 The screen should now show the first eight fields of the first record in the file to meet the Query condition of AMT > 350.00.

When the last such record is displayed, the display will not advance any further.

To quit the Query, move the top highlight to **Exit.** Press **Return** to Exit the Query and **Save** the Query criterion.

Step 5: Quit dBASE.

To end this session, move the highlight to **Set Up** and move the cursor down to **Quit dBASE III Plus.** Press **Return.** The ending message appears:

```
*** END RUN    dBASE III PLUS
A>
```

This action has also saved your database, storing it on the disk so you can retrieve it at your next session.

Turn off the computer to conclude this session. You have just created your first database, produced a listing on the screen and on a printer, created a Query criterion, and displayed the records that meet the logical condition of the Query. Finally, you have saved the Query and the database and have properly ended a dBASE III Plus session. In the tutorial in Lesson 10 you will retrieve this database, add more records to it, edit it, and produce various reports.

SUMMARY

A database is an orderly collection of one or more related files containing data related to a specific type of application. Each file is composed of records and fields. A record is a collection of data about one entity (person, place, or thing), and a field is a set of spaces holding one item of data. A key field holds data, such as a person's social security number or a part number, that uniquely labels or identifies an entity.

A database management system is a software tool that aids in the design, creation, updating, searching, and rearranging of a database and the reporting from a database. In designing a new database, principles that users should follow include minimizing redundant data and maintaining the integrity of the data.

Potential database applications typically involve large quantities of data, repetitive use of that data, frequent revision of the data, and a need to produce specialized or ad hoc reports using the stored data. A single-file, flat-file database is the simplest type of database, and it resembles a spreadsheet made up of rows and columns. A relational database can cross-reference multiple flat files, and a programmable database system also allows the user to write programs to further process the data.

The eight major command functions found in most database systems are creating, data entry, editing, retrieving and reporting, modifying, organizing, pointing, and file handling. Creation of a new database includes naming the database and naming and describing each of the fields within each of the record structures. Fields can be described as numeric, character, date, logical, or memo fields. Fields also need to be described in terms of the number of spaces in the field and, if numeric, the number of spaces to the right of the decimal point.

An important distinction between saving database records and saving word processing documents or spreadsheets is that database software typically does not have a Save command. However, it is important to quit each database session properly, so that the data are properly saved and the files are closed.

EXERCISES

1. Define the following terms:

database	character field	sorting
key	numeric field	copy
computerized database	date field	modifying
DBMS	logical field	pointing
file	Boolean field	positioning
record	memo field	pointer
field	data field width	file handling
networking	data entry	sequencing
single-file database	editing	physical sorting
flat file	retrieve and report function	logical indexing
command driven	relational operators	reporting
menu driven	logical operators	report format file
multiple-file database	mathematical operators	pull-down menus
relational database	organizing	action line
programmable database system	indexing	status bar
creation		navigation line
alphanumeric field		message line

2. Matching

_____	collection of one or more related files	a.	book index
_____	example of a database	b.	database
_____	field that uniquely identifies	c.	redundancy
_____	dBASE III Plus	d.	DBMS
_____	orderly collection of data fields about one subject	e.	key
_____	set of spaces containing data about one entity	f.	record
_____	maintaining same data on multiple files	g.	field

_____	specialized report produced on request	h. networking
_____	multiple users can access database	i. ad hoc

3. Matching

_____	data that can be organized into files	a. relational database
_____	file organized in rows and columns	b. Codd
_____	can cross-reference multiple flat files	c. programmable DBMS
_____	inventor of relational database concept	d. alphanumeric
_____	allows user to write programs to further process the data	e. creation
_____	describing and naming the contents of the database	f. structured data
_____	includes both alphabetic and numeric characters	g. flat file
_____	1 or 0	h. Boolean variables
_____	T or F	i. logical field

4. Matching

_____	holds miscellaneous information that cannot be manipulated later	a. <>
_____	changing, replacing, or deleting contents of records	b. <=
_____	not equal to	c. .NOT.
_____	less than or equal to	d. indexing
_____	logical *not*	e. file handling
_____	creates another file holding the key field and the prescribed order	f. pointer
_____	contains address or location of the next record in sequence	g. memo field
_____	housekeeping	h. editing

5. Identify which of the following are examples of databases and which are not and explain why:
   a. an index at the end of a book
   b. a card catalog in a library
   c. the daily stock market report in the *Wall Street Journal*
   d. the business section of a newspaper
   e. an accounting textbook

6. Consider a filing system a business might use for payroll purposes. With this system in mind, describe each of the following:
   a. key field
   b. type of field for hourly rate
   c. type of field for employee name
   d. type of field for eligible for overtime or not
   e. type of field for street address and number
   f. width of the field for hourly rate if the maximum rate is $45.00
7. Practice using dBASE III Plus by completing the tutorial "Creating a Database with dBASE III Plus" within this lesson. Then revise the tutorial to include the following changes:
   a. Make a copy of the database file, giving the database a unique name, such as CLIENTSA. (Do not use CLIENTSA; it is just an example.)
   b. With the Append Command, add five additional records to the copied database. Make sure the attributes are unique and satisfy field definitions.
   c. Continue with the tutorial, producing a printed listing.
8. Use dBASE III Plus to create a database with a single file containing the following:

STUDENT NAME	YEAR IN COLLEGE	GPA
Brown, Donald	4	3.33
Ellis, Bonnie	3	3.50
Farney, Charles	2	2.75
Garrels, Gerald	1	2.00
Howland, Richard	4	3.90
Kohler, Margaret	4	3.80
Metz, Steve	3	2.90
Metz, Teresa	2	4.00
Nussbaum, Donald	3	3.00
Nussbaum, Mary	3	3.10
Traub, Edward	1	2.75

Assume that all the students listed above belong to the same club (the Clubbers) and that you have been assigned the task of awarding prizes to those with the highest grade point averages in each class. You have also been asked to list all the students in order by GPA and alphabetically by year in college.

To describe each field, use the following:

NAME OF FIELD	TYPE OF FIELD	WIDTH	DEC
Name	Character	25	
Year	Numeric	1	0
GPA	Numeric	4	2

When you have finished creating the database, enter exactly the names, years, and GPAs listed above. Then create the following printed reports using the Query function.

a. All seniors
b. All juniors
c. All sophomores
d. All freshmen
e. All members with GPA greater than 3.0
f. All members with GPA less than 2.5

9. Use dBASE III Plus to create a database called FIT containing a single flat file called SUBJECTS. The purpose of the database is to hold records of the subjects of an experiment regarding people's sex, age, height, weight, and resting pulse rate. Each record contains the following fields:

FIELD NAME	TYPE	WIDTH	DEC
NAME	CHARACTER	25	0
SEX	CHARACTER	1	0
AGE	NUMERIC	3	0
HEIGHT	NUMERIC	2	0
WEIGHT	NUMERIC	3	0
PULSE	NUMERIC	3	0

Use the following data:

NAME	SEX	AGE	HEIGHT	WEIGHT	PULSE
JACKSON, JERRY	M	25	60	200	100
JENSEN, JAMES	M	42	61	250	150
JENSEN, BONNIE	F	35	57	125	120
FITZPATRICK, EDWARD	M	67	64	200	160
WEAVER, CONNIE	F	36	57	150	150
HILL, MARVIN	M	35	57	180	167
KIETERLEN, EDWARD	M	45	55	150	140
KIETERLEN, ANN	F	42	52	100	100
ANDERSEN, ELLEN	F	35	55	130	129
SMITH, LYLE	M	51	56	180	110
SMITH, DIANNE	F	40	55	140	140
DUNLOP, TIM	M	37	56	190	160

Create the following reports:

a. All subjects listed in alphabetical order.
b. All subjects listed in order by age, youngest first.
c. All subjects over 40 years old, listed in order, youngest first.

10. A family with several children wants to maintain a database of baby sitters. They have decided the fields should be these:

FIELD NAME	TYPE	WIDTH	DEC
NAME	Character	25	
PHONE	Character	8	
ADDRESS	Character	30	
RATE	Character	4	2
AVAIL	Character	10	

Create a database called SITTERS using the following data:

NAME	PHONE	ADDRESS	RATE	AVAIL
Missy Kieterlen	777-5021	202 Linden	2.00	Evenings
Gail Willey	777-5670	201 W Highland	3.50	Evenings
Nancy Parks	777-0011	47 N First	4.00	Days
Robert Williams	777-0987	123-1/2 Hillcrest	4.00	Weekends
Tina Maris	777-0112	456 W Taylor	4.00	Weekends
Mary Robertson	777-3330	201 N Rivercrest	4.75	Days
Jerry Hanson	777-2323	567 Nashua	5.00	Weekends
Katie Gallagher	777-1234	89 S Elm	5.00	All
Luann Cullison	777-6275	23 W Forrest Rd.	5.00	Evenings
Shirley Swenson	777-7770	890 W Maple	5.00	Weekends

List the records on the printer using the Retrieve-List-Execute the command sequence. When prompted to direct the output to the printer, answer Y for Yes.

11. A small sporting goods mail order business wants to create a database of its customers using the following fields:

FIELD NAME	TYPE	WIDTH	DEC
ACCTNO	Numeric	3	0
LASTNAME	Character	10	
FSTNAME	Character	10	
STATE	Character	2	
SINCE	Date	8	
BALANCE	Numeric	10	2

Create a database called CUSTOMER using the following data:

ACCTNO	LASTNAME	FSTNAME	STATE	SINCE	BALANCE
201	Swetten	George	MA	01/10/88	400.00
303	Jones	William	NJ	03/15/86	200.00
304	Roberts	Larry	CT	03/23/88	300.00
403	Smith	Loren	MA	12/15/87	100.00
500	Clark	Jerry	IL	03/23/86	200.00
505	Young	William	IL	12/20/86	500.00
508	Johnson	Steven	TX	05/20/86	475.00
551	Mitchel	Sharon	TX	05/20/85	245.00
381	York	Jill	IL	02/15/87	500.00
701	Gallagher	Patrick	IL	02/02/87	300.00
299	Clarkson	Jim	CT	02/02/87	475.00

Add one more record, ACCTNO=001, and use your LASTNAME, FSTNAME, and STATE. For SINCE enter today's date and for BALANCE enter 100.00.

Using The Assistant, move to highlight Position and Go to Record and then press Return. When TOP is highlighted, press Return. Then, using the left arrow key, move to highlight Update. Move down to highlight Browse and press Return. Now view and edit the fields using the commands shown in the Help menu at the top of the screen. Press Esc when you have finished. Using the right arrow key, highlight Retrieve and List. Press Return twice and answer Y to the prompt for printer output.

12. Create a database called BOOKS to file references for books about dBASE III Plus using the following design:

FIELD NAME	TYPE	WIDTH	DEC
AUTHOR	Character	30	
TITLE	Character	50	
PUBLISHER	Character	40	
CITY	Character	20	
YEAR	Numeric	4	0

Use the following data plus other books you find that are helpful:

AUTHOR	TITLE	PUBLISHER	CITY	YEAR
Chou, George	dBASE III Plus Handbook, Second Edition	Que	Indianapolis	1986
Liskin, Miriam	Advanced dBASE III Programming and Techniques	Osborn/ McGraw-Hill	Berkeley	1986
Bharacha, Kerman	dBASE III Plus A Comprehensive User's Manual	Tab Books Inc.	Blue Ridge Summit	1986
Baker, Richard	Advanced dBASE III Applications	Tab Books Inc.	Blue Ridge Summit	1985
Dinerstein, Nelson	dBASE III for the Programmer	Scott, Foresman	Glenview	1985
Prague, Cary	Programming with dBASE III Plus	Tab Books Inc.	Blue Ridge Summit	1986
Krumm, Rob	dBASE III Plus Power Tools	MIS: Press	Portland	1986
Simpson, Alan	Understanding dBASE III	SYBEX	Berkeley	1985
Simpson, Alan	Simpson's dBASE III Library	SYBEX	Berkeley	1986
Hallam, Teresa	Microcomputer Use	Harcourt Brace Jovanovich	San Diego	1989
Weber Systems Inc. Staff	dBASE III User's Handbook	Balantine Books	New York	1985

Display the listing of books using the Retrieve-Display-Specify scope-ALL-Execute the command sequence on The Assistant. Then create a printed listing using the Retrieve-List-Execute command-Y sequence.

13. Use dBASE III Plus to create a database similar to the one you created using Lotus 1-2-3 in the tutorial in Lesson 8. Name the database WORKERS and use the following design:

FIELD NAME	TYPE	WIDTH	DEC
NAME	Character	25	
DEPT	Character	10	
STATUS	Character	8	
OFFICE	Numeric	3	0
SALARY	Numeric	10	2

Use the following data:

NAME	DEPT	STATUS	OFFICE	SALARY
Jensen, Bonnie	Adm	Parttime	208	30000.00
Monsell, Gloria	Adm	Fulltime	306	40000.00
Kiederlen, Ed	Sales	Fulltime	201	50000.00
Brown, Pat	R&D	Parttime	205	35000.00
Maris, Tina	Sales	Parttime	206	20000.00
Jensen, James	Sales	Fulltime	207	60000.00
Anderson, Ellen	R&D	Fulltime	301	40000.00
Kiederlen, Ann	Adm	Fulltime	303	50000.00
Monsell, Randy	R&D	Fulltime	305	45000.00

Use the List command in The Assistant to list the WORKERS. Use the Browse command to examine the records and correct any typing errors. Then use the Retrieve-Display-Build a search condition-Dept-=Equal To-Adm-No more conditions-Execute the command sequence to display the workers in the Adm department. Use a similar sequence of commands to display the workers who have salaries greater than or equal to 30000. Try out several other conditions, and then use the Append command to add a record containing your own name. List the entire file on a printer.

10
Database Applications

LESSON OUTLINE

Lesson 9 introduced several important concepts essential to your understanding and use of database management software. In Lesson 10 we will expand on some of these concepts and apply these concepts in the tutorial.

DATABASE MANAGEMENT SOFTWARE FUNCTIONS

In Lesson 10 you will use some of the more sophisticated features of database management software to edit, organize, modify, and retrieve information from an existing database. Let's briefly review and expand on each of these functions of dBASE III Plus database management software.

Editing

Editing is the changing, replacement, or deletion of the contents of a data record. It usually involves the computer searching a database file to find the record or records the user desires, displaying the records on the screen in some predetermined order, and then allowing the user to make changes using commands similar to the editing features in a word processing software system. dBASE III Plus offers sophisticated editing capabilities, primarily through the two commands Edit and Browse. Both commands are available through the Update menu of Assist. The Edit command causes records to appear on the screen one at a time, while Browse allows several records to appear on the screen at once. Figure 10-1(*a*) is an example of the Edit command using the CLIENTS database, while (*b*) is an example of Browse. Notice that the Browse feature of showing several records at once makes the screen look much like a spreadsheet. Each line contains one record. The editing commands used with Browse are similar to those used with Edit. You can remove the editing commands from the screen by pressing [F1]. Because the width of the record may be longer than the width of the screen, Browse offers the Pan command. Like scrolling with electronic spreadsheets, the Pan command allows you to see fields that extend beyond the screen.

Since several records appear on the screen at one time, some navigational commands are needed to let the user move through the file to edit particular fields. Notice the top line in Figure 10-1(*b*), listing the Browse options. With Browse you can move the highlight to the *Bottom* of the file, the *Top* of the file, or a specified record number. The *Lock* option holds the display of certain fields fixed at the left side of the screen, even if

FIGURE 10-1 *(a)* **An example of the Edit command using the CLIENTS database. Each record appears individually on the screen, with all fields visible on one screen.** *(b)* **An example of the same record, using the Browse command. Notice that each record is one line on the screen but that not all of the records can be seen at once. The Pan command lets the user scroll to the fields that extend beyond the screen.**

```
CURSOR    <--  -->  |            UP     DOWN  |     DELETE       | Insert Mode:    Ins
 Char:       ←  →   | Field:     ↑      ↓     | Char:     Del    | Exit/Save:      ^End
 Word:   Home  End  | Page:    PgUp   PgDn    | Field     ^Y     | Abort:          Esc
                    | Help:     F1            | Record:   ^U     | Memo:           ^Home

ACCTNO          101
FNAME           Craig
INITIAL         A
LNAME           Abbott
ADDRESS1        1512 Margaret Lane
CITY            DeKalb
STATE           IL
ZIP             60115
AMT                500.00
PAYDATE         01/15/88
```

(a)

```
EDIT           |<B:>|CLIENTS                  |Rec: 1/20      |     |

Bottom        Top        Lock        Record No.        Freeze  11:27:51 am
CURSOR    <--  -->  |            UP     DOWN  |     DELETE       | Insert Mode:    Ins
 Char:       ←  →   | Record:    ↑      ↓     | Char:     Del    | Exit        :   ^End
 Word:   Home  End  | Page:    PgUp   PgDn    | Field     ^Y     | Abort:          Esc
 Pan:       ^← ^→   | Help:     F1            | Record:   ^U     | Set Options     ^Home
ACCTNO FNAME----- INITIAL LNAME----------  ADDRESS1-----------------
   101 Craig      A       Abbott           1512 Margaret Lane
   102 Ellen      P       Anderson         213 River Drive
   103 Barbara    K       Bickle           1732 Raintree Court
   104 Robert     M       Harkness         350 South Malta Road
   105 Elizabeth  M       George           315 North Maple
   106 Dalia      H       Bach             9 Moraine Terrace
   107 Curt       P       Behrens          317 Joanne Lane
   108 Helen      L       Bishop           102 Ridge Drive
   109 Carol      H       Brown            1315 Gifford
   110 Clifford   T       Cleland          404 South Fourth Street
   111 Anne       H       Cole             1107 Normal Road #2

BROWSE         |<B:>|CLIENTS                  |Rec: 1/20      |     |
             Position selection bar with ↔.  Select with ↵.
                       Go to end of the file.
```

(b)

you "pan" or move to the fields on the right. The *Freeze* option lets you specify a single field for editing. The cursor will not move to the beginning of the next record but rather remains in the same field when it moves to the next record.

Organizing

Organizing is the physical or logical rearrangement or duplication of a database file. The major types of dBASE commands to help organize a database are Sort and Index.

Sorting is the physical rearranging of the records in a database in a specified sequence, such as alphabetic or numeric order. After sorting the database, the computer creates a new database, identical in structure and size to the original file, but with the records physically rearranged in the specified sequence. When sorting, the user is required to designate one or more key fields on which to reorder the database. For example, if you were to sort the CLIENTS database by last name, you would designate the field LNAME as the key field.

Indexing is the creation of another file holding only the key field and the sequencing order. The records contained in the file are not physically rearranged or changed. Once an index is created and activated, it affects all subsequent commands—the records on the master database (for

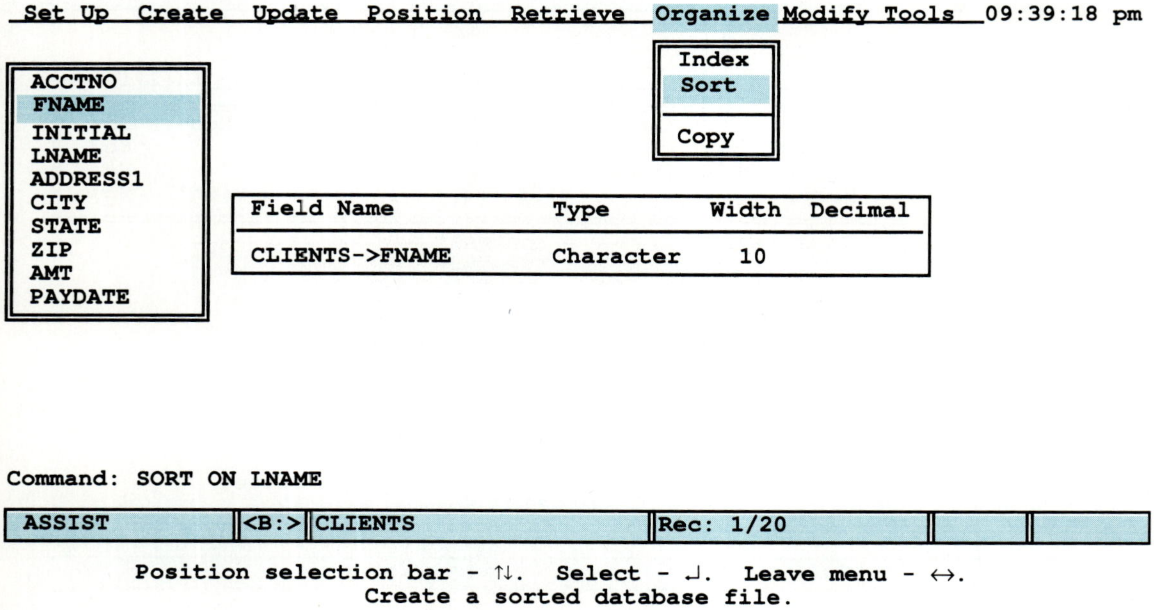

FIGURE 10-2 dBASE III Plus permits users to sort files quickly and easily using the Assist menu and selecting the proper options. Sorting a file creates a new, sorted file.

example, CLIENTS) are processed in the logical order of the index; the file can be printed or otherwise processed in the indexing order. An index is associated with a particular master file.

dBASE III Plus allows sorting through the Organize menu of Assist and through direct commands. When you are using Assist, a sort is always in ascending order and based on one or more key fields. For example, in Figure 10-2, if you want to sort a file such as CLIENTS in order of last name and then first name, you would designate LNAME as the first key field and FNAME as the second. Sorting creates a new file, so if you want to use the sorted field, you must open it using the Set Up menu. Note that the Sort command will sort deleted records that have not yet been packed. **Packing** is the removal of records marked for deletion from the database.

Indexing is also offered through the Organize menu of Assist and through direct commands. With Assist, when indexing a file, the user is prompted for the filename to be indexed, the field to be used for indexing, and the index name. Figure 10-3 is an example of dBASE prompting for the key field. When indexing with Assist, the user can designate only one key field. Both indexing and sorting provide, on command ([F10]), on the left side of the screen, a list of field names to remind the user of the available fields.

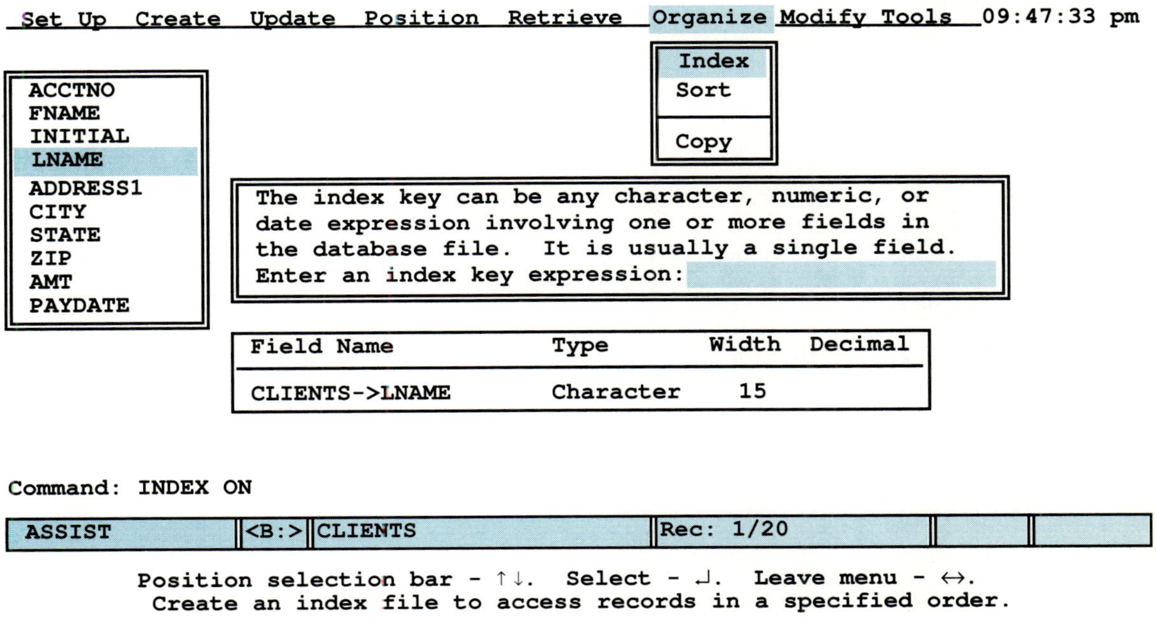

FIGURE 10-3 **An example of dBASE III Plus prompting for the key field to be used when indexing the file. Indexing a file creates an index file that contains the key field (LNAME) and the sequencing order.**

Indexing is a vital part of using databases effectively. It has several significant advantages over sorting databases.

1. Active indexes are automatically updated if the key field values in the associated master file are changed or altered. For example, if you add new records to a database that has an active index, the new records are automatically placed in their proper logical sequence in the indexed file. While the new record is physically placed at the bottom of the file, it is logically placed in the indexed sequence. A sorted file would not reorder the new records until the file is sorted again.
2. Once a master file has an active index, you can locate an individual record almost instantly using the Seek command on the Position menu. The **Seek command,** which will work only with an indexed file, does a very rapid record search, locating in an indexed database file the first record with a key field that matches the search expression. The record is then displayed using the Display option of the Retrieve menu.
3. Indexing is generally twice as fast as sorting.
4. Indexing has the ability to relate one file to another. We will discuss such linked databases in Lesson 11.

Since indexing and sorting accomplish the same task, when should you index and when should you sort? You should index when you need fast, automatic rearranging. For example, if an office has a file in which clients' records are updated and referred to several times a day, then indexing makes sense. You should sort when the data require only occasional rearranging and when the logical or mathematical processing can be done more rapidly if the file has been sorted before the processing begins, such as in producing a monthly payroll report.

Modifying

Modifying is the revision of the structure of the database currently in use. Users modify the various names and characteristics in database files, records, and fields. Report formats and field relationships may also be modified.

The Modify submenu in dBASE III Plus lets users conveniently change several database functions, including the structure of the database file, query statements, report formats, and label formats. Figure 10-4 is an example of how a database structure is revised in dBASE III Plus. Any changes are entered on the screen and saved. The contents of the original file are then automatically copied to the revised file for those fields with identical field names. If the modification includes adding a new field, of course, the new field is empty. If a field is deleted, the contents of the

FIGURE 10-4 Modifying a database structure with dBASE III Plus. Notice that the user can edit the field definitions.

```
                                                          Bytes remaining:   3908
+---------------------+---------------+---------------+---------------------------+
| CURSOR  <--   -->   |    INSERT     |    DELETE     | Up a field:      ↑        |
|  Char:    ←    →    | Char:   Ins   | Char:    Del  | Down a field:    ↓        |
|  Word:  Home  End   | Field:  ^N    | Word:    ^Y   | Exit/Save:       ^End     |
|  Pan:     ^←   ^→   | Help:   F1    | Field:   ^U   | Abort:           Esc      |
+---------------------+---------------+---------------+---------------------------+
     Field Name  Type       Width  Dec              Field Name  Type      Width  Dec
     =====================================          =====================================
  1  ACCTNO      Numeric        3    0          9   AMT         Numeric       8
  2  FNAME       Character     10              10   PAYDATE     Date          8
  3  INITIAL     Character      1
  4  LNAME       Character     15
  5  ADDRESS1    Character     25
  6  CITY        Character     15
  7  STATE       Character      2
  8  ZIP         Character      5

MODIFY STRUCTURE ||<B:>||CLIENTS            ||Field: 1/10        ||      ||
                              Enter the field name.
Field names begin with a letter and may contain letters, digits and underscores
```

copied field are lost. Fields that are shortened may lose some characters in the transfer. For example, if you decide that you need to increase the width of the Zip code field from 5 spaces to 10 to accommodate the newer 10-digit Zip codes, just move the highlight to the ZIP field, move the cursor across the line to the width specification, type 10, and press Return. You save the changes by pressing ^ End.

Retrieving

Retrieve commands cause the database software to search the records in one or more files within the database, extracting those particular records requested by the user and reporting them to the user either by displaying them on the screen or by printing them. The desired records must be described by certain conditions such as file and record names, field names, and relational and logical operators.

dBASE III Plus offers a variety of Retrieve commands, including List, Display, Report, and Label. **List** displays specified records and fields from the currently selected database. The user can request a printed copy of the list. The listing is like a rough draft, headings are the field names, and spacing is determined by the field width. You can pause the listing by pressing ^ S. You used the List command in the Lesson 9 tutorial.

The **Display** command shows on the screen one or more records from the currently selected database. Usually it shows only the record where the pointer is currently located, but users can specify optional

FIGURE 10-5 The Display command permits users to locate and show individual records on the screen.

```
 Set Up  Create  Update  Position  Retrieve  Organize Modify Tools  10:17:17 am
                                  List
                                  Display     Execute the command
                                  Report      Specify scope
                                  Label       Construct a field list
                                  ------      Build a search condition
                                  Sum         Build a scope condition
                                  Average
                                  Count                  Default scope
                                                         ALL
                                                         NEXT
                                                         RECORD
                                                         REST

Command: DISPLAY
 ASSIST           |<B:>|CLIENTS               |Rec: 1/20       |     |

                    Position selection bar - ↑↓.  Select - ↵.
                               Process all records.
```

scopes or conditions to include more records. Figure 10-5 is an example of the Display command.

With the **Report** option of the Retrieve menu, users can recall a previously created report form and produce a report that combines the report form with the currently selected database. Reports are created with the Create Report option. For example, to report from the CLIENTS database, you would have to first create a report form and then, with the Retrieve command, use the previously created report form to report from the database. The tutorial at the end of this lesson gives you the opportunity to create and use a report form.

Label is a quick and easy way to produce mailing labels from a database. Like Report, the label form must have been previously created before it can be used to Retrieve data. Figure 10-6 is an example of the Label Create function.

dBASE III PLUS COMMANDS

Although the Assistant menus are very helpful, in some cases they are long and tedious. For example, if you had to enter client records every day, using the same commands in the same sequence, soon you would be looking for a way to automate the command sequence. Maybe you are tired of hearing dBASE beep every time you reach the end of a field, or maybe

FIGURE 10-6 **Mailing labels can be created quickly and easily with the Create Label command. Users are given several choices for label sizes and options.**

```
Options                        Contents                          Exit  08:24:09 pm

 Predefined size:          3 1/2 x 15/16 by 1

 Label width:               35
 Label height:               5
 Left margin:                0
 Lines between labels:       1
 Spaces between labels:      0
 Labels across page:         1


CURSOR   <-- -->   Delete char:  Del   Insert row:      ^N   Insert:     Ins
  Char:   ←  →     Delete word:  ^T    Toggle menu:     F1   Zoom in:   ^PgDn
  Word: Home End   Delete row:   ^U    Abandon:        Esc   Zoom out:  ^PgUp

CREATE LABEL    <B:> B:CLLABEL.LBL          Opt: 1/7                     Caps
        Position selection bar - ↑↓.   Select - ↵.   Leave menu - ↔´.
       Select a standard label size: (Width x Height by Number across).
```

you would like to prevent the cursor from moving to the next field automatically. You can do either of these with dBASE commands. In fact, dBASE III Plus is one of the most popular programming languages used for business applications. It is beyond the purpose of this book to teach you programming with dBASE. However, we would like to give you a taste of this powerful, versatile feature of dBASE III Plus. Remember, until dBASE III was introduced in the early 1980s, dBASE required the use of commands. All of the commands you have used with The Assistant are available at the dot prompt.

To give commands, first exit The Assistant by pressing the Esc key. The dot prompt will appear as a "." on the screen just above the status line. You type in all commands at the dot prompt and enter them by pressing Return.

After the dot prompt appears, enter a command name and any of the parameters that come after it. For example, the statement **LIST lname FOR age > 30** contains the command **LIST** and the parameters **lname FOR age > 30** to limit the listed fields to the last name **(lname)** and limit the records on the database and the value contained in the age field to greater than 30. These parameter values determine the action of the command.

Commands and parameters may be entered in upper or lower case. However, most dBASE programmers put the dBASE commands in upper case (as in **LIST** and **FOR**) and put the parameters in lower case. Commands vary in the amount and complexity of syntax. If you make an error while entering a command, a prompt will appear asking if you want any help. If you press Y, a Help menu appears; pressing N returns you to the dot prompt.

Set commands control or set up the operational environment of dBASE. For example, if you want to turn off that annoying beep, just enter the command SET BELL OFF at the dot prompt. If you want to suppress the automatic movement of the cursor to the next field, enter the command SET CONFIRM ON. If you want to change the disk drive to B, just enter SET DEFAULT TO B:.

The list of Set commands is extensive. Fortunately, dBASE also offers a menu to change the Set commands. At the dot prompt type SET and press Return. A menu of Set options will appear on the screen (see Figure 10-7). Set commands must be reentered each time you load dBASE. However, Set commands may be placed in a program file that is executed when dBASE is loaded or upon command. Program files are constructed in dBASE with the

```
 Options    Screen   Keys   Disk   Files   Margin   Decimals  09:57:48 pm
 Alternate   OFF
 Bell        ON
 Carry       OFF
 Catalog
 Century     OFF
 Confirm     OFF
 Deleted     OFF
 Delimiters  OFF
 Device      SCREEN
 Dohistory   OFF
 Escape      ON
 Exact       OFF
 Fields      OFF
 Fixed       OFF
 Heading     ON
 Help        ON
 History     ON
 Intensity   ON

SET          ||<A:>||                 ||Opt: 1/25          ||        ||
  Position selection bar - ↑ ↓.  Change - ↵.  Leave menu - ↔.  Exit - Esc.
                 Specify the dBASE III environment options.
```

FIGURE 10-7 The Set menu permits users to customize their operating environment.

Modify Command command. You enter command statements in the file, save them, and later execute them by invoking the filename. For example, if we want to construct a small program called SETME to turn off the bell, set the disk drive to B, and set the Confirm on, we would enter the following:

```
.MODIFY COMMAND SETME
```

A new screen would appear showing various editing commands (see Figure 10-8). This text editor allows users to enter, edit, and save program statements. We would enter

```
set bell off
set default to B
set confirm on
```

and press ^W to save the file. To execute the program file, we would enter, at the dot prompt,

```
do setme
```

A convenient way to execute the program is to type

```
A>dbase setme
```

The program is automatically executed after dBASE is loaded. Table 10-1 lists some of the most commonly used set commands and their functions.

Now that we've discussed some of the more advanced features and applications of database management software, let's apply them in the following tutorial.

```
Edit: SETME.prg                                          Caps
┌──────────────────────┬────────────────────┬───────────────┬──────────────────────┐
│ CURSOR:  <--  -->    │          UP  DOWN  │    DELETE     │ Insert Mode:     Ins │
│  Char:      ←  →     │ Line:     ↑    ↓   │ Char:     Del │ Insert line:     ^N  │
│  Word:   Home End    │ Page: PgUp  PgDn   │ Word:     ^Y  │ Save: ^W  Abort:Esc  │
│  Line:     ^←  ^→    │ Find:    ^KF       │ Line:     ^Y  │ Read file:       ^KR │
│  Reformat: ^KB       │ Refind: ^KF        │               │ Write file:      ^KW │
└──────────────────────┴────────────────────┴───────────────┴──────────────────────┘
```

FIGURE 10-8 The editing commands available with the Modify Command command permit users to edit dBASE programs without needing an additional text editor.

Table 10-1 dBASE III PLUS COMMONLY USED SET COMMANDS

*Command**	*Function*
SET	Loads SET menu
SET BELL ON/off	Bell RINGS/does not ring during data entry
SET CONFIRM on/OFF	Requires/DOES NOT REQUIRE that you press the Return to place an entry in a field
SET DATE	Determines the date format
SET DEFAULT TO	Designates the default disk drive for file search
SET DELETED on/OFF	Does not display/DISPLAYS the records marked for deletion
SET FUNCTION TO	Sets Function key values
SET HELP ON/off	PROMPTS/does not prompt for help when error occurs
SET INDEX TO	Opens named INDEX files
SET MARGIN TO	Sets the left margin of the printer
SET MENUS ON/off	DISPLAYS/does not display a menu during full-screen commands
SET MESSAGE TO	Displays on the bottom line of the screen a user-defined character string enclosed in quotes
SET RELATION	Links two open database files according to a key field or expression that is common to both files
SET SAFETY ON/off	PROMPTS/does not prompt when a file is about to be overwritten
SET SCOREBOARD ON/off	Program messages APPEAR/do not appear on the status line
SET STATUS ON/off	DISPLAYS/does not display the status line from the dot prompt
SET TALK ON/off	SENDS/does not send the results of commands to the screen

*The default settings are in capital letters.

TUTORIAL: RETRIEVING AND REVISING AN EXISTING DATABASE USING dBASE III PLUS

For this tutorial you need the following:

- MS-DOS system disk or MS-DOS on the dBASE disk
- dBASE III Plus disk
- The data disk used in Lesson 9 containing CLIENTS
- A printer connected to the microcomputer

While completing this tutorial you will learn how to

- Retrieve an existing database
- Use Append to add records to the database
- Index the file
- Edit records to correct errors in the data
- Create a report file and produce reports

Step 1: Load the operating system and dBASE III Plus.

a. Load the operating system using the procedures described in earlier lessons.

b. If necessary, insert the dBASE III Plus system disk into drive A and the data disk containing the CLIENTS database created in Lesson 9 into drive B.

c. At the system prompt, enter

```
dbase
```

Press Return. After dBASE has been loaded, press Return again to load The Assistant. If the dot prompt (.) appears, type

```
assist
```

Press **Return.**

Step 2: Load the CLIENTS database.

Before running any database operation, you must specify which file is to be used.

a. After The Assistant has been loaded, if necessary, select **Set Up** by moving the highlight on the menu line. At the next menu option, select the option of **Database file.** Press **Return.** Move the cursor down to **B:.**

Press **Return.**

b. A submenu appears, containing the names of the files that are on the logged disk drive (see Figure 10-9). Notice that in our figure there are several files. If your data disk contains more than one database file, then each filename will be listed. If CLIENTS is the only database you have saved on this disk, then it will be the only one on the list. Highlight **CLIENTS.** Press **Return.** The following prompt appears:

FIGURE 10-9 The screen as it appears after The Assistant has been loaded. Your screen may list only one file.

```
Set Up  Create  Update  Position  Retrieve  Organize Modify Tools  09:33:05 am

 Database file              MUCFIG.DBF
                            TRADEMK.DBF
 Format for Screen          CLIENTS.DBF
 Query                      FIGURES.DBF
                            NEW.DBF
 Catalog                    CLIENTSO.DBF
 View                       NEIGHBOR.DBF
                            EMPLOYEE.DBF
 Quit dBase III PLUS




Command: USE B:
ASSIST      |<B:>|                 |Opt: 3/8    |     |     |
          Position selection bar - ↑ ↓.  Select - ↵.
                    Select a database file.
```

```
Is the file indexed? [Y/N]
```

Since we have not yet indexed the file, press **N** for No. The CLIENTS database file is retrieved from the disk and loaded into primary storage for use by the database.

Step 3: Add data to the database.

a. To move the highlight to Update, press **U.** Notice that the highlight moves without your needing to press the arrow key. The top choice in the Update submenu Append is also highlighted. The Append command is used to add new records to a database. Select the **Append** command and press **Return.**

A new screen appears, similar to the screen on which you entered data when the database was first created (see Figure 9-17). The highlighted areas represent the width of the fields in the records.

b. Enter the following new records. Remember the procedures for entering data, discussed earlier.

ACCT NO	FNAME	INITIAL	LNAME	ADDRESS	CITY	STATE	ZIP	AMT	PAYDATE
106	Dalia	H	Bach	9 Moraine Terrace	DeKalb	IL	60115	100.00	01/05/88
107	Curt	P	Behrens	317 Joanne Lane	DeKalb	IL	60115	1000.00	12/15/87
108	Helen	L	Bishop	102 Ridge Drive	DeKalb	IL	60115	750.00	01/15/88
109	Carol	H	Brown	1315 Gifford	DeKalb	IL	60115	450.00	12/15/87
110	Clifford	T	Cleland	404 South Fourth Street	DeKalb	IL	60115	450.00	12/15/87
111	Anne	H	Cole	1107 Normal Road #2	DeKalb	IL	60115	150.00	01/15/88
112	Dee G.	S	Coover	803 Normal Road	DeKalb	IL	60115	850.00	01/15/88
113	William	P	Cummings	1621 Sleepy Hollow Ln.	DeKalb	IL	60115	1500.00	11/15/87
114	John	J	Engstrom	115 W. Exchange Street	Sycamore	IL	60178	500.00	11/15/87
115	Edward	P	Fitzgerald	217 Laurel Lane	DeKalb	IL	60115	850.00	11/15/87
116	Norma	P	Fitzgerald	217 Laurel Lane	DeKalb	IL	60115	500.00	01/15/88
117	Mary Lou	J	Flemal	433 Normal Road	DeKalb	IL	60115	500.00	12/15/87
118	Eva	H	Leonard	121 Park Avenue	DeKalb	IL	60115	500.00	01/15/88
119	Robert	H	McFadden	309 Fairmont Drive	DeKalb	IL	60115	2500.00	11/15/87
120	Jan	J	Bach	9 Moraine Terrace	DeKalb	IL	60115	500.00	01/15/88

Press **Return** to complete the inputting of records. Look at the status bar to see the location of the pointer and the total number of records.

Step 4: Index the file.

Since the file is larger than it was, we need to organize it so that records can be located quickly and easily.

a. Create an Index file. Select **Organize** by pressing **O.** Since the highlight is on Index, press **Return.**

A prompt appears:

```
The index key can be any character, numeric,
or date expression involving one or more
fields in the database file. It is usually a
single field.
Enter an index key expression:
```

Enter the name of the field on which the CLIENTS file will be rearranged. Since we want to keep track of the CLIENTS by last name, enter the name of the field containing the last name. If you cannot remember the exact field name, press **[F10].** A list of fields will appear.

Move the cursor to **LNAME** and press **Return.** After LNAME has been placed in the box, press **Return** again.

A prompt appears asking you to designate the disk drive in which the index is to be stored. Move the highlight to **B:** and press **Return.**

Notice that a command line (Command: INDEX ON LNAME TO B:) is being constructed on the action line.

A new prompt appears:

```
Enter a file name (consisting of up to 8
letters or digits) followed by a period and
a filename extension (consisting of up to 3
letters or digits.)
Enter the name of the file:
```

Enter the name of the file in which the index is to be stored. We have chosen a name that includes part of the database filename and the field that the index uses to rearrange the file. Type

```
CLLNAME
```

Press **Return.** dBASE III Plus will supply the extension .NDX.

Within a few seconds the index is constructed and the CLIENTS file is indexed according to the client's last name.

b. Select the **Retrieve** menu and select the **List** command. Press **Return**. At the submenu

```
Execute the command
Specify scope
Construct a field list
Build a search condition
Build a scope condition
```

move the highlight to **Construct a field list.** Press **Return.** A list of fields appears in a submenu.

With the highlight on **ACCTNO,** press **Return.** Then move the highlight to **LNAME** and press **Return.** Notice the action line above the status bar. Through Assist you are constructing a series of commands for dBASE to execute.

Exit the field selection by pressing either ← or →.

Move the highlight to **Execute the command** and press **Return.**

Answer **N** to the prompt.

A list of records will appear on the screen. Notice that the records are now in order by the last name rather than the account number.

What happens if you need to look at the file in account number order? Just construct a new index.

Press any key to leave the list.

c. Create a new index. Select **Organize** and press **Return** to select **Index.**

At the prompt for key expression, enter the name of the account number field:

```
ACCTNO
```

Press **Return** and store the index file on drive **B.**

Name the index file

```
CLACCTNO
```

Press **Return.**

d. After the file has been indexed, list it following the steps above. Notice that the file has been reordered in account number order.

e. Since we need to have our file in order by client's last name, let's change the index back to CLLNAME.

Move the highlight to **Set Up** and press **Return** to select **B:.** Press **Return.** Select **CLIENTS.DBF** and press **Return.** At the prompt

```
Is the file indexed? [Y/N]
```

type **Y.**

Notice that a new listing appears with the two indexes you created. Since the index to be used is selected from a list of filenames, you can see how important it is to give the index file a name that will remind you of the associated file and field used. Select the index file using the LNAME field **CLLNAME,** and press **Return.**

Use the ← or → key to leave the index listing.

The index has been reactivated. To deactivate an index, go back to Set Up and reopen the database file without naming an index.

Step 5: Edit the file.

Now that the file has been organized using Index, let's use the Edit and Browse commands to change some records on the database.

a. Use the Seek command to move the pointer to the **Robert H McFadden** record. Seek looks for a specified field value in an indexed database. It works on the contents of the key field of only the primary or master index, such as LNAME in the CLIENTS database. If the specified value is found, the pointer is moved to the corresponding record in the database. If the value is not found, the message "No find" appears on the screen.

Move the highlight to **Position.** With the menu option highlight on **Seek,** press **Return.** A prompt appears:

```
Enter an expression:
```

The expression is the field value to be located. It can be a literal string of characters, such as a specific name, or it can be a numeric value or a name of a value. Character strings must be enclosed in single quotes or in brackets. However, before an expression can be sought, it must be in the key field of the master index.

Since we are looking for a particular client, and client's last name is the key field in the index, type

```
'McFadden'
```

Press **Return.** Remember to put the quotes around the field contents. If you have entered the value correctly, the screen will look unchanged and no error messages will appear. In the meantime, however, the pointer has moved within the file. Look at the record number on the status bar. That number indicates where the pointer is currently located—at the record containing the value 'McFadden'.

b. Edit the record. Press the ← key to move to **Update.** Then move the menu option highlight to **Edit.** Press **Return.** McFadden's record will appear on the screen, ready for editing.

Notice, at the top of the screen, the menu that has the editing commands. Use the up and down arrow keys to move from field to field within a record. Use the left and right arrow keys to move one character to the left or right. Use the Del key to delete a character. If you need to delete a record, press ^U. Remember, deleted records must be *packed* before they are removed from the database. The Pack command is also available through the Update menu.

Save the changes to the record by pressing **^End.** If you decide you do not want to save any of the changes to the record, press Esc before going to the next record.

c. Enter the following changes by seeking the needed record and using the editing commands displayed across the top of the screen. Use only the entries in the indexed field (LNAME) to locate the record. Remember to save the changes and exit the record by pressing **^End.**

1. Change Robert H McFadden's address to 517 Fastexit Lane, Sycamore, IL 60178.
2. Change Carol Brown's amount from $450.00 to $400.00
3. Change Curt Behrens' amount from $1000.00 to $1750.00.
4. Change Dalia H Bach's amount from $100.00 to $50.00

Edit can also be used without the Seek option. Just select Update and Edit. Use the PgUp and PgDn keys to locate individual records. However, this approach would not be very practical if you are using a large database with many records.

d. After the Assist menu reappears, select **Update** and **Browse** from the menu option. Notice that Browse shows several records on the screen at one time. Remember, however, that if the width of the database is larger than the screen, you must use the Pan command to move to the other fields.

Press ^→ to scroll to the fields on the right.

Press **[F10]** to see the navigational commands at the top of the screen.

Try out the Freeze command. Move the command highlight to **Freeze** and press **Return.** A prompt appears on the screen, asking for the name of the field the computer is to freeze.

```
Enter field name to freeze:
```

Type

```
ADDRESS1
```

Notice that the highlight shrinks to the size of the specified field. If you try to move the highlight to another field, you cannot. It stays only in the ADDRESS1 column. This feature is handy when you want to make a series of changes in the same field in a database.

Remove the Freeze command. Press **[F10]** and select **Freeze.** At the prompt press **Return.** The full width of the highlight will be restored.

Use the Browse command to find and correct any typing errors. Remember to pan over to the fields you need to correct before pressing Return.

e. After you complete any corrections, use Browse to add new records. Move the highlight to the last field of the last record and press **Return** until the following prompt appears at the bottom of the screen:

```
====>Add new records? (Y/N)
```

Press **Y.**

Directly below the last record an empty highlight appears, ready to accept a new record. Enter the next account number (ACCTNO), your name, and your address. Do NOT press Return.

Then press the **Pan** command (^→) *three times* to move the screen over. The PAYDATE column should appear on the screen.

Press **Return** to move the CITY column.

Enter your city, state, Zip code, an amount due of **$100.00,** and today's date. Press **Return** to move to the next record. Press **Return** until you reach the end of the empty record and the added record is placed within the file. Watch what has happened to your entry. Because the file is indexed, the newly entered name is automatically moved to the proper place in the file. If you made an error and cannot find the record, use the Find option. To do so, press **[F10].** Move the highlight to **Find.** Press **Return.** A prompt will appear:

```
Enter search string:
```

Type a string or set of characters contained in the field that is contained in the index file. You do not need to put quotation marks around the characters when using Find. Since our index contains client's last name, type a set of characters found in the LNAME field of the record you are seeking. For example, to find the record for McFadden, type Mc.

Remember to use the Pan command to see the remaining fields of the record.

End the editing session. Press ^ **End.**

Step 6: Design a report and print it.

Now it is time to design a dBASE III Plus report using the database you have designed, input data to, saved, appended more data to, and edited.

a. Move the highlight to **Create,** move the cursor down to **Report,** and press **Return.** A submenu appears, listing the choices of disk drives.

Move the cursor down to **B:** and press **Return.** At the prompt

```
Enter the name of the file:
```

type

```
Report1
```

Press **Return.** The extension .FRM will automatically be added to the filename. The report creation screen appears.

Notice at the bottom of the screen the menu containing various editing commands. The combination of the Control key and character keys forms a command. To use such commands, remember to press and hold down the Control key, and then press the character key.

b. Set the page options. The submenu options offer a list of **page formatting options,** including options for a title at the top of the report, the width of the page, left and right margins, spacing, page ejection, and the **plain page** command, which will remove the heading that normally appears at the top of each page. To the right of each option is the current value setting.

The default values for width, margin, and line options are set up for a standard $8\frac{1}{2}$ by 11-inch page. To change any of these options, use the ↑ and ↓ arrow keys to move the corresponding highlight bar within the box until it is on the option to be selected. Press **Return.** Depending on the option you choose, an arrow (▶) will appear in the highlight bar. Enter the new value for the option and then press **Return** again to complete the change. The last option, Plain Page, has settings of Yes and No (the default). If you select No, the date, page number, and report heading (if inserted) appear at the top of each page of the report. Yes will suppress these items.

The first option is **Page title.** This is the title to appear on the top of the report. Up to four lines of text may be inserted as a title.

With the highlight on **Page title,** press **Return.**

After the window opens, enter the following title, pressing **Return** after the word "to" so the title is on two lines.

```
Report of Clients Owing Money to
Hallam, Hallam, & Hallam
```

Press ^**End** to end and save the page title. The Page Options menu reappears.

Change the **Page eject** before printing option from Yes to No. You will set up your printer with the first page ready for printing, and you will not want to waste a page of paper by having it automatically eject before the report begins. You know how careful school computer labs must be about excess expenditures on paper!

Using the **down arrow,** move the highlighted area to **Page eject before printing.**

Press **Return.** The setting will change to **No.**

c. Now that we've specified the page format, we will define the contents of the report by using the Columns command. Move to the **Columns** command. Press the **right arrow** *twice.*

The **Columns menu** is used to define the contents and structure of the report columns. **Contents** is an option used to specify the names of the fields that are to appear in the report.

Press **Return.** A small arrow (▶) appears in the submenu option for Contents. Enter the exact name of the field in which the first names are stored. What? You say you forgot their names! Fortunately, dBASE realizes that most users need some help. Press **[F10]** to get a menu listing the field names for the CLIENTS file.

Move the highlight down to **FNAME** and press **Return.** The listing of the field names disappears, and FNAME appears in the highlighted area for Contents.

Press **Return** again to close the Contents highlight.

Move the highlight to **Heading** and press **Return.** A box opens. You can type into it a heading to go above the FNAME column in the report. Type

```
Client's;Name:
```

Press ^ **End.**

Notice that the column heading appears in the Report Format template, while the X's on the bottom of the box indicate the width specified for the FNAME field. The semicolon (;) instructs dBASE to print the heading on two lines.

Expert Tips:

1. If the heading is wider than the width specified for the column, dBASE automatically increases the column width to match the heading width. If you want the contents of a field to wrap around, move the highlight down to the width option, press Return, and insert a width less than that of the field.
2. Make sure to press Return before entering a column heading or dBASE will interpret the heading characters as commands. dBASE requires the user to open the option before typing the heading characters.

To call up a menu of editing commands, press **[F1].**

Move to the selection of the next field by pressing the **PgDn** key. Press **Return.**

At the Contents ▶ prompt, type

```
INITIAL
```

Press **Return.**

Move on to the next field by pressing **PgDn.** Then press **Return** and type in

LNAME

Press **Return** again.

Press **PgDn** and press **Return.** Type in

AMT

Press **Return.** Notice the line that reads

```
Total this column is now set to Yes.
```

dBASE will now sum all the values for AMT and print the total at the bottom of the column on the report. This amount will be the total owed to Hallam, Hallam, & Hallam.

Move the highlighted area to **Heading** and press **Return.** A highlighted box appears. Type

```
Amount;Owed:
```

Press **^End, PgDn,** and **Return** consecutively. Type

PAYDATE

Press **Return.**

Move the cursor down to **Heading** and press **Return.** In the box, type

```
Date of;Last Payment:
```

Press **^End.** Your screen should be similar to the one in Figure 10-10. Press the **right arrow** *twice* to highlight **Exit** and **Save.** Press **Return** to save this report file called Report1.

d. Use the report form to retrieve information. Move the top highlighted area to **Retrieve** and move the lower highlighted area to **Report.** Press **Return.**

Another menu highlights **B:.** Press **Return.**

A listing of the various report files appears in another menu. If this is your very first report, then only REPORT1.FRM will appear. If there are more than one in the list, use the arrow key to highlight REPORT1.FRM. Then press Return.

FIGURE 10-10 The screen as it appears after the last field in Report1 has been defined. Notice how the report is displayed in the Report Format box. The report headings appear on the screen as they will on the page. "Client's Name:" appears as "lients name:" because the width of the report is wider than the screen. The X's represent the width of the character fields, the #'s represent the width of numeric fields, and the mm/dd/yy indicates a date field.

```
 Options          Groups          Columns          Locate          Exit  12:49:27 pm

                     Contents                      PAYDATE
                     Heading                       Date of;Last Payment:
                     Width                          12
                     Decimal places
                     Total this column


   Report Format
 lient's                                Amount        Date of       -------------
 ame:                                   Owed:         Last Payment:


 XXXXXXXXX     X XXXXXXXXXXXXXXX      #####.## mm/dd/yy

 CREATE REPORT   <B:> B:REPORT1.FRM           Column: 5
   Position selection bar - ↑↓.  Select - ↵.  Prev/Next column - PgUp/PgDn.
     Enter up to four lines of text to display above the indicated column.
```

Notice that dBASE added the extension .FRM to REPORT1. ".FRM" is an abbreviation for "form," so you can distinguish report forms from other kinds of files. After the file is retrieved, another menu appears on the screen with **Execute the command** highlighted. At this point you could specify which records to use in the report, such as all clients owing less than $200 or clients with Zip codes = 60115. However, since we want to include all the records on the file, press **Return** to execute the command.

A new prompt appears:

```
Direct the output to the printer? [Y/N]
```

Since we want to take a look at the report before committing it to paper, press **N.** The report will scroll on the screen. Use **^S** to stop the scrolling of the screen so you can read the beginning of the report. Press **^S** again to resume the scrolling so you can see the bottom half of the report.

e. Print the report. If you are satisfied with the appearance of the report, prepare your printer by turning it on and making sure the paper is aligned. Then press **Return** and repeat the steps in d. above, starting with pressing **Return** to select **Retrieve Report.** But at the prompt

```
Direct the output to the printer? [Y/N]
```

press **Y.** The report will be printed on your printer.

f. Notice the large gaps between the first name, initial, and last name. dBASE offers syntax commands to improve report appearance. These include **Trim** to remove unneeded spaces, the plus mark (+) to combine two or more fields in one column, single quote marks (' ') to insert spaces and other characters in the column, and semicolons (;) to print on multiple lines.

Step 7: Modify the report.

To change the report form, REPORT1.FRM, we need the Modify command. The **Modify** command can be used to change an existing database file or function, such as the database structure or a report form.

a. With the arrow key, select **Modify** from the Assist menu; then select **Report.**
Press **Return** and select disk drive **B:.** Press **Return.**
Select **REPORT1.FRM** from the list of report formats.
Press **Return.**

b. Change the column contents. A screen similar to the Report Create appears. With the arrow keys, select **Columns.**

Contents should be FNAME. Press **Return** to open the Contents line. Move the cursor to the beginning of the line and type

```
TRIM(FNAME)+' '+INITIAL+'.'+' '+LNAME
```

where

`TRIM`	removes all the extra blank spaces after the field FNAME.
+	combines multiple fields within the same column.
`' '`	(single quotes around a single space) inserts a blank space in the column.
`'.'`	inserts a period (.) after the field INITIAL.

Press **Return.**

c. Delete two columns. Use **PgDn** to go to the next column containing INITIAL. Press ^**U.** The column will be deleted. Repeat the same steps in the column containing LNAME.

d. Insert an extra blank column after PAYDATE to improve the spacing of the columns. Use the **PgDn** key to move to the column containing PAYDATE. Press ^**N.**

Press **Return** to open the Contents line. Type

```
' '
```

(a single quote, a blank space, and another single quote). You press the Space bar once to insert a single blank space between two single quotes.

Press **Return.**

e. Change the width of a column. To do so, move the highlight to **Width** and press **Return.** Change the width of the column to 5 by typing **5.** Press **Return.**

f. Select **Exit** and **Save.** Press **Return** to return to the Assist Menu.

Step 8: Review the revised report.

Select **Retrieve** and **Report** and press **Return.** Select drive **B:** and press **Return.** Select **REPORT1.FRM** and press **Return** *twice* to execute the command. At the prompt

```
Direct the output to the printer? [Y/N]
```

type **N.**

Check your report. If necessary, return to the Modify submenu and revise REPORT1.FRM until your output looks similar to Figure 10-11. The differences will be that you have added your name and address and the amount. Your list should be in alphabetical order by last name.

After the report is completed, print it out. Select **Retrieve** and **Report** and press **Return.** Direct the output to the printer.

Step 9: Search and report each of those clients whose account is 60 days overdue.

Once you have defined a report form, it can be used a variety of ways to retrieve valuable information, including searching for particular records.

a. After the printing is completed, press **Return** *twice* to select **Retrieve** and **Report.** Select disk drive **B:** and **REPORT1.FRM.**

FIGURE 10-11 An example of the printed report defined by report form Report1.

```
Page No.     1
03/21/88
                              Report of Clients Owing Money to
                                 Hallam, Hallam, & Hallam

Client's                                Amount       Date of
Name:                                    Owed:       Last Payment:


Craig A. Abbott                         500.00       01/15/88
Ellen P. Anderson                       200.00       02/15/88
Dalia H. Bach                            50.00       01/15/88
Jan J. Bach                             500.00       01/15/88
Curt P. Behrens                        1750.00       12/15/87
Barbara K. Bickle                       250.00       02/15/88
Helen L. Bishop                         750.00       01/15/88
Carol H. Brown                          400.00       12/15/87
Clifford T. Cleland                     450.00       12/15/87
Anne H. Cole                            150.00       01/15/88
Dee G. S. Coover                        850.00       01/15/88
William P. Cummings                    1500.00       11/15/87
John J. Engstrom                        500.00       11/15/87
Edward P. Fitzgerald                    850.00       11/15/87
Norma P. Fitzgerald                     500.00       01/15/88
Mary Lou J. Flemal                      500.00       12/15/87
Elizabeth M. George                     450.00       12/15/87
Robert M. Harkness                      975.00       12/15/87
Eva H. Leonard                          500.00       01/15/88
Robert H. McFadden                     2500.00       11/15/87
*** Total ***
                                      14125.00
```

b. Construct a search condition. We want to locate all the clients who have bills more than 60 days overdue. At the submenu options

```
Execute the command
Specify scope
Construct a field list
Build a search condition
Build a scope condition
```

highlight **Build a search condition** and press **Return.**

A list of field names will appear. Move the **arrow key** to select **PAYDATE.** Press **Return.**

A list of relational conditions appears:

```
=  Equal To
<= Less Than or Equal To
<  Less Than
>  Greater Than
>=Greater Than or Equal To
<>Not Equal To
```

Move the arrow key down to highlight **<= Less Than or Equal To.** Press **Return.**

At the prompt

```
Enter a date value:
```

type

```
12/15/87
```

We are assuming that any payment dates on or before (equal to or less than) December 15, 1987, are 60 days overdue as of February 15, 1988, the date on which we are preparing our report.

Press **Return** again to select **No more conditions.**

c. Produce the report. Move the highlight to **Execute the command** and press **Return.** At the prompt

```
Direct the output to the printer? [Y/N]
```

Press **N** so the report will be displayed on the screen.

Print a list of the names, addresses, and amounts owed so that Bruno, our bill collector, will be able to call on each of these clients.

Press **Return** to return to the Assistant screen.

d. Create a new report for clients with overdue bills. Move the top highlighted area to **Create.** Select **Report** and press **Return** *twice* to select **B:.** Then enter

```
OVERDUE
```

for the name of the file.

Press **Return** to select **Page title.** Type

```
Clients 60 Days Overdue
```

Press **Return.**
Type

```
Bruno Collection
```

Press **Return.**
Type

```
So we can pay our rent
```

Press ^ **End.**

Double space the report. Move the highlight to the line **Double space report** and press **Return.**

Move to the **Columns** command and, using the steps explained previously, enter the following fields in the columns:

Column 1: `TRIM(LNAME)-','+' '+TRIM(FNAME)+' '+INITIAL+'.'`

Column 2: `ADDRESS1+';'+TRIM(CITY)+','+' '+STATE+' '+ZIP`

Column 3: `AMT`

Set **Total this column** to **No.**

Move to **Exit** and **Save** and press **Return** to save this report format.

Move to **Retrieve** and select **Report.**

Press **Return** *twice* to select **B:.**

Move the highlighted area to **OVERDUE.FRM** and press **Return.**

Move the highlighted area to **Build a search condition** and select **PAYDATE.** Press **Return.**

Select **<= Less Than or Equal To** and enter

```
12/15/87
```

Press **Return** to select **No more conditions.**

Select **Execute the command** and press **N** to preview the report on the screen. If the report is correct, repeat the above steps starting with **Retrieve** and **Report.** Answer **Y** to the prompt about printing. When the printing is finished, press **Return.**

Check the report carefully for errors. When the report is complete, move to **Set Up** and select **Quit dBASE III Plus.** The dBASE session should end with this or a similar screen message:

```
*** END RUN   dBASE III PLUS
A>
```

Turn off the microcomputer. Remove the reports from the printer and turn off the printer.

SUMMARY

This lesson presented some of the more sophisticated features of database management software for editing, organizing, modifying, and retrieving information from an existing database. Editing is defined as the changing, replacement, or deletion of the contents of a data record. The main dBASE III Plus commands for editing are Edit and Browse. The Edit command causes records to appear on the screen one at a time, while Browse allows several records to appear on the screen at once. Both allow the user to edit the displayed records using editing commands similar to those found with most word processing software.

Organizing is the physical or logical rearrangement or duplication of a database file. The main dBASE III Plus organizing commands are Sort and Index. Sorting creates a new file with the records physically rearranged in a specified manner, such as in alphabetical or numeric order. Indexing does not create an entirely new file containing all the database records, but rather creates a file holding only the key field and the sequencing order. The records are not physically rearranged or changed. Indexing is generally preferred to sorting because indexing is faster, doesn't use as much disk storage space, and is required for various other operations such as relating one file to another file.

Modifying is the revision of the structure, rather than the data contents, of the database currently in use. In dBASE III Plus, the Modify command lets you conveniently change the structure of the database file, query statements, report formats, and label formats.

Retrieving causes the database software to search the records in one or more files within the database, extracting those particular records requested by the user and reporting them either by displaying them on the screen or by printing them. The dBASE III Plus commands for retrieving include List, Display, Report, and Label. List provides a rough draft report format that is handy for a quick look on the screen or on paper. Display presents one or more records on the screen. Report is the more formal way to present data. The Report command uses a two-step approach in which first a report format is completely defined and then a database file is retrieved and printed out using the report format.

Label provides a quick and easy way to produce mailing labels using data from a database. Like Report, the label form must have been previously created before it can be used to retrieve data.

After dBASE III Plus users become skilled in using Assistant menus, they often desire a faster method. By pressing Esc one or more times, you can leave The Assistant and face a screen that displays only a single dot. This dot prompt is your signal that The Assistant is gone and you are on your own to type in commands. Entire programs can be written using the extensive set of dBASE III Plus programming commands. Some of the more commonly used commands are the Setup commands, such as SET BELL OFF and SET DEFAULT TO B:. The tutorial provides an opportunity to retrieve and revise an existing database and practice several commands described in this lesson.

EXERCISES

1. Define the following terms:

editing	List	page title
organizing	Display	page eject
sorting	Report	columns menu
indexing	Label	contents
packing	Set commands	Modify command
seek	page formatting options	trim
modifying	plain page	
Retrieve		

2. Matching

_____	changing, replacement, or deletion of the contents of a data record.	a. packing
_____	the physical rearranging of the records in a database in a specified sequence.	b. list
_____	the creation of another file holding only the key field and the sequencing order used for the logical rearranging of records in a database in a specified sequence.	c. seek
_____	a very rapid record search of an indexed record file, locating the first record with a key field that matches the search expression.	d. indexing
_____	revision of the structure of the database currently in use.	e. sorting

_____	the searching of records in one or more files within the database, extracting those particular records requested by the user and reporting them to the user.	f. modifying
_____	shows one or more records from the currently selected database on the screen.	g. set
_____	removal of records marked for deletion from the database.	h. displaying
_____	commands that control or set up the operational environment of dBASE.	i. editing

3. What is the difference between the dBASE III Plus commands Browse and Edit?

4. What is the difference between indexing and sorting? List at least two reasons for using indexing over sorting.

5. Practice using dBASE III Plus by completing the tutorial "Retrieving and Revising an Existing Database Using dBASE III Plus" within this lesson. Then revise the tutorial to include the following changes:
   a. Make a copy of the database file, giving the database a new unique name, such as CLIENTSB. (Do not use this name; it is just an example.)
   b. With the Append command, add five new records to the copied database. Make sure the attributes are unique and satisfy field definitions.
   c. Continue with the tutorial.
   d. In Step 6, for the report title "Report of Clients Owing Money to Hallam, Hallam, and Hallam," add an additional line to be printed on a new line—"Produced by ____________________" —inserting your name.
   e. In addition to the report of clients whose accounts are 60 days overdue (Step 9), produce a report of clients whose accounts are 90 days overdue.
   f. Create a new report for clients with bills that are 90 days overdue. Remember to give the report a title to reflect the contents of the report. Name it OVERDUE9.

6. In Lesson 9, exercise 8, you used dBASE III Plus to create a single-file database. If you have not already done so, complete this exercise. Then make the following revisions.
   a. Use the Append command to add five new records to this database.
   b. Index the file by GPA.
   c. Produce a report of all the students in grade point average order.

Include on the report only the student's name and grade point average. The report title should be on the first line: "Members in Grade Point Average Order." For the second line use "Produced by ____________________" and insert your name. Include a heading for each column.

d. Use the Trim command to format the report so there are only three spaces between the Student Name column and the GPA column.

e. Print the report on the printer.

7. In Lesson 9, exercise 9, you used dBASE III Plus to create a single-file database called FIT. If you have not already done so, complete this exercise. Then make the following revisions.
   a. Using the Append command, add five new records to the database.
   b. Using the Sort command, create a sorted file.
   c. With the sorted file, produce a printed report with the following specifications:
      - Include the name, sex, and age of each subject.
      - Add a report title, including a description of the report contents and your name.
      - Add column headings.
      - Use the Trim command to format the report. There should be no more than five spaces between each column in the report.

8. In Lesson 9, exercise 10, you used dBASE III Plus to create a single-file database called SITTERS. Revise this exercise to include the following changes:
   a. Add three new records.
   b. Create a report to list the sitters in alphabetical order.
   c. Include appropriate titles and headings in the report.
   d. Produce a printed report listing all the sitters who are available during the evening.

9. Create a database of students in the class. Include fields for last name, first name, address, phone number, and date of birth. Index the file by last name. Create a report including a descriptive title, your name, the date, and column headings. Use Trim and other report formatting commands to concisely print the data on the report. Print the report.

10. In Lesson 9, exercise 11, you used dBASE III Plus to create a single-file database called CUSTOMERS. Revise and complete this exercise to include the following changes:
   a. Use the Modify Structure command to add a new field to the

database file. This field will be the date of entry into the database. Give the field an appropriate name, and the Date field type.

b. Using the Browse/Freeze command, add the new date to each existing record.

c. Insert a new record, including your name and appropriate data for each field.

d. Create and print a report. Include in the report a heading describing its contents, your name, and the date of the report. Also include column headings and appropriate concise lines, using the report formatting commands. Records should be in alphabetical order by last name.

11. Create a small dBASE program to turn the bell off, set the default disk drive to B, and set Confirm on.

11
Advanced Database Applications

LESSON OUTLINE

BUILDING A RELATIONAL DATABASE

To understand how to build a relational database, we will define such a database and then discuss essential terms and concepts. Several examples will help you understand how to distinguish between a spreadsheet application and a relational database application. Further, we will examine how to define relations within a relational database and construct logical conditions involving multiple files within a database. Later in the lesson, we will address the issue of comparing and selecting a database management software package by using the general analysis and design process described in Lesson 2 (see Figure 2-10). A checklist is also presented as a general guide to database software selection. Features of some of the most popular database management software packages are summarized. The tutorial leads you through the steps of creating a relational database, and producing a report.

Like word processing and electronic spreadsheet software, database management software should be selected to fit the user's particular needs. Once you understand how such software works and what its potential is, you may want to purchase one of the many commercial packages for your personal or professional use. Even if you are not in the market to purchase database software right now, the information and guidelines presented in this lesson will help you understand the main features of and differences among commercial database management software packages. The potential of this tool is so great that most knowledgeable microcomputer users eventually become frequent database management software users. This lesson will better equip you to take advantage of these expanding opportunities.

What Is a Relational Database?

Remember, a **relational database** is a database that allows the user to reference more than one file in the construction of reports and selected other database operations by utilizing the logical relationships or connections between the files. Relational databases consist of multiple files called relations in the terminology of relational mathematics, the foundation of relational database theory. Recall from the introductory discussion of relational database concepts in Lesson 9 that the relational database software of today is based upon the field of relational algebra, and the terminology used today is a combination of terms common to data processing and to relational algebra. Each file is a *flat file* or table organized

FIGURE 11-1 A relational database is similar to a collection of logically connected spreadsheets.

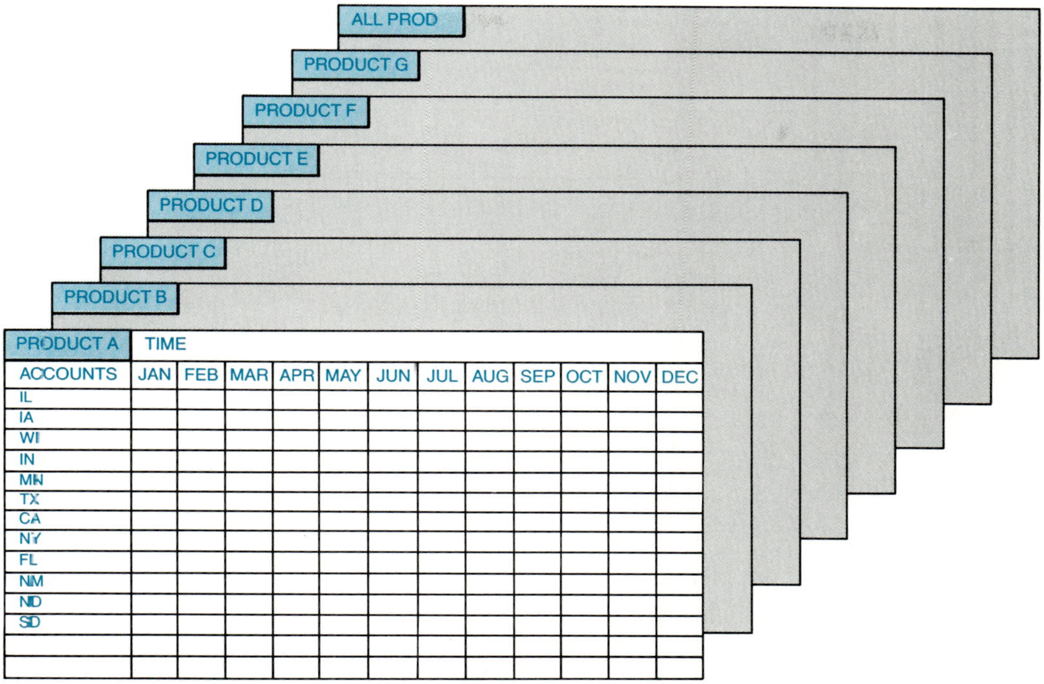

into rows and columns much like a spreadsheet. You might like to think of a relational database as a collection of spreadsheets (see Figure 11-1).

Each row within a flat file is called a **tuple** (rhymes with *couple*), and each column is called an **attribute.** A tuple is simply another term for a record. An attribute is simply another term for a field. Although it may seem a little confusing to use these words rather than the more familiar terms of record and field, it is important for you to know what they mean, so when you read articles describing relational database concepts you will not be confused by the terminology. The concepts are really quite simple, and your experience with spreadsheets will make it easier to comprehend these relational database concepts. Each tuple is equivalent to a row, while each attribute is equivalent to a column. In fact, simplicity is the main feature of relational databases. Figure 11-2 illustrates tuples and attributes.

In the general theory of relational database design, a **relation** is another name for a single file consisting of an ordered set of fields called attributes. *Attributes* contain data that identify (key fields) or describe entities. For example, in Figure 11-2 the attributes are IDNO, NAME, DEPT, SKILL, and ED. In the CLIENTS database described in Lessons 9 and 10,

FIGURE 11-2 In a relational database, the rows are called tuples and the columns are called attributes. In this example, each tuple represents one employee, and the attributes are called IDNO, NAME, DEPT, SKILL, and ED.

Attributes

IDNO	NAME	DEPT	SKILL	ED
101	ABBOTT, CRAIG	4	4	MS MATH
102	BROWN, WILBUR	2	3	BS HIST
103	DRAYTON, MARY	4	4	HS
104	KELLEY, ANN	5	3	PHD BUS
105	MURRY, ED	2	2	MBA
106	NORDQUIST, TOM	3	3	HS
107	ROBERTS, TOM	3	1	HS
108	WILLIAMS, KAREN	4	3	MS ENG

1 Tuple (Record)

some database management systems would refer to the file we called CLIENTS as a relation and the fields we called ACCTNO, FNAME, INITIAL, LNAME, ADDRESS1, CITY, STATE, ZIP, AMT, and PAYDATE as attributes.

However, in dBASE III Plus, specifically, a single flat file is called a database and a relation is defined as a link or tie between two databases. In dBASE III Plus the linkage must be based upon a field held in common between the two databases. For example, if we were to create a dBASE III Plus database called CASES to hold information about the individual cases the attorneys of the law firm Hallam, Hallam, & Hallam are handling for their clients, then we could use a common field such as ACCTNO to link the two databases together.

Returning to the general theory of relational database design, a file is commonly referred to as an **ordered set** of fields or attributes. The arrangement or order of the fields is important to maintaining the structure of the database. In the example in Figure 11-2 the field IDNO must always be the first field, NAME the second, and so on. In the CLIENTS database you created in Lesson 9, the field called ACCTNO must always be the first field, FNAME the second, INITIAL the third, and so on.

Databases hold data about entities. Remember, an **entity** is a person, place, or thing that is identified and described by the fields or attributes in a record. In Figure 11-2 the entities are employees. In CLIENTS the entities are the clients. The attribute called ACCTNO uniquely identifies each entity (client), and the other attributes (FNAME, INITIAL, LNAME, ADDRESS1, CITY, STATE, ZIP, AMT, and PAYDATE) further describe each entity. An attribute that uniquely identifies records within a file is called a **key field.** Several clients may have the same AMT or PAYDATE, and it is even possible for two of the firm's clients to have exactly the same last name (such as Smith, for example). But we must assign each client a unique account number (see Figure 11-3). The account number will be the key field.

Defining Relations

Once a relational database is built, most people find it easy to use. However, suppose you were faced with the task of starting from the beginning. How would you know that a relational database is what is needed? How would you distinguish between a spreadsheet application and a database application? How would you know what to include in the database, and what relational connections are needed? What principles or guidelines should you follow so the resulting database is as useful as possible to decision makers? The following paragraphs provide guidelines for defining files in relational databases.

Distinguish between Spreadsheet and Database Applications To create a new database, we need to develop the ability to visualize the data organized into a series of flat files, each resembling a spreadsheet. A flat file, like a spreadsheet, is a table of rows and columns. In fact, some people use spreadsheets for some of their database needs. Many applications overlap.

With a spreadsheet, you will recall, the intersection of a row and a column is called a cell. A cell can hold a label or text, a formula, a reference to another cell location, or a value. In contrast, many database management systems do not provide for the storage of formulas within the fields of the database. A field can hold alphabetic, numeric, logical, date, or memo data. Although some database software provide for mathematical operations such as addition, subtraction, multiplication, and division, (usually as part of the reporting procedures), many provide for only the addition of a column, and most are not as versatile with mathematical operations as spreadsheets are.

In general, if your data are mostly numeric and you need to be able to manipulate them mathematically, then a spreadsheet is probably what you want. On the other hand, if the data are primarily alphabetic and your needs center around being able to select particular records and display them on the screen or in printed reports, then a database is more appropriate. Many software packages provide a means to transfer data back and forth between a spreadsheet and a database, allowing a user to use the spreadsheet when complex mathematical computations are needed and the database management system software when reports are to be prepared, using logically defined subsets of the database.

Anticipate Users' Questions The ability to design good relational databases depends largely on the designer's ability to anticipate the types of questions the users might want to answer using data from the database. If the person creating the database is not the person who will be using it, then it is important for the creator to discuss with the potential users just what questions they hope to answer with the database.

One relation or file

Ten attributes or fields

Key field

ACCTNO	FNAME	INITIAL	LNAME	ADDRESS1	CITY	STATE	ZIP	AMT	PAYDATE
101	Craig	A	Abbott	1512 Margaret Lane	DeKalb	IL	60115	500.00	01/15/88
102	Ellen	P	Anderson	213 River Drive	DeKalb	IL	60115	200.00	02/15/88
103	Barbara	K	Bickle	1732 Raintree Court	Sycamore	IL	60178	250.00	02/15/88
104	Robert	M	Harkness	350 South Malta Road	Malta	IL	60150	975.00	12/15/87
105	Elizabeth	M	George	315 North Maple	Waterman	IL	60556	450.00	12/15/87
106	Dalia	H	Bach	9 Moraine Terrace	DeKalb	IL	60115	50.00	01/15/88
107	Curt	P	Behrens	317 Joanne Lane	DeKalb	IL	60115	1750.00	12/15/87
108	Helen	L	Bishop	102 Ridge Drive	DeKalb	IL	60115	750.00	01/15/88
109	Carol	H	Brown	1315 Gifford	DeKalb	IL	60115	400.00	12/15/87
110	Clifford	T	Cleland	404 South Fourth Street	DeKalb	IL	60115	450.00	12/15/87
111	Anne	H	Cole	1107 Normal Road #2	DeKalb	IL	60115	150.00	01/15/88
112	Dee G.	S	Coover	803 Normal Road	DeKalb	IL	60115	850.00	01/15/88
113	William	P	Cummings	1621 Sleepy Hollow Ln.	DeKalb	IL	60115	1500.00	11/15/87
114	John	J	Engstrom	115 W. Exchange Street	Sycamore	IL	60178	500.00	11/15/87
115	Edward	P	Fitzgerald	217 Laurel Lane	DeKalb	IL	60115	850.00	11/15/87
116	Norma	P	Fitzgerald	217 Laurel Lane	DeKalb	IL	60115	500.00	01/15/88
117	Mary Lou	J	Flemal	433 Normal Road	DeKalb	IL	60115	500.00	12/15/87
118	Eva	H	Leonard	121 Park Avenue	DeKalb	IL	60115	500.00	01/15/88
119	Robert	H	McFadden	517 Fastexit Lane	Sycamore	IL	60178	2500.00	11/15/87
120	Jan	J	Bach	9 Moraine Terrace	DeKalb	IL	60115	500.00	01/15/88

One tuple or record

FIGURE 11-3 **Each row (tuple) contains attributes about a single entity. Some columns (attributes) uniquely identify the entity (key field), while others provide descriptive data.**

For example, a personnel department may need to quickly answer such questions as "What are the names of our employees who speak Spanish?" or "Which employees have been with the company over ten years?" or "Which employees are not U.S. citizens?" A credit department may need answers to such questions as "What is the current account status for John Smith?" or "What are the names and addresses of our customers whose accounts are overdue?" or "What is the name of the city where most of our customers live?" All these types of questions indicate the need for a database.

However, the following questions suggest the need for a spreadsheet. "What is the forecasted profit from the sale of the new product we are planning to produce?" "What would the monthly schedule of payments be for a loan of $10,000 at 10 percent interest for a period of five years?" "How much should we charge a client given that we know the number of hours spent by the senior lawyer in the firm, the number of courtroom appearances, the number of hours spent by the law clerk, and the number of secretarial hours expended on this client's case plus the charge-out rates for each of those categories?"

Notice that the questions suggesting a spreadsheet involved mostly numeric data and the solution of formulas. In contrast, the database questions involved the selection of records from a file based upon some logical condition. The issue of whether to use a spreadsheet or a database is not always clear-cut. Some human judgment is required.

Logically Connect Files A relational database really shines when we need to logically connect two or more files to obtain the answer to a user's question. Before relational databases were invented, often a user would ask a question that required the use of more than one file, and the data processing department would reply that it was unable to answer the question, or the user would get two or more reports that would require digging through a mountain of data for the answer. Users would often comment that the data processing department was not serving their needs and would use the phrase "Their right hand doesn't know what their left hand is doing!" What seemed so logical and easy for a human to do was difficult, if not impossible, for the database management system to do. Relational database software packages, however, are specifically designed to logically connect two or more files. The design of such a database does require some planning during the creation of the database and some understanding about how to write the commands that logically connect the files.

To see the effect of a second file in a relational database, we will create a second relation, or file, in the database called CLIENTS. Let's assume we also want to maintain information about the types of cases the attorneys are handling for each of the clients. The entity of interest to us is a client, and we can again identify each client by his or her account number. To allow us to easily relate the data in this new file to the already existing file called CLIENTS, we should name the common field using exactly the same name and description as used before. The field ACCTNO needs to be a numeric field three positions in length with no positions to the right of the decimal point.

Now that we have one field (ACCTNO) that is described the same in both files and will contain exactly the same data, we can refer to ACCTNO as the **linking field.** That is, when we are talking about a particular client, Craig Abbott, for example, that entity's ACCTNO will be 101 in both files. This fact allows the database management system to relate or connect records from one file to records in the other file. For example, we could have the computer search the CLIENTS file to find those cases being handled by a particular attorney.

Minimize Redundant Data Recall that **data redundancy** is defined as keeping the same data in more than one file. A database designer may be tempted to create a very large file containing all possible fields in order to minimize redundant data. However, actual business applications may simply become too large to be efficiently handled in a single file.

Further, trying to put all the fields in one file may result in many fields being blank. For example, in the CLIENTS database we may have some clients for whom the law firm is handling only one case, perhaps a house closing. However, we may have other clients who see the firm's attorneys for tax preparation, a house closing, a divorce, and several court appearances. This second example is referred to as a **one-to-many** relationship because for one client there may be many cases. If the database designer wants to include all the fields in a single file, then it would be necessary to anticipate the largest number of cases the firm would handle for one client and reserve fields to hold the needed information for each of those possible cases.

Therefore, the solution is to create a separate file for cases and build a relation between records in the CASES file and records in the CLIENTS file. There would be some data redundancy because at least one field must be held in common between the two files—the ACCTNO field in the example of the CLIENTS and CASES files. However, this data redundancy would be minor compared to what could be found. Some firms keep customer addresses in several different files, or duplicate part numbers in several different files, or list inventory items in more than one file, resulting in wasted data storage and a higher possibility of error.

Maintain Data Integrity **Data integrity** is defined as maintaining the accuracy and consistency of the data throughout a total information system. Lack of data integrity occurs when, for example, one file shows a client's address to be 223 West Locust and another file says the same client lives at 408 North First. Perhaps the client moved, and one file was updated but the other one was not.

You may compare data integrity to personal integrity; people with integrity always tell the truth, even when doing so may not be as convenient as telling a falsehood. A database with integrity also provides the same accurate data in response to users' inquiries, even though the updating procedure may sometimes be tedious. Minimizing data redundancy reduces the tediousness of the updating procedure. A system with low data redundancy requires less updating because, ideally, updating the data once results in the data being accurate and consistent throughout the system. For example, changing a client's address from 223 West Locust to 408 North First on one file should result in the new address being displayed in all subsequent reports or inquiries into the database. This requires that all reports using the client's address either use the one file or use a relation that refers to that file.

MULTIPLE FILES IN dBASE III PLUS

So far you have used only one flat file at a time. But what if part of the information you want is on one file and part is on another?

Join

dBASE III Plus allows you to **join** or merge two or more files into another file (see Figure 11-4). Let us consider two very simple files. FILE1 contains an employee ID number, NAME, and ADDRESS. FILE2 contains an employee ID number, DEPT, and PHONE. Let's also assume that the files are already created and contain data. We get a request to produce a list of employee names and phone numbers.

It is simpler here to leave The Assistant and type in the commands from the dot prompt. Remember, pressing Esc one or more times will cause dBASE III Plus to leave The Assistant and display only the dot

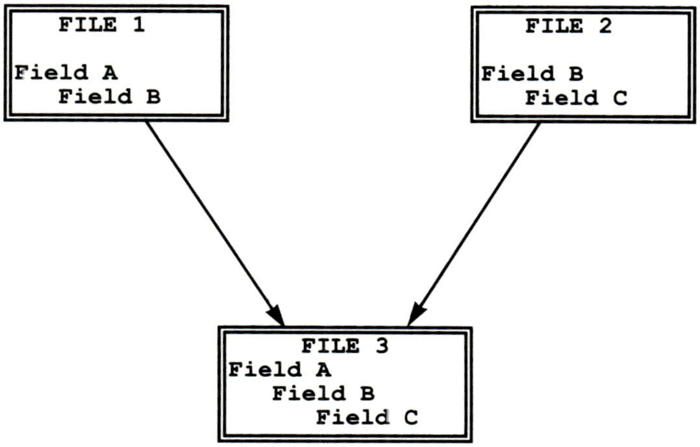

FIGURE 11-4 One or more files can be merged using the Join command, provided they share a common field, in this case, Field B. A new file is created containing fields from both files.

prompt. Now we need to make both files active by using them at the same time. dBASE III Plus allows this through the Select command. The **Select** command allows up to ten areas (numbered 1 to 10 but also referred to as A, B, C, . . . J), each able to contain a dBASE III Plus file. One file is placed in area 1, for example, and another file in area 2; then they can be joined and the result placed in a third file. Suppose, for example, we have the following data in FILE1 and FILE2:

FILE1

ID	NAME	ADDRESS
101	Bill Jones	123 Elm Street
102	Susan Smith	345 Locust
103	Joe Diller	908 Maple
104	Mary Nice	621 Elm Street
105	Terry O'Brien	202 Normal Rd.

FILE2

ID	DEPT	PHONE
101	Accounting	712-1234
102	Production	712-7654
103	Production	712-4090
104	Sales	756-4512
106	Sales	756-0099

Notice that records with ID's 101–104 are in both files but ID=105 is in FILE1 only and ID=106 is in FILE2 only. When files are joined, only those that match will be put into the merged file. Thus ID=105 and ID=106 will not be in FILE3.

Now suppose we press Esc to change from The Assistant to the dot prompt mode and then enter the following commands:

```
select 1
use FILE1
select 2
use FILE2
select 1
join with FILE2 to FILE3 for ID=FILE2->ID fields NAME, PHONE
```

Taken all together these commands instruct the computer to join FILE1 from area 1 with FILE2 from area 2 and call the resulting file FILE3. The files are to be joined where there is a match of the field called ID in FILE1 and ID in FILE2. The fields in the newly created file will be NAME and PHONE. The FILE2−>ID means the field ID found in FILE2.

dBASE III Plus will provide a message telling how many records were joined. Now use FILE3 for the report:

```
use FILE3
display all
```

dBASE III Plus will display on the screen the new file created from this merger:

RECORD#	NAME	PHONE
1	Bill Jones	712-1234
2	Susan Smith	712-7654
3	Joe Diller	712-4090
4	Mary Nice	756-4512

This example may not seem significant, but remember that our purpose was to illustrate the concept using a very simple case. A firm may have numerous files that, prior to the development of relational database management systems, could not easily be joined. Further, the types of questions management must answer frequently require information from more than one file. The ability to do the simple operation shown above represents, on a small scale, the tremendous usefulness of relational database management.

Set Relations

In addition to the Join command, dBASE III Plus offers the **Set Relation** command, which allows the user to draw fields from two different files but does not produce a new file. As with the Join command, the user must first place the two original files into separate work areas using the Select command. There must be at least one field held in common between the two files and that field (or fields) must be indexed (see Figure 11-5).

To continue with the previous simple example, the following commands would create a relation between FILE1 and FILE2:

```
select 1
use FILE1
index on ID to FILE1
select 2
use FILE2
index on ID to FILE2
set relation to ID into FILE1
list PHONE, FILE1->NAME for ID=FILE1->ID
```

FILE1 has been put into working area 1 and FILE2 into working area 2. Both are indexed on the field they hold in common, ID. The Set Relation command tells dBASE to create a link between the current file (FILE2 because it is the one most recently mentioned in a USE command) and FILE1, using ID as the linking field. The List command tells dBASE to list on the screen the following:

FIGURE 11-5 The Set Relation command links files using a common field. Unlike Join, it does not create a new file, but permits users to draw data from both fields for lists, reports, and other data retrieval operations.

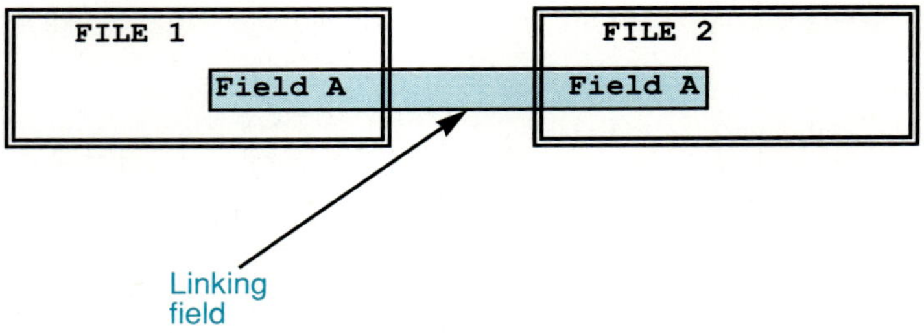

RECORD#	PHONE	FILE1→NAME
1	712-1234	Bill Jones
2	712-7654	Susan Smith
3	712-4090	Joe Diller
4	756-4512	Mary Nice

This listing is exactly the same as that obtained when we used the Join command discussed earlier. The field PHONE came from FILE2 and the field NAME came from FILE1. The phones and names listed were only those for which the ID's matched in both files. How does the Join function differ from the Set Relation function? Obviously, it is possible to obtain exactly the same results from either; however, the Join command created a new file whereas the Set Relation did not. Therefore, Set Relation is more efficient in terms of storage space used, lessens the possibility of data redundancy, and reduces the potential problem of data integrity discussed earlier in this lesson. However, there are times when a new file is exactly what a user needs. For example, the newly created FILE3 in the Join example can be stored on a separate disk and given to a user who needs that particular combination of data fields. The tutorial at the end of this lesson provides you with hands-on experience in using both the Join and the Set Relation commands in dBASE III Plus.

COMPARING AND SELECTING SOFTWARE

When we discussed the selection of word processing and spreadsheet software, we first employed the general four step problem-solving approach. Once again, this approach can guide us in selecting the best database management software.

Define Goals and Constraints

To define and put in writing your database *goals,* you first need to understand your information needs. **Information** is data that have been processed so that they are meaningful and useful to a decision maker. List the questions that the decision maker (yourself, if the database is for you) wants to be able to answer. List the data items that need to be in the database in order to answer those questions. Determine how the data items are related. Will a single file be sufficient, or will you need a database containing several integrated files? Once you have a good idea of your information needs and the type of database that could address them, it is time to gather data about the various database software packages available on the market.

As with any software, you must recognize limitations on your selection. Such constraints can include your budget, the microcomputer hardware you plan to use, and compatibility with other software or hardware systems you plan to use. Everyone has budgetary limitations. There is a variety of database management software available today with a wide range of prices and features. At the low-cost extreme, some single-file database software such as PC-File are the shareware. **Shareware** is software that can be copied, and if the user finds the software is useful, he or she pays a voluntary fee to the author. Shareware fees are very reasonable, ususally less than $100, whereas other popular packages, such as dBASE III Plus and PFS:Professional File, are priced in the range of $400 to $700. Although price is not always directly correlated with features, usually you get what you pay for. The higher priced packages, in general, offer more features and better documentation plus customer support.

Gather Data

After you have considered your needs, *gather data* about the software that is compatible with your hardware and software systems. Find out the costs, features, and limitations of these packages. Fortunately, just as when you are choosing word processing and spreadsheet packages, current magazine articles are one of your best sources of up-to-date information. Magazines such as *Byte, Business Computing, InfoWorld, PC,* and *PC World* offer a variety of database articles.

People you know who already use a database software package on a microcomputer are another valuable source of advice. You will probably find that database use is not quite as common as word processing and electronic spreadsheet use, but the number of users is growing rapidly. In fact, there may be a local user's group in which people share their experiences about dBASE, Perfect Filer, R:base, Clout, Paradox, and other packages.

Another information source is your local computer store. Of course, you must realize the store has a special interest in promoting the brands of software it carries and is familiar with. Still, a responsible computer retail store operator will be knowledgeable about different brands and will want to gain and maintain satisfied customers. Of course, remember that database management systems require not only a commitment of money for purchasing the package, but also a large commitment of time and talent to implement the system.

Test Alternatives

Testing possible solutions or alternatives regarding database software may prove a little more difficult than testing word processing or spreadsheet software. In some cases, however, you may find it possible to take a small database application (such as a tutorial from this book) along with you to use in a "test drive" of the database software at your local computer store. Also, you can read about other test drives in the software review sections of microcomputer magazines.

Even if you buy one of the commonly available database software packages and find, after some initial testing, that it is not what you need, you probably have not wasted more than a few hundred dollars. That may be substantial for your personal budget, but it is usually not a major expense for even a small company. Most database systems retail for less than $1,000.

Implement the Best Solution

Implementation of database software involves training time plus time to experiment with designing databases. No matter how "user friendly" packages are advertised to be, there is no substitute for investing time in studying the documentation and practicing with some sample databases.

If you are going to be responsible for a database once it is created, then you have to consider a systematic way to update and maintain it. In a large data center where mainframe computers and many computer professionals are employed, very elaborate systems exist for maintaining the data in an accurate and up-to-date fashion. Users of personal databases often forget about the long-term upkeep needed for proper database maintenance.

It is also important to consider the dynamic nature of the database software selection process. Your information needs will change, and the needs of your organization will change. Also, the availability of new database software packages changes almost weekly. Your choice of a database software package should not be considered a long-term choice. Surely within the next few years many new systems will be marketed with capabilities far beyond what is currently available. However, if you have information needs today that could be served by a database system, you cannot wait for the perfect system to be invented. You must make a rational choice today, knowing that within a year or less it may no longer be the best choice.

One way to approach the selection problem in a systematic manner is to use the following checklist of database software features.

A DATABASE SOFTWARE CHECKLIST

Use this checklist as a general guide in the systematic search for the database software package that will most closely meet your needs. The checklist is organized around the categories of (1) general features, (2) capacity issues, (3) compatibility, and (4) miscellaneous issues.

Put a check mark by the item if the database software package you are testing has that feature. You may want to mark some features that are very important to you with double check marks.

General Features

_____ Is the software menu driven?

_____ Is the software command driven?

_____ Does it require a hard disk?

_____ Does it support multiuser networking?

_____ Is it a single-file system?

_____ Are multiple files per database allowed?

_____ Are relational features supported?

Capacity Issues

_____ Is the maximum number of characters per record adequate?

_____ Is the maximum number of fields per record adequate?

_____ Is the maximum number of records per file adequate?

_____ Is the maximum number of files per database adequate?

_____ Is your current primary storage capacity sufficient?

_____ Will your current disk capacity be sufficient?

Compatibility

_____ Will the database software operate on your operating system?

_____ Is the database compatible with your word processing software?

_____ Does it read files created by other software you currently use?

_____ Does it write files you can use on other software you currently use?

Miscellaneous Issues

_____ Does it offer reporting features you need?

_____ Does it offer back-up and file security features?

_____ Is an on-screen tutorial provided?

_____ Are on-screen helps provided?

_____ Will it provide the needed data calculations?

_____ Does it provide the added programming capabilities needed?

_____ Are satisfied users available for consultation?

Cost of the software: $_____ versus Your Budget: $_____

POPULAR DATABASE PACKAGES

We will first examine some simple single-file, flat-file database managers for MS-DOS–based microcomputers and then move on to relational database systems. Recall that a single-file, flat-file manager (also known as a flat-file manager or simply a file manager) requires data to be organized inside a single file. A flat file can be visualized as two-dimensional or flat, hence the name. A flat file is similar to a table or a spreadsheet and can be viewed as a set of rows and columns. Each row is a record, and each row must have exactly the same number of columns, meaning that each record in the file must have exactly the same number of fields.

Relational databases, by contrast, provide the flexibility to link within one database, the data stored in several different files. In general, relational databases are more powerful, more complex, more difficult to use, and more expensive than file managers. People turn from file managers to relational databases when they find that the questions decision makers want answered require the flexibility of linking several files together to create relations among those files. As relational database systems become more popular, they are also becoming more inexpensive and easier to use.

Table 11-1 summarizes features of several of the more popular database software systems. Terms presented in Table 11-1 that have not been previously defined are briefly described here. **Record size** is the maximum size of each record in the database, expressed in bytes. Recall that one byte is used to store one ASCII character, so, in general, a record size limit of 4,000 bytes means you can store 4,000 characters in a single record. Data entry rules may require certain fields, such as record number, to be included on a database or may not allow blank fields (the system states, "Must fill field"). **Data conversion** is the ability to change the format of such fields as the date field. For example, the format MM/DD/YY (month, day, year) could be changed to YY/MM/DD (year, month, day). **Forced upper case** permits the database to change characters typed in as lower case to upper case without the need to reenter the field contents. **Automatic data entry** permits certain data, such as record numbers or dates, to be placed in a field without additional data entry. Most programmable databases require specific program statements to automatically place data in a field. **Calculated fields on entry screen** is a feature that places the result of a formula in a field.

The **data import and export** feature permits the computer to exchange data between different software packages without first converting the data into another format. **Data import** is the ability of the software to read such files, whereas **data export** is the ability to write to such files. As discussed in Lesson 1, **ASCII** is a code commonly used to store text data. Most database software can easily exchange ASCII formatted files. .DBF, .SDF, and .WKS are the three-character extensions following the filename. **.DBF** is the extension for files stored in the standard database format; **.SDF** is the extension for files stored in the *system data file* format; and **.WKS** and **.WK1** are the extensions for files stored in the format of Lotus 1-2-3 files.

Data manipulation is the changing, extraction, or organizing of data in the database. **Indexing** uses one or more data fields as a key field or fields on which to generate an index file. The index file is then used to reorganize the contents of the database file while reporting or listing the database file. Unlike the Sort command, the Index command does not physically rearrange the database itself. **Sorting** arranges the data records in the database in ascending or descending order according to the contents of a key field or fields. The data records in the database file are rearranged as specified in the Sort command. **Multiple-record deletions and updates** permits a number of records to be changed in the database through only one command. **Table merging** or **joining** is the combining of information from two or more files that are currently open in separate work areas. The merged information is then saved in a new file.

Command strategy is the approach the software takes for prompting and accepting commands. Four general types of menus are used on most database software packages: horizontal bar menus, pull-down menus, pop-up windows, and vertical menus. **Horizontal bar menus** place the command options along the top or bottom of the screen, much like the Lotus 1-2-3 menu. Many database management software packages use the Lotus 1-2-3 menu as a model. **Pop-up windows** instantly appear on the screen in small boxes when a command key is pressed. **Pull-down menus** appear, usually in a small window, from the menu bar when a particular menu option is chosen. **Vertical menus** display the command choices in a form much like a multiple choice quiz. The cursor goes from line to line until all the needed choices have been made. In addition to menus, databases may use **typed commands,** in which whole words or abbreviations of commands are given or placed in statements.

Input facilities specify the capabilities of the database software to accept data to be placed in the file. The input screen can be **user defined,** created by the user; **automatic,** created by the software; or **programmed,** created by the user with program statements.

Output facilities specify the capabilities of the database software to define and generate reports. Most can do a variety of arithmetic and statistical functions on the data while reporting. **Multiple-file reports** can integrate information from two or more files from one database into a single report. **Predefined mailing labels** conveniently allow the user to produce standard mailing labels without additional programming or specifications.

Among the special features of database software are **query capabilities,** allowing the user to request information from the files by simply asking questions, and **user-access security provisions,** which may include **passwords** (secret words that allow access only to properly informed and authorized users), **data encryption** (changing the characters into a secret code so others cannot understand the data), or other file restrictions.

Table 11-1 A COMPARISON OF POPULAR DATABASE MANAGEMENT SOFTWARE PACKAGES

SOFTWARE NAME	*dBASE III Plus*	*R:base System V*	*Paradox*
DATABASE TYPE	relational	relational	relational
HARDWARE REQUIREMENTS			
Minimum RAM	256K	512K	410K
Requires hard disk	recommended	yes	recommended
Total number of distribution disks	7	11	5
Number of disks required to run program	2	10	2
FILE STRUCTURE LIMITS			
Number of fields per record	128	400	255
Record size (bytes)	4000	4096	4K
Number of records per data file	1 billion	unlimited	65000
Number of records per database	10 billion	unlimited	unlimited
Field size (bytes)	254	4092	255
DATA TYPES AND SIZES			
Character	yes	yes	yes
Numeric	yes	yes	yes
Floating decimal point	yes	yes	yes
Logical (Boolean)	yes	no	yes
Date	yes	yes	yes
DATA ENTRY AND EDITING			
Required fields	no	yes	yes
Must fill field	no	yes	yes
Forced upper case	yes	no	yes
Date conversions	yes	yes	yes
Automatic data entry	no	yes	no
Calculated fields on entry screen	yes	yes	yes
DATA IMPORT/EXPORT			
ASCII	both	both	both
.DBF	both	both	both
.SDF	both	both	none
.WKS	both	both	both
DATA MANIPULATION			
Indexing	yes	yes	yes
Sorting	yes	no	yes
Maximum number of open files	10	80	unlimited
Multiple-record deletions and updates	yes	yes	yes
Table merging (joining)	yes	yes	yes
Maximum number of tables merged	2	2	unlimited
COMMAND STRATEGY			
Menu type	pull-down pop-up windows	vertical horizontal bar pull-down pop-up windows	horizontal bar
Typed commands:			
Whole words	yes	yes	no
Abbreviations	yes	yes	no

PFS:Professional File	*Q&A*	*Reflex*
flat file	flat file	flat file
256K	512K	384K
no	no	no
1	6	3
1	4	2
3200	2400	250
61000	16780	63500
29500	16 million	65500
64	not applicable	65550
1919	1678	254
yes	yes	no
yes	yes	yes
no	yes	no
no	yes	no
no	yes	yes
no	yes	no
no	no	no
no	yes	no
no	yes	yes
no	yes	yes
yes	yes	yes
both	both	both
no	both	import
no	both	both
yes	both	import
yes	yes	no
yes	yes	yes
1	1	1
yes	yes	no
no	no	yes
none	none	16
vertical horizontal bar pull-down pop-up windows	vertical	horizontal bar pull-down pop-up windows
no	no	no
no	no	no

Table 11-1 (*continued*)

SOFTWARE NAME	*dBASE III Plus*	*R:base System V*	*Paradox*
INPUT FACILITIES			
Screen definition:			
User defined	yes	yes	yes
Automatic	yes	yes	yes
Programming	yes	yes	yes
OUTPUT FACILITIES			
Report generation:			
Arithmetic functions	yes	yes	yes
Statistical functions	no	yes	yes
Multiple-file reports	yes	yes	no
Predefined mailing labels	yes	yes	no
Report definition methods:			
User defined	yes	yes	yes
Automatic	no	yes	yes
Programming	yes	yes	yes
Stored report definitions	yes	yes	yes
SPECIAL FEATURES			
Query capabilities	yes	yes	yes
Multiple-file access	yes	yes	yes
Macros	yes	yes	yes
User-access security provisions	yes	yes	yes
Network support	extra cost	yes	no
LIST PRICE	$695	$700	$695

Selected Flat-File Database Managers

PFS: Professional File This is a simple-to-use, menu-driven flat-file database that allows users to read from or write to files created with Lotus 1-2-3 without conversion. The software includes a report writing feature for crosstab reports. A **crosstab report** summarizes or cross-tabulates data in a specified field relative to one or two other fields of a file. See Table 11-1 for further information about PFS:Professional File.

Reflex: The Analyst This is a low-cost, flat-file database system for MS-DOS machines. Like PFS:Professional File, Reflex can read and further process Lotus 1-2-3 files and has a cross-tabulation feature that allows users to cross-reference information. One of the unique features of Reflex is a large collection of built-in functions (4 for financial forecasting, 16 for data manipulation, 3 for logical programming, and 13 for special purposes such as calculating data from different records). Reflex also includes a graphics module that can print scatter, line, bar, stacked bar, and pie charts using fields from individual records or summaries of fields from a number of records. Reflex's menu types include a menu bar, a pull-down menu, and a pop-up window. Since Reflex uses a graphics screen for both text and

PFS:Professional File	*Q&A*	*Reflex*
yes	yes	yes
no	no	no
no	no	no
yes	yes	yes
no	no	yes
no	no	no
no	with Write	no
yes	yes	yes
no	no	no
no	no	no
yes	yes	yes
yes	Intelligent Assistant	yes
no	no	no
yes	yes	no
no	no	no
through other software	yes	no
$249	$349	$150

graphs, it can show both text and graphics on the screen at one time. Table 11-1 contains further information about Reflex.

Q&A This is another flat-file database with some important enhanced features. It includes a built-in word processor, called Write, that contains such features as a spelling checker and column/row math capabilities. One of the unique features of Q&A is the Intelligent Assistant, which lets you query the database with ordinary English-language phrases. Most database software require strict rules of syntax to extract information from the database files, but the Intelligent Assistant lets you use simple English phrases to query, generate reports, and create, change, or delete forms from a file. See Table 11-1 for more information about Q&A.

Selected Relational Database Managers

Now let's examine a few multiple-file, relational database systems for MS-DOS computers. In general, these software packages are more expensive and require more training for users to become effective, but they offer more features.

dBASE III Plus By Ashton-Tate, this is currently the best-selling database for the personal computer. dBASE III Plus is based upon the previously best-selling database system, dBASE II, also by Ashton-Tate. A feature of dBASE III Plus called Assist provides pull-down menus and on-line help features, so beginners can perform tasks without programming. A screen painter feature helps users create custom screens to aid in data entry. An advanced query system provides an English-based method for searching and retrieving specific information. A view feature lets users see two or more files on the same screen, and the applications generator enables users to create custom applications without programming. dBASE III Plus can also be used in a local area network (LAN), so multiple users can access a single database. In its network mode, dBASE III Plus offers password protection, encryption of files and fields, and commands to limit access to specific files and records.

Paradox This database offers both ease of use and powerful features. The word *paradox* means something with seemingly contradictory qualities. The Paradox database package meets that definition. Like its chief competitors, dBASE III Plus and R:base System V, Paradox offers power and flexibility to create and use large, complex databases. However, Paradox is very easy to start using, especially for someone already familiar with a spreadsheet package such as Lotus 1-2-3. Paradox provides a Lotus-like menu structure and displays database files on the screen as though the files were spreadsheets. Across the top of the screen, the data field names are displayed as if they were column headings. Each record in the file is shown as if it were a row. Multiple files can be displayed by way of a horizontal window, thus providing the user with a visual display of files unlike most of the other database packages. Users can select, combine, and summarize information by checking off columns and setting criteria to select records. Reports can be designed onscreen, and data files can be easily transferred to and from other systems such as Lotus 1-2-3, Symphony, dBASE, PFS:File, and VisiCalc. Table 11-1 contains further information about Paradox.

R:base System V Sold by Microrim Incorporated, this is the latest version of the R:base family of software. It offers many advanced features. The less powerful version, R:base 5000, is designed to run on a microcomputer with just 256K of RAM and two floppy disk drives. It is relational and also provides an easy-to-use applications generator that guides the user through the steps of creating a database. R:base 5000 is designed for one-user systems. In contrast, R:base System V is available in both single-user and multiuser versions. Complex applications can be developed using simple menus rather than programming statements. Users can select and retrieve specific information from a database by using a query-by-example feature. Another feature of R:base System V is its ability to transfer data back and forth between mainframe databases as well as between other microcomputer software systems. R:base System V requires 512K RAM and a hard disk. See Table 11-1 for more information about R:base System V.

Other relational databases for MS-DOS computers include **Condor 3** by Condor Computer Corporation, **DAC-Easy Base** by Dac Software, **Oracle** by Oracle Corporation, and **Ingres for Personal Computers** by Relational Technology.

ON YOUR OWN

Now that you have learned some basic terminology regarding database applications, design and creation, and use, you are about ready to strike out on your own to create relational databases, perhaps for your personal use or as part of your professional career. The tutorial in Lesson 9 led you through the steps to create and use a single-file database. In Lesson 10 and in the Lesson 11 tutorial to follow shortly, you are led through the steps needed for multiple-file database design. Now you need to consider the more lifelike situation in which you are not told whether the problem to be solved is really a database application. You have to ask others what specific questions are to be answered by the database; the definition of the data entities is unclear; and it is not evident whether you should design the database as one large file or as several small files.

Is It a Database Application?

Earlier, we discussed some of the characteristics of database applications and how potential database applications differ from spreadsheet applications. In general, spreadsheet applications are more involved with numeric calculations and formulas. Database applications, in general, are more involved with alphabetic and alphanumeric data, and, instead of using formulas to do lots of calculations, database applications usually involve arranging data in alphabetic or numeric order, selecting certain records that meet some logical condition, and responding to users' queries about the status of data fields within selected records.

Sometimes it is also necessary to distinguish between word processing applications and database applications. Many word processing packages have mail-merge functions designed to facilitate the creation of mailing labels and to insert individual inside addresses and greetings on form letters. If the application is basically a mailing list, then a word processor would be simpler to use than a database.

To further complicate this issue, several software vendors now market integrated packages (such as Framework and Symphony) that simultaneously provide some, if not all, of the features of word processors, spreadsheets, and databases. In fact, Lotus 1-2-3, the most popular spreadsheet package, actually has a database feature that provides many of the standard database functions. It's very possible, as software gets more and more sophisticated, that the distinction between word processing, spreadsheets, and database management will become more and more blurred, especially as personal computers are introduced with larger RAM, and hard disks become standard. For now, however, it is still necessary to use some human judgment when determining whether a particular problem can be solved with a database package or with some other tool. Think of the characteristics of a database application, the common functions of a database management system, and the particular features and limitations of the hardware and software at your disposal.

What Questions Should the Database Answer?

In the tutorials and exercises presented so far in this book, you have been told which reports to create and have been led through the logical conditions and report statements needed to produce those reports. In industry the situation is likely to be much less clear. A manager may have a feeling that he or she needs more information to make a particular decision but may not be able to accurately and concisely express those needs in terminology that can easily be translated into file and data field definitions and well-formed logical conditions. Instead, what typically happens is better described as a repetitive trial and error process. A certain level of understanding is reached; a database is designed with some sample data; and a set of reports is produced. The decision maker, who with a personal computer may well be the same person who designed the database, will examine the reports and express a need for revisions. The process is often frustrating, but nevertheless common, even if the database designer and the decision maker are the same person.

People who design databases as a career become skilled at asking the right questions about just how the planned database will be used. Many use a process known as **prototyping** to quickly develop a small database and a few reports with a small amount of sample data as a preliminary step. Sometimes the reports are just **mock-ups** or simulations of the actual report. The benefit of this approach is that it allows the decision maker to look at something concrete and make suggestions for change. A good database system will allow the creator the flexibility to change the design of files and data fields and copy the data from the old structure into the new one, thus eliminating the need to rekey the data.

What Is the Entity or Entities?

Earlier, we discussed the difficulty of exactly defining the entity (person, place, or thing described by a record in a file). In simple situations the entity is easy to see. In an inventory application, each item that has a separate inventory number is an entity. In a personnel application, each employee is an entity. However, if you are dealing with projects involving employees, supervisors, budgets, vendors, and customers, there may be multiple entities, and it may not always be clear just how to identify and describe each record. Recall that a key field is a data field within a record that uniquely identifies that record, such as a social security number or a serial number.

Today's culture has made one area particularly difficult to define. What is the identifying field for a family or a household? A few years ago it was standard practice to use the husband's name to identify a household entity. Today that is not considered proper. One approach is to use the family's last name, but today some women keep their maiden names when they marry. Some people, like the first author of this book, hyphenate their last names, thus creating names that, in some cases, contain too many characters for the data field. The designer of a database must use human judgment to designate a key field that uniquely defines each record in a database; the decision is not automatic. When more than one field seem to be good candidates for the key field, this is a clue that more than one file may be needed in the database, and yet a third file may be needed to relate the two key fields to each other, thus creating the ability to cross-reference the files.

Create One Large File or Several Small Files?

Consider a university that needs to keep various items of information about each of its students. If it keeps all the items it needs about each student in a single file, the number of data fields in each record would be several hundred. If a flat-file database is used, each record in the file would have the same number of data fields, even if many of the fields are blank. Therefore, a record for a freshman who has just been admitted would need to be the same size as for a graduate student who has completed over 100 courses. Clearly, such a file design would be awkward and waste disk space. However, if the university keeps information about a single student on many different files, there can easily be problems of data redundancy and a lack of data integrity.

Recall that data redundancy is one of the things database designers try to minimize. Attempting to keep the same data item, such as a student's current address, in several different files also makes it difficult to maintain data integrity. When a student changes his or her address, as students frequently do, it is always possible that the change may be made to some of the files but not all of them. At that point the total information system lacks integrity. To the outside world it looks as if the organization maintaining the information system is confused and inaccurate.

In many cases, the answer to this paradox is a relational database system comprising several smaller files related to each other through clever design and software. The key is to understand how to cross-reference the various files. If two files need to be related, either they must share a common data field, or a narrow file must be created using one field from each of the two files. A third approach is to provide a path the software can follow from file to file that eventually connects the needed files.

Other Issues

Today many database users are interfacing with mainframe database systems, local area networks, and telecommunication systems. Going from a PC to a mainframe DBMS presents some new and interesting challenges. Whenever more than one user at a time will use a database, the software to manage that database system needs to be more sophisticated. For example, some files may be confidential and require a **lock-out** system to prevent unauthorized users from seeing or in any way altering the data in them. Users may identify themselves with account numbers and passwords. **Account numbers** are used to allocate computer-use charges to the proper budget. **Passwords** are secret signals that authorized users memorize and keep confidential, thereby preventing unauthorized use. If the user does not enter the proper password when asked, the computer logs off the user instead of allowing access to the files. At some military installations, entry of an improper password causes a hidden camera to take a photo of the user and triggers a siren to alert guards who arrest the unauthorized user.

Another interfacing problem occurs when a PC user wants to analyze data in a file stored on the mainframe. A typical approach is to provide the PC user with a copy of all or part of the file from the mainframe database. The copy is then stored on the PC disk, and the PC user utilizes a database management system to search and retrieve selected data records. However, while the PC user is working with this copy of the file, the mainframe database is constantly being updated with new data. This again raises the issue of data integrity. The data in one part of a firm's information system are different from the data in another part. Firms must establish suitable procedures to regulate PC users, but PC users are known as an independent lot who do not take kindly to rules that appear to inhibit their freedom. One approach some large firms use is to require all reports generated from a database to contain dates indicating when the data was extracted from the mainframe database and when the database was last updated. The reports should also caution the reader about possible discrepancies caused by more recent updates to the file.

TUTORIAL: BUILDING AND USING A DATABASE WITH MULTIPLE FILES USING dBASE III PLUS

To complete this tutorial you need the following:

- MS-DOS system disk or MS-DOS on the dBASE disk
- dBASE III Plus disk
- A data disk
- A printer connected to the microcomputer

While completing this tutorial you will learn how to

- Create four separate files
- Create a relation on the files
- Produce a report using the relation

A wholesale sport shoes store, Hallam's Sport Shoes, wants you to create a database system of four files: ITEM, to hold information about each item in their inventory; CUSTOMER, to hold information about each of their customers; ORDERS, to hold information about each order received; and ORDERITM to tell what quantity of each item was ordered for each order. In actual practice each file would contain more data, but for this tutorial we are simplifying the file structure to minimize the amount of typing needed yet still illustrate the important concepts. The structure for each file is as follows:

ITEM			
ITEMNO	NUMERIC	4	
DESC	CHARACTER	30	
PRICE	NUMERIC	6	2
CUSTOMER			
CUSTNO	NUMERIC	4	
NAME	CHARACTER	20	
STREET	CHARACTER	20	
CITY	CHARACTER	15	
STATE	CHARACTER	2	
ZIP	CHARACTER	5	
ORDERS			
ORDNO	NUMERIC	4	
CUSTNO	NUMERIC	4	
ORDER DATE	DATE	8	
ORDERITM			
ORDNO	NUMERIC	4	
QTY	NUMERIC	3	
ITEMNO	NUMERIC	4	

Using dBASE III Plus with The Assistant, create each database file and input the following data in each file:

ITEM

ITEMNO	DESC	PRICE
1001	10K Running Shoes	45.00
1002	Marathon Shoes	75.00
1003	Basketball Shoes	45.00
1004	Track Shoes	35.00
1005	Football Shoes	50.00

Index the ITEM file on ITEMNO using Assist or the command

```
index on ITEMNO to ITEM
```

CUSTOMER

CUSTNO	NAME	STREET	CITY	STATE	ZIP
0001	John Smith	202 Park Ave.	DeKalb	IL	60115
0002	Pat Delaney	123 Elm	Sycamore	IL	60178
0003	Don Kieso	780 Lakeshore	Lake Holiday	IL	60345
0004	Richard Baker	789 Billings	Sycamore	IL	60178
0005	Mark Martinet	404 W. Pine	DeKalb	IL	60115

Index the CUSTOMER file on CUSTNO using Assist or the command

```
index on CUSTNO to CUSTOMER
```

Enter the following data:

ORDERS (Remember, do not enter slashes; they will be inserted automatically.)

ORDNO	CUSTNO	ORDERDATE
0001	0001	01/15/88
0002	0004	01/23/88
0003	0005	01/29/88
0004	0002	02/01/88
0005	0003	02/03/88
0006	0005	02/07/88
0007	0004	02/15/88
0008	0002	02/18/88

Index the ORDERS file on ORDNO and CUSTNO, using Assist or entering the commands

```
index on ORDNO to ORDERS
index on CUSTNO to ORDERS2
```

Enter the following data:

ORDERITM

ORDNO	QTY	ITEMNO
0001	10	0001
0001	2	0002
0002	4	0002
0003	40	0001
0003	10	0005
0004	6	0004
0005	10	0004
0006	12	0003
0007	25	0005
0007	45	0002
0008	12	0003
0008	12	0005

Index ORDERITM on ORDNO and ITEMNO, using Assist or entering the commands

```
index on ORDNO to ORDERITM
index on ITEMNO to ORDERITM
```

Now create a relation and produce a report, using the commands

```
select 1
use ORDERITM
select 2
use item
select ORDERITM
set relation to ITEMNO into ITEM
list ORDNO, QTY, ITEM->DESC, ITEM->PRICE, QTY*ITEM->PRICE OFF
```

This sequence of commands tells the computer to produce a list on the screen, using the ORDNO and QTY from the file called ORDERITM, but to get the DESC and the PRICE from the file called ITEM and multiply the QTY by the PRICE. OFF turns off the record number. The report should look like the one in Figure 11-6.

The report in Figure 11-6 used the ORDNO from the ORDERITM file, the QTY from the ORDERITM file, the DESCription from the ITEM file, and the PRICE from the ITEM file, and then multiplied the QTY from the ORDERITM file by the PRICE from the ITEM file, a feat nearly impossible without a relational database management system such as dBASE III Plus.

Now let's examine how we can use the Join command to produce another report, this time to match order numbers (ORDNO) with customer numbers (CUSTNO) and order dates (ORDERDATE). Use the following commands:

```
clear all
select 1
use ORDERS
select 2
use ORDERITM
select 1
join with ORDERITM to ORDREP for
ORDNO=ORDERITM->ORDNO fields ORDNO, CUSTNO, ORDERDATE, QTY, ITEMNO
```

```
ORDNO QTY ITEM->DESC             ITEM->PRICE  QTY*ITEM->PRICE
    1  10 10K Running Shoes            45.00           450.00
    1   2 Marathon Shoes               75.00           150.00
    2   4 Marathon Shoes               75.00           300.00
    3  40 10K Running Shoes            45.00          1800.00
    3  10 Football Shoes               50.00           500.00
    4   6 Track Shoes                  35.00           210.00
    5  10 Track Shoes                  35.00           350.00
    6  12 Basketball Shoes             45.00           540.00
    7  25 Football Shoes               50.00          1250.00
    7  45 Marathon Shoes               75.00          3375.00
    8  12 Basketball Shoes             45.00           540.00
    8  12 Football Shoes               50.00           600.00
```

FIGURE 11-6 The report produced by the command list ORDNO,QTY,ITEM->DESC,ITEM->PRICE,QTY*ITEM->PRICE OFF

FIGURE 11-7 The display produced when ORDERS is joined with ORDERITM.

```
ORDNO CUSTNO ORDER DATE
    1      1 01/15/88
    2      4 01/23/88
    3      5 01/29/88
    4      2 02/01/88
    5      3 02/03/88
    6      5 02/07/88
    7      4 02/15/88
    8      2 02/18/88
```

These tell the computer to join ORDERS with ORDERITM, making a new file called ORDREP in which the field called ORDNO in ORDERS is equal to the field called ORDNO in the file called ORDERITM. It will then put into this new file (called ORDREP) the fields called ORDNO, CUSTNO, ORDERDATE, QTY, and ITEMNO.

After you press **Return** you should see the message

```
12 records joined
```

Enter the command

```
display all off
```

The report should look like the one in Figure 11-7.

Try other relations and joins. When you think you have mastered the technique, enter

```
quit
```

to end this session.

SUMMARY

The standard problem-solving method of defining goals, gathering data, testing alternatives, and implementing the best solution can be applied to the problem of selecting the best database software to fit your needs or the needs of your employer. To define the user's goals, start with a list of the questions the user wants the finished database to be able to answer. Magazines, experienced users, and vendors can all supply information about alternative software packages, but nothing beats a "test drive" in which the user actually tries out the software using a small but representative database application. The tutorials found within this book can be used to test the various packages, and the checklist of features in this lesson also provides a list of considerations.

Flat-file database managers—such as PFS:Professional File, Q&A, and Reflex—provide low-cost, simple database management software. Relational database managers—such as dBASE III Plus, Paradox, and R:base System V—offer more advanced features and the ability to cross-reference two or more files within a database.

You have now reached the end of the lessons on word processing, spreadsheets, and databases and should be ready to tackle several microcomputer applications on your own. When you are dealing with real-life problems, rather than textbook tutorials and exercises, you need to use judgment to determine if a particular problem really is a database application area or not. Sometimes the choice of the proper microcomputer software tool is unclear, but the concepts presented in each of these lessons and in the various tutorials and exercises should provide some general guidelines and examples to consider. Often the process of defining the user's needs, creating a database system for the user to try, and revising the database system is a very repetitive process because of the difficulty most people have clearly defining their needs and understanding how a database can aid the decision-making process. Being able to quickly create a small database using sample data and mock-up reports greatly facilitates this design process.

Currently, many database users are dealing with the issue of integrating their personal computer database software with their firm's mainframe database system and/or local area network system. This step forces users to give more thought to security issues, passwords, lock-outs, and account numbers because several users may now have access to what previously was private information. The database management area promises to be one of great potential as more and more people realize the power of selecting and retrieving the right information to aid decision making.

EXERCISES

1. Define the following terms.

relational database	Set Relation command	.DBF
tuple	information	.SDF
attribute	shareware	data manipulation
relation	record size	indexing
ordered set	data conversion	sorting
entity	forced upper case	multiple record deletions and updates
key field	automatic data entry	table merging/joining
linking field	calculated fields on screen entry	command strategy
data redundancy	data import	horizontal bar menus
one-to-many	data export	pop-up menus
data integrity	ASCII	vertical menus
Join		typed commands
Select command		

input facilities	predefined mailing labels	data encryption
user defined	query capabilities	crosstab report
automatic	user-access security provisions	prototyping
programmed	passwords	mockups
output facilities		lock-out
multiple-file reports		account numbers

2. For the following database software packages, indicate whether each is a single-file system or a multiple-file system and name at least one other distinguishing feature of each package:
   a. Reflex
   b. Q&A
   c. dBASE III Plus
   d. R:base System V
   e. Paradox
   f. PFS: Professional File
3. List the four general problem-solving steps and discuss how they apply to the issue of selecting the proper database management system for a microcomputer.
4. Use the database software selection checklist to review four database management software systems. Use WordPerfect to write a report about what you found out and your conclusions. Which database management software system would you buy for yourself? Which would you buy for a business?
5. Assume that you work for a small nonprofit organization whose sole source of income is donations. Develop a database system for keeping track of donors and gifts. The DONORS file structure looks like the following:

FIELD NAME	TYPE	WIDTH	DEC
DONORID	N	3	
TITLE	C	4	
FIRST	C	10	
LAST	C	10	
ADDRESS1	C	20	
ADDRESS2	C	20	
ZIP	N	5	
TOTGIVING	N	10	2

The DONORS file is kept in numeric order by the DONORID number. The records of each gift are kept in chronological order by date of donation, and the GIFT file structure looks like the following:

FIELD NAME	TYPE	WIDTH	DEC
DONORID	N	3	
DATE	D		
AMOUNT	N	10	2

Use data supplied by your instructor or make up your own data for approximately 25 donors and 100 gifts. Make various reports, such as the following:

a. List the donors who gave more than $100.

b. List the donors within a certain Zip code area.

c. List the donors who did not give during this month.

d. Select and retrieve the records of gifts of particular donors.

6. Create a new database called CASES and relate it to the CLIENTS database used in Lessons 9 and 10. The structure of the CASES database is as follows:

FIELD	NAME	TYPE	WIDTH	DEC
1	CASENO	Numeric	3	0
2	ACCTNO	Numeric	3	0
3	DESC	Character	40	
4	ATTY	Character	10	
5	HOURS	Numeric	5	1

Enter the following data:

CASENO	ACCTNO	DESC	ATTY	HOURS
201	101	Tax Prep	TAH	2.0
202	102	Will & Estate	SFH	3.0
203	102	Court Appearance	SFH	1.0
204	103	House Closing	JAH	1.0
205	104	Tax Prep	TAH	2.0
206	105	Will & Estate	SFH	2.0

Use the Join command to merge the CLIENTS database with the CASES database and create a third database called NEWFILE in which the ACCTNOs for both CLIENTS and CASES match. Using NEWFILE, create a listing that shows the ACCTNO, CASENO, and LNAME of each client with a case listed in CASENO.

Use the Set Relation command to define a relation between the two files based on ACCTNO and create the same listing as requested above.

7. Complete Exercise 9-3, creating the database called CUSTOMER. After more careful examination, the user has decided that what is needed is two files—a master file containing the names and addresses of the customers and a transaction file containing the items ordered. The two files can be linked by a customer account number.

Design the two file structures and enter the existing data from Exercise 9-3 plus at least ten transactions in which each transaction represents an order from a customer for one or more items.

8. Complete Exercise 9-4. Then create a similar database called BOOKS123 to file references for books about Lotus 1-2-3. Use the following data as a start:

AUTHOR	**TITLE**	**PUBLISHER**	**CITY**	**YEAR**
Cobb, Douglas F.	1-2-3 for Business	Que	Indianapolis	1984
Lotus Books	The Lotus Guide to 1-2-3 Advanced Macro Commands	Addison-Wesley	Reading	1986
Adams, Eddie	Command Performance Lotus 1-2-3	Microsoft Press	Bellevue	1986
Lotus Books	The Lotus Guide to Learning 1-2-3	Addison-Wesley	Reading	1985
Person, Ron	1-2-3 Business Formula Handbook	Que	Indianapolis	1986
Molloy, James F., and Dennis P. Curtin	Business Problem Solving with Lotus 1-2-3	Curtin & London	New York	1984
Hallam, Teresa, et al.	Microcomputer Use	Harcourt Brace Jovanovich	San Diego	1988

Prepare a report, based on the relation between the two files, that lists books written by the same author.

9. Examine Exercise 9-5, in which a database called WORKERS was created. Consider the employee information needs of a firm that employs approximately 100 workers. The master file of the firm's database should contain those fields that will need to be updated least frequently—for example, the employee identification number, name, date of start of employment with firm, and level of education. A transaction file may contain fields of number of hours worked in the current pay period, pay adjustments due to overtime or bonus pay conditions, and other information needed to produce the weekly or monthly paycheck. Still another file may contain fields about each employee's skill levels in various categories, on-the-job training courses completed, and other information of interest to someone in the personnel department who might be seeking a person with particular skills for a position. Find a local small business or organization and request permission to interview the manager about his or her personnel database needs. Create a database to fulfill as many of those needs as your time and talent will allow.

10. Create your own database containing multiple files. What entities are important in the model, and what relationships link the entities together? Create various reports that draw information from several files.

FIVE
OTHER MICROCOMPUTER SOFTWARE

Part V examines some of the thousands of other microcomputer applications that are being used and developed. Although you may not use these applications as immediately as word processing, electronic spreadsheets, and database management, you will no doubt utilize these new and exciting microcomputer applications in the future. Lesson 12 describes data communications and public-access databases. Lesson 13 examines statistical and graphics software. Lesson 14 surveys a variety of applications in management. These areas have been chosen for further discussion because of their increasing popularity and potential.

12
Data Communications

LESSON OUTLINE

The preceding lessons introduced you to three of the most popular uses of personal computers: word processing, spreadsheets, and databases. To many people, however, the most useful application of the microcomputer is none of these; it is, instead, *data communications.* These people use their microcomputers to communicate with large mainframe computers, with other microcomputers, and with each other. The basic tools in a microcomputer data communications system include a microcomputer, a modem (hardware), a data communications software package (software), and telephone lines (communication channel). With such a system, you can also use several of the services provided by public-access databases. This lesson introduces you to these and other aspects of data communications.

Imagine sitting at home and having access to some of the largest, most sophisticated computer databases in the world. You decide to get a listing of all the articles published in the last two years about computer simulation of manufacturing processes. After giving some short, simple commands and waiting a few minutes, you get a listing of hundreds of articles. Perhaps you want to make an airline reservation or find out how your stock investments are doing. You also might discuss the state of the world with people located hundreds or thousands of miles away, or transmit a manuscript to a coauthor, or share a database, or access specialized equipment. All of these data communications capabilities exist today.

Since this book focuses on the microcomputer, we are going to describe and discuss the data communications system as it specifically relates to the microcomputer. Of course, large computers also play a major role in many data communications systems. Often they are the hub of a large network of terminals, microcomputers, minicomputers, and other mainframes, all communicating with each other in a complex system of data communications. Developing a comprehensive understanding of such complex systems is beyond the scope of this book, but we can discuss some of the basic concepts involved in becoming a knowledgeable user of a variety of data communications systems.

WHAT IS DATA COMMUNICATIONS?

Data communications is the transmission of digital data from one location to another. Today, most of that transmission is over telephone lines. A data communications system that uses telephone lines for data transmission is referred to as a **telecommunications system.**

Data communications systems are made up of hardware and software that permit the transmission of the data. The hardware in most data communications systems include computers (mainframes, minicomputers, or microcomputers), terminals, modems, and communications channels (see Figure 12-1).

DATA COMMUNICATIONS HARDWARE

A **terminal** is a device used to send and receive data. With the proper hardware and software, a microcomputer can serve as a terminal in a communications system. A **communications channel** is a bi-directional data path between input/output devices and the main memory in a computer. The most common communications channel is a telephone line.

In a microcomputer-based communications system, the transmission of data starts with someone entering a message at a microcomputer. The electrical impulses produced are translated into digital signals (0's and 1's) by the microcomputer. For these signals to be transmitted to another computer, communications software must be installed in the microcomputer so that it acts as a terminal, and some connection must be made between two or more locations. There are a variety of data transmission

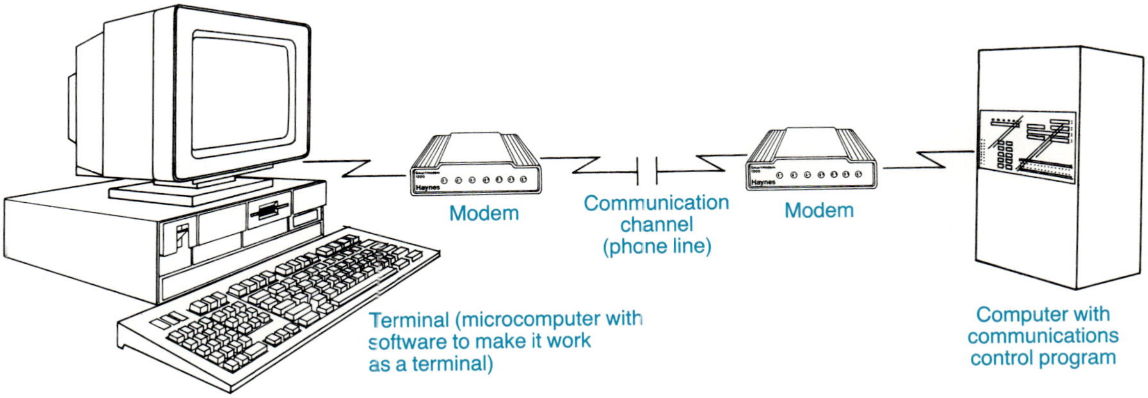

FIGURE 12-1 The hardware used in a data communications system: a terminal (a microcomputer with communications software to emulate a terminal), modems (to convert the signals from digital to analog and back to allow transmission over a phone line), a communications channel (usually a phone line), and a computer with a communications control program (a mainframe, minicomputer, or microcomputer).

mediums, including coaxial cable, radio signals, fiber optic cable, and microwave. **Coaxial cable** is a transmission cable made up of a conducting outer metal tube enclosing and insulating a core conductor. **Fiber optic cable** is made up of hair-thin glass fibers that allow light beams to be bent and reflected with low levels of signal loss and interference.

Although telephone lines are the most common connecting medium for communications network systems, there is a fundamental problem in the transmission of data over phone lines. Telephone lines are not designed to carry the digital impulses produced by the computer. They are designed primarily to carry the human voice as **analog** signals, a modulating wave representing sound. This problem is solved through the use of modems.

Modems

A **modem** is a device for converting the digital impulses coming from the computer into the signals that can be transmitted over telephone lines. The word *modem* is a contraction of *MO*dulation and *DEM*odulation. **Modulation** is the conversion of the digital, direct-current pulses used by the computer system into an analog signal containing the same information. This analog signal can then be transmitted through the voice-only channels of the telephone system. **Demodulation** is the reverse process (see Figure 12-2). Modems are necessary because normal telephone links will not allow digital, direct-current signals to pass. Modems, therefore, are essential links between phone lines and computers. They both modulate (when sending) and demodulate (when receiving) signals. One is needed at each end of the data transmission.

There are two basic categories of modems: direct connect and acoustic. With a **direct-connect modem,** the phone line is connected to the modem through a modular phone jack that plugs into a modem, forming an electrical connection. There are two types of direct-connect modems: external, or stand alone, and internal. An **internal modem** is placed within the microcomputer main system unit, usually in an expan-

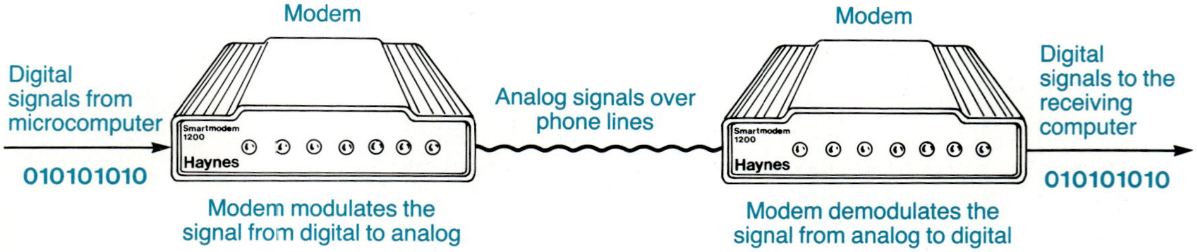

FIGURE 12-2 The modem performs the essential job of converting transmission from digital to analog signals and back so phone lines can be used for data communications.

sion slot, whereas external modems have the circuitry in a separate unit outside the microcomputer. Internal modems can be purchased and added on by the user or installed by the manufacturer. Internal modems are usually in the form of a board or card that is inserted into the expansion board in the microcomputer.

An **external modem** is a small box containing the modem circuitry connected to the microcomputer with a cable through the serial port in the back of the microcomputer. A **port** is a channel through which data flows in and out of the microcomputer for the connection of a specific circuit or piece of peripheral equipment such as a modem, printer, or external disk drive. The phone line is connected to the modem through a modular phone jack that plugs directly into the modem.

Acoustic modems use an acoustic coupler to link a modem and a standard desktop telephone by sound waves rather than by an electrical connection. The acoustic coupler converts the analog signals made by the modem into sounds that are picked up by the microphone in the telephone handset and passed through the telephone network again as electrical signals. A microphone in the acoustic coupler picks up the sounds emitting from the earpiece of the handset, converts them to analog electrical signals, and supplies them to the modem. Most couplers have two rubber cups that surround the mouthpiece and earpiece of the telephone handset. Acoustic couplers were invented before telephone regulations permitted individuals to connect modems directly to their telephone lines. They are used today because they can be easily connected and disconnected from nonmodular telephones that have no direct access to the system wiring, such as pay phones or certain hotel room phones. In addition, acoustic couplers are usually low in price because they do not require the elaborate circuitry of direct-connect modems. However, an acoustic coupler is not as reliable or as fast as a direct-connect modem. The receiver used in an acoustic coupler may also pick up noise that interferes with accurate data transmission.

Figure 12-3 illustrates a common type of acoustic modem, an external direct-connect modem, and an internal direct-connect modem on an expansion board. All modulate and demodulate communications signals for transmission over telephone lines.

The speed of transmission of the data is measured in terms of individual **bits per second (bps)**. Remember, a bit is a binary digit (0 or 1). This is commonly referred to as the **baud rate,** even though the term *bps* is technically more correct. Most data communications involving microcomputers currently use a transmission rate of either 300 bps or 1,200 bps, but 2,400-bps and 9,600-bps modems are becoming more popular. The higher the bps rate, the faster the data transmission. At a rate of 1,200 bps, for example, a 40-page document can be transmitted in approximately 10 to 15 minutes. As the data transmission speed increases, the quality of the telephone line becomes more critical. Mainframe computers transmit data over dedicated data lines, such as cables between other mainframes

FIGURE 12-3 An acoustic modem *(a)* uses an acoustic coupler to link a modem and a standard telephone by sound waves rather than by an electrical connection. A direct-connect modem has the phone line plugged directly into the modem. An external direct-connect modem *(b)* has the circuitry in a separate unit outside the microcomputer. An internal direct-connect modem *(c)* is placed within the microcomputer main system unit, usually in an expansion slot.

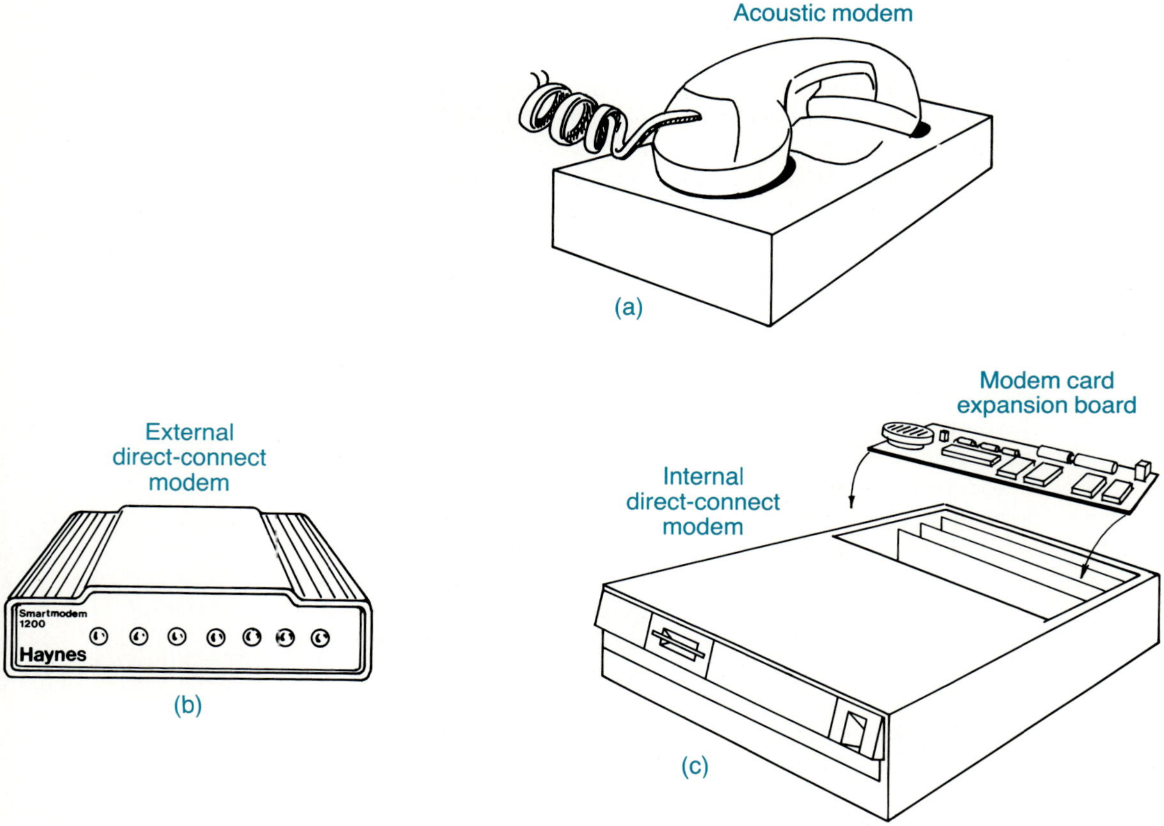

and minicomputers, at even higher rates since they do not have to deal with the telephone line noise.

Networks

For frequent long-distance transmissions, there are other networks in addition to public telephone networks available to microcomputer users. These include *value-added networks* and *private telephone networks.*

Value-added networks include Tymnet and Telenet telephone systems. These systems use hardware and software with a technique called **packet switching** to route the data on leased telephone circuits between the network connections. These telephone systems also provide back-up equipment, alternative data routing, and error-checking of the transmissions to insure better data transmission than through the public telephone system. In addition to producing high-quality data transmissions, these value-added networks are usually less expensive than the public telephone system. However, these networks are not offered in some rural areas.

A **local area network** usually does not use telephone lines but instead employs coaxial cable, fiber optic cable, or other direct lines. Such systems use a combination of specialized hardware and software to connect computers within a local area, such as one building or a series of buildings owned by one firm. Such networks are becoming an increasingly popular way to share expensive computer equipment, such as laser printers, or to exchange messages through electronic mail.

The second major category of telephone system alternatives is **private telephone networks,** such as MCI and Sprint. Their main advantage is that they are less expensive than regular public telephone long distance, a consideration that grows in importance when one becomes a heavy user of data communications over long-distance telephone lines.

DATA COMMUNICATIONS SOFTWARE

In addition to a microcomputer, a modem, and a communications channel, a data communications system also needs software. **Data communications software** directs a microcomputer to emulate a terminal so that it can send and receive data. **Emulate** means to imitate, or operate as another piece of hardware. Normally, microcomputers take the data and commands input from the keyboard or disk file and process them. Once data communications software is loaded into the microcomputer, the microcomputer is "tricked" into thinking that it is a terminal, so it can communicate with other computers. Commands given at the keyboard are transmitted to the remote computer for execution, rather than being processed by the local microcomputer.

Most popular data communications software packages have a wide range of sophisticated features to help users, including **online help,** the additional explanation of commands when requested; menus and function key commands; **auto-dialing,** the automatic dialing of a phone number a specified number of times until a connection is established; **auto-log-on,** the automatic registration of the user with the remote computer, including any necessary account numbers and passwords; **data capture,** the collection of incoming data in RAM and then saving it to a disk file; **file transfer,** the coordinated transmission and receipt of files directly from disk by using predefined protocols. **Protocols** are established sets of rules for data communications. Protocols may include rules for modem frequency, speed, and type of modulation; **flow-control protocol** specifies the characters used to tell the sending computer to stop when the receiving computer is busy; and **error-checking protocol** establishes ways to acknowledge receipt of data or to request the resending of data.

Data communications software provides an automatic verification process to check the accuracy of the data transmission in various ways, including sending two copies of the message and comparing the two transmissions to be sure they are identical. In another approach, the software adds up the value of the 0's and 1's sent and compares that sum to the sum of the 0's and 1's in the original document. This verification process prevents "garbage" (erroneous characters) from being transmitted undetected. The data communications software not only checks for possible errors in transmission but also converts the format of a Macintosh file, for example, into a file readable by an IBM PC and back again, so the message can be processed by both computers. In fact, some people use data communications systems to handle the problem of incompatible computer systems between different users. For example, users of CompuServe, a popular public-access database to be described later in this lesson, regularly use a variety of incompatible personal computers, such as Apples, IBMs, and Commodores, to exchange messages and text files despite hardware differences.

DATA COMMUNICATIONS AND THE WORK WORLD

Data communications is actually changing the nature of work for many people. Some people work at home and use data communications systems to transmit their work to their employers. It is even possible to use a battery-powered microcomputer and do work while traveling or while camping in the woods. Handicapped people can use such devices to communicate even though they may be unable to travel to work or hear or speak. In fact, when people discuss the transmission rate of data communications, they use the term *baud rate,* named after **Emile Baudot,** a Frenchman who was deaf. Over a hundred years ago Baudot used printing telegraphy to communicate with other deaf people.

Data communications has already changed the nature of the work world for many people and will, no doubt, affect the way many more people work in the future. For some, data communications makes it possible to earn a living where it was impossible or extremely difficult before. For others, it provides freedom and flexibility not previously available. Another service made possible by the field of data communications is access to publicly available databases.

ONLINE DATABASES

An **online database** is a collection of files and services available electronically. With over 3,000 online data bases, you can find information on almost any topic imaginable by using a microcomputer, a modem, and a telephone. For example, you can search electronic versions of encyclopedias, examine *Books in Print,* investigate the *Readers' Guide to Periodical Literature,* find out the weather forecast for any location in the world, check the latest news and stock quotes, and make hotel and airline reservations. You can exchange electronic mail instantly, participate in a forum to discuss the latest events with friends with similar interests, share computer software, and find help for any problem from medical questions to computer hardware queries. Services such as Cupcake's Column on CompuServe offer the latest gossip about the online social scene.

A wide variety of services are available, from narrowly focused databases such as the law database Lexis to very broad databases such as The Source. Basically there are three types of services: communications, database, and videotext.

Communications-oriented services, such as MCI Mail and EasyLink by Western Union, offer electronic mail, message, bulletin board, and some gateway services, primarily for business users. **Electronic mail** is the private electronic exchange of correspondence between specific individuals. Usually both the sender and the receiver must be members of the service, although some offer mailing services for nonmembers. A **bulletin board** is a public area, much like the traditional company bulletin board, where members exchange messages, ask for and give opinions, and get information. When an online database offers the members access to other databases, it is offering a **gateway service.**

Database services, such as Dialog and BRS (Bibliographic Retrieval Service), offer a vast collection of information, from listings of books in print to Census Bureau information to magazine bibliographies. Such services are marketed toward business and academic users.

Videotext services, such as CompuServe and The Source, have a wide variety of database, communications, shopping, game, and other services appealing primarily to home, business, and educational users.

Making the best choice for an online database depends on your interests, needs, experience, and finances. For example, if your needs are primarily for academic research, then Dialog may be what you need. Of course the $1 per minute average charge may make it impractical. Fortunately, many of the Dialog databases are available through less expensive services. No matter which service a user chooses, online databases open a new wide world of computing. Let's look at some of the more popular online databases.

Communications Services

Communications services, such as Easylink and MCI Mail, provide electronic mail and bulletin board services, usually to businesses. Many corporations find such services essential for communications between geographically separated groups. Some organizations have their own in-house electronic mail and bulletin board systems. However, this requires sophisticated hardware, software, and communication lines, which may not be cost effective. Many groups find that, by contracting with communication services, they can have the convenience of electronic mail without the overhead expense.

EasyLink A service of Western Union, **EasyLink** gives users access to a range of sophisticated electronic message options. **Mailbox** lets EasyLink subscribers exchange messages with other users of the system. **Telex**

permits EasyLink users to send Telex messages to over 200,000 businesses in the United States, Canada, and Mexico with Telex terminals. **Overseas Telex** offers access to the over 1.5 million subscribers to the Worldwide Telex network. **Mailgrams** are inexpensive overnight letters that can be sent to anyone in the United States, Puerto Rico, and Canada. The electronic message is transmitted to a location where it is printed and sent through the postal service with the next day's mail. If an EasyLink subscriber needs to send a message to a domestic location quickly, then the **Telegram** service may be the answer. The user enters the message electronically, and the Western Union operators then deliver a telegram by phone in a few hours to any location in the United States. A printed copy is mailed if the recipient requests it. **Cablegrams** can be delivered overnight to overseas locations not served by Telex. **Express Document** gives EasyLink users the option of having documents electronically transmitted and then delivered within two hours or overnight as letter-quality documents.

In addition to the sophisticated electronic communications, EasyLink also offers **FYI,** a business and consumer database that includes news, stock quotes, and airline information; and **InfoMaster,** a database service offering access to over 700 databases.

MCI Mail A subsidiary of MCI Communications, the long-distance phone company, **MCI Mail** offers a wide range of sophisticated electronic mail options with some additional database services. MCI Mail offers four classes of domestic mail service: electronic mail (messages are sent and received electronically between users' mailboxes); printed copy with four-hour delivery (provided your recipient lives within 25 miles of a MCI Mail postal center); printed copy with overnight delivery; and regular letters (after being laser printed at an MCI Mail postal center, the letter is put in the nearest mailbox and delivered by the U.S. Postal Service). Regular letters can be printed on letterhead stationery for an extra fee. International correspondence is sent electronically to special MCI Mail centers and delivered by the destination country's postal service or by courier. Like EasyLink, MCI Mail also offers communications through Telex.

MCI Mail has a variety of services for high-volume users, including automatic electronic mailing lists, custom-printed mailings with inserts, and company-specific bulletin boards. Additional database services include access to Dow Jones News/Retrieval Service as well as CompuServe E-Mail systems.

Database Services

Database services are large public-access databases that specialize in the type of information you would normally find in an encyclopedia. These are also known as **encyclopedic utilities.**

Bibliographic Retrieval Service **BRS** was started in 1976 and offers over 125 databases through three services—BRS/After Dark, BRS/Brkthru, and BRS/Search Service—providing business and educational references to approximately 15,000 users. Each offers a different selection of databases and services. *BRS/After Dark* offers evening access to 35 of the most popular BRS databases. *BRS/Brkthru* offers nearly the same databases with the convenience of menu-assisted searching. Both BRS/Search and BRS/Brkthru are for business-hour searching. *BRS/Search* offers command-driven, direct access to a wide variety of databases. It contains many of the same sources that you will find in Dialog, another encyclopedic database. The main difference between Bibliographic Retrieval Service and Dialog is that Bibliographic Retrieval Service is a *full-text* service. It has, for example, the complete text for the *Harvard Business Review.* Bibliographic Retrieval Service lets subscribers access the news portion of the Dow Jones News/Retrieval System. Users can also access other information services, such as the *New York Times* Information Bank II.

BRS/After Dark and BRS/Brkthru have a one-time $75 registration fee, whereas BRS/Search charges a $75 annual registration fee. Basic online costs are approximately $50 per year plus 58 cents per minute and for BRS/Search, a database royalty fee averaging $1 per minute. BRS/After Dark charges approximately 10 cents to 52 cents per minute with a $12 per month minimum. Brkthru menu service is billed at various hourly rates. Other costs include document charges and telecommunication charges. Support services include user instructions, a magazine, and optional guides. BRS, like Dialog, offers full- and half-day training seminars for a fee as well as toll-free telephone support.

Dialog One of the most comprehensive encyclopedic databases available, **Dialog Information Services** emphasizes business, professional, and educational applications. Dialog is a subsidiary of Lockheed Missile and Space Corporation. The system was designed originally to supply NASA with a computerized documentation program on U.S. space activities. Dialog now offers access to more than 250 databases with an estimated 115 million items available online. Such databases are excellent for professional researchers as well as for the individual home computer user. Dialog has approximately 70,000 members, and even more users have access through educational and corporate memberships. Dialog is command oriented, requiring users to thoroughly understand the search command structures. However, Dialog offers training classes and documentation to help new users. In addition, search software is available from other vendors.

Information is presented to the user in two forms: bibliographic citations or abstracts. The bibliographic information tells you the subject of the material in the book, article, magazine, or other item being researched, and then you must locate the material in a library or book store. The abstract form of information provides a summary of the item being researched, including most of the facts and figures you would need. The full text of the document is generally not available online.

As a part of Dialog, the *Knowledge Index* is presented as a low-cost, limited service designed for the home personal computer user who wants less expensive access during non-prime-time (evening) hours. Knowledge Index charges a set hourly fee instead of the variable fee charged by Dialog. In addition, Knowledge Index allows credit card billing. *Business Connection,* another Dialog-associated service, offers custom business databases according to the individual user's needs. Such databases have information concerning corporate intelligence, financial screening, products, and markets. The user selects which business-oriented Dialog databases are needed and then accesses them through custom menus.

There is no initial registration fee for Dialog; however, there are charges for the user's guide ($50), for the orientation and training courses ($55 to $125 per day), and for the basic online time ($1 per minute on average). In addition, some databases have additional charges for displaying found records. Business Connection charges a $145 registration fee that includes software and $100 worth of free connect time, a $1.40 per minute online fee, and a surcharge for displaying records. Knowledge Index has a registration fee of $35, a 40 cents per minute basic online fee, and surcharges for displaying records from some databases. The electronic mail service Dialmail costs 20 cents per minute.

Videotext Services

Remember, *videotext services* offer a wide variety of online services, including access to encyclopedic databases and to communications, shopping, game, and other services. In contrast to Dialog and BRS, such services are aimed primarily at home and business users. Among the most popular videotext services are The Source and CompuServe.

The Source

Founded in 1979 by Telecommunication Corporation of America (TCA) in McLean, Virginia, **The Source** was sold to Reader's Digest in 1980. Reader's Digest invested millions to make The Source an information utility that, like the popular *Reader's Digest* magazine, provides over 100,000 people with self-help information at a reasonable cost to aid them in personal and business decisions. It is targeted at business, professional, and home users. Today The Source provides more than 1,200 different features, including special interest groups (SIGs), news services, communications, and online shopping as well as online live conferencing (Participate). The different divisions of services provided by The Source are charted in Figure 12-4.

One of the unique features of The Source is *Chat.* You can "chat" with anyone logged onto The Source. Your typed message will appear on the person's screen. This is similar to the "chats" CB users have on their citizens band radios. All you need to know is your "good buddy's" user number, which is easily available by asking for a list of users currently logged onto the system. The list can be narrowed down by geographic

FIGURE 12-4 The major divisions of services offered by The Source.

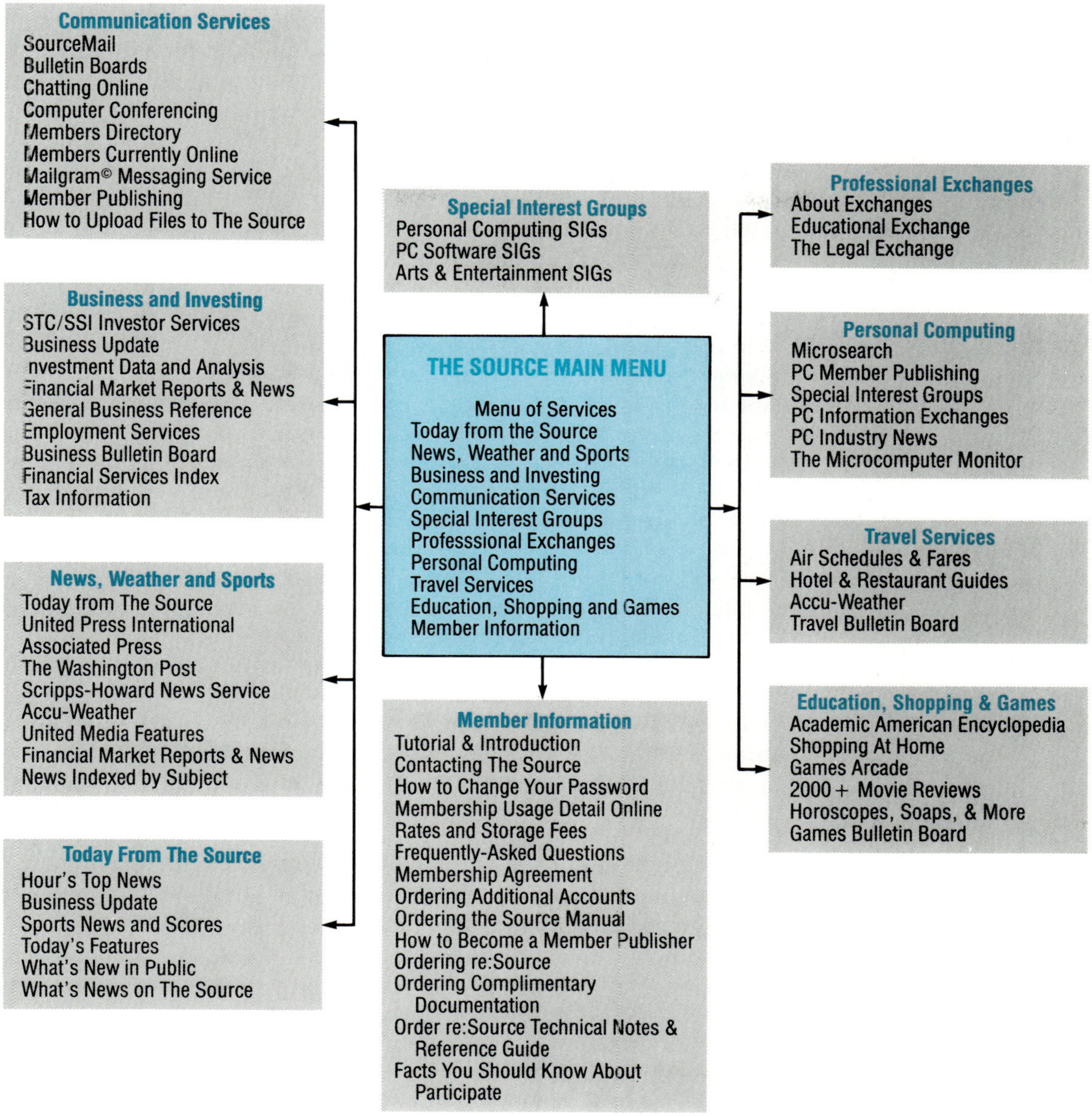

location (you've always wanted to talk to somebody from Alaska). If you are using The Source and do not want to be interrupted by a chat, you can turn off the chat option.

The Source charges a registration fee of approximately $30, or $45 with a user's manual. Basic online costs include a $10 per month or a $95 per year usage minimum. The standard time online charges are 18 cents per minute, rising to 43 cents per minute during prime time. Additional telecommunication charges are assessed for 1,200-bps and 2,400-bps service as well as access from Alaska, Hawaii, and Canada. The Source offers online help as well as toll-free telephone support.

CompuServe One of the biggest and oldest videotext services, **CompuServe** was established in 1969. Now over 380,000 subscribers use the wide variety of business, professional, educational, and home services. CompuServe is based in Columbus, Ohio, and is a subsidiary of H&R Block. It started as a remote time-sharing service, but H&R Block soon found that it had excess time on the huge DEC computers. So CompuServe decided to make its idle computer time available to hobbyists and anyone else interested in buying computer time after business hours. For a very modest fee, a person could sign on and use vast amounts of computer space. Soon, CompuServe made electronic mail services available to its subscribers. Shortly thereafter, other features, such as stock market quotations, news, weather, and even some magazine articles, were added. By 1980, a separate CompuServe Information Service (CIS) was formed. Today, some of the many services available to the thousands of CompuServe subscribers include bulletin boards, databases, electronic mail, shopping, references, and special interest groups. The Executive Information Service offers enhanced business services, including financial information such as Standard & Poor's, earnings and growth from I/B/E/S, stock market highlights and quotes, Value Line, Disclosure II, Stevens Business Reports, and The Business Wire. A clipping service is also offered. A **clipping service** automatically places information concerning particular topics and/or companies requested by a user into a private file to be read when convenient.

One of the most popular and dynamic areas on CompuServe is the five forums (Software, Hardware, Communications, New User, and Jr.) of the IBM Network. With approximately 15,000 members, it is the world's largest IBM PC user's group. It has over 80 megabytes of files in the data libraries, with programs and information about a wide variety of topics. Approximately 4,000 people use the forums each month. The most active forum is the IBM Software Forum, with over 500 messages left on the bulletin board each day.

Hundreds of other forums serve the interests of CompuServe users, including the Apple User's Group, Atari Forums, Commodore User's Group, Kaypro Forum, Tandy User's Network, Ashton-Tate Forum, Computer Consultant Forum, Lotus Forum, Programmers Forum, Broadcast Professional Forum, International Entrepreneurs Network, The Legal Forum, Work from Home Forum, Aquarium and Tropical Fish Forum, Comic Book Forum, Disabilities Forum, Educator Forum, WordPerfect Forum, and Student Forum—just to name a few.

Other services provided by CompuServe include electronic banking, computerized conferencing, games, and encyclopedic search. One of the most useful services for researchers is **IQuest,** which gives CompuServe users access to over 800 publications, databases, and indexes of business, government, research, news, and sports. It is menu-based, accessing databases through online services such as Dialog, BRS, NewsNet, and Vu/Text. CompuServe users have access to all these high-powered databases through one set of commands and one membership with CompuServe. Users can get live human assistance simply by typing "SOS" at the prompt. Figure 12-5 summarizes the services available on CompuServe.

CompuServe charges a one-time registration fee of $39.95 with no usage minimum. The basic online cost is $6 per hour for 300-bps service and $12.50 for 1,200-bps service. Support features include a user's guide and magazine at no additional cost and an almanac. Like all online services, there are additional charges for telephone line access. The charge to access a line or *node* on the CompuServe network is a minimal 25 cents per hour. Charges through Telenet and Tymnet are from $5 to $10 per hour. Several stores, including some book shops, sell the CompuServe starter kits that include the user's guide, account number, password, current rate structure, and $25 worth of connect time.

Specialized Videotext Services

Specialized videotext services feature more focused offerings, including services for business and legal professions.

Dow Jones News/Retrieval Service **Financial utilities** are online databases that are designed primarily for users interested in financial information. The best-known financial utility is the **Dow Jones News/Retrieval Service** (DJNS), a news and financial database service. DJNS is owned by Dow Jones & Company, the publishers of the *Wall Street Journal,* and was started in 1974 as a stock market information reporting service available only to stock brokerage houses and professional investors. By 1979, Dow Jones had reorganized the service into a broader information utility. It now provides electronic and surface mail through MCI's mail service, national weather, movie reviews, sports, and online shopping. However, the primary service provided is still current stock and investment information. Other services include in-depth company reports from Disclosure, Investext, and Standard & Poor's as well as business and general news drawn from the *Wall Street Journal* and *Barron's.* The service provides information on more than 6,000 companies and more than 50 different industries. The service also covers some 700 Canadian companies from the Toronto Stock Exchange. Dow Jones News/Retrieval Service provides its service worldwide, and it is updated almost continuously. For the user who wants to keep abreast of the most timely information throughout the world, one command will bring up the top five current news stories. DJNS is available from a variety of other services through gateways. The Dow Jones

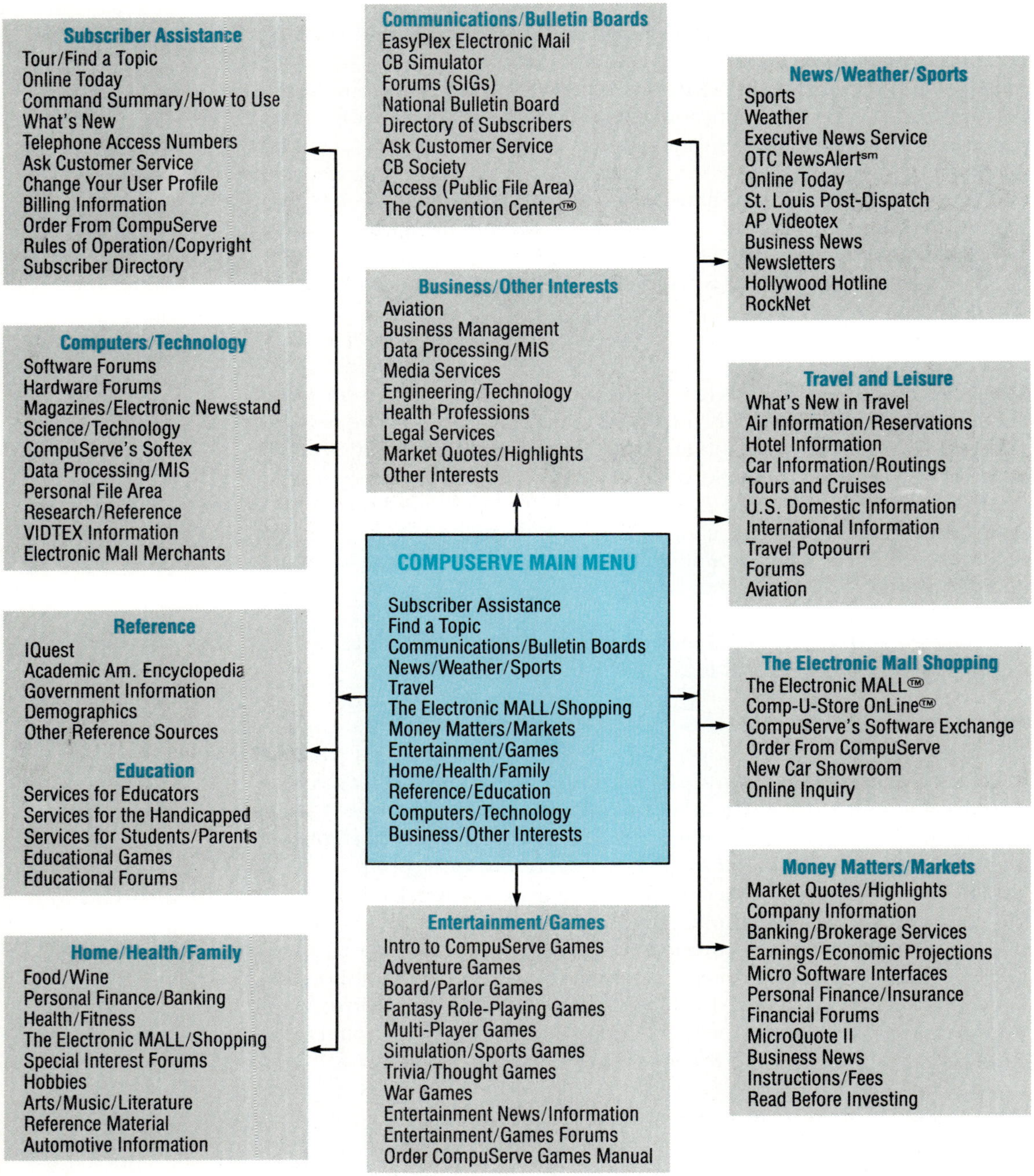

FIGURE 12-5 **A summary of services available on CompuServe. Notice the differences between these and The Source services in Figure 12-4.**

service is essentially command driven with optional menus available when needed.

The cost of using the Dow Jones News/Retrieval Service is a little more complicated to determine than the cost for other similar services. There is a start-up fee of approximately $50. As with most public databases, discounts may be available when you purchase communications hardware or software. The hourly rate for Dow Jones News/Retrieval Service is dependent upon the time of day and the specific service you use. Standard fees are 10 cents to $1.76 per minute with a 30 cents per minute surcharge for prime-time use. Additional costs include a monthly charge of $18.50 for real-time stock quotes, $5 per month for the Dow Jones tracking service (a clipping service), and a QuickSearch company reports charge of $2 to $39 each. Additional support features include a user's manual, online help, newsletters, and a magazine. Dow Jones News/Retrieval Service does not provide the Visa or MasterCard billing option that is provided by a number of information utilities. Dow Jones News/Retrieval Service bills subscribers directly.

There are at least two ways to start receiving the Dow Jones News/Retrieval Service. First, if you have already purchased a modem or software package that includes Dow Jones News/Retrieval Service membership, merely call the customer service number provided and disclose certain information contained in the sealed envelope included with your purchase. You will be operational within about 30 minutes. The second way to get started is to call or write to Dow Jones News/Retrieval Service directly and ask for an application.

Lexis **Law utilities** specialize in providing electronic databases for the legal profession. **Lexis** is a full-text service from a specialized legal database. Mead Data Control both generates the legal database and offers the service for a fee. Attorneys and accountants use this utility to do computerized bibliographic searches regarding legal matters. Lexis is a special, limited-purpose database with a vast library of legal information, including both federal and state codes as well as millions of court opinions.

Bulletin Board Services

A **bulletin board service (BBS)** is a computerized method of leaving messages. It is like having a cork bulletin board in your home for public notices. The first such bulletin board service was started by Ward Christensen and Randy Suess in Chicago, Illinois, in 1978. They set up a computer system whereby local computer club members could leave messages for other club members. Currently there are 10,000 to 20,000 bulletin boards in use in the United States. Some of the typical features offered by a computerized bulletin board include the following:

Leave message—to leave a message for an individual.

Scan messages—to scan messages on the bulletin board and retrieve those you want.

Retrieve messages—to retrieve specific messages.

Kill message—to delete a message.

Userlog—to see a log of the recent users and locations.

Bulletins—to access information left by the operator of the system.

Information—to find out how the bulletin board operates.

Help—to view a list of command options.

Download—to download, or retrieve, files from the bulletin board. Many public domain programs are found on bulletin boards. Not all bulletin boards can download.

Upload—to place programs or data files on the bulletin board for anyone to use.

Setting up a computerized bulletin board is not complicated; however, maintaining and expanding services can be a demanding but rewarding hobby. To run a BBS you need a personal computer with a communications card, at least one disk drive, and a modem that will automatically answer the phone. BBS software can cost from $75 to $150.

Using a BBS is even less complicated. You need a phone, a modem, and a microcomputer with software to turn it into a terminal. Computerized bulletin boards, especially those maintained by user's groups, have been called the greatest resource a microcomputer user can have. Remember, a *computer user's group* is an organization of people who use or have interest in a particular brand of microcomputer or software. They share information, swap public domain software, and, in general, help each other.

There seems to be an endless variety of computerized bulletin boards now available. Many organizations offer bulletin boards through CompuServe or The Source. Some users find a challenge in running their own bulletin board. Using your personal computer as a bulletin board is a modern-day phenomenon. In addition to being useful, it is inexpensive and enjoyable. As a user, you can be as up-to-date as possible on a wide variety of topics.

SUMMARY

Data communications is the transmission and reception of messages sent by a computer over some distance. The hardware needed is a microcomputer to serve as a terminal, a modem, and a telephone line or other communications channel.

Data communications software allows your computer to send and receive data communications messages. The software can dial the phone, answer the phone, and check the data transmission for errors.

Data communications has changed the work environment for many people. The handicapped and others may now work at home and transmit their work to their employers via data communications.

Online databases enable you to obtain information from some of the world's largest databases. These include The Source, CompuServe, Dow Jones News/Retrieval Service, Dialog, Bibliographic Retrieval Service, and Lexis.

EXERCISES

1. Find and read articles about data communications from several microcomputer magazines. Prepare a report mentioning recent developments beyond those discussed in this lesson.

2. If a public-access database such as The Source, CompuServe, or Dow Jones News/Retrieval Service is available to you, sign on and try several features. Prepare a report describing those features.

3. Visit a local computer store and obtain a listing of the types of data communications hardware and software available. Inquire about the cost of a modem and a data communications software package.

4. Find out if your school or employer uses data communications and, if so, for what purpose. What hardware and software are used? Which public-access databases are used?

5. Define the following terms:

data communications
telecommunications system
terminal
communications channel
coaxial cable
fiber optic cable
analog
data communications software
emulate
online help
auto-dialing
auto-log-on
data capture
file transfer
protocols
flow control protocol
error-checking protocol
Emile Baudot
online database
communications-oriented services
modem
modulation
demodulation
direct-connect modem
internal modem
external modem
port
electronic mail
bulletin board
gateway service
database services
videotext services
EasyLink
Mailbox
Telex
Overseas Telex
Mailgrams
FYI
InfoMaster
MCI Mail
encyclopedic utilities
Bibliographic Retrieval Service (BRS)
acoustic modem
bits per second
baud rate
value-added network
packet switching
local area network
private telephone network

Dialog Information Services
The Source
CompuServe
clipping service
IQuest
specialized videotext services
financial utilities
Dow Jones News/Retrieval Service
law utilities
Lexis
bulletin board service (BBS)

13
Statistical and Graphics Software

LESSON OUTLINE

STATISTICAL SOFTWARE

Statistics is the science of collecting, analyzing, interpreting, and presenting data. The statistical process generally involves four problem-solving steps:

1. Formulate a clear problem statement in the form of a hypothesis.
2. Collect and analyze data.
3. Prove or disprove the original hypothesis.
4. Communicate the results.

This chapter examines some microcomputer applications that address Steps 2 and 4. Statistical software packages aid in the analysis of data, and graphics software packages aid in the effective communication of results. It is the responsibility of people to formulate a clear problem statement in the form of a hypothesis and to decide whether or not the statistical results truly prove or disprove the original hypothesis.

Today, powerful software packages can do almost any type of statistical calculation. All the user needs is a microcomputer, the software package, and a collection of meaningful and accurate data.

This does not mean everyone can stop studying statistics. In fact, it is more important than ever to have a fundamental understanding of statistics to properly interpret what the computer produces. Because the computer makes statistical analysis so easy to do, much more statistical analysis is now being done. Today, employers look to recent college graduates to provide the statistical expertise to go along with this new capacity for computerized statistical analysis.

Also, do not fall victim to the error of assuming that what the computer produces is necessarily the correct analysis. Computers will produce erroneous results just as rapidly as correct results. Users can generally rely on the computational accuracy of the computer, but the computer has no ability to determine which statistical test is appropriate or how we should interpret the results. This lesson looks at microcomputer software for statistical analysis, but we recommend that you study statistics to understand the fundamental concepts involved.

COMPONENTS OF STATISTICAL SOFTWARE

A **statistical software package** is a set of programs used to describe, store, and analyze data and report the results of the analysis. Packages such as the Statistical Analysis System (SAS) and the Statistical Package for the Social Sciences (SPSS) have long been available for large computers, but statistical packages for microcomputers are recent.

Spreadsheet packages such as Lotus 1-2-3, VP-Planner, and Excel can be used to calculate the average of a range of numbers, compute squares and square roots, and, given the proper formula, handle practically any statistical procedure. For example, the Data Table feature of Lotus 1-2-3 Release 2 includes a command for simple and multiple regression. The user merely provides the cell ranges for the variables to be included and enters the Regression command, and the formulas for regression are executed. Using a spreadsheet to do statistics allows the user to convert the data into other units, such as dollars or units of production. However, statistical software packages are much easier to use because the statistical formulas are already built in. The user merely describes the data and selects the statistical procedure to be applied from an extensive list or menu of statistical techniques.

Describing and Storing Data

With a statistical software package, users can describe their data once and then apply several different types of procedures. There is no need to describe the data differently for each type of analysis. Before today's more advanced statistical software packages, describing data was a common problem. Utilizing a series of unrelated computer programs, each with the ability to do a particular statistical analysis, users had to describe their data to each program and set up a separate data file for each program. Modern statistical software packages greatly simplify the data description process.

What you have already learned about data fields and variable names can be applied to the use of statistical software. The software normally requires the user to describe each variable as a data field, supply a name for the data field, and specify how many columns wide the field will be and how many positions will be to the right of the decimal point. Each package has rules governing the number of letters that can be used in a variable name, the width of each field, and the way decimal precision is described. Many also have a maximum data capacity expressed in the number of variables accepted and the maximum number of values each variable may have.

Statistical Procedures

The series of statistical procedures is sometimes referred to as a **library** or collection of statistical tests. These tests summarize the data, compare groups of data to other groups of data, and relate the observed distribution of data to expected distributions.

On the simple end of the statistical spectrum, the user may want to know the measures of central tendency of the data, such as the **mean** (the arithmetic average), the **median** (the middle value), or the **mode** (the most frequently observed value). Measures of the spread of the data include the range of values, the highest and lowest values, the variance, and the standard deviation. These measures help describe the data and are often referred to as simple **descriptive statistics.**

Hypothesis testing involves the comparison of statistical measures to test an assumption about the data. For example, the researcher might test the assumption that the means of two groups of data are the same. This does not indicate that the means are exactly the same. Rather, it tests the assumption that the means are so close in value that the slight difference can be caused by normal and expected variation in the data. Statistical hypothesis testing helps us separate the normal slight variations from the abnormal or caused variations. When only a few observations are available, the ***t*-test** is often used. For larger numbers of observations, ***Z*-scores** are used to test the difference between means. Procedures to calculate *t*-tests and *Z*-scores are found in practically all statistical software packages.

A common use of statistical analysis is to analyze data collected from a survey to see if particular groups of people answered questions in a similar manner. **Cross-tabulation** is a common statistical technique to compare data collected from one group to data from another group. As the title implies, a table is used to tabulate the results. The rows of the table may represent the different questions asked, and the columns may represent groupings of people who responded. The statistical question usually asked is whether or not the groups are different in their responses. Because all people are different to some extent, some differences can normally be expected. The job of the analyst is to determine the probability that the observed differences are simply the result of this normal variance rather than the result of some fundamental differences between the groups.

This question normally suggests the field of statistics referred to as **analysis of variance,** statistical procedures that examine the amount and types of variation found in the data and compare the observed variations to what could normally be expected. The use of analysis of variance is so common that the phrase is often shortened to **ANOVA** (ANalysis Of VAriance). Most statistical packages offer several types of analysis of variance procedures.

Often the researcher will try to determine which of many factors are really the most important. A field of statistics known as **factor analysis** looks at similar themes in all the variables and then produces a smaller number of common traits or factors. For example, a researcher may begin with over 100 variables and, through application of factor analysis, be able to reduce that cumbersome number to nine or ten common traits. This technique has many applications in market research, where people try to determine which factors are most important in a consumer's decision to buy a particular product. There may be hundreds of minor factors, but just a few, such as price, quality, and convenience, may prove to be the most important. Other variables may be measured as part of the main factors.

All businesses want to predict future sales or income levels. Most business people have a rather good idea of what factors affect sales for their products, but a more precise understanding is often valuable in budget planning and planning for personnel and inventory needs. Often, thousands or even millions of dollars can be wasted if the sales forecast is inaccurate. One field of statistics that attempts to predict results given a collection of variables is known as **regression. Linear regression** results in an equation that produces a straight (linear) line through a scattering of data values. The line represents a forecast of some variable (called the dependent variable) given the values of one or more other variables (called the independent variables). If there is only one independent (predictor) variable, the process is referred to as **simple linear regression.** If two or more independent variables must be used to make the forecast, **multiple regression** is used. Statistical software packages typically include software to perform both simple and multiple linear regression.

Linear regression should only be used when it seems reasonable that the relation should be a straight line. That is, for every increase in the value of the independent variable, the dependent variable will increase or decrease by some constant rate. In **nonlinear regression,** the relation between the independent variables and the dependent variable may not necessarily be one that can be expressed as a straight line. Curved lines are examined. That is, for every increase in the value of the independent variable, the dependent variable may increase or decrease at some different rate.

One common example of such a curved relationship is the progress a student might make in the learning of a new skill. At first there is not much improvement. As time passes and the student practices the skill, the level of ability improves. Then, at a certain level, the rate of improvement tapers off. This is referred to as the "learning curve." Consumer acceptance of a new product often follows such a pattern. At first, only a few customers buy an item. Then it becomes popular for a period of time and eventually reaches some point at which the rate of increase levels off. Some, but not all, statistical packages allow you to use nonlinear regression to deal with this and other types of nonlinear relations.

Reporting Features

After the data have been described to the statistical software package and it has read and analyzed the data using one or more statistical tests, then the package must produce a report showing the results. On the simple end of the spectrum, the software package may show the answer on the screen or print it out on a printer. On the other end, elaborate graphics options may be included as part of the statistical package. (The area of graphics will be discussed more fully later in this lesson.) Most statistical packages provide some simple graphics, such as cross-tabulations, bar charts, histograms, scatter diagrams, and plots of simple linear regression lines.

In general, microcomputer statistical packages offer a collection of the most commonly used statistical procedures. Some packages cost less than $100 and offer 10 to 20 different procedures. Among the most elaborate are microcomputer versions of SPSS and SAS, two of the major mainframe statistical packages. Also, statistical software packages vary in the number of variables they can handle and the number of different values each variable can have. The following section provides a brief description of some popular statistical software packages currently on the market.

AVAILABLE STATISTICAL SOFTWARE PACKAGES

Most statistical packages come on one or more floppy disks and include a user's manual. Most assume that the user already has a fundamental understanding of statistics and is capable of properly selecting the correct statistical procedure and interpreting the results. As you study the following brief descriptions, keep in mind that prices and features change rapidly.

1-2-3 Forecast!

As the name implies, this package is related to the popular spreadsheet package Lotus 1-2-3. With **1-2-3 Forecast!,** users can create a forecast using data from a Lotus 1-2-3 spreadsheet. The screen contains a menu across the top, similar to the Lotus 1-2-3 menu. To select any option, the user either moves the cursor to locate the option and presses Return or enters the first character of the desired option. Once the user has entered a set of data, either by reading in a column or an area of a spreadsheet or by directly keying in the data, a long list of possible forecasting options are available, including

Simple trend analysis

Trends of seasonally adjusted data

Exponential smoothing

Simple regression analysis

Multiple regression analysis

1-2-3 Forecast! is the brainchild of Bruce Gates, a statistics professor who markets the product himself for $89.95. Don't let the low price and simple marketing technique fool you; this is no toy. Many large businesses prefer 1-2-3 Forecast! to packages costing thousands of dollars. Currently, the product's major limitation is that it can handle only ten independent variables and a maximum of 150 observations. Its strongest point, aside from the accuracy of its formulas, is how easy it is for a Lotus 1-2-3 user to move from a simple Lotus 1-2-3 spreadsheet to a forecasting model. All the user does is select menu choices. There are even some error messages designed to prevent the user from making certain statistical errors, such as forecasting too far ahead with insufficient historical periods. 1-2-3 Forecast! comes on a single $5\frac{1}{4}$-inch floppy disk and includes a brief user's manual and an onscreen tutorial.

Microstat

Microstat can also be used to do time-series analysis, but it includes much more and requires a knowledge of basic statistics. Microstat will do descriptive statistics, such as the mean, median, mode, and standard deviation, plus hypothesis testing, crosstabs, chi-square, and other frequently used procedures. It is completely menu driven and is marketed by Ecosoft for $375. Microstat comes on a single $5\frac{1}{4}$-inch floppy disk, can run on practically any version of MS-DOS, and requires only 128K RAM.

Exec*U*Stat

Exec*U*Stat is similar to the other packages in many features, but one special feature is its ability to *teach* the user some of the principles involved in each statistical procedure. Exec*U*Stat is designed for the busy executive with little background in statistics. For example, some statistical packages simply list the names of statistical procedures and expect the user to know which procedure fits the problem and the data. Instead, Exec*U*Stat briefly describes the purpose of each testing option. For example, instead of simply listing the Wilcoxon test as an option, Exec*U*Stat lists this procedure on the menu as "testing for a difference between two samples." Statistical experts would quickly recognize the Wilcoxon test as a nonparametric signed-rank test for paired samples, but the typical executive or manager would much prefer a brief explanation rather than just the word *Wilcoxon* on a menu. This package is marketed by Exec*U*Stat, Inc., for $495 and requires 320K RAM, MS-DOS 2.0 or later, and a color graphics card.

Minitab

Minitab is similar to Exec*U*Stat in that both teach the user about statistics in addition to actually performing useful statistical procedures. It is marketed by Minitab, Inc., at a list price of $1,000, but a more fundamental version is available for $500. Because this package was originally developed in 1972 and is used at many colleges and universities, considerable educational material has been developed to help students learn Minitab, including a student handbook called *Minitab* and a textbook called *Statistics for Business with Minitab.* Instructional material is necessary with Minitab because it is not menu driven. Instead, it is similar to large statistical packages available for mainframes and assumes that the user does not need to be prompted with a series of multiple choices.

One of the features recently added to Minitab is the **Box-Jenkins methodology,** a technique that identifies possible useful modeling methods and checks each in turn against the time-series data until it finds the model that best fits. Minitab requires 320K RAM, two disk drives, and MS-DOS 2.0 or later.

Other Statistical Packages

Several other statistical packages and their current prices are listed in Table 13-1. Of course, there are also microcomputer versions of the commonly used mainframe statistical packages, such as **SPSS** (Statistical Package for the Social Sciences) and **SAS** (Statistical Analysis System). These packages

Table 13-1 STATISTICAL PACKAGES

Package	*Company*	*Approximate Cost*
SmartForecasts	Smart Software	$695
Statpro	Penton Software	$795
SYSTAT	SYSTAT	$595
BMDPC	BMDP Statistical Software	$450 to $1500 (depending on modules selected)
RATS (Regression Analysis of Time Series)	VAR Econometrics	$200
GAUSS	Applied Technical Systems	$250
Forecast Master	Scientific Systems	$795
ESP	Economica	$795

cost over $1,000 each for the basic software plus several hundred dollars per module or statistical procedure needed. Although these packages are much more expensive than the ones previously listed, they do provide a full range of statistical procedures and allow the professional researcher the convenience of using a personal computer. Because it takes a large amount of disk storage to hold the various modules that make up these packages, they are commonly run on a hard disk system.

STATISTICAL SOFTWARE SELECTION

In selecting statistical software, some of the factors to consider include

Compatibility with your computer and operating system.

Maximum capacity of data file in terms of number of variables and number of values per variable.

The specific statistical tests included.

The availability and usefulness of manuals and other documentation.

Compatibility with your word processing, spreadsheet, database, and graphics software.

Cost.

Currently, many statistical software packages incorporate several features of graphics software. Let's take a look at the field of graphics software to get a better understanding of this new and interesting application.

GRAPHICS SOFTWARE

Today, the fastest-paced, most imaginative corner of the microcomputer world is that of graphics software. Imagine yourself giving a presentation using nothing but lists of numbers. How long do you think you would hold the attention of the audience? Although your numbers may be valid and important, it is difficult to make your point using only printed numbers. After electronic spreadsheets became popular, information overload became a problem. There were too many numbers to comprehend and not enough usable information. Computer graphics offer a solution.

Graphics software is a set of programs that takes data contained in a computer file and interprets them graphically on a screen, printer, or plotter. The purpose of such graphics is to communicate information more clearly and concisely. There is a wide range of computer graphics software. Some are used for sophisticated art and animation, whereas others are used primarily for simple presentations. We will discuss the more commonly used graphics for business and other professional presentations.

When prepared manually by an artist, charts and graphs used for a professional presentation could easily cost $100 or more each. Now graphics packages costing less than $500 are available for nearly all microcomputers.

There are two basic types of presentation graphics: personal presentation aids and general presentation aids. **Personal presentation aids** are graphics that appear on the screen of a microcomputer. **General presentation aids** are designed to be shown to groups and include computer-produced flipcharts, transparencies for overhead projection, and slides. General presentation graphics require sophisticated equipment for preparation and presentation.

Personal presentation aids require less specialized equipment, but a more expensive monitor (screen) and a graphics interface board are usually required. For printed graphics, a simple dot matrix printer is often sufficient, but the user may want to select a printer with more advanced graphics capabilities or a plotter. Remember, a **plotter** draws lines and circles on paper using one or more pens and can draw much more elaborate graphics than a simple dot matrix printer.

Some very simple graphic presentation features are available on certain spreadsheet and statistical software packages. If these features are sufficient, you will not need to purchase additional graphics software. However, if you need additional features, you may want to buy a graphics software package. A graphics software package allows the user to easily enter labels, legends, and other descriptive headings on the graphics produced. Some of the more common graphics capabilities include

Line chart—plotted data points connected by straight lines.

Pie chart—the total of the data entered is calculated as 100 percent, and then each classification of data is assigned a slice of the pie in proportion to its share of the total.

Scattergram—data points scattered on a graph with no connecting lines.

FIGURE 13-1 *(a)* is an example of a bar chart created using Harvard Graphics. *(b)* is a combination of pie and bar charts created using Harvard Graphics.

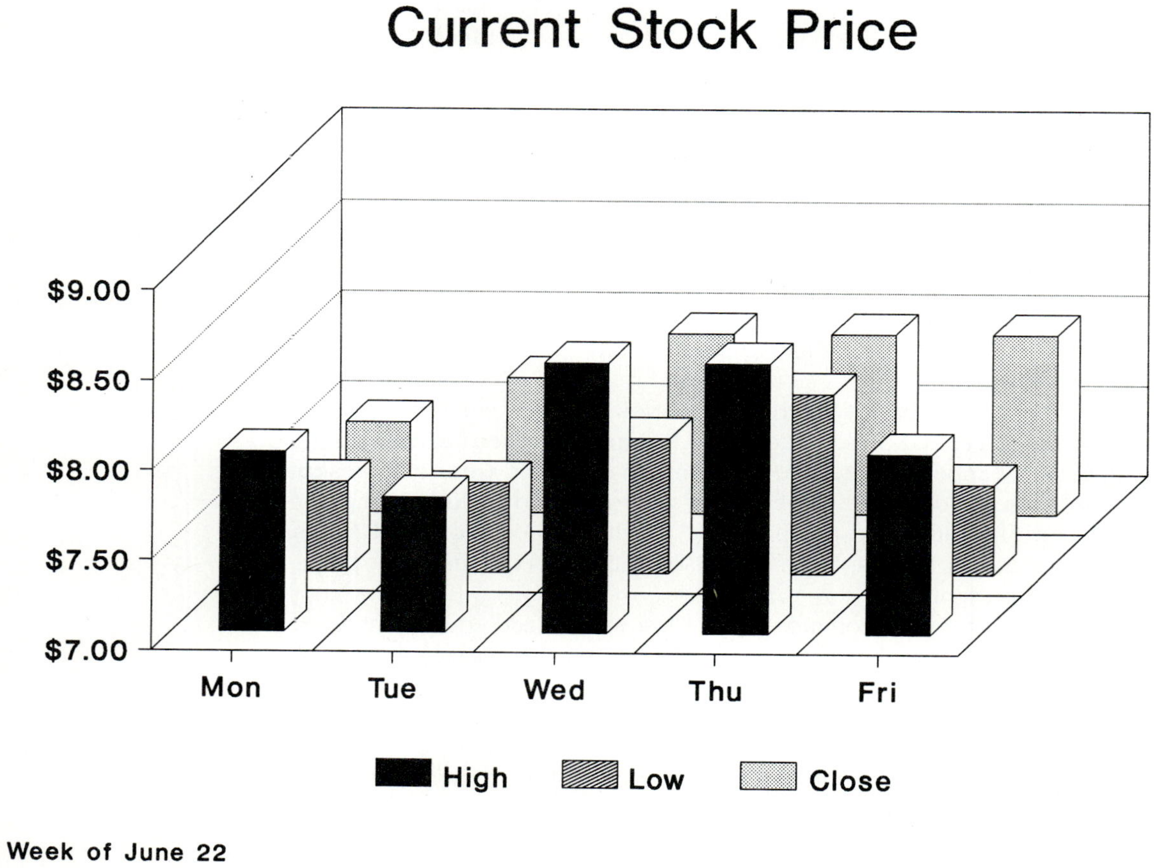

(a)

Bar chart—a series of horizontal or vertical bars represent the data.

Least-square trend—a straight line plotted through a collection of data points. This type of graph is particularly effective when analyzing trends.

Superimposition—one image placed on top of another image for comparison.

Split screen—two images shown side by side on the screen.

Colors—highlight and emphasize to produce dramatic effects.

Labels—describe the graphics, so users can better understand the contents. Graphics software differ on how much labeling is printed.

FIGURE 13-1 (Continued)

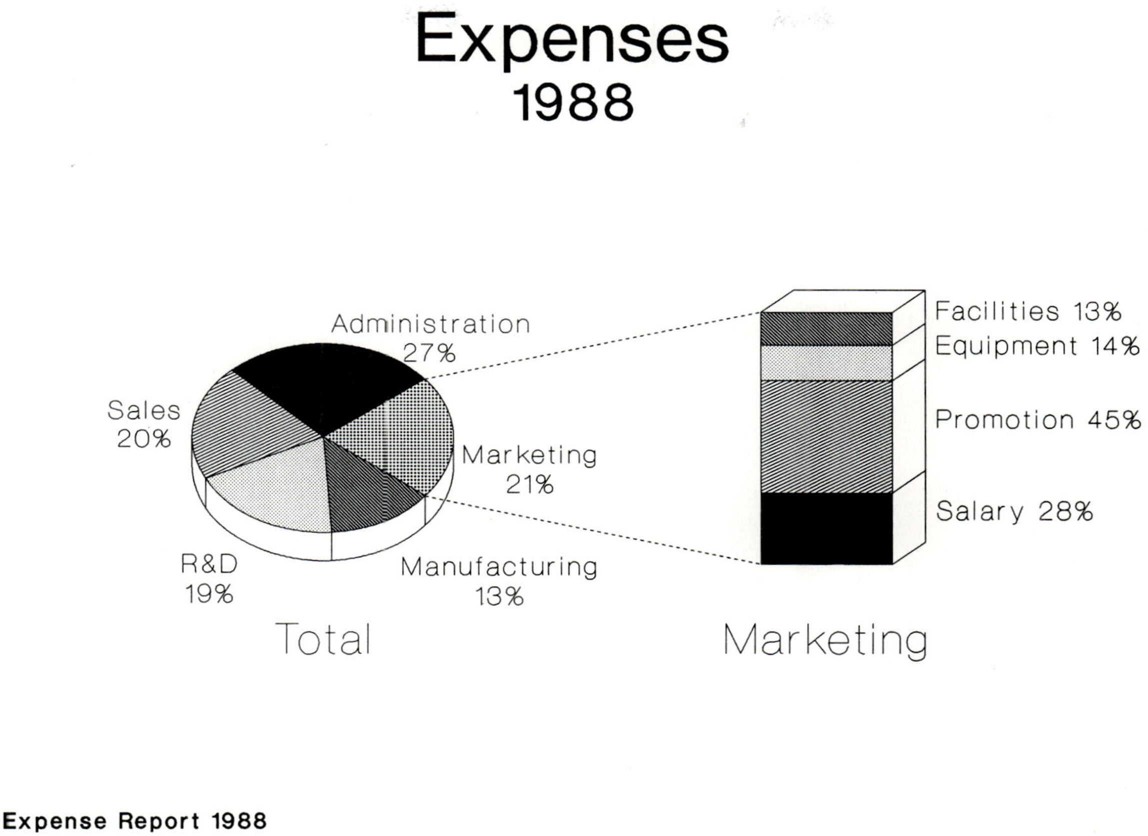

(b)

Figure 13.1 shows two examples of the enhanced graphics available with graphics software.

GRAPHICS OUTPUT DEVICES

The combination of a good color monitor and a graphics adapter board inside the microcomputer can produce beautiful graphics on the user's screen. Remember, the two types of graphics adapter boards most commonly used today are the **Color Graphics Adapter,** commonly called a **CGA** board, and the **Enhanced Graphics Adapter,** commonly called an **EGA** board. The CGA board can display four colors in resolutions of 640 dots by 200 lines and 320 dots by 200 lines. The EGA board displays 16 colors at a resolution of 640 by 350. The higher the resolution, the sharper the image.

Two major systems are used to create graphic images on a screen: bit-mapping and vector graphing. **Bit-mapping,** sometimes referred to as

raster graphics, uses a consistent number of bits in the computer's memory to define each individual pixel of display memory. Remember, a **pixel** is the smallest point that can be displayed on the screen. All screen images are combinations of pixels. The word *pixel* is a contraction of "picture element." Bit-mapping systems define each pixel, assigning each a place on the screen and a color.

Vector graphics uses shapes such as circles and rectangles instead of individual pixels. Vector graphics, sometimes called an **object-oriented system,** requires less memory and is faster than bit-mapping. Further, vector graphing is more flexible because mathematical calculations can be performed on the images, causing the shapes to increase or decrease in size, to rotate about an axis to show 3-D images, or to become taller or shorter. However, such systems do not enable the user to perform detailed editing of individual pixels.

Graphics software and hardware together determine the number of colors and the resolution of graphics output. For example, a simple dot matrix color printer typically uses a ribbon with three colors plus black and can use combinations of those colors to produce 14 colors. In contrast, some plotters use up to eight different pens, giving the user a wider variety of colors for the graphics output. There are a number of plotters on the market selling for less than $2,000. The user has a wide variety of plotters from which to chose, both in terms of price and in terms of whether the printing will be on paper, Mylar, or some other substance. In Lesson 1, the different types of plotters were described.

Special cameras can also be used for output of microcomputer graphics. Both the Digital Research Imagemaker and the Polaroid Palette produce 35mm slides at a rather low cost. They are also capable of making $3\frac{1}{4}$-by-$4\frac{1}{4}$-inch instant pictures of the graphics output.

AVAILABLE GRAPHICS SOFTWARE PACKAGES

The key to good graphics is in the software. It is the software that ties the computer to the output tools. Prices and features change rapidly, but the following discussion will provide a general idea of some of the packages currently available.

Harvard Graphics

Software Publishing Corporation's **Harvard Graphics** retails for approximately $395 and is completely menu driven. It asks the user to select the type of chart desired and then presents a fill-in-the-blank template. Choices are text, pie, bar/line, area, high-low, and organizational charts. The user is also prompted to insert titles and labels. Pressing [F1] provides help in the form of detailed explanations about menu selections. Pressing [F2] commands the program to draw the chart onscreen. Various other commands allow the user to adjust text sizes and specify font attributes such as italic or boldface. Data and charts from other software packages such as Lotus 1-2-3 can be transferred to Harvard Graphics. In addition to the regular types of charts, Harvard Graphics provides overlapping and stacked bars, pies with removable slices, and 3-D bar charts.

Freelance Plus

Produced by Lotus Development Corporation, **Freelance Plus** retails for approximately $495 and allows the user to create most common business chart formats, including vertical or horizontal bar charts and line, pie, and scatter charts. In addition, charts can be enhanced with free-form images created by using computerized versions of the tools common to a professional graphics artist. Included is a predefined library of more than 500 common symbols, including maps of each of the 50 states. For an added fee ($145), the user can obtain optional symbol sets that furnish maps of the United States divided by county, major city, or three-digit zip code boundaries. With a mouse, the user can trace existing images, including logos or diagrams, and add them to any screen. The user can enter data directly into Freelance Plus or import files created by Lotus 1-2-3, Symphony, or dBASE III. Freelance Plus supports most popular dot matrix printers and plotters plus several film recorders, including the Polaroid Palette and Matrix PCR, allowing output to 35mm slides.

PFS:Graph

Inexpensive, easy to learn, and easy to use, **PFS:Graph** is offered by Software Publishing Corporation for $140 and provides simple menus for clear, one-step choices of the program's most significant functions and features. It is especially easy to learn for someone who is already a user of any of the PFS series of packages. Despite its low price, it offers a good selection of bar, line, and pie charts plus area and stacked bar charts in a choice of colors, shades, or hatch patterns to differentiate among data groupings. It requires 128K of RAM and DOS 2.0 or later and supports the IBM Monochrome Adapter, CGA, and the Hercules monochrome/graphics card. For output, it supports dot matrix, ink-jet, and laser printers plus various plotters.

Table 13-2 lists a sampling of other graphics software currently available.

Table 13-2 GRAPHICS PACKAGES

Package	*Company*	*Approximate Cost*
Chart-Master	Ashton-Tate	$375
Decision Graphics	Samna	$450
GEM Graph	Digital Research	$249 ($896 with all options)
KeyChart	Softkey Software	$149
GrafTalk	Software Solutions	$695
Graphics Express	Bell & Howell	$1,200
Show Partner	Brightbill-Roberts/The Marketing Channel	$79
PC Storyboard	IBM	$275

GRAPHICS SOFTWARE SELECTION

As you can see from Table 13-2, there are many different graphics software packages available. Questions to ask when selecting presentation graphics software include

Is the program menu driven with user-selected defaults?

Are the software and its output compatible with your word processing and spreadsheet system?

Can the type styles and sizes be changed? Are they appropriate for the planned uses?

Will the software produce the graphs and charts you need?

Does the software work with the hardware available?

Does the software offer sufficient shading options or color options for your needs?

Does the software work with the programs manipulating the data?

Will you need to input the data independently, or can it be accessed through your existing software?

SUMMARY

Statistics is the science of collecting, analyzing, interpreting, and presenting data. Most statistical software packages include procedures to describe and store the data, to perform a variety of statistical tests, and to report the results of the analysis. The availability of easy-to-use statistical software packages for microcomputers makes it even more important to study statistics and gain a fundamental understanding of statistical analysis. The computer cannot select the proper statistical test and cannot interpret the true meaning of the results. Because the computer has made it so easy to perform statistical calculations, the use of statistics is increasing.

Practically all statistical packages include routines to calculate means, standard deviations, tests of means, cross-tabulations, simple regression, and analysis of variance. Some also include more advanced and specialized statistical tests. Statistical packages also vary in their capacity, both in terms of the number of different variables they can handle per file and the number of values each variable can have. Many statistical packages include features commonly found in separate graphics packages.

Graphics can help you interpret and present information in a meaningful way. The two types of presentation graphics are personal presentation and general presentation. Personal presentation graphics allow you to see results of numeric processing in graphic form on the screen of the computer. General presentation graphics are used when you need to make a professional presentation to several or more people.

Computer graphics is the next logical step for a microcomputer user who has already mastered word processing, spreadsheets, and databases. Graphics help you communicate by illustrating your presentations with charts and graphs.

EXERCISES

1. Read recent articles concerning statistical packages from several microcomputer magazines and answer the following questions:
   a. What new packages are available?
   b. What do they cost?
   c. What hardware and software do they use?
   d. What statistical procedures do they provide?

2. Read recent articles regarding computer graphics. What new software is available? Describe the software in terms of hardware and software requirements, cost, features, and ease of use.

3. Interview several people who regularly use statistical packages or graphics packages and answer the following questions:
   a. What packages do they use and why?
   b. What features would they look for if they were going to purchase another software package now?

4. Visit a local computer store and ask what statistical and graphics packages are available, and answer the following:
   a. Which packages are selling best and why?
   b. What do the packages cost?
   c. What additional software and/or hardware would be needed to utilize each package?
   d. Ask for a demonstration of the various graphics packages available. Prepare a report describing your findings.

5. If a statistical package such as Microstat or Minitab is available, use it to make a sales forecast for a firm, given eight quarters worth of data about the firm's sales, advertising expenditures, and research expenditures. Predict the firm's sales using multiple regression where advertising expenditures and research expenditures are considered the independent variables and the sales amount is the dependent variable.

6. If a graphics package is available, produce several graphs from the data used in Exercise 7. Use a bar chart to show the level of sales for each of the eight periods. If the package is capable of producing a plot of the regression line computed in Exercise 7, display the plot on the screen and, if possible, also print it.

7. Define the following terms:

statistics	mode	graphics software
statistical software package	Exec*U*Stat	personal presentation aids
library of statistical tests	Minitab	descriptive statistics
mean	Box-Jenkins methodology	hypothesis testing
median	SPSS	*t*-test
	SAS	*Z*-score

cross-tabulation
analysis of variance (ANOVA)
factor analysis
general presentation aids
plotter
Color Graphics Adapter (CGA)
Enhanced Graphics Adapter (EGA)
bit-mapping
raster graphics
regression
linear regression
simple linear regression
multiple regression
nonlinear regression
1-2-3 Forecast!
Microstat
pixel
vector graphics
object-oriented system
Harvard Graphics
Freelance Plus
PFS:Graph

14
Management Applications Software

LESSON OUTLINE

In a sense, all the software discussed in this book can be considered software for management applications. Certainly, managers use word processing, spreadsheet, database, data communications, statistical, and graphics software packages. In addition to those, there are four areas of special interest to managers: project management, decision support systems, financial management, and artificial intelligence. Within each area we will discuss the general nature of the application and the features offered by software packages currently available in that area.

PROJECT MANAGEMENT

A **project management software package** is designed to aid managers in the planning, monitoring, and tracking of projects that involve multiple tasks and relationships. **Project planning** involves identifying the tasks needed to complete a project and laying out the tasks according to the proper sequence and schedule. Resources, such as personnel and equipment, have to be assigned to specific tasks within any project, and those resources have to be at the right place at the right time. Project planning takes place *before* a project starts. **Project monitoring** takes place *during* the project and involves changes that happen while the project is in progress, such as delays, price adjustments, and design modifications. Revised completion dates and revised costs are projected. During a project is when project management software really shines; changes and subsequent revisions in the budget and schedule are easily handled. **Project tracking** takes place *after* a project is completed and evaluates a project to break down costs and to study how future projects could be improved. Construction companies and other businesses that are constantly managing one or more major projects can use the project tracking feature to improve project management.

Project Management Techniques

Most project management software packages relate to the paper and pencil tools of project management, such as Gantt charts, Critical Path Method (CPM) charts, or Project Evaluation and Review Technique (PERT) charts.

Gantt, PERT, and CPM Charts A **Gantt chart** graphically represents the starting and completion dates for each planned activity (see Figure 14-1).

FIGURE 14-1 A Gantt Chart.

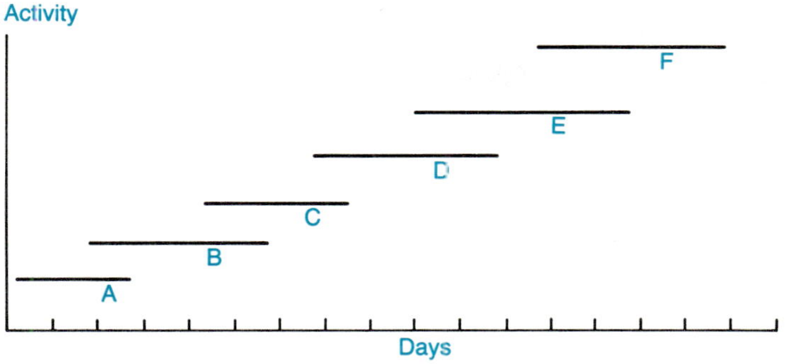

A **PERT chart** and a **CPM chart** are similar. Both depict a project as a network of connecting activities. Each activity is identified with a unique label and given a duration time. In addition, the label of the activity that must be completed before each activity can begin is indicated. The first time a user completes the steps necessary to use project management software to do a PERT chart, he or she will probably conclude it would have been easier to draw the chart by hand, especially if the project is not a complex one. However, when numerous projects must be managed or when a project is complex, project management software is the most efficient method.

In some cases, planners using PERT indicate three different potential task durations: a pessimistic time, an optimistic time, and a most likely time. Some software allow the user to designate probabilities to associate with each estimated time, so the schedule is presented not as absolute times but as a range of estimated starting and completion dates. This feature recognizes the uncertainty caused by unpredictable events, such as bad weather, labor strikes, and equipment failure. During the monitoring stage of the project, planned times are replaced with actual times as specific activities are completed. These changes affect the future planned completion dates plus all the planned starting dates for tasks still to begin. The manager can then reschedule personnel and equipment according to the revised schedule.

The CPM approach focuses on the path through the network of activities that is the longest from beginning to end. Any delay along that path will cause a delay in the planned completion date. Because that path is so critical to the completion of the project on schedule, it is called the **critical path** (see Figure 14-2). Most project management software includes a graphics feature that draws a proposed PERT chart on the screen or on paper given the duration and sequence of each task. Most also identify the critical path using a special colored line or a double line, so the critical path stands out within the total PERT chart.

FIGURE 14-2 A PERT chart with the critical path marked in color.

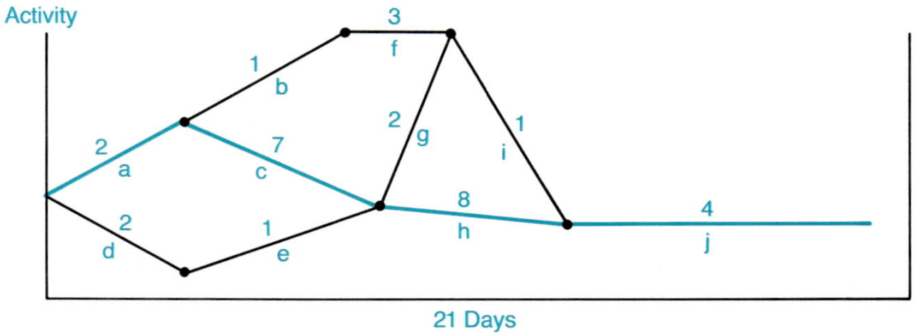

Critical path activity = a,c,h,j Critical path days = 2 + 7 + 8 + 4 = 21 days

Available Project Management Software

Several project management software packages are available for microcomputers, ranging in price from approximately $1,000 for rather elaborate packages (such as Project/Manager Workbench from Applied Business Technology) to simple ones retailing for less than $100.

SuperProject and Harvard Total Project Manager Among the most popular packages are SuperProject from Computer Associates and Harvard Total Project Manager from Software Publishing. Both are priced under $500 and run on the IBM PC and compatibles with MS-DOS 2.0 or later and 256K RAM. **SuperProject** can handle approximately 1,800 tasks and 180 resources per project. The user can select time units in terms of hours, days, weeks, or months. **Harvard Total Project Manager** allows users to designate time in units as short as a minute or as long as a year. Both packages contain built-in calendars lasting at least 20 years. Standard holidays and weekends are built in as nonwork days, but the user can alter this setup if the business plans to work overtime or on weekends or holidays. Other nonwork days can also be designated by the user.

Users can think of each task in a project as a record in a file. The project management software prompts the user to insert data about each task, such as task identification number, task name, description, task that must be done before this task begins, length of time this task will take, and resources that will be assigned to this task.

Resources are also described as records within the resource file. Each resource, such as a truck, a carpenter, a plumber, or a crane, must have a resource identification number, a name, a description, and a cost per hour or day. Some project management software allow various projects to share one resource file. When a project calls for a particular resource such as a crane but the crane is scheduled to be busy on another project, the software provides the manager with a warning that there is a conflict in the scheduling of resources. The manager can then either rearrange the scheduling or obtain another crane. The important thing is that the manager is alerted to this problem *before* the projects are in progress, while there is still time to do something, so the projects will not be delayed.

DECISION SUPPORT SYSTEMS

Decision support systems (DSS) are used to create, revise, check, and utilize decision models. A **decision model** is any quantitative or logical abstraction of reality that is created and used to help someone make a decision. The model helps the decision maker keep track of details, perform calculations rapidly, and revise and recompute with ease. A good DSS does not make decisions but rather supports the human decision maker by taking care of the details of calculations, so the decision maker can concentrate on human judgment.

In a broad sense, a spreadsheet software package such as Lotus 1-2-3 is a decision support system. However, most people think of a DSS as a package that allows the user to communicate in English-like expressions, is able to access a database to obtain the values that go into the model, has easy-to-use graphics for displaying the results, and contains powerful computational and statistical features for activities such as "What if?" analysis, sensitivity analysis, goal seeking, forecasting, risk analysis, and optimization.

Optimization is a mathematical technique for finding the best solution among a limited or constrained set of possible solutions. Linear programming is the most commonly used optimization technique in business. It locates the best-fitting straight line expression of the goal or objective that can be found within an area bounded by straight line expressions of the constraints. The more sophisticated DSSs allow the decision maker to deal with ill-structured problems and extend and enhance the person's own understanding and judgment rather than providing a unique solution. At this end of the spectrum, a DSS borders on the field of artificial intelligence and expert systems, topics to be considered later in this lesson.

FINANCIAL MANAGEMENT SOFTWARE

A **financial management software package** is a set of programs to help managers plan and budget resources. Advertisements for home computers often claim that the computer will solve your home financial management problems—balance your checkbook, do your home budgeting, keep track of your investments, forecast your cash needs, analyze potential investment opportunities, and calculate loan payments or mortgages. Although software is available to do all those things, for most people, the time it would take to enter the data is too long for what they perceive to be the benefits.

However, when it comes to running a business, proper financial management is a very serious matter. For very large businesses, the budgeting and planning processes have been aided by financial management systems operating on mainframe computers.

Interactive Financial Planning System

One such planning tool is the **Interactive Financial Planning System** (IFPS) by Execucom, retailing for several thousand dollars. In 1984, Execucom introduced **IFPS/Personal,** a smaller version of the mainframe package for the IBM PC and compatibles, selling for just a few hundred dollars.

Users of IFPS and similar packages will see some resemblance to electronic spreadsheets. Users can think of the system as a set of rows and columns. Usually each column will represent a period of time, such as a month or a quarter. Each row holds a formula in the financial model. In simple cases, the rows look very similar to the rows of a spreadsheet used for an income statement, a balance sheet, or a funds flow statement. However, the big difference comes in the way the user creates the spreadsheet. With IFPS the user does not create formulas by referring to the column and row coordinates; instead, he or she uses the row and column labels and other regular words common to financial planning. For example, the spreadsheet version of a formula to compute net income might be

```
C15-@SUM(C20.C30)
```

whereas the IFPS version would look like

```
NET INCOME = GROSS INCOME - TOTAL EXPENSES
```

Some of the functions of IFPS/Personal include

"What if?"—the ability to make one change in the model and see the results of that change on the entire model. Unlike changes made in most spreadsheets, the "What if?" change does not permanently change the original model.

Goal-seeking—the ability to make the model work backwards to tell you what input is needed to achieve a desired output. The user defines a goal as a specific value to be achieved in a certain row and column and indicates which variables should be allowed to change, and IFPS calculates what it would take to reach the desired goal. Again, the original model is not altered, and several target goals can be tested to see which is most feasible.

Analyze—provides a stepwise trace back through model logic to help the user determine dependency relationships among model variables. This feature combines some of the statistical functions described in Lesson 13 as functions of statistical software packages. For example, a decision maker may want to know the relation between markup and sales. Such information is critical to future pricing decisions.

Sensitivity—determines the relative sensitivity in a given model's values to changes in the values of other model variables. For example, you might want to know how sensitive your profit is to the price you charge for your product. It can help decision makers find answers to questions such as "If we increase our price by 5 percent, what would be the percentage increase or decrease in net sales?"

Although IFPS/Personal is capable of doing almost everything the mainframe version can do, the mainframe version will continue to be the software package used by large corporations to combine the various divisional financial models into one corporate-wide model. The mainframe version of IFPS is capable of linking to a firm's accounting system and gathering the financial information it needs for the financial model. Further, it contains optimization and Monte Carlo simulation as built-in features. **Monte Carlo** is a simulation technique in which risk and uncertainty are expressed as probabilities, and alternatives are selected on the basis of those probabilities. Instead of a roulette wheel, as might be found in a Monte Carlo casino, a computer program is used to simulate randomness.

A common use of this powerful package is to simulate a company's merger with or acquisition of another firm and project the result of such a move upon the income statement, balance sheet, and financial ratios of the company. Many complex alternatives can be tested, and the results instantly presented in easy-to-understand graphic form. Mergers and acquisitions among large firms can involve millions or even billions of dollars in combined assets, and executives need a powerful and reliable modeling tool to consider the feasibility of such major decisions. For the small business, however, the introduction of IFPS/Personal makes computerized financial management affordable. The small factory owner or the corner retailer can now benefit from the same tool used by the industrial giants.

Other Financial Planning Packages

Since 1984, when IFPS/Personal became available, several more vendors have introduced financial planning software at prices that bring the world of financial modeling and planning well within the reach of practically all firms. Other software packages with features similar to IFPS include

- System W by Comshare
- Stratagem by Integrated Planning
- IMPACT by MDCR
- CUFFS by CUFFS Planning and Models
- Express by Management Decision Systems
- MBA by Context Management Systems

ARTIFICIAL INTELLIGENCE

Artificial intelligence (AI) is a subfield of computer science, mathematics, and symbolic logic that is concerned with the concepts and methods of symbolic inference by a computer and the symbolic representation of the knowledge to be used in making inferences. Artificial intelligence is currently a mostly academic field of study aimed at pursuing the possibility that a computer can be made to act in ways that humans recognize as "intelligent" behavior. Three practical areas that have developed from the study of artificial intelligence are natural language processors, robotics, and expert systems.

Natural Language Processors

Natural language processors allow computer systems to accept input and produce output in a conventional language like English. Currently, systems can be built that will accept typed natural language input within strictly defined limits. Some voice input is also being used in limited areas. An example is the use of query languages that permit users to instruct a database management system to retrieve items from a database by using English-like statements rather than programming statements.

Robotics

Robotics is the science of enabling computers to "see" and "manipulate" objects in their surrounding environment. Artificial intelligence contributes to the area of robotics by developing **heuristics** (rules of thumb or good judgment). These heuristics allow the robots to function in a flexible manner while interacting with a constantly changing environment. Robotics is a dramatic example of the practical consequences of the theoretical study of artificial intelligence. Currently, numerous manufacturers are installing robots in their factories as they strive to modernize production facilities and compete in a global market.

Expert Systems

Expert systems is a category of computer programs that addresses problems normally thought to require human specialists for their solution. For example, TAXADVISOR is capable of advising a client regarding the tax consequences of alternative investment approaches. MYCIN diagnoses infections. PROSPECTOR aids geologists in evaluating mineral sites. INTERNIST simulates the process a physician uses to diagnose illnesses in a patient. SACON provides engineers with advice on structural analysis.

Some claim that expert systems can be used to do the following functions and more:

advise	consult	explain
analyze	design	explore
categorize	diagnose	forecast
form concepts	learn	retrieve
identify	manage	schedule
interpret	monitor	test
justify	plan	tutor

Expert systems are developed with the help of human experts who reveal their thought processes as they solve specific problems. Most experts solve problems in a manner that, on the surface, does not appear to be straightforward. Also, they solve problems that seem to be unstructured and ill defined. However, most experts do use heuristics that enable them to eliminate possible solutions that are not feasible in a specific case and narrow in on the correct solution Many such rules follow the format of

IF a certain condition is true

THEN this action must be taken

OTHERWISE a different action must be taken

A human expert is able to deal with a particular set of possible conditions and is aware of a particular set of possible actions to take. He or she combines a series of IF–THEN–OTHERWISE rules to arrive at an expert opinion. The opinion is not quite the same as the single solution to a well-defined mathematical problem. Another expert may consider the same problem and come up with a different opinion. However, a client or patient may be willing to pay for the expert's opinion because of the expert's reputation.

TK!Solver is a microcomputer-based software package designed to provide a general framework for building expert systems in science, engineering, and other disciplines. It has no built-in knowledge of any particular discipline, but it provides a framework in which a user with specialized knowledge can construct an expert system. Although much of the work to date with expert systems has been with mainframe computers, watch for this exciting new area to expand with the introduction of such products for microcomputers.

SUMMARY

A variety of software applications packages are available in the general field of management. Specific applications include project management, decision support systems, financial management, and artificial intelligence.

Software for project management aids in the planning and control of activities in a major project by using techniques such as CPM, PERT, and Gantt charts. The user creates a task or activity file in which each record is a task to be completed in the project. A resource file contains data about the various resources, such as personnel and equipment, that are to be assigned to the tasks in the project. A built-in calendar is used to consider weekends and holidays and other scheduled events that may interrupt the project. Project management software is especially useful in the construction business or in other businesses where several complex projects need to be scheduled at the same time and where project scheduling is frequently repeated. Scheduling conflicts and unavailability of resources can be predicted and avoided.

Decision support systems help decision makers test alternative solutions. DSS software combines many of the features of spreadsheets, statistical packages, and graphics packages into an easy-to-use tool that provides support for the person who must make decisions in complex situations.

Financial management software helps managers plan for their financial needs and avoid sudden emergencies caused by cash shortages and other financial mistakes.

The field of artificial intelligence addresses the types of problems that are not solved by exact formulas but by some vaguely defined problem-solving approach. Expert systems attempt to mimic the problem-solving approach of human experts. Until recently, this area was reserved just for academic research. Firms have now begun to actually market a few such systems, and some people suggest this type of problem solving can even be accomplished using microcomputers rather than giant mainframes. Science fiction stories about computers that seem to reason on a level equal to or above human intelligence may become reality.

EXERCISES

1. Define the following terms:

   - project management software package
   - project planning
   - project monitoring
   - project tracking
   - Gantt chart
   - PERT chart
   - CPM chart
   - critical path
   - SuperProject
   - Harvard Total Project Manager
   - decision support systems
   - decision model
   - optimization
   - financial management software package
   - Interactive Financial Planning System
   - IFPS/Personal
   - "What if?"
   - goal-seeking
   - analyze
   - sensitivity
   - Monte Carlo
   - artificial intelligence
   - natural language processors
   - robotics
   - heuristics
   - expert systems

2. Read recent articles describing project management, decision support systems, financial management, or artificial intelligence software packages *for mainframe computers.* Write a short report describing features and applications.

3. Read recent articles regarding project management, decision support systems, financial management, or artificial intelligence software *for microcomputers.* Write a short report describing features and costs.

4. Examine literature about the field of artificial intelligence and answer the questions on page 501.

a. In what ways can computers be considered capable of human intelligence?

b. What forms of human intelligence cannot be duplicated by computers?

c. What social implications do you see regarding this new computer applications area?

APPENDIXES

A
Word Processing Tutorials Using WordStar

WordStar is one of the most popular word processing packages available for microcomputers today. It offers many of the word processing features discussed in Lessons 3, 4, and 5 For those students who will be using WordStar for word processing, we repeat here major portions of the tutorials contained in Lesson 3, 4, and 5, with the instructions revised to include WordStar version 4.0 commands. Students should review the tutorials within the lessons for conceptual material, such as how back-up files are made. Note: If you are using WordStar Version 4.0, the function key commands in the tutorials should be available. However, WordStar Version 3.3 offers different function key commands. Students should refer to the documentation accompanying the software for more information about those function key commands. Also, unfortunately, earlier versions of WordStar, including 3.3, do not offer the Undo or Unerase command.

LESSON 3 TUTORIAL: CREATING AND PRINTING A LETTER

To complete this tutorial you need the following:

- WordStar disk
- A blank formatted disk
- A printer connected to the microcomputer

While completing this tutorial you will learn how to do the following:

- Load WordStar
- Create, edit, and save a letter
- Print a letter

In this tutorial you will create a cover letter written by a student applying for a summer job at the imaginary NewSoft Corporation.

Create the Document

There are four basic steps in creating a new document using a word processor: (1) loading the operating system into primary storage, (2) loading the word processing software into primary storage, (3) opening the document using a unique filename, and (4) inserting new text into the document.

Step 1: Load the operating system (MS-DOS) into primary storage.

In order to use any applications software, including a word processor, you must first load the operating system into primary storage. Some microcomputer systems permit you to place an abbreviated version of the operating system on the same floppy disk that contains the applications software. Others require the operating system to reside on a separate floppy disk that must be inserted into the disk drive every time the microcomputer is started or reset. It is usually more convenient to have the operating system on the applications software disk because it reduces floppy disk handling.

The details of loading the operating system were covered in Lesson 2, but if you need a review, follow the instructions below.

a. Insert in disk drive A the MS-DOS disk or the WordStar disk that contains the system. Remember that the disk is usually inserted label side up with the write-protect notch on the left.

b. Turn the microcomputer and the monitor on. If the computer is already on, simultaneously press the three keys labeled Ctrl, Alt, and Del.

c. After the system checks the keyboard and memory status, if the system requires manual setting of the time and date, enter the required information. Remember to use the 24-hour clock. For example, April 29, 1989, would be entered as 04-29-89 and 1:15 p.m. would be entered as 13:15. Press the Enter key at the end of each entry. When you see the MS-DOS system prompt of A>, you have completed loading the operating system and are ready to load WordStar.

Step 2: Load the word processing software into primary storage.

a. If necessary, remove the MS-DOS disk from drive A and insert the WordStar disk in drive A and the blank formatted disk in drive B. Latch the disk drive doors.

b. Enter the command to load WordStar:

WS

Press **Return.**

A copyright notice will appear on the screen. If necessary, press the **Space bar** to continue.

The WordStar Opening Menu will appear on the screen. Your screen will be similar to Figure A-1. Remember that there will be some slight differences between the different versions of WordStar.

Since we are going to store files on disk drive B, change the logged disk drive. Type

L

A screen appears, giving further explanation of the Log command and the drives that can be specified with the Log command. Type

B

Press **Return.**

Step 3: Open the new document, using a unique filename.

Enter the name of the new document. At this point the operating system and the word processing software are loaded into primary storage and you are logged on to disk drive B for file storage. At the Opening Menu, type

D

to open a document.

```
                    WordStar Professional Release 4
================== O P E N I N G   M E N U ===================
      D open a document                 L change logged drive/directory
      N open a nondocument              C protect a file
      P print a file                    E rename a file
      M merge print a file              O copy a file
      I index a document                Y delete a file
      T table of contents               F turn directory off
      X exit WordStar                 Esc shorthand
      J help                            R run a DOS command
DIRECTORY   Drive A:\   112k free
 .4k BOX             .1k CHAPTER1.DOC    .1k CHAPTER2.DOC    .1k CHAPTER3.DOC
3.5k DIARY.DOC      8.3k LASER1.DOC     3.1k LASER2.DOC      80k PATCH.LST
5.5k PRINT.TST       94k README.TXT      .9k RULER.DOC       .6k SAMPLE1.DOC
 .4k SAMPLE2.DOC     .3k SAMPLE3.DOC     .1K SS5489.LET      .9k TABLE.DOC
5.5k TEXT.DOC       1.8k WS3KEYS.PAT    1.5k WSINDEX.XCL
```

FIGURE A-1 WordStar Opening Menu and directory of files.

A new prompt appears, asking for the name of the document to be opened. When you create a file, you must assign it a name. Some word processing software, such as WordPerfect, require that a document be named when it is saved; others, such as WordStar, require the assignment of a filename before the file is opened.

Remember, a filename should be unique to that particular disk, yet follow a convention or series of rules and guidelines to help you determine the type and content of the document when you look at the directory of filenames that you call up on the disk using either the MS-DOS directory command DIR or the WordStar Opening Menu. For example, you may decide to start all your correspondence with the initials of the recipient and the date. A letter sent to John Doe on May 4, 1989, would be named JD5489.LET.

1. Use extensions (suffixes) that describe the nature of the contents, such as .LET for letter, .DOC for document, or .RPT for report.
2. Avoid using restricted extensions such as .BAK (backup files created by WordStar), .DBF (database files created by dBASE III Plus), and .WKS, .WK1, .PRN, and .CAL (common extensions used by such spreadsheet software as Lotus 1-2-3 and SuperCalc4).
3. The name should begin with a letter or a number and be no more than 8 characters long.
4. Avoid using special symbols and punctuation marks in the name.
5. Do not use blank spaces within the name!

Since the logged disk drive has already been changed to B, we do not need to specify a filename prefix for the disk drive. Remember, word processing software used on MS-DOS accepts either upper- or lower-case letters in filenames and suffixes and automatically changes lower-case commands or filenames into upper case.

Be aware that backup files and other files automatically created by the software can use up disk space faster than you might realize. Making a backup file, for example, automatically doubles the amount of disk space needed to store a file. Figure 3-17 is an illustration of how backup files are created.

Notice also that editing an existing file causes the software to automatically create a copy of your old file, giving you two files where previously you had only one. These backup files are stored on the same disk, so if that disk is lost, damaged, or destroyed, both the original file and the backup will be gone. To prevent such disasters, make a copy of the file on a separate floppy disk.

What happens if you give an improper filename? That depends on the word processing software. Some refuse to use it and will give you an error message. For example, WordStar will truncate the entry and use only the first eight characters for the filename.

For your first document, use a complete file specification of SS5489.LET. At the prompt

```
Document to open?
```

enter the name

```
SS5489.LET
```

Press **Return.**

WordStar will accept the filename and open a document file. The Edit Menu, ruler line, and blank screen will then appear, indicating that WordStar is ready to accept text (see Figure A-2).

Step 4: Insert text into the document.

a. Examine the screen features. At this point, let's assume that you have properly loaded the operating system and the word processing soft-

```
  A:LETTER.DOC        P01 L01 C01 Insert Align
=============================== E D I T   M E N U ===============================
    CURSOR       SCROLL         ERASE      OTHER                 MENUS
 ^E up       ^W up          ^G char     ^J help              ^O onscreen format
 ^X down     ^Z down        ^T word     ^I tab               ^K block & save
 ^S left     ^R up screen   ^Y line     ^V turn insert off   ^P print controls
 ^D right    ^C down       Del char     ^B align paragraph   ^Q quick functions
 ^A word left   screen      ^U unerase  ^N split the line   Esc shorthand
 ^F word right                          ^L find/replace again
L----!----!----!----!----!----!----!----!----!----!----!--------R
                                                                          ^
                                                                          ^
                                                                          ^
                                                                          ^
                                                                          ^
                                                                          ^
                                                                          ^
                                                                          ^
                                                                          ^
                                                                          ^
                                                                          ^
                                                                          ^
 Display Center  ChkRest ChkWord Del Blk HideBlk MoveBlk CopyBlk Beg Blk1End Blk
1Help   2SaveRt 3Undrlin4Bold   5DelLine6DelWord7Align  8Ruler  9Save & 0Done
```

FIGURE A-2 The WordStar screen ready to accept text.

ware and have created the new, blank document. By your opening the document, the word processing software has established a blank space or storage area in primary storage and is now ready to accept data into the file.

Think of this screen as a page. Unlike a printed page, however, the screen has features unique to word processing.

The line at the top of the screen is a **status line,** which shows what file you are using (B:SS5489.LET); the current page (P01); the line and column numbers (L01 and C01); the character insert status (Insert); and the alignment status (Align).

Because it is a disk-based word processor, WordStar reads and writes information to the disk *while* collecting a document. This feature sometimes slows down operations because time is needed to access the disk, but it permits larger documents. With WordStar, the maximum length of a single document is determined by the amount of disk space available. However, remember that backup files and other file operations require disk space; always leave sufficient room on your disks.

The **ruler line,** another feature on the screen, shows the left (indicated by L) and right (indicated by R) margins and the tab stops (indicated by the !). Margins can be adjusted through the following commands:

Action	*Command*
Change left margin	^O L *or* ^[F5]
Change right margin	^O R *or* ^[F6]

After you give a command, a prompt appears asking you to type in the new margin column number or to press Escape, which will set the margin to the current cursor column. The margin is unchanged if you give the cancel command (^U). Newly entered text is automatically adjusted to the revised margins. You can adjust existing text using the align paragraph command, ^B.

Note that WordStar starts printing text in column 1 on the screen. However, this is really column number 10 on the paper, leaving a 1-inch left margin.

A **tab** is a point indicated on the ruler line by an exclamation mark (!) where the cursor will stop when the Tab key is pressed. In WordStar the default setting for tab stops is every 5 spaces. You set or remove tab stops using the ^I command. Note that the spaces inserted with the Tab key are interpreted as "hard" spaces, just as if a letter or a number were entered. "Soft" spaces are spaces inserted by the word processing software for page appearance. Since they are soft, they can be automatically adjusted by the software. In contrast, hard spaces and carriage returns must be deleted or changed by the user, if changes are needed.

Word processing software packages generally have default settings for margins and page width. **Default** means that the word processor has particular automatic settings for certain commands (for example, margins, tabs, page numbering). If the user does not specify a setting, say, for margins, the software will automatically use the default margin settings. Most default settings are the ones used for general business correspondence. We will use those default settings for this tutorial.

As you examine the WordStar screen, notice the Menus listed in the upper right-hand corner. The caret symbol (^) indicates that you should press the Control key while pressing the letter. For example, when you enter ^P, the Print Controls Menu appears.

The Edit Menu serves as a reminder of which commands move the cursor, scroll the screen, erase characters, unerase the previous delete, and perform miscellaneous other commands, and which commands display the other help menus.

A series of Help menus are available to remind you of word processing commands. The Onscreen Format Menu contains reminders about the commands that change the appearance of the document on the screen, including margins, line spacing, centering, and print control displays. The Block and Save Menu contains information on the commands that save files; perform block operations; and perform file operations such as Copy, Print, Rename, and Erase. Reminders about the commands for print enhancements are contained on the Print Controls Menu. The Quick Functions Menu contains the quick cursor movement commands, find and replace, spelling, and scrolling commands.

The Edit Menu can be left onscreen if the Help level is set to 3. The Help level has four settings. At level 3 all menus are always on. At level 2, the Edit Menu is turned off while the submenus for other operations, such as Block and Quick commands, are left on. At level 1, the Edit Menu, submenus, and command confirmations are turned off. Level 0 turns off all menus, status lines, and confirmations. Other menus stay on the screen only until you press any key, but you can call any one of them again by holding down the Control key and pressing the other required key. Use the menus to remind you about commands, or just to get more information.

For more general help about WordStar features, press ^J.

At the bottom of the screen is a list of Function key commands. Table A-1 lists the available Function key commands.

b. Type the letter exactly as shown in Figure A-3, including the spelling and typing errors (maybe you'll add a few of your own). Later we will describe how to correct them.

Table A-1 FUNCTION KEY COMMANDS IN WORDSTAR

Function Key		*With Control Key*	*With Shift Key*	*With Alt Key*
[F1]	Help	Find	Display On/Off	│
[F2]	Undo	Find and Replace	Center	─
[F3]	Underline Beg/End	Find Again	Check Spelling of Rest of Document	┌
[F4]	Boldface Beg/End	Go to Page	Check Spelling of Word	┐
[F5]	Delete Line	Left Margin	Delete Block	└
[F6]	Delete Word Right	Right Margin	Hide Block	┘
[F7]	Align Paragraph	Paragraph Margin	Move Block	┬
[F8]	Insert Ruler	Insert Page Break	Copy Block	┴
[F9]	Save/Continue	Left End of Line	Begin Block	├
[F10]	Save/Done	Right End of Line	End Block	┤

Remember to use your Tab key to move the cursor to the proper columns for the inside address. Use the Return key only as a marker for the end of paragraphs. **Do not press the Enter key or the Return key at the right margin! Let the word wrap feature handle this.** If you are accustomed to using a regular typewriter, you will be in the habit of listening for the bell indicating the right margin and you may find it difficult to break the habit of pressing the Return key at the right margin. With a word processor, use the Return key to start a new paragraph, not a new line. This is the error beginners most commonly make, so do not feel bad if it takes some practice to get used to letting the word wrap feature do its job.

Edit the Document

One of the handiest features of word processing is the ability to edit documents quickly. To show this, let's edit the letter you just entered.

Step 1: Correct the errors.

Make the corrections, either by deleting the errors and typing in the corrections or by typing over the errors. Use the arrow keys to move the cursor on the screen to locate and correct errors. Remember to use the following commands:

Action	*Command*
Delete the current cursor character	^G *or* Del
Delete character to the left of the cursor and backspace	Backspace
Delete the current word	^T *or* [F6]
Delete the current line	^Y *or* [F5]
Insert On/Off (Typeover)	Ins *or* ^V
Undo delete	^U *or* [F2]

Column 40

Press the TAB key 8 times → 123 East Street Apt. 21 RETURN
Iowa City, Iowa 52204 RETURN
(402) 555-9876 RETURN
May 4, 1989 RETURN RETURN

Column 1 on screen

Ms. Shirley Swanson RETURN
Vace President for Personnel RETURN
NewSoft Corporation RETURN
56 High Tech Drive RETURN
Naperville, Illinois 60234 RETURN RETURN

Dear Ms. Swanson: RETURN RETURN

Yaur ad in the Chicago Tribune on Aprol 30 stated you are looking for persom with experience using ward processing, spreasheets, and date bases plus a fundamantal understanding of IBM PC-compatible hardwere and software. The ad further states the position will be available begining June 1 and will continue full-time throughout the summer. I believe your position describes my qualifications and employment interests perfectly. RETURN RETURN

My resume is enclosed for your consideration. The resume does not explain that I have just completed a curse where I was required to do several projects using word processing, spreadshets, and data base management software. While enrolled in that course I decided to use the extra money earned last summer working for TechMARK as a microcomputer salesperson to purchase my own microcomputer system. I have installed several expansion boards and have become even more acquainted with the hardware and software. This semester I am enrolled in two microcomputer related courses: Computer Graphics and Data Communications. I hove also completed the course called Systems Analysis and Design. RETURN RETURN RETURN

By June 1 I will have completed my jnior year at the University of Iowa and will be living in Naperville with my parents. I will be returning to Iowa for my senior year starting the last week in August. RETURN RETURN

With my previous work experience, courses at Iowa, and personal experience with my own microcomputer, I think I can be of service to NewSoft. Your consideration of may application is appreciated. I will be calling in a few days to answer any additional questions you may have concerning my qualifications and supply references. Please call me if you have any questions. RETURN RETURN

Press the TAB key 8 times → Sincerely, RETURN
RETURN
RETURN
RETURN
Pat Allen RETURN

FIGURE A-3 The letter, complete with errors.

Step 2: Reformat the paragraphs.

While inserting new material between existing words, you may see the line extend beyond the right margin. To realign a paragraph according to the set margins and tab stops, set the cursor at the beginning of the paragraph and press the Reform command

^B *or* **[F7]**

The paragraph will be realigned to the current margins.

Step 3: Add a Print Format command.

Add the dot command .OP to turn off the page number. Move the cursor to the first line, first column. Press

^Q R

Press **Return.**
Move the cursor back up to the first line, first column.
Starting in the first column, type

.OP

The dot must be in column 1.

Step 4: Proofread the document carefully.

It is more difficult than you may imagine to find all your errors as you proofread. Your mind plays tricks on you and you "see" what you think you typed, not necessarily what you really did type. You may want to print the letter, since some people find it easier to locate errors on a printed document than on the screen. Some expert proofreaders actually read a manuscript backwards, making it more difficult for their minds to trick them into "seeing" what isn't really there. Others read the material out loud or have someone else read it out loud to them. Still others use a piece of paper to cover up all but one line as they proofread. Learn to develop good proofreading techniques. It doesn't do much good to learn to use a word processor if you then fail to find and correct mistakes.

Once you are sure that all errors have been corrected, you are ready to save the document.

Save the Document

One lesson most students learn the hard way is the importance of periodically saving their work on their disk. A document is saved when the text contained in **working storage** (the contents of primary memory RAM) is written into **permanent storage** (disk). Remember, until you save your letter on a disk, it is stored only in volatile primary storage. Your letter can disappear if there is any interruption in the electrical supply or if you shut off the computer. When you save a document or a file on a disk, the computer actually makes a copy of what is currently in primary storage and places the copy on the disk. At that moment, two copies of your file exist—one on the disk (a form of secondary storage) and one in the primary storage area of the microcomputer.

We recommend that you save your work every 10 minutes. In this way, if something should happen to accidentally erase your working storage you will have lost only the last 10 minutes worth of effort. To save the document and return to editing, use the command ^KS or [F9]. This command saves the text on the disk and allows you to return to the document for further work.

Remember, as you make changes on the screen, that the only copy being changed is the one in primary storage. This version of the file is referred to as the *working storage version* or the *working copy*. When you finish making all the needed changes in the working storage file, you will need to again save that file on a disk, or in permanent storage. If you save the file using *exactly* the same name as you previously used, then the newly revised version will totally replace the older version on the disk. If you use a slightly different filename, two versions will exist on the disk—the old, unedited version and the newly edited version. If your files are long, you will rapidly use up your available disk file space. Also, you may get confused about which file on the disk is the latest version.

A common, but troublesome, oversight is to fail to save the latest working storage version. It is easy to forget that you are working on a primary storage copy of the file and not directly on the file stored on the disk. You can avoid this problem by remembering to always save your latest working storage version on a disk before quitting and turning off the computer.

There are three ways to save a document using WordStar:

Action	*Command*
Save text and exit to WordStar Opening Menu	^K D *or* [F10]
Not save text and exit to WordStar Opening Menu	^K Q
Save text and return to the document for editing	^K S *or* [F9]

Since you have completed editing your document, enter the command

^K D *or* **[F10]**

Print the Document

Before entering a Print command, be certain your computer is properly connected to a printer and the printer is turned on and ready. There are two basic steps to printing a document: (1) accessing the main menu and (2) producing the document on a printer.

Step 1: Access the main menu.

In WordStar you can print a document by first saving the document (^K D) and then returning to the Opening Menu.

Step 2: Print the document.

Press

```
P
```

The Print Utility will be loaded and a prompt will appear on the screen:

```
Document to print?_
```

One of the handy features of WordStar 4.0 is the ability to move the cursor to the filename listed on the file directory. Use the arrow keys to move to SS5489.LET, or type the filename. Press **Return.**

If the printer is properly connected and is turned on, the letter should be printed quickly.

Step 3: Proofread the printed document.

Step 4: Correct any remaining errors.

If the letter still contains errors, reload the document and make the needed corrections.

Quit WordStar

As fundamental as this may sound, it is very important to quit WordStar properly to make sure files are properly saved and closed. Always return to the system prompt before removing the WordStar disk or turning the microcomputer off.

When you are satisfied with your letter, save it, return to the Opening Menu, and type

```
X
```

to quit.

Remove the disk, close the disk drive doors, and turn off the microcomputer.

LESSON 4 TUTORIAL: CREATING A RESUMÉ

To complete this tutorial you need the following:

- MS-DOS system disk
- WordStar program disk

- Disk containing the files from Lesson 3
- A standard printer connected to the microcomputer

While completing this tutorial you will learn how to use

- boldfacing
- block operations
- format commands for margins, page breaks, tabs, indent, and centering
- print options
- file retrieval

In this tutorial you will create a resumé for Pat Allen, the same fictitious person who wrote the cover letter in Lesson 3.

Overview of the Tutorial

We will assume you have already learned how to load the MS-DOS operating system, load WordStar, and create a new document name. This tutorial will introduce techniques for centering text, highlighting text using the boldface option, moving blocks of text, setting margins, setting and using tab stops, inserting unconditional page breaks, merging one document into another document, and using the print options of WordStar.

Create the Document

As explained in Lesson 3, there are four basic steps for creating a new document: (1) load the operating system into primary storage, (2) load the word processing software into primary storage, (3) open the document using a unique filename, and (4) insert the new text into the document. Below we will briefly review the steps. If necessary, refer to Lesson 3 for more detailed information.

Step 1: Load the operating system into primary storage.

Load the operating system and, if necessary, set the time and date. The system prompt (A>) will appear on the screen. At that point, if you are using a separate MS-DOS disk, remove the MS-DOS disk from disk drive A.

Step 2: Load WordStar into primary storage.

Insert the WordStar disk in drive A and the files disk (the disk on which you stored your files from Lesson 3) in drive B. Latch the disk drive doors. Type

```
WS
```

to load WordStar.

At the Opening Menu, change the logged disk drive to B. Type

```
L
```

At the prompt, type

```
B
```

Press **Return.**

Step 3: Open the new document.

At the Opening Menu, press

```
D
```

to open a document. Type

```
RESUME.DOC
```

Press **Return.**

Remember, since you have already declared disk drive B as the drive holding your work files, that WordStar automatically will locate and store files on drive B. RESUME is a name you created that starts with a letter, contains no blanks or punctuation characters, has eight characters or fewer, and reminds you of the contents of the file. .DOC is a suffix you added to remind you that this is a document file rather than a worksheet or a database file.

Step 4: Insert text into the document.

After you have entered the filename you created, you will again be shown a new editing screen.

a. Enter the heading. The heading is centered and boldfaced to improve appearance and to get the reader's attention.

1. Enter the command to boldface the heading. Press

   `^PB` *or* **[F4]**

   The boldface code (^B) will appear on the screen. The P does not appear on the screen, and the code will not appear on the printed page. The characters will be shifted over two spaces to the left when the text is printed. Feel free to substitute the function key command, [F4], when boldfacing.
2. Enter the title of the document. Press the **Caps Lock key** and type

   ```
   RESUME
   ```

Remember, if you use the Shift key while the Caps Lock key is on, characters will be printed as lower case. Notice that the appearance of entered characters may be distinctive. Installation options permit users to specify whether boldfaced and underlined characters will appear as such on the screen.

3. End the boldfacing by repeating the boldface code. Press

   ```
   ^PB
   ```

   again. It is very important to remember that you end the boldfacing by repeating the command. If you do not repeat it, the computer will continue the boldfacing until it encounters the next ^PB.

4. Center the text. Make sure the cursor is on the line that you want centered. Press

   `^OC` *or* **Shift-[F2]**

   The text will be centered instantaneously, saving you much time and aggravation.

   The cursor will remain at the end of the centered line. Press **Return.**

5. Repeat the same steps to boldface and center the name. To boldface the name, press

   ```
   ^PB
   ```

   Type

   ```
   PAT ALLEN
   ```

   Turn off the boldfacing by pressing

   ```
   ^PB
   ```

   Center the text by typing

   `^OC` *or* **Shift-[F2]**

   If the centered line doesn't turn out the way you wanted and you would like to delete the entire line and start over, use the line delete command (^Y). Be careful to have the cursor on the exact line you want to delete. WordStar has a feature that you can use if you delete the wrong line. Just press ^U and the deleted line returns. WordStar temporarily saves the last item you delete and allows you to retrieve it if you find you need to. Some people like to refer to this as the Oops! feature.

The boldfaced title and name normally appear on the screen centered and in a different shading or color. This is an example of onscreen formatting. Note that you can instantly tell whether the text has been properly boldfaced. Check to be sure the ^B symbol appears at the *end* as well as the beginning of the area you want boldfaced.

b. Enter the address headings. The headings HOME ADDRESS and SCHOOL ADDRESS are created using the boldface command (^PB or [F4]), the Caps Lock key, and the Tab key.

1. Insert two blank lines so the address headings begin two lines below the name heading. Press **Return** *twice.*

2. With the Caps Lock on, type

```
^PBHOME ADDRESS:
```

3. Press the Tab key *five times.* Your cursor should be on column 36. Type

```
SCHOOL ADDRESS: ^PB
```

Press **Return.** Press the **Caps Lock key.**
In WordStar the tab stops are automatically fixed at five-space intervals. However, you can change the tab settings using the tab clear and set commands. Let's set the tabs to make the addresses quicker and easier to enter.

4. Delete all tabs. Type

```
^ON A
```

Press **Return.** Notice that the ruler line is now clear except for the margins.

5. Set the new tab stops for columns 5 and 40. Type

```
^OI 5
```

Press **Return.**
Repeat the Set Tabs command. Type

```
^OI 40
```

Press **Return.** Notice the new tab stops placed on the ruler line.

6. To type the data for the home and school addresses, first move to the tab stops we just set. Press **Tab** before entering each line of the addresses.
   Press **Tab** and type

   ```
   880 West Elm Street
   ```

   Press **Tab** and type

   ```
   123 East St. Apt. 21
   ```

   Press **Return.**
   Press **Tab** and type

   ```
   Naperville, Illinois 60234
   ```

   Press **Tab** and type

   ```
   Iowa City, Iowa 55204
   ```

   Press **Return.**
   Press **Tab** and type

   ```
   (312) 555-1234
   ```

   Press **Tab** and type

   ```
   (402) 987-9876
   ```

   Press **Return** *twice.*

c. Enter the sections. Section headings are used to highlight the areas of interest on a resumé. Each heading will be typed in upper case and boldfaced.

1. Press the **Caps Lock key.** Use the boldfacing command before and after each heading. Type

   ```
   ^PBEMPLOYMENT OBJECTIVE:^PB
   ```
   Press **Return.**
2. Press the **Caps Lock key.** Press the temporary indent command

   ```
   ^OG
   ```
   When you give the temporary indent command, the text in the paragraph will be indented as it is typed until you press Return to

signal the start of a new paragraph, press ^B to align the paragraph, or press ^OL to change the left margin. **Do not use the Return key to move to the next line. Let word wrap do the work!** Type

```
Seeking full-time summer position working
with microcomputer hardware and software.
```

Press **Return** *twice.*

3. Press the **Caps Lock key.** Type

```
^PBEDUCATION: ^PB
```

Press **Return.** Press the **Caps Lock key.** Press the temporary indent command

```
^OG
```

Type

```
Currently pursuing B.S. in Business
Administration, University of Iowa.
Expected graduation date May 20, 1989.
Majoring in Management Information
Systems. Overall GPA 3.4 on 4.0 scale and
3.5 in courses in major.
```

Press **Return** *twice.*

4. Repeat the temporary indent command

```
^OG
```

and type

```
High school diploma from Naperville High
School, 1985 with 3.88 GPA (top 10 percent
of class). Member National Honor Society,
and Computer Club. Participated in band
and yearbook.
```

Press **Return** *twice.*

5. Press the **Caps Lock key.** Type

```
^PBHONORS AND AWARDS^PB
```

6. Press the **Caps Lock key.** Press **Return.** Press the temporary indent command

```
^OG
```

and type

```
The University of Iowa Dean's List, 1988.
```

Press **Return** *twice.*
Press the temporary indent command

```
^OG
```

and type

```
Elected president of Lincoln South
Residence Hall, 1987 and 1988.
```

Press **Return** *twice.*

7. Press the **Caps Lock key.** Type

```
^PBEMPLOYMENT RECORD:^PB
```

8. Press the **Caps Lock key.** Press **Return.** Press the temporary indent command

```
^OG
```

and type

```
Current: Computer Lab Assistant, Business
Microcomputer Laboratory, University of
Iowa. Assist students in lab in using
IBM-compatible microcomputers and software
including Lotus, dBASE III, and WordStar.
```

Press **Return** *twice.*

9. Press the temporary indent command

```
^OG
```

and type

```
Summer 1988: Sales Representative,
TechMARK Incorporated. Sold various models
of microcomputers and helped customers set
up hardware and software for home and
small business use. Gained experience
dealing with people in addition to
handling a variety of technical problems.
```

Press **Return** *twice.*

9. Press the temporary indent command

```
^OG
```

and type

```
Summer 1987: Sales Clerk, Kay's Department
Store. Sold women's dresses and luggage.
Gained experience meeting people and
handling money.
```

Press **Return** *twice.*

10. Press the **Caps Lock key.** Type

```
^PBREFERENCES FURNISHED UPON REQUEST^PB
```

Press **Return.**

Your document should be similar to Figure 4-13 (p. 144) without the hanging margins.

Step 4: Save the document and return to editing.
Use the Save/Continue command

`^KS` *or* **[F9]**

to save the document and return to editing.

Step 5: Format the document.

a. Change the margins. As explained in Lesson 3, the margins (the amount of blank space on either side of the paper when the document is printed) are indicated on the ruler line. The left margin (indicated by the letter L) is column 1 on the screen but actually starts printing in column 10 on the page, while the right margin (indicated by the letter R) is column 65 on the screen and column 75 on the printed page. Since 10 spaces equals one inch, the current margin settings would provide a one-inch margin on the left side and the right side.

Let's experiment with the appearance of the resumé by adjusting the margins.

1. Move the cursor to the top of the document. Press

   ^QR

2. Type the left margin command

   ^OL

   The status line will change to the prompt

   `New left margin?_`

   WordStar is asking for a left margin setting. If you press the Escape key, the left margin will be set at the *current cursor column.* You can also enter the column number for the new left margin. For example, if you want to set the left margin at 10 spaces (a printed margin 20 spaces or 2 inches wide on the left side of the printed page), you would type "10" and press Return. If you want to keep the current margins, just press the Space Bar.
3. Since we want the new left margin to begin in column 15 on the printed page, type

   5

   Press **Return.**

   Notice that the left side of the ruler line now starts in column 5. All newly entered and realigned text will be aligned with the new margins.
4. Realign the previously entered text by first placing the cursor on the first character of the first line of the title (RESUME). Then press

   ^B

   to realign the line to the new margins. Notice that the title is moved to the current margin after you give the align paragraph command. This command will not affect the paragraphs entered with the temporary indent command.

5. Return to the previous margins by moving the cursor to line 1, column 1. Press

```
^OL
```

Press **Escape.**
With the cursor on the same line as the title (RESUME), press

```
^B
```

b. Add a Print Format command. Since your resumé is a single page, you will not want a page number printed at the bottom of the page. A Print Format command is used to turn off the automatic page numbering.

Move the cursor to line 1, column 1, of the document using one of the quick movement commands. Press **Home.** Insert the dot command for turning the page numbering off. First, insert a blank line to make room for the dot command. Press **Return.** Use the **up arrow key** to move the cursor back up to line 1, column 1. After the cursor is in the proper position, type, in upper or lower case,

```
.OP
```

The dot command must start in column 1 to be effective. If you accidentally place the dot command on the same line with text, the text will not be printed.

Normally, when the document is printed the pages will automatically be numbered at the bottom. The dot command .OP turns off the page numbering for this particular document. You can turn the page numbering back on by using the command .PN on the page where you want the numbering resumed. Specify the page number by the command .PN *n,* where *n* is the page number.

Step 6: Save the document and return to editing.

Now is a good time to save the document and return to editing. Type

`^KS` *or* **[F9]**

The document will be saved on the disk in drive B and WordStar will return to editing.

Edit the Document

Although you have a complete resumé, you may want to improve the appearance, emphasize particular areas, or change the order of information. Word processing is perfect for editing without the time-consuming job of retyping, and WordStar has a full range of commands to make editing quick and easy. Some of the handiest tools for effective editing are block operations, which we will examine at length in Step 3.

Step 1: Proofread the document.

Now is the time to *carefully* proofread the document. Do not be concerned if it takes you a few tries to get the resumé perfect. A resumé is not something you do every day, and accuracy is more important than speed.

Step 2: Correct all errors.

Use the arrow keys and the Delete and Insert commands to correct any errors. If you need a reminder of these commands, refer to the on-screen menus.

Step 3: Mark and move a block of text.

Move the EMPLOYMENT RECORD section to before EDUCATION to highlight the employment history. To rearrange the document, you will need to define the section called EMPLOYMENT RECORD as a block and then move the block where you want it.

a. Mark the block. You must instruct the word processing software where the block begins and ends. This is called *marking a block.* To complete a Block command, you must insert both block markers in the text and be sure they are visible

To place a set of block markers, use the arrow keys to move the cursor to where you want the block to begin. Place the cursor on the first character (^) in the title ^BEMPLOYMENT RECORD^B. Press

^KB *or* **Shift-[F9]**

The first character of the block is moved over by a <B> to indicate the beginning of the block.

Mark the end of the block by using the arrow keys to move the cursor to the last character of the block (space after the period at the end of the word *money.*). Press

^KK *or* **Shift-[F10]**

The last character of the block is replaced by a <K> to indicate the end of the block. Please note that not all screens will show the second block marker, but will show the block in a distinctive shading or reverse video.

b. Move the block.

1. Using the arrow keys, move the cursor to the blank line directly above the title ^BEDUCATION^B in column 1. Press **Return** to insert a blank line.
2. Type the command

   `^KV` *or* **Shift-[F7]**

   to move the block.
3. Check the document to be sure all the spacing is correct. Press **Return** to move the paragraph down one line. Check carefully the number of blank lines between the section titles and the sections. There should be one blank line above each section title. If there are too many lines, delete the blank lines by placing the cursor on the blank line directly above the REFERENCES line, in column 1. Press

   `Del` *or* `^Y`

   The extra line will disappear and the section title will move up one line. Delete as many lines as necessary to have only one blank line between the section title and the preceding section.

c. Save the document using the Save/Continue command

`^KS` *or* **[F9]**

The resumé will be saved on the disk in drive B.

d. Merge two documents. Merge the cover letter completed in the tutorial for Lesson 3 with the resumé so they can be printed together. The cursor will be moved to the end of the document, the letter file will be read and retrieved, and then the revised resumé will be stored, using a new filename so that the original resumé will be preserved.

1. Move the cursor to the bottom of the document. Press

   `^QC`

   If necessary, press **Return** to insert a blank line. Your cursor should be in column 1 of the blank line at the bottom of the document.

   Insert a hard page break. Type

   `.PA`

   Press **Return.**

A dashed line will appear on the screen, indicating the beginning of a new page.

2. Read the letter onto the new page. Use the Insert a File command. Press

   ^KR

   and, at the prompt

   Document?_

   type the needed filename,

   SS5489.LET

   Or use the arrow key to move the cursor to the filename and press **Return.**

3. Change the date in the letter to today's date.

4. Save the file using a new name. To do this, first move the cursor to the beginning of the document—line 1, column 1 (^QR).

   Type the Block Mark Begin command

   ^KB *or* **Shift-[F9]**

   Move the cursor to the end of the document by typing

   ^QC

   Press **Return** to insert a line.

   Type the Block Mark End command

   ^KK *or* **Shift [F10]**

   Press the Block Write command to save the file to a new filename. Type

   ^KW

   At the prompt

   Name?_

   type

```
B:RESLET.DOC
```

to indicate that you have combined the resumé and the letter.
To remove the block markers, type

```
^KH
```

5. Quit the file without saving. Type

```
^KQ
```

At the prompt asking you if you are sure that you want to abandon the changes, type

```
Y
```

Print the Document

Before entering the Print command, be certain that your computer is properly connected to a printer and the printer is turned on and ready. Some software also require you to properly configure the software for your printer. **Configure** means to customize the software for your specific model of printer. Some software have command "codes" that permit special printing characteristics on particular printers.

At the Opening Menu, type

```
P
```

At the prompt

```
Document to print?
```

enter the filename, or use the arrow keys to move the cursor to the filename and press **Return.** Press **Escape** to accept the default settings.

Quit WordStar

After printing is completed, the WordStar menu will reappear on the screen. Press

```
X
```

to quit.

Remove the disk, close the disk drive doors, and turn off the microcomputer.

In addition to using a word processor to type your resumé perfectly, you can also customize parts of your resumé to fit the job you are applying for. You may want to slightly change the section on employment objectives to more nearly match those of the job or you may want to emphasize or deemphasize particular courses or experiences, depending on the position you are considering. In this way you can send out many resumés, and each can seem custom made. Also, each can be an original, rather than a copy.

An interesting method for customizing documents is the use of **boiler-plate** paragraphs. For example, a section of your resumé may be particularly appropriate if you are applying for a sales position. Rather than retyping it every time you make up a custom resumé, save the section in a file, such as B:RESALES.DOC, and recall or read the file into a new file whenever it is needed.

LESSON 5 TUTORIAL: PLANNING AND WRITING A TERM PAPER

For this tutorial you need the following:

- WordStar disk
- Files disk used in Lessons 3 and 4
- An installed printer connected to the microcomputer

While completing this tutorial you will learn how to

- Use formatting commands, including margins, headings, page numbers, centering, and double spacing
- Use Search and Replace

So far you have learned how to use word processing to edit, format, save, and print short documents. This tutorial uses a report as an example of a longer and more complicated document. As we have seen, editing and revising, especially on longer documents, are easier using word processing.

Suppose you have been asked to investigate and discuss the topic of the history of word processing software. The report you produce should meet the following standards of style:

- The report must be double spaced and have a 1-inch top margin, a $1\frac{1}{2}$-inch left margin, and a 1-inch right margin. The first page of text should have a top margin of $1\frac{1}{2}$ inches.
- A title page is required. The title of the paper should be centered in the middle of the page, followed by your name, the course name and number, and the instructor's name, each centered.
- Each page of the report should have a page heading that includes the title of the report, the date, and the page number.

- The report is to contain reference notes with at least five references. The notes are to be printed at the end of the document as endnotes.

You already know how to load the operating system and word processing software into your computer. If you need a reminder, see Lesson 3 or Lesson 4. Name the new file B:TERM*tah,* substituting your initials for *tah.*

Create and Format the Report

If you have properly opened a new file, the next step is to format, or set up, the document according to the required standards of style. As we discussed earlier, some word processing software permit very flexible formatting. All margins (top, bottom, right, and left) are adjustable through formatting commands. Most word processing software packages have default settings for formatting requirements. The default format settings are usually the common settings for a standard business letter. Therefore, if you add no formatting commands on your own, the document you create will be formatted according to the default settings.

Step 1: Create the cover page.

Since the settings will be different from the default settings, you need to use the format commands to change the format of the title and text pages. The onscreen format dot commands are listed in Table A-2.

a. Title pages are usually not numbered. Since most word processors automatically number each page, you will need to turn off this feature for the title page. With the cursor in column 1, type

```
.OP
```

b. Enter the titles.

1. Move the cursor to the center of the page. Press **Return** until you reach line 20. Watch the status line at the top of the page. It will tell you which line you are on.
2. Type the title on line 20. Type

```
A SHORT HISTORY OF WORD PROCESSING
```

3. Center the title. For centering text, an alternative command is available with the Shorthand Menu with WordStar 4.0. Press Esc and, after the Shorthand Menu appears, press

```
C
```

The title on that line will be centered automatically. Remember all those times you had to center text by counting the

Table A-2 COMMONLY USED DOT COMMANDS IN WORDSTAR

Dot Command	*Action*
.PA	Unconditional page break
.CP*n*	Conditional page break
.RR	Embedded ruler line
.PM*n*	Starts the first line of paragraph in column *n*
.LM*n*	Sets the left margin at column *n*
.RM*n*	Sets the right margin at column *n*
.IG *or* ..	Comment
.PN*n*	Sets page number to *n*
.PL*n*	Sets page length to *n* lines
.MT*n*	Sets the top margin to *n* lines
.MB*n*	Sets the bottom margin to *n* lines
.LH*n*	Sets the line height to $\frac{n}{48}$ inch
.OP	Omits page numbers from the bottom of each printed page
.PG	Restores the page numbers on each printed page
.PC*n*	Prints page numbers at column *n*
.HE text	Prints text on this line as page header
.H1 text	Same as .HE
.H2 text	Second line of a header
.H3 text	Third line of a header
.F0 text	Print text as a footer
.F1 text	Same as .F0
.F2 text	Second line of footer
.F3 text	Third line of footer
.LS*n*	Sets the line spacing to *n* where 1=single, 2=double, 3=triple spacing.

number of characters in a title and then backspacing? Most word processors have line centering, although some require print formatting commands rather than onscreen formatting to center text.

4. Press **Return** *twice.*
5. Type and center

```
by
```

Press **Return** *twice.*

6. Type and center your name.
7. Press **Return** *four times.*
8. Type and center

```
Prepared for
```

9. Press **Return** *twice.*
10. Type the lines below and center them. Press **Return** after each line.

```
Introduction to Information Systems
Information Systems 110
Dr. Joseph Baumgart
Spring 1990
```

11. Insert today's date. Press

```
Esc @
```

The Esc key recalls the Shorthand Menu. The @ is the shorthand command to insert the current system date.

12. Center it and press **Return.**

c. Start a new page. Type the new page command

```
.PA
```

Step 2: Format the text pages.

The text pages are to be double spaced, with margins of $1\frac{1}{2}$ inches on the left and 1 inch on the right. The top margin is to be $1\frac{1}{2}$ inches on the first page and 1 inch on subsequent pages. Each page is to have a heading made up of the title of the paper, today's date, and a page number.

a. Insert the formatting codes to change the left margin to $1\frac{1}{2}$ inches. Since there are 10 spaces to an inch and the margin is already set for 1 inch, the dot command .LM 6 will cause the text on the page to be printed beginning in column 16. With the cursor in column 1, line 1, of the new page, type

```
.LM 6
```

b. Turn the page numbering back on to start at page number 1. On line 2, column 1, type

```
.PN 1
```

c. Insert the formatting code to place the top margin at $1\frac{1}{2}$ inches. Since 6 lines equals 1 inch, to set the top margin at $1\frac{1}{2}$ inches, we will set it at 9 lines. On line 3, column 1, type

```
.MT 9
```

d. Set the line spacing to double spacing. On line 4, column 1, type

```
.LS 2
```

Step 3: Enter the text.

As the text is entered, you will mark the footnotes using the superscript command. You will then place the footnotes at the end of the document.

a. Type the text as it is written below. Remember to use the Tab when necessary and to let word wrap do its work. Use the Return key only at the end of paragraphs.

```
    At what point in history did word
processing begin? It depends on how word
processing is defined. To quote the authors
of THE NAKED COMPUTER, a humorous almanac of
computer lore, "One of the most common and
useful applications for a personal computer
is writing, called word processing."
```

Do not press Return.

1. Insert a reference note. Press the superscript command

   ```
   ^PT
   ```

   The symbol ^T appears on the screen. Any text after the ^T is highlighted, and the new text you type is also highlighted. Type

   ```
   1
   ```

   and repeat the superscript command

   ```
   ^PT
   ```

to end the superscripting. Remember to insert two line spaces after every note by pressing the space bar twice.

2. Continue with the paper. Do not press Return before entering the following text. It should be in the same paragraph as the text preceding the footnote.

```
They say the term grew out of data
processing, which is a computer working
with numerical information as opposed to
the written language. "Next to liquor,
word processing is a writer's best
friend," says one writer we know.
```

3. Insert a reference note. Follow the same directions as above to superscript the note number, substituting *2* for *1* since this is the second note.

4. Press **Return.**

   Insert the command to change the top margin back to 1 inch. Type

```
.MT 6
```

   Press **Return.**

5. Insert the commands to have headings at the top of each page, including page number.

   On a new line, with the cursor in column 1, type

```
.HE A Short History of Word Processing Page #
```

Press **Return.**

The "#" in "Page #" indicates where the page number should be inserted. The # should be placed in column 68 to compensate for the three spaces taken up by the dot command (.HE). Since the dot command will not be printed, the page number will be printed in column 65, at the right margin.

On the next line, in column 1, type

```
.H2 Your name
```

Press

```
Esc @
```

By pressing Esc @, you cause the Shorthand Menu to insert today's date in the heading. Press **Return.**

6. Continue typing the paper.

```
    One way to mark the beginning is to
consider some developments in typewriting
technology in the 1960's. In July 1961,
IBM first presented its Selectric
typewriter, a speedy electric model with
changeable print balls that gave users
more control over the typeface and type
size in their documents.
```

7. Insert a reference note. Repeat the commands for superscripting text, making this note number 3.
8. Continue with the paper. Do not press Return; continue with the same paragraph.

```
In 1971, a full ten years later, Wang Labs
introduced Wang 1200, a typing workstation
with a small screen and the ability to
store up to 133,000 characters on cassette
tape.
```

9. Insert a reference note. Repeat the commands for superscripting text, making this note number 4.
10. Continue with the paper. Do not press Return; continue with the same paragraph.

```
Five years later Wang introduced a system
it called the WPS, which stood for Word
Processing System, and the term was born.
```

11. Insert a reference note, making this note number 5.
12. Continue with the paper. Do not press Return; continue with the same paragraph.

```
Also in 1976, Michael Shrayer produced
Electric Pencil, the first popular word
processing program for microcomputers.
```

13. Insert a reference note, making this note number 6.
14. Continue with the paper. Press **Return** and type as follows:

```
    Following those initial steps in the
1960's and '70's, a flood of developments
hit. WordStar was born in 1979, IBM
Displaywriter in 1980, Volkswriter,
EasyWriter, and WangWriter in 1981,
MultiMate with WordMate, and Wordperfect
in 1982, Microsoft Word, PFS:Write, and
Version 3.3 of WordStar were all
introduced in 1983, and since then
practically every product mentioned has
introduced one or more major new versions.
```

15. Insert a reference note, making this note number 7.
16. Continue with the paper. Press **Return** and type

```
    Today journals such as PERSONAL
COMPUTING, BYTE, PC MAGAZINE, FAMILY &
HOME-OFFICE COMPUTING, and many more
feature new word processing software
reviews practically every month. Some,
such as INFOWORLD and COMPUTING WORLD, are
produced in newspaper-style format and
manage to fill approximately 100 pages per
week with articles and ads concerning new
developments.
```

Press **Return** *twice.* Continue with the paper.

```
WHO USES WORD PROCESSING?
    Some folks may still view personal
computers and word processing as the tools
of secretaries and technical nerds only,
and not executives and other high-ranking
professionals. However, even arch
conservative William F. Buckley, Jr., is a
regular user. Buckley says those who say
you cannot love the written word unless
you set it down by pencil on a legal pad
are just foolish.
```

17. Set off the quote below using the temporary indent and single-space dot commands.

    Press **Return.** In column 1, type

```
.LS 1
```

Press **Return.**

Press

```
^OG
```

and type

```
Writing is menial work. It is not
artistic, unless one is a calligrapher. So
then, why not attempt to abbreviate that
work? . . . Progressive conservatives should
pass a law making it unlawful not to use a
computer.
```

18. Insert a reference note using the superscript command, making this note number 8.
19. Return to double spacing and the original margins. Press **Return** *twice.* In column 1, type

```
.LS 2
```

20. Continue with the paper. Press **Return** and type

```
    Numerous other surveys and reports
indicate top executives are using word
processing to help them prepare speeches,
draft reports and memorandums, and, with
the aid of spelling checkers and grammar
checkers anc outline processors, improve
the quality of their writing. Former
President Jimmy Carter tells of the sheer
fun he had learning to use his new word
processor after he left the White House
and began to write a series of books.
```

21. Insert a reference note, making it note number 9.
22. Continue with the paper. Do not press Return; continue with the same paragraph.

```
Professionals in practically all walks of
life have found that using a PC and a word
processing package does more than merely
speed up the typing process. It actually
aids their ability to communicate.
    Word processing traces its roots back
into data processing and typewriting, but
```

```
it was the invention of the transistor in
1948 by John Bardeen, Walter Brattain, and
William Shockley of Bell Laboratories and
its use in the microcomputer in the early
1970's that really propelled word
processing into its current state of
popularity. That current state includes
numerous vendors retailing word processing
software; in fact, the February 29, 1988,
issue of PC MAGAZINE reviews 55 packages.
With so many products to choose from, how
does the potential buyer know which to
select? One approach is to go with the
industry standard, the so-called IBM of
word processing software.
```

Press **Return** *twice.* Continue with the paper.

```
THE INDUSTRY STANDARD?
    A few years ago WordStar was the
standard in American offices. Its
mail-merge and spelling checker came at an
additional cost, but today its vendor,
MicroPro, offers those features and many
others as part of the standard package
called WordStar Professional, retailing at
$395.00. Currently the industry leader in
sales is Wordperfect, by Wordperfect
Corp., selling for $495.00.
```

23. Insert a reference note, making it note number 10.
24. Continue with the paper. Do not press Return; continue with the same paragraph.

```
Wordperfect is described as featuring easy
import of files created in other leading
programs, mail-merge, outlining,
red-lining, table of authorities,
unlimited toll-free telephone support,
plus an energetic Wordperfect forum on
CompuServe offering on-line advice,
utilities, and free updates of program
add-ons.
```

25. Insert a reference note, making it note number 11.

26. Continue with the paper. Do not press Return, continue with the same paragraph.

```
Despite the recent surge in the popularity
of Wordperfect, WordStar remains an
industry standard too. Recent versions
have added many features missing from
earlier versions, and when WordStar
Professional, Release 4.0 was released in
February 1987, it sold 170,000 copies
within six months. Version 5.0 has also
been successful. In all, MicroPro has sold
more than three million copies of the
various versions of WordStar.
```

27. Insert a reference note, making it note number 12.
28. Continue with the paper. Press **Return** *twice* and type

```
SUMMARY AND CONCLUSION
    Word processing can trace its recent
history from the early 1970's and has been
greatly affected by the boom in personal
computer sales, especially since the
introduction of the IBM PC in August of
1981. The IBM PC legitimized the
microcomputer industry to the rest of the
world and established the preeminence of
the Intel 8086 family of processors and
the Microsoft MS-DOS operating system.
```

29. Insert a reference note, making it note number 13.
30. Continue typing the paper. Do not press Return; continue with the same paragraph.

```
Since then dozens of word processing
packages have been marketed and word
processing has spread from the secretary's
desk to the desk of the executive and the
home office worker. Wordperfect and
WordStar are now the industry standards
but many others are also popular. The
laser printer and desktop publishing
software now make it possible for
individuals to produce high-quality
documents with just a few hundred dollars
worth of hardware and software.
```

Press **Return** *twice.*

31. Type the notes at the end of the document. Remember to insert the superscript command before and after the note number. Press **Return** *twice* after each note. Type

[1]Rochester, Jack B., and John Gantz, The Naked Computer (New York: William Morrow, 1983), p. 29.

[2]Ibid.

[3]Ellison, Carol, "The Trek from Typewriters," PC Magazine, Feb. 29, 1988, p. 96.

[4]Ibid.

[5]Ibid.

[6]Williams, Gregg, and Mark Welch, "A Microcomputing Timeline," Byte, Sept. 1985, p. 200.

[7]Ibid.

[8]Buckley, William F., "The Conservative Computer," in Digital Deli, Steve Ditlea, (New York: Workman Publishing, 1984), pp. 362-363.

[9]Carter, Jimmy, and Rosalynn Carter, Everything to Gain, (New York: Random House, 1987), p. 18.

[10]Seymour, Jim, "Word Processing: Fast, Flexible, and Forward Looking," PC Magazine, Feb. 29, 1988, pp. 92-104.

[11]Ibid, p. 324.

[12]Brown, Bruce, "WordStar Professional," PC Magazine, Feb. 29, 1988, p. 326.

[13]Williams and Welch, p. 205.

Step 4: Save the document.
Press

`^KS` *or* **[F9]**

Edit the Document

Step 1: Spell-check the document to find spelling errors.

The commands for using the WordStar spelling corrector appear on the Quick Menu (^Q). These include ^QL to check the spelling of the entire document. To use it, place the cursor at the start of the document and press **^QL.** If you want to interrupt the spell check, press **^U.** ^QN will check the spelling of the word where the cursor is currently placed. ^QO allows you to enter a word and check its spelling. If for some reason the spell-checking files are not on your WordStar disk, WordStar will prompt for the disks to be placed in the disk drive. After you load the spell-checker, a full menu will appear with the command options.

Step 2: Do a global find and replace the word "Wordperfect" with "WordPerfect" without confirmation of each word replacement.

a. Move to the beginning of the document.

b. Press

`^QA`

At the prompt

`Find what?`

type

`Wordperfect`

Press **Return.**

c. At the prompt

`Replace with?`

type

`WordPerfect`

Press **Return.**

d. The prompt changes to

`Options(s)?`

Press

WGN

to find only whole words (where the characters are not embedded in another word), replace all of the correct matches in the entire document, and replace them without asking for each matched word.

Press **Return.**

Within a few seconds the word is replaced and you can continue editing.

Step 3: Print the document.

a. Save the document and return to the Opening Menu. Press

^KD

b. Print the document. Press

P

At the prompt, enter the document name. Press **Return** and press **Esc.**

Step 4: Proofread the document.

Check the document carefully and mark any errors and any awkward page breaks.

Step 5: Correct any errors.

a. Use the Insert and Delete commands to correct any errors.

b. If necessary, insert a conditional page break. For example, if the page break comes directly under the subsection title SUMMARY AND CONCLUSION, as on page 541, place the cursor on the line directly above the title, in the first column. Type .CP 10 for the total number of lines to keep together and press Return. The page break will be placed directly above the title.

Save the Document

To save the document, type

^KD

Print the Document

Before printing the term paper, check the paper alignment in the printer for proper spacing. Make sure you use a printer ribbon with enough ink to print a clear image. Use paper that is as close to standard typing paper as possible. Wide "green bar" paper (computer paper with green bars) should be avoided. If you need to use bond paper and your printer will not accept single sheets of paper, some stores carry continuous-feed computer bond paper with connected sheets of paper for printers. If you use continuous-feed paper, you will need to "burst" or separate the perforated pages for your printed report. Be sure to make a copy of your report before submitting it.

Step 1: Select the Print options.

a. At the Opening Menu, press

```
P
```

b. Print two copies of the document.

1. At the prompt

   ```
   Document to print?
   ```

   type the filename or move the cursor to the filename in the directory. Press **Return.**
2. At the prompt

   ```
   Number of copies?
   ```

   type

   ```
   2
   ```

3. Press Esc to accept the other default options.

Exit WordStar

After you have printed the document successfully, exit WordStar using the Exit command. Press

```
X
```

After the system prompt has reappeared, remove your disks from the disk drive.

B
Using Educational Versions of Software

INTRODUCTION

Harcourt Brace Jovanovich, Inc., the publisher of this textbook, has contracted with various software firms to provide educational versions of WordPerfect 4.2, VP-Planner Plus Version 2, and dBASE III Plus at reduced cost to adopters of this textbook. The publisher and software producers will strive to provide the latest, most up-to-date versions of the various software products. Also, the particular combinations of software chosen may differ, with one college using the educational version of WordPerfect, for example, and the commercial version of Lotus 1-2-3. Therefore, the following instructions and guidelines may need to be modified slightly to match the particular combination of software available at your college. In general, the current educational versions differ from the commercial versions in the following ways.

WORDPERFECT

The educational or training version of the software licensed with this textbook is WordPerfect 4.2, with the following restrictions:

- The Help is limited to only the template ([F3][F3]).
- The spell checker and thesaurus file contains few words and is specially constructed to check and look up words contained in a file named README.WP (contained on the disk), although it can be tried with other WordPerfect files.
- The software is configured to send output to printers through the LPT 1 port only.

- Font changes and the use of ASCII characters are not available.
- The characters *WPC appear occasionally within a document.
- File size is restricted to 50K, or approximately 30 double-spaced pages.
- Files cannot be transferred between the educational version and the Commercial version of WordPerfect 4.2.

Otherwise, the educational version of WordPerfect contains all of the features of the commercial version of WordPerfect 4.2.

Regardless of what version of WordPerfect you are using, it is especially important to properly exit WordPerfect using [F7]. Do not remove the WordPerfect disk until you receive the DOS prompt (A>, B>, C>, or D>). Failure to properly exit WordPerfect can eventually result in a DISK FULL error message.

VP-PLANNER PLUS

The educational or training version of the software licensed with this textbook is VP-Planner Plus Version 2, with the following restrictions:

- The worksheet matrix is limited to 64 columns by 256 rows (16,384 cells).
- No access to multi-dimensional database functions is available.

Otherwise, the educational version of VP-Planner Plus licensed to be used with this book contains all the advanced features of VP-Planner Plus, including graphics, report generation, priority recalculation, and undo and redo features.

Some users of VP-Planner and VP-Planner Plus may experience problems using the View command, which will require you to change the hardware video default setting by using /Worksheet Global Default Hardware Video and selecting the appropriate video display for your computer. You then execute the Update command to make the change permanent. With VP-Planner, to properly display graphs using the Hercules graphics option, execute the HGC.COM file before starting. VP-Planner Plus does not require any other programs.

dBASE III PLUS

The educational version of dBASE III Plus licensed with this textbook has all the advanced features of the commercially sold dBASE III Plus, with the following restrictions:

- Each file is limited to 31 records.
- The word "demo" appears before the dot prompt.

Please note that dBASE does not warn users when they have created more than 31 records in a file. If the 31-record limitation is exceeded, access to the file is denied when the user later attempts to use a file. If a commercial version is available, that version can be used to access the file and delete the excess records. Each record can contain up to 256 fields. There is no restriction on the number of files.

Installing dBASE Using the Educational Version of dBASE III Plus

This version of dBASE III Plus requires a special routine for installing and using the software on the microcomputer of your choice. It may be necessary to install dBASE before you use it on the microcomputer for the *first* time. However, it is not necessary to repeat the installation routine unless you change the type of microcomputer you are using with dBASE III Plus.

To install:

1. Load the operating system by inserting a system disk in disk drive A. Turn on the microcomputer or reset the machine using the Ctrl + Alt + Del command. If necessary, set the time and date. The system prompt (A>) should appear on your screen.
2. If necessary, remove the system disk from the drive and place the dBASE III Plus Educational Version Disk 1 in drive A. dBASE refers to this disk as Sampler Disk 1.
3. Type **install** and press **Return.**
4. A new screen will appear, listing various memory and drive selections.

```
dBASE III  PLUS SAMPLER INSTALLATION

            MEMORY AND DRIVE SELECTION

  A. 256K and 2 floppy drives
  B. More than 256K and 2 floppy drives
  C. 256K and 1 floppy drive and 1 harddisk
  D. More than 256K and 1 floppy drive and 1 harddisk

Type the letter corresponding to your computer's configuration:
```

5. Find the configuration for the microcomputer you are now using and press the appropriate letter.
6. A new prompt will appear on the screen. Place dBASE Disk 1 in drive A and the MS-DOS system disk that you will use with dBASE in drive B. dBASE will place a CONFIG.SYS file on the MS-DOS disk that will permit it to properly run your version of dBASE.

7. Press any key to continue.
8. After dBASE has properly installed the CONFIG.SYS file, a new screen will appear. Place the newly configured MS-DOS disk in disk drive A.
9. Press **Ctrl + Alt + Del** to reboot the system.
10. After the system prompt reappears (A>), remove the MS-DOS system disk from drive A and replace it with dBASE Disk 1.
11. Type **dbase** and press **Return** *twice* to load the software and agree to the licensing agreement.
12. A new prompt will appear. Remove dBASE Disk 1 from drive A and replace it with Sampler Disk 2. Place a data disk to store your files in drive B. Press **Return.**

Loading dBASE III Plus Educational Version

After the software has been installed, follow these steps to load dBASE III Plus.

1. Insert the MS-DOS disk containing the operating system that has been properly configured for dBASE III Plus Educational Version.
2. Turn the computer on, or press **Ctrl + Alt + Del.**
3. If necessary, set the date and time at the prompts.
4. The system prompt (A>) will appear, indicating that the operating system has been loaded.
5. Remove the system disk from drive A and place dBASE III Plus Disk 1 (Sampler Disk 1) in drive A.
6. Type **dbase** and press **Return.**
7. After the first part of dBASE III Plus has been loaded into RAM, at the prompt, insert Sample Disk 2 (dBASE III Plus Disk 2) into drive A and a data disk into drive B. Press **Return.**
8. The rest of dBASE III Plus will load and the Assistant menu will appear. dBASE is now ready to use.
9. To exit dBASE III Plus, move the highlight to **Set Up – Quit dBASE III PLUS** or press **Esc** and at the dot prompt, ((DEMO).), type **quit.**
10. If a prompt appears on the screen asking for a disk with COMMAND.COM, place any disk containing the operating system in drive A and press any key. The system prompt will reappear.

C
WordPerfect Command References

WORDPERFECT VERSION 4.2

Feature	*Keystrokes*
Advance Line	Shift-[F1]*
Advance Up/Down	Shift-[F1]
Alignment Character	Shift-[F8]
Append Block (Block on)	Ctrl-[F4]
Auto Rewrite	Ctrl-[F3]
Backspace	←**
Binding Width	Shift-[F7] 3
Block	Alt-[F4]
Block, Cut/Copy (Block on)	Ctrl-[F4]
Block Protect (Block on)	Alt-[F8]
Bold	[F6]
Cancel	[F1]
Cancel Hyphenation	[F1]
Cancel Print Job(s)	Shift-[F7] 4
Case Conversion (Block on)	Shift-[F3]
Center	Shift-[F6]
Center Page Top to Bottom	Alt-[F8]
Change Directory	[F5] ↵***
Change Print Options	Shift-[F7]
Colors	Ctrl-[F3]
Column, Cut/Copy (Block on)	Ctrl-[F4]
Columns, Text	Alt-[F7]
Column Display	Alt-[F7]
Conditional End of Page	Alt-[F8]
Copy (List Files)	[F5] ↵
Create Directory	[F5] =
Ctrl/Alt Key Mapping	Ctrl-[F3]
Date	Shift-[F5]
Delete	Del
Delete (List Files)	[F5] ↵
Delete Directory (List Files)	[F5] ↵
Delete to End of Line (EOL)	Ctrl-End
Delete to End of Page (EOP)	Ctrl-PgDn
Delete Word	Ctrl-←
Display All Print Jobs	Shift-[F7] 4
Display Printers and Fonts	Shift-[F7] 4†
DOS Text File	Ctrl-[F5]
Endnote	Ctrl-[F7]

*Function key.

**←, →, ↑, ↓: Left, right, up, and down arrow keys, respectively.

***↵: Return.

†Not in L-WP 4.2.

Feature	*Keystrokes*
Enter (or Return)	↵
Escape	Esc
Exit	[F7]
Extended Tabs	Shift-[F8]
Flush Right	Alt-[F6]
Font	Ctrl-[F8]
Footnote	Ctrl-[F7]
Full Text (Print)	Shift-[F7]
Generate	Alt-[F5]
"Go" (Resume Printing)	Shift-[F7] 4
Go to DOS	Ctrl-[F1]
Hard Page	Ctrl-↵
Hard Return	↵
Hard Space	Home Space Bar
Headers or Footers	Alt-[F8]
Help	[F3]
Home	Home
Hyphen	-
Hyphenation On/Off	Shift-[F8] 5
H-Zone	Shift-[F8] 5
▶Indent	[F4]
▶Indent◀	Shift-[F4]
Index	Alt-[F5]
Insert Printer Command	Ctrl-[F8]
Justification On/Off	Ctrl-[F8]
Line Draw	Ctrl-[F3]
Line Format	Shift-[F8]
Lines per Inch	Ctrl-[F8]
List Files	[F5] ↵
List (Block on)	Alt-[F5]
Locked Documents	Ctrl-[F5]
Look	[F5] ↵
Macro	Alt-[F10]
Macro Def	Ctrl-[F10]
◀Margin Release	Shift-⇆
Margins	Shift-[F8]
Mark Text	Alt-[F5]
Math	Alt-[F7]
Merge	Ctrl-[F9]
Merge Codes	Alt-[F9]
Merge E	Shift-[F9]
Merge R	[F9]

*Function key.
**←, →, ↑, ↓: Left, right, up, and down arrow keys, respectively.
***↵: Return.
†Not in L-WP 4.2.

Feature	*Keystrokes*
Minus Sign	Home -
Move	Ctrl-[F4]
Name Search	[F5] ↵
New Number (Footnote)	Ctrl-[F7]
New Page Number	Alt-[F8]
Number of Copies	Shift-[F7] 3
Outline	Alt-[F5]
Overstrike	Shift-[F1]
Page Format	Alt-[F8]
Page Length	Alt-[F8]
Page Number Column Positions	Alt-[F8]
Page Number Position	Alt-[F8]
Page (Print)	Shift-[F7]
Paragraph Number	Alt-[F5]
Pitch	Ctrl-[F8]
Print	Shift-[F7]
Print (List Files)	[F5] ↵
Print a Document	Shift-[F7] 4
Print Block (Block on)	Shift-[F7]
Print Format	Ctrl-[F8]
Printer Control	Shift-[F7]
Printer Number	Shift-[F7] 3†
Proportional Spacing	Ctrl-[F8] 1
Rectangle, Cut/Copy (Block on)	Ctrl-[F4]
Redline	Alt-[F5]
Remove	Alt-[F5]
Rename (List Files)	[F5] ↵
Replace	Alt-[F2]
Retrieve	Shift-[F10]
Retrieve (List Files)	[F5] ↵
Retrieve Column (Move)	Ctrl-[F4]
Retrieve Rectangle (Move)	Ctrl-[F4]
Retrieve Text (Move)	Ctrl-[F4]
Reveal Codes	Alt-[F3]
Rewrite	Ctrl-[F3] Ctrl-[F3]
Rush Print Job	Shift-[F7] 4
Save	[F10]
Screen	Ctrl-[F3]
▶Search	[F2]
◀Search	Shift-[F2]
Select Print Options	Shift-[F7] 4
Select Printers	Shift-[F7] 4
Sheet Feeder Bin Number	Ctrl-[F8]
Shell	Ctrl-[F1]
Soft Hyphen	Ctrl--

Feature	*Keystrokes*
Sort	Ctrl-[F9]
Sorting Sequences	Ctrl-[F9]
Spacing	Shift-[F8]
Spell	Ctrl-[F2]†
Split Screen	Ctrl-[F3] 1
Stop Printing	Shift-[F7] 4
Strikeout (Block on)	Alt-[F5]
Super/Subscript	Shift-[F1]
Suppress Page Format	Alt-[F8]
Switch	Shift-[F3]
Tab	⭾
Tab Align	Ctrl-[F6]
Tab Ruler	Ctrl-[F3] 1
Table of Contents (Block on)	Alt-[F5]
Tab Set	Shift-[F8]
Text in (List Files)	[F5] ↵
Text In/Out	Ctrl-[F5]
Text Lines	Alt-[F8] 4
Thesaurus	Alt-[F1]†
Time	Shift-[F5] 2
Top Margin	Alt-[F8]
Typeover	Ins
Type-thru	Shift-[F7]

Feature	*Keystrokes*
Undelete	[F1]
Underline	[F8]
Underline Style	Ctrl-[F8]
Widow/Orphan	Alt-[F8]
Window	Ctrl-[F3]
Word Count	Ctrl-[F2]
Word Search	[F5] ↵
Cursor Control	
Go To	Ctrl-Home
Word Left	Ctrl ←
Word Right	Ctrl →
Screen Left	Home ←
Screen Right	Home →
Screen Down	+ *or* Home ↓
Screen Up	− *or* Home ↑
Page Down	Pg Dn
Page Up	Pg Up
Beginning of Text	Home Home ↑
End of Text	Home Home ↓
Beginning of Line (text)	Home Home ←
Beginning of Line (codes)	Home Home Home ←
End of Line	Home Home →

*Function key.
**←, →, ↑, ↓: Left, right, up, and down arrow keys, respectively.
***↵: Return.

†Not in L-WP 4.2.

WORDPERFECT VERSION 5.0

Feature	*Keystrokes*
Advance	Shift-[F8] 4 1*
Appearance Attributes	Ctrl-[F8] 2
Automatic Reference	Alt-[F5] 1
Automatically Format and Rewrite	Shift-[F1] 3 1
Backspace	← (Backspace)**
Backup	Shift-[F1] 1
Base Font	Ctrl-[F8] 4
Beep Options	Shift-[F1] 5 1
Binding	Shift-[F7] B
Block	Alt-[F4]
Block Protect (Block on)	Shift-[F8]
Bold	[F6] *or* Ctrl-[F8] 2 1
^ C (Text from Keyboard)	Shift-[F9] C
Cancel	[F1]
Print Job(s)	Shift-[F7] 4 1
Cartridges and Fonts	Shift-[F7] S 3 5
Case Conversion (Block on)	Shift-[F3]
Center	Shift-[F6]
Center Page Top to Bottom	Shift-[F8] 2 1
Colors/Fonts/Attributes	Shift-[F1] 3 2
Columns (Text and Parallel)	Alt-[F7]
Compose	Ctrl-2
Concordance	Alt-[F5] 5 3
Conditional End of Page	Shift-[F8] 4 2
Control Printer	Shift-[F7] 4
Copy File	[F5] ↵ 8 ***
Create Directory	[F5] =
^ D (Date)	Shift-[F9] D
Date	
Code	Shift-[F5] 2
Format	Shift-[F5] 3
Text	Shift-[F5] 1
Date/Outline	Shift-[F5]
Decimal/Align Character	Shift-[F8] 4 3

*Function key.
**←, →, ↑, ↓: Left, right, up, and down arrow keys, respectively.
***↵: Return.

Feature	*Keystrokes*
Define (Mark Text)	Alt-[F5] 5
Delete	
Character Left	Backspace
Character Right	Del
Directory	[F5] ↵ 2
File	[F5] ↵ 2
to End of Line (EOL)	Ctrl-End
to End of Page (EOP)	Ctrl-PgDn
Word	Ctrl-Backspace
Word Left	Home Backspace
Word Right	Home Delete
Display All Print Jobs	Shift-[F7] 4 3
Display Pitch	Shift-[F8] 3 1
Display Setup	Shift-[F1] 3
Document Comments	Ctrl-[F5] 5
Document Compare	Alt-[F5] 6 2
Document Format	Shift-[F8] 3
Document Summary	Shift-[F8] 3 4
DOS Text File	
Retrieve (CR/LF to [HRt])	Ctrl-[F5] 1 2
Retrieve (CR/LF to [SRt])	Ctrl-[F5] 1 3
Save	Ctrl-[F5] 1 1
Double Underline	Ctrl-[F8] 2 3
^ E (End of Record)	Shift-[F9] E
Edit Table of Authorities Full Form	Alt-[F5] 5 5
Endnote	Ctrl-[F7] 2
Endnote Placement Code	Ctrl-[F7]3
Enter (or Return)	↵
Exit	[F7]
Extra Large Print	Ctrl-[F8] 1 7
^ F (Field)	Shift-[F9] F
Fast Save	Shift-[F1] 4
Figure (Graphics)	Alt-[F9] 1
Filename on Status Line	Shift-[F1] 3 4
Fine Print	Ctrl-[F8] 1 3
Flush Right	Alt-[F6]
Footers	Shift-[F8] 2 4
Footnote	Ctrl-[F7] 1
Force Odd/Even Page	Shift-[F8] 2 2
Format	Shift-[F8]
Forms	Shift-[F7] S 3 4
^ G (Start Macro)	Shift-[F9] G

Feature	*Keystrokes*
Generate (Mark Text)	Alt-[F5] 6
Generate Tables, Indexes etc.	Alt-[F5] 6 5
Generic Word Processor Format	Ctrl-[F5] 3
"Go" (Start Printer)	Shift-[F7] 4 4
Go to DOS	Ctrl-[F1] 1
Graphics	Alt-[F9]
Graphics Quality	Shift-[F7] G
Graphics Screen Type	Shift-[F1] 3 5
Hard	
Page	Ctrl-←
Return	↵
Return Display Character	Shift-[F1] 3 6
Space	Home Space Bar
Headers	Shift-[F8] 2 3
Help	[F3]
Home	Home
Horizontal Line (Graphics)	Alt-[F9] 5 1
Hyphenation	Shift-[F8] 1 1
Hyphenation Zone	Shift-[F8] 1 2
▶Indent	[F4]
▶Indent◀	Shift-[F4]
Index	
Define	Alt-[F5] 5 3
Mark	Alt-[F5] 3
Initial Settings (Format)	Shift-[F8] 3 2
Initial Settings (Setup)	Shift-[F1] 5
Insert	Ins
Insert, Forced	Home Home Ins
Italics	Ctrl-[F8] 2 4
Justification	Shift-[F8] 1 3
Kerning	Shift-[F8] 4 6 1
Keyboard Layout	Shift-[F1] 6
Language	Shift-[F8] 4 4
Large Print	Ctrl-[F8] 1 5
Line	
Draw	Ctrl-[F3] 2
Format	Shift-[F8] 1
Height	Shift-[F8] 1 4
Numbering	Shift-[F8] 1 5

*Function key.
**←, →, ↑, ↓: Left, right, up, and down arrow keys, respectively.
***↵: Return.

Feature	*Keystrokes*
Spacing	Shift-[F8] 1 6
List	
Define	Alt-[F5] 5 2
Mark (Block on)	Alt-[F5] 2
List Files	[F5]↵
Location of Auxiliary Files	Shift-[F1] 7
Look	[F5] ↵ 6
Macro	Alt-[F10]
Macro Define	Ctrl-[F10]
◀Margin Release	Shift-Tab
Margins	
Left/Right	Shift-[F8] 1 7
Top/Bottom	Shift-[F8] 2 5
Mark Text	Alt-[F5]
Master Document	
Condense	Alt-[F5] 6 4
Expand	Alt-[F5] 6 3
Subdocument	Alt-[F5] 2
Math/Columns	Alt-[F7]
Menu Letter Display	Shift-[F1] 3 7
Merge	Ctrl-[F9] 1
Codes	Shift-[F9]
Move	Ctrl-[F4]
Block (Block on)	Ctrl-[F4] 1
Page	Ctrl-[F4] 3
Paragraph	Ctrl-[F4] 2
Rectangle (Block on)	Ctrl-[F4] 3
/Rename (List Files)	[F5] ↵ 3
Sentence	Ctrl-[F4] 1
Tabular Column (Block on)	Ctrl-[F4] 2
^N (Next Record)	Shift-[F9] N
Name Search (List Files)	[F5] ↵ N
New Page Number	Shift-[F8] 2 6
Normal Text (Turn off Attributes)	Ctrl-[F8] 3
Number of Copies	Shift-[F7] N
^O (Display Message)	Shift-[F9] O
Other Directory	[F5] ↵ 7
Outline	Shift-[F5] 4
Outline (Attribute)	Ctrl-[F8] 2 5
Overstrike	Shift-[F8] 4 5
^P (Primary File)	Shift-[F9] P
Page Format	Shift-[F8] 2
Page Numbering	Shift-[F8] 2 7
Paragraph Number	Shift-[F5] 5
Paragraph Numbering	

Feature	*Keystrokes*
Definition	Shift-[F5] 6
Paper Size/Type	Shift-[F8] 2 8
Password	Ctrl-[F5] 2
Print	Shift-[F7]
Block (Block on)	Shift-[F7] Y
Color	Ctrl-[F8] 5
Full Document	Shift-[F7] 1
List Files	[F5] ↵ 4
Page	Shift-[F7] 2
Printer	
Command	Shift-[F8] 4 6 2
Settings	Shift-[F7] S 3
^Q (Stop Merge)	Shift-[F9] Q
^R (End of Field)	Shift-[F9] R
Redline	Ctrl-[F8] 2 8
Redline Method	Shift-[F8] 3 3
Remove Redline/ Strikeout	Alt-[F5] 6 1
Repeat Value	Esc
Replace	Alt-[F2]
Replace, Extended	Home Alt-[F2]
Retrieve	
Block (Move)	Ctrl-[F4] 4 1
Document	Shift-[F10]
List Files	[F5] ↵ 1
Rectangle (Move)	Ctrl-[F4] 4 3
Tabular Column (Move)	Ctrl-[F4] 4 2
Reveal Codes	Alt-[F3]
Rewrite	Ctrl-[F3] 0
Rush Print Job	Shift-[F7] 4 2
^S (Secondary File)	Shift-[F9] S
Save	[F10]
Screen	Ctrl-[F3]
▶Search	[F2]
▶Search, Extended	Home [F2]
◀Search	Shift-[F2]
◀Search, Extended	Home Shift-[F2]
Select Printer	Shift-[F7] S
Setup	Shift-[F1]
Shadow	Ctrl-[F8] 2 6
Shell	Ctrl-[F1]

*Function key.

**←, →, ↑, ↓: Left, right, up, and down arrow keys, respectively.

***↵: Return.

Feature	*Keystrokes*
Side-by-side Column Display	Shift-[F1] 3 8
Size Attribute	Ctrl-[F8] 1
Small Caps	Ctrl-[F8] 2 7
Small Print	Ctrl-[F8] 1 4
Sort	Ctrl-[F9] 2
Spell	Ctrl-[F2]
Split Screen	Ctrl-[F3] 1
Stop Printing	Shift-[F7] 4 5
Strikeout	Ctrl-[F8] 2 9
Style	Alt-[F8]
Subscript	Ctrl-[F8] 1 2
Superscript	Ctrl-[F8] 1 1
Suppress (Page Format)	Shift-[F8] 2 9
Switch	Shift-[F3]
^T (Send to Printer)	Shift-[F9] T
Tab Align	Ctrl-[F6]
Tab Set	Shift-[F8] 1 8
Table (Graphics)	Alt-[F9] 2
Table of Authorities	
Define	Alt-[F5] 5 4
Edit Full Form	Alt-[F5] 5 5
Full Form (Block on)	Alt-[F5] 4
Short Form	Alt-[F5] 4
Table of Contents	
Define	Alt-[F5] 5 1
Mark (Block on)	Alt-[F5] 1
Text Box (Graphics)	Alt-[F9] 3
Text In (List Files)	[F5] ↵ 5
In/Out	Ctrl-[F5]
Text Quality	Shift-[F7] T
Thesaurus	Alt-[F1]
Thousand's Separator	Shift-[F8] 4 3
Type Through	Shift-[F7] 5
Typeover	Ins
Typeover, Forced	Home Ins
^U (Rewrite Screen)	Shift-[F9] U
Undelete	[F1]
Underline	[F8] or Ctrl-[F8] 2 2
Underline Spaces/Tabs	Shift-[F8] 4 7
Units of Measure	Shift-[F1] 8
User-Defined Box (Graphics)	Alt-[F9] 4
^V (insert merge code)	Shift-[F9] V
Vertical Line (Graphics)	Alt-[F9] 5 2
Very Large Print	Ctrl-[F8] 1 6
View Document	Shift-[F7] 6

Feature	*Keystrokes*
Widow/Orphan Protection	Shift-[F8] 1 9
Window	Ctrl-[F3] 1
Word/Letter Spacing	Shift-[F8] 4 6 3
Word Search	[F5] ↵ 9
Word Spacing Justification Limits	Shift-[F8] 4 6 4
WordPerfect 4.2 Format	Ctrl-[F5] 4
Cursor Control	
Beginning of Document	Home Home ↑
Beginning of Line (Before Codes)	Home Home Home ←
Beginning of Line (Before Text)	Home Home ←
Character Left	←

Feature	*Keystrokes*
Character Right	→
End of Document	Home Home ↓
End of Line	Home Home → *or* End
Go To	Ctrl-Home
Line Down	↓
Line Up	↑
Page Down	PgDn
Page Up	PgUp
Screen Down	Home ↓ *or* + (Num Pad)
Screen Left	Home ←
Screen Right	Home →
Screen Up	Home ↑ *or* − (Num Pad)
Word Left	Ctrl-←
Word Right	Ctrl-→

*Function key.
**←, →, ↑, ↓: Left, right, up, and down arrow keys, respectively.
***↵: Return.

D
WordStar Command References

Feature	Keystrokes
Opening Menu Commands	
Change logged drive/directory	L
Directory on/off	F
Help	J *or* [F1]
Memory usage	?
Open a document file	D
Open a nondocument file	N
Print a file	P
Merge print a file	M
Rename a file	E
Copy a file	O
Delete a file	Y
Protect a file	C
Index a document	I
Create a table of contents	T
Shorthand	Esc
Run a program/DOS command	R
Exit WordStar	X
Commands to Use at Prompts	
Safely cancel a command or an operation	^U* *or* [F2]**
Delete answer	^Y *or* [F5]
Repeat previous answer	^R
Other Menus (from the Edit Menu)	
Block and Save Menu	^K
Onscreen Format Menu	^O
Print Controls Menu	^P
Quick Menu	^Q
Shorthand Menu	Esc
Help	
Get help with specified command	^J *or* [F1]
Change help level	^J ^J *or* [F1] [F1]
Help with screen layout	^J? *or* [F1]?
Help with dot commands	^J. *or* [F1].
Move Cursor	
Right one character	^D *or* →
Left one character	^S *or* ←
Up one line	^E *or* ↑
Down one line	^X *or* ↓
Right one word	^F *or* ^→
Left one word	^A *or* ^←
To tab right	^I *or* Tab
To top of screen	^QE *or* Home
To right end of last onscreen line	^QX *or* End

*^: Ctrl Key.
**F: Function key.

Feature	*Keystrokes*
To beginning of document	^QR *or* ^Home
To end of document	^QC *or* ^End
To right end of line	^QD *or* ^[F10]
To left end of line	^QS *or* ^[F9]
To beginning block marker	^QB
To end block marker	^QK
To marker 0–9	^Q0–9
To specified page (document)	^QI *or* ^[F4]
To specified line (nondocument)	^QI
To previous cursor position	^QP
To last find/replace or block	^QV
Forward to specified character	^QG
Back to specified character	^QH
Scroll (Move Screen)	
Up one line	^W *or* ^PgUp
Down one line	^Z *or* ^PgDn
Up one screen	^R *or* ^PgUp
Down one screen	^C *or* ^PgDn
Up screen continuously	^QW
Down screen continuously (Use 0–9 to control speed; 0 is fastest)	^QZ
Delete and Insert	
Delete character at cursor	^G *or* Del
Delete character left	^H *or* Backspace
Delete word at cursor	^T *or* [F6]
Delete line	^Y *or* [F5]
Delete line to right	^QY
Delete line to left	^Q Del
Delete to next specified character	^QT
Delete a block	^KY
Erase a file	^KJ
Insert on/off	^V *or* Ins
Insert carriage return (split line)	^N
Unerase (restore deleted text)	^U *or* [F2]
Tabs and Margins	
Change left margin	.LM *or* ^[F5]
Change right margin	.RM *or* ^[F6]
Use a new ruler line	.RR

* ^: Ctrl Key.
**F: Function key.

Feature	*Keystrokes*
Ruler line characters	
L left margin	
R right margin	
P paragraph margin	
! tab stop	
# decimal tab stop	
– space	
Margin at top of page	.MT
Margin at bottom of page	.MB
Paragraph margin	.PM *or* ^[F7]
Set left margin	^OL
Set right margin	^OR
Release margins	^OX
Set ruler from text	^OF
Embed current ruler line as a .RR	^OO *or* [F8]
Set tab stop	^OI
Clear tab stop	^ON
Temporary indent	^OG
Set tab interval (nondocument)	^O
Eight-column tab	^PI
Page Layout/Format	
Conditional page	.CP
Page break	.PA *or* ^[F8]
Line height	.LH
Change page number	.PN
Page length	.PL
Page offset	.PO
Line spacing	.LS
Omit page number	.OP
Restore default page numbers	.PG
Page number column	.PC
Center line	^OC *or* Shift-[F2]
Set line spacing	^OS
Justification	^OJ
Display of Text While Editing	
Print control display	^OD *or* Shift-[F1]
Preview mode	^OP
Ruler display	^OT
Display block markers	^KH
Soft-space display	^OB
Alignment of Text	
Alignment/word wrap	.AW
Justification	.OJ
Microjustification	.UJ

Feature	Keystrokes
Proportional spacing	.PS
Print time formatting	.PF
Word wrap	^OW
Align paragraph	^B
Align rest of paragraphs (document)	^QU *or* [F7]
Align text at column number	^P@
Hyphen help	^OH
Enter soft hyphen	^OE
Printer Commands	
Bidirectional printing	.BP
Change sheet feeder bin	.BN
Letter quality print	.LQ
Subscript/superscript roll	.SR
Character width	.CW
Continuous underline	.UL
Display message while printing	.DM
Clear screen while printing	.CS
Insert file at print time	.FI
Print file *n* times	.RP
Redefine custom print ^PQ	.XQ
Redefine custom print ^PW	.XW
Redefine custom print ^PE	.XE
Redefine custom print ^PR	.XR
Redefine form feed character ^PL	.XL

Character Pitch/Line Height Conversion Tables

Pitch (Characters per inch)	*Dot Command*	*Lines per Inch*	*Dot Command*
5	.CW24	2.0	.LH24
6	.CW20	2.4	.LH20
7	.CW17	2.6	.LH18
8	.CW15	3.0	.LH16
10	.CW12***	4.0	.LH12
12	.CW10	4.8	.LH10
15	.CW8	5.3	.LH9
20	.CW6	6.0	.LH8***
24	.CW5	6.8	.LH7
30	.CW4	8.0	.LH6
		9.6	.LH5

* ^: Ctrl Key.
**F: Function key.
***Use command at beginning and end of text to be included.

Feature	Keystrokes
Headers and Footers	
Footer (first line)	.F1 *or* .F0
Footer (second line)	.F2
Footer (third line)	.F3
Header (first line)	.H1 *or* .HE
Header (second line)	.H2
Header (third line)	.H3
Header margin	.HM
Footer margin	.FM
Alternate position odd/even pages	^PK
Design the Printed Page	
Bold	^PB*** *or* [F4]
Double strike	^PD***
Underline	^PS*** *or* [F3]
Strikeout	^PX***
Subscript	^PV***
Superscript	^PT***
Italics/color	^PY***
Overprint character	^PH
Overprint line	^P ↵
Binding space	^PO
Phantom space	^PF
Phantom rubout	^PG
Alternate pitch	^PA
Normal pitch	^PN
Print pause	^PC
Line feed without carriage return	^PJ
Form feed	^PL
Custom print functions	^PQ, ^PW, ^PE, ^PR
Shorthand	
Use a shorthand definition	Esc
Display and/or change definitions	Esc?
Type result from last ^QM or ^KM math	Esc =
Enter formatted number	Esc$
Enter last ^QM equation	Esc#
Enter today's date	Esc@
Enter current time	Esc!
Block Operations	
Mark block beginning	^KB *or* Shift-[F9]
Mark block end	^KK *or* Shift-[F10]
Hide/display marked block	^KH *or* Shift-[F6]

Feature	*Keystrokes*
Column mode	^KN
Column replace mode	^KI
Copy block	^KC *or* Shift-[F8]
Delete block	^KY *or* Shift-[F5]
Move block	^KV *or* Shift-[F7]
Block math	^KM
Convert block to lower case	^K'
Convert block to upper case	^K"
Write block to disk	^KW
Set/remove marker 0–9	^K0–9
File Operations	
Insert a file from disk	^KR
Copy a file	^KO
Rename a file	^KE
Print or merge print a file	^KP
Erase a file	^KJ
Run a program/DOS command	^KF
Change logged drive/ directory	^KL
Save Files	
Save and resume edit	^KS *or* [F9]
Save, return to Opening Menu	^KD *or* [F10]
Save and exit WordStar	^KX
Quit without saving	^KQ
Save and print	^KDP^R *or* ^PrtSc
Find and Replace	
Find text	^QF *or* ^[F1]
Find/replace text	^QA *or* ^[F2]
Strings	
^P Enter Ctrl sequence that follows	
? Wild card	
Options	
W Whole words	
B Look backwards	
G Start from beginning or end	
U Ignore case	
? Use ? as wild card	
A Align paragraph after replacement	
N Replace without asking approval	
R Replace for rest of document	
Find/replace text again	^L *or* ^[F3]
Forward to specified character	^QG

* ^: Ctrl Key.
**F: Function key.

Feature	*Keystrokes*
Back to specified character	^QH
Cursor to last find/replace	^QV
Math	
Onscreen calculator	^QM
Functions	
+ add	
− subtract	
* multiply	
/ divide	
^ exponentiate	
int integer	
ln base e log	
log base 10 log	
exp e ^ x	
sqr square root	
sin sine (in degrees)	
atn arctangent	
cos cosine	
tan tangent	
Block math	^KM
Set variable to result of equation	.MA
Merge Printing	
Set variable	.SV
Set variable to result of equation	.MA
Ask for data for variable	.AV
Read variables from data file	.RV
Define data file for .RV	.DF
Variables	
Substitute data	& *var* &
Remove line if variable is empty	& *var* /O&
Substitute variable using format *F* (Use .SV to define format)	& *var* /F&
Substitute current page number	&#&
Substitute current line number	&_&
Substitute today's date	&@&
Substitute current time	&!&
Conditional print	.IF
Operators: (For numeric comparisons, precede operators with #)	
= Equal to	
> Greater than	
< Less than	
>= Greater than or equal to	
<= Less than or equal to	
<> Not equal to	
Do if last .IF is not true	.EL

Feature	*Keystrokes*
End of .IF condition	.EI
Go to top/bottom of document	.GO
Index/Table of Contents	
Mark beginning/end of index entry	^PK
Define index entry	.IX
Define table of contents entry	.TC
Define entry for tables 1–9	.TC 1–9
Spelling	
Check rest of document	^QL *or* Shift-[F3]
Check word at cursor	^QN *or* Shift-[F4]
Enter word to check	^QO
Options	
I Ignore, check next word	
A Add to personal dictionary	
B Bypass this time only	
E Enter correction	
T Auto-alignment	
G Global replace	
^U Quit spelling check	

Feature	*Keystrokes*
Miscellaneous	
Insert carriage return	^M *or* ↵
Repeat following command or character	^QQ
Display character count to cursor	^Q?
Change hard return to soft (document)	^6
Strip high-order bits from line (nondocument)	^B
Strip high-order bits from file (nondocument)	^QU
Comment (not printed)	.IG *or* ..
Line and Box Drawing	
Alt-[F1]	│
Alt-[F2]	─
Alt-[F3]	┌
Alt-[F4]	┐
Alt-[F5]	└
Alt-[F6]	┘
Alt-[F7]	┬
Alt-[F8]	┴
Alt-[F9]	├
Alt-[F10]	┤

* ^: Ctrl Key.
**F: Function key.

E
Lotus 1-2-3 Release 2 Brief Command Summary

Lotus 1-2-3 Release 2 provides a worksheet grid made up of 8,192 horizontal rows and 256 vertical columns. Each intersection of a row and a column forms a cell in which you can store numeric values, text labels, formulas, and other miscellaneous items. Lotus 1-2-3 provides ten main commands, each of which has numerous subcommands or options. The commands are used to change the appearance of the worksheet and to work with the data stored within the cells. Generally you can enter the commands and their subcommands and option choices by moving the highlighted pointer to the selection and pressing Return or by typing the first letter of each selection and pressing Return. The brief descriptions provide a quick summary of the main Lotus 1-2-3 commands. Command options are indicated by the indentation directly below the command or by the parentheses or brackets directly after the command.

After turning on the microcomputer, loading MS-DOS, and loading Lotus 1-2-3 by entering 123, the user is presented with a menu of the following ten choices:

/Worksheet	/Print
/Range	/Graph
/Copy	/Data
/Move	/System
/File	/Quit

/WORKSHEET

In general, /Worksheet commands affect the entire worksheet, whereas /Range commands affect only selected parts of the worksheet. Among the most common uses of the /Worksheet command are setting global (worksheet-wide) format commands, changing the way Lotus recalculates the worksheet formulas after new data have been entered, and dividing the screen into various types of windows. Following are the main choices available within the /Worksheet command.

/Worksheet

Global
- Format (Fixed Scientific Currency ,*(comma)* General +/− Percent Date [Time] Time Text Hidden)
- Label-Prefix (Left Right Center) Column-Width
- Recalculation (Natural Columnwise Rowwise Automatic Manual Iteration)
- Protection (Enable Disable)
- Default
  - Printer (Interface Auto-LF Left Right Top Bottom Pg-Length Wait Setup Name Quit)
  - Directory
  - Status
  - Update
  - Other (International [Punctuation Currency Date Time Quit] Help)
  - Clock
  - Quit
  - Zero

Insert (Column Row)

Delete (Column Row)

Column (Set-Width Reset Width Hide Display)

Erase

Titles (Both Horizontal Vertical Clear)

Window (Horizontal Vertical Sync Unsync Clear)

Status

Page

/RANGE

The /Range command and its set of choices are used to manipulate ranges of cells. A range is any rectangular block of one or more cells. One of the most frequent uses of the /Range command is to change the format of a particular cell, row, or column. /Range is also used to name a block of cells containing a macro (series of worksheet instructions to be performed as a unit or "program"), thus allowing the macro to be performed when the macro name is entered.

/Range

Format (Fixed Scientific Currency General
+/− Percent Date Text Hidden Reset)

Label (Left Right Center)

Name (Create Delete Labels Reset Table)

Justify

Protect

Unprotect

Input

Value

Transpose

/COPY

The /Copy command creates either absolute or relative copies of existing cell entries. If a formula to be copied is in *absolute* cell address form, then the copied formula will be exactly like the original. If *relative* cell addresses are used in the original formula, then Lotus 1-2-3 can adjust the copies to relate to the new row and column addresses. This process is similar to describing a simple mathematical process to a human assistant and then telling that assistant to continue the process in a similar manner across other rows or columns on the worksheet.

/Copy

Enter range to copy FROM (Enter range to
copy TO)

/MOVE

/Move transfers existing cell entries to a new location. If you move data to an area of the worksheet that already contains data, then the new data replaces the old data and the original cells are left empty.

/Move

Enter range to move FROM (Enter range to
move TO)

/FILE

The /File command allows you to save an existing worksheet to a disk file, retrieve a previously saved worksheet, incorporate part of one worksheet into another, save part of a worksheet in a separate worksheet file, erase files from a disk, import a print file into the current worksheet, and produce a directory of the names of worksheet files previously stored on the logged disk drive.

/File

Retrieve

Save (Cancel Replace)

Combine
- Copy (Entire-File Named/Specific Range)
- Add (Entire-File Named/Specific Range)
- Subtract (Entire-File Named/Specific Range)

Xtract (Formulas Values)

Erase (Worksheet Print Graph Other)

List (Worksheet Print Graph Other)

Import (Text Numbers)

Directory

/PRINT

/Print commands let you create printed copies of a worksheet. The first choice offered is to either print the worksheet on a printer or save a copy of the print file on a disk. Saving a print file on a disk lets you print the file from DOS or use the file in another program, such as a word processing program. You must specify the range of the worksheet to be printed. You are given the options of setting margins and creating headings for the top of each printed page and footings for the bottom. After you have made all the choices you desire for the printed output, you must then select Go to actually begin the printing process.

/Print

Printer
- Range
- Line
- Page
- Options
  - Header
  - Footer
  - Margins (Left Right Top Bottom)

Borders (Columns Rows)
Setup
Pg-Length
Other (As-Displayed
Cell-Formulas
Formatted Unformatted)
Clear (All Range Borders Format)
Align
Go
Quit

/GRAPH

The /Graph commands allow you to represent data on the worksheet in five different types of graphs: line, bar, XY, stacked bar, and pie charts. Line graphs are especially useful in showing changes in data over time, bar graphs emphasize differences among data items, XY graphs show relationships between two sets of data, and pie charts compare parts to the whole.

/Graph

Type (Line Bar XY Stacked Bar Pie)

X A B C D E F

Reset (Graph X A B C D E F Quit)

View

Save

Options
Legend (A B C D E F)
Format (Graph A B C D E F Quit)
Titles (First Second X-Axis Y-Axis)
Grid (Horizontal Vertical Both
Clear)
Scale
Y Scale (Automatic Manual
Lower Upper
Format Indicator Quit)
X Scale (Automatic Manual
Lower Upper
Format Indicator Quit)
Skip
Color
B&W
Data-Labels (A B C D E F Quit)
Quit

Name (Use Create Delete Reset)

/DATA

The /Data commands permit you to use Lotus 1-2-3 to perform certain database functions. When you use 1-2-3 as a database, all entries in a single row constitute one record, each column comprises one field, and each cell in the first row of a database contains a label, called a field name, that identifies the category of information in the column below. Once a worksheet has been set up as a database, the entered data can be designated as the input range and a criterion range can be used to establish criteria for finding or extracting selected data from the input range. Extracted data is copied into another designated area of the worksheet called an output range.

In addition to the database functions mentioned above, the /Data command can be used to perform regression analysis. You can specify up to 16 independent variables for multiple regression. Regression analysis allows you to statistically predict the value of a dependent variable based upon other values for one or more independent variables.

/Data

Fill

Table (1 2 Reset)

Sort (Data-Range Primary-Key
  Secondary-Key Reset Go Quit)

Query (Input Criterion Output Find
  Extract Unique Delete [Cancel Delete]
  Reset Quit)

Distribution

Matrix (Invert Multiply)

Regression (X-Range Y-Range

  Output-Range Intercept [Compute Zero]
  Reset Go Quit)

Parse

/SYSTEM

/System lets you leave Lotus 1-2-3 temporarily to use DOS commands and then return to your Lotus 1-2-3 worksheet. The values entered in the worksheet are not lost and there is no need to restart 1-2-3. After using the desired DOS commands, type EXIT and press Return to return to 1-2-3. **Warning:** External DOS commands that load another program into RAM, such as Print or Setclock, do not permit you to return to 1-2-3. To be safe, it is a good idea to use /File Save to save your work before using /System.

/QUIT

/Quit lets you leave 1-2-3. It does *not* automatically save your work when you leave the program, so *always save your work first.* It does provide a safeguard against accidentally entering /Quit and leaving 1-2-3 when you do not want to. It prompts you to enter Yes before actually leaving.

FUNCTIONAL COMMAND SUMMARY

The following is handy if you know what you want to do but are not sure which command to use.

Analyzing Data

Change formulas into values	/Range Value
Place a series of numbers in a range	/Data Fill
Graph data	/Graph
Do linear regression	/Data Regression
Sort rows of data	/Data Sort

Changing the Appearance of the Worksheet

Align specific labels	/Range Label
Format specific cells	/Range Format
Change the default alignment of labels	/Worksheet Global Label-Prefix
Change the default appearance of numbers	/Worksheet Global Format
Change the default column width	/Worksheet Global Column Width
Change the width of a specific column	/Worksheet Column Set-Width
Copy cell contents	/Copy
Display values as formulas	/Range Format Text
Erase worksheet from screen	/Worksheet Erase
Erase specific cell contents from screen	/Range Erase
Hide columns	/Worksheet Column Hide
Insert new blank rows or columns	/Worksheet Insert
Freeze row or column headings onscreen	/Worksheet Titles
Move data within the worksheet	/Move
Remove rows or columns from the worksheet on the screen	/Worksheet Delete
Split the worksheet into two windows	/Worksheet Window

Copying Data

Copy data from one location of the worksheet to another	/Copy
Copy data, transposing rows and columns	/Range Transpose
Copy formulas so the new copy is values	/Range Value
Import data from a text (ASCII)file	/File Import
Include data from another worksheet file	/File Combine

Erasing Data

Remove a row or column of data	/Worksheet Delete
Erase a file from the disk	/File Erase
Erase specific cell contents from the screen	/Range Erase
Erase worksheet from the screen	/Worksheet Erase

Graphing Data

Add titles, labels, and other descriptive text to the graphs	/Graph Options Legend;/Graph Options Titles
Cancel graph settings	/Graph Reset
Display the current graph on the screen	/Graph View
List the graph files on the current directory	/File List Graph
Label data points on graph	/Graph Options Data-Labels
Show horizontal and/or vertical grid lines on the graph	/Graph Options Grid
Print the graph	Load the PrintGraph program
Save the current graph file for later printing with PrintGraph	/Graph Save
Select the data to graph	/Graph X, A–F
Change graph settings	/Graph Options
Determine kind of graph	/Graph Type
Save and/or use named set of graph settings	/Graph Name

Hiding Data

Hide column	/Worksheet Column Hide
Hide range	/Range Format Hidden
Display hidden column	/Worksheet Column Display
Hide values of zero on the worksheet	/Worksheet Global Zero

Loading Data

Import data from a text (ASCII) file	/File Import
Include data from another worksheet file	/File Combine
Load an existing worksheet file	/File Retrieve

Printing

Move the paper up one line	/Print Printer Line
Move the paper up one page	/Print Printer Page
Start printing	/Print Printer(File) Go
Change printer settings for this session only	/Print Printer(File) Options
Save current printer settings as the default settings	/Worksheet Global Default Printer
Print formulas instead of values	/Print Printer(File) Options Other Cell-Formulas
Print a graph	The PrintGraph program
Clear current printing settings	/Print Printer(File) Clear
Print the worksheet as a text file to be saved on disk	/Print File

Set options for the printed page, including headings, footings, and margins	/Print Printer(File) Options
Set paper to top-of-page	/Print Printer Align
Define the range to print	/Print Printer(File) Range

Protecting Data

Assign a password to a file	/File Save
Protect specific cells	/Range Protect
Remove protection from certain cells	Range Unprotect
Protect or unprotect the entire worksheet	/Worksheet Global Protection

Saving Worksheets

Extract and save a portion of the worksheet	/File Xtract
Save a graph for later printing	/Graph Save
Save a worksheet	/File Save
Save a worksheet as a text (ASCII) file	/Print File

Database Functions

Reset database settings	/Data Query Reset
Search and copy selected records	/Data Query Extract
Search and highlight selected records	/Data Query Find
Sort specified records	/Data Sort
Specify ranges of the worksheet for a database	/Data Query Input/Criterion/Output

File Operations

Check available disk space for logged disk	/File List
List file names in current directory	/File List
Erase a file from a disk	/File Erase
Extract a portion of a worksheet and save it on a file	/File Xtract
Import a text (ASCII) file into the worksheet	/File Import
Include part of a worksheet file in the current worksheet	/File Combine
Load a worksheet file from disk into RAM	/File Retrieve
Save data as a text file on disk	/Print File
Save current worksheet settings as the default settings in the configuration file	/Worksheet Global Default Update
Save a graph file for later printing	/Graph Save
Save a worksheet file on a disk	/File Save
Specify the directory where files are to be retrieved and stored for the current session	/File Directory
Specify the directory where files are to be retrieved and stored for current and future sessions	/Worksheet Global Default Directory Update

Label Operations

Change alignment of labels within a range	/Range Label
Change column width	/Worksheet Column Set-Width
Change default setting for alignment of labels	/Worksheet Global Label-Prefix
Name a range using existing labels	/Range Name Labels

Named Range Operations

Delete a range name	/Range Name Delete
Delete all range names	/Range Name Reset
List all range names	/Range Name Table
Name a range	/Range Name Create
Name a range using existing labels	/Range Name Labels

Number Operations

Change the appearance of specific numbers in a range	/Range Format
Increase the width of the column if the numbers are displayed as asterisks	/Worksheet Column Set-Width
Change the default settings for the appearance of numbers on the worksheet	/Worksheet Global Format
Convert formulas to values	/Range Value
Show the recalculation setting	/Worksheet Status
Place a series of numbers in a range	/Data Fill
Name a range	/Range Name Create
Change when and how formulas are recalculated	/Worksheet Global Recalculation
Hide values equal to zero	/Worksheet Global Zero

Miscellaneous Operations

Break up lines of data into individual cell entries	/Data Parse
Show the amount of memory remaining in RAM	/Worksheet Status
Display the configuration settings for printer, current directory, etc.	/Worksheet Global Default Status
Display worksheet settings for display format, column width, protection, etc.	/Worksheet Status
Quit 1-2-3	/Quit
Restrict movement of the cell pointer	/Range Input
Change configuration settings for printer, current directory, etc.	/Worksheet Global Default
Change recalculation settings	/Worksheet Global Recalculation
Change the way Help is used	/Worksheet Global Default Other Help
Define worksheet settings (display format, column width, protection, etc.)	/Worksheet Global
Go to the operations system temporarily	/System

@FUNCTIONS

Lotus 1-2-3 offers a wide variety of @functions. These are built-in formulas that perform a wide variety of specified functions, from adding a column of numbers to performing statistical operations. The general format or syntax of an @function is

```
@function name(argument1, argument2 . . . )
```

The function name determines which calculations are to be performed. The arguments are the values used in the calculations of the functions. For example, in the function @MAX(R5.R12), 1-2-3 will locate the maximum (highest) value in the cell range of R5 through R12 and return the value. In the listing below, the function name is in upper case and the arguments are in italics. Functions can be entered in upper or lower case. All functions will return a single value in the cell.

Rules for entering functions include the following:

- Enclose the function arguments in parentheses.
- Do not put any spaces between the function name and the arguments. For example, @SUM(A2.A14).
- Use a comma or a semicolon to separate multiple arguments in a function, such as @MIN(5,B10,B12). There should be no spaces between these arguments.
- Use double quotes ("") around the string (text) values in arguments. For example, @LENGTH("Employee Benefits").
- When 1-2-3 detects an error in the function argument, it will place the value "ERR" in the cell where you placed the function.
- When a function name is entered incorrectly or is entered in an incorrect format, 1-2-3 will beep and enter the EDIT mode.

SELECTED FUNCTIONS LISTED BY TYPE

Financial Functions

These functions make it easy to do financial calculations. Definitions are as follows: *periods*—a unit of time between equal payments, such as one month; *rate*—interest rate period (if period is one month and annual interest rate is .12 [12%], then rate in formula is .01 [.12/12]); *term*—number of periods; *payment*—amount paid per period; *present value*—value of investment or loan at start of term; *future value*—value of investment or loan at end of term.

@CTERM(int,fv,pv)	compounding periods for an investment of present value (pv) to grow to future value (fv), earning a fixed period interest rate (int)
@DDB(cost,salvage,life,period)	double declining balance
@FV(payment,rate,term)	future value
@IRR(guess,range)	internal rate of return

@NPV(rate,row/colrange)	net present value
@PMT(present value,rate,term, period)	annuity payment
@PV(payment,rate,term)	annuity present rate
@RATE(future value,present value,term)	periodic interest rate
@SLN(cost,salvage,life)	straight line
@SYN(cost,salvage,left,period)	sum-of-the-years digit
@TERM(payment,rate,future,value)	periods to achieve future value

Statistical Functions

These functions use lists of values for calculations.

@AVG(list)	mean average
@COUNT(list)	formula cell count
@MAX(list)	maximum value
@MIN(list)	minimum value
@STD(list)	standard deviation
@SUM(list)	total value
@VAR(list)	variance

Mathematical Functions

These functions use numeric values in their calculations. *x* is a numeric value or a cell containing a value.

@ABS(*x*)	absolute (positive) value
@INT(*x*)	integer
@RAND	a random number between 0 and 1
@ROUND(*x*,*n*)	*x* rounded to *n* places
@SQRT(*x*)	the positive square root of *x*

Logical Functions

These functions produce values based on the result of a conditional statement.

@IF(*cond*,*x*,*y*)*x*	*x* if *cond* is TRUE, and *y* if *cond* is FALSE
@TRUE	returns 1 for true
@FALSE	returns 0 for false
@ISERR(*x*)	returns 1 (true) if the cell reference *x* contains the value ERR; otherwise, returns 0 (false)
@ISNA(*x*)	returns 1 (true) if the cell reference *x* contains the value NA; otherwise, returns 0 (false)
@ISNUMBER(*x*)	returns 1 (true) if the cell reference *x* contains a numeric value; otherwise, returns 0 (false)
@ISSTRING(*x*)	returns 1 (true) if the cell reference *x* contains a string value (characters); otherwise, returns 0 (false)

Date and Time Functions

These functions return the serial date and time numbers.

@DATE(yy,mm,dd)	the date number
@DATEVALUE(date string)	the date number of date string
@NOW	current date and time
@TIME(hr,min,sec)	the time number of hr,min,sec
@TIMEVALUE(time string)	the time number of time string

The following functions use the serial date and time numbers.

@DAY(date number)	the day number of date number
@HOUR(time number)	the hour number of time number
@MINUTE(time number)	the minute number of time number
@MONTH	the month number of date number
@SECOND	the second number of time number
@YEAR(date number)	the year number of date number

Data Management Statistical Functions

These functions perform statistical calculations on a database. The database is defined as the input range. The criterion range must be defined to select the records from the database that each function uses. The definitions are as follows: *input*—the range, which must include all the database records and their field names; *offset*—the column number containing the field. The first column of the input range is field 0, the second column is field 1, the third column is field 2, and so on; *criterion* is the criterion range. The first row in the input range and the criterion range must contain the field names of each column.

@DAVG(input,offset field,criterion)	data management average
@DCOUNT(input,offset field, criterion)	data management formula cell count
@DMAX(input,offset,criterion)	data management maximum
@DMIN(input,offset,criterion)	data management minimum
@DSTD(input,offset,criterion)	data management standard deviation
@DSUM(input,offset,criterion)	data management total value
@DVAR(input,offset,criterion)	data management variance

FUNCTION KEY COMMANDS

[F1]	Help
[F2]	Edit
[F3]	Name
[F4]	Abs
[F5]	Goto
[F6]	Window
[F7]	Query
[F8]	Table
[F9]	Calc
[F10]	Graph
Alt + [F1] *or* [F11]	Compose
Alt + [F2] *or* [F12]	Step

F
dBASE III Plus Brief Command Summary

COMMAND SYNTAX

lower case—User-supplied information

UPPER CASE—dBASE III Plus commands

< >	Angle brackets mean that the enclosed item is to be used by the user. The brackets are not included as part of the command.
[ ]	Square brackets enclose optional items. The brackets are not included as part of the command.
^	Indicates the control key. Press the Control key and hold it down while pressing another key.
/	Slash indicates a choice between options.
<exp>	Indicates a combination of constants, variables, and operators that return a value.
<field>	An individual data item in a record within a database file.
<scope>	Specifies the amount of the database to which the command applies. It may be RECORD N (a single record); NEXT N (*n* records beginning with the current record); ALL (all records in the file); and REST (from the current record to the end of the file).

SELECTED COMMANDS AND FUNCTIONS GROUPED BY FUNCTION

Assistant submenus follow in parentheses.

Commands

Change Data Content

APPEND [BLANK]
Adds record to the database file currently in use. (Update)

BROWSE [FIELDS <field list>]
Adds or edits records of the file currently in use, using full screen editing. (Update, or press [F9] at the dot prompt.)

EDIT [n]
Edits selected records of the database currently in use. (Update or press [F10] at the dot prompt.)

DELETE [<scope>][FOR<exp>]
Marks a selected record for deletion. When the record is marked for deletion, an asterisk (*) appears next to the record or the message "DEL" appears on the status line. (Update)

RECALL [<scope>][FOR<exp>]
Recovers records previously marked for deletion but not yet Packed. (Update)

REPLACE [<scope>]<field>WITH<exp>[FOR<exp>]
Replaces the value of the specified field of specified records with stated values. (Update)

PACK
Removes marked records from the file. (Update)

ZAP
Remove all records from the current database file.

Change Files (Database and Ancillary)

MODIFY LABEL <.lbl filename>
Loads the LABEL menu that permits the user to change the LABEL (.lbl) file. (Modify)

MODIFY QUERY <.qry filename>
Loads the QUERY menu that permits the user to change the QUERY (.qry) file. (Modify)

MODIFY REPORT <.frm filename>
Loads the REPORT menu that permits the user to change the REPORT (.frm) file. (Modify)

MODIFY SCREEN <.scr filename>
Loads the SCREEN menu that permits the user to change the SCREEN (.scr) file. (Modify—Format)

MODIFY STRUCTURE
Lets the user change the field structure of an existing database using a full-screen mode. Fields can be added, changed, or deleted.

Close Files

CLEAR ALL

Closes all database and related files, releases all memory variables, and selects work area 1.

QUIT

Closes all files, stops dBASE and returns control to the operating system. *Always QUIT dBASE before turning off the computer.* (Set Up)

USE <filename> [INDEX <file list>]

Opens a database in the current work area. Any open database in the work area is closed. The user may optionally select an index when the USE command is given. USE with no parameters closes the active database and index files in the currently selected work area. (Set Up)

Create Ancillary Files

CREATE LABEL <.lbl filename>

Activates the LABEL menu which lets the user create and modify LABEL (.lbl) files. The LABEL FORM command uses these files to produce labels from the contents of database files. (Create)

CREATE QUERY <.qry filename>

Activates the QUERY menu that permits users to create and modify QUERY (.qry) files. (Create)

CREATE REPORT <.frm filename>

Activates the REPORT menu that permits users to create REPORT FORM (.frm) files. The REPORT FORM command uses these files to prepare reports from the contents of database files. (Create)

CREATE SCREEN <.scr filename>

Loads the SCREEN menu that permits users to create SCREEN (.scr) files, which in turn create and modify FORMAT (.fmt) files. (Create—Format)

INDEX ON <index key field> TO <filename>

Creates and opens an index file for the current active database. Contains only the index key values and pointers to corresponding records in the database. (Set Up)

MODIFY COMMAND <filename>

Loads a text editor to create or modify an ASCII text file, including dBASE command files. Edited files are given a .prg extension.

Create Database Files

COPY TO <target file> [<scope>] [FIELDS <field list>] [FOR <condition>] [WHILE <condition>] [TYPE <file type>]

Copies all or part of the current active database to a target file. (Organize)

CREATE <filename>

Defines a new database structure. The user specifies the name, type, and width for each field. (Create)

JOIN WITH <alias> TO <newfile> FOR <condition> [FIELDS <field list>]

The active database (which is open in the current work area) merges with the database specified in the JOIN command (which is open in another work area) to create a third database named by the TO clause and including those records that meet the FOR condition. (Organize)

SORT [<scope>] ON <keyfield> TO <fieldname> [ASCENDING] or [DESCENDING]

Creates a new, sorted database containing records copied from the active database. (Organize)

Data Display

AVERAGE [<scope>] [<field list>] [TO <variable list>] [FOR <condition>] [WHILE <condition>]

Computes and displays the average value of each expression in the expression list. (Retrieve)

COUNT [<scope>] [TO <variable>] [FOR <condition>] [WHILE <condition>]

Counts the number of records in the current active database that meet the specified scope or condition. (Retrieve)

DISPLAY [<scope>] [<field list>] [FOR <condition>] [WHILE <condition>] [OFF] [TO PRINT]

Displays, one screen at a time, selected records from the database file currently in use. (Retrieve)

LABEL FORM <.lbl filename> [<scope>] [FOR <condition>] [WHILE <condition>] [SAMPLE] [TO PRINT] [TO FILE <filename>]

Produces labels from the contents of the current active database using a label form created using the MODIFY LABEL command. (Retrieve)

LIST [<scope>] [<field list>] [FOR <condition>] [WHILE <condition>] [OFF] [TO PRINT]

Displays on the screen a continuous listing of the records on the active database. (Retrieve, or press [F3] at the dot prompt.)

REPORT FORM <filename> [<scope>] [FOR <condition>] [WHILE < condition>] [PLAIN] [HEADING <character string>] [NOEJECT] [TO PRINT] [TO FILE <filename>] [SUMMARY]

Produces reports based on existing .FRM file report forms created using CREATE REPORT. (Retrieve)

SUM [<scope>] [<expression list>] [TO <variable list>] [FOR <condition>] [WHILE <condition>]

Calculates and displays the total value of each expression in the expression list for the specified records. If no expressions are listed, then the sum is computed for each numeric field in the active database. (Update)

Data Entry

APPEND

See definition above. (Update)

BROWSE

See definition above. (Update)

EDIT

See definition above. (Update)

File Operation

COPY FILE <source filename> TO <target filename>
Copies a source file, which must not be open, to a target file. (Organize)

DIRECTORY [<drive>] [<path>] [<file delimiter>]
(abbreviated as DIR) DIR with no file delimiter displays the name, record count, and date of the last change for every file with a .DBF extension in the current directory. File delimiters can include the wild card symbols of * and ?. (Tools)

DISPLAY MEMORY [TO PRINT]
Displays, one screen at a time, information about the current memory variables. (Press [F7] at the dot prompt.)

DISPLAY STATUS [TO PRINT]
Displays, one screen at a time, information about the current data and processing conditions. (Press [F6] at the dot prompt.)

DISPLAY STRUCTURE [TO PRINT]
Displays, one screen at a time, the structure of the current database. (Tools—List Structure, or press [F5] at the dot prompt.)

ERASE <filename>
Erases a closed file from the current directory. The command must include the full filename, including the file extension. (Tools)

RENAME <filename> TO <new filename>
Renames a specified file with a new name. The file must be closed and the new filename must include the complete filename, including extensions. (Tools)

SELECT <alias>, SELECT <work area>
Selects a work area containing an open database by using the database's alias; or by selecting from the 10 work areas, using the numbers 1 through 10 or the letters A through J.

Interface to Other Programs

APPEND FROM <source file> [FOR <condition>] [TYPE <file name>]
Copies records from a closed source file to the active database. The newly copied records are added to the end of the active database, and all open index files are updated.

COPY TO
See definition above. (Organize)

Open Files

DO <program name> [WITH parameter list]
Executes the specified program or procedure.

USE
See definition above. (Set Up)

Printer Operation

EJECT
Sends a form feed to the printer. (Retrieve)

Record Selection

CONTINUE

Continues the search for the next record that matches the condition expressed in the last LOCATE command issued. (Position)

FIND <character string> <number>

Searches the controlling index for the first record whose index key matches the specified character string or number. The character string must be enclosed with delimiters (single quotes, double quotes, or square brackets).

GO[TO] <record number> <TOP> <BOTTOM>

Moves the record pointer to a specific record, the first logical record, or the last logical record. (Position)

LOCATE [<scope>] [FOR <condition>] [WHILE <condition>]

Searches the current active database for the first record that matches the conditions and then displays the record number. The next match can be found using the CONTINUE command. (Position)

SEEK <expression>

Searches the controlling index for the first record that has an index key that matches the expression and then places the record pointer on that record. If no match is found, the record pointer is moved to the end of the file.

SKIP [n]

Move the record pointer backwards and forwards by the value of *n*. *n* can be positive or negative. When *n* is omitted, the record point is advanced one record. (Position)

Miscellaneous

ASSIST

The menu-driven Help program that permits the user to use dBASE without entering commands. Novice users can use the database management system without having to learn the programming language. However, not all dBASE commands or custom features are available through ASSIST. To load Assist: at the dot prompt type Assist, or press [F2].

Sorting and Indexing

INDEX

See definition above. (Organize)

REINDEX

Rebuilds all open index files to reflect changes to records in the database.

SORT

See definition above. (Organize)

Selected Functions

DATE()

Shows the system date as a date value.

EOF()

End-of-file function that returns the logical value .T. (true) if the user attempts to move the record pointer after the last logical record in the current work area; otherwise, .F. (false) is returned.

LTRIM(character string)
Shows the character string with the leading blank spaces removed.

TRIM(character string)
Shows the character string with all trailing blank spaces removed.

UPPER(character string)
Shows all alphabetic characters in the character string in upper case.

Selected SET Commands

SET
Provides a full-screen, user-interactive menu system to display and control SET parameters.

SET ALTERNATIVE TO [filename]
Captures screen output and places it in the named file.

SET BELL <ON/OFF>
ON enables the system bell to beep when the wrong data type is entered in a field or when a typed entry fills a field template. OFF disables the system bell.

SET CARRY <ON/OFF>
ON copies all data forward from record to record when records are added using APPEND, BROWSE, and INSERT. OFF is the default setting.

SET CONFIRM <ON/OFF>
ON requires that you press the Return key to place an entry in a field when the system is in full-screen entry mode. OFF is the default setting.

SET DATE <date style>
Determines a format for displaying dates. Styles include mm/dd/yy (American), dd/mm/yy (British or French), dd.mm.yy (German), dd-mm-yy (Italian), and yy.mm.dd (ANSI).

SET DECIMALS TO [<n>]
Determines the display of the number of decimal places in calculations.

SET DEFAULT TO [<drive>]
Sets the default disk drive. If the drive is not specified, the drive from which you loaded dBASE is set as the default disk drive.

SET DELETED <ON/OFF>
ON hides the records marked for deletion, but not yet PACKED, from standard operations. OFF is the default setting.

SET FILTER TO [FILE <query filename>]
Hides records in the current work area that do not meet specified filter conditions.

SET FUNCTION <key> TO <character string>
Assigns a character string to a function key. You must enclose the function key name (2–10 or F2–F10) and the character string in delimiters. Function key [F1] cannot be reprogrammed and is reserved for Help.

SET HELP <ON/OFF>
ON displays "Do you want some help? (Y/N)" if you make an error when entering a command.

SET INDEX TO [<index file list>]
Opens as many as seven index (.ndx) files. The index listed first controls the order in which the database is accessed. SET INDEX TO without a parameter closes all open indexes in the current work area.

SET MARGIN TO <n>
Sets the left-hand margin of the printer to <n>.

SET MENU <ON/OFF>
ON displays a Help menu in full-screen modes. You can turn the Help menu on and off using the [F1] function key.

SET MESSAGE TO [<character string>]
Displays on the bottom line of the screen a user-defined character string of up to 79 characters. The character string must be delimited with double quotes, single quotes, or square brackets, unless the character string is in a memory variable. SET STATUS must be ON.

SET ORDER TO <n>
Selects the controlling index from open index files where *n* = 1–7, indicating the position of the index file in the index file list. Using SET ORDER TO 0 or omitting the number causes the database to be used in physical record order.

SET PATH TO <directory list>
Determines the directories to be searched if a file is not in the current directory. dBASE path is independent of the system path command.

SET RELATION TO [key expression INTO alias]
Links two open databases by a key expression, which can be a field name, a numeric expression, or the function RECNO().

SET SAFETY <ON/OFF>
ON requires confirmation when a file is about to be overwritten or all data records are about to be destroyed. The ERASE command does not require confirmation.

SET SCOREBOARD <ON/OFF>
ON displays the top line of the screen and the messages on the status line.

SET STATUS <ON/OFF>
ON displays a status line on screen line 21 at all times and reserves lines 22–24 for messages. OFF does not turn off the status line of the full-screen commands of ASSIST, BROWSE, CREATE, MODIFY STRUCTURE, or SET, or any of the CREATE/MODIFY commands.

SET TALK <ON/OFF>
ON displays messages that show that an action has taken place.

Operators

Logical operators (in order of precedence)

()	Parentheses for grouping
.NOT.	Logical *not*
.AND.	Logical *and*
.OR	Logical *or*
$	Substring operator

Arithmetic operators

()	Parentheses for grouping
/	Division
*	Multiplication
+	Addition
−	Subtraction

Relational operators

<	Less than
>	Greater than
=	Equal to
<>	Not equal to
<=	Less than or equal to
>=	Greater than or equal to

String operator

+	String concatenation

File Types

Data can be interchanged between dBASE and other software packages using the APPEND FORM and COPY TO commands. Use one of the following file types when copying records to or from different file formats and dBASE.

DELIMITED [WITH <delimiter>]
Used to transfer to or from an ASCII file. Commas, separate fields, and the specified delimiter are used to separate character fields. If *With delimiter* is not included in the command line, the default delimiter of character fields is a double quote (").

DELIMITED WITH BLANK
Used to transfer to or from an ASCII file. Blanks are used to separate all fields.

SDF (System Data Format)
Used to transfer to or from an ASCII file. No field separators are used. Data is assigned to fields in the database file by the position of the character within the source record.

DIF
Used to transfer to or from a VisiCalc format file with the suffix .DIF. Each row in the source file becomes a record and each column a field.

SYLK
Used to transfer to or from a Multiplan file. Each row in the source file becomes a record and each column a field.

WKS
Used to transfer to or from a Lotus file with the suffix .WKS. Each row in the source file becomes a record and each column a field.

Cursor Movement Commands

Create and Modify Structure

Key	Cursor movement
Right arrow	character right
Left arrow	character left
Up arrow	field definition up
Down arrow	field definition down
^Y	Delete item in field definition
^U	Delete field definition
Ins	Insert or typeover characters
^N	Insert template line for new field definition
Esc	Exit without saving definition
^End	Exit, saving definition

Append and Edit

Key	Cursor movement
Right arrow	character right
Left arrow	character left
Up arrow	field up
Down arrow	field down
PgUp	Previous record
PgDn	Next record
^ PgDn	Edit current memo field
^ End	Save current memo field
^ Y	Delete contents of field template
^ U	Mark or unmark current record for deletion
Ins	Insert or typeover characters
Esc	Exit without saving record
^ End	Exit, saving current record
Return *or* Enter	Exits Append when cursor is in the first position of the first field

Browse

Key	Cursor movement
Right arrow	character right
Left arrow	character left
End	field right
Home	field left
Up arrow	record up
Down arrow	record down
^ Right arrow	Pan right
^ Left arrow	Pan left
^ Y	Delete to the right of cursor within a field
^ U	Mark or unmark record for deletion. *DEL* appears on the screen for marked record
Ins	Insert or typeover characters
Esc	Exit BROWSE without saving new edits in the current record. Other changes will be saved.
^ End	Exit BROWSE and save all changes
^ Home *or* [F10]	Activate the BROWSE menu
[F1]	Activate the list of control keys

Function Keys at Dot Prompt

[F1]	Help
[F2]	Assistant
[F3]	List
[F4]	Directory of .DBF files
[F5]	Display structure
[F6]	Display staus
[F7]	Display memory
[F8]	Display
[F9]	Append
[F10]	Edit

Glossary

Absolute replication A spreadsheet process in which formulas are copied from the source range and duplicated exactly in the target range.

Account number A specially assigned group of numbers used to allocate computer-use charges to the proper budget.

Acoustic modem A type of modem that uses an acoustic coupler to link a modem and a standard desktop telephone by sound waves rather than by an electrical connection. The standard phone handset is placed in rubber cups on the modem.

Action line On the database screen, the line that displays the command being generated by the menu or submenu selection.

Add-on Software developed to work with another software package and purchased separately. Examples include 1-2-3 Forecast!, a Lotus add-on that provides numerous common forecasting techniques for statistical analysis, and HAL, another Lotus add-on that allows spreadsheet users to give English-like commands.

Address The description of the location of a cell on a worksheet as determined by the coordinates of the column and the row for that cell. An address may be relative, absolute, or mixed.

Alphanumeric or character fields A field type in database management systems that generally includes alphabetic or alphanumeric data, such as names, addresses, or descriptive information. Fields that are to be alphabetically sorted must be defined as character fields. Such fields cannot be included in mathematical operations.

Analog signals Signals transmitted in a modulating wave representing sound.

Applications software A set of programs that directs the computer to solve particular problems or to perform certain tasks. Applications software is *user oriented.* Examples include word processing, electronic spreadsheet, and database management systems software.

Arithmetic and logic unit (ALU) The part of the computer that carries out addition, subtraction, multiplication, division, and logical comparison.

Artificial intelligence (AI) A field of study related to computer science, mathematics, and symbolic logic concerned with the concepts and methods of thinking. AI uses symbolic inference and symbolic representation of knowledge to create computer programs with many of the properties of human intelligence.

ASCII (American Standard Code for Information Interchange) A 7-bit code used in computers to represent numbers, letters, and special characters. It is used to exchange information between software packages and to communicate between different hardware devices.

Attributes In relational database terminology, the parts of a tuple or record commonly called data fields. Attributes describe or identify entries in a relation.

Auto-dialing A feature of data communications software packages that automatically dials a phone number a specified number of times until a connection is established.

Auto-log-on Software feature that provides automatic registration of the user with the remote computer, including any necessary account numbers and passwords.

Automatic recalculation A feature of spreadsheet software that updates the results of the worksheet formulas each time a value is entered or changed.

Auxiliary storage Storage outside of the central processing unit. Magnetic disk and magnetic tape devices are the most common forms of auxiliary storage. Also called *secondary storage* or *permanent storage.*

BASIC (Beginners All-Purpose Symbolic Instruction Code) A language processor commonly used to program microcomputers. It is hardware and software independent, interactive, and easy to learn.

Batch files A feature of MS-DOS that permits files with the .BAT suffix to contain a list (batch) of DOS commands or program commands to be executed when the batch filename is invoked.

Baud rate An approximation of the number of *bits per second* (bps) being transmitted in a data communications activity. Common rates are 300, 1200, and 2400.

Binary numbering system System of "on" and "off" switches through which all microcomputer data and instructions are expressed. "On" is represented by 1, "off" by 0. Combinations of 1's and 0's are used to represent letters, numbers, and other characters and symbols.

Bit A contraction for *binary digit.* One unit of binary code, either a 0 or a 1, stored in a computer as a charge of electricity. Usually 8 bits are used to make 1 *byte,* or *character of data.*

Bit-mapping A method of graphics display that uses a consistent number of bits in the computer's memory to define each individual pixel of display memory, assigning each a location and a color on the screen. Also called *raster graphics.*

Bits per second (bps) A measurement of the speed of transmission of data. Commonly referred to as the *baud rate.* The most common rates are 300, 1200, and 2400 bps.

Block In word processing, a segment of text, such as a line, a paragraph, or a page.

Block printing The printing of a group of adjacent cells that make up partial rows and/or partial columns on a spreadsheet. Also called *range printing.*

Boldfacing A printing enhancement in which a character is struck twice in a slightly different location on the paper to darken the image.

Border The edges of the spreadsheet that define the rows and columns. The border is located near the top and left side of the spreadsheet.

Buffer A temporary storage area or device between two other devices, such as a computer and a disk or a printer. Buffers allow the two devices to operate at different speeds and still communicate smoothly with each other.

Bugs Errors or mistakes in a program. (An early computer malfunctioned because a moth became trapped within the electrical wiring. When the moth was removed, the computer operator recorded that the machine had been "debugged," and the term stuck.)

Built-in functions Formulas that are already stored in a spreadsheet program and are used by placing the function name and conditions in the appropriate cell. Examples include SUM<range>(sum), MAX<range>(maximum number in a range), and SQRT<value>(square root of a value). Lotus 1-2-3 and VP-Planner require the @ sign before built-in functions.

Bulletin board A storage area within an online database where users store messages to each other, exchange opinions, and get information.

Bulletin board service (BBS) A computerized method of exchanging messages in which users access a database of messages through telecommunications.

Bundled software Software that is included or sold as a package along with the microcomputer hardware.

Bus A group of parallel wires used as a path over which data can be transferred to and from the microprocessor, primary storage, disks, printers, modems, and any other device used as part of the microcomputer system. Bus size and architecture are factors in computer processing speed.

Bus controller The part of the microcomputer that regulates the movement of data to and from primary storage.

Byte The fundamental storage unit in a computer. A byte is normally made up of 8 bits. A byte can store an individual character (a letter of the alphabet, a digit, or a punctuation symbol). A byte is sometimes referred to as a *character of data.*

C A language processor that is the favorite language for software developers of programs for IBM and IBM-compatible microcomputers. C permits programs to be portable and structured, and to direct special operations of the computer.

Cell A location on an electronic spreadsheet formed by the intersection of a row and a column. A cell can store a value, a formula, or a label. Each cell has an address determined by the coordinates of the column and row, such as A1 for column A, row 1.

Central processing unit (CPU) The part of the computer where the processing of data and instructions is performed using a three-step process: (1) fetch data from primary storage, (2) alter the data, and (3) store the altered data in primary storage. In a microcomputer, the CPU is essentially contained on the microprocessor.

Character Any letter, number, or symbol typed on a keyboard or input through other computer hardware.

Character of data The symbol stored in 1 byte. The smallest unit of data a user can manipulate through programming language commands.

Chip A collection of integrated semiconductor circuits contained within a wafer-thin slice of silicon. A microcomputer has 20 or more chips.

Circular reference When the formula to calculate one cell depends on the results of a formula in a second cell and the formula of the second cell also depends on the results in the first cell.

Clone Software or hardware that imitates well-known software or hardware by appearing or operating nearly identically to the original. VP-Planner and Quattro are clones of Lotus 1-2-3.

Coaxial cable A transmission cable made up of a conducting outer metal tube enclosing and insulating a core conductor.

Code Program statements written in a computer language.

Coding The actual writing of a computer program.

Column In electronic spreadsheets, a vertical area from top to bottom on a spreadsheet, usually designated by an alphabetic character. For example, the first column would be A, the second B, and so on.

Command strategy The approach the software takes for prompting and accepting commands. See *menu.*

Communications channel A bi-directional data path between input/output devices and the primary storage of the computer. The most common is a telephone line.

Communications services A type of online database that emphasizes electronic mail and bulletin board services. Two such services are EasyLink and MCI Mail.

Compatibility The ability of hardware and/or software to interact without special adapters or other devices. For example, IBM-compatible microcomputers can use software written for the IBM PC without the software code having to be altered. *Incompatibility* is when, for example, the diskettes of two systems cannot be interchanged because the systems use different operating systems.

Compiler A category of language processor that changes an entire high-level program (the source code) into machine language (the object code) at one time.

Compressed print A printing option in which characters are printed smaller, usually 14 to 17 characters per inch instead of the standard 10 to 12.

Concordance file A file containing all the words and phrases to be searched for and marked as index entries.

Contents In dBASE, an option to specify the names of the fields that are to appear in the report.

Control key A key on the microcomputer keyboard that causes other keys to have a different meaning or use. The use of the control key is often indicated by the symbol ^ or CTRL.

Control panel A term used by Lotus 1-2-3 and other electronic spreadsheet software packages for the area on an electronic spreadsheet containing the status line, entry line, and prompt line. Also called the *prompt area.*

Coordinates In electronic spreadsheets, used to indicate the address of the cell on the spreadsheet. The cell address of B1 has the coordinates B and 1.

Co-processor A type of chip designed to work with a microprocessor for specialized functions. The most popular is the mathematics co-processor chip, which takes over the mathematics functions normally done by the microprocessor, thereby speeding up processing.

Copy The duplication of a file. Also, a command that directs DOS to duplicate one file or a group of files to another disk as defined by the command. The MS-DOS command is COPY [source <drive> filename] [destination <drive> filename].

Copy protection A feature built into the software to restrict or prohibit its being copied.

CP/M-80 (Control Program for Microcomputers) A microcomputer operating system written by Digital Research and used in microcomputer systems based on the 8-bit, Z80 chip. Programs written in languages using CP/M-80 are not compatible with those using MS-DOS.

Creating A function or category of commands common to word processing, electronic spreadsheet, and database software that causes the computer to establish a new file with specific content descriptions. It includes commands to open a document and enter the contents. In word processing, it may also include naming the document. In database management software, it includes describing the database contents to the database management software.

Current cell In electronic spreadsheets, the cell where the cell pointer is currently located. Also called the *active* cell.

Cursor A blinking line, small box, triangle, or other special character that marks the entry position on the screen. It shows the position where a character is to be corrected or data inserted. In electronic spreadsheets, there are two cursors: one on the entry line in the prompt area and one on the worksheet. The worksheet or cell cursor indicates the current cell where entries will be placed, whereas the entry line cursor indicates the position where the user is typing. Also called *pointer.*

Cursor control keys The arrow keys and optional cursor control keys that move the cursor around on the screen. *Arrow keys,* marked with arrows, move the cursor up, down, right, or left one character or cell at a time. *Optional cursor control keys* are regular keys on the keyboard that, when combined with the Control or Escape key, have command power to move the cursor anywhere on the screen.

Cursor direction after data entry Feature of SuperCalc that causes the cursor to automatically move to the "next" cell after data is entered. Cursor direction is determined by the direction of the latest cell movement.

Cursor movement Moving the cursor around on the screen with the cursor control keys.

Daisy wheel printer A letter-quality printer that uses a solid-font printing mechanism shaped like a flower. At the end of each "petal" is the shape of a letter, number, or symbol, which, when pressed against the printer ribbon and paper, creates a printed character.

Data Unprocessed facts or figures that can, if properly processed by a computer, be converted into meaningful information. Although the word *data* is technically plural (the singular is *datum*), in common practice *data* is used for both the singular and plural forms.

Database An orderly collection of one or more related files containing data related to a specific type of application. A *computerized database* is a collection of one or more related files stored compactly and electronically on a disk and accessed through a computer. A *single-file* database provides the customary functions of a database but consists of only one file. A *multiple-file* database performs all the functions of a single-file database but can contain more than one file.

Database management system (DBMS) Software designed to aid in the design, creation, updating, searching, and rearranging of a database and reporting from a database.

Database services A type of online database that markets reference or encyclopedic services. Also known as *encyclopedic utilities.* Two such services are Dialog and Bibliographic Retrieval Services (BRS).

Data capture Collecting incoming data in RAM and then saving it to a disk file. Commonly used in data communications to quickly store transmitted data to disk for later offline retrieval.

Data communications The transmission of digital data from one location to another.

Data conversion Changing the format of a file so that it can be read or used by a different software package.

Data entry An electronic spreadsheet feature that includes the process of putting labels, formulas, and values into cells. In database management software, a function or category of commands that includes the placing of data into defined fields in the records in the database file. *Automatic data entry* is an option that permits certain data, such as record numbers or dates, to be placed in a field without additional data entry.

Data import and export A feature in electronic spreadsheet and database management software that permits data to be exchanged between different software packages without first converting the data into another format.

Data integrity The accuracy and consistency of data throughout the total information system. A database lacks integrity if data in one file contradicts data stored in another file. Such problems usually arise because of improper or unsystematic updating procedures.

Data management In Lotus 1-2-3 and some other spreadsheet software packages, the use of electronic spreadsheet commands to sort, search, and extract selected data contained within a spreadsheet.

Data manipulation The changing, extraction, or organizing of data in a database.

Data query commands Commands that let the user search a database for a particular record, copy records from a database to a separate part of the worksheet, extract records with no duplication, and remove selected records.

Data redundancy Keeping the same data in more than one file.

Data fields A database field type that holds calendar dates. The field format is determined by the software.

Decision support system (DSS) A system used to create, revise, check, and utilize decision models. A DSS aids a decision maker by providing a model to test various "What if?" scenarios. Users can typically take advantage of statistical, graphics, and English-like command features built into the DSS software, making the system easy to use without extensive technical training.

Default setting The setting the software automatically uses if the user does not give other instructions. For example, in word processing, the margins are set at specific columns (i.e., 10 on the left, and 65 on the right) when the software is loaded and until the user makes any changes.

Deletion An editing feature of word processing software that permits the removal of a specified character or group of characters from a document.

Demodulation The process of transforming an analog signal that can be transmitted over voice-only telephone lines into digital, direct-current pulses that can be used by a computer.

Desktop publishing A system of hardware and software—usually including scanners, laser printers, page composition software, and word processing software—that permits the production of high-quality brochures, newsletters, and other documents by applying the basic principles of typography, graphics, and aesthetic page layout.

Destructive write The process of destroying the contents of a byte of storage by entering, or writing, a new character in the same byte. The new character replaces the character that was originally in the byte.

Dictionary An electronically stored list of properly spelled words, used by the spell checker program to find and correct misspellings in a word processing document.

Direct-connect modem A category of modem in which the phone line is connected through a modular phone jack that plugs into the modem, forming an electrical connection. There are two types of direct-connect modems: internal and external.

Directory A list of files available on the logged disk and their attributes, including file size as well as date and time of origin or modification. The MS-DOS command is DIR <drive> <option>, where the available options are /p (page) and /w (wide). Also a command available in dBASE and Lotus 1-2-3.

Disk A platter-shaped, nonvolatile medium used for secondary storage. Disks come in a variety of types, sizes, and storage capacities, including hard disks, minifloppies, and microfloppies.

DISPLAY command In dBASE, a command that shows on the screen one or more records from the currently selected database.

Document In word processing, a large grouping of characters input on a keyboard or through some other device. Examples include memorandums, letters, term papers, reports, and manuscripts.

Document handling In word processing, a function or category of commands for copying, deleting, or renaming entire files.

Documentation Procedures and other program descriptions explaining how to use the software.

Doping The process of adding impurities to silicon to give it conducting and nonconducting properties.

DOS (disk operating system) The term used for the operating system when the microcomputer uses a disk drive. Also a common expression for either PC-DOS or MS-DOS. The operating system is loaded into RAM from a disk.

Dot command A type of print formatting command used by Wordstar to control the format of the text when it is printed. Dot commands are typed in the document and begin with a period, or dot, in column one, followed by a two-letter code.

Dot matrix printer A printer that produces characters with dots formed by pins in the printing head. Such printers can print a variety of type styles and graphics.

Double-density disk A disk that permits the storage of more data per disk because the data is stored more compactly.

Double-sided disk A disk on which data can be written and read from both the top and bottom sides.

Double striking A print enhancement in which a character is printed twice in the same location on the paper to darken the image.

Editing A category of commands used for the correction of stored data, including text, after it has been entered into a file. Editing commands in word processing software include deletion, overwriting, and insertion of text. Electronic spreadsheet editing commands include deletion, overwriting, and insertion of the previously stored cell contents. Database management editing commands include changing, replacing, or deleting the contents of a data record.

Electronic bulletin board The electronic version of a community bulletin board where people can leave messages, ask for assistance, advertise hardware and software for sale, etc.

Electronic mail Private electronic exchange of correspondence between specific individuals who are members of a data communications system. This contrasts with a bulletin board service, in which the messages are not private.

Electronic spreadsheet An electronic version of a paper spreadsheet consisting of a system of rows and columns where each intersection of a row and column is a cell that can hold data, a formula, a label, or a command. Additional features such as increased size, recalculation, replication, and formatting make the electronic spreadsheet an effective tool. Popular electronic spreadsheet software packages include Lotus 1-2-3, Microsoft Excel, Jazz, Quattro (a Lotus clone), and SuperCalc4.

Electronic thesaurus Software containing a list of alternative terms—including synonyms, antonyms, and related terms—to help the user find the most appropriate way to say something.

Emulation When one piece of hardware is designed to imitate, or operate as, another piece of hardware. Data communications software directs a computer to emulate a terminal so that it can send and receive data.

Encryption Changing the characters of a database into a secret code so unauthorized users cannot understand the data.

Entity An item, a person, or an activity around which data is grouped into records. Each record describes one entity. For example, in a database of all the students enrolled in a school, each student is an entity.

Entry line A line in the prompt area or control panel of an electronic spreadsheet where newly typed or edited labels, formulas, or values appear before they are placed in the current cell.

Expansion board A printed circuit board that is plugged into expansion ports in the main system unit of the microcomputer. Used to provide additional features such as extended color graphics, data communications, networking, or additional primary storage.

Expert systems A category of computer programs that approaches a problem-solving situation by mimicking the processes used by people who are experts in that type of problem solving. Often follows the IF-THEN-ELSE format of rules.

Extension A suffix added by either the user or the software to the end of a filename after the period (.) to further describe the file.

External DOS commands A type of MS-DOS system command that can be executed only while the utility program files are present on the disk currently being used.

External modem A modem in which circuitry is housed in a separate unit outside the microcomputer. The modem is connected by a cable through the serial port in the back of the microcomputer.

Fiber optic cable A transmission cable made up of hair-thin glass fibers that allow light beams to be bent or reflected with low levels of signal loss and interference.

Field A set of spaces containing data describing or identifying one entity, such as a customer's name, a client's account number, a student's grade, or the amount of a sales transaction. Several related fields make up one record or tuple. *Field names* are the labels used to describe and name the columns in a database.

File An orderly collection of related records. May also be called a *relation* in a relational database.

File handling Performing operations upon entire files. In electronic spreadsheet software, includes commands for the copying, deletion, consolidation, and loading of files. In database management software, includes file drive designation, erasing files, file back-up, structure listing, and file interchange.

File transfer The coordinated transmission and receipt of files directly from the disk of one computer to the disk of another.

Financial management software package A set of programs, such as the Interactive Financial Planning System (IFPS), used to help managers solve problems commonly found in the area of finance.

Fixed part A part of a document or spreadsheet that does not change as other parts change. For example, in a form letter, the fixed part is the text common to all the letters, and the variable part is the name, address, and salutation.

Flat file A two-dimensional file that is organized in rows and columns. Each row contains the same number of columns. All files within a relational database must be flat files.

Floppy disk A small disk made of flexible Mylar plastic and coated with a substance that can be magnetized. Used for secondary storage, the most popular disks for microcomputers include *minifloppy* disks ($5\frac{1}{4}$-inch) and *microfloppy* ($3\frac{1}{2}$-inch) disks. Floppy disks can be easily removed from the computer's disk drive by the user, whereas hard disks are permanently mounted in the disk drive.

Forced upper case Option that permits the database to change to upper case any characters typed in as lower case, without the need to reenter the field contents.

Format A command that directs DOS to prepare blank disks to accept files by giving addresses for tracks and sectors on the disk. These addresses will be used by the computer to save and later locate files. The disk is also checked to make sure it is usable. The MS-DOS command for the procedure is FORMAT <drive>.

Formatting A function or category of commands in word processing and electronic spreadsheets that provides a neat and professional appearance to a spreadsheet or word processing document. In word processing, includes the adjustment or positioning of margins, line spacing, page breaks, and other placement options. In electronic spreadsheets, includes the adjustment of the display of cell contents, such as numeric display, precision, column width, and the display of label borders and formulas in a spreadsheet. With both, some formatting commands refer to screen appearance and some refer to the appearance of printed output

Formula The symbolic expression of a rule or principle or calculation, such as D12*A2, used in electronic spreadsheets. Normally only the result of the formula is visible in the cell containing the formula. Also called an *expression* because it is understood that the result of the expression will be placed in the current cell, thus completing the formula.

Formula-driven spreadsheets Electronic spreadsheets designed to depend as much as possible on formulas rather than typed-in data values, thus providing greater flexibility.

Forward reference When a formula being calculated depends upon the result of another formula that has not yet been calculated.

Fully formed graphics Graphics software, within word processing software, that lets the user make charts and graphs within the word processing document.

Function keys Special keys on the keyboard that are defined by the software or by programmed instructions stored in the microcomputer. Sometimes called *soft keys* and typically labeled [F1], [F2], [F3], and so on.

Gateway service Offers users of one online data base service access to other online data bases, such as the large encyclopedic utilities of BRS and Dialog.

Grammar checker Software that scans a document and flags suspected errors in punctuation and grammar. It can also rate the reading level of a document.

Global formatting command A command that enables a certain format or function to be carried out throughout the entire file. For example, in electronic spreadsheets, global format commands affect the appearance of the entire spreadsheet.

Global replacement A word processing feature that changes all occurrences of a particular word or phrase throughout the document.

Graphics adapter board A type of expansion card that allows microcomputer screens to display graphics. The most common types are CGA (Color Graphics Adapter), EGA (Enhanced Graphics Adapter), and VGA (Video Graphics Array).

Graphics software A set of computer programs that takes data stored in the computer and interprets them graphically on a screen, plotter, printer, or other output device. There are two general types of graphics: *personal presentation aids,* which appear on the screen of the microcomputer, and *general presentation aids,* which are produced using specialized equipment for showing to groups.

Hard copy Printed copy of a file.

Hard disk An aluminum-alloy disk that is coated with continuous magnetic film, covered by an overcoat, and sealed within an air-tight container. Is faster and holds much more data than a floppy disk. Available as an expansion card or as a disk unit. A hard disk cannot be removed from the disk drive.

Hard spaces Spaces inserted by the user with the space bar, as between words in a sentence.

Hardware The physical computer equipment and its related parts.

High-density disk drives Disk drives capable of using disks that can store a larger amount of data than regular disks. For example, the $5\frac{1}{4}$-inch high-density disk can store up to 1.2 megabytes while the $3\frac{1}{2}$-inch high-density disk can store up to 1.44 megabytes per disk.

Impact printer A general classification of printers that form a character on the page by using a typing mechanism that directly strikes the ink ribbon and the paper. Examples include daisy wheel and most dot-matrix printers.

Indexing The logical, but not physical, rearrangement of a database file. The database management software uses one or more data fields as a key field or fields on which to generate an index file. The index file is then used to reorganize the contents of the database file while reporting or listing the database file. Unlike *sorting,* indexing does not physically rearrange the file.

Information Data that have been processed so that they are meaningful and useful to a decision maker.

Information centers Locations set up by organizations, such as corporations, schools, or colleges, to provide users with information about and hands-on experience with hardware and software.

Ink-jet printer A nonimpact printer that sprays ink in either a continuous stream or droplets onto the paper to form characters.

Insert function A function that enables text to be entered. If the insert function is on, inserted characters are placed between already existing material, pushing the existing material to the right. If the insert function is off, new material replaces the original material rather than pushing it to the right. Usually controlled by the Insert key.

Insertion Newly typed characters are placed next to the previously typed characters, moving the old characters over.

Integrated circuit A collection of thousands of miniature junctions on a chip.

Interactive An attribute of certain programming languages in which the program can be written to prompt the user for data, have the user enter data, and then process the supplied data—all while the program is executing.

Internal control unit The part of the microprocessor that regulates the speed and timing of the execution of instructions within the CPU.

Internal DOS commands System commands that can be executed whenever MS-DOS has been loaded into primary storage, even if the MS-DOS disk has been removed.

Internal modem A modem placed within the microcomputer main system unit, usually in an expansion slot.

Interpreter A type of language processor that reads a high-level program and converts it statement by statement into machine language.

Junction A location on a chip that acts like an on/off switch, permitting the flow of electricity when on and stopping the flow of electricity when off.

Justification The alignment or realignment of text in a document to specific margins. Newspaper columns are commonly justified on both the right and left sides.

K The abbreviation for *kilobyte*. One K, or kilobyte, is equal to 2^{10}, or 1,024, bytes. It is usually rounded off to 1,000 bytes.

Key A field or attribute, such as a social security number or invoice number, that uniquely identifies a specific record. Also called *key field*.

Label Any descriptive text used primarily to provide headings for rows and columns on a spreadsheet.

Language processor A type of systems software that reads a program written in a high-level programming language and converts it into machine language the computer can execute.

Laser printer A type of nonimpact printer that uses a laser beam to trace an image onto a photosensitive drum that transfers the image to paper.

Letter-quality printer A character printer, such as a daisy wheel printer, that produces output resembling typewritten text suitable for formal business correspondence.

Line spacing The distance between lines of text.

Linking field A field that acts as a link or a bridge between two or more files in a relational database. The field is described the same in each file and contains exactly the same data, such as an individual's social security number or an inventory part number.

LIST command dBASE command that displays specified records and fields from the currently selected database.

Local area network (LAN) A system that uses a combination of specialized hardware and software to connect microcomputers within a local area, such as one building or a series of buildings owned by one firm, in order to share software, data, and/or hardware.

Lock-out system System to prevent unauthorized users from seeing or in anyway altering the data in a file.

Logged disk drive The disk drive accessed automatically by the microcomputer when a file action, such as saving a file, takes place.

Logical field A field type in database management systems that generally accepts only one character to indicate a true or false value. Sometimes called a *Boolean field.* The field is set up to have the value of 1 if a condition is true and 0 if the condition is false, or T if true and F if false, or Y for yes and N for no.

Machine language The actual binary code used by a computer.

Macro A set of commands, instructions, or text stored as a group and executed either by pressing a few keys or by invoking the macro name. *Internal macros* are stored within an individual worksheet and are applicable to only that worksheet. *External macros* are stored in a separate file and can be recalled for use in any worksheet. The *macro body* is the entire list of commands within a given macro, stored in spreadsheet cells like numbers, labels, and formulas.

Macro commands In Lotus 1-2-3, commands enclosed in braces and used only within macros to simplify various cursor movements, simulate pressing of a function key, or perform other specific functions.

Magnetic disk A device used in computers to magnetically store data that can be retrieved directly. Data and instructions are stored as a pattern of magnetic spots recorded on and read from tracks on the disks. Such storage is nonvolatile.

Magnetic tape A tape coated with magnetic material and used to store data and instructions in a series of magnetic spots. It is often used for the low-cost backup of disk data.

Mail merge A feature found with word processing software that permits variable parts to be merged with a document. A common use for this feature is to merge names and addresses with form letters.

Manual recalculation The recalculation of the worksheet formulas upon command by the user, as opposed to automatically with each data entry.

Margin The amount of space left between the edges of the paper and the text printed on the paper.

Marking a block The process of putting a block marker at the beginning and end of a block of text for word processing block operations.

Megabyte (M or MB) 1,048,576 bytes, or approximately 1 million bytes of memory.

Memo fields A field type in database management systems that holds large amounts of descriptive text. Such fields cannot be manipulated but can be associated with specific records in a database file.

Menu A listing of the commands available to the user. Menu types include *on-demand, pull-down, pop-up windows, vertical,* and *horizontal bar.*

Message line On the database screen, the line that provides an explanation of the current menu option and any action required of the user if that option is chosen.

Microfloppy disk A $3\frac{1}{2}$-inch disk enclosed in a hard plastic shell. Increasingly popular, especially with laptop computers and the IBM PS/2 line of microcomputers.

Microprocessor A silicon chip containing the central processing unit of a microcomputer. It contains four parts: *arithmetic and logic unit, registers, internal control unit,* and *bus controller.*

Mockup Simulation of an actual report.

Model A symbolic representation or example used to help visualize or test something that cannot be directly observed. Spreadsheets are sometimes called models, especially if they are mostly formula driven and used to test various "What if?" questions. In business management, a *decision model* is any quantitative or logical abstraction of reality that is created and used to help someone make a decision.

Modem A device for converting digital impulses coming from the computer into analog signals and vice versa, to permit transmission of data over ordinary telephone lines. A contraction of the words *MO*dulation and *DEM*odulation. There are two categories of modems: *direct connect* and *acoustic.*

Modifying A function or category of database management commands, including revision of the database already in use.

Modulation The conversion of the digital, direct-current signals used by the computer system into analog signals for transmission through the voice-only channels of the telephone system.

Module A program or program segment that is a discrete unit that can be combined with other program units to perform common computer operations such as input, output, and printing.

Monitor A TV-like screen used for video display. Sometimes called a cathode ray tube (CRT) or a video display terminal (VDT). There are two basic varieties: color and monochrome.

Monochrome A monitor that uses only one color (white, green, or red) against a dark background.

Motherboard The main system board. All other boards must connect to the motherboard.

Mouse A small hand-held pointing device used to move images on the screen, edit or format text, draw or change graphics, and choose commands in certain mouse-supported applications.

MS-DOS (Microsoft Disk Operating System) The most popular operating system for 16-bit and 32-bit microcomputers. The IBM PC operating system is a variation of MS-DOS called *PC-DOS.*

Multiple concurrent communications sessions When the microcomputer transmits and receives data from several sources at the same time.

Multiple-file database A database that performs all the functions of a single-file database, but can contain more than one file, with the ability to link those files together.

Multiple record deletions and updates Database software feature that permits a number of records to be changed in the database through only one command.

Multiple file reports Reports that integrate information from two or more files from one database into a single report.

Multitasking The ability to run two or more software applications at one time.

Natural language processor A system of software that allows computers to accept input and produce output in a conventional language such as English.

Navigation line On the dBASE III Plus screen, the line that provides instruction for moving from one menu option or submenu to another.

Networking The interconnection of multiple microcomputers in which more than one user can access hardware, software, and/or files simultaneously while coordinating concurrent processing.

Newspaper-style columns Text is continuously written down the first column until it reaches the bottom of the page, and then the text continues at the top of the second column. Columns are both right and left justified.

Nonimpact printer A general classification of printers that form a character on the page by using a mechanism that does not touch the paper. Examples include laser and ink-jet printers.

Numeric fields A field type in database management systems that generally contains numeric data to be used in mathematical operations such as adding and subtracting.

Object code The code that results when a compiler converts high-level program, or *source code,* to machine language.

Online database A collection of files and services available electronically using telecommunications.

Online help A software feature to supply on the screen additional explanations of commands at the user's request.

Onscreen formatting A word processing feature that causes the text to appear on the screen essentially as it will be printed.

Operating system A set of programs that supervises the processing of applications programs and all input and output operations of the microcomputer system.

Operating system prompt A signal to the user that the operating system has been loaded and is ready to be used. On several microcomputers it appears as A> if the logged disk drive is A.

Order of recalculation The sequence or order that the electronic spreadsheet uses when it recalculates the formulas and functions, such as natural, column by column, or row by row.

Organizing A function or category of commands in database management software that includes the physical or logical rearrangement or duplication of database files.

Orphan The last line of a paragraph when it appears alone as the first line of a page with all the preceding text of the paragraph at the bottom of the preceding page.

OS/2 (Operating System/2) A recent variation of the MS-DOS operating system for IBM PS/2 models of microcomputers. Features include enhanced menus, virtual memory, multiuser and multitasking capabilities, networking, and sophisticated graphics.

Outline processor Software that can automatically construct and maintain an outline as it is created and edited.

Overstriking A printing enhancement in which one character, such as a slash, is typed over another character.

Overwriting A technique for replacing letters in a document by placing the new characters over the previous characters. The previous text is removed from primary storage and from the screen. Usually controlled by the *insert function.*

Packing Removing from the database any records marked for deletion.

Page break A word processing command to end a page of printing and start a new page. There are two types: *conditional* (a page break will be inserted if a specified number of lines of text do not remain on a page) and *unconditional* (a page break will be inserted on the page regardless of text location).

Page footing The title or other text printed at the bottom of a page. Also called a *footer.*

Page heading The title or other text printed at the top of the page. Also called a *header.*

Page number omission Shuts off the automatic page numbering. Usually used on single-page word processing documents.

Page number setting A word processing feature that allows the user to start numbering printed pages at some number other than one.

Page offset A word processing feature that allows the left margin of the document to be shifted on the printer.

Parallel columns Text, such as lists and command descriptions, is printed across columns.

Parallel port A connection point commonly used to connect printers to microcomputers. Parallel interfaces transfer data by sending all the bits that are contained in a byte of storage at one time—whereas a serial port sends out only one bit at a time, resulting in a series or stream of bits. The most common type of parallel port is the Centronics port.

Pascal A popular standardized computer language designed primarily for instructional use. Pascal is a structured language so it can easily be broken into independent modules or procedures.

Passwords Secret signals or words that authorized users memorize, keep confidential, and use to reply to computer prompts, thereby preventing unauthorized computer access.

Permanent storage A medium, such as a floppy disk, on which data is saved and stored for retrieval and use later. Also called *secondary* or *auxiliary* storage.

Pirating The copying of a floppy disk whose programs are protected by the Copyright Law.

Pixel A tiny dot on a computer screen capable of being turned on or off or set to a color. All screen images are composed of pixels.

Plotter A device to draw graphs and other pictures by moving pens, in electronically driven holders, across the paper to produce an image. The types of plotters include *flatbed, drum,* and *roller bed.*

Pointer In electronic spreadsheets, another name for the worksheet cursor. In database management systems, the address or location of the next record in the file.

Pointing A method of entering cell references into a formula or command. Rather than keying in cell references, the user activates the pointer; the cursor is moved to the desired cell; the necessary key is pressed; and the cell reference then appears on the entry line. Also, a function common to database management software that includes the movement of the pointer (location of the next logical record) anywhere in the database file. Pointing is also called *positioning.*

Port A connection point or interface used to connect various peripheral devices such as printers and modems to the microcomputer. Channels through which data flow in and out of the computer. The most common are *parallel* and *serial* ports.

Predefined mailing labels A software feature that allows users to produce standard mailing labels without additional programming or specifications.

Primary disk drive The drive where the operating system and the applications software are normally located. On most microcomputers, the primary disk drive is designated as drive A.

Primary storage Commonly called *RAM* (random access memory). The part of the computer in which data and instructions are internally stored immediately before and after processing. The amount of storage is expressed in K (kilobytes). This area is sometimes called *internal storage, primary memory,* or *main memory.*

Print formatting Instructions in a word processing document that adjust the text for the printer but not necessarily on the screen. Instructions can be embedded in the text file or in commands given when the document is printed.

Print spooling The word processing software permits a document to be printed while the user continues to edit documents with the word processing software.

Printer A device used to transform the binary digits in the microcomputer into hard copy on paper.

Printing Producing paper output of a document, a spreadsheet, or a database report.

Private telephone network A company, such as MCI or SPRINT, that sells telephone services competing with public telephone companies, such as AT&T.

Procedures Instructions on the use and operation of the computer system. User's manuals are a form of procedures. Sometimes called *documentation.*

Processing Sorting, coding, editing, calculating, moving, storing, retrieving, summarizing, and other manipulation of data into information.

Program A set of instructions in a specific order designed to accomplish a specific task with a computer. Programs are written in a language, such as BASIC, FORTRAN, COBOL, C, or Pascal. Using applications packages, such as word processing, spreadsheet, and database management software, also has some of the elements of programming.

Programmable database system A type of database management software that combines the functions of both flat-file and relational databases and also allows the user to write programs to further process the data and create custom-designed reports.

Programming The act of writing a set of instructions that causes the computer system to perform specific actions.

Project management software Software designed to aid managers in the planning, monitoring, and tracking of projects that involve multiple tasks and relationships. Examples include Harvard Project Manager, SuperProject, and TimeLine.

Prompt area The part of a spreadsheet that displays information about the current, or active, cell. It contains the status line, the entry line, and the prompt line. Lotus 1-2-3 calls this area the *control panel.*

Prompt line A line in the prompt area of an electronic spreadsheet that displays the available commands. The content of the prompt line changes with each level of command.

Proportional printing A feature found in some word processing packages that relates the amount of space allocated to a printed character to the size of that character, thereby providing a neater and more professional appearance to the printed output.

Protocols Established set of rules for data communications. May include rules for modem frequency, speed and type of modulation, flow control, and error checking.

Prototyping A tool used in systems analysis and design in which a planned database management system is quickly developed and tested using a small database and a few reports with a small amount of sample data. Then the user and developer go through several trial and error models to eventually develop a system that meets the needs of the user.

Pure binary The storing of numbers in the exact binary format.

Query capabilities The ability to request information from the files by simply asking questions.

RAM (random access memory) The common term for primary storage within a microcomputer. RAM capacity is expressed in K (kilobytes).

Random access memory (RAM) A type of semiconductor storage in the microcomputer. Stores the data and instructions while they are actively being processed or executed in the microcomputer. RAM capacity is expressed in K (kilobytes). Also called *primary storage, primary memory,* and *working storage.* Acts as an electronic scratch pad.

Range A group of adjoining cells in an electronic spreadsheet that form a square or rectangular pattern specified by the address of the first and last cells in the group. Similar to a block in word processing. In Lotus 1-2-3 database applications, the *input range* is the area of the worksheet to be searched. It must include the row of field names. The *output range* is a designated place on the worksheet where selected records are copied and placed as they meet the stated criterion in the criterion range.

Read-only memory (ROM) A type of semiconductor storage in the microcomputer that is nonvolatile. Stores instructions that can be used or read, but cannot be altered or erased by the user. Commonly used to store frequently used instructions that can be changed only by the computer manufacturer.

Read-write heads A device within the disk drive unit to read and/or write magnetic spots to or from a disk.

Recalculation The repeated calculation of the formulas on an electronic spreadsheet after the values in the cells have been entered or changed. Recalculation mode may be *automatic* or *manual.*

Record An orderly collection of data fields about one subject, or entity, such as one client, one student, or one transaction. An orderly collection of related records is a file. Record size is the maximum size of each record in a database, expressed in bytes.

Register Small storage areas used to temporarily hold data being processed within the microcomputer.

Relation An orderly collection or set of tuples or records. A term commonly used in relational databases to mean essentially the same thing as a *file.*

Relational database A type of database management software that has the ability to cross-reference, or link two or more flat-files through at least one common field. A relational database is capable of searching and retrieving data from more than one of the flat files within the database, provided there is a defined relationship between the files.

Relational operators Symbols such as > (greater than) and < (less than) plus the colon (:) (to indicate a link between two relations or files).

Relative replication A type of copying of cell contents in electronic spreadsheets. When formulas are copied using relative replication, the references to other cells are adjusted to their new positions on the spreadsheet.

Rename A command that directs DOS to rename an existing file. The MS-DOS command is RENAME [<drive> old filename] [<drive> new filename].

Reporting The database process involving the creation of a report format file for later printing.

Report format file The database file that describes each report in terms of report headings, column headings, fields to be included, grouping of records within the report, and fields to be totaled.

Replication A spreadsheet command that copies the cell contents from one cell or a range of cells to another cell or range of cells.

Reset command The command used to restart the computer. The contents of primary storage are lost, and the operating system must be reloaded. On the IBM PC and compatibles, the Reset command is a combination of three keys: Ctrl + Alt + Del. Some IBM compatibles have reset buttons.

Restore command The WordPerfect command that will cancel a deletion and restore the deleted characters at the *current* location of the cursor.

Retrieving and reporting A function or category of commands in database management software that causes the database software to search a database for records requested by the user and report those records to the user either by displaying them on the screen or by printing them.

Revisions Adjustments made to a file to reflect changes in external factors affecting the file.

Robotics Study of using computers to see and manipulate objects in their surrounding environment.

ROM (read-only memory) A type of semiconductor storage that is nonvolatile and used to store instructions that cannot be altered by the user.

Row A horizontal area across a page or a spreadsheet. In electronic spreadsheets, rows are designated by numbers.

Ruler line A feature on the screen used with several word processing software packages. The line shows the left margin (L), the right margin (R), and any tab stops (!).

Saving The process of placing a copy of the contents of primary storage onto a disk file.

Scanners Specialized input devices that let users electronically store text or graphic images.

Screen A TV-like screen that is sometimes called a cathode ray tube (CRT), video display terminal (VDT), or *monitor.*

Scrolling The movement of a portion of a document or spreadsheet up, down, or from side to side, so that other parts of the document or worksheet can be seen on the screen.

Search and replace A word processing editing feature that allows the user to conduct an electronic search through a document and systematically correct an error or substitute one word or phrase for another.

Secondary storage Storage outside of the central processing unit, sometimes called *auxiliary storage.* Magnetic disk and magnetic tape devices are the most common forms of secondary storage used with microcomputers.

Sector A wedge-shaped portion of a disk. A *soft-sectored* disk has sectors that are determined by the software; a *hard-sectored* disk has sectors that are determined by the holes in the disk.

Semiconductor A substance capable of carrying electricity at a very low energy level.

Sensitivity analysis A specialized type of "What if?" analysis in which the user determines how sensitive results are to a minor change in just one value or variable.

Separate formatting program Word processing software that requires the user to run the program that formats the document file before printing.

Serial port A connection point commonly used to connect microcomputers to communication devices. Serial interfaces transfer data 1 bit at a time. The most common type of serial port is the RS-232.

SET commands Commands that control or set up the operational environment of dBASE—for example, turning off the automatic beep that sounds at the ends of fields or changing the disk drive.

SET RELATION command Allows the dBASE user to draw fields from two different files without producing a new file.

Shareware Software that can be copied and, if the user finds the software useful, a voluntary fee paid to the author.

"Shrink-wrap" license The user automatically agrees to the licensing requirements of a software package by breaking the plastic shrink wrap enclosing the package.

Silicon A common element (sand) used to make semiconductors by adding small amounts of impurities through a process called *doping.*

Single-file database A simple type of database management software that provides the customary functions of creating, updating, searching, and reporting; however, the data in the database are stored, organized, and retrieved sequentially, and the database consists of just one file, a *flat file.*

Slash command A type of spreadsheet command entered by typing a / (slash) and a letter indicating a specific function. Also called *extended* commands.

Soft spaces Spaces inserted by the software for formatting purposes in word processing.

Software house A company that develops and sells software for standard, rather than custom, applications.

Soft words Words stored electronically as opposed to physically (such as on paper). The words stored within the primary memory of a word processing system (the microcomputer system) are termed soft because they are not in a physical form.

Software Instructions that direct a computer to process data. There are two general categories of software: *systems software* and *applications software.*

Software package A set of prewritten commands that accomplish a task. Generally the package is purchased so that users do not have to spend the time and effort to write their own programs.

Sorting The physical rearrangement of a database file in ascending or descending order according to the contents of a key field or fields. The typical sorting function causes the software to actually create a copy of the original file, but the new file is in the desired sorting order. The new file then replaces the old file.

Source code A program written in a high-level compiler language, such as COBOL, BASIC, or FORTRAN, to be converted into object code (machine language) before execution.

Source range A cell or group of spreadsheet cells to be copied to the destination or target range.

Special print features Word processing print enhancements such as boldfacing, double striking, underlining, and overprinting.

Specialized videotext services A type of online database that emphasizes specialized offerings for particular interests and professions, such as business and law. Such services include Dow/Jones News Retrieval Service, a financial utility, and Lexis, a law utility.

Spell checker Software that compares each word in a word processing document to an electronic dictionary. Each misspelled or missing word is marked for the user to review. Words can be corrected, ignored, or added to the dictionary.

Spreadsheet auditing The careful checking of an electronic spreadsheet for errors, incompleteness, and inaccuracy.

Statistical software package A set of programs used to describe, store, and analyze data and report the results of the analysis. Commercial statistical software packages include 1-2-3 Forecast!, Microstat, Exec*U*Stat, and Minitab.

Statistics The science of collecting, analyzing, interpreting, and presenting data.

Status area A term used with some electronic spreadsheet packages for the prompt area or control panel on a spreadsheet.

Status line or bar In word processing, a feature that indicates which file is being used, the current page number, the line number, the column number, the character insert status, and how much room remains in primary memory to collect text. In electronic spreadsheets, a feature that indicates the location of the cursor on the worksheet. Some electronic spreadsheet software also use the status line to show primary storage use at loading, the cursor position, and cell contents.

Structured programming A modern programming technique that generally uses only simple logic structures (including sequential, conditional, and looping structures), has only one entrance and one exit from a structure, has minimal use of branching instructions such as GOTO, and uses the top-down approach.

Style sheet A group of preset format commands that can be used with any document.

Subscripting Typing one character below another.

Superscripting Typing one character above another character.

System command A communication to the microcomputer's operating system to ask it to carry out a function, such as giving a disk directory, deleting a file, or saving a file.

System prompt An indication on the screen, usually A>, that the operating system has been loaded into primary storage.

Systems analysis The examination and study of an activity or problem to determine the purposes or goals and how they should be achieved.

Systems design The definition of the system and the working relationships involving parts of the system. May include the programming of the software needed in the system or at least a detailed description that a programmer can follow.

Systems software A set of commands that coordinate the operations of the various hardware components. It is computer-oriented. Systems software is usually purchased from a software developer and supplied by the computer manufacturer with the hardware. There are three types of systems software available: operating systems, utilities, and language processors.

Tab A point where the cursor will stop when the Tab key is pressed. Used for indenting text and lining up columns.

Table merging/joining The combining of information from two or more files that are currently open in separate work areas. The merged information is then saved in a new file.

Table of authorities A list of all the citations referred to in a legal document.

Table of contents An outline, including page numbers, of the contents of a long document.

Target range The location on an electronic spreadsheet where copied cells are to be placed.

Telecommunications system A data communications system that uses telephone lines for data transmission.

Template A standardized format for an electronic spreadsheet. A template may contain all the labels, formulas, and other fixed parts for a particular application, leaving only a small amount of data entry for the user.

Terminal A device used to send and receive data, but typically with little or no processing capability. With proper hardware and software, a microcomputer can be used as a terminal in a data communications system.

Text Characters (information) entered in a word processing, electronic spreadsheet, or database file.

Title lock A command used with electronic spreadsheets that locks or freezes designated rows and/or columns in place on the screen. Once a row and/or column has been defined as a title, the worksheet can be scrolled past the fixed set of titles and they will remain on the screen, regardless of their relative position on the worksheet. Also called *titling*.

TRIM A dBASE syntax command to improve report appearance by removing unneeded spaces.

Tuple A relational database term commonly used interchangeably with *record*. In a relational database, each row within a flat file is called a tuple. It is a collection of attributes about one entity.

Turnkey software Software that requires no user programming.

Typeover In word processing, the replacement of previously typed characters with new characters. Also called *overwriting*.

Unconditional page breaks Word processing command instructing the printer to start printing on a new page.

Underlining A printing enhancement in which specified text is underlined.

Undo A word processing feature for retrieval of the last deletion that was made.

Unix A multiuser, multitasking, portable operating system originally developed by Bell Labs as a program development tool. In recent years, increasingly adapted and used in microcomputer systems.

User defined format codes A combination of format codes used to format a spreadsheet or area of a spreadsheet. The user can select a predefined set or alter any of the format settings.

Users groups Clubs of people who share an interest in a particular brand of hardware and/or software.

Utilities Programs supplied within the operating system to support the user in the operation of the computer system. Includes such functions as copying disks, copying files, formatting disks, listing file directories, erasing and renaming files, and other routine activities. Such utilities may also be available through applications software modules.

Value A number that is entered into a cell in a spreadsheet as data. Values are entered directly into the worksheet and are not the result of a formula.

Value-added networks A communications network that uses software and hardware to route data on leased public telephone circuits between the network connections.

Variable part A part of a document or file that is subject to frequent alteration as the result of some other change.

Variables Quantities that are the result of a calculation by a formula in a spreadsheet. In statistical applications in particular, the *dependent variable* is the variable whose value is to be predicted. The *independent variable* is the variable whose value is known and will be used to help determine the dependent variable.

Vector graphics A method of graphics display that holds entire shapes, such as circles and rectangles, instead of individual pixels. Also called an *object-oriented* system.

Videotext services A type of online database that offers a variety of consumer-oriented services, including encyclopedic databases, communications, shopping, and games. Two such services are CompuServe and The Source.

Virtual memory A technique that transfers data and commands between primary and secondary storage. Software can use secondary storage as if it were primary storage, greatly increasing the amount of primary storage available.

Volatile storage Storage that depends upon a constant flow of electricity.

Warm boot Restarting the microcomputer after it is already in use by using the Reset command (Control + Alt + Delete keys in MS-DOS).

"What if?" analysis A technique used with electronic spreadsheets to test the effect of changes.

Widow A first line of a paragraph appearing alone at the bottom of a page, with the rest of the paragraph appearing at the top of the following page.

Wildcard characters Characters that permit commands to affect several files or words with one command. In MS-DOS, the wildcard character replaces a group of characters, and ? replaces any single character.

Window The portion of the document or spreadsheet currently visible on the screen. Some software permit multiple windows. *Multiple windows* can be *synchronized* (cursor movement in one window causes a similar movement in the other window) or *unsynchronized* (cursor movement in one window does not affect the other window).

Word processing The automated processing or manipulation of words using specialized applications software designed to help compose, revise, print, and file written documents. Popular word processing packages include WordStar and WordPerfect.

Word wrap A word processing feature in which the text being inserted is automatically moved to a new line when it goes past the right margin.

Working storage Another name for primary storage.

Worksheet The portion of the spreadsheet where the actual work of the spreadsheet is done. The worksheet contains the border and the cells.

Write-protect notch A notch on the side of a floppy disk that when covered will prevent data from being erased from or written on the disk.

WYSIWYG (What you see is what you get) A term used in word processing when the text on the screen is shown as it will appear on the printed page.

Trademark Acknowledgments

True BASIC is a registered trademark of **Addison-Wesley Publishing.** Alpha/three is a registered trademark of **Alpha Software Corporation.** Paradox is a registered trademark of **Ansa Software,** a Borland Company. Apple II GS, Apple IIe, MacDOS, Macintosh, and ProDOS 16 are registered trademarks of **Apple Corporation.** Project/Manager Workbench is a registered trademark of **Applied Business Technology.** GAUSS is a registered trademark of **Applied Technical Systems.** Chart-Master, Framework, Framework II, Multimate, dBASE II, dBASE III, dBASE III Plus, and dBASE IV are registered trademarks of **Ashton-Tate.** Graphics Express is a registered trademark of **Bell & Howell.** Unix is a registered trademark of **Bell Labs.** BMDPC is a registered trademark of **BMDP Statistical Software.** Lightning, Quattro, Reflex: The Database Manager, Reflex: The Analyst, and Turbo BASIC are registered trademarks of **Borland International Inc.** Show Partner is a registered trademark of **Brightbill-Roberts/The Marketing Channel.** Bank Street Writer is a registered trademark of **Broderbund Software.** BRS, PC Outline is a registered trademark of **Brown Bag Software.** BRS, BRS/After Dark, BRS/Brkthru, BRS/Search and Bibliographic Retrieval Service are registered trademarks of **BRS Information Technologies.** PC-File III and PC-File/R are registered trademarks of **Buttonware Inc.** TOTAL is a registered trademark of **CINCOM Corporation.** CompuServe and IQuest are registered trademarks of **CompuServe.** Easy Writer II, Super SpellGuard, SuperCalc, Super Calc2, SuperCalc4, and SuperProject are registered trademarks of **Computer Associates.** System W is a registered trademark of **Comshare.** Condor 3 is a registered trademark of **Condor Computer Corporation.** MBA is a registered trademark of **Context Management Systems.** Revelation is a registered trademark of **Cosmos.** CUFFS is a registered trademark of **CUFFS Planning and Models.** IDMS/R is a registered trademark of **Cullinet.** DAC-Easy Base is a registered trademark of **Dac Software.** DataEase is a registered trademark of **DataEase International.** Business Connection, Dialog, and Knowledge Index are registered trademarks of **Dialog Inc.** Random House Proofreader is a registered trademark of **Digital Marketing.** CP/M-80, Digital Research Imagemaker, and GEM Graph are registered trademarks of **Digital Research.** Barron's, Dow Jones News/Retrieval Service, and The Wall Street Journal are registered trademarks of **Dow Jones & Company.** Nota Bene is a registered trademark of **Dragonfly Software.** ESP is a registered trademark of **Economica.** IFPS/Personal and Interactive Financial Planning are registered trademarks of **Execucom.** Exec*U*Stat is a registered trademark of **Exec*U*Stat Inc.** 1-2-3 Forecast! is a registered trademark of **Bill L. Gates.** Telenet is a registered trademark of **GTE Telenet Communications Corp.** Personal Computing is a registered trademark of **Hayden Publishing Company Inc.** Hercules monochrome adapter is a registered trademark of **Hercules Computer Technologies.** Infoworld is a registered trademark of **Infoworld Publications.** Stratagem is a registered trademark of **Integrated Planning.** 80287, 8087, 80286, and 80386 are registered trademarks of **Intel.** Color/Graphics Adapter, DB2, Enhanced Graphics Adapter, IBM, AT, IBM Enhanced Keyboard, IBM PC, IBM PS/2 Model 30, IBM PS/2 Model 50, IBM PS/2 Model 60, IBM PS/2 Model 80, IBM Personal System/2, IMS, OS/2, PC Storyboard, PC-DOS, PS/2, SQL/DS, and Video Graphics Array are registered trademarks of **International Business Machines Corporation.** Javelin is a registered trademark of **Javelin Software.** Volkswriter 3 is a registered trademark of **Lifetree Software Inc.** Think Tank is a registered trademark of **Living Videotext.** Freelance, Freelance Plus, HAL, Jazz, Lotus 1-2-3, Manuscript, Symphony, and VisiCalc are registered trademarks of **Lotus Development Corporation.** Express is a registered trademark of **Management Decision Systems.** MCI Mail is a registered trademark of **MCI.** IMPACT is a registered trademark of **MDCR.** Lexis is a registered trademark of **Mead Data Control.** Knowledgeman is a registered trademark of **Micro Database Systems Inc.** CorrectStar, Easy, WordStar, WordStar 2000, WordStar 4.0, and WordStar Professional are registered trademarks of **Micropro.** Clout, R:base 5000, and R:base System V are registered trademarks of **Microrim.** BASICA, Excel, GW-BASIC, MS-DOS, Microsoft, Microsoft Mouse, Multiplan, Quick BASIC, Word, and Xenix System V are registered trademarks of **Microsoft.** Minitab is a registered trademark of **Minitab Inc.** MC68020 and Motorola 68000 are registered trademarks of **Motorola.** Oracle is a registered trademark of **Oracle Corporation.** VP-Planner/VP-Planner Plus are registered trademarks of **Paperback Software.** Personal Pearl is a registered trademark of **Pearlsoft Inc.** Statpro is a registered trademark of **Penton Software.** VisiTrend/Plot is a registered trademark of **Personal Software.** Polaroid Palette is a registered trademark of **Polaroid.** Ingres and Ingres for Personal Computers are registered trademarks of **Relational Technology Inc.** Decision Graphics, Samna Plus, and Samna Word IV are registered trademarks of **Samna Corporation.** Statistical Analysis System (SAS) is a registered trademark of **SAS Institute.** Forecast Master is a registered trademark of **Scientific Systems.** Webster's New World Spelling Checker is a registered trademark of **Simon & Schuster Software.** SmartForecasts is a registered trademark of **Smart Software.** KeyChart is a registered trademark of **Softkey Software.** ADABAS is a registered trademark of **Software AG of North America.** Harvard Graphics, Harvard Total Project Manager, PFS:Graph, PFS:Professional File, and PFS: Professional Write are registered trademarks of **Software Publishing Corporation.** Graf'Talk is a registered trademark of **Software Solutions.** Chat and The Source are registered trademarks of **The Source Telecomputing Corporation.** Q&A is a registered trademark of **Symantec Corp.** SYSTAT is a registered trademark of **SYSTAT.** Perfect Filer is a registered trademark of **Thorn/EMI Computer Software Inc.** TK!Solver is a registered trademark of **Universal Technical Systems.** RATS (Regression Analysis of Time Series) is a registered trademark of **VAR Econometrics.** EasyLink, FYI, and InfoMaster are registered trademarks of **Western Union Telegraph Service.** WordPerfect is a registered trademark of **WordPerfect Corporation.** PC Magazine is a registered trademark of **Ziff-David Publishing Company.**

Some of the product names mentioned in this textbook are used for identification purposes only and may be trademarks of their respective companies.

Index

A 9
B 0
C 1
D 2
E 3
F 4
G 5
H 6
I 7
J 8

F1 Shell **Super/Subscript** *Thesaurus* CANCEL	F2 Spell **◄Search** *Replace* ►SEARCH
F3 Screen **Switch** *Reveal Codes* HELP	F4 Move **►Indent◄** *Block* ►INDENT
F5 Text In/Out **Date** *Mark Text* LIST FILES	F6 Tab Align **Center** *Flush Right* BOLD
F7 Footnote **Print** *Math/Columns* EXIT	F8 **Format** Print **Line** *Page* UNDERLINE
F9 Merge/Sort **Merge E** *Merge Codes* MERGE R	F10 Macro Def **Retrieve** *Macro* SAVE

Key: WordPerfect 4.2
Control + Function Key
Shift + Function Key
Alt + Function Key
FUNCTION KEY ALONE

F1 Shell **Setup** *Thesaurus* CANCEL	F2 Spell **◄Search** *Replace* ►SEARCH
F3 Screen **Switch** *Reveal Codes* HELP	F4 Move **►Indent◄** *Block* ►INDENT
F5 Text In/Out **Date/Outline** *Mark Text* LIST FILES	F6 Tab Align **Center** *Flush Right* BOLD
F7 Footnote **Print** *Math/Columns* EXIT	F8 Font **Format** *Style* UNDERLINE
F9 Merge/Sort **Merge Codes** *Graphics* MERGE R	F10 Macro Def. **Retrieve** *Macro* SAVE

Key: WordPerfect 5.0
Control + Function Key
Shift + Function Key
Alt + Function Key
FUNCTION KEY ALONE

Alt + Key	
Compose	Step
Help F1	Edit F2
Name F3	Abs F4
GoTo F5	Window F6
Query F7	Table F8
Calc F9	Graph F10

Lotus® 1-2-3®

Help F1	Assist F2
List F3	Dir F4
Display Struc F5	Display Status F6
Display Memory F7	Display F8
Append F9	Edit F10

dBASE III Plus™

WordPerfect 4.2

F1	F2	F3	F4	F5	F6	F7	F8	F9	F10
Shell	Spell	Screen	Move	Text In/Out	Tab Align	Footnote	Font	Merge/Sort	Macro Define
Thesaurus	**Replace**	**Reveal Codes**	**Block**	**Mark Text**	**Flush Right**	**Math/Columns**	**Style**	**Graphics**	**Macro**
Setup	*◀Search*	*Switch*	*▶Indent◀*	*Date/Outline*	*Center*	*Print*	*Format*	*Merge Codes*	*Retrieve*
CANCEL	▶SEARCH	HELP	▶INDENT	LIST FILES	BOLD	EXIT	UNDERLINE	MERGE R	SAVE

Key: Control + Function Key **Shift + Function Key** *Alt + Function Key* FUNCTION KEY ALONE

WordPerfect 5.0

F1	F2	F3	F4	F5	F6	F7	F8	F9	F10
Shell	Spell	Screen	Move	Text In/Out	Tab Align	Footnote	Print Format	Merge/Sort	Macro Def
Super/Subscript	**◀Search**	**Switch**	**▶Indent◀**	**Date**	**Center**	**Print**	**Line Format**	**Merge E**	**Retrieve**
Thesaurus	*Replace*	*Reveal Codes*	*Block*	*Mark Text*	*Flush Right*	*Math/Columns*	*Page Format*	*Merge Codes*	*Macro*
CANCEL	▶SEARCH	HELP	▶INDENT	LIST FILES	BOLD	EXIT	UNDERLINE	MERGE R	SAVE

Key: Control + Function Key **Shift + Function Key** *Alt + Function Key* FUNCTION KEY ALONE

Lotus® 1-2-3®

F1	F2	F3	F4	F5	F6	F7	F8	F9	F10
Help	Edit	Name	Abs	GoTo	Window	Query	Table	Calc	Graph
Compose	Step								
Alt + Key									

dBASE III Plus™

F1	F2	F3	F4	F5	F6	F7	F8	F9	F10
Help	Assist	List	Dir	Display Struc	Display Status	Display Memory	Display	Append	Edit